The Manager's Book of Quotations

The Manager's Book of Quotations

Lewis D. Eigen
Jonathan P. Siegel

amacom
American Management Association

This book is available at a special discount when ordered in bulk quantities.
For information, contact Special Sales Department,
AMACOM, a division of American Management Association,
135 West 50th Street, New York, NY 10020

Library of Congress Cataloging-in-Publication Data

The manager's book of quotations.

    Includes index.
    1. Management--Quotations, maxims, etc.
I. Eigen, Lewis, D. II. Siegel, Jonathan P.
(Jonathan Paul), 1944-   .
HD38.M31875 1989   658   88-48030
ISBN 0-8144-5839-4

Printing number

10 9 8 7 6 5 4 3 2 1

Contents

Contents

Preface

Everyone who works either manages, is managed, or is trying to avoid either or both of these conditions. Management affects our lives continually—not just at work, but also in our private worlds and in the public arena. Our standard of living, the movement of traffic, the conduct (or misconduct) of foreign policy, and even the ethics of our companies and the body politic reflect directly upon management. Because more than anything else, "managers manage people," and people make almost everything else happen.

Managers are the fastest growing professional class in our society. According to the Census Bureau, there are approximately fifteen million managers in the United States in business, government, and nonprofit and service institutions. They do many of the same things—motivating, budgeting and accounting, training, personnel selection, supervision, performance measurement, and performance evaluation, just to name a few. Managers in many occupations and industries face similar problems, issues, and concerns—leadership, labor relations, computers, office politics, management style, marketing, growth, and communications. Often, the manager needs a concise, clear insight—a well-formulated position, a "peg" on which to hang a thought or a decision or a statement. Occasionally, he needs the information yesterday.

The Manager's Book of Quotations is a first-line resource in the contemporary manager's quest for relevant and timely information; it is the largest (and we hope the most useful) collection of applicable and interesting quotes ever assembled for the manager. We have drawn these quotes from a wide range of modern, classical, and traditional sources. We have arranged them topically in forty-seven chapters, to be perused for insight and stimulation in the best tradition of the English commonplace book. Many of the quotes will provide focused thought-units for speeches, training sessions, newsletters, and correspondence; some will help the manager formulate appropriate written and oral explanations and discussions of new or existing managerial policies and practices. Simply browsing through the management thoughts of thousands of individuals who have faced similar challanges can provide a perspective to our own daily activities.

Scope

This compilation of Quotations is designed for the manager. It encompasses management and the management aspects of buisness as opposed to finance or economics. As a result there are quotes on budgeting but not on investment, on quantitative methods but not finance. *The Manager's Book of Quotations* does not attempt to deal with material on the stock market for example, although there are many quotes on the management aspect of running a firm from Wall Street and some views of investment banking house managers. As a result, many pithy quotes are not included herein. For example, the oil tycoon, J. Paul Getty said, "The meek shall inherit the earth, but they shall not acquire the mineral rights." The quotation is marvelous, but it is not really relevant to management per se. *The Manager's Book of Quotations* incorporates quotes from professionals of many fields. It includes some politicians, but the quotations refer to their roles as mangers and leaders—not politicians per se. Likewise, for scientists, physicians, educators, and others.

Management Literature

The formal, "official" literature on management is vast, and not easily accessible in its totality to busy managers. There is also another "literature"—speeches, television interviews, press conferences—that has management significance, but is ephemeral unless recorded and presented succinctly for later use. Some of the best management quotations come from minutes of company meetings, internal memos, sales meetings, and other activities not usually associated with "management literature." We have included much material from the unofficial literature as well as the more formal.

There are persons, living and dead, not usually primarily associated with "management" who have said or written things worthwhile for managers. Often they, too, had some managerial function or were the beneficiaries or victims of managers. We have considered all these resources in compiling *The Manager's Book of Quotations*. Our only principle of selection was, "Is it a good management quote?"

Quality Quotations

What makes a good management quote? Foremost in our view is the intellectual quality of the quotation. The clear expression of useful and interesting ideas for practicing managers was the primary criterion for inclusion in *The Manager's Book of Quotations*. For that reason we did not restrict ourselves to quoting only contemporary management writers in this volume. Readers will find many quotations from the Bible, Shakespeare, philosophers, poets, restauranteurs, presidents, scientists, journalists, airport managers, monks, physicians, sitcom stars, athletes and their managers, and many others—all with something to say about managing people, projects, and budgets.

There were several criteria of inclusion.

Literary quality. The same idea is often expressed with differential eloquence by different people. Given the option, we included the "better" version.

Succinctness. Some quotations effortlessly express the essence of a complex idea or situation in just a few words. Not surprisingly, many of these quotes came from professional writers rather than managers.

Source. Successful managers are sometimes very eloquent writers. Andrew Grove, the president of Intel Corporation, is an example. While many of his management ideas are not unique, his expression of management concepts is so good and so concise that he and others like him are quoted extensively.

Historical considerations. A quotation which has modern management relevance becomes even more interesting when we realize that it was first expressed over a thousand years ago, or that it was uttered or written by a person known outside the management arena, such as William Shakespeare, Abraham Lincoln, or Polly Adler. Throughout recorded history men and women have successfully managed projects that required the cooperative effort of several or many people. Their observations have merited inclusion in *The Manager's Book of Quotations*. Not only were many of these good management quotes, but they helped us overcome some of the limitations and biases of the "official" management literature.

Regardless of the field, the "one-liners" are usually the favorite quotations of most people, including us. We have included over a thousand of these. Ideally, all relevant quotes would be short, sweet, and to the point. In recognition of this factor, we have also included longer quotes that may require a little more reader concentration than the one liners.

Sources

All quotations originate somewhere. In compiling *The Manager's Book of Quotations* we have consulted thousands of sources from the classic and modern literature—formal and informal. We wish to express our appreciation to the persons quoted and their various publishers and disseminators. In the contemporary periodical literature, we wish to particularly acknowledge newspapers such as *The New York Times* and *The Washington Post*; journals like the *Harvard Business Review*; and magazines like *Inc.*, *Black Enterprise*, *Working Woman*, *Success*, *Hispanic Business*, *Forbes*, *Fortune*, and *Nation's Business*. While there are many specialized financial magazines and journals, and business coverage in almost all newspapers, there is a profound difference between covering business and financial matters and writing about the management aspects of these things. The effect of a change in the prime interest rate is, in many ways, much easier to cover than the operational effect of the change on R&D teams. Yet the latter may be of much more profound importance than the former. We are especially appreciative of these and other publications that regularly include much material on modern management techniques, issues, and problems.

Bias

Over the years there have been persistent, albeit frequently inadvertent, biases in the totality of writings and speeches on management. Generally the extent of coverage favors the management practices of the large organization over those of the small, the profit-making over the nonprofit, the manufacturing firm over the service enterprise, and the established over the recent. However, half of America's workers are managed in small enterprises rather than large, and smaller companies are creating most of the country's new jobs as well as the new technologies that are so crucial to our nation's competitive position. The quality of management of our service organizations has a far more profound effect on the nation today than ever before. The number of managers in various service industries, in government, and nonprofit organizations has long since eclipsed that of the manufacturing sector.

Public vs. Private Management

Most managers have heard of Thomas Watson, Jr., and are somewhat familiar with some of IBM's management practices. But how many of us think of Secretary of Defense Frank Carlucci or Admiral Grace Hopper in managerial as opposed to political contexts? Yet Carlucci's management philosophy and practices may have had much more impact than even those of Watson and IBM. Carlucci served as secretary of defense as well as the chief managerial officer of many other federal government agencies. As an exemplary manager, his influence extended over many years to countless federal agencies, state and local governmental entities, foreign governments, and private corporations throughout the world. Watson's managerial influence, incidentally, extended not only through IBM, but through government as he served as the U.S. Ambassador to Russia. The line between public and private management has blurred considerably, both in techniques and personage.

Admiral Grace Hopper brought the navy into the age of computers, beginning in the 1940s. Although she was a skilled programmer and systems analyst, she made her real mark—and her greatest contributions— as a leader and manager of large-scale projects. Her influence on managers should be extended because she exemplifies the position that managing information is also managing people, a theme that runs through *The Manager's Book of Quotations*.

Production vs. Knowledge Work

Until the 1960s, management was usually synonymous with managing production workers. Today, even in manufacturing facilities, the management of professional "knowledge workers" has become equally, if not more critical. One of the nation's largest and otherwise most successful law firms disintegrated recently. Spectacular growth was mismanaged, human and financial resources were squandered, interpersonal conflicts were out of control, and many people suffered needlessly. Growth is not simply changes of numbers; organizations have to change with growth, and that change has to be managed. But by whom? Lawyers, engineers, scientists, salespeople, and even artists face management challenges in the modern world. These areas have contributed much to the management literature that is useful to all. The teambuilding required of a concert string quartet is not dissimilar to that which is required in other, more traditional management fields. *The Manager's Book of Quotations* therefore, contains quotations from a wide variety of fields and professions.

Gender and Ethnic Bias

Modern, as well as older, management literature is male gender biased to a high degree. Feminine pronouns are among the rarest of words in this field, reflecting the assumption that managers were and are always male. One cannot help but speculate on the cumulative cost to Western Civilization of this loss of half the society's potential managerial talent. Fortunately, recent business and organizational practices have led to an improvement in this area. This change is reflected in many of the selections found in *The Manager's Book of Quotations* from the last decade or so, as well as earlier sources. It is further emphasized by the inclusion of many recent quotations from contemporary, successful female managers. However, we made no effort to edit the sexist language or tone of other quotations cited in *The Manager's Book of Quotations*. The ignorance of early managers with respect to gender issues does not obviate the value of *all* of their views any more than Sir Isaac Newton's ignorance of the effects of relativity vitiates the contributions of his calculus.

Racial religious and ethnic biases, as they have existed in Western society in general, reflect in the management literature, but not to the same degree as the gender bias, where the masculine and feminine nouns and pronouns inherent in the English language constantly call attention to the problem. In the modern management literature, Blacks and other groups, traditionally underrepresented in management ranks, begin to appear regularly. These appearances are included in this volume when they have met the other criteria of selection.

Also, our management literature is primarily English language based. We have made an effort to reflect management points of view from other cultures and parts of the world by citing relevant proverbs as well as some of the contemporary management thoughts of European, Asian, and other non-American managers and leaders.

Organization

The more than 5,000 quotations in *The Manager's Book of Quotations* are organized into forty-seven separate chapters reflecting major areas of management. Within each chapter the quotes are presented in alphabetical order of the persons quoted. Anonymous quotes appear at the end of each chapter. Proverbs and sayings appear in the normal alphabetical order. "Turkish proverb" would appear under "T," for example.

For many quotes there was some ambiguity as to which of our forty-seven chapters would be most appropriate. Does a quotation on the motivating effect of bonus payments belong in the "Remuneration" chapter or in

"Motivation?" In most cases we have made our best judgment, but our own frequent disagreement indicates that there is much subjectivity involved in this process. The reader is, therefore, urged to consult other conceptually related chapters for material on a particular subject or concept.

Citations

Each quotation in *The Manager's Book of Quotations* is referenced with sufficient, accurate information so that a diligent researcher could find the material with little trouble. However, sometimes our references are secondary, and in those cases we have not made any attempt to find, verify, or cite the primary reference. Publishers and dates of publication are cited for most of the modern works. For more classical material, which may over the years have been published many times, only the title is provided.

A large proportion of the quotes are from contemporary, living people—mostly managers. Since the average American executive remains in his position only a short time, and frequently changes organizational affiliation, the accuracy of the titles and affiliations of the persons quoted are of limited currency. We have used the rule of thumb of citing the title and affiliation for "public figures" as those which are most recognizable to the public. As such, Thomas J. Watson, Jr., is cited as the CEO of IBM and the U. S. Ambassador to Russia. His many other positions and affiliations are not included.

For sources not generally known to the public, we have used either their title and affiliation at the time the quote was made or, absent that, their title and affiliation at the time we compiled this work. By the time the reader sees the material, the individual quoted may often be affiliated with a different organization and hold a different title or position from that cited in this book.

For persons no longer living, we have tried to include years of birth and death. This provides the reader with some temporal perspective. However, some of the contemporary sources may have passed away between the time of their quote and the present moment.

For modern quotees we have designated the national origin of their organizational affiliation *only if it is not American.*

Multiple Sources

Just as teamwork has become a modern management practice, management writing has in recent years also shown this trend. A fair proportion of the current literature is written by two or even more authors. There are those who hold that a quotation that comes from a group somehow is rendered weaker by the lack of singular attribution. We do not concur with this view, and quotes with multiple authorship were not automatically precluded from *The Manager's Book of Quotations*. We simply attributed the quote to the pair or the group. Our first principle "Is it a good management quote?" took precedence over problematics of citation.

Editorial Material

At various points in *The Manager's Book of Quotations* we have added editorial material to place the quote in some context. This material is always placed in brackets so that the reader may distinguish between our writing and the source's material. Regular parentheses are used within a quote when the material belongs to the person quoted. So are italics.

Several quotes were originally written in Latin and are often quoted that way. In these few cases, we have presented the English translation and the original Latin in square brackets.

Context

All quotations, by definition, are to some extent out of context or at least devoid of most context. The reader is urged to keep this in mind when perusing this or any other book of quotations. It is obviously impossible to make a judgment of a person's beliefs, capabilities, or intellectual positions on the basis of a single or even a group of quotations. The benefit of reading quotes comes from the stimulation of the ideas expressed therein. Judgments of the person quoted, or his or her positions, should be made on a more extensive study of the writings and accomplishments of the individual. Also, although most of the quotees were affiliated with organizations at the time the quotes were written or uttered, it is not necessarily the case that the affiliated organizations subscribe now or ever concurred with the statements or views of the individual quotee.

Content of Quotations

There is little agreement on many of the aspects of management. This lack of consensus is reflected throughout this work in the often contradictory quotes within a given category. We have striven to provide quotations reflecting the major points of views that exist. This practice, of course, produces a certain inconsistency of viewpoint within *The Manager's Book of Quotations.* We have not used consistency with our own or any other views of management as a criterion of inclusion. Nor, do we necessarily personally concur with many of the points of view herein expressed. Indeed, several are offensive to one or both of us. However, we have tried to present a sample of the entire spectrum of viewpoint of modern and traditional management.

We have not—and could not—read everything that has ever been written that pertains to management. *The Manager's Book of Quotations* is derived from thousands of sources. Certainly, we have inadvertently overlooked or omitted many worthy quotations. We welcome suggestions and quotes from all readers and managers to help us strengthen future editions of *The Manager's Book of Quotations.*

Finally, we would like to suggest that the quotations herein are but nuggets of ideas, usually expressed by the author in much greater detail and richness in the original work. For example, Tom Peters, the management writer, has a great gift for producing quotable statements as do Peter Drucker, Andrew Grove, Norman Augustine, and many others. As good as these quotes are, however, they are no substitute for the insight that can be gleaned by reading the books and articles of the writers where the reader may benefit from the context, background, and explanation of the concepts behind the quote. We, therefore, recommend the reading of the referenced works as much as possible. Without the thousands of writers and thinkers quoted herein, this work would obviously not be possible. The wealth of their myriad contributions is but hinted at in the *The Manager's Book of Quotations.*

Alphabetization

The quotations in this work are, for the most part, alphabetized in each chapter. Anonymous quotations appear at the end of each chapter. Quotations from religious sources appear as follows: The New Testament, Luke 12:5-8. In such an instance, the book name (Luke, in this example) is the element relative to the alphabetization.

Technological Acknowledgment

A work of this magnitude presented many organizational, research, informational, management, and production challenges. There are two technological tools that saved us enormous amounts of work in producing *The Manager's Book of Quotations.* In retrospect, it is almost impossible to conceive of this project being completed in reasonable time without the productivity enhancement provided by them. First, are the 3M Post-it notes. Without these to mark appropriate materials in thousands of books, magazines, and newspapers, it is painful to imagine the alternative of producing this work the way we used to compile material before their invention. Then there is *Microsoft Word* and *Quick Basic*—software that not only served as the computerized word processor for this project, but enabled us to sort, classify, revise, organize, and index this extensive amount of complex material. Without a program that is capable of data base functions and macro programming, it is hard to imagine completing this work in the time that we did.

To the inventors and developers of these two marvelous tools, our thanks and appreciation for the savings of what would have otherwise been thousands of hours of routine work.

On Quotations

The superior man acquaints himself with many sayings of antiquity and many deeds of the past,
In order to strengthen his character thereby.

I Ching: Book of Changes
China, c. 600 B.C.

It is a good thing for an uneducated man to read books of quotations.

Winston Churchill, 1874–1965
English Prime Minister, writer, and soldier
My Early Life

Do not neglect the discourse of wise men,
But busy yourself with their proverbs;
For from them you will gain instruction,
And learn to serve great men.

Apocrypha, Wisdom of Ben Sira 8:8

Nothing gives an author so much pleasure as to find his works respectfully quoted by other learned authors.

Benjamin Franklin, 1706–1790
American printer and statesman
Pennsylvania Almanack

Hang these fellows, who have said all our good things before us!

Quoted by James Russell Lowell, 1819–1891
Professor of Poetry, Harvard University,
and U. S. Ambassador to Spain and England
Speech, London, July 4, 1883

I love them, because it is a joy to find thoughts one might have, beautifully expressed with much authority by someone recognizedly wiser than oneself.

Marlene Dietrich
German-American actress and singer
Marlene Dietrich's ABC
(Doubleday, 1961)

A great man quotes bravely, and will not draw on his invention when his memory serves him with a word so good.

Ralph Waldo Emerson, 1803–1882
American essayist and poet
Quotation and Originality

He ranged his tropes, and preached up patience;
Backed his opinion with quotations.

Matthew Prior, 1664–1721
English poet and diplomat
Paulo Purganti and His Wife

[Making up presidential quotes] ... is not lying.... When you're a press secretary, you develop a bond of understanding with the President so that you think like the President.... I knew those quotes were the way he felt.

Larry Speakes
President Ronald Reagan's
former Press Secretary
Quoted in *The Washington Post,*
April 12, 1988

Acknowledgments

Grateful acknowledgment is hereby made to the following for permission to reprint selections included in *The Manager's Book of Quotations*:

Doubleday & Co.: excerpts from *Managing* by Harold Geneen. Copyright © 1984. Reprinted by permission of Doubleday & Co.

Peter F. Drucker: excerpts from *The Changing World of the Executive* by Peter F. Drucker. Copyright © 1982 by Peter F. Drucker. Reprinted with permission of the author and Quadrangle Books, Inc.

E. P. Dutton: excerpts from *The Supermanagers* by Robert Heller. Copyright © 1984 by Heller Arts Ltd. Reprinted by permission of the publisher, E. P. Dutton, a division of NAL Penguin, Inc.

Harper & Row, Publishers, Inc.: excerpts from *People and Performance* by Peter F. Drucker. Copyright © 1980 by Peter F. Drucker. Reprinted by permission of Harper & Row, Publishers, Inc. *Management in Turbulent Times* by Peter F. Drucker. Copyright © 1980 by Peter F. Drucker. Reprinted by permission of Harper & Row, Publishers, Inc. *How to Motivate People: The Team Strategy for Success* by Fran Tarkenton. Copyright © 1986 by Harper & Row, Publishers, Inc. Reprinted by permission of Harper & Row, Publishers, Inc.

Alfred A. Knopf, Inc.: excerpts from *Up the Organization*. Copyright © 1970 by Robert Townsend. Reprinted by permission of Alfred A. Knopf, Inc. Excerpts from *Further Up the Organization*. Copyright © 1970, 1984 by Robert Townsend. Reprinted by permission of Alfred A. Knopf, Inc. Excerpts from *Thriving on Chaos: Handbook for a Management Revolution* by Tom Peters. Copyright © by Excel, a California Limited Partnership. Reprinted by permission of Alfred A. Knopf, Inc.

Prentice-Hall, Inc.: excerpts from Paul Hersey/Kenneth Blanchard, *Management of Organizational Behavior*, 4th edition, © 1982. Reprinted by permission of Prentice-Hall, Inc., Englewood Cliffs, New Jersey.

The Putnam Publishing Group: excerpts from *One-On-One With Andy Grove* by Andrew S. Grove. Copyright © 1987 by Andrew S. Grove. Reprinted by permission of The Putnam Publishing Group.

Random House, Inc.: excerpts from *High Output Management* by Andrew S. Grove. Copyright © by Random House, Inc. Reprinted with the permission of the publisher. Excerpts from *A Passion for Excellence* by Tom Peters and Nancy Austin. Copyright © by Random House, Inc. Reprinted with permission.

Simon & Schuster, Inc.: excerpts from *How Managers Make Things Happen* by George S. Odiorne. Copyright © 1982 by Prentice-Hall. Used by permission of the publisher, Prentice-Hall, Inc., Englewood Cliffs, New Jersey. Excerpts from *The Art of Japanese Management* by Richard T. Pascale and Anthony G. Athos. Copyright © 1981 by Simon & Schuster, Inc. Excerpts from *Managing Up, Managing Down* by Mary Ann Allison and Erik Allison. Copyright © 1984 by Simon & Schuster, Inc.

Warner Books, Inc.: excerpts from *Megatrends* by John Naisbitt. Copyright © 1982 by John Naisbitt. Reprinted by permission of Warner Books/New York. Excerpts from *Re-Inventing the Corporation* by John Naisbitt and Patricia Aburdeen. Copyright © 1985 by Megatrends, Inc. Reprinted by permission of Warner Books/New York.

The Manager's Book of Quotations

1

Accounting & Budgeting

Whatever you have, spend less.

In God we trust—all others pay cash.

American saying

Gold is where you find it.

American saying

The budget is our guide. It tells us what we're supposed to do for the year. We couldn't get along without it.

Jim Bell
Plant Manager, International Steel Products Co.
Tosi and Carroll, *Management* (Wiley, 1976)

Let giving and receiving all be in writing.

Apocrypha, Wisdom of Ben Sira 42:7

Money is like promises—easier made than kept.

Josh Billings
(Henry Wheeler Shaw), 1818–1885
American writer and auctioneer
Josh Billings: His Book

The principal difference between a luxury and a necessity is the price.

Josh Billings
(Henry Wheeler Shaw), 1818–1885
American writer and auctioneer
Josh Billings: His Book

Accountancy—*that* is government!

Louis Dembitz Brandeis, 1856–1941
U. S. Supreme Court Justice
Testimony, House Committee on Interstate and
Foreign Commerce, January 30, 1914

In determining the value of a business, as between buyer and seller, the good will and earning power due to effective organization are often more important elements than tangible property.

Louis Dembitz Brandeis, 1856–1941
U. S. Supreme Court Justice
Galveston Electric Co. v. *Galveston* (1921)

Mere parsimony is not economy..,. Expense, and great expense, may be an essential part of true economy. Economy is a distributive virtue, and consists not in saving but selection. Parsimony requires no providence, no sagacity, no powers of combination, no comparison, no judgment.

Edmund Burke, 1729–1797
English statesman, orator, and writer
Letter to a Noble Lord

It has been said that the love of money is the root of all evil. The want of money is so quite as truly.

Samuel Butler, 1835–1902,
English novelist and translator
Erewhon

All progress is based upon a universal innate desire on the part of every organism to live beyond its income.

Samuel Butler, 1835–1902
English novelist and translator
Note-Books of Samuel Butler

I have always taught them [my children] that *on domestic management depends the preservation or dissipation of their fortunes.*

Jeanne Louise Campan, 1752–1822
First lady of the bedchamber to Marie Antionette
Familiar Letters to her Friends

[A sound cost accounting system]... not only reveals our mistakes—it shows us who's doing a good job!

Bror R. Carlson
Director of Accounting,
International Minerals & Chemicals Co.
Managing for Profit (IMC, 1961)

The budget evolved from a management tool into an obstacle to management.

Frank C. Carlucci
U. S. Secretary of Defense
Frank Carlucci on Management in Government
(Center for Excellence in Government, 1987)

There are but two ways of paying debt—increase of industry in raising income, increase of thrift in laying out.

Thomas Carlyle, 1795–1881
Scottish essayist and historian
Past and Present

In contrast to the traditional budgeting approach of incrementing the new on the old, zero-base budgeting demands a total rejustification of everything from zero. It means chopping up the organization into individual functions and analyzing each annually, regardless of whether it is 50 years old or a brand-new proposal for a future program. The budget is broken into units called decision packages, prepared by managers at each level. These packages cover every existing or proposed activity of each department. They include analyses of purpose, costs, measures of performance and benefits, alternative courses of action, and consequences of disapproval.

Jimmy Carter
Thirty-ninth President of the United States
Nation's Business, January 1977

He who can predict [winning] numbers should not set off fire crackers.

Chinese proverb

The higher mind has no need to concern itself with the meticulous regimentation of figures.

Winston Churchill, 1874–1965
English Prime Minister, writer, and soldier
Remark, 1924

Put your money where your need is.

Madeline E. Cohen
Staff trainer, American Greetings Corp.
Training and Development Journal,
January 1988

The very best financial presentation is one that's well thought out and anticipates any questions ... answering them in advance.

> Nathan Collins
> Executive Vice President,
> Valley National Bank
> *CFO,* August 1985

When articles rise [in price] the consumer is the first that suffers, and when they fall, he is the last that gains.

> Charles Caleb Colton, c. 1780–1832
> English cleric, sportsman, and wine merchant
> *Lacon*

The wise man understands equity; the small man understands only profits.

> Confucius, c. 551–c. 479 B.C.
> Chinese philosopher and teacher
> *Analects*

If you can only cover costs, capitalism is irrelevant.

> Ernest F. Cooke
> University of Baltimore
> Remark in class, 1983

One difficulty in developing a good [accounting] control system is that quantitative results will differ according to the accounting principles used, and accounting principles may change.

> Ernest Dale
> The Wharton School
> *Readings in Management*
> (McGraw-Hill, 1970)

Debt is a prolific mother of folly and of crime.

> Benjamin Disraeli, 1804–1881
> English Prime Minister and novelist
> *Henrietta Temple*

Business? It's quite simple—it's other people's money.

> Alexandre Dumas (Dumas *fils*), 1824–1895
> French playwright and novelist
> *The Question of Money*

They were so broke that they couldn't even pay attention.

> John R. Du Teil
> Investment advisor, TJM Securities, Inc.
> Remark, April 25, 1988

[Answering a question about a new showroom the company had opened:] I've never actually seen it. I only know how much it costs and what sales it generates.

> Morris Eigen
> President, Heiser-Egan, Inc.
> Speech, New York City, August 1986

Farming looks mighty easy when your plow is a pencil and you're a thousand miles from a cornfield.

> Dwight David Eisenhower, 1890–1969
> Thirty-fourth President of the United States
> Speech, September 25, 1956

Money is of no value; it cannot spend itself. All depends on the skill of the spender.

> Ralph Waldo Emerson, 1803–1882
> American essayist and poet
> *The Young American*

Pay as you go is the truest economy.

> *Farmers' Cabinet,* 1840

Money is like an arm or a leg—use it or lose it.

> Henry Ford, 1863–1947
> American industrialist and car manufacturer
> *The New York Times,* November 8, 1931

If you would know the value of money, go and try to borrow some.

> Benjamin Franklin, 1706–1790
> American printer and statesman
> *The Way to Wealth*

Never ask of money spent
Where the spender thinks it went.
Nobody was ever meant
To remember or invent
What he did with every cent.

> Robert Frost, 1874–1963
> American poet
> *The Hardship of Accounting*

Public accounting taught me analytical approaches to business problems, objective reasoning, and the highest order of discipline in making factual presentations.

> Harold Geneen
> CEO, IT&T
> *Managing* (Doubleday, 1984)

Gresham's Law: Bad money drives out good money.

> Thomas Gresham, 1519–1579
> English financier

No man is rich whose expenditures exceed his means; and no one is poor whose incomings exceed his outgoings.

> Thomas Chandler Haliburton, 1796–1865
> Canadian jurist and humorist
> *Sam Slick's Wise Saws*

A national debt, if it is not excessive, will be to us a national blessing.

> Alexander Hamilton, 1755–1804
> First Secretary of the U. S. Treasury
> Letter to Robert Morris, April 30, 1781

Accountants are the witch doctors of the modern world.

> J. Harman, 1894–1970
> English jurist
> *Miles* v. *Clarke* (1953)

In an era in which the misdeeds of the powerful and the established are trumpeted in almost daily headlines, the accounting profession is among the best regarded institutions in the country.

> Louis Harris
> Public opinion pollster
> *The New York Times*, September 20, 1987

Those who try to paint a management picture "by the numbers" will always be amateurs.

> James L. Hayes
> President, American Management Association
> *Memos for Management: Leadership*
> (AMACOM, 1983)

Many financial measurements which are useful and valid in steady-state or static situations are strategic traps in growth situations.

> Bruce Henderson
> CEO, Boston Consulting Group, Inc.
> *Henderson on Corporate Strategy* (Abt, 1979)

He that has lost his credit is dead to the world.

> George Herbert, 1593–1633
> English clergyman and poet
> *Jacula Prudentum*

When it's your own money, you tend to spend it more wisely.... Don't borrow any money.... You sleep better that way.

> George Hernandez
> President, Del Ray Chemical, Inc.
> *Hispanic Business,* June 1987

Little to little added, if oft done,
In small time makes a good possession.

> Hesiod, eighth century B.C.
> Greek poet
> *Works and Days*

Put not your trust in money, but put your money in trust.

> Oliver Wendell Holmes, 1809–1894
> American physician and popular writer
> *The Autocrat of the Breakfast Table*

Whenever decisions are made strictly on the basis of bottom-line arithmetic, human beings get crunched along with the numbers.

> Thomas R. Horton
> President and CEO,
> American Management Association
> *Management Review*, January 1987

No man's credit is as good as his money.

> Edgar Watson Howe, 1853–1937
> American journalist, editor, and publisher
> *Sinner Sermons*

The only absolutely safe way to double your money is to fold it once and put it in your pocket.

> Frank McKinney ("Kin") Hubbard, 1868–1930
> American caricaturist and humorist
> *Abe Martin Hoss Sense and Nonsense*

It is not hard to be stingy.

> Jabo proverb

I am one of those who do not believe that a national debt is a national blessing, but rather a curse to a republic; inasmuch as it is calculated to raise around the administration a moneyed aristocracy dangerous to the liberties of the country.

> Andrew Jackson, 1767–1845
> Seventh President of the United States
> Letter to T. H. Colman, April 26, 1824

I sincerely believe that banking establishments are more dangerous than standing armies, and that the principle of spending money to be paid by posterity, under the name of funding, is but swindling futurity on a large scale.

> Thomas Jefferson, 1743–1826
> Third President of the United States
> Letter to Elbridge Gerry, January 26, 1799

Cost accounting is the number one enemy of productivity.

> H. Thomas Johnson and Robert S. Kaplan
> *Relevance Lost: The Rise and Fall of Management Accounting*
> (Harvard Business School, 1987)

Whatever you have, spend less.

> Samuel Johnson, 1709–1784
> English lexicographer and essayist
> Letter to Dr. Boswell, December 7, 1782

Any jackass can draw up a balanced budget on paper.

> Lane Kirkland
> President, AFL-CIO
> *U. S. News & World Report*, May 19, 1980

[In response to a question regarding the "bottom line" implication of a new product:] You think that the only thing that counts is the bottom line! What a presumptuous thing to say. The bottom line is in heaven.

> Edwin Land
> Founder, Polaroid
> Remark at Shareholders Annual Meeting, 1977

It bugs us when there is no real ambition to translate ... thoughts into numbers.... A company must run the numbers on a proposal to see if they work.

James Lientz
President, Citizens & Southern Bank
CFO, August 1985

You don't need an M.B.A. from Harvard to figure out how to lose money.

Royal Little
Founder, Textron
Best of Business Quarterly, 1987

There went out a decree from Caesar Augustus that all the world should be taxed.

New Testament, Luke 2:1

It is the duty of the auditor to see that the authority to charge is not made a pretext for extravagence or favouritism.

J. Lush, 1807–1881
English jurist
R. v. *Cumberlege* (1877)

I have enough money to last me the rest of my life, unless I buy something.

Jackie Mason
Comedian
Jackie Mason's America

The only thing that matters is cash flow—not the cash flows they use today, but the old cash flows that laid out the source and application of funds—where it's coming from and where it's going and how much is left over. No company has ever gone bankrupt because it had a loss on its P&L.

William G. McGowan
Chairman, MCI Communications Corp.
Inc. Magazine, August 1986

Insolvency is not a very thrilling or amusing subject.

Lord Mishcon
Speech, House of Lords, 1985

A public fund is [to be] collected by no less than two, and disbursed by no less than three [persons].

The Mishna, Peah

[W]e like to depreciate as much as possible even though we sacrifice our profits the first year.... We were very much surprised that American management does not want to have such a fast depreciation because as an American partner told me, he did not want to sacrifice his profit to his successor.

Akio Morita
CEO, Sony Corp. (Japan)
Cherry Blossoms and Robotics
(Young Presidents' Organization, 1983)

In Parliament he [Cobden] again pressed the necessity of reducing expenditure. Friends warned him that he was flogging a dead horse.

John Morley, 1838–1923
English statesman and political biographer
Richard Cobden

Few have heard of Fra Luca Parioli, the inventor of double-entry bookkeeping; but he has probably had more influence on human life than has Dante or Michelangelo.

Herbert J. Muller
Economist and historian
The Uses of the Past

The high cost of managing is now perceived as an expense that can be scrutinized and controlled.

Phil Nienstedt
Manager of Human Resource Programs
and Richard Wintermantel
Director of Organization and Human Resources
Motorola Corp.
Management, January 1987

Sins and debts are always more than we think they are.

Old Farmer's Almanack (1797)

I would rather have my people laugh at my economies than weep for my extravagance.

Oscar II, 1829–1907
King of Sweden
Attributed

Expenditure rises to meet income.... Individual expenditure not only rises to meet income but tends to surpass it ... [and] what is true of individuals is also true of governments.

C. Northcote Parkinson
University of Malaya
The Law and the Profits, 1960

Parkinson's Law of Triviality: The time spent on any item of the agenda will be in inverse proportion to the sum involved.

C. Northcote Parkinson
University of Malaya
Parkinson's Law and Other Studies in Administration, 1957

Kickbacks must always exceed bribes.

John Peers
President, Logical Machine Corp.
1,001 Logical Laws (Doubleday, 1979)

Inspiring visions rarely (I'm tempted to say never) include numbers.

Tom Peters
Business writer
Thriving on Chaos (Knopf, 1987)

Most of the troubles accountants have in ... judging soundness of accounting practices are caused by an inevitable conflict in the need for figures which are both realistic and objectively measurable.

G. Edward Phillips
University of California
The Accounting Review, October 1963

It is important [for an entrepreneurial manager] to become associated with at least one accountant, especially if he or she is the one who assembles the budget and reports your number progress.

Gifford Pinchot III
The International Institute of Intrapreneurs
Intrapreneuring (Harper & Row, 1986)

We don't have a staff of business analysts in our headquarters.... Those financial people can only crunch numbers. They can't add any original thinking.

Robert Pritzker
President, Marmon Group
Tomasko, *Downsizing* (AMACOM, 1987)

After great getters come great spenders.

Barber, *The Book of 1000 Proverbs* (1876)

The borrower is servant to the lender.

Old Testament, Proverbs 22:7

Financial accounting helps the manager to "keep score" for the firm. It watches the flow of resources and lets those who have an interest in them know where they stand.

Managerial accounting calls attention to problems and the need for action. It also aids in planning and decision making. It is aimed more at *control* and less at *valuation* than financial accounting.

> John A. Reinecke
> University of New Orleans
> and William F. Schoell
> University of Southern Mississippi
> *Introduction to Business*
> (Allyn and Bacon, 1983)

If accountants don't understand that all double-entry bookkeeping today is computer driven, they don't understand the accounting environment.

> Anthony M. Santomero
> The Wharton School
> *Working Woman*, March 1988

More money tends to buy more of the same.

> Lyle E. Schaller
> Yokefellow Institute
> *The Change Agent* (Abingdon, 1972)

Under budgetary pressure (arbitrary or not) it is truly remarkable how many options one discovers one can do without.

> James R. Schlesinger
> U. S. Secretary of Defense
> Memorandum to Senate Committee on
> Government Operations, April, 1968

A well constructed numerical estimate can be worth a thousand words.

> Charles L. Schultze
> Director, U. S. Bureau of the Budget
> Senate Testimony, August 23, 1967

Creativity is great—but not in accounting.

> Charles Scott
> CEO, Intermark
> *Inc. Magazine's Guide to
> Small Business Success*, 1987

I can get no remedy against this consumption of the purse; borrowing only lingers and lingers it out, but the disease is incurable.

> William Shakespeare, 1564–1615
> English dramatist and poet
> *Henry the Fourth*

No reckoning made, but sent to my account With all my imperfections on my head.

> William Shakespeare, 1564–1616
> English dramatist and poet
> *Hamlet*

And, how his audit stands, who knows, save heaven?

> William Shakespeare, 1564–1616
> English dramatist and poet
> *Hamlet*

Words pay no debts.

> William Shakespeare, 1564–1616
> English dramatist and poet
> *Troillus and Cressida*

I don't know any CEO who doesn't love numbers.

> Jeffrey Silverman
> CEO, Ply Gem Industries, Inc.
> *Nation's Business*, December 1987

Solvency is entirely a matter of temperament and not of income.

> Logan Pearsall Smith, 1865–1946
> American-born English writer
> *The Wealth of Nations*

Profit is the most important thing, and the way you get profit is through gross margins.

> Arthur F. F. Snyder
> Vice Chairman, United States Trust Co.
> *CFO*, August 1985

Take care of the pence, for the pounds will take care of themselves.

> Philip Dormer Stanhope, 1694–1773
> English Secretary of State
> *Letters of Lord Chesterfield to His Son*

A good part of the problem [poor productivity] ... lies with the current accounting system, which sort of makes overhead disappear—it simply gets added into the cost of a product, like a tax.

> Paul Strassmann
> Former Vice President, Xerox
> *Inc. Magazine*, March 1988

Alwayes those that dance must pay the musicke.

> John Taylor, 1580–1653
> English pamphleteer and inn-keeper
> *Taylor's Feast*

While the total U.S. economic output rose only 15 percent from 1978 to 1985, the number of accountants on corporate staffs increased by 30 percent.

> Lester C. Thurow
> Dean, Sloan School of Management, M. I. T.
> Tomasko, *Downsizing* (AMACOM, 1987)

Deals aren't usually blown by principals; they're blown by lawyers and accountants trying to prove how valuable they are.

> Robert Townsend
> Former CEO, Avis
> *Further Up the Organization* (Knopf, 1984)

Development participative management ... calls for some creative insulation from the effects of accounting and reporting.

> Robert Townsend
> Former CEO, Avis
> *Further Up the Organization* (Knopf, 1984)

Accountants can be smarter than anybody else or more ambitious or both, but essentially they are bean counters—their job is to serve the operation. They can't run the ship.

> Robert Townsend
> Former CEO, Avis
> *Further Up the Organization* (Knopf, 1984)

To contract new debts is not the way to pay old ones.

> George Washington, 1732–1799
> First President of the United States
> Letter to James Welsh, April 7, 1799

Treat ... financial controls as liberating.

> Robert H. Waterman
> Management consultant and writer
> *The Renewal Factor* (Bantam, 1987)

He smote the rock of the natural resources, and abundant streams of revenue gushed forth.

> Daniel Webster, 1782–1852
> American statesman and orator
> Speech on Alexander Hamilton,
> March 10, 1831

Reform, economize. You may reason, speculate, complain, raise mobs, spend life in railing at Congress and your rulers, but unless you import less than you export, unless you spend less than you earn, you will be eternally poor.

> Noah Webster, 1758–1843
> American lexicographer and writer
> *New Haven Gazette*, December 14, 1786

It is an axiom of program budgeting that the budget should facilitate the process of alternative methods of obtaining objectives.

Chester Wright
Director, Financial Management Training,
U. S. Civil Service Commission
Program Budgeting and Cost Benefit Analysis
(Goodyear, 1969)

2

Career Development

*It takes twenty years
to make an overnight success.*

Seek till you find, and you will not lose by the toil.

Aesop, c. 620–c. 560 B.C.
Greek fabulist
The Field of Corn

Management skills are only part of what it takes.... Managers must also be corporate *warriors* or leaders. These unique individuals are the problem identifiers. They possess a strong sense of vision; view firefighting as an opportunity to do things differently and smarter; and are business strategists who help identify key corporate growth issues. [The author is referring to Black managers, but the import is general.]

John W. Aldridge
President, Aldridge Associates
Management Review, December 1987

Mentors ... guide their disciples ... imparting the wisdom they have acquired over many years.... Godfathers (sometimes called "rabbis") are in a position to intervene on your behalf; by definition, they are powerful people with an interest in your career.

Mary Ann Allison
Vice President, CitiCorp
and Eric Allison
Financial writer
Managing Up, Managing Down
(Simon & Schuster, 1984)

Try as far as possible to pass on information rather than your conclusions. Your conclusions, if they are right, are part of your competitive advantage. If they are wrong and you pass them on they may come back to haunt you.

Mary Ann Allison
Vice President, CitiCorp
and Eric Allison
Financial writer
Managing Up, Managing Down
(Simon & Schuster, 1984)

Preserve thy tongue from answering thy superior/And guard thyself against reviling him.

Do not make him cast his speech to lasso thee/Nor make too free with thy answer.

Amen Em Opet I, 1991–1962 B.C.
Egyptian Pharaoh
The Wisdom of Amen Em Opet

[Referring to his mentor, Charles Tandy:] If he didn't push you, he didn't like you.

Bernard Appel
President, Radio Shack
Computer & Software News, December 7, 1987

If you're not a white male, consider sales seriously. Most employers, regardless of how sexist or racist they may be, will pay for any sales they can get. And they care little for the color or gender of the person who brings that business to the firm. Most will be glad to get the business even if it comes from a green, bisexual Martian. And in sales you're usually not exposed to subjective or biased performance appraisal systems. Either you're bringing in the business or you're not.

Ramona E. F. Arnett
President, Ramona Enterprises, Inc.
Speech, New York City, June 6, 1971

A wise man will make more opportunity than he finds.

Francis Bacon, 1561–1624
Lord Chancellor of England
Of Ceremonies and Respects

He who puts up at the first inn he comes across, very often passes a bad night.

Filippo Baldinucci, 1634–1696
Florentine art historian
La Veglia

I must not rust.

Clara Barton, 1821–1912
Founder, The American Red Cross
Quoted in *American Heritage*, April 1988

The greater the rate of company expansion, the easier it is to find valuable new jobs for people.

Ed Bersoff
Founder, BTG, Inc.
Inc. Magazine, December 1987

If our people develop faster than a competitor's people, then they're worth more.

James M. Biggar
CEO, Nestle Enterprises
USA Today, March 10, 1988

A winner is someone who recognizes his God-given talents, works his tail off to develop them into skills, and uses these skills to accomplish his goals.

Larry Bird
Professional basketball player
Bird on Basketball (Addison-Wesley, 1986)

To be a manager, you have to start at the bottom—no exceptions.

Henry Block
CEO, H&R Block
Inc. Magazine, December 1987

As consultants, we frequently observe the phenomenon of a wide range in the quality of the relationships among boss and subordinates. But when we talk with individual members, we have often discovered that this range of relationships does not closely reflect the actual competence levels of the subordinates.... [P]eople with high ability but irritating styles are pushed away and underused. "Brilliant but impossible" and "competent but defensive" are labels often used to isolate talented subordinates.

David L. Bradford
Stanford University School of Business
and Allan R. Cohen
Babson College
Managing for Excellence (Wiley, 1984)

All men that are ruined are ruined on the side of their natural propensities.

> Edmund Burke, 1729–1797
> English statesman, orator, and writer
> *Letters on a Regicide Peace*

I awoke one morning and found myself famous.

> George Gordon Byron, 1788–1824
> English poet and satirist
> Moore, *Life of Byron*

It takes twenty years to make an overnight success.

> Eddie Cantor, 1892–1964
> American comedian and writer
> *The New York Times*, October 20, 1963

The American system of ours, call it Americanism, call it Capitalism, call it what you like, gives each and every one of us a great opportunity if we only seize it with both hands and make the most of it.

> Al Capone, 1899–1947
> American gangster
> Cockburn, *In Time of Trouble*

It is the first of all problems for a man to find out what kind of work he is to do in this universe.

> Thomas Carlyle, 1795–1881
> Scottish essayist and historian
> Address at Edinburgh University

The folly of that impossible precept, "Know Thyself"; till it be translated into this partially possible one, "Know what thou canst work at."

> Thomas Carlyle, 1795–1881
> Scottish essayist and historian
> *Sartor Resartus*

Many of the best jobs do not really exist until someone is hired for them.

> James E. Challenger
> President, Challenger, Gery, & Christmas
> *Working Woman*, March 1988

In order to be irreplaceable one must always be different.

> Coco Chanel, 1883–1971
> French fashion designer
> *Coco Chanel, Her Life, Her Secrets*

You do not rise by the regulations, but in spite of them. Therefore in all matters of active service the subaltern must never take "No" for an answer. He should get to the front at all costs.

> Winston Churchill, 1874–1965
> English Prime Minister, writer, and soldier
> *Ian Hamilton's March*

The family motto of the House of Marlborough from which I descend is *Faithful but Unfortunate*. But I, by my enterprise, nay daring, have reversed the motto, to *Faithless but Fortunate*.

> Winston Churchill, 1874–1965
> English Prime Minister, writer, and soldier
> Halle, *Irrepressible Churchill*

Let a man practice the profession which he best knows.

> Cicero, 106–43 B.C.
> Roman orator and statesman
> *Tusculanarum Disputationum*

I caught on to the finance stuff really fast. There are things that you like to do, and then there are things that you are very good at. I would love to be a Broadway star, but I am not Bernadette Peters. I *am* very good at finance.

> Deborah A. Coleman
> Vice President and CFO, Apple Computer Co.
> *Working Woman*, December 1987

Career advancement is much like marketing; your objective is to position yourself as the ideal solution to an organizational need. Self-marketing requires the basic textbook approach, including recognition of the need, target marketing, positioning, pricing and development of a communications strategy.

> J. Paul Costello
> President, Costello Erdlen & Company
> *Management World*, September/October 1987

One never rises so high as when one does not know where one is going.

> Oliver Cromwell, 1599–1658
> Lord Protector of England
> Reported by Cardinal de Retz, *Memoires*

If you have ever been in business for yourself, it's hard to stop. Once you have been bitten, you can't go back to being somebody else's employee.

> Casey Cummins
> Owner, Precision Tune (franchise)
> *U.S. News & World Report*, December 21, 1987

Every member of the staff knew that if he aspired to higher office, he must make a record for himself, a good part of which would be a reputation among upper line officers of ability to "understand" their informal problems without being told.

> Melville Dalton
> University of California
> *American Sociological Review*, June 1950

We've entered an era when very good, competent people aren't getting jobs. One remedy is to stand out, to self-promote. If you do, you're going to get the nod over some co-worker.

> Jeffrey P. Davidson
> Marketing consultant
> *The Washington Post*, May 20, 1985

A consistent man believes in destiny, a capricious man in chance.

> Benjamin Disraeli, 1804–1881
> English Prime Minister and novelist
> *Vivian Grey*

To blame a promotion that fails on the promoted person, as is usually done, is no more rational than to blame a capital investment that has gone sour on the money that was put into it.

> Peter F. Drucker
> Management consultant and writer
> *Management in Turbulent Times*
> (Harper & Row, 1980)

The mature woman ... after having raised her children has been a "chief executive officer" at home for ten years or more. No one told her whether to dust first or make the beds first—and both chores got done. Yet when she starts working, she is put under a "supervisor" who treats her as a moron who has never done anything on her own before when what she needs is a teacher and an assistant.

> Peter F. Drucker
> Management consultant and writer
> *Management in Turbulent Times*
> (Harper & Row, 1980)

A job in which young people are not given real training—though, of course, the training need not be a formal "training program"—does not measure up to what they have a right and a duty to expect.

> Peter F. Drucker
> Management consultant and writer
> *People and Performance*
> (Harper & Row, 1977)

There are two kinds of stones, as everyone knows, one of which rolls.

> Amelia Earhart, 1898–1937
> American aviator, social worker, and writer
> *20 Hours: 40 Minutes*

The workers and professionals of the world will soon be divided into two distinct groups. Those who will control computers and those who will be controlled by computers. It would be best for you to be in the former group.

> Lewis D. Eigen
> Executive Vice President,
> University Research Corp.
> Lecture, Columbia University, May 12, 1961

Hitch your wagon to a star.

> Ralph Waldo Emerson, 1803–1882
> American essayist and poet
> *Civilization*

Make yourself necessary to someone.

> Ralph Waldo Emerson, 1803–1882
> American essayist and poet
> *Considerations by the Way*

As long as a man stands in his own way, everything seems to be in his way.

> Ralph Waldo Emerson, 1803–1882
> American essayist and poet
> *Journals* (quoting Henry David Thoreau)

First say to yourself what you would be; and then do what you have to do.

> Epictetus, c. 60
> Greek philosopher
> *Of Such as Read and Dispute Ostentatiously*

Plough deep while sluggards sleep.

> Benjamin Franklin, 1706–1790
> American printer and statesman
> *Poor Richard's Almanack*

No gain without pain.

> Benjamin Franklin, 1706–1790
> American printer and statesman
> *Poor Richard's Almanack*

By working faithfully eight hours a day you may eventually get to be a boss and work twelve hours a day.

> Robert Frost, 1874–1963
> American poet
> Rowes, *The Book of Quotes* (Dutton, 1979)

The longer you're in a new job, the more you develop a personal sense of comfort.

> John J. Gabarro
> Harvard Business School
> *The Dynamics of Taking Charge*
> (Harvard Business School, 1987)

Know that thou shouldst be more prompt to do what thou hast not promised, than to promise what thou wilt not do.

> Solomon ibn Gabirol, 1021–1069
> Spanish poet and grammarian
> *The Improvement of the Moral Qualities*

In the business world, everyone is paid in two coins: cash and experience. Take the experience first; the cash will come later.

> Harold Geneen
> CEO, IT&T
> *Managing* (Doubleday, 1984)

Going to work for a large company is like getting on a train. Are you going sixty miles an hour, or is the train going sixty miles an hour and you're just sitting still?

> Jean Paul Getty, 1892–1976
> Chairman, Getty Oil Co.
> *The Official MBA Handbook of Great Business Quotations* (Simon & Schuster, 1984)

If you wish in this world to advance,
Your merits you're bound to enhance;
You must stir it and stump it,

And blow your own trumpet,
Or trust me, you haven't a chance.

William Schwenck Gilbert, 1836–1911
English playwright
Ruddigore

Keep your affairs in suspense.
Make people depend on you.
Avoid victories over your superiors.
Control your imagination.
Know how to take and give hints.
Know how to be all things to all men.
Without lying, do not tell the whole truth.
Be a man without illusions.
Behave as if you were watched.
—*In a word, be a saint.*

Baltasar Gracián, 1601–1658
Spanish priest and popular writer
Oraculo Manual

If you think your boss is stupid, remember:
You wouldn't have a job if he was any
smarter.

Albert A. Grant
President, American Society of Civil Engineers
Speech, Washington, D. C., May 30, 1988

I have given them [the directors] quantitative
goals that they can measure me by within
specific time periods. The fact that I've done
this over the last five years in all the major
business segments is what has earned me the
presidency. It's not because people like me.
Not because I've been around here for almost
20 years. I'm a manager and I'm a teacher and
I understand banking, and for that reason I am
president of this bank.

Rosemarie Greco
President, Philadelphia Fidelity Bank
Working Woman, December 1987

The best business you can go into you will
find on your father's farm or in his workshop.
If you have no prospect or friends to aid you

there, turn your face to the great West, and
there build up a home and fortune.

Horace Greeley, 1811–1872
American journalist and politician
To Aspiring Young Men

It seems that woman has more likelihood of
success the higher she pitches her sights.

Germaine Greer
Writer and feminist
The Female Eunuch (Bantam, 1970)

The way these things often work in the real
world, particularly in bigger organizations, is
that the promotional opportunity will probably surface in a different department from the
one in which you work. This gives your current boss a different role. While he
undoubtedly wishes you well, your opportunity means a new problem for him. If you
move on to take a higher position, he must find
a replacement. So, that promotion is not quite
yours yet ...

Andrew S. Grove
CEO, Intel Corp.
One-On-One With Andy Grove
(G. P. Putnam's Sons, 1987)

A résumé is a balance sheet without any
liabilities.

Robert Half
President, Robert Half International
Robert Half on Hiring (Crown, 1985)

A Requiem for Joe:

His company wanted the impossible and expected Joe to get it.

Joe gave his company what they asked for but
not what they expected.

Poor Joe, he did the right thing for the wrong

reason and was fired for the wrong thing for the wrong reason.

Bruce Henderson
CEO, Boston Consulting Group, Inc.
Henderson on Corporate Strategy (Abt, 1979)

In ways to greatness, think on this,
That slippery all ambition is.

Robert Herrick, 1591–1674
English poet
Hesperides

By far the most valuable possession is skill. Both war and the chances of fortune destroy other things, but skill is preserved.

Hipparchus, second century B.C.
Greek mathematician and astronomer
Commentaries

Job mobility is connected to job competence, and vice versa.

Harold S. Hook
Chairman and CEO, American General Corp.
Forbes, October 19, 1987

It is much easier to apologize than to ask permission.

Grace Murray Hopper
Admiral, U. S. Navy (retired)
60 Minutes (CBS TV), 1986

I don't in a day at my desk ever once think about what my sex is. I'm thinking about my job.

Karen N. Horn
CEO, Cleveland Federal Reserve Bank
Working Woman, March 1988

In talking with successful CEOs of large companies, I hear one recurrent theme: "the willingness to pay the price." This phrase implies an intense motivation, a burning desire to become chief executive. The price includes not just consistently long hours and longer days, but grueling travel schedules, emotional stress, loss of privacy, putting one's reputation on the line, guilt for the neglect of spouses and children, and little time, if any, left over for oneself.

Thomas R. Horton
President and CEO,
American Management Association
Management Review, December 1987

It is not book learning young men need, nor instruction about this and that, but a stiffening of the vertebrae which will cause them to be loyal to a trust, to act promptly, concentrate their energies, do a thing—"carry a message to Garcia."

Elbert Hubbard, 1856–1915
American writer, printer, and editor
A Message to Garcia

High positions must be fought for inch by inch, and held by a vigilance that never sleeps.

Elbert Hubbard, 1856–1915
American writer, printer, and editor
The Philosophy of Elbert Hubbard

You are your first product, so positioning yourself in the market as an individual is extremely important.

Portia Isaacson
Founder, Future Computing, Inc.
Management, April 1987

[Referring to the development of the Macintosh computer:] Opportunities like this don't come along very often.... And it's being done by a bunch of people who are incredibly talented but who in most organizations would be working three levels below the impact of the decisions they're making in this organization.... It won't last forever.... It's more important than their personal lives right now.

> Steven Jobs
> Cofounder, Apple Computer Co.
> *Macworld*, 1981

He is no wise man that would quit a certainty for an uncertainty.

> Samuel Johnson, 1709–1784
> English lexicographer and essayist
> Preface, *Dictionary of the English Language*

Some luck lies in not getting what you thought you wanted but getting what you have, which once you have got it, you may be smart enough to see it's what you would have wanted had you known.

> Garrison Keillor
> Host, *A Prairie Home Companion*
> American Public Radio, 1986

When they [workers] choose a company, they often choose a way of life. The [corporate] culture shapes their responses in a strong, but substantial way. Culture can make them fast or slow workers, tough or friendly managers, team players or individuals. By the time they've worked for several years, they may be so well conditioned by the culture they might not even recognize it. But when they change jobs they may be in for a big surprise.

> Terrence E. Deal and Allan A. Kennedy
> Harvard Business School
> *Corporate Cultures* (Addison-Wesley, 1982)

[Mr. President, how did you become a war hero?]
It was absolutely involuntary. They sank my boat.

> John Fitzgerald Kennedy, 1917–1963
> Thirty-fifth President of the United States
> Reply to a little boy's question
> Adler, *The Kennedy Wit* (Bantam, 1962)

Be entrepreneurial. What one needs in government, as in the private sector, is imagination. If you can come up with something a little different in the way of understanding a problem, or approaching it in a way that combines different resources, then ... you won't have to wait for opportunities; you'll make your own.

> Alan Keyes
> U. S. Assistant Secretary of State
> *Management*, 1987

Put your emotional life in order.... It's a great help in climbing toward the higher rungs of the career ladder, to be happy in life, rather than find yourself mired in emotional crisis. It's hard enough to succeed without taking on personal problems that sap your energy and divert your attention.

> Michael Korda
> Editor-in-Chief, Simon & Schuster
> *Success!*, March 1985

When I hear a man talk about how hard he works, and how he hasn't taken a vacation in five years, and how seldom he sees his family I am certain that this man will not succeed in the creative aspects of business ... and most of the important things that have to be done are the result of creative acts.

> Herman C. Krannert
> Chairman, Inland Container Corp.
> *The Forum*, Spring 1969

A woman politician [executive] learns to operate on two levels: a gender-neutral level, focussing on the issue, and a gender-sensitive level, always alert to the signals.

> Madeleine Kunin
> Governor of Vermont
> *The Journal of State Government*,
> September/October 1987

[Computer and other technical managers] ... must become business managers or risk landing on the technological rubbish heap.

Jim Leeke
Business and computer writer
PC Week, December 8, 1987

The common remark of top managers, "It's up to you here" or "You can't keep a good man down" is often a cloak for the fact that promotion is completely chancy and that merit plays a subordinate role simply because no system for assessing performance by men in junior and middle management exists.

Roy Lewis and Rosemary Stewart
The Boss (Phoenix House, 1958)

The way for a young man to rise is to improve himself every way he can, never suspecting that anybody wishes to hinder him.

Abraham Lincoln, 1809–1865
Sixteenth President of the United States
Letter to William Henry Herndon, July 1848

To get ahead ... learn from others with proven success and experience. Don't be afraid to adopt key parts of their styles.

Sharron Lipscomb
Special Assistant, U. S. Department of Justice
Management, 1987

I attribute the little I know to my not having been ashamed to ask for information, and to my rule of conversing with all descriptions of men on those topics that form their own peculiar professions and pursuits.

John Locke, 1632–1704
English philosopher
Some Thoughts Concerning Education

The Gods implore not,
Plead not, solicit not; they only offer
Choice and occasion, which being once passed
Return no more.

Henry Wadsworth Longfellow, 1807–1882
American poet
Masque of Pandora

My difficulties [in being nominated by the Senate as Ambassador to Brazil] go back some years when Senator [Wayne] Morse [of Oregon, who opposed the nomination] was kicked in the head by a horse.

Clare Boothe Luce, 1903–1987
Congresswoman, playwright, and diplomat
Press conference, Washington, D. C., 1957

We're going to see a lot more young people entering entrepreneurial ventures.

Fredric V. Malek
President, Marriott Corp., Hotel Division
Business Week, August 24, 1987

Love the trade which thou hast learned, and be content therewith.

Marcus Aurelius, 121–180
Roman Emperor and Stoic philosopher
Meditations

Our opportunities to do good are our talents.

Cotton Mather, 1663–1728
American theologian
The New Dictionary of Thoughts, 1957

Some of the best-known management schools have become virtual closed systems in which professors with little interest in the reality of organizational life teach inexperienced students the theories of mathematics, economics, and psychology as ends in themselves. In these management schools, management is accorded little place.

Henry Mintzberg
McGill University School of Management
Harvard Business Review on Human Relations, 1986

If corporations can no longer achieve success by doing only one thing, workers hired by those companies can no longer believe that they will have lifetime employment by having only one skill or assignment. People are going to have to be prepared, not only to change jobs within a corporation, but to change companies, and perhaps careers as well.

> Barbara Morgenstern
> Corporate consultant
> *The Washington Post*, November 22, 1987

I know how I got here. It was mostly happenstance.... When I first came to Boston looking for a job, this was the only company that would hire me.

> James Morton
> CEO, John Hancock Insurance Co.
> Quoted on *Pinnacle* (CNN TV), January 1988

A closed door policy not only shuts you [the manager] in, it shuts out the career growth paths of those who can benefit from you.

> Jack L. Most
> Former General Counsel, Revlon
> Letter, April 25, 1988

What I need as a publisher is first-line leadership that understands the newspaper business. Editors have no theoretical or practical experience to help them to take the step across the threshold to management.

> Reg Murphy
> Publisher, *The Baltimore Sun*
> *Presstime*, March 1988

Jump at opportunities to take on responsibilities. People should try new things—that's how to grow.

> Kevin Murray
> Deputy Director, Office of Information,
> U. S. Department of Agriculture
> *Management*, 1987

By the time you rise through the ranks, the culture of homogenization has bred the spirit and imagination out of you.

> Ralph Nader
> Consumer advocate
> *Best of Business Quarterly*, Winter 1986

You may end up in a staff job, but the line jobs are the ones that give you the training that you need.

> Richard Neblett
> President, National Action Council for
> Minorities in Engineering
> *Black Enterprise*, August 1987

If you would go up high, then use your own leg! Do not get yourself carried aloft; do not seat yourself on other peoples backs and heads!

> Georg Wilhelm Nietzsche, 1844–1900
> German philosopher
> *Thus Spake Zarathustra*

Understand the culture of the new company [with which you are joining or negotiating] and its standards of what is reasonable.

> James C. Nunan
> Vice President for Systems Control, SCICON
> and Thomas J. Hutton
> Partner, Pierce/Hutton Associates
> *Personnel Journal*, November 1987

One quality that has brought many executives up to their present positions is their ability to handle emergencies and to work under pressure. But an executive, in order to grow and endure, will soon find it imperative to concentrate on the elimination of emergencies.

> E. B. Osborn
> President, Economics Laboratory, Inc.
> *Executive Development Manual* (ELI, 1959)

Before I was a genius I was a drudge.

> Ignace Paderewski, 1860–1941
> Polish concert pianist and statesman
> Remark to reporters, 1936

When your employer says sales are down this year and there won't be a raise, you're not supposed to look around and say, "Well, where would I be better off?" But it also means that when the company is hurting, it doesn't start firing people. Loyal employees have to believe that the company will support them [in bad times] and I don't find very many employees who believe that anymore.

> Mark Pasten
> Arizona State University
> *The Washington Post*, January 5, 1988

The squeaky wheel doesn't always get greased; it often gets replaced.

> John Peers
> President, Logical Machine Corp.
> *1,001 Logical Laws* (Doubleday, 1979)

'Tis a wise saying, Drive on your own track.

> Plutarch, c. 46–c. 120
> Greek biographer and philosopher
> *Of the Training of Children*

In every enterprise consider where you would come out.

> Publilius Syrus, c. 42 B.C.
> Roman writer
> *Maxims*

The way to subject all things to thyselfe, is to subject thyselfe to reason: thou shalt govern many if reason govern thee: wouldst thou be crowned the monarch of a little world? commend thyselfe.

> Francis Quarles, 1592–1644
> English poet and chronologer
> *Enchiridion*

Professional education in America is putting progressively more emphasis on the manipulation of symbols to the exclusion of other sorts of skills—how to collaborate with others, to work in teams, to speak foreign languages, to solve concrete problems—which are more relevant to the new competitive environment. And more and more, America's best students have turned to professions that allow them to continue attending to symbols, from quiet offices equipped with a telephone, telex, and a good secretary. The world of truly productive people, engaged in the untidy and difficult struggle with real production problems, is becoming alien to America's best and brightest.

> Robert B. Reich
> JFK School of Government, Harvard University
> *The Next American Frontier*, 1983

I am married to my business.

> Betty Rivera
> CEO, American Toyota Dealership
> *Hispanic Business,* June 1987

I never had a boss that tried to sit on me, and I think that's essential. If you expect people to develop, you have to give them the responsibility, you have to tell them what their objectives are and you have to let them do it.

> David M. Rodman
> Chairman, U.S. Steel
> *Sky*, June 1, 1984

The skills that make technical professionals competent in their specialties are not necessarily the same ones that make them successful within their organizations.

> Bernard Rosenbaum
> President, MOHR Development, Inc.
> *Training*, November 1986

I was lucky, not a genius.

> Julius Rosenwald, 1862–1932
> Chairman of Sears, Roebuck & Co.
> *Time*, 1932

If you can do nothing with yourself, others are not likely to do better.

> Dagobert D. Runes
> Editor, publisher, and philosopher
> *A Book of Contemplation*

The best way for a young man who is without friends or influence to begin is: first, to get a position; second, to keep his mouth shut; third, observe; fourth, be faithful; fifth, make his employer think he would be lost in a fog without him; sixth, be polite.

> Russell Sage, 1816–1906
> American financier and philanthropist
> Quoted in *Elbert Hubbard's Scrap Book*

Never allow your sense of self to become associated with your sense of job. If your job vanishes, your self doesn't.

> Gorden Van Sauter
> Former President, CBS News
> *Working Woman*, February 1988

Let this be your motto,—Rely on yourself!
For, whether the prize be a ribbon or throne,
The victor is he who can go it alone!

> John Godfrey Saxe, 1818–1887
> American newspaper publisher and editor
> *The Game of Life*

Implementers aren't considered bozos anymore.

> John Sculley
> CEO, Apple Computer Co.
> Peters, *Thriving on Chaos* (Knopf, 1987)

It is common practice to keep promoting personnel from jobs in which they performed competently to higher positions until they have reached a level at which they are incompetent (the Peter principle). To prevent this, the best technique I have been able to develop has been to ask an employee temporarily to substitute for one in a higher position (to avoid disappointment by concealing my wish to promote him); I have then offered the higher post only after he has shown his competence for it.

> Hans Selye
> University of Montreal
> *The Stress of Life* (McGraw-Hill, 1976)

A man must be upon the place and deliberate upon circumstances, and be not only present, but watchful, to strike in the very nick of the occasion.

> Seneca, 4 B.C.–A.D. 65
> Roman writer and rhetorician
> *Epistles to Lucilius*

... 'tis the curse of service,
Preferment goes by letter and affection,
And not by old gradation, where each second
Stood heir to the first.

> William Shakespeare, 1564–1616
> English dramatist and poet
> *Othello*

Who seeks, and will not take, when once 'tis offered,
Shall never find it more.

> William Shakespeare, 1564–1616
> English dramatist and poet
> *Antony and Cleopatra*

Our executive development programs take place on the job, not in a bunch of classrooms.

> Joseph Shersen
> Director
> Advanced Management Development, IBM
> *Management*, 1987

Energy enables a man to force his way through irksome drudgery and dry details and carries him onward and upward to every station in life.

Samuel Smiles, 1812–1904
Scottish physician and popular writer
Self-Help

The difference of intellect in men depends more upon the early cultivation of this *habit of attention*, than upon any great disparity between the powers of one individual and another.

Samuel Smiles, 1812–1904
Scottish physician and popular writer
Self-Help

The demand for men, like that of any other commodity, necessarily regulates the production of men.

Adam Smith, 1723–1790
Scottish political economist
Inquiry into the ... Wealth of Nations

Yesterday I was a dog.
Today I am a dog.
Tomorrow I'll probably still be a dog.

Snoopy

Today, in order to have job security, you've got to have a broader range of knowledge that enables you to handle a broader range of assignments and to work for more than one company.

Anthony P. St. John
Vice President for Human Resources,
Chrysler Corp.
The Washington Post, November 22, 1987

It doesn't matter where you start as long as you have a road map and consider every work day as training along the way.

Deborah Steelman
Associate Director,
U. S. Office of Management and Budget
Management, 1987

"It has always seemed strange to me," said Doc. "The things we admire in men, kindness and generosity, openness, honesty, understanding and feeling are the concomitants of failure in our system. And those traits we detest, sharpness, greed, acquisitiveness, egotism and self-interest are the traits of success. And while men admire the quality of the first they love the produce of the second."

John Steinbeck, 1902–1968
American novelist
Cannery Row

Mutiny and riot were not the best ways of conveying a soldier's aspirations to his sovereign.

Tacitus, c. 55–117
Roman orator, politician, and historian
Annals of the Julian Emperors

A full-rounded, well-negotiated employment contract is more in the employee's favor than the employer's.

John Tarrant
Business consultant and writer
Perks and Parachutes
(Simon & Schuster, 1985)

[Referring to a previous job which he lost and suffered a period of unemployment:] I made a play to be president of the firm, and lost.

Henry Brown Turner
Chairman, Ardshiel, Inc.
The New York Times, April 12, 1988

All my life people have said I wasn't going to make it.

> Ted Turner
> CEO, Turner Enterprises
> TV interview, 1984

One does not gain much by mere cleverness.

> Marquis de Vauvenargues, 1715–1747
> French soldier and moralist
> *Reflections and Maxims*

The secret of business success is not who you know. It's what you know.

> *The Wall Street Journal*
> TV advertisement, 1987

Let down your bucket where you are.

> Booker T. Washington, 1856–1915
> Principal, Tuskegee Institute
> Opening address, Atlanta Exposition, 1895

There's always room at the top.

> Daniel Webster, 1782–1852
> American statesman and orator
> Motto

The people who get into trouble in our company are those who carry around the anchor of the past.

> John Welch
> CEO, General Electric Co.
> Tomasko, *Downsizing* (AMACOM, 1987)

Every man who takes office in Washington either grows or swells, and when I give a man office I watch him carefully to see whether he is growing or swelling.

> Woodrow Wilson, 1856–1924
> Twenty-eighth President of the United States
> Speech, May 15, 1916

If you only do things you know well and do comfortably, you'll never reach higher goals.

> Linda Tsao Yang
> California Savings and Loan Commissioner
> *Working Woman*, February 1988

Don't be irreplaceable. If you can't be replaced, you can't be promoted.

> Anonymous

The image of the [Harvard] business school is that it produces the captains of industry. But now it's producing the incredibly well-paid lieutenants of Wall Street.

> Anonymous Harvard MBA
> *Fortune*, November 9, 1987

3

Change

The universe was dictated but not signed.

===============================

The future comes one day at a time.

Dean Acheson, 1893–1971
U. S. Secretary of State
Remark, 1966

We're trying to change the habits of an awful lot of people. That won't happen overnight, but it will bloody well happen.

John Akers
CEO, IBM
Business Week, February 15, 1988

[To produce change:] Rub raw the sores of discontent.

Saul Alinsky
Community organizer
Rules for Radicals (Random House, 1970)

The future is made in the present.

Kelly Andrews
Project Director, U. S. Labor Department
Personnel Journal, March 1988

It is perhaps elementary that those holding authority should resist diminution of their freedom to act. But opposition to change is not limited to those in power. Many of those over whom authority is exercised raise the strongest voice for the *status quo*.

Kenneth J. Arrow
Nobel laureate in economics
The Limits of Organization (Norton, 1974)

Why this reluctance to make the change? We fear the process of reeducation! Adults have invested endless hours of learning in growing accustomed to inches and miles; to February's twenty-eight days; to "night" and "debt" with their silent letters; to qwertyuiop; and to all the rest. To introduce something altogether new would mean to begin all over, to become ignorant again, and to run the old, old risk of failing to learn.

Isaac Asimov
Science writer and biochemist
Machines that Think
(Holt, Rinehart and Winston, 1983)

People fear change because it undermines their security.

Thomas R. Bennett III
Planning For Change
(Leadership Resources, 1961)

I've been in this business a long time. I was on television when it was radio.

Milton Berle
American comedian and television star
Variety, 1978

Modern business must have its finger continually on the public pulse. It must understand the changes in the public mind and be prepared to interpret itself fairly and eloquently to changing opinion.

Edward L. Bernays
Pioneer American publicist
Propaganda (Liveright, 1928)

The man who never alters his opinion is like standing water, and breeds reptiles of the mind.

William Blake, 1757–1827
English poet and artist
The Marriage of Heaven and Hell

[When conditions change] the same rules that worked so well in steadier times can misinform management and derail effective responses to new conditions. Unless the company is endowed with ... individuals who challenge old practices and, when necessary, violate company rules and policy—it won't be able to meet the difficult challenge of changing conditions.

Thomas V. Bonoma
Harvard Business School
Harvard Business Review,
November/December 1986

[Fifty reasons why we/it/they/ can't change:]
(1) We've never done it before. (2) Nobody else has ever done it. (3) It has never been tried before. (4) We tried it before. (5) Another company/person tried it before. (6) We've been doing it this way for 25 years. (7) It won't work in a small company. (8) It won't work in a large company. (9) It won't work in our company. (10) Why change—it's working OK. (11) The boss will never buy it. (12) It needs further investigation. (13) Our competitors are not doing it. (14) It's too much trouble to change. (15) Our company is different. (16) The ad dept. says it can't be done. (17) The sales dept. says it can't be sold. (18) The service dept. won't like it. (19) The janitor says it can't be done. (20) It can't be done. (21) We don't have the money. (22) We don't have the personnel. (23) We don't have the equipment. (24) The union will scream. (25) It's too visionary. (26) You can't teach an old dog new tricks. (27) It's too radical a change. (28) It's beyond my responsibility. (29) It's not my job. (30) We don't have the time. (31) It will obsolete other procedures. (32) Customers won't buy it. (33) It's contrary to policy. (34) It will increase overhead. (35) The employees will never buy it. (36) It's not our problem. (37) I don't like it. (38) You're right, but ... (39) We're not ready for it. (40) It needs more thought. (41) Management won't accept it. (42) We can't take the chance. (43) We'd lose money on it. (44) It takes too long to pay out. (45) We're doing all right as it is. (46) It needs committee study. (47) Competition won't like it. (48) It needs sleeping on. (49) It won't work in this department. (50) It's impossible.

E. F. Borisch
Product Manager, Milwaukee Gear Co.
Product Engineering, July 20, 1959

[Humanities graduates] achieved the best overall performance, and were most suited for change, which is the leading feature of the high-speed, high-pressure, high-tech world we now occupy.

Charles L. Brown
Chairman, AT&T
Personnel Journal, February 1986

Fate proceeds inexorably ... only upon the passive individual, the passive people.

> Pearl S. Buck, 1892–1973
> Pulitzer Prize author and
> Nobel laureate in literature
> Address to Nobel Prize winners,
> New York, December 10, 1942

Decay is inherent in all compounded things. Strive on with diligence.

> Buddha (Prince Siddhartha), 563?–483? B.C.
> Indian philosopher and founder of Buddhism
> Last words

If past history was all there was to the game, the richest people would be librarians.

> Warren Buffett
> Financier and investor
> *The Washington Post,* April 17, 1988

Custom reconciles us to everything.

> Edmund Burke, 1729–1797
> British statesman and political writer
> *On the Sublime and Beautiful*

Well, well—the world must turn upon its axis;
And all mankind turn with it, heads or tails;
And live and die, make love and pay our taxes,
And, as the veering wind shifts, shift our sails.

> George Gordon Byron, 1788–1824
> English poet and satirist
> *Don Juan*

[Immediately after airline deregulation:] We were going around gaga.

> Donald J. Carty
> Senior Vice President, American Airlines
> *The New York Times,* April 12, 1988

[Referring to the changing times:] A great wind is blowing, and that gives you either imagination or a headache.

> Catherine II ("The Great"), 1729–1796
> Empress of Russia
> *Correspondence avec le Baron F. M. Grimm*

There was never a moment when it was possible to say that a tank had been "invented". There never was a person about whom it could be said "this man invented the tank". But there was a moment when the actual manufacture of the first tanks was definitely ordered, and there was a moment when an effective machine was designed as the direct outcome of this authorisation.

> Winston Churchill, 1874–1965
> English Prime Minister, writer, and soldier
> *The World Crisis*

To improve is to change; to be perfect is to change often.

> Winston Churchill, 1874–1965
> English Prime Minister, writer, and soldier
> Speech, House of Commons, 1925

Only the wisest and the stupidest of men never change.

> Confucius, 551?–479? B.C.
> Chinese philosopher and teacher
> *Analects*

Many of the obstacles for change which have been attributed to human nature are in fact due to the inertia of institutions and to the voluntary desire of powerful classes to maintain the existing status.

> John Dewey, 1859–1952
> American philosopher and educator
> *Encyclopedia of Unified Sciences,* 1938

Even the gods cannot strive against necessity.

> Diogenes Laertius, c. 200–250
> Greek historian and writer
> *Lives and Opinions of Eminent Philosophers:*
> *Pittacus*

The future never just happened. It was created.

> Will Durant, 1885–1981
> and Ariel Durant, 1898–1981
> Historians and popular writers
> *The Lessons of History*

People do not change easily or all at once. Most of us need a chance to try out new ways and to become familiar with new procedures.

> William G. Dyer
> Brigham Young University
> *Strategies for Managing Change*
> (Addison-Wesley, 1984)

The by-product is sometimes more valuable than the product.

> Havelock Ellis, 1859–1939
> English scientist and author
> *Little Essays of Love and Virtue*

Science changes its aspect as every new investigator gains sufficient publicity to discredit his predecessors.

> Ford Madox Ford, 1873–1939
> English writer and poet
> *Return to Yesterday*

Sober-minded managers accept [change as a] fact of business life and are constantly on the lookout for those subtle trends and tides before their competition spots them. A healthy development of this temporal view of things prevents being caught unawares or languishing in undue optimism.

> William H. Franklin, Jr.
> Georgia State University
> *Financial Strategies*, Fall 1987

Most of the change we think we see in life/Is due to truths being in or out of favor.

> Robert Frost, 1874–1963
> American poet
> *The Black Cottage*

The enemy of conventional wisdom is not ideas but the march of events.

> John Kenneth Galbraith
> Economist and diplomat
> *The Affluent Society* (Houghton Mifflin, 1958)

You cannot fight against the future.

> William Ewart Gladstone, 1809–1898
> English Prime Minister and author
> Speech in Parliament, 1866

Change can come with breathtaking speed, leaving a company on the defensive and in financial trouble when it's forced to catch up.

> Gary Goldstick and George Schreiber
> Principals, Goldstick & Schreiber
> *Inc. Magazine Guide to Small Business Success,*
> 1987

If we are to perceive all the implications of the new, we must risk, at least temporarily, ambiguity and disorder.

> J. J. Gordon
> Founder of the "Brainstorming" process
> *Creative Computing*, October 1983

Clearly no group can as an entity create ideas. Only individuals can do this. A group of individuals may, however, stimulate one another in the creation of ideas.

> Estill I. Green
> Vice President, Bell Telephone Laboratories
> *Effective Administration of Research Programs*
> (Cornell University Press, 1958)

Make no mistake: realizing significant improvements in the quality of a product or service ... is *hard, hard work* involving a serious amount of grunting and sweating and heavy lifting on the part of *all employees*. It will mean "doing things better," but it will also mean "doing things differently"—which is to say, it will mean *change*.

> John Guaspari
> Management writer
> *Management*, March 1987

All organizations do change when put under sufficient pressure. This pressure must be either external to the organization or the result of very strong leadership.

> Bruce Henderson
> CEO, Boston Consulting Group, Inc.
> *Henderson on Corporate Strategy* (Abt, 1979)

It is rare for any organization to generate sufficient pressure internally to produce significant change in direction. Indeed, internal pressure is likely to be regarded as a form of dissatisfaction with the organization's leadership.

> Bruce Henderson
> CEO, Boston Consulting Group, Inc.
> *Henderson on Corporate Strategy* (Abt, 1979)

Panta rei—all is flux.... [Therefore] you cannot step twice into the same river.

> Heraclitus, 535?–475? B.C.
> Greek philosopher
> *On the Universe*

The concept of progress acts as a protective mechanism to shield us from the terrors of the future.

> Frank Herbert
> Science fiction writer
> *Dune* (Chilton, 1965)

Not only ought fortune to be pictured on a wheel, but every thing else in this world.

> George Herbert, 1593–1633
> English clergyman and poet
> *Jacula Prudentum*

If managers are able to understand, predict, and direct change and control behavior, they are essentially applied behavioral scientists.

> Paul Hersey
> California American University
> and Kenneth H. Blanchard
> University of Massachussetts
> *Management of Organizational Behavior*
> (Prentice-Hall, 1982)

Certainty generally is illusion, and repose is not the destiny of man.

> Oliver Wendell Holmes, Jr., 1841–1935
> U. S. Supreme Court Justice
> *The Path of the Law*

Mack truck theory: A key employee can be lost at any time (killed by a Mack truck or through resignation), so managers should always be prepared for sudden and permanent personnel changes.

> Harold S. Hook
> Chairman and CEO, American General Corp.
> *Forbes*, October 19, 1987

Custom, then, is the great guide of human life.

> David Hume, 1711–1776
> English philosopher
> *An Enquiry Concerning Human Understanding*

There is a certain relief in change, even though it be from bad to worse; as I have found travelling in a stagecoach, that it is often a comfort to shift one's position and be bruised in a new place.

> Washington Irving, 1783–1859
> American essayist and novelist
> *Tales of a Traveller*

There are two kinds of taste, the taste for emotions of surprise and the taste for emotions of recognition.

Henry James, 1843–1916
American novelist
Partial Portraits

Change is not made without inconvenience, even from worse to better.

Samuel Johnson, 1709–1784
English lexicographer and critic
Preface, *The English Dictionary*

You can change behavior in an entire organization, provided you treat training as a process rather than an event.

Edward W. Jones
Training Director, General Cinema Beverages
Training, December 1986

Change is the law of life. And those who look only to the past or present are certain to miss the future.

John Fitzgerald Kennedy, 1917–1963
Thirty-fifth President of the United States
Speech, Frankfurt, West Germany,
June 25, 1963

Provide ample advance notice of change—whether the change is favorable or unfavorable.

Donald L. Kirkpatrick
University of Wisconsin
How to Manage Change Effectively
(Josey-Bass, 1985)

Times change, and we change with them.
[*Tempora mutantur et nos mutamur in illis.*]

Latin proverb

Times don't change. Men do.

Sam Levenson, 1911–1980
Teacher and comedian
You Don't Have to be in Who's Who to Know What's What (Simon & Schuster, 1979)

The dogmas of the quiet past are inadequate to the stormy present. The occasion is piled high with difficulty, and we must rise with the occasion. As our case is new, so we must think anew and act anew. We must disenthrall ourselves.

Abraham Lincoln, 1809–1865
Sixteenth President of the United States
Message to Congress, December 1, 1862

Men like the opinions to which they have become accustomed from youth; this prevents them from finding the truth, for they cling to the opinions of habit.

Moses Maimonides, 1135–1204
Egyptian physician and philosopher
Guide for the Perplexed

Observe constantly that all things take place by change, and accustom thyself to consider that the nature of the Universe loves nothing so much as to change the things which are, and to make new things like them.

Marcus Aurelius, 121–180
Roman Emperor and Stoic philosopher
Meditations

The only [management] practice that's now constant is the practice of constantly accommodating to change.

William G. McGowan
Chairman, MCI Communications Corp.
Inc. Magazine, August 1986

One of the best lessons children learn through video games is standing still will get them killed quicker than anything else.

Jinx Milea
University of Southern California
and Pauline Lyttle
President, Operational Politics, Inc.
Why Jenny Can't Lead, 1986

People who want to stay in business should learn how to cope with change.

Barbara Morgenstern
Corporate consultant
The Washington Post, November 22, 1987

Change occurs only when there is a confluence of changing values and economic necessity.

John Naisbett and Patricia Aburdene
Business writers and social researchers
Re-inventing the Corporation (Warner, 1985)

It is also said of me that I now and then contradict myself. Yes, I improve wonderfully as time goes on.

George Jean Nathan, 1882–1958
American editor and critic
The Theatre in the Fifties

Potential users are quick to adapt to change— they like learning new software tools which have a direct impact on how they do "work."

Bridget O'Conner
New York University
Administrative Management, September 1987

There are only two ways to get people to support corporate change. You should give employees the information they need to understand the reasons for change, and put

enough influence behind the information to [gain their] support.

Carla O'Dell
President, O'Dell & Associates
CFO, October 1987

It is one thing to be stiff and another to be steady in an opinion. The steady man changes when reason requires it, but the stiff-necked is at war with all reason.

Old Farmer's Almanac (1812)

Once you have created a market, you are faced with the necessity of re-creating it continually.

William Olsten
CEO, Olsten Services Corp.
Success, February 1988

One thing that is new is the prevalence of newness, the changing scale and scope of change itself, so that the world alters as we walk in it.

J. Robert Oppenheimer, 1904–1967
Physicist and Director of the Manhattan Project
The Dynamics of Change (Prentice-Hall, 1967)

Manage the opportunities change offers.

Performance Sciences Corp.
Advertisement, 1986

Winners [successful business managers] must learn to relish change with the same enthusiasm and energy that we have resisted it in the past.

Tom Peters
Business writer
Nightly Business News (PBS TV),
September 2, 1987

Today, loving change, tumult, even chaos is a prerequisite for survival, let alone success.

Tom Peters
Business writer
Thriving on Chaos (Knopf, 1987)

Constant change by everyone requires a dramatic increase in the capacity to accept disruption.

Tom Peters
Business writer
Thriving on Chaos (Knopf, 1987)

Success breeds conservatism, and that means a love affair with the status quo and an aversion to change.

Frank Popoff
CEO, Dow Chemical Co.
The New York Times, November 22, 1987

[T]echnology always fosters radical social change.

Neil Postman
New York University
Conscientious Objections (Knopf, 1988)

People are asking more cogent questions, and they're observing behavior that begins to be amenable to the ideas of chaotic dynamics.

James Ramsey
New York University
The New York Times, November 22, 1987

People's minds are changed through observation and not through argument.

Will Rogers, 1879–1935
American actor and humorist
Will Rogers (Hallmark, 1969)

Changes are impossible to bring off when managers and unions are adversaries.

Dean M. Ruwe
Senior Vice President, Copeland Corporation
and Wickham Skinner
Harvard Business School
Harvard Business Review, May/June 1987

Radical change was the hallmark of the industrial revolution—yet we managed to adapt to it successfully. We have reconciled ourselves to the startlingly different concept of the atomic age. We are beginning to master the complexities of the space age and all the novelties it embodies.

David Sarnoff, 1891–1971
Founder and President, RCA
Wisdom of Sarnoff and the World of RCA

Reversals are inevitable.

Gorden Van Sauter
Former President, CBS News
Working Woman, February 1988

In normal times, and under normal conditions the pace of change tends to be slow. During a crisis, it is relatively easy to accelerate the pace of change.... It matters more whether a crisis is percieved than whether a crisis really exists.

Lyle E. Schaller
Yokefellow Institute
The Change Agent (Abingdon, 1972)

A method for hastening the pace of planned change is to deliberately encourage an increase in the level of discontent with the status quo.

Lyle E. Schaller
Yokefellow Institute
The Change Agent (Abingdon, 1972)

Fortune turns on her wheel the fate of kings.
[*Praecipites regum casus fortuna rotat.*]

Seneca, 4 B.C.–A.D. 65
Roman writer and rhetorician
Agamemnon

All things are ready, if our minds be so.

William Shakespeare, 1564–1616
English dramatist and poet
Henry the Fifth

I always loved change, something new.
Change is a challenge, an excitement.

Dawn Sibley
Executive Vice President, Ally & Gargano
Working Woman, May 1988

The great man is the man who does a thing for
the first time.

Alexander Smith, 1830–1867
Scottish poet
On the Importance of a Man to Himself

So much has been written about employees'
resistance to change that we are sometimes
tempted to forget that they can also react
favorably.

Nathaniel Stewart
Director, Management Development Center,
U. S. Agency for International Development
Leadership in the Office (AMACOM, 1963)

It's a giant step between hearing what other
people are doing and doing it ourselves.

Dick Thompson
General, U. S. Army
Government Executive, January 1987

Things do not change; we change.

Henry David Thoreau, 1817–1862
American poet, naturalist, and essayist
Walden

A competitive world has two possibilities for
you. You can lose. Or, if you want to win,
you can change.

Lester C. Thurow
Dean, Sloan School of Management, M. I. T.
60 Minutes (CBS TV), February 7, 1988

The stone that is rolling can gather no moss,
For master and servant oft changing is loss.

Thomas Tusser, c. 1524–1580
English versifier on agriculture
Hunderedth Good Points of Husbandrie

All experience shows that even smaller technological changes than those now in the cards
profoundly transform political and social
relationships. Experience also shows that
those transformations are not *a priori* predictable and that most contemporary "first
guesses" concerning them are wrong. For all
these reasons, one should take neither present
difficulties nor presently proposed reforms
too seriously.... To ask in advance for a complete recipe would be unreasonable. We can
specify only the human qualities required:
patience, flexibility, intelligence.

John Von Neumann, 1903–1957
Father of the serial computer
Fortune, June 1955

Markets change, tastes change, so the companies and the individuals who choose to
compete in those markets must change.

Dr. An Wang
Founder and CEO, Wang Laboratories
Nation's Business, December 1987

Our stomachs quiver at the prospects of
change. But today's leaders and managers
have no choice.

Robert H. Waterman
Management consultant and writer
The Renewal Factor (Bantam, 1987)

Habit breaking, the prerequisite for change and renewal, needs more than a simple decision. It takes motivation, desire and will. Crisis can provide that and all too often is the sole force for change.

Robert H. Waterman
Management consultant and writer
The Renewal Factor (Bantam, 1987)

The time you save in not making changes and taking risks can be used to perfect current practices. Your employees will be grateful to you for letting them know exactly where they stand—and will reward you by being unimaginative, uninspired and unhappy.

Donald C. Whitham
Supervisory Special Agent, FBI Academy
The National Sheriff, August/September 1986

It is personalities not principles that move the age.

Oscar Wilde, 1854–1900
Irish poet, playwright, and novelist
The Picture of Dorian Gray

Once you decide to make a change in a particular area, it often means a change in people, and that's most often where things bog down.

Q. T. Wiles
Turnaround Operations consultant
Inc. Magazine, February 1988

Not choice
But habit rules the unreflecting herd.

William Wordsworth, 1770–1850
English poet
Grant that by this

Change ... has a well-structured, short-term, operational component and an ill-structured, long-term, strategic component.... Operational change is short or medium term, with a 1- to 3-year horizon. It focuses on methods and procedures, personnel assignments, and use of materials.... Strategic change is long-term, usually 3 to 10 years. It focuses on values, goals, policies, organizational structure, and investments of capital and other resources.

Dale E. Zand
New York University
Information, Organization, and Power
(McGraw-Hill, 1981)

We are living in the first period of human history for which the assumption that the time-span of major cultural change is greater than the life-span of an individual is false. Today this time-span is considerably shorter than that of human life, and accordingly our training must prepare individuals to face a novelty of conditions.

Alfred North Whitehead, 1861–1947
English mathematician and philosopher
Introduction to Donam, *Business Adrift*

4

Communications

*None love the messenger
who brings bad news.*

You people [his subordinates] are telling me what you think I want to know. I want to know what is actually happening.

> Creighton Abrams
> Commander of American forces in Vietnam
> *Time*, March 8, 1971

[To improve communications practices of computer departments] ... you have to break the back of the bureaucracy you've established.

> Michael Albrecht, Jr.
> Principal, Nolan, Norton & Co.
> *PC Week*, December 8, 1987

[Prime Minister William] Gladstone speaks to me as if I were a public meeting.

> Alexandrina Victoria, 1819–1901
> Queen of Great Britain and Ireland
> Attributed

Managers who are skilled communicators may also be good at covering up real problems.

> Chris Argyris
> Harvard Graduate School of Education
> *Harvard Business Review*,
> September/October 1986

Reading maketh a full man; conference a ready man; and writing an exact man.

> Francis Bacon, 1561–1624
> Lord Chancellor of England
> *Of Superstition*

It is generally better to deal by speech than by letter.

> Francis Bacon, 1561–1624
> Lord Chancellor of England
> *Of Negotiating*

[When communicating to a large or mass media audience:] I imagine I'm talking to a single person.

> Red Barber
> Sportscaster and commentator
> National Public Radio, February 18, 1988

[T]he first function of the executive is to develop and maintain a system of communication.

> Chester I. Bernard, 1886–1961
> President, USO
> *The Functions of the Executive* (Harvard, 1938)

The great art in writing well, is to know when to stop.

> Josh Billings
> (Henry Wheeler Shaw), 1818–1885
> American writer and auctioneer
> *Josh Billings: His Book*

Nothing is real unless it happens on television.

> Daniel J. Boorstin
> Historian and Librarian of Congress
> *The New York Times*, February 19, 1978

Proofread EVERYTHING, dummy!

> Thomas "Wayne" Brazell
> U. S. Army Materiel Command
> Training session, February 18, 1988

Incomprehensible jargon is the hallmark of a profession.

> Kingman Brewster, Jr.
> President, Yale University
> Speech, December 13, 1977

[Referring to baseball manager Leo Durocher's lectures:] They often made up in energy what they lacked in clarity.

> Heywood Hale Broun
> American sports journalist
> *Merriment*, 1979

Self-expression must pass into communication for its fulfillment.

> Pearl S. Buck, 1892–1973
> Pulitzer Prize author and
> Nobel laureate in literature
> In Hull, *The Writer's Book*

[Electronic Mail] advocates love to push the benefits of direct communication. Managers send and receive messages on a one-to-one basis. Now that secretaries don't fix their sloppy writing, the whole world wonders how they passed English 1A.

> David J. Buerger
> Santa Clara University
> *Infoworld*, February 22, 1988

[On communicating with foreign construction workers:] I learned to point in Spanish.

> James Burke
> Construction manager
> Remark, Kensington, Maryland, April 1988

Merchants know perfectly well what they mean when they express themselves, not in the language of lawyers, but in the language of courteous mercantile communication.

> Hugh McCalmont Cairns, 1819–1885
> English jurist
> *Shepherd* v. *Harrison* (1871)

Thoughts unexpressed may sometimes fall back dead; but God himself can't kill them when they're said.

> William McKendree Carleton, 1845–1912
> American poet
> *First Settler's Story*

The Orator persuades and carries all with him, he knows not how; the Rhetorician can prove that he ought to have persuaded that he carried all with him.

Thomas Carlyle, 1795–1881
Scottish essayist and historian
Characteristics

Take care of the sense, and the sounds will take care of themselves.

Lewis Carroll
(Charles Lutwidge Dodgson), 1832–1898
English mathematician and writer
Alice's Adventures in Wonderland

Words are what hold society together.

Stuart Chase, 1888–1985
Economist and founder, Consumers' Research
The Power of Words

This report, by its very length, defends itself against the risk of being read.

Winston Churchill, 1874–1965
English Prime Minister, author, and soldier
Remark at a Cabinet meeting

Too often the strong, silent man is silent because he does not know what to say.

Winston Churchill, 1874–1965
English Prime Minister, writer, and soldier
Speech, London School of Economics, 1924

Telecommunications enables companies to move information rather than people.

Eric K. Clemons
The Wharton School
and F. Warren McFarlan
Harvard Business School
Harvard Business Review, July/August 1986

That writer does the most who gives his reader the most knowledge, and takes from him the least time.

Charles Caleb Colton, c. 1780–1832
English cleric, sportsman, and wine merchant
Lacon

In language it is simply required that it conveys the meaning.

Confucius, c. 551–c. 479 B.C.
Chinese philosopher and teacher
Analects

Literature is the art of writing something that will be read twice and journalism what will be grasped at once.

Cyril Vernon Connolly, 1903–1974
English editor and critic
Enemies of Progress

Seeing then that we have such hope, we use great plainness of speech.

New Testament, II Corinthians 3:12

You can never over coordinate.

Cle Cox
Management Training Center, FAA
Meeting, August 15, 1987

It is much easier to be critical than to be correct.

Benjamin Disraeli, 1805–1881
English Prime Minister and novelist
Speech in Parliament, January 24, 1860

Many of our communications difficulties arise because we attack problems like James Thurber's dog Jeannie, who tried to get out of a garage by digging through the concrete floor with one paw. We constantly think other people will be persuaded by our intelligent presentation of the facts or the force of our convictions—when in reality these glance off them like raindrops off a car roof. We have totally ignored the need to prepare the ground for the emotional climate which will make people listen to us, trust us and be persuaded by us.

Eli Djeddah
Employment counselor
Now That I Know Which Side Is Up
(Ten Speed Press, 1976)

[Referring to joke telling in the office:] It's a fine line. You don't want to tell too many and seem like you're trying to act like one of the boys.

Theresa Dowling
Vice President, Hoare Govett
Forbes, November 2, 1987

The good time users among managers spend many more hours on their communications up than on their communications down. They tend to have good communications down, but they seem to obtain these as an effortless by-product. They do not talk to their subordinates about their problems, but they know how to make the subordinates talk about theirs.

Peter F. Drucker
Management consultant and writer
People and Performance
(Harper & Row, 1977)

Learn to write well, or not to write at all.

John Dryden, 1631–1700
English poet
Essay on Satire

Listen. Don't explain or justify.

William G. Dyer
Brigham Young University
Strategies for Managing Change
(Addison-Wesley, 1984)

Blessed is the man who, having nothing to say, abstains from giving in words evidence of the fact.

George Eliot (Marian Evans), 1819–1880
English novelist, essayist, and editor
Impressions of Theophrastus Such

When I attended church, and the man in the pulpit was all clay and not of tuneable metal, I thought that if men would avoid that general language and general manner in which they strive to hide all that is peculiar, and would say only what was uppermost in their own minds, after their own individual manner, every man would be interesting.

Ralph Waldo Emerson, 1803–1882
American essayist and poet
Journals

Eloquence is the power to translate a truth into language perfectly intelligible to the person to whom you speak.

Ralph Waldo Emerson, 1803–1882
American essayist and poet
Eloquence

The hearing ear is always found close to the speaking tongue.

Ralph Waldo Emerson, 1803–1882
American essayist and poet
English Traits

We all, in one way or another, send our little messages to the world.... And rarely do we send our messages consciously. We act out our state of being with nonverbal body language. We lift one eyebrow for relief. We rub our noses for puzzlement. We clasp our arms to isolate ourselves or to protect ourselves. We shrug our shoulders for indifference, wink one eye for intimacy, tap our fingers for impatience, slap our foreheads for forgetfulness. The gestures are numerous, and while some are deliberate.... [T]here are some, such as rubbing our noses for puzzlement or clasping our arms to protect ourselves, that are mostly unconscious.

Julius Fast
Psychologist
Body Language (Pocket Books, 1971)

Television has the power to transmit the experience itself.

Reuven Frank
President, NBC News
Television (PBS TV), February 15, 1988

It is the part of wisdom, particularly for judges, not to be victimized by words.

Felix Frankfurter, 1882–1965
U. S. Supreme Court Justice
Shapiro v. *United States* (1948)

The learned fool writes his nonsense in better language than the unlearned, but still 'tis nonsense.

Benjamin Franklin, 1706–1790
American printer and statesman
Prochnow, *The Toastmaster's Treasure Chest*
(Harper & Row, 1979)

[T]he most important element in establishing a happy, prosperous atmosphere was an insistence upon open, free, and honest communications up and down the ranks of our management structure.

Harold Geneen
CEO, IT&T
Managing (Doubleday, 1984)

Today practically anybdy, anywhere, can talk at any time of the day or night with anybody anywhere else.

Walter S. Gifford
President, AT&T
Speech to Chicago Chamber of Commerce, 1930
Quoted in E. M. Forster's *Commonplace Book*

When ideas fail, words come in very handy.

Johann Wolfgang von Goethe, 1749–1832
German poet and dramatist
Faust

Communicate unto the other guy that which you would want him to communicate unto you if your positions were reversed.

Aaron Goldman
CEO, The Macke Company
Sign given to all managers

How well we communicate is determined not by how well we say things but by how well we are understood.

Andrew S. Grove
CEO, Intel Corporation
One-On-One With Andy Grove
(G. P. Putnam's Sons, 1987)

The worse the news, the more effort should go into communicating it.

Andrew S. Grove
CEO, Intel Corp.
One-On-One With Andy Grove
(G. P. Putnam's Sons, 1987)

[T]he information most useful to me ... comes from quick, and often casual verbal exchanges. This usually reaches a manager much faster than anything written down. And usually the more timely the information is, the more valuable it is.

Andrew S. Grove
CEO, Intel Corp.
High Output Management
(Random House, 1983)

An energetic myth, a permanent motive to which the masses adhere and which the mass elaborates upon solidify vague conceptions into figures, notions into judgments and formulas; and though they may rarely create the language of history, they often create its legends and proverbs.

Friedrich Gundolf (Gundelfinger), 1880–1931
German writer and translator
Essays in Antiquity

Not knowing the question,
It was easy for him
To give the answer.

Dag Hammerskjöld, 1905–1961
Secretary-General of the United Nations
Markings

A social collectivity is patterned communicative behavior; communicative behavior does nor occur *within* a network of relationships but is that network.

Leonard C. Hawes
Quarterly Journal of Speech, December 1974

Spell well, if you can.

Lucy Hay, 1599–1660
English author and wit
Thoughts

Employees must be with Heath at least three years before they can answer the phone. The policy ensures that customers are greeted by someone who knows the ropes. It's had a very positive effect.

Janice Heath
President, Heath Electronic Manufacturing Co.
Inc. Magazine, August 1987

All propaganda has to be popular and has to accomodate itself to the comprehension of the least intelligent of those whom it seeks to reach.

Adolf Hitler, 1889–1945
Führer of the Third German Reich
Mein Kampf

Rudeness is the weak man's imitation of strength.

Eric Hoffer, 1902–1983
Writer, longshoreman, and critic
The Passionate State of Mind

No generalization is wholly true, not even this one.

Oliver Wendell Holmes, Jr., 1841–1935
U. S. Supreme Court Justice
Attributed

But words once spoke can never be recalled.

Horace, 65–8 B.C.
Roman poet
Ars Poetica

Crisis in dialogue occurs when the participants ... fail to really address each other but turn away defensively, each within himself, for the purposes of self-justification.

Reuel Howe
American theologian
The Miracle of Dialogue (Seabury, 1963)

The right to be heard does not automatically include the right to be taken seriously. To be taken seriously depends entirely upon what is being said.

Hubert Horatio Humphrey, 1911–1978
Vice President of the United States
Speech, University of Wisconsin at Madison,
August 23, 1965

When high words confuse the talk, low words will untangle it.

Jabo proverb

How forcible are [the] right words!

Old Testament, Job 6:25

Our ability is to hear all the chatter [of patients, physicians and health insurance companies] out there and come up with a clear focus.

David Jones
CEO, Humana Inc.
The Renewal Factor (Bantam, 1987)

Words are, of course, the most powerful drug used by mankind.

Rudyard Kipling, 1865–1936
Nobel laureate in literature (England)
Speech, February 14, 1923

Whenever possible, information should go directly from sender to receiver.

Donald L. Kirkpatrick
University of Wisconsin
How to Manage Change Effectively
(Josey-Bass, 1985)

To be able to really listen, one should abandon or put aside all prejudices.... When you are in a receptive state of mind, things can be easily understood.... But, unfortunately, most of us listen through a screen of resistance. We are screened with prejudices, whether religious or spiritual, psychological or scientific; or, with daily worries, desires, and fears. And with these fears for a screen, we listen. Therefore we listen really to our own noise, our own sound, not to what is being said.

Jiddu Krishnamurti, 1895–1986
Indian philosopher and writer
The First and Last Freedom (Harper, 1954)

Words fly, writings remain.
[*Litera scripta manet, verbum ut inane perit.*]

Latin proverb

Sometimes you have to be silent to be heard.

Stanislaw J. Lec
Polish writer and aphorist
Unkempt Thoughts (St. Martin's Press, 1962)

The finest eloquence is that which gets things done.

David Lloyd George, 1863–1945
British Prime Minister
Prochnow, *The Toastmaster's Treasure Chest*
(Harper & Row, 1979)

Every person seems to have a limited capacity to assimilate information, and if it is presented to him too rapidly and without adequate repetition, this capacity will be exceeded and communication will break down.

R. Duncan Luce
University of Pennsylvania
Developments in Mathematical Psychology
(The Free Press, 1960)

People don't read today; they flip.

John Lyons
Advertising and communications writer
The Best of Bohannin (radio program),
Mutual Broadcasting System, January 3, 1988

The object of oratory alone is not truth, but persuasion.

Thomas Babington Macaulay, 1800–1859
English historian and author
Essay on the Athenian Orators

Men are never so likely to settle a question rightly as when they discuss it freely.

Thomas Babington Macaulay, 1800–1859
English historian and author
Southey's Colloquies

It is a foolish thing to make a long preface to the history, and to be short in the story itself.

Apocrypha, II Maccabees 2:32

There is no quicker way for two executives to get out of touch with each other than to retire to the seclusion of their offices and write each other notes.

R. Alec Mackenzie
Management consultant
The Time Trap (McGraw-Hill, 1972)

A supervisor has to be able to talk sufficiently well at the level of those with whom he deals that they can understand him.

Milton M. Mandell
Management consultant
Leadership in the Office (AMACOM, 1963)

He who has ears to hear, let him hear.

New Testament, Mark 4:9

Communication is not just words, paint on canvas, math symbols or the equations and models of scientists; it is the interrelation of human beings trying to escape loneliness, trying to share experience, trying to implant ideas.

William M. Marsteller
Advertising executive
Mandell, *Advertising* (Prentice-Hall, 1984)

We were so internally focused that we lost touch [with customers].

Whitney McFarlin
President, Everest & Jennings International
Forbes, February 9, 1987

It is ironic, but true, that in this age of electronic communications, personal interaction is becoming more important than ever.

Regis McKenna
Marketing consultant and writer
The Regis Touch (Addison-Wesley, 1986)

Everyone is accustomed to watching television, being entertained and informed through the eyes. Therefore, use a slide carousel, flip charts, overhead projector, a tape recorder, even videotape.

Robert L. Montgomery
President, R. L. Montgomery & Associates
How to Sell in the Nineteen Eighties
(Prentice-Hall, 1980)

Anonymity and withdrawal are part of the CEO's inventory of power. The reverse of anonymity is visibility, which brings with it an expectation of accountability. If you want to operate without accountability, you make yourself difficult to reach.

Ralph Nader
Consumer advocate
Best of Business Quarterly, Winter 1986

Television can be a distorting mirror.

Edwin R. Newman
Journalist and author
Television (PBS TV), February 15, 1988

Everyone knows that listening is important to communication.... But few organizations listen carefully to their employees and their customers.

William Nickels
University of Maryland
Marketing Communication and Promotion
(John Wiley & Sons, 1984)

Many managers find themselves reading [all] this stuff coming into their in box in order to determine whether they ought to be reading it at all.

Frank Nunlist
Assistant Postmaster General
Mackenzie, *The Time Trap*
(McGraw-Hill, 1972)

[Referring to telephone conferences:] People act and respond more openly in a phone meeting than they would in memos or one-on-one meetings with their boss.

Ron Owens
Vice President, Houghton Mifflin
Administrative Management, September 1987

A communication style is a particular, distinctive, or characteristic mode, manner, or tone of expressing and responding.

R. Wayne Pace
Brigham Young University
Organizational Communication
(Prentice-Hall, 1983)

Ask yourself: How often are brute integrity and explicit communication worth the price of the listener's goodwill, openmindedness, and receptivity to change? Explicit communication is a cultural assumption; it is not a linguistic imperative. Skilled executives develop the ability to vary their language along the spectrum from explicitness to indirection depending on their reading of the other person and the situation.

Richard T. Pascale
Stanford University School of Business
and Anthony G. Athos
Harvard Business School
The Art of Japanese Management
(Simon & Schuster, 1981)

Man's great power of thinking, remembering, and communicating are responsible for the evolution of civilization.

Linus Pauling
Nobel laureate in chemistry and peace
To Live as Man (Fund for the Republic, 1965)

The chain of command is an inefficient communication system. Although my staff and I had our goals, tasks, and priorities well defined, large parts of the organization didn't know what was going on. Frequent, thorough, open communication to every employee is essential to get the word out and keep walls from building within the company. And while face-to-face communication is more effective than impersonal messages, it's a good idea to vary the medium and the message so that no one (including top management) relies too much on "traditional" channels of communication.

William H. Peace
Vice President, KRW Energy Systems, Inc.
Harvard Business Review, March/April 1986

Speak properly, and in as few Words as you can, but always *plainly;* for the End of Speech is not Ostentation, but to be understood.

William Penn, 1644–1718
Founder of Pennsylvania
Fruits of Solitude in Reflections and Maxims

If thou thinkest twice, before thou speakest once, *thou* wilt speak twice the better for it.

William Penn, 1644–1718
Founder of Pennsylvania
Fruits of Solitude in Reflections and Maxims

Written reports stifle creativity.

H. Ross Perot
Founder, Electronic Data Systems
Peters, *Thriving on Chaos* (Knopf, 1987)

Communication is everyone's panacea for everything.

Tom Peters
Business writer
Thriving on Chaos (Knopf, 1987)

People, including managers, do not live by pie charts alone—or by bar graphs or three inch statistical appendices to 300 page reports. People live, reason, and are moved by symbols and stories.

Tom Peters
Business writer
Thriving on Chaos (Knopf, 1987)

Rhetoric is the art of ruling the minds of men.

Plato, 427–327 B.C.
Greek philosopher and teacher
Plutarch, *The Parallel Lives: Pericles*

We know more than we can tell.

Michael Polanyi
Scientist and writer
The Tacit Dimension
(Doubleday/Anchor, 1966)

The first rule of style is to have something to say. The second rule of style is to control yourself when, by chance, you have two things to say; say first one, then the other, not both at the same time.

George Polya
Hungarian mathematician
How to Solve It

If you don't get the reader's attention in the first paragraph, the rest of your message is lost.

Public relations maxim

Care should be taken, not that the reader *may* understand, but that he *must* understand.

Quintilian, c. 35–c. 95
Roman rhetoric teacher and advocate
De institutione oratoria

[A] member of any organization is, in large measure, the kind of communicator that the organization compels him to be.

W. Charles Redding
Communications specialist
Business and Industrial Organization
(Harper & Row, 1964)

[General Eisenhower] and I didn't discuss politics or the campaign. Mostly we talked about painting and fishing. But what I remember most about the hour and a half I spent with him was the way he gave me all his attention. He was listening to me and talking to me, just as if he hadn't a care in the world, hadn't been through the trials of a political convention, wasn't on the brink of a presidential campaign.

Norman Rockwell
American artist
The Saturday Evening Post, April 2, 1960

Franklin [Delano Roosevelt] had a good way of simplifying things. He made people feel that he had a real understranding of things and they felt they had about the same understanding.

Eleanor Roosevelt, 1884–1962
American statesman and humanitarian
Interview, April 6, 1947

The exact words that you use are far less important than the energy, intensity and conviction with which you use them.

Jules Rose
Vice President, Sloan Supermarkets
Training session, July 1954

A rumor is an unverified assertion; as soon as you verify it, it is no longer a rumor. Gossip can be unverified or not, but it's always about people, whereas a rumor need not be about people. The grapevine is the information communications network that operates in an organizational setting.

Ralph L. Rosnow
Temple University
Rumor and Gossip

To communicate, put your thoughts in order; give them a purpose; use them to persuade, to instruct, to discover, to seduce.

William Safire
Columnist, *The New York Times*
Reader's Digest, December 1987

We are in the communications business, the business of conveying messages to the human brain. No man is wise enough to know which avenue to the brain is best. Therefore, the sensible idea is to make all avenues available for carrying the message—whether it be a message of religion, education, entertainment, news, or whatever information the instrumentalities can carry and deliver to human beings.

David Sarnoff, 1891–1971
Founder and President, RCA
Wisdom of Sarnoff and the World of RCA

Communication is the deep exchange of experience that brings the two parties to a full understanding of each other, including the understanding that they understand each other. People actually go out of their way to not communicate with people with whom they feel out of harmony.

Kenneth and Linda Schatz
Leadership and organization consultants
Managing by Influence (Prentice-Hall, 1986)

Against stupidity the very gods themselves struggle in vain.

Johann von Schiller, 1759–1805
German poet and playwright
The Maid of Orleans

As it becomes bigger, the tendency of a corporation is to create pockets of bureaucracy that love to write memorandums. I'm just not a memo writer. I like to look someone in the eye and say, "Let's talk."

Peter L. Scott
Chairman, Emhart Corp.
Sky, August 1, 1987

Conscious of mutual sincerity, by a sort of intellectual communication, through which individuals are led to understand each other better, perhaps, in delicate circumstances, than by words.

Walter Scott, 1771–1832
Scottish poet, novelist, and biographer
Woodstock

It is not the quantity, but the pertinence [of your words] that does the business.

Seneca, 4 B.C.–A.D. 65
Roman writer and rhetorician
Epistles to Lucilius

Therefore,—since brevity is the soul of wit,
And tediousness the limbs and outward flourishes,—
I will be brief.

William Shakespeare, 1564–1616
English dramatist and poet
Hamlet

It is the disease of not listening, the malady of not marking, that I am troubled withal.

William Shakespeare, 1564–1616
English dramatist and poet
King Henry IV

But men are men; the best sometimes forget.

William Shakespeare, 1564–1616
English dramatist and poet
Othello

Memos just don't move the heart and the soul.

> Ervin Shames
> General Foods Co.
> *Fortune,* September 28, 1987

[Referring to the office "grapevine":] With the rapidity of a burning powder train, information flows like magic out of the woodwork, past the water fountain, past the manager's door and the janitor's mop closet. As elusive as a summer zephyr, it filters through steel walls, bulkheads, or construction glass partitions, from the sub-basement to the rafters, from office boy to executive.... It carries good news and bad, fact as well as fancy, without discrimination. It cares nothing for reputation, nothing about civil rights; it will carve up and serve the big brass, the shop foreman, and the stenographer with fine impartiality.

> Joseph K. Shepard
> Journalist
> *Leadership in the Office* (AMACOM, 1963)

There is a significant distinction between the orator and the writer. The orator must be prepared to move a mass of men at once. The writer addresses himself to one man at a time.

> Stuart Pratt Sherman, 1881–1926
> American critic
> Zenker, *Mastering the Public Spotlight*
> (Dodd Mead, 1983)

Hurried speech is a form of deference.

> Earl Shorris
> Manager and writer
> *Power Sits at Another Table* (Fireside, 1986)

Whatever people think, is.

> Otis Singletary
> Chancellor, University of Kentucky,
> and Director, U. S. Job Corps
> Speech, Washington, D.C., January 1966

None love the messenger who brings bad news.

> Sophocles, c. 496–406 B.C.
> Greek dramatist
> *Antigone*

Bigger organizations spend too much time and overhead on internal communications.

> Jim Swiggett
> CEO, Kollmorgen Corp.
> *Inc. Magazine*, February 1987

There is nothing which cannot be perverted by being told badly.

> Terence, c. 190–159 B.C.
> Roman playwright
> *Phormio*

The ability to speak is a short cut to distinction. It puts a man in the limelight, raises him head and shoulders above the crowd, and the man who can speak acceptably is usually given credit for an ability out of all proportion to what he really possesses.

> Lowell Thomas, 1892–1981
> Radio broadcaster and journalist
> Introduction to Dale Carnegie's
> *How to Win Friends and Influence People*
> (Simon & Schuster, 1936)

We cannot ignore tone of voice or attitudes. These may be just as important as the words used.

> Maurice S. Trotter
> New York University
> *Supervisor's Handbook on Insubordination*
> (Bureau of National Affairs, 1967)

I never give 'em hell. I just tell the truth and they think it's hell.

> Harry S. Truman, 1884–1972
> Thirty-third President of the United States
> *Look*, April 3, 1956

A picture may instantly present what a book could set forth only in a hundred pages.

> Ivan Turgeniev, 1818–1883
> Russian novelist
> *Fathers and Sons*

It usually takes me more than three weeks to prepare a good impromptu speech.

> Mark Twain
> (Samuel Langhorne Clemens), 1835–1910
> American author and riverboat captain
> Prochnow, *The Toastmaster's Treasure Chest*
> (Harper & Row, 1979)

I like the way you always manage to state the obvious with a sense of real discovery.

> Gore Vidal
> American writer
> *The Best Man*

A great many people think that polysyllables are a sign of intelligence.

> Barbara Walters
> TV reporter and commentator
> *How to Talk with Practically Anybody About Practically Anything* (Dell, 1971)

[S]ubmit your sentiments with diffidence. A dictorial Stile, though it may carry conviction, is always accompanied with disgust.

> George Washington, 1732–1799
> First President of the United States
> Letter to Bushrod Washington,
> November 10, 1787

We tell them [salesmen] exactly what to say, when to say it, and how to say it.

> Ben Watkins
> New England Sales Manager, Cole & Wiley
> Tosi and Carroll, *Management* (Wiley, 1976)

You don't hear things that are bad about your company unless you ask. It is easy to hear good tidings, but you have to scratch to get the bad news.

> Thomas J. Watson, Jr.
> CEO, IBM, and U. S. Ambassador to Russia
> *Fortune*, 1987

Ask any anthropologist who has worked in deepest, darkest corporate America: people at cross-purposes are probably struggling to cross cultural boundaries. Members of each group are trying to get past their own cultural mind-set and preconceptions, all the while seeming to defend them. At the same time, they are seeking admission to the other group's belief system and perceptions of reality.

> Gerald M. and Daniella Weinberg
> Computer consultants and writers
> *Journal of Information Systems Management*,
> Winter 1985

Humans, if they are machines at all, are vastly general-purpose machines and ... they understand communications couched in natural languages (e.g. English) that lack, by very far, the precision and unambiguousness of ordinary programming languages.

> Joseph Weizenbaum
> American computer scientist
> *Computer Power and Human Reason*
> (Penguin, 1984)

Seek simplicity, and distrust it.

> Alfred North Whitehead, 1861–1947
> English mathematician and philosopher
> *Science and the Modern World*

Whenever one has anything unpleasant to say, one should always be quite candid.

> Oscar Wilde, 1854–1900
> Irish poet, wit, and dramatist
> Prochnow, *The Toastmaster's Treasure Chest*
> (Harper & Row, 1979)

The CFO was a disaster. After 17 years he was still telling the CEO what he thought the CEO wanted to hear.

Q. T. Wiles
Turnaround Operations consultant
Inc. Magazine, February 1988

Everything that can be thought at all can be thought clearly. Everything that can be said can be said clearly.

Ludwig Wittgenstein, 1889–1951
Austrian philosopher
Tractatus Logico-Philosophicus

Anyone who isn't confused here doesn't really understand what's going on.

Nigel Wrench
English journalist and commentator
Belfastman

I wish I had some way to make a bridge from man to man.... Man is all we've got.

Richard Wright, 1908–1960
American author
The Outsider

Talk too much and you talk about yourself.

Yiddish proverb

Extroverts stand a far better chance of capturing and holding a listener's attention.

Arnold Zenker
Managing Director, Arnold Zenker Associates
Mastering the Public Spotlight
(Dodd Mead, 1983)

One should address another person in language which [the other person] understands: He should not use a literary form of speech to an uneducated person, nor vulgar [common] language to the learned.

The Zohar

The most important words in the English language:

5 most important words: *I am proud of you*!
4 most important words: *What is your opinion*?
3 most important words: *If you please.*
2 most important words: *Thank you.*
1 most important word: *You.*

Anonymous manager
Quoted by Kirkpatrick,
How to Manage Change Effectively
(Josey-Bass, 1985)

A closed mouth gathers no feet.

Anonymous

ESCHEW OBFUSCATION!

Anonymous

5

Competitiveness

*There's no column on the scorecard
headed 'remarks.'*

We were fairly arrogant, until we realized the Japanese were selling quality products for what it cost us to make them.

> Paul A. Allaire
> President, Xerox
> *The New York Times*, February 21, 1988

Suppose that a football reformer observed the obvious fact that the object of the game is to make touchdowns. This would lead immediately to the important discovery that if the two teams would only cooperate, hundreds of touchdowns could be made in a game, while only one or two of them are made when each opposes the other.

> Thurman Wesley Arnold, 1891–1969
> American attorney, jurist, and writer
> *The Folklore of Capitalism*

The principle of competition is, as Hesiod pointed out long ago, built into the very roots of the world; there is something in the nature of things that calls for a real victory and a real defeat.

> Irving Babbitt, 1865–1933
> Harvard University
> *Democracy and Leadership*

One of the only ways to compete is with technology.

> John H. Beakes
> Cofounder, RWD Technologies
> *The Washington Post*, March 14, 1988

The toughest thing about success is that you've got to keep on being a success.

> Irving Berlin, 1888–1988
> American songwriter
> *Theatre Arts*, February 1958

No man loves to get beat, but it's better to get beat than to be wrong.

Josh Billings
(Henry Wheeler Shaw), 1818–1885
American writer and auctioneer
Josh Billings: His Book

Formerly when great fortunes were only made in war, war was a business; but now when great fortunes are only made by business, business is war.

Christian N. Bovee, 1820–1904
Author and editor
The New Dictionary of Thoughts, 1957

Undoubtedly competition involves waste. What human activity does not?.... There are wastes of competition which do not develop, but kill. These the law can and should eliminate, by regulating competition.

Louis Dembitz Brandeis, 1856–1941
U. S. Supreme Court Justice
In Fraenkel, *The Curse of Bigness*

No system of regulation can safely be substituted for the operation of individual liberty as expressed in competition.

Louis Dembitz Brandeis, 1856–1941
U. S. Supreme Court Justice
Mason, *Brandeis: A Free Man's Life*

Competition is a task master that protects the public. But there are penalties as well as rewards in a competitive society.... Business must accept the penalties of failure.

Courtney C. Brown
Columbia University School of Business
Dun's Review, August 1979

Everybody's got a little competitive spirit in them.

Stephen Burns
Machine Operator, Tenneco
Tosi and Carroll, *Management* (Wiley, 1976)

The company with the second best organization ends up second place in the market.

D. Wayne Calloway
CEO, PepsiCo.
Harvard Business Review,
September/October 1987

I have to convince the 160,000 people who work for Peugeot about how terrifying the competition is.... We will just have to be a little faster.

Jacques Calvert
Chairman, Peugeot Automobile Group (France)
The New York Times, March 20, 1988

Now *here*, you see, it takes all the running *you* can do to keep in the same place. If you want to get somewhere else, you must run at least twice as fast as that.

Lewis Carroll
(Charles Lutwidge Dodgson), 1832–1898
English mathematician and writer
Alice's Adventures in Wonderland

In my view he who goes ahead is always the one who wins.

Catherine II ("The Great"), 1729–1796
Empress of Russia
Correspondence avec le Baron F. M. Grimm

In war you do not have to be nice—you only have to be right.

Winston Churchill, 1874–1965
English Prime Minister, writer, and soldier
Quoted in Halle, *Irrepressible Churchill*

Thou shalt not covet; but tradition
Approves all forms of competition.

Arthur Hugh Clough, 1819–1861
English poet and educator
The Latest Decalogue

The most important thing in the Olympic Games is not winning but taking part.... The essential thing in life is not conquering but fighting well.

> Pierre de Coubertin, 1863–1937
> First President,
> International Olympic Committee
> Speech, London, July 24, 1908

All things being equal, the career person who is going to get ahead is not going to get ahead because he does great work. That is a given. We expect that. What will get him ahead is the edge he creates.

> Jeffrey P. Davidson
> Marketing consultant
> *The Washington Post*, May 20, 1985

Man is not the creature of circumstances. Circumstances are the creatures of men.

> Benjamin Disraeli, 1805–1881
> English Prime Minister and novelist
> *Vivian Grey*

To vie is not to rival.

> Benjamin Disraeli, 1804–1881
> English Prime Minister and novelist
> *The Young Duke*

The way to conquer the foreign artisan, is, not to kill him, but to beat his work.

> Ralph Waldo Emerson, 1803–1882
> American essayist and poet
> *Worship*

[The most successful companies at maintaining their competitive edge are] ... close to ruthless in cannibalizing their current products and processes just when they are the most lucrative and begin the search again,

over and over. The best abandon the skills and products that have bought them success.

> Dick Foster
> Director, McKinsey & Co.
> Peters, *Thriving on Chaos* (Knopf, 1987)

It is a silly game where nobody wins.

> Thomas Fuller, 1608–1661
> Chaplain in extraordinary to Charles II
> *Gnomologia*

There is a persistent and never–ending competition between what is relevant and what is merely acceptable. In this competition, while a strategic advantage lies with what exists, all tactical advantage is with the acceptable. Audiences of all kinds most applaud what they like best.

> John Kenneth Galbraith
> Economist and diplomat
> *The Affluent Society* (Houghton Mifflin, 1958)

Our [America's] competitors have learned how to do what we invented *better* and *faster* than we do.

> Stanley C. Gault
> CEO, Rubbermaid, Inc.
> Speech, New York City, October 29, 1987

In the business world, everyone is always working at legitimate cross purposes, governed by self interest.

> Harold Geneen
> CEO, IT&T
> *Managing* (Doubleday, 1984)

It is not sufficient that I succeed—all others must fail.

> Genghis Khan, 1162–1227
> Mongol conqueror
> Quoted in *The New York Times*,
> February 28, 1988

The ability to learn faster than your competitors may be the only sustainable competitive advantage.

Arie P. de Geus
Head of Planning, Royal Dutch/Shell
Harvard Business Review, March/April 1988

You must either conquer and rule or serve and lose, suffer or triumph, be the anvil or the hammer.

Johann Wolfgang von Goethe, 1749–1832
German poet and dramatist
Der Gross-Cophta

Who is a lion in his words,
Is ofttimes in his deeds a hare.

Carlo Goldoni, 1707–1792
Italian dramatist
La Pelarina

You may fight to the death for something in which you truly believe, but keep such commitments to a bare minimum.

Albert A. Grant
President, American Society of Civil Engineers
Speech, Washington, D. C., May 30, 1988

Our technological standing will continue to decline without the discoveries that come only from basic research.

Phillip A. Griffiths
Provost, Duke University
High Technology, August 1987

"America's competiveness is declining—largely because of the performance of U.S. managers." Almost 90% [of the survey respondents] place the burden on the shoulders of U.S. management.

Survey of readers
Harvard Business Review,
September/October 1987

Planning and competition can be combined only by planning for competition, but not by planning against competition.

Friedrich A. Hayek
Nobel laureate in economics
The Road to Serfdom
(University of Chicago, 1944)

Don't look for the secrets of Japanese management: look for Japan's use of Western methods to achieve Western-style objectives—and copy that.

Robert Heller
Editor, *Management Today*
The Supermanagers (Dutton, 1984)

Concentrate your strength against your competitor's relative weakness.

Bruce Henderson
CEO, Boston Consulting Group, Inc.
Henderson on Corporate Strategy (Abt, 1979)

Good businessmen should know their competitors.... It is absolutely essential to know the character, attitudes, motives and habitual behavior of a competitor if you wish to have ... advantage.

Bruce Henderson
CEO, Boston Consulting Group, Inc.
Henderson on Corporate Strategy (Abt, 1979)

Competition and cooperation go hand in hand in all real-life situations. Otherwise, conflict could only end in extermination of the competitor. There is a point in all situations of conflict where both parties gain more or lose less from peace than they can hope to gain from any foreseeable victory. Beyond that point cooperation is more profitable than conflict.

Bruce Henderson
CEO, Boston Consulting Group, Inc.
Henderson on Corporate Strategy (Abt, 1979)

There is no doubt that the most competitive manufacturers are those who have learned to produce more with fewer people.

Edward L. Hennessy, Jr.
Chairman, Allied Signal, Inc.
The New York Times, March 13, 1988

At the game's end we shall see who gains.

George Herbert, 1593–1633
English clergyman and poet
Jacula Prudentum

Danger itself is the best remedy for danger.

George Herbert, 1593–1633
English clergyman and poet
Jacula Prudentum

Our management has to be superior to that of for-profit organizations. We have little margin for error.

Frances Hesselbein
Executive Director, Girl Scouts U.S.A.
Management, April 1987

He who fails to act, must succumb. There is only one alternative: either you must be a hammer, or you will be made into an anvil.

Paul von Hindenburg, 1847–1934
General, statesman, and President of Germany
Ybarra, *Hindenburg*

Seize the day and put the least possible trust in tomorrow.
[*Carpe diem quam minimum credula a postero.*]

Horace, 65–8 B.C.
Roman poet and satirist
Ars Poetica

Man ... is simply the most formidable of all the beasts of prey, and, indeed, the only one that preys systematically on its own species.

William James, 1842–1910
American psychologist
Remarks at Peace Banquet, October 7, 1904

We've come a third of the way to regaining competitiveness by slashing costs and improving productivity, but clearly we have not done enough.

Jerry J. Jasinowski
Senior Vice President,
National Association of Manufacturers
The New York Times, February 21, 1988

If you have run with footmen and they have wearied you, then how can you contend with horses?

Old Testament, Jeremiah 12:5

Your levellers wish to level *down* as far as themselves; but they cannot bear levelling *up* to themselves.

Samuel Johnson, 1709–1784
English lexicographer and critic
Boswell's Life of Dr. Johnson

High pay does not equal good service, and, as McDonald's has shown, low pay need not result in poor service.... High-quality service depends on high-quality management. If U.S. providers fail to learn this lesson, they should not be surprised if Americans have accounts at Japanese banks, fly Singapore Airlines or eat in French-owned restaurants.

Robert E. Kelley
Carnegie-Mellon University
The Wall Street Journal, October 12, 1987

When times get tough, it just gets down to who can outdo the other fellow.

> W. Duke Kimbrell
> CEO, Parkdale Mills
> *Forbes*, November 2, 1987

We cut each others' throats—almost.... But it's not an underhanded, dog-eat-dog environment.

> Lawrence Kichen
> Chairman, Lockheed
> *High Technology Business,* April 1988

Contrary to what you may think, your company will be a lot more productive if you refuse to tolerate competition among your employees.

> Alfie Kohn
> Management lecturer and author
> *No Contest: The Case Against Competition*
> (Houghton Mifflin, 1987)

There's no column on the scorecard headed "remarks."

> Sidney Lansburgh, Jr.
> Financier and developer
> *The Baltimore Evening Sun*, March 22, 1979

He who limps is still walking.

> Stanislaw J. Lec
> Polish writer and aphorist
> *Unkempt Thoughts* (St. Martin's Press, 1962)

The duPonts and Cornings have succeeded not primarily because of their product or research orientation but because they have been thoroughly customer-oriented also. It is constant watchfulness for opportunities to apply their technical know-how to the creation of customer-satisfying uses which accounts for their prodigious output of successful new products.

> Theodore Levitt
> Editor, *Harvard Business Review*
> *HBR*, September/October 1975

You are ambitious, which, within reasonable bounds, does good rather than harm.

> Abraham Lincoln, 1809–1865
> Sixteenth President of the United States
> Letter to General Joseph Hooker,
> January 26, 1863

Winning isn't everything, but wanting to win is.

> Vince Lombardi, 1913–1970
> Coach, New York Giants
> *Esquire*, November 1962

Not failure, but low aim, is crime.

> James Russell Lowell, 1819–1891
> Professor of Poetry, Harvard University, and
> U. S. Ambassador to Spain and England
> *For an Autograph*

In the land of the blind the one-eyed man is king.

> Niccolò Machiavelli, 1469–1527
> Florentine statesman and philosopher
> *La Mandragola*

The battle of competition is fought by the cheapening of commodities.

> Karl Marx, 1818–1883
> German political philosopher
> *Capital*

Young boys often play "king of the hill," where one child physically overcomes the others to get to the top. His reward? The others try to push him off.

Jinx Milea
University of Southern California
and Pauline Lyttle
President, Operational Politics, Inc.
Why Jenny Can't Lead, 1986

He who knows only his own side of the case, knows little of that.

John Stuart Mill, 1806–1873
English philosopher and economist
On Liberty

When you win, nothing hurts.

Joe Namath
Professional football player
The Official MBA Handbook of Great Business Quotations (Simon & Schuster, 1984)

Show me a good loser and I'll show you a loser.

Wallace "Chief" Newman
Football coach, Whittier College
The Memoirs of Richard Nixon

When you lose get mad—but get mad at yourself, not your opponent.

Wallace "Chief" Newman
Football coach, Whittier College
The Memoirs of Richard Nixon

A man is not finished when he's defeated; he's finished when he quits.

Richard Milhous Nixon
Thirty-seventh President of the United States
Remark to reporters, November 11, 1960

I don't compete with other discus throwers. I compete with my own history.

Al Oerter
Olympic discus thrower
Garfield, *Peak Performers (*Avon, 1986)

Without competitors there would be no need for strategy.

Kenichi Ohmae
The Mind of the Strategist
(McGraw-Hill, 1982)

Whoever is winning at the moment will always seem to be invincible.

George Orwell (Eric Blair), 1903–1950
English novelist, essayist, and critic
Shooting an Elephant

When a society is perishing ... recall it to the principles from which it sprung.

Pope Leo XIII (Giacchino Pecci), 1810–1903
Encyclical Letter on Labor,
May 15, 1891

In the private or public sector, in big buisness or small, we observe that there are only two ways to create and sustain superior performance over the long haul. First, take exceptional care of your customers ... via superior service and superior quality. Second, constantly innovate. That's it. There are no alternatives in achieving long-term superior performance, or sustaining strategic competitive advantage.

Tom Peters and Nancy Austin
Management consultants and writers
A Passion for Excellence
(Random House, 1985)

We must compete in new ways if we are to prosper.

Thomas G. Plaskett
CEO, Pan Am
Telex to all employees, January 1988

Even a nod from a person who is esteemed is of more force than a thousand arguments or studied sentences from others.

> Plutarch, c. 46–c. 120
> Greek biographer and philosopher
> *The Parallel Lives: Phocion*

There is no greater proof of the abilities of a general than to investigate, with the utmost care, into the character and natural abilities of his opponent.

> Polybius, c. 202–120 B.C.
> Greek historian
> *History*

'Tis a hard winter when one wolf eats another.

> Barber, *The Book of 1000 Proverbs*, 1876

Two dogs strive for a bone, and the third runs away with it.

> Barber, *The Book of 1000 Proverbs*, 1876

Compete not with evil-doers.

> Old Testament, Psalms 37:1

Free enterprise is a rough and competitive game. It is a hell of a lot better than a government monopoly.

> Ronald Wilson Reagan
> Fortieth President of the United States
> Speech to the
> National Association of Manufacturers,
> New York, December 8, 1972

The industries in which the United States can retain a competitive edge will be based not on huge volume and standardization, but on producing relatively smaller batches of more specialized, higher-valued products—goods that are precision engineered, that are custom-tailored to serve individual markets, or that embody rapidly evolving technologies. Such

products will be found in high-value segments of more traditional industries (speciality steel and chemicals, computer-controlled machine tools, advanced automobile compolnents) as well as in new high-technology industries (semiconductors, fiber optics, lasers, biotechnology, and robotics).

> Robert B. Reich
> JFK School of Government, Harvard University
> *The Next American Frontier*, 1983

"Rejoice not at thine enemy's fall"—but don't pick him up either.

> Religious proverb

I don't meet competition. I crush it.

> Charles Revson
> Founder, Revlon, Inc.
> *Time*, June 16, 1958

Although we feel very strongly about competitive spirit, we feel it should be vented against our real competition outside, not within, the company.

> Francis P. Rich, Jr.
> President, Action Equipment Co.
> *Inc. Magazine*, February 1988

There is great ability in knowing how to conceal one's ability.

> François de La Rochefoucauld, 1613–1680
> French politician, writer, and philanthropist
> *Maxims*

Far and away the best prize that life offers is the chance to work hard at work worth doing.

> Theodore Roosevelt, 1858–1919
> Twenty-sixth President of the United States
> Labor Day speech, Syracuse, N.Y., 1903

In life as in a football game, the principle to follow is: Hit the line hard.

> Theodore Roosevelt, 1858–1919
> Twenty-sixth President of the United States
> *The Strenuous Life*

None ever got ahead of me except the man of one task.

> Azariah Rossi, 1513–1578
> Italian physician and religious writer
> *Light of the Eyes*

It may be that the race is not always to the swift, nor the battle to the strong—but that's the way to bet.

> Alfred Damon Runyon, 1880–1946
> American journalist and writer
> Quoted by Allen, *More Than Somewhat*

Government and co-operation are in all things the law of life; anarchy and competition the laws of death.

> John Ruskin, 1819–1900
> English art critic and historian
> *Unto This Last*

The thrill, believe me, is as much in the battle as in the victory.

> David Sarnoff, 1891–1971
> Founder and President, RCA
> *Youth in a Changing World*, June 12, 1954

The minute you start talking about what you're going to do if you lose, you have lost.

> George Schultz
> U. S. Secretary of State
> *This Week* (TV program), January 21, 1988

The breakfast of champions is not cereal, it's the opposition.

> Nick Seitz
> Editor, *Golf Digest*, and sports commentator
> *Best Sports Stories of 1978*

Fight for your highest attainable aim
But never put up resistance in vain.

> Hans Selye
> University of Montreal
> *The Stress of Life* (McGraw-Hill, 1976)

Do as adversaries in law, strive mightily,
But eat and drink as friends.

> William Shakespeare, 1564–1616
> English dramatist and poet
> *Taming of the Shrew*

Two stars keep not their motion in one sphere.

> William Shakespeare, 1564–1616
> English dramatist and poet
> *King Henry IV*

There's no such sport, as sport by sport
o'erthrown;
To make theirs ours, and ours
none but our own.

> William Shakespeare, 1564–1616
> English dramatist and poet
> *Love's Labour Lost*

Advantage is a better soldier than rashness.

> William Shakespeare, 1564–1616
> English dramatist and poet
> *King Henry V*

Many managers set out to increase the intensity of competition among the striving equals below them.... They do so believing, as Stalin said he did, that efficiency would be improved and skills would be heightened.... [M]any businessmen use this tactic of totalitarianism in the sincere belief that it will produce better results than a co-operative spirit.

Earl Shorris
Manager and writer
The Oppressed Middle
(Anchor/Doubleday, 1981)

Cutting [costs and personnel] isn't the answer—that can be done by stupid arbitrary judgements. Competitive companies must understand how to motivate people to be productive, and that is hard as hell.

Andrew C. Sigler
Chairman, Champion International, Inc.
The New York Times, February 21, 1988

Treating a competitor's brand as if it didn't exist doesn't mean your customers will do the same.

Margie Smith
Senior Vice President, Mark Ponton Corp.
Working Woman, December 1987

The best thing the Japanese did for us, they made us work closer with our own people, and the other way around, too. It made our people understand. The guy in Flint, he thought his competition was over in Dearborn. His competition isn't Dearborn. His competition is sitting over there in Toyota City, and now they realize that, and maybe they didn't before.

Roger B. Smith
CEO, General Motors Corp.
The Washington Post, October 11, 1987

A wise player ought to accept his throws and score them, not bewail his luck.

Sophocles, c. 496–406 B.C.
Greek tragic playwright
Fragments

He loses not, nor wins, who never jousts.

Gaspara Stampa, d. 1554
Italian poet
Rime

Those who endeavour to excel all, are at least sure of excelling a great many.

Philip Dormer Stanhope, 1694–1773
English Secretary of State
Letters of Lord Chesterfield to His Son

We don't do anything on the basis of what the competition is doing.

Richard G. Starmann
Senior Vice President, McDonald's
The New York Times, March 13, 1988

Business organizations have certain characteristics—strengths—which make them uniquely adapted to carry out their tasks. Conversely, they have other features—weaknesses—which inhibit their abilities to fulfill their purposes. Managers who hope to accomplish their tasks are forced to evaluate the strengths and weaknesses of the organization.

Howard H. Stevenson
Sloan Management Review, Spring 1976

Free competition means a free and open market among both buyers and sellers for the sale and distribution of commodities.

Harlan F. Stone, 1872–1946
U. S. Supreme Court Justice
Maple Floors Manufacturers Association
v. *U. S.* (1924)

The reason America is not competitive is not because of a disadvantage in direct costs such as labor or materials.... What's outrageous are the overhead costs.

Paul Strassmann
Former Vice President, Xerox
Inc. Magazine, March 1988

I like to win.

L. Margarita Tarabay
Owner, Aztech Industrial Supply Corp.
Hispanic Business, August 1987

Every profession is becoming more competitive, and that's a good thing. We all do a better job. That's why we're always experimenting with new methods.

John Templeton
Investment counselor and market analyst
Forbes, January 25, 1988

If we had to point to one single notion which is calculated to damage our industrial performance, to prevent us from competing effectively in the world and ultimately to undermine the basis of a free and diverse society, it is the idea that profit is somehow wrong.

Margaret Thatcher
English Prime Minister
Speech, May 4, 1976

A competitive world has two possibilities for you. You can lose. Or, if you want to win, you can change.

Lester C. Thurow
Dean, Sloan School of Management, M. I. T.
60 Minutes (CBS TV), February 7, 1988

The trouble with the rat race is that even if you win, you're still a rat.

Lily Tomlin
Comedienne and actress
Omni, April 1988

Business is war!

Jack Tramiel
Former CEO, Commodore Computers
Garfield, *Peak Performers* (Avon, 1986)

[Referring to predictions that he would lose by a landslide to Thomas Dewey:] It isn't important who is ahead at one time or another in either an election or a horse race. It's the horse that comes in first at the finish that counts.

Harry S. Truman, 1884–1972
Thirty-third President of the United States
Speech, October 17, 1948

It is not true that equality is a law of nature. Nature has no equality. Its sovereign law is subordination and dependence.

Marquis de Vauvenargues, 1715–1747
French soldier and moralist
Reflections and Maxims

I do not think that winning is the most important thing. I think winning is the only thing.

Bill Veeck
President, Chicago White Sox
Attributed

Success nourished them; they seemed to be able, and so they were able.

Virgil, 70–19 B.C.
Roman poet
Aeneid

Women are freer to express their competitiveness now. Women's competitiveness in the past has been limited to competing for men, but those days are over. It's no longer a totally negative thing.

Judy Wenning
Social worker and women's sports advocate
The Los Angeles Times, April 23, 1974

He only is exempt from failures who makes no efforts.

Richard Whatley, 1787–1863
Archbishop of Dublin and Professor of
Political Economy, Oxford University
Introductory Lectures on Political Economy

Whatever women do they must do twice as well as men to be thought half as good. Luckily this is not difficult.

> Charlotte Whitton, 1896–1975
> Mayor of Ottawa (Canada)
> Sign in office

As long as the machine has beaten the man who programmed it in checkers, it will in some sense compete with human intelligence over a limited scope.

> Norbert Wiener, 1894–1964
> Pioneer computer scientist
> Greenberger, *Management and the Computer of the Future* (M. I. T., 1962)

Nothing succeeds like excess.

> Oscar Wilde, 1854–1900
> Irish poet, playwright, and novelist
> *A Woman of No Importance*

While competition cannot be created by statutory enactment, it can in large measure be revived by changing the laws and forbiding the practices that killed it.

> Woodrow Wilson, 1856–1924
> Twenty-eighth President of the United States
> Speech, August 7, 1912

He got there first, damn him! Wouldn't that give you a pain in the neck!

> P. G. Wodehouse, 1881–1975
> English humorous writer
> *Leave it to Psmyth*

Adam Smith was wrong. Individuals working for their own best interests are not good for the whole country. American management and labor are only hurting each other and themselves by adopting adversarial roles. While Americans are fighting with each other, the rest of the world will walk right by us economically.

> Anonymous respondent
> Competitiveness Survey
> *Harvard Business Review*,
> September/October 1987

On a country hike, two city kids saw a grizzly bear. One kid sat down to put on a pair of sneakers and make ready to run. The other kid said, scoffing, "I've read all there is to read about grizzly bears, and no man alive can outrun a grizzly." The first kid looked up and said, "I don't care about outrunning the bear. I just want to outrun you!"

> Anonymous (but probably from Brooklyn)

If your enemy surrenders, it's only because he couldn't kill you.

> Anonymous sign on a Pentagon office door

6

Computers & Robots

Control over computing belongs with users.

Control over computing belongs with users.

Brandt Allen
University of Virginia
Harvard Business Review,
January/February 1987

If arithmetical skill is the measure of intelligence, then computers have been more intelligent than all human beings all along. If the ability to play chess is the measure, then there are computers now in existence that are more intelligent than any but a very few human beings. However, if insight, intuition, creativity, the ability to view a problem as a whole and guess the answer by the "feel" of the situation, is a measure of intelligence, computers are very unintelligent indeed. Nor can we see right now how this deficiency in computers can be easily remedied, since human beings cannot program a computer to be intutitive or creative for the very good reason that we do not know what we ourselves do when we exercise these qualities.

Isaac Asimov
Science writer and biochemist
Machines that Think
(Holt, Rinehart and Winston, 1983)

In science fiction, the robot is created in full bloom. In real life, however, what we now call the "industrial robot" is little more than a complex and computerized arm, bearing no resemblance to a human being. It is, therefore, much more easily visualized as a complex machine than as a pseudoperson, and is feared for its effect on jobs rather than for its blasphemous imitation of ourselves.

Isaac Asimov
Science writer and biochemist
Machines that Think
(Holt, Rinehart and Winston, 1983)

I do not fear computers. I fear the lack of them.

Isaac Asimov
Science writer and biochemist
Rowes, *The Book of Quotes* (Dutton, 1979)

The Three Laws of Robotics:

1) A robot may not injure a human being or, through inaction, allow a human being to come to harm.

2) A robot must obey orders given to it by a human being except where such orders would conflict with the First Law.

3) A robot must protect its own existence as long as such protection does not conflict with the First or Second Law.

> Isaac Asimov
> Science writer and biochemist
> *I, Robot* (Doubleday, 1950)

Supercomputers are as significant to pioneering research today as calculus was to Newton.

> Ron Bailey
> Chief,
> Numerical Aerodynamic Simulation Program,
> NASA Ames Research Center
> *Time*, March 28, 1988

A tool is but the extension of a man's hand, and a machine is but a complex tool. And he that invents a machine augments the power of a man and the well-being of mankind.

> Henry Ward Beecher, 1813–1887
> American preacher and lecturer
> *Proverbs from Plymouth Pulpit*

The factory of the future will have only two employees, a man and a dog. The man will be there to feed the dog. The dog will be there to keep the man from touching the equipment.

> Warren G. Bennis
> President, University of Cincinnati
> University of Maryland symposium,
> January 21, 1988

It has become clear not only that the number of neurons in the brain is very much larger than the number of components in a computer but also that the basic principles of organization must be very different. A computer is constructed according to a precise predetermined plan ... [and] exhibits very little "redundancy" [in memory].... On the other hand ... there is considerable redundancy in the brain.... [N]eurons are not connected together according to a rigorous wiring diagram.... [I]t is quite likely that most of the connections among the neurons in the brain develop at random.

> Jeremy Bernstein
> Physicist and writer
> *The Analytical Engine* (Random House, 1963)

The computer is in some ways a grand machine in the Western mechanical-dynamic tradition and in other ways a tool-in-hand from the ancient craft tradition.... A machine is characterized by sustained, autonomous action.... A tool, unlike a machine, is not self-sufficient or autonomous in action. It requires the skill of a craftsman and, when handled with skill, permits him to reshape the world in his way.... However, the computer is not really a tool-in-hand; it is designed to extend the human brain rather than the hand, to allow the manipulation of mathematical and logical symbols at high speed. Yet is can be used with a kind of mental dexterity and reminds us of the craftsman's hand.

> David J. Bolter
> American computer scientist
> *Turing's Man*
> (University of North Carolina Press, 1984)

Any sufficiently advanced technology is indistinguishable from magic.

> Arthur C. Clarke
> English science fiction writer and scientist
> Peers, *1,001 Logical Laws* (Doubleday, 1979)

[Functional managers] must participate actively in the development of the computer system they will be using, just as you would work along with an architect to build a new house. If you tell the architect to call you when the house is completed and then walk away, you aren't going to be very pleased with the results. You might not even live in it.

Joseph F. Clayworth
Physicians Association of Clackamas County
Harvard Business Review,
November/December 1986

"Labor saving" means more work.

Ruth Schwartz Cowan
State University of New York at Stony Brook
American Heritage of Invention and Technology
(American Heritage, 1987)

Few companies that installed computers to reduce the employment of clerks have realized their expectations.... [T]hey now need more, and more expensive, clerks even though they call them "operators" or "programmers."

Peter F. Drucker
Management consultant
Management in Turbulent Times
(Harper & Row, 1980)

If you look at the introduction of railroads, automobiles, air travel, escalators, elevators—all the ways in which technology touches people's lives have been associated with both with transient anxiety-fear reactions, and with real phobic reactions. What happens in the population is that as the technology becomes more widely experienced, the fears tend to go away and one is left with a residual phobic category.

Robert DuPont
Washington Center for Behavioral Medicine
The Washington Post, December 29, 1985

Computers certainly contributed in a logistical way to making the sheer volume and speed of the [1987 stock market] fall possible.... In a more fundamental way ... computers led people to focus too much on the numbers and not enough on the things that computers can't

yet measure—quality of management, of product, of financial soundness.

Esther Dyson
Editor and publisher, *Release 1.0*
Forbes, November 30, 1987

[Referring to "Expert Systems" software's ability to make business and management decisions:] Not genius. Consistency.

Esther Dyson
Editor and publisher, *Release 1.0*
Forbes, November 2, 1987

A computer won't clean up the errors in your manual of procedures.

Sheila M. Eby
Business writer
*Inc. Magazine's Guide to
Small Business Success*, 1987

A computer will not make a good manager out of a bad manager. It makes a good manager better faster and a bad manager worse faster.

Edward M. Esber
CEO, Ashton-Tate
Fortune, March 2, 1987

The robot ... is capable of performing a variety of tasks, or a sequence of tasks, but the choice of tasks at any particular moment is determined not only by a pre-set program, but also by some information *fed into it from the outside world which is relevant to the task it is performing.* The information it absorbs is fed into it through sensing devices attached to its own structure, and not by command signals from a human.

Christopher Evans
Psychologist and computer scientist
The Micro Millenium (Pocket Books, 1979)

There are close to four times as many personal computers as there are managers in this country.

Roxane Farmanfarmaian
Technology Editor, *Working Woman*
Working Woman, April 1988

[Of artificial intelligence and "expert systems":] When you reach the edge of its expertise it falls off from very good to very bad.

Edward Feigenbaum
Stanford University
Forbes, October 19, 1987

The types of jobs industrial robots handle well are not the types of jobs that provide people with a high level of motivation ... material handling, welding, spray painting and assembly.... About 85% of all manual labor in the United States [is assembly] ... represent[ing] the most dramatic example of robotic potential and also why most anti-robot, anti-automation forces have directed their efforts toward assembly applications.

Terry Feulner
Section Head, Hughes Aircraft Co.
and Brian H. Kleiner
California State University
Personnel Journal, February 1986

In many instances, a properly motivated person can outperform a robot. That high level of performance, however, could never, and likely should never, be sustained by a person day in and day out.

Terry Feulner
Section Head, Hughes Aircraft Co.
and Brian H. Kleiner
California State University
Personnel Journal, February 1986

I really don't care that I don't have what's current [in computer technology] because whatever is at the moment, it will be infinite-

ly better in a few months and even better months later.

William Fink
Superintendent, U. S. Park Service
Personal Computing, September 1987

It works better if you plug it in.

Free advice

[The computer] will alter the entire nervous system of social organization.

French government study
McNitt, *The Art of Computer Management*
(Simon & Schuster, 1984)

Computers can automate the mechanics of work of all kinds—whether they generate payroll checks or perform sophisiticated statistical analyses. So far they cannot even come close to doing the kind of work that involves *judgment* on the part of managers.

Andrew S. Grove
CEO, Intel Corp.
One-On-One With Andy Grove
(G. P. Putnam's Sons, 1987)

Factory work must be adapted to people, not people to machines.

Pehr G. Gyllenhammar
Managing Director, Volvo (Sweden)
Schleicher, *Volvo: New Directions in Work Technology* (Hitchcock, 1977)

It [the personal computer] takes the drudgery out of your job.

Elaine Harrison
Secretary, Southern Union Co.
The New York Times, April 27, 1988

The use of [a] model or any of the mathematical techniques of the operations researcher does not imply management by computer.

James C. Hetrick
Operations Researcher, Arthur D. Little, Inc.
In Bursk and Chapman,
New Decision Making Tools for Managers
(New American Library, 1963)

What is this proverbial distinction between *software* and *hardware*? It is the distinction between programs and machines—between long complicated sequences of instructions, and the physical machines which carry them out. I like to think of software as "anything you could send over the telephone lines," and hardware as "anything else." A piano is hardware, but printed music is software. A telephone set is hardware but a telephone number is software.

Douglas R. Hofstadter
American computer scientist
Gödel, Escher, Bach (Random House, 1980)

In the early days of this country, when people wished to move heavy objects they used oxen. If one ox could not do the job they did not try to grow a bigger ox, but used two oxen. Their approach tells us something. When we need greater computer power, the answer is not to get a bigger computer, but to get *another* computer, as common sense would have told us. We must build systems of computers and operate them in parallel.

Grace Murray Hopper
Rear Admiral, U. S. Navy (retired)
Speech, Washington, D.C., February 1987

It is said that one machine can do the work of fifty ordinary men. No machine, however, can do the work of one extraordinary man.

Tehyi Hsieh
Chinese educator, writer, and diplomat
Chinese Epigrams Inside Out and Proverbs

Not until a machine can write a sonnet or compose a concerto because of thoughts and emotions felt, and not by the chance fall of symbols, could we agree that machine equals brain—that is, not only write it but know that it had written it. No mechanism could feel (and not merely artificially signal, an easy contrivance) pleasure at its successes, grief when its valves fuse, be warmed by flattery, be made miserable by its mistakes, be charmed by sex, be angry or depressed when it cannot get what it wants.

G. Jefferson
Royal Medical Society Lister Oration
British Medical Journal, 1949

The personal computer is a tool that can amplify a certain part of our inherent intelligence.

Steven Jobs
Cofounder, Apple Computer Co.
Sign in a computer store, Rockville, Maryland

In five years we'll see computers that gather information the way a good research assistant does.

Mitchell D. Kapor
Founder, Lotus Development Corp.
The New York Times, February 21, 1988

In computers, every "new explosion" was set off by a software product that allowed users to program differently.

Alan Kay
Massachusetts Institute of Technology
The New York Times, February 21, 1988

Man is still the most extraordinary computer of all.

John Fitzgerald Kennedy, 1917–1963
Thirty-fifth President of the United States
Speech, May 21, 1963

Training is probably the most important aspect of buying a computer system.

Barry Knowles
Owner, Valcom Computer Center
Inc. Magazine, November 1987

"Our computer's down." This is another great [business] lie. Unfortunately, it is true so often that you seldom can attack it head on.

Charles W. Kyd
Financial consultant and author
Inc. Magazine, August 1987

I am a firm believer that it is far easier to teach the creative business person something about computers than it is to teach the programmer something about business.

Pete Lawson
CEO, Brenton Management Corp.
McNitt, *The Art of Computer Management*
(Simon & Schuster, 1984)

The real definition of a supercomputer is a machine that is just one generation behind the problems it is asked to solve.

Neil Lincoln
Computer architect
Time, March 28, 1988

The broad availability and low cost of computer and telecommunications equipment provides both the *impetus* and the *means* to perform new record-keeping functions. These functions can bring the individual substantial benefits, but there are also disadvantages for the individual. On one hand, they can give him easier access to services that make his life more comfortable or convenient. On the other, they also tempt others to demand, and make it easier for them to get access to, information about him for purposes he does not expect and would not agree to if he were asked.

David F. Linowes
Chairman, Congressional Privacy Protection
Study Commission
Personal Privacy in an Information Society,
Washington, D.C., 1977

Given a multilevel organization having component groups which perform a variety of functions in order to accomplish a unified objective, an MIS [Management Information System] is an integrated structure of data bases and information flow over all levels and components, whereby information collection and transfer is optimized to meet the needs of the organization.

Larry E. Long
Management Information Systems consultant
*Manager's Guide to Computers and
Information Systems* (Prentice-Hall, 1983)

The Analytical Engine [of Charles Babbage, 1792–1871] has no pretensions whatever to originate anything. It can do whatever we know how to order it to perform. It can follow analysis; but it has no power of anticipating any analytical relations or truths. Its province is to assist us in making available what we are already acquainted with.

Ada Augusta Lovelace, 1815–1852
English mathematician
Morrison, *Charles Babbage and his
Calculating Engines* (Dover, 1961)

[T]he machine will still not be an adequate model of the mind. We are trying to produce a model of the mind which is mechanical— which is essentially "dead"—but the mind being in fact "alive," can always go one step better than any formal, ossified dead system can.... [T]he mind always has the last word.

J. R. Lucas
American computer scientist
Minds and Machines (Prentice-Hall, 1964)

[Computers] can also do other things that human beings can't do at all, because they wouldn't live long enough to complete the calculations with a pencil or a desk calculator, or couldn't complete them in time for the answers to be of much use.

William E. Mahaffay
Group Vice President, Whirlpool Corp.
Speech, Chicago, November 1967

Your own computer experts may be on the salesman's side instead of on yours, because they like to have the latest equipment to play with, and because they may be relying too heavily upon the manufacturer for their knowledge.

William E. Mahaffay
Group Vice President, Whirlpool Corp.
Speech, Chicago, November 1967

Can we design an artificial intelligence that improves upon human discretion for some decisions? I don't know—today. I do know, however, that we will never develop that capacity if we always accept a negative answer, and don't devote the resources necessary to investigate and develop better approaches.

T. Allen McArtor
Administrator, FAA
Speech, Washington, D.C., August 18, 1987

When a program grows in power by an evolution of partially understood patches and fixes, the programmer begins to lose track of internal details, loses his ability to predict what will happen, begins to hope instead of know, and watches the results as though the program were an individual whose range of behavior is uncertain.... This is already true in some big programs ... developed and modified by several programmers, each testing them on different examples from different [remotely located computer] consoles and inserting advice independently. The program will grow in effectiveness, but no one of the programmers will understand it all.... Now we see the real trouble with statements like 'It only does what its programmer told it to do.' There isn't any one programmer.

Marvin M. Minsky
American computer scientist
Design and Planning II
(Hastings House, 1967)

Earlier devices—looms, engines, generators—resisted at critical points human ignorance and stupidity. Overloaded, abused, they stopped work, stalled, broke down, blew up; and there was the end of it. Thus they set clear limits on man's ineptitude. For the computer ... the limits are not so obvious. Used in ignorance or stupidity, asked a foolish question, it does not collapse, it goes on to answer a fool according to his folly. And the questioner, being a fool, will go on to act on the reply.

E. E. Morison
Massachusetts Institute of Technology
Greenberger, *Management and the Computer of the Future* (M. I. T., 1962)

The technology of the computer allows us to have a distinct and individually tailored arrangement with each of thousands of employees.

John Naisbitt
Chairman, Naisbitt Group
Megatrends (Warner, 1984)

We created the hierarchical, pyramidal, managerial system because we needed to keep track of people and the things people did; with the computer to keep track, we can restructure our institutions horizontally.

John Naisbitt
Chairman, Naisbitt Group
Megatrends (Warner, 1984)

People don't want to understand all the components; they just want to make it [the technology] happen.

Bernadine Nicodemus
Information Center Supervisor, Rockport Co.
PC Week, December 8, 1987

Machines should work. People should think.

John Peers
President, Logical Machine Corp.
1,001 Logical Laws (Doubleday, 1979)

Who needs new computers if there's nothing to run on them?

Jerry Pournele
Computer columnist
Infoworld, February 22, 1988

Many people have thought of computers strictly as "number crunchers".... In fact, though, the most common use for professional computers is word-processing; that is, more individual computer owners use their machines primarily for textual work than for numbers.

T. R. Reid
Writer, "Personal Computing"
The Washington Post, February 1, 1988

Computer technology has, quite simply, not delivered its long awaited productivity payback.

Stephen S. Roach
Senior economist, Morgan Stanley
PC Week, December 8, 1987

What is new is that a class of technicians has managed to remove large data processing expenditures from the control of corporate management and the rule of common sense.

Richard S. Rubin
Telecommunications manager, Citibank
Harvard Business Review, July/August 1986

Always remember what you originally wanted the system to accomplish. Having the latest, greatest system and a flashy data center to boot is not what data processing is supposed to be all about. It is supposed to help the bottom line, not hinder it.

Richard S. Rubin
Telecommunications manager, Citibank
Harvard Business Review, July/August 1986

Machines are worshipped because they are beautiful and valued because they confer power; they are hated because they are hideous and loathed because they impose slavery.

Bertrand Russell, 1872–1970
English mathematician and philosopher
Skeptical Essays

There is no Ghost in the Machine.

Gilbert Ryle
Oxford University
The Concept of Mind

A machine is not a genie, it does not work by magic, it does not possess a will, and [Norbert] Wiener to the contrary, nothing comes out which has not been put in, barring of course, an infrequent case of malfunctioning.... The "intentions" which the machine seems to manifest are the intentions of the human programmer, as specified in advance, or they are subsidiary intentions derived from these, following rules specified by the programmer.... The machine will not and cannot do any of these things until it has been instructed as to how to proceed.... To believe otherwise is either to believe in magic or to believe that the existence of man's will is an illusion and that man's actions are as mechanical as the machine's.

Arthur L. Samuel
American computer scientist
Science, September 16, 1960

Replacing workers on their present jobs with machines is not the major function of automation. Its greater promise is its ability to do new things, to create new products, new services and new jobs, and to meet the increasing requirements of a growing population.

David Sarnoff, 1891–1971
Founder and President, RCA
Wisdom of Sarnoff and the World of RCA

It is dangerous to push affinities and analogies to excess.... The stuff of life transcends, in its complexity, the most ambitious inventions man can imagine, let alone construct. Even the most elaborate man-made apparatus is primitive when matched against a living creature. The largest electronic computer, for example, may have one million storage elements, whereas the human brain has perhaps a hundred billion cells.

David Sarnoff, 1891–1971
Founder & President, RCA
Wisdom of Sarnoff and the World of RCA

Knowledge representation ... is the study of how one portrays the things one knows. This is a hot research area in artificial intelligence because how knowledge is represented determines what kind of symbols and relationships a computer can process. To put it crudely, knowledge representation is the software of software.

Michael Schrage
Writer, "Personal Computers"
The Washington Post, November 3, 1986

The hardware and the software are only a small part—certainly less than half—of the true costs of bringing PC's into the organization.

Jim Seymour
Syndicated computer columnist
PC Week, December 8, 1987

Cyberphobia—"fear of computers." Characterized by panic, terror, heart palpitations, breathing difficulties, dizziness, trembling, going crazy or losing control.

Jonathan P. Siegel
Information Communications Associates
Inner Guide to Office Automation, 1988

Computers do only what you program them to do in exactly the same sense that humans do only what their genes and their cumulative experience program them to do. This assertion leaves little room for free will in either computer or human, but it leaves a great deal of room in both for flexible, adaptive, complex, intelligent behavior.

Herbert A. Simon
Carnegie-Mellon University
Anshen and Bach, *Management and Corporations 1985* (McGraw Hill, 1960)

Programs do not merely substitute brute force for human cunning. Increasingly, they imitate—and in some cases improve upon—human cunning.

Herbert A. Simon
Carnegie-Mellon University
Anshen and Bach, *Management and Corporations 1985* (McGraw-Hill, 1960)

The mathematical and computing techniques for making programmed decisions replace man but they do not generally simulate him.

Herbert A. Simon
Carnegie-Mellon University
Anshen and Bach, *Management and Corporations 1985* (McGraw-Hill, 1960)

In the future, most all nonviolent crime against small business will be computer-related or [will] use the computer as a masking tool.... [B]ecause the use of computers for business applications in small business will be so pervasive ... it will be impossible to commit a nonviolent crime except in the presence of computers.

Report
Computer Security Advisory Council
U. S. Small Business Administration, 1987

I am asking whether we are now running into a position where only those who are concerned with the computer, who are formulating its decision rules, are going to be knowledgeable about the decision.

Charles Percy (C. P.) Snow, 1905–1980
English physicist, critic, and diplomat
Greenberger, *Management and the Computer of the Future* (M. I. T., 1962)

I suspect that computers in government are going to get into the hands of persons with mildly defective or canalized judgement and become gadgets. It will be astonishing if that does not happen.

Charles Percy (C. P.) Snow, 1905–1980
English physicist, critic, and diplomat
Greenberger, *Management and the Computer of the Future* (M. I. T., 1962)

Too many companies have beautiful, elegant computer systems that create more problems than they solve.

Susan E. Steele
The Wharton School
CFO, December 1987

The reverence of persons can be appropriately given only to that which itself is at least personal.

William Temple, 1881–1944
Archbiship of Canterbury
Nature, Man and God

Men have become the tools of their tools.

Henry David Thoreau, 1817–1862
American naturalist and writer
Walden

The next major explosion is going to be when genetics and computers come together. I'm talking about an organic computer—about biological substances that can function like semiconductors.

Alvin Toffler
Futurist and writer
The New York Times, February 21, 1988

It may be possible to produce computational systems which model various aspects of consciousness, emotion and so on, but a computer running a program which models consciousness is clearly quite a different thing from a computer which, by virture of the program it is running, is conscious.

Steven Torrance
American computer scientist
Gill, *Artificial Intelligence for Society*
(John Wiley & Sons, 1986)

Most of the computer technicians ... are complicators, not simplifiers.... They're building a mystique, a priesthood, their own mumbo-jumbo ritual to keep you from knowing what they—and you—are doing..

Robert Townsend
Former CEO, Avis
Further Up the Organization (Knopf, 1984)

We can no longer plunk a machine [computer] in front of a guy and make him more productive. Those days are over.

Paul Trotter
Information System manager, Chemical Bank
PC Week, December 8, 1987

I suppose when it [the computer] gets to that stage we shan't know how it does it.

Alan Turing, 1912–1954
English mathematician and computer scientist
Bernstein, *The Analytical Engine*
(Random House, 1963)

The facts as set forth by plaintiff suggest an Orwellian nightmare of computer control which breaks down through mechanical and programmers' failures and errors.... [The individual] is confronted by an impersonal bureaucracy held together by computers, wherein inefficiency and a resultant high level of error are the norm, and unresponsiveness or "run-arounds" the only answer to his inquiries.

Harold R. Tyler
Judge, Federal District Court, Manhattan
Bronson v. *Consolidated Edison Co.* (1972)

Support anyone in your office who develops an interest in computers. It's not uncommon that a little tinkering can solve a problem, saving the delay of waiting for a service visit.

Unsigned report
Law Office Management and Administration,
July 1986

The machine rules. Human life is rigorously controlled by it, dominated by the terribly precise will of mechanisms. These creatures of man are exacting. They are now reacting on their creators, making them like themselves. They want well-trained humans; they are gradually wiping out the differences between men, fitting them into their own orderly functioning, into the uniformity of their own regimes. They are thus shaping humanity for their own use, almost in their own image.

Paul Ambroise Valéry, 1871–1945
French poet and philosopher
Fairy Tales for Computers (Eakins, 1969)

A system of logical instructions that an automaton can carry out and which causes the automaton to perform some organized task is called a code.... The use of a modern computing machine is based on the user's ability to develop and formulate the necessary complete codes for any given problem that the machine is supposed to solve.

John von Neumann, 1903–1957
Father of the serial computer
The Computer and the Brain (Yale, 1958)

[U]sers is a term people never apply to themselves; it is given them by people on the other—that is, technical—side. Groups we've known who buy and use computer systems have called themselves bankers, scientists, or marketing people, reflecting the business they're in or the work they do. Systems analysts, on the other hand, often see themselves as professionals, managers, or engineers.

Gerald and Daniella Weinberg
American computer consultants
Journal of Information Systems Management,
Winter 1985

There is a myth that computers are today making important decisions of the kind that were earlier made by people. Perhaps there are isolated examples of that here and there in our society. But the widely believed picture of managers typing questions of the form "What shall we do now?" into their computers and then waiting for their computers to "decide" is largely wrong. What is happening instead is that people have turned the processing of information on which decisions must be based over to enormously complex computer systems. They have, with few exceptions, reserved for themselves the right to make decisions based on the outcome of such computing processes.

Joseph Weizenbaum
American computer scientist
Computer Power and Human Reason
(Penguin, 1984)

The connection between a model and a theory is that a model *satisfies* a theory; that is, a model obeys those laws of behavior that a corresponding theory explicity states or which may be derived from it.... Computers make possible an entirely new relationship between theories and models.... A theory written in the form of a computer program is ... both a theory and, when placed on a computer and run, a model to which the theory applies.

Joseph Weizenbaum
American computer scientist
Computer Power and Human Reason
(Penguin, 1984)

An interpreter of programming-language texts, a computer, is immune to the seductive influence of mere eloquence.... Words like "obviously" are not represented in the primitive vocabularies of any computers.... To write a program is to legislate the laws for a world one first has to create in imagination. Only very rarely does any designer, be he an architect, a novelist, or whatever, have so coherent a picture of the world emergent in his imagination that he can compose its laws without criticism from that world itself. This is precisely what computers may provide.

Joseph Weizenbaum
American computer scientist
Computer Power and Human Reason
(Penguin, 1984)

Man is not an appropriate model for a machine. If we abandon that model, we are free to take a totally different approach to a task, as Howe did with sewing, and end up with a new definition of it as well as a new way of doing it. Only when we have studied the task and understood its requirements can we properly decide what the machine or robot for that job should be like.... Robots are not mechanical people; they are parts of an integrated manufacturing system.

Daniel E. Whitney
American roboticist
Harvard Business Review, May/June 1986

An intelligent understanding of [a machine's] mode of performance may be delayed until long after the task which [it has] been set has been completed.... This means that, though

machines are theoretically subject to human criticism, such criticism may be ineffective until long after it is relevant.

Norbert Wiener, 1894–1964
Pioneer computer scientist
Science, May 6, 1960

Render unto man the things which are man's and unto the computer the things which are the computer's. This would seem the intelligent policy to adopt when we employ men and computers together in common undertakings. It is a policy as far removed from that of the gadget worshipper as it is from the man who sees only blasphemy and the degradation of man in the use of any mechanical adjuvants whatever to thoughts. What we need now is an independent study of systems involving both human and mechanical elements. This system should not be prejudiced either by a mechanical or antimechanical bias.

Norbert Wiener, 1894–1964
Pioneer computer scientist
God and Golem, Inc. (M. I. T., 1964)

As long as the machine has beaten the man who programmed it in checkers, it will in some sense compete with human intelligence over a limited scope.

Norbert Wiener, 1894–1964
Pioneer computer scientist
Greenberger, *Management and the Computer of the Future* (M. I. T., 1962)

Every representation of knowledge is an interpretation.

Terry Winograd and Fernando Flores
Stanford University
Understanding Computers and Cognition
(Ablex, 1987)

If computers did help accelerate the [1987] Black Monday [stock market] slide, they were not responsible for it. As an IBM executive once said: "Computers don't kill stock markets. People do."

Anonymous IBM executive
Time, November 2, 1987

Managerial achievement in human organization is not dependent on mechanical devices nor routine methods.... We are leading men, not handling robots.

Anonymous manager
Quoted in *American Management Review*,
November 1923

The relationship between input and output is sometimes—when input is incorrect—tersely noted by the expression "garbage in, garbage out" [GIGO].

Glossary of Automated Typesetting
and Related Computer Terms
(Composition Information Services, 1975)

7

Conflict &
Conflict Resolution

*When angry, count to four;
when very angry, swear.*

Humor is a social lubricant that helps us get over some of the bad spots.

Steve Allen
Writer and comedian
The Center Magazine, January/February 1971

Swifter is speech when the heart is hurt.

Amen Em Opet I, 1991–1962 B.C.
Egyptian Pharaoh
The Wisdom of Amen Em Opet

Power and violence are opposites; where the one rules absolutely, the other is absent. Violence appears where power is in jeopardy, but left to its own course it ends in power's disappearance.

Hannah Arendt, 1906–1975
German-American philosopher and critic
Crises of the Republic
(Harcourt Brace Jovanovich, 1972)

The man who is angry at the right things and with the right people, and, further, as he ought, when he ought, and as long as he ought, is praised.... For the good-tempered man tends to be unperturbed and not to be led by passion, but to be angry in the manner, at the things, and for the length of time, that the rule dictates.

Aristotle, 384–322 B.C.
Greek philosopher and teacher
Nicomachean Ethics

Revolutions are not about trifles, but spring from trifles.

Aristotle, 384–322 B.C.
Greek philosopher and teacher
Politics

The existence of sanctions is not a sufficient condition for obedience to authority.... Individuals exercising authority may be and are removable even in the absence of legal means.

Revolution is an ever-present possibility, and in mild forms, can occur in a wide variety of organizations.

Kenneth J. Arrow
Nobel laureate in economics
The Limits of Organization (Norton, 1974)

It is not necessary to understand things in order to argue about them.

Pierre Beaumarchais, 1732–1799
French playwright and arms merchant
Prochnow, *The Toastmaster's Treasure Chest*
(Harper & Row, 1979)

If God lived on earth, people would break His windows.

Belfast maxim

As a general rule, if you want to get at the truth—hear both sides and believe neither.

Josh Billings
(Henry Wheeler Shaw), 1818–1885
American writer and auctioneer
Josh Billings: His Book

Progress flows only from struggle.

Louis Dembitz Brandeis, 1856–1941
U. S. Supreme Court Justice
Business—A Profession

I'm not one to waste energy and time having arguments.

Richard Branson
Chairman, Virgin Group (England)
Inc. Magazine, November 1987

The best strategy for resolving a personal feud between two key members of your organization is remarkably simple: *take one side or the other*.... The best method of handling an alleged persecution [is:] *delegate responsibility for investigating and settling the complaint to an impartial agent*.... About the only way to put a stop to a boundary dispute is to *reorganize the departments or the disputed territory so that the boundary is unmistakable*.... The strategy for resolving a schism in an organization may be stated thus: *Bring the factions together, force them to work out a mutually acceptable compromise, and then throw all your weight behind the compromise*.

Theodore Caplow
Managing an Organization
(CBS College Publishing, 1983)

Democracy exists just as long as the lower level of management follows the precepts of top management; whenever a conflict develops, it is top management that wins and lower management that either gives in or moves out.

William T. Carnes
Chairman,
Airlines Electronic Engineering Committee
Effective Meetings for Busy People—Let's Decide It and Go Home (McGraw–Hill, 1983)

Parliament can compel people to obey or to submit, but it cannot compel them to agree.

Winston Churchill, 1874–1965
English Prime Minister, writer, and soldier
Speech in Parliament, September 27, 1926

I do not resent criticism, even when, for the sake of emphasis, it parts for the time with reality.

Winston Churchill, 1874–1965
English Prime Minister, writer, and soldier
Speech in Parliament, January 22, 1941

When your argument has little or no substance, abuse your opponent.

Cicero, 106–43 B.C.
Roman orator and statesman
Rhetorica

The competent executive is able to consider many points of view.... An executive's life consists of reconciling points of view that often seem, and sometimes are, irreconcilable.

> Abram T. Collier
> CEO, New England Mutual
> *Harvard Business Review*,
> January/February 1987

In answering an opponent, arrange your ideas but not your words.

> Charles Caleb Colton, c. 1780–1832
> English cleric, sportsman, and wine merchant
> *Lacon*

Wise men do not quarrel with each other.

> Danish proverb

Proud Prelate—You know what you were before I made you what you are now. If you do not immediately comply with my request [to read the English litany in London churches], I will unfrock you, by God!

> Elizabeth I, 1533–1603
> Queen of England and Ireland
> Letter to Bishop Richard Cox, 1559

The only sin which people never forgive in each other is a difference of opinion.

> Ralph Waldo Emerson, 1803–1882
> American essayist and poet
> *Journals*

We boil at different degrees.

> Ralph Waldo Emerson, 1803–1882
> American essayist and poet
> *Literary Ethics*

There was never a good war or a bad peace.

> Benjamin Franklin, 1706–1790
> American printer and statesman
> Letter to Josiah Quincy, September 11, 1773

Contradiction should awaken Attention, not Passion.

> Thomas Fuller, 1608–1661
> Chaplain in extraordinary to Charles II
> *Gnomologia*

I guess there are two schools of thought about this—yours and mine.

> Ernest Gallo
> CEO, Gallo Wineries
> *The New York Times,* May 2, 1988

Those who in quarrels interpose
Must often wipe a bloody nose.

> John Gay, 1685–1732
> English poet, dramatist, and fabulist
> *Fables*

In the business world, everyone is always working at legitimate cross purposes, governed by self interest.

> Harold Geneen
> CEO, IT&T
> *Managing* (Doubleday, 1984)

The free expression of opinion, as experience has taught us, is the safety-valve of passion. The noise of the rushing steam, when it escapes, alarms the timid; but it is the sign that we are safe. The concession of reasonable privilege anticipates the growth of furious appetite.

> William Ewart Gladstone, 1809–1898
> English Prime Minister and author
> *The New Dictionary of Thoughts*, 1957

Bad blood among board members or senior managers can threaten a firm's stability if allowed to go unchecked.

> Gary Goldstick and George Schreiber
> Principals, Goldstick & Schreiber
> *Inc. Magazine's Guide to*
> *Small Business Success*, 1987

When a man is wrong and won't admit it, he always gets angry.

> Thomas Chandler Haliburton, 1796–1865
> Canadian jurist and humorist
> *The Attaché, or Sam Slick in England*

Be calm in arguing; for fierceness makes
Error a fault and truth discourtesy.

> George Herbert, 1593–1633
> English clergyman and poet
> *Antiphon*

Fools bite one another, but wise men agree together.

> George Herbert, 1593–1633
> English clergyman and poet
> *Jacula Prudentum*

Force, and fraud, are in war the two cardinal virtues.

> Thomas Hobbes, 1588–1679
> English philosopher
> *Leviathan*

Deep-seated preferences can not be argued about.

> Oliver Wendell Holmes, Jr., 1841–1935
> U. S. Supreme Court Justice
> *Natural Law*

If you can't answer a man's arguments, all is not lost; you can still call him vile names.

> Elbert Hubbard, 1856–1915
> American writer, printer, and editor
> *Elbert Hubbard's Scrap Book*

Nobody ever forgets where he buried the hatchet.

> Frank McKinney ("Kin") Hubbard, 1868–1930
> American caricaturist and humorist
> *The Indianapolis News*, January 4, 1925

It is difficult to settle a town riot.

> Jabo proverb

An association of men who will not quarrel with one another is a thing which never yet existed, from the greatest confederacy of nations down to a town-meeting or a vestry.

> Thomas Jefferson, 1743–1826
> Third President of the United States
> Letter to John Taylor, 1798

A little rebellion now and then is a good thing.

> Thomas Jefferson, 1743–1826
> Third President of the United States
> Letter to James Madison, January 30, 1787

For anger killeth the foolish man.

> Old Testament, Job 5:2

Words wound. But as a veteran of twelve years in the United States Senate, I happily attest that they do not kill.

> Lyndon Baines Johnson, 1908–1973
> Thirty-sixth President of the United States
> Speech, Denver, August 26, 1966

We will have differences. Men of different ancestries, men of different tongues, men of different colors, men of different environments, men of different geographies do not see everything alike. Even in our own country we do not see everything alike. If we did, we would all want the same wife—and that would be a problem, wouldn't it?

> Lyndon Baines Johnson, 1908–1973
> Thirty-sixth President of the United States
> Speech, February 11, 1964

Organizations ought to thrive on most personal and professional differences, because in the long run they account for the dynamics of organizational growth.

> Stephen S. Kaagan
> Management consultant
> *Personnel Journal*, February 1978

I never fight except against difficulties.

> Helen Keller, 1880–1968
> American writer and lecturer
> *The Story of My Life*

A real diplomat is one who can cut his neighbor's throat without having his neighbor notice it.

> Trygve Halvdan Lie, 1896–1968
> Secretary-General of the United Nations
> Prochnow, *The Toastmaster's Treasure Chest*
> (Harper & Row, 1979)

Be not deceived. Revolutions do not go backward.

> Abraham Lincoln, 1809–1865
> Sixteenth President of the United States
> Speech, May 19, 1856

We should have a great many fewer disputes in the world if words were taken for what they are, the signs of our ideas only, and not for things themselves.

> John Locke, 1632–1704
> English philosopher
> *Essay concerning human understanding*

I have heard speakers use the phrase, "I can say without fear of contradiction ..." Anyone who says this in a modern democracy, or to the shareholders of a modern company, should see the doctor.

> Oliver Lyttleton
> (Viscount Chandos), 1893–1980
> English banking and metals executive
> *Memoirs of Lord Chandos*
> (New American Library, 1963)

The most common and durable source of faction has been the various and unequal distribution of property.

> James Madison, 1751–1836
> Fourth President of the United States
> *The Federalist Papers*

Opinions cannot survive if one has no chance to fight for them.

> Thomas Mann, 1875–1955
> German novelist and essayist
> *The Magic Mountain*

Agree with thine adversary quickly while thou art in the way with him.

> New Testament, Mark 5:25

Deeds of violence in our society are performed largely by those trying to establish their self-esteem, to defend their self-image, and to demonstrate that they, too, are significant.... Violence arises not out of superfluity of power but out of powerlessness.

> Rollo May
> American psychologist and therapist
> *Love and Will*

It is impossible to defeat an ignorant man in argument.

> William Gibbs McAdoo, 1863–1941
> Railroad executive and U. S. Senator
> Remark to President Woodrow Wilson

Our differences are policies, our agreements principles.

> William McKinley, 1843–1901
> Twenty-fifth President of the United States
> Speech, Des Moines, 1901

Some people mistake weakness for tact. If they are silent when they ought to speak and so feign an agreement they do not feel, they call it being tactful. Cowardice would be a much better name. Tact is an active quality that is not exercised by merely making a dash for cover. Be sure, when you think you are being extremely tactful, that you are not in reality running away from something you ought to face.

> Frank Medlicott
> English solicitor
> *Reader's Digest*, July 1968

It doesn't take a majority to make a rebellion; it takes only a few determined leaders and a sound cause.

> Henry Louis Mencken, 1880–1956
> Editor, author, and critic
> *Prejudices*

Where there is much desire to learn, there of necessity will be much arguing, much writing, many opinions; for opinion in good men is but knowledge in the making.

> John Milton, 1608–1674
> English poet
> *Areopagitica*

Willfully to strive and obstinately to contest in words are common qualities most apparent in basest minds.

> Michel Eyquem de Montaigne, 1533–1592
> French philosopher and essayist
> *Essays*

For it must needs be that there is an opposition in all things. If not so ... righteousness could not be brought to pass; neither wickedness; neither holiness nor misery; neither good nor bad.

> Book of Mormon, 2 Nephi 1:81–82

A man or woman who, believing that the public interest overrides the interest of the organization he serves, publicly "blows the whistle" if the organization is involved in corrupt, illegal, fraudulent, or harmful activity.

> Ralph Nader, Peter J. Petkas, and Kate Blackwell
> Public interest advocates
> *Whistle Blowing* (Grossman, 1972)

He who fights with monsters might take care lest he thereby become a monster.

> Georg Wilhelm Nietzsche, 1844–1900
> German philosopher
> *Beyond Good and Evil*

Like everybody else, once in a while we have a desk pounding or two.

> James Ortega
> Partner, Best Western Paving Co.
> *Hispanic Business,* June 1987

"Acceptance time" is a powerful antidote to conflict in Japanese organizations. The things a person believes in are often more important belongings than physical possessions.... Even less compelling beliefs reach back into a person's past and forward into his future. When new ideas or facts come along, however compelling they may be, it is felt that people need time let go gradually of the old before they can accept the new.

> Richard Tanner Pascale
> Stanford University School of Business
> and Anthony G. Athos
> Harvard Business School
> *The Art of Japanese Management*
> (Simon & Schuster, 1981)

Quarreling dogs come halting home.

Barber, *The Book of 1000 Proverbs,* 1876

He is wise that can make a friend of a foe.

Barber, *The Book of 1000 Proverbs,* 1876

Many get into a dispute well that cannot get out well.

Barber, *The Book of 1000 Proverbs,* 1876

Where there is no wood a fire goes out;
And where there is no whisper a quarrel dies down.

Old Testament, Proverbs 26:20

He that keepeth his mouth keepeth his life; but he that openeth wide his lips shall have destruction.

Old Testament, Proverbs 13:3

The inherent conflict between managers and professionals results basically from a clash of cultures: the corporate culture, which captures the commitment of managers, and the professional culture, which socializes professionals.

Joseph A. Raelin
Boston College School of Management
Clash of Cultures: Managers and Professionals
(Harvard Business School, 1986)

People need a chance to see how much agreement is possible between seemingly intractable opponents.

Robert Redford
Actor and entrepreneur
Harvard Business Review, May/June 1987

It makes me nervous when someone says, "I agree with everything you say." Not even *I* agree with everything I say.

Jeremy Rifkind
Director, Foundation on Economic Trends
The Washington Post, January 17, 1988

Quarrels would not last long if the fault was only on one side.

François de La Rochefoucauld, 1613–1680
French politician, writer, and philanthropist
Reflections, or Sentences and Moral Maxims

Handle people with gloves, but issues, barefisted.

Dagobert D. Runes
Editor, publisher, and philosopher
A Book of Contemplation

Anger is never without an Argument, but seldom with a good one.

George Savile (Lord Halifax), 1633–1695
English politician and statesman
Moral Thoughts and Reflections

The easiest, the most tempting, and the least creative response to conflict within an organization is to pretend it does not exist.

Lyle E. Schaller
Yokefellow Institute
The Change Agent (Abingdon, 1972)

[Intra-organizational conflict] exists because as groups become more committed to their own goals and norms, they are likely to become competitive with one another and seek to undermine their rivals' activities, thereby becoming a liability to the organization as a whole. The overall problem, then, is how to establish high-productive, *collaborative* intergroup relations.... The basic strategy of reducing conflict, therefore, is to find goals upon which groups can agree and to reestablish valid communications between the group.

Edgar H. Schein
Massachusetts Institute of Technology
Organizational Psychology
(Prentice-Hall 1980)

"Winning" in a conflict does not have a strictly competitive meaning; it is not winning relative to one's adversary. It means gaining relative to one's own value system; and this may be done by bargaining, by mutual accomodation, and by the avoidance of mutually damaging behavior.

Thomas C. Schelling
The Strategy of Conflict (Harvard, 1960)

[In adversarial processes:] The emphasis tends to shift to a search for the winning argument as opposed to the correct conclusion.

James R. Schlesinger
U. S. Secretary of Defense
Memorandum to Senate Committee on
Government Operations, April 1968

In a world of finite men, conflict is inevitably associated with creativity. Without conflict there is no major personal change or social progress. On the other hand, runaway conflict (as in modern war) can destroy what men intended to save by it. Conflict management then becomes crucially important. This involves accepting or even encouraging such conflict as is necessary, but at the same time doing everything possible to keep it to the minimum essential to change, to confine it to the least destructive forms, and to resolve it as rapidly and constructively as possible.

Harvey Seifert
Social scientist
and Howard Clinebell, Jr.
Pastoral counselor
Personal Growth and Social Change
(Westminster, 1969)

[The two Indian chiefs] came to an agreement and buried two axes in the ground, which ceremony to them is more significant and binding than all the Articles of Peace, the hatchet being the principal weapon.

Samuel Sewall, 1652–1730
American jurist
Diaries

It is an irrepressible conflict between opposing and enduring forces.

William Henry Seward, 1801–1872
Governor of New York and U. S. Senator
Speech in Congress, October 25, 1858

I understand a fury in your words,
But not the words.

William Shakespeare, 1564–1616
English dramatist and poet
Othello

Two stars keep not their motion in one sphere.

William Shakespeare, 1564–1616
English dramatist and poet
King Henry IV

You can't argue your way back into the job.

Earl Shorris
Manager and writer
The Oppressed Middle
(Anchor/Doubleday, 1981)

For souls in growth, great quarrels are great emancipations.

Logan Pearsall Smith, 1865–1946
American essayist and biographer
All Trivia

[In the corporations he studied:] Covert power struggles are permissible but open conflict is settled by eliminating the weaker.

Ross Stagner
Michigan State University
Business Topics (MSU, Winter 1965)

Socializing with other executives outside of office hours improves communication and mutual understanding. Unfortunately, there was considerable friction manifest in some firms where socializing was particularly common. It may be ... that real understanding may just intensify friction.

Ross Stagner
Michigan State University
Business Topics (MSU, Winter 1965)

There is no such test of a man's superiority of character as in the well-conducting of an unavoidable quarrel.

Henry Taylor, 1800–1886
English poet and Colonial administrator
The Statesman

Compromise is usually bad. It should be a last resort. If two departments or divisions have a problem they can't solve and it comes up to you, listen to both sides and then ... pick one or the other. This places solid accountability on the winner to make it work. Condition your people to avoid compromise.

Robert Townsend
Former CEO, Avis
Up the Organization (Knopf, 1975)

If you're the boss and your people fight you openly when they think you're wrong, that's healthy. If your people fight each other openly in your presence for what they believe in, that's healthy. But keep all conflict eyeball to eyeball.

Robert Townsend
Former CEO, Avis
Further Up the Organization (Knopf, 1984)

A distinction must be drawn between presenting arguments in a positive manner and being argumentative.

Maurice S. Trotter
New York University
Supervisor's Handbook on Insubordination
(Bureau of National Affairs, 1967)

Intense feeling too often obscures the truth.

Harry S. Truman, 1884–1972
Thirty-third President of the United States
Speech, October 19, 1948

Too much fault-finding with rulers brings disgrace; with friends, it brings estrangement.

Tzu Hsia, 1834–1908
Dowager Empress of China
Words and Sayings

When angry, count to four; when very angry, swear.

Mark Twain
(Samuel Langhorne Clemens), 1835–1910
American author and riverboat captain
Pudd'nhead Wilson's Calendar

It were not best that we should all think alike; it is difference of opinion that makes horse-races.

Mark Twain
(Samuel Langhorne Clemens), 1835–1910
American author and riverboat captain
Pudd'nhead Wilson's Calendar

Let us work without disputing; it is the only way to render life tolerable.

François Marie Voltaire, 1694–1778
French writer
Candide

I remember that a wise friend of mine did usually say, "that which is everybody's business is nobody's business."

Izaak Walton, 1593–1683
English biographer and businessman
The Compleat Angler

One can distinguish between resolution and control as different goals of conflict management. The principals themselves or a third party may attempt to gain *resolution*, so that the original differences or feelings of opposition no longer exist, or they may attempt to merely *control* conflict, so that the negative consequences of the conflict are decreased, even though the opposing preferences and antagonisms persist.

Richard Walton
Organizational consultant
Interpersonal Peacemaking
(Addison-Wesley, 1969)

It is much easier to avoid disagreement than to remove discontents.

George Washington, 1732–1799
First President of the United States
Letter to John Sullivan, May 11, 1781

If you're going to be a bridge, you've got to be prepared to be walked upon.

Roy A. West
Principal,
Mosby Middle School, Richmond, Virginia
The Washington Post, May 8, 1988

Arguments are to be avoided; they are always vulgar and often convincing.

Oscar Wilde, 1854–1900
Irish poet, wit, and dramatist
Prochnow, *The Toastmaster's Treasure Chest*
(Harper & Row, 1979)

A man once reproached another, who then made no reply. They asked him, "Why do you not reply?" He answered, "I will enter no quarrel where the victor suffers defeat."

Joseph ibn Zabara, c. 1150
Spanish physician and writer
The Book of Delight

Managers in business and government in the United States appear to be insulating themselves from views that differ from their own. Harmony and amiability are so highly valued that many organizations operate with ineffectual policies because managers are reluctant to risk unpleasantness by speaking up.

Dale E. Zand
New York University
Information, Organization, and Power
(McGraw-Hill, 1981)

8

Corporate Culture

Experience tells you only so much about a company; its culture tells more.

The [quality control] issue has more to do with people and motivation and less to do with capital and equipment than one would think. It involves a cultural change.

Michael Beer
Harvard Business School
The Washington Post, October 11, 1987

[T]he price of continued deviation from a group norm is rejection.

Robert J. Blake and Jane S. Mouton
Scientific Methods, Inc.
Productivity: The Human Side
(AMACOM, 1981)

To be a manager, you have to start at the bottom—no exceptions.

Henry Block
CEO, H&R Block
Inc. Magazine, December 1987

The conclusion our study produced is that *employee timidity leads to mediocrity and the eventual stagnation of the firm.*

Srully Blotnick
Management consultant
The Corporate Steeplechase
(Facts On File, 1984)

Silicon Valley is like an individual running around in front of a steamroller. You can out-run the steamroller on any given day. But if you ever sit down you get squashed.

Bob Boschert
High-tech entrepreneur
Hickman and Silva, *Creating Excellence*
(New American Library, 1984)

Organizational culture is ... built in countless small ways, on a daily basis. The manager's interactions with others ... all help establish the department's norms about what is valued and how things are done.

David L. Bradford
Stanford University School of Business
and Allan R. Cohen
Babson College
Managing for Excellence (Wiley, 1984)

[Speaking of Thomas Watson, Sr., founder of IBM:] Let him discourse on the manifest destiny of IBM, and you are ready to join the company for life.... Everybody in the organization is expected to find the ubiquitous THINK sign a constant source of inspiration, as the weary travelers of old found new strength in the wayside crucifixes.

Gil Burck
Business writer and reporter
Fortune, January 1940

Manners are of more importance than laws.

Edmund Burke, 1729–1797
English statesman, orator, and writer
Letters on a Regicide Peace

Organizational values are best transmitted when they are acted out, and not merely announced, by the people responsible for training, or by the people who become role-models for recruits. The manager of an organization is a role-model *ex officio* and may have an astonishing ability to communicate organizational values to recruits in fleeting contacts with them. That is the age-old secret of successful generalship, and it is applied every day by charismatic leaders in other fields, whose commitments to their roles is so dramatic that they strike awe into the recruits who observe them in action.

Theodore Caplow
Managing an Organization
(CBS College Publishing, 1983)

Business papers should never be displayed in the common rooms of the first, second and third floors.

Century Club of New York
The Spirit and the Letter, 1985

We have a maxim in the House of Commons, and written on the walls of our house, that old ways are safest and surest ways.

Edward Coke, 1552–1634
English politician and jurist
Speech in Parliament, May 9, 1628

Custom, that unwritten law,
By which the people keep even kings in awe.

William D'Avenant, 1606–1668
English poet and dramatist
Circe

The individual in the large organization ... like the uncalculating animals, is also a defenseless creature who calculatingly practices deception for safety's sake against the invisible threats around him.

Melville Dalton
American sociologist
Men Who Manage (Wiley, 1959)

These builders [of the great early American corporations like IBM, Procter & Gamble, and Johnson & Johnson] saw their role as creating an environment—in effect a culture—in their companies in which employees could be secure and thereby do the work necessary to make the business a success.

Terrence E. Deal and Allan A. Kennedy
Harvard Business School
Corporate Cultures (Addison-Wesley, 1982)

It is often possible to track company statements over time and watch how its culture evolves, a procedure called content analysis. It can be done by simply tabulating the number of times a particular phrase or belief is articulated in the annual report. The surprise is that even such a simplistic analysis will show a clear trend in the evolution of a company's beliefs about itself.

Terrence E. Deal and Allan A. Kennedy
Harvard Business School
Corporate Cultures (Addison-Wesley, 1982)

A culture is its heroes, values, networks. It has all these things, but something else besides. Culture is a money-in-pocket investment—for CEO's, financial analysts, even job seekers. Experience tells you only so much about a company; its culture tells more.... CEO's and senior managers can read a culture for early warning signals of people out of synch with the aims of their business. Investment analysts can turn to culture for greater accuracy in forecasting. Even executives in search of new opportunities would do well to match-make their personality to that of a company.

Terrence E. Deal and Allan A. Kennedy
Harvard Business School
Corporate Cultures (Addison-Wesley, 1982)

After examining hundreds of corporations and their business enviornments, we have come to see that many companies fall into four general categories or types of cultures.... The tough-guy, macho culture.... The work hard/play hard culture.... The bet-your-company culture.... The process culture.... No company we know today precisely fits into any one of these categories. In fact, within any single real-world company, a mix of all four types of cultures will be found. Marketing departments are tough-guy cultures. Sales and manufacturing departments work hard and play hard. Research and development is a world of high risk and slow feedback. And accounting sits squarely in the upper reaches of bureaucratic life.

Terrence E. Deal and Allan A. Kennedy
Harvard Business School
Corporate Cultures (Addison-Wesley, 1982)

When they [workers] choose a company, they often choses a way of life. The [corporate] culture shapes their responses in a strong, but substantial way. Culture can make them fast or slow workers, tough or friendly managers, team players or individuals. By the time they've worked for several years, they may be so well conditioned by the culture they might not even recognize it. But when they change jobs they may be in for a big surprise.

Terrence E. Deal and Allan A. Kennedy
Harvard Business School
Corporate Cultures (Addison-Wesley, 1982)

There is a written and an unwritten law. The one by which we regulate our constitutions in our cities is the written law; that which arises from custom is the unwritten law.

Diogenes Laertius, c. 200–250
Greek historian and writer
Lives and Opinions of Eminent Philosophers:
Xenocrates

A want of tact is worse than a want of virtue.

Benjamin Disraeli, 1804–1881
English Prime Minister and novelist
The Young Duke

"Management" means, in the last analysis, the substitution of thought for brawn and muscle, of knowledge for folkways and superstition, and of cooperation for force. It means the substitution of responsibility for obedience to rank, and of authority of performance for authority of rank.

Peter F. Drucker
Management consultant and writer
People and Performance
(Harper & Row, 1977)

[Employed professionals] see themselves as the successors to yesterday's independent professional; but they are employees.... These people are not "bosses"; but they are also not "subordinates." They "report" to someone rather than "take orders." They work for an institution rather than for a person. They constitute a new social class, a new social phenomenon that does not fit our perceptions, or for that matter, their own self-perceptions.

> Peter F. Drucker
> Management consultant and writer
> *Management in Turbulent Times*
> (Harper & Row, 1980)

We live in a world where corporate executives believe they can spend the assets of ... corporations for their own creature comforts. Those executives ... have created a high flying world of undisclosed corporate perks, including private jets, corporate apartments, hunting lodges, country clubs, and martini infused lunches, all unwarranted and all paid for by unknowing shareholders.

> Asher B. Edelman
> General Partner, Plaza Securities Co.
> *The New York Times*, November 22, 1987

The smaller the role of marketing, the greater the possibility that the firm operates its marketing activities on a project, crisis, and fragmented basis.

> Joel R. Evans and Barry Berman
> Hofstra University
> *Essentials of Marketing* (Macmillan, 1984)

You've got to have an atmosphere where people can make mistakes. If we're not making mistakes we're not going anywhere.

> Gordon Foward
> President, Chaparral Steel
> Peters, *Thriving on Chaos* (Knopf, 1987)

These men of the technostructure are the new and universal priesthood. Their religion is business success; their test of virtue is growth and profit. Their bible is the computer printout; their communion bench is the committee room. The sales force carries their message

to the world, and a message is what it is often called.

> John Kenneth Galbraith
> Economist and diplomat
> *The Age of Uncertainty*

A strong corporate culture is the invisible hand that guides how things are done in an organization. The phrase, "You just can't do that here," is extremely powerful, more so than any written rules or policy manuals.

> Andrew S. Grove
> CEO, Intel Corp.
> *One-On-One With Andy Grove*
> (G. P. Putnam's Sons, 1987)

I want workers to go home at night and say "I built that car."

> Pehr G. Gyllenhammar
> Chairman, Volvo (Sweden)
> *Administrative Management*, September 1987

It is no accident that 80 percent of the businessmen who comprise today's chief executive officers told *Fortune* magazine ... that football was their favorite spectator sport.... College textbooks often introduce business management subjects to inexperienced students by using the illustration of a football platoon.... Top management in business feels an intense affinity to the head coach of a football team; their problems seem almost identical.... Sports metaphors abound in business talk ... back—up team or bench strength ... coach ... disqualified player ... end run ... huddle ... jock, Monday morning quarterback ... punt ... quarterback ... tackle the job.

> Betty Lehan Harragan
> Business writer
> *Games Mother Never Taught You*
> (Warner, 1977)

A corporation prefers to offer a job to a man who already has one, or doesn't immediately need one. The company accepts you if you are already accepted. To obtain entry into paradise, in terms of employment, you should be in a full state of grace.

> Alan Harrington
> Advertising executive and manager
> *Life in the Crystal Palace* (Knopf, 1959)

All the forces of corporate culture are set against change.

> Bruce Henderson
> CEO, Boston Consulting Group, Inc.
> *Henderson on Corporate Strategy* (Abt, 1979)

Strong corporate cultures, like strong family cultures, come from within, and they are built by individual leaders, not consultants.

> Craig R. Hickman
> President, Bennett Information Group
> and Michael A. Silva
> President and CEO, Bennett Enterprises
> *Creating Excellence*
> (New American Library, 1984)

The act of becoming a member [of a corporation] is something more than a contract, it is entering into a complex and abiding relation.

> Oliver Wendell Holmes, Jr., 1841–1935
> U. S. Supreme Court Justice
> *Modern Woodman* v. *Mixer* (1924)

EVER ONWARD—EVER ONWARD.

That's the spirit that brought us fame!
We're big, but bigger we will be.
We can't fail for all can see,
That to serve humanity has been our aim.
Our products are now known in every zone.
Our reputation sparkles like a gem.
We've fought our way through, and new
Fields we're sure to conquer too.
Forever onward IBM.

> IBM Company Song

As long as people do their jobs well, I see no reason why they shouldn't have as much fun as they possibly can.

> Andy Jacobs
> Cofounder, Jacobs Bros. Bagels
> *Brown Alumni Monthly,* April 1988

Most company presidents show an immediate understanding of what President William Howard Taft had in mind when he said after he had been in the White House several months, "Nobody ever drops in for the evening."

> J. Elliott Janney
> *Harvard Business Review*, May/June 1952

We know more about the motives, habits, and most intimate arcana of the primitive peoples of New Guinea or elsewhere, than we do the denizens of the executive suites in Unilever House.

> Roy Lewis and Rosemary Stewart
> *The Boss* (Phoenix House, 1958)

With economic success, a change in emphasis from innovation to tightened administration tends to create an increasingly rigid culture. The new culture inhibits the rapid changes often necessary to respond to a rapidly changing business environment.

> Peter Lorange
> The Wharton School
> and Robert T. Nelson
> Management consultant
> *Sloan Management Review*, Spring 1987

I watched two strong, old male baboons assaulting each other in earnest for a minute. A moment later, one of them fled, hotly pursued by the other, who finally chased him into a corner. Unable to escape, the loser ran after him and presented his colorful hindquarters, so persistently that the stronger one eventually "acknowledged" his submissiveness by mounting him with a bored expression and performing a few perfunctory copulatory movements. Only then was the submissive one apparently satisfied that his rebellion had been forgiven.

Konrad Lorentz
Anthropologist and writer
On Aggression
(Harcourt, Brace & World, 1966)

Employees are most apt to deal with their problems when they believe that they will be helped in good faith.

Paul V. Lyons
Partner, Foley, Hoag & Eliot
Management, March 1987

For some reason, Wall Street is highly joke-tolerant. There, humor—in many guises—is not only an antidote to stress but frequently the excuse to call a customer.

Dyan Machan
Writer, "Careers"
Forbes, November 2, 1987

Diffused knowledge immortalizes itself.

James Mackintosh, 1765–1832
Scottish physician, judge, and historian
Vindiciae Gallicae

The dress of a wise man must be free of stains; he should not wear the apparel of princes, to attract attention; nor the raiment of paupers, which incurs disrespect.

Moses Maimonides, 1135–1204
Egyptian physician and philosopher
Mishneh Torah

I favor a very democratic, open, egalitarian atmosphere combined with a slightly mysterious, benevolent authority.

Fritz Maytag
President, Anchor Brewing Co.
Harvard Business Review, July/August 1986

We believe that our activities should be governed by the needs and desires of our customers rather than by our internal requirements and insights.

Eugene F. McCabe
Vice President of Marketing,
Merke Sharpe & Dohme
Management, January 1987

It [financial services] wasn't their [Westinghouse's headquarters executives] thing. It doesn't hum, it doesn't rotate and you don't plug it in.

John McClester
Chairman, Westinghouse Financial Services
Forbes, April 4, 1988

We had been a proud group who felt that people who knew nothing were telling us what to do. It took us a long time to realize that regulators, legislators, even environmentalists had a right to ask questions.

Keith R. McKennon
President, Dow Chemical USA
The New York Times, November 22, 1987

Culture itself is neither education nor law-making: it is an atmosphere and a heritage.

Henry Louis Mencken, 1880–1956
Editor, author, and critic
Minority Report

In declining organizations, pathology and dysfunctioning are more widespread than in organizations displaying neurotic organizational behavior.

Uri Merry and George I. Brown
The Neurotic Behavior of Organizations
(Gestalt Institute of Cleveland, 1987)

Disclosure, frankness, and revelation are not useful tactics in any male sport for they tend to be obstructive and ineffective. For this reason many females consider businessmen and politicians devious and deceitful. But we have little experience with quarterback sneaks and closely held cards. Women promote "honesty," by which we mean the right to say whatever we feel about someone without having to pay the consequences.

> Jinx Milea
> University of Southern California
> and Pauline Lyttle
> President, Operational Politics, Inc.
> *Why Jenny Can't Lead*, 1986

The achievement of excellence can occur only if the organization promotes a culture of creative dissatisfaction.

> Lawrence M. Miller
> Business consultant
> *American Spirit* (William Morrow, 1984)

When white-collar people get jobs, they sell not only their time and energy, but their personalities as well. They sell by the week, or month, their smiles and their kindly gestures, and they must practice that prompt repression of resentment and aggression.

> C. Wright Mills, 1916–1962
> American sociologist
> *White Collar* (Oxford, 1956)

Ultimately, vision gets translated into sales and profit growth and return on investment, but the numbers come after the vision. In the old-style companies, the numbers are the vision.

> John Naisbett and Patricia Aburdene
> Business writers and social researchers
> *Re-inventing the Corporation* (Warner, 1985)

Companies that cling to a "go it alone" mentality are in danger of going the way of the dinosaur as we move toward the 21st century.

> Lorenze Necci
> President, EniChem (Italy)
> *Management*, March 1987

Individual managers ... are all different, but they share a management culture ... and values: economic efficiency, growth, short-term profitability, loyalty to the system.

> James O'Toole
> University of Southern California
> *Making America Work* (Continuum, 1981)

New ideas ... are not born in a conforming environment.

> Roger von Oech
> President, Creative Think, Inc.
> *A Whack on the Side of the Head*
> (Warner, 1983)

[Referring to the trend of people working at home:] It's against corporate culture not to have people on site. Executives want to own their employees.

> Margreth Olson
> Director,
> Center for Research on Information Systems
> *Working Woman*, March 1988

What we saw [by comparing us to the Japanese] was that generally we were very similar on all the "hard-ball" S's—strategy, structure, and systems. Our major differences are in the "soft-ball" S's—skills, style, staff, and superordinate goals. Their culture gives them advantages in the "softer" S's because of its approach to ambiguity, uncertainty, and imperfection, and to interdependence as the most approved mode of relationship.

> Richard T. Pascale
> Stanford University School of Business
> and Anthony G. Athos
> Harvard Business School
> *The Art of Japanese Management*
> (Simon & Schuster, 1981)

Organizations tend to grow through stages, face and surmount crises, and along the way learn lessons and draw morals that shape values and future actions. Usually these developments influence assumptions and the way people behave. Often key episodes are recounted in "war stories" that convey lessons about the firm's origins and transformations in dramatic form. Eventually, this lore provides a consistent background for action. New members are exposed to the common history and acquire insight into some of the subtle aspects of their company.;

Richard T. Pascale
Stanford University School of Business
and Anthony G. Athos
Harvard Business School
The Art of Japanese Management
(Simon & Schuster, 1981)

The first EDSer to see a snake kills it. At GM, the first thing you do is organize a committee on snakes. Then you bring in a consultant who knows a lot about snakes. Third thing you do is talk about it for a year..

H. Ross Perot
Founder, Electronic Data Systems
Peters, *Thriving on Chaos*
(Knopf, 1987)

Generally the American executive does not take to doctrines, theories, or systems.... The dominant proportion of establishments ... have managements representing inherited patterns modified by casual imitation.

H. S. Person
Early management writer
Scientific Management in American Society,
1929

Most hierarchies were established by men who now monopolize the upper levels, thus depriving women of their rightful share of opportunities for incompetence.

Laurence J. Peter
University of Southern California
The Peter Principle (William Morrow, 1969)

Nothing reveals more of what a company really cares about than its stories and legends.... Listening to a company's stories is the surest

route to determining its real priorities and who symbolizes them.

Tom Peters and Nancy Austin
Management consultants and writers
A Passion for Excellence
(Random House, 1985)

You won't reduce the paperwork in a lasting fashion until you remove the underlying cause for it—mistrust and adversarial relations.

Tom Peters
Business writer
Thriving on Chaos (Knopf, 1987)

Excellent firms don't believe in excellence—only in constant improvement and constant change.

Tom Peters
Business writer
The Washington Post, October 4, 1987

Success breeds conservatism, and that means a love affair with the status quo and an aversion to change.

Frank Popoff
CEO, Dow Chemical Co.
The New York Times, November 22, 1987

Corporate culture has rarely encouraged female participation throughout history.

Shirley Quastler
Executive Vice President,
Quastler Advertising, Inc.
Inc. Magazine, September 1986

[Quoting St. Ambrose:] When I am at Milan, I do as they do at Milan; but when I go to Rome, I do as Rome does.

St. Augustine, 354–430
Early Christian church father and philosopher
Epistles

There has been an enormous amount of pain and trauma. And the culture's not completely changed yet.

J. Phillip Samper
Vice Chairman, Kodak
The New York Times, March 6, 1988

If the prevailing culture about attendance in the organization is one that values good attendance, then the attendance levels of most employees will be good.

Paul Sandwith
Senior Consultant, Alpha Association (Canada)
Personnel Journal, November 1987

The sources of innovation and the requirements for innovation tend to create a climate favorable to an ethic of change.

Lyle E. Schaller
Yokefellow Institute
The Change Agent (Abingdon, 1972)

[The chief executive's role is]... instilling an attitude of quality ... creating a common purpose and corporate identity.

Erich Mittleson Scheid
German industrialist
Washington Business Week, October 19, 1987

Culture [is] a pattern of basic assumptions—invented, discovered, or developed by a given group as it learns to cope with its problems of external adaptation and internal integration—that has worked well enough to be considered valid and, therefore, to be taught to new members as the correct way to perceive, think, and feel in relation to those problems.

Edgar H. Schein
Massachusetts Institute of Technology
Organizational Culture and Leadership
(Jossey-Bass, 1985)

Employees are not only members of the organization which employs them, they are also members of society, other organizations, unions, consumer groups, and so on. From these various other roles they bring with them demands, expectations and cultural norms which often conflict with the internal norms of the employing organization.

Edgar H. Schein
Massachusetts Institute of Technology
Human Problems in Organization
(Prentice-Hall, 1980)

The customer comes first, employees second and stockholders third.

Elliot Sclar
Chairman, Franklin Research & Development
Vital Speeches of the Day, March 1, 1988

Jails, like other places, have their ancient traditions, known only to the inhabitants, and handed down from one set of the melancholy lodgers to the next who occupy their cells.

Walter Scott, 1771–1832
Scottish poet, novelist, and biographer
The Heart of Midlothian

Implementers aren't considered bozos anymore.

John Sculley
CEO, Apple Computer Co.
Peters, *Thriving on Chaos* (Knopf, 1987)

[Referring to Tandy, his previous employer:] There are no secrets. Everybody knows what everybody else is doing. The store manager who makes a quarter of a million dollars stands up in front of everybody and gets handed a plaque with a replica of a check on it. Everybody knows this guy made more money than most vp's. It's that kind of culture.

John Shirley
President, Microsoft Corp.
Computer & Software News, December 7, 1987

[Referring to the executives in the American copper industry:] They finally got off the golf course and tried to figure out what they could do to improve the situation.

> William G. Siedenburg
> Analyst, Smith Barney, Harris Upham & Co.
> *The Washington Post*, January 17, 1988

An institution cannot be explained in terms of principles alone. Human energy is required to give life and purpose and direction to principles. Certain principles have been kept alive during the 70 years of the concern's existence because various men at various times performed certain tasks, or endured certain trials, or took certain risks, or dedicated themselves to certain causes.... The spirit of an institution will inevitably be a reflection of the persons who formulate and direct its policies.

> John H. Sorrells
> Executive Editor, Scripps Howard Newspapers
> *A Handbook of Scripps Howard*, 1948

You can't tell people you trust them—and be believed—if you have a lot of inspectors and auditors running around.

> Louis Springer
> CEO, Campbell Soup
> *Government Executive*, January 1987

Courtesy is as important within an organization as in dealing with outsiders.

> Swift and Company
> *Employee Relations Manual*, 1921

Professionals have dual loyalties. They respond both to the needs of their employers and the influence of their professions.

> Robert M. Tomasko
> Principal, Temple, Barker & Sloane, Inc.
> *Downsizing* (AMACOM, 1987)

In statesmanship get the formalities right, never mind about the moralities.

> Mark Twain
> (Samuel Langhorne Clemens), 1835–1910
> American author and riverboat captain
> *Pudd'nhead Wilson's New Calendar*

If it moves, salute it.
If it doesn't move, pick it up.
If you can't pick it up, paint it.

> United States Army

Conservatism means the maintenance of conventions already in force. The business classes are conservative ... but such a conservative bent is not peculiar to them. These occupations are not the only ones whose reasoning ... moves on a conventional plane. Indeed, the intellectual activity of other classes, such as soldiers, politicians, the clergy, and men of fashion, moves on a plane of still older conventions, so that if the training given by business employment is to be characterized as conservative, that given by these other, more archaic employments should be called reactionary.

> Thorstein Veblen, 1857–1929
> American political economist and sociologist
> *The Theory of Business Enterprise*

[Explaining her honor system for production workers' time cards:] It works both ways. I don't want them to think we don't trust them; they don't nickle and dime us either.

> Nancy Vetrone
> President, Original Copy Centers, Inc.
> *Inc. Magazine*, March 1988

I understand why some American companies fail to gain the loyalty and dedication of their employees. Employees cannot care for an employer who is prepared to take their livelihood away at the first sign of trouble.

Samadi Wada
Vice President, Sony of America
Tomasko, *Downsizing* (AMACOM, 1987)

A worker is, first of all, a person who must fit into the social community in which he works.

Guy M. Wadsworth, Jr.
Employment Test developer
Studies in Personnel Policy 32
(National Industrial Conference Board, 1941)

It's important for me to get on the cafeteria line like everyone else.

Ralph E. Ward
CEO, Chesebrough-Pond, Inc.
Management, January 1987

You have to have your heart in the business and the business in your heart.

Thomas J. Watson, Sr., 1874–1956
Founder and first President, IBM
Favorite saying

I'd have to say that [before the events of the past four years] our culture in the Ford Motor Company said that there's one central objective in our business, and that's to earn a return on our investment. I think we've now learned there's something else that's central—and that profits will fall to you if you view this as central: *Serve the customer.* You have to have your costs right, quality right, all those other things that have to be done. But we must always think the customer is the middle of the thrust of what we're trying to do. I think that's what we've learned. I don't think it's much more complicated than that, and I would suggest it to you for your consideration.

Edson P. Williams
Vice President, Ford Truck Operations
Peters and Austin, *A Passion for Excellence*
(Random House, 1985)

Acquire, too, a habit of observation on men and manners, without which you can never secure the knowledge of the world essential to success in practical life.

Martha Wilson, 1758–1848
Friend of George Washington
Letter to C. S. Stewart, May 31, 1814

We decided to create an open and dialogue-intensive corporate culture. This generates creativity and motivation and brings out entrepreneurs at all levels. This is the true power and success of Bertelsmann.

Mark Woessner
CEO, Bertelsmann Group (West Germany)
The Washington Post, November 22, 1987

Personal values are influenced by prevailing company norms—the company's local culture. Typically, one or a few strong, respected senior executives set the tone. Their values become widely known, mostly through their actions. Risks that should be taken, attention to the environment, the precedence of the bottom line over customer or employee relations, and similar matters are likely to be treated in a manner congruent with values endorsed by the tone-setters.

Boris Yavitz
Director, Federal Reserve Bank of New York
and William H. Newman
Columbia University School of Business
Strategy in Action (The Free Press, 1982)

One critical source of knowledge is an understanding of how your organization formulates policies.

Dale E. Zand
New York University
Information, Organization, and Power
(McGraw-Hill, 1981)

9
Counseling & Advice

We may give advice,
but we cannot inspire the conduct.

If you need to talk [about a personal crisis], find a confidant outside the office [instead of discussing your problems with a colleague] or see a counselor.

Patricia G. Abelson
Director of Employee Counseling Services,
Jewish Family and Children's Services
Working Woman, April 1988

Beware of the counsel of the unfortunate.

Aesop, c. 620–c. 560 B.C.
Greek fabulist
The Fox Who Lost His Tail

Advice is like a stranger—if welcome, he stays the night; if not welcome, he returns home that day.

African proverb

If you must deal in criticism, confine your practice to self-criticism.

The Little Red Book of Alcoholics Anonymous
(Coll-Webb, 1955)

We generally need someone to show us things which should be apparent to the eyes of all.

Francisco Algarotti, 1712–1764
Italian writer and scientist
An Essay On Opera

One often hears the remark "He talks too much," but when did anyone last hear the criticism "He listens too much"?

Norman R. Augustine
President, and CEO, Martin Marietta Corp.
Augustine's Laws (Penguin, 1987)

Ineffective leaders often act on the advice and counsel of the last person they talked to.

Warren G. Bennis
President, University of Cincinnati
University of Maryland symposium,
January 21, 1988

Make sure you have someone in your life from whom you can get reflective feedback.

> Warren G. Bennis
> President, University of Cincinatti
> University of Maryland symposium,
> January 21, 1988

Most of the advice we receive from others is not so much evidence of their affection for us, as it is evidence of their affection for themselves.

> Josh Billings
> (Henry Wheeler Shaw), 1818–1885
> American writer and auctioneer
> *Josh Billings: His Book*

Who cannot give good counsel? 'Tis cheap, it costs them nothing.

> Robert Burton, 1577–1640
> Vicar of St. Thomas's, Oxford
> *The Anatomy of Melancholy*

It is quite natural that your son, who is probably young and energetic, wants to keep up with the times.... We are of the opinion that if your husband is near the age when he will be ready to turn the whole business over to his son he should now, little by little, give him a chance to show what he can do. But if he is not yet thinking of retiring and is absolutely opposed to making changes in the business, then the son must not be hindered from looking for something else.

> Abraham Cahan, 1860–1951
> Journalist and newspaper editor
> *A Bintel Brief* (Doubleday, 1971)

A leader must have the courage to act against an expert's advice.

> James Callaghan
> English Prime Minister
> *Harvard Business Review*,
> November/December 1986

You don't want to get the same kind of advice from everyone on your board.

> Ruben Cardenas
> Attorney and Director, Southwestern Bell
> *Hispanic Business,* August 1987

In those days Mr. Baldwin was wiser than he is now; he used frequently to take my advice.

> Winston Churchill, 1874–1965
> English Prime Minister, author, and soldier
> Speech in Parliament, May 22, 1935

Advice is judged by results, not by intentions

> Cicero, 106–43 B.C.
> Roman orator and statesman
> *Ad Atticum*

Personal counseling requires professional training and experience, and even qualified counselors would probably refer their own employees to another source in order to keep the supervisor-employee relationship clear of counseling complexities.

> William F. Cone
> Manager of Professional Development,
> Hughes Aircraft
> *Supervising Employees Effectively*
> (Addison-Wesley, 1974)

Be always sure you're right—then go ahead.

> David Crockett, 1786–1836
> American pioneer and soldier
> Motto

There is no wisdom like frankness.

> Benjamin Disraeli, 1804–1881
> English Prime Minister and novelist
> *Sybil*

I know they are most deceived that trusteth most in themselves.

> Elizabeth I, 1533–1603
> Queen of England
> Letter to Lord Protector Edward Seymour,
> February 21, 1549

Bad counsel confounds the advisor.

> Ralph Waldo Emerson, 1803–1882
> American essayist and poet
> *Compensation*

Criticism should not be querulous and wasting, all knife and root-puller, but guiding, instructive, inspiring, a south wind, not an east wind.

> Ralph Waldo Emerson, 1803–1882
> American and essayist and poet
> *Journals*

Keep counsel of thyself first.

> English proverb

Endure and abjure.

> Epictetus, c. 100
> Stoic philosopher
> *Discourses*

If err we must, let us err on the side of tolerance.

> Felix Frankfurter, 1882–1965
> U. S. Supreme Court Justice
> *The New York Times*, November 23, 1952

He that won't be counseled can't be helped.

> Benjamin Franklin, 1706–1790
> American printer and statesman
> *Poor Richard's Almanack*

None is so perfect that he does not need at times the advice of others. He is an incorrigible ass who will never listen to anyone. Even the most surpassing intellect should find a place for friendly counsel.

> Baltasar Gracián, 1601–1658
> Spanish priest and popular writer
> *The Art of Worldly Wisdom*

[B]ecause God has endued thee with so violent a spirit, as that whatever you want, you want very strongly; therefore by so much the more it behooveth thee to deliberate what thou undertakest.

> Elizabeth Grymeston, c. 1563–1603
> English writer
> *Miscelanea*

None ever has the right to flee advice.

> Marco Guazzo, 1496–1556
> Italian writer
> *Errori d'Amore*

Know when to speak; for many times it brings Danger to give the best advice to kings.

> Robert Herrick, 1591–1674
> English poet
> *Hesperides*

That man [is] far best who can conceive and carry out with foresight a wise counsel; next in order [is one] with the sense to value and heed such [wise] counsel; while he who can neither initiate it [counsel] nor avail himself of it when thrown in his way, is to all intents and purposes worthless and good for nothing.

> Hesiod, eighth century B.C.
> Greek poet
> *Works and Days*

The advice of elders to young men is very apt to be as unreal as a list of the hundred best books.

> Oliver Wendell Holmes, Jr., 1841–1935
> U. S. Supreme Court Justice
> *The Path of the Law*

Whatever advice you give, be brief.

Horace, 65–8 B.C.
Roman poet and satirist
Ars Poetica

Never make a decision. Let someone else make it and then if it turns out to be the wrong one, you can disclaim it, and if it is the right one you can abide by it.

Howard R. Hughes, 1905–1976
Founder, Hughes Tool Co.
The Hughes Legacy: Scramble for the Billion
(Time, 1976)

No one's head aches when he is comforting another.

Indian proverb

True words are not fine; fine words are not true.

Lao-Tzu, c. 604–c. 531 B.C.
Chinese philosopher and founder of Taoism
Precepts and Sayings

Employees are most apt to deal with their problems when they believe that they will be helped in good faith.

Paul V. Lyons
Partner, Foley, Hoag and Eliot
Management, March 1987

People ask you for criticism, but they only want praise.

W. Somerset Maugham, 1874–1965
English novelist and playwright
Of Human Bondage

It is the dull man who is always sure, and the sure man who is always dull.

Henry Louis Mencken, 1880–1956
Editor, author, and critic
Prejudices

'Tis the worst counsel
To take no counsel.

Pietro Antonio Metastasio, 1698–1782
Italian poet and dramatist
Demafoonte

[The Japanese] spend seemingly endless time analyzing the situation, studying the problem, and looking at all avenues of the decision-making process before making a decision. Everyone has a say before the decision is made. Typically, they then move much faster in getting the decision implemented than we do in our American system.

R. Henry Miglione
Oral Roberts University
An MBO Approach to Long-Range Planning
(Prentice-Hall, 1983)

Part of our drive for explicitness stems from the Western notion that it's a matter of honor to "get the cards on the table." The assumption is that no matter how much it hurts, the "truth" is good for you, and it is a sign of strength and maturity to give and take negative feedback.... The evidence would suggest that for most of us being pushed *too* hard and crowded into a corner is counterproductive. Great honesty is seldom helpful without empathetic compassion, skillfully expressed in private, by someone assumed to care about the other person's well-being.

Richard T. Pascale
Stanford University School of Business
and Anthony G. Athos
Harvard Business School
The Art of Japanese Management
(Simon & Schuster, 1981)

They have a Right to censure, that have a *Heart* to help: The rest is Cruelty, not Justice.

William Penn, 1644–1718
Founder of Pennsylvania
Fruits of Solitude in Reflections and Maxims

Enquire *often*, but Judge *rarely*, and thou wilt not often be mistaken.

> William Penn, 1644–1718
> Founder of Pennsylvania
> *Fruits of Solitude in Reflections and Maxims*

Before you take on the counseling role, ask yourself if the situation really calls for it ... give the individual a reasonable chance to turn things around under his or her own power, with your wholehearted support, without your interference. Counseling is *not* meddling— "involvement without the right or an invitation." Too soon is as disastrous as too late. You have the right to counsel only when you're invited, or performance problems threaten to undermine an individual's ability to contribute over time in spite of conscientious education and coaching.

> Tom Peters and Nancy Austin
> Management consultants
> *A Passion for Excellence*
> (Random House, 1985)

Give me money, not advice.

> Portugese proverb

For want of counsel a people will fall;
But safety lies in a wealth of counselors.

> Old Testament, Proverbs 11:14

Reprove your friends in secret, praise them in public.

> Publilius Syrus, c. 42 B.C.
> Roman writer
> *Maxims*

Many receive advice; few profit by it.

> Publilius Syrus, c. 42 B.C.
> Roman writer
> *Maxims*

We may give advice, but we cannot inspire the conduct.

> François de La Rochefoucauld, 1613–1680
> French politician, writer, and philanthropist
> *Reflections, or Sentences and Moral Maxims*

Advice should be given by the example of the accomplished, not by one's own meager experience.

> Dagobert D. Runes
> Editor, publisher, and philosopher
> *A Book of Contemplation*

Consult your friend on all things, especially on those which respect yourself. His counsel may then be useful where your own self love might impair your judgment.

> Seneca, 4 B.C.–A.D. 65
> Roman orator and rhetorician
> *Epistles to Lucilius*

Friendly counsel cuts off many foes.

> William Shakespeare, 1564–1616
> English dramatist and poet
> *King Henry IV*

It can be no dishonor to learn from others when they speak good sense.

> Sophocles, c. 496–406 B.C.
> Greek tragic playwright
> *Antigone*

I know how to listen when clever men are talking. That is the secret of what you call my influence.

> Hermann Sudermann, 1857–1928
> German playwright and novelist
> *The Joy of Living*

A friend advises in his interest, not yours.

> Turkish proverb

He had only one vanity, he thought he could give advice better than any other person.

Mark Twain
(Samuel Langhorne Clemens), 1835–1910
American author and riverboat captain
The Man that Corrupted Hadleyburg

Reason and emotion are each the other's counsellor and complement.... Whoever takes counsel of one of them only, and neglects the other, is thoughtlessly forfeiting a part of the aid that has been granted for our guidance.

Marquis de Vauvenargues, 1715–1747
French soldier and moralist
Reflections and Maxims

Time may unfold more, than prudence ought to disclose.

George Washington, 1732–1799
First President of the United States
Letter to Henry Lee, July 21, 1793

Confidence is a thing not produced by compulsion. Men cannot be forced into trust.

Daniel Webster, 1782–1852
American statesman and orator
Speech, U. S. Senate, 1833

(1) Never pay any debt that can possibly be avoided; (2) Never do anything to-day that can by any possibility be avoided; (3) Never do anything [yourself] which you can get anybody else to do [for you].

Daniel Webster, 1782–1852
American statesman and orator
Quoted by Emerson, *Journals*

All cruel people describe themselves as paragons of frankness.

Tennessee Williams, 1914–1983
American playwright and novelist
The Milk Train Doesn't Stop Here Anymore

Words should be weighed and not counted.

Yiddish proverb

When you give advice, remember that Socrates was a Greek philosopher who went around giving good advice. They poisoned him.

Anonymous
Prochnow, *New Speaker's Treasury of Wit and Wisdom* (Harper & Brothers, 1958)

No distance is greater than that between advice and help.

Anonymous

10

Decision Making

Second thoughts are invariably wiser.

One of the problems in the United States, with government and business, is the very short-term, expedient approach to problems.

William Agee
Chairman, Bendix Corp.
The Washington Post, January 17, 1982

[Paul Kruger (1825–1904), President of the Transvaal, once decided a dispute between two brothers about an inheritance of land in South Africa:] Let one brother divide the land, and let the other have first choice.

Edward Frank Allen
Modern Humor for Effective Speaking
(Citadel, 1945)

An error is the more dangerous in proportion to the degree of truth which it contains.

Henri Frédéric Amiel, 1821–1881
Swiss journalist and critic
Journal intime

A wise man sometimes changes his mind, but a fool never.

Arabic proverb

They were not just intelligent, but prided themselves on being "rational...." They were eager to find formulas, preferably expressed in a pseudo-mathematical language, that would unify the most disparate phenomena with which reality presented them; that is, they were eager to discover *laws* by which to explain and predict political and historical facts as though they were as necessary, and thus as reliable, as the physicists once believed natural phenomena to be.... [T]hey did not *judge*, they calculated.... [A]n utterly irrational confidence in the calculability of reality [became] the leitmotif of the decision making.

Hannah Arendt, 1906–1975
German-American philosopher, and critic
Crises of the Republic
(Harcourt Brace Jovanovich, 1972)

Some management groups are not good at problem solving and decision making precise-

101

ly because the participants have weak egos and are uncomfortable with competition.

Chris Argyris
Harvard Graduate School of Education
Harvard Business Review,
September/October 1986

Because the executives [trying to avoid inter-personal problems] don't say what they really mean or test the assumptions they really hold, their skills inhibit a resolution of the important intellectual issues.... Thus the meetings end with only lists and no decisions.... People's tendency to avoid conflict, to duck tough issues, becomes institutionalized and leads to a culture that can't tolerate straight talk.

Chris Argyris
Harvard Graduate School of Education
Harvard Business Review,
September/October 1986

Information may be accumulated in files, but it must be retrieved to be of use in decision making.

Kenneth J. Arrow
Nobel laureate in economics
The Limits of Organization (Norton, 1974)

Unadvised hasty judgment is a token apparent of a very slender wit.

Anne Askew, 1520–1546
English Protestant martyr
Testimony before the Inquisition
Quoted by Foxe, *The Book of Martyrs*

One may be tempted to see the great man instead of the logic of the question.

Babylonian Talmud, Bava Metzia

Professionalism is friendly to the qualified performance of precise tasks, but unfriendly to those accommodations and bargains that give coherence and direction to general public objectives.

Stephan K. Bailey
President,
American Society of Public Administration
Agenda For the Nation
(The Brookings Institution, 1968)

Nothing creates more self-respect among employees than being included in the process of making decisions.

Judith M. Bardwick
University of California at San Diego
The Plateauing Trap (AMACOM, 1986)

Participative management is, simply stated, involving the right people at the right time in the decision process.

Wayne Barlow
Regional Administrator, FAA
MTS Digest, April/June 1987

If you get all the facts, your judgment can be right; if you don't get all the facts, it can't be right.

Bernard Mannes Baruch, 1870–1965
Presidential advisor and investment broker
St. Louis Post-Dispatch, June 21, 1965

The fine art of executive decision consists in not deciding questions that are not now pertinent, in not deciding prematurely, in not making decisions that cannot be made effective and in not making decisions that others should make.

Chester I. Bernard, 1886–1961
President, U. S. O.
The Functions of the Executive (Harvard, 1938)

We know what happens to people who stay in the middle of the road. They get run over.

Aneurin Bevan, 1897–1960
English Labour leader and Minister of Health
Speech, House of Commons, April 2, 1946

It is such a delight now [that I'm no longer working for a large corporation] to make decisions based on one criterion only; is it a good decision, in both the short term and the long term? When you are making a decision in a large corporation, you also ask that question. But then, in parallel and with virtually no exceptions, you have to ask yourself, how will this decision look at corporate headquarters? Can it be defended against attack? If it goes wrong, what is the recovery procedure? God, what a pain in the ass that was!

Charles J. Bodenstab
CEO, Battery & Tire Warehouse, Inc.
Inc. Magazine, August 1987

Take time to deliberate, but when the time for action has arrived, stop thinking and go in.

Napoleon Bonaparte, 1769–1821
Emperor of France
Maxims

The logic of words should yield to the logic of realities.

Louis Dembitz Brandeis, 1856–1941
U. S. Supreme Court Justice
DeSanto v. *Pennsylvania* (1926)

Most of our executives make very sound decisions. The trouble is many have them have turned out not to have been right.

Donald Bullock
Training Director, C&P Telephone Co.
Seminar, Washington, D.C., December 1980

The easiest person to deceive is one's own self.

Edward George Bulwer-Lytton, 1803–1873
English novelist and playwright
The Disowned

You can never plan the future by the past.

Edmund Burke, 1729–1797
English statesman, orator, and writer
Letter to a Member of the National Assembly

Shelving hard decisions is the least ethical course.

Adrian Cadbury
Chairman, Cadbury Schweppes (England)
Harvard Business Review,
September/October 1987

Some people, however long their experience or strong their intellect, are temperamentally incapable of reaching firm decisions.

James Callaghan
English Prime Minister
Harvard Business Review,
November/December 1986

The closeness of the decision attests the measure of the doubt.

Benjamin Nathan Cardozo, 1870–1938
U. S. Supreme Court Justice
People ex rel. Hayes v. *McLaughlin* (1927)

Deliberate with caution, but act with decision and promptness.

Charles Caleb Colton, c. 1780–1832
English cleric, sportsman, and wine merchant
Lacon

There are only two ways to be quite unprejudiced and impartial. One is to be completely ignorant. The other is to be completely indifferent. Bias and prejudice are attitudes to be kept in hand, not attitudes to be avoided.

Charles P. Curtis
Attorney and Member,
The Harvard Corporation
A Commonplace Book
(Simon & Schuster, 1957)

Market research will always tell you why you can't do something. It's a substitute for decision making, for guts.

> Laurel Cutler
> Vice Chairman, FCB/Leber Katz Partners
> *Inc.*, November 1987

Timorous minds are much more inclined to deliberate than to resolve.

> Cardinal de Retz, 1614–1679
> French ecclesiastic and politician
> *Political Maxims*

A precedent embalms a principle. The principle may be right or may be wrong—that is a question for discussion; but at the first glance it is right to conclude that it is a principle that has been acted upon and recognised by those who preceded us.

> Benjamin Disraeli, 1804–1881
> English Prime Minister and novelist
> Speech in Parliament, February 22, 1848

Ignorance never settles a question.

> Benjamin Disraeli, 1804–1881
> English Prime Minister and novelist
> Speech, House of Commons, May 14, 1866

You can and you can't,
You shall and you shan't;
You will and you won't;
You'll be damned if you do,
And you'll be damned if you won't.

> Lorenzo Dow, 1777–1834
> American evangelist
> Definition of Calvinism

Clear thinking without knowledge will not guarantee a sound decision and extensive knowledge without clear thinking is no better.... A sound decision is the healthy child of a marriage between clear thinking and relevant knowledge.

> A. R. C. Duncan
> Queens University (Canada)
> Lecture, Executive Development Group, 1964

It is useless to make a formal decision with which group members informally disagree.

> William G. Dyer
> Brigham Young University
> *Strategies for Managing Change*
> (Addison-Wesley, 1984)

You should buy [airtime and advertising] from us because we're good, not because we're black.

> Mark Dyson
> President, WGCI FM (Chicago)
> *The Wall Street Journal*, March 23, 1988

Compromise is but the sacrifice of one right or good in the hope of retaining another, too often ending in the loss of both.

> Tryon Edwards, 1809–1894
> American theologian
> *The New Dictionary Of Thoughts*, 1957

The majority of decisions that reach a high level executive will have to be made on the basis of insufficient information. If sufficient information were available in time, the decision would have been clear and made at a lower level. If sufficient information is available and the decision is bucked up, you can be sure it's a political hot potato. Now this is as it should be, for who else should be most equipped to make these decisions other than the high-priced help.

> Lewis D. Eigen
> Executive Vice President,
> University Research Corp.
> *Microcomputers for Executive Decision-Making*
> (FAA, 1986)

All the mistakes I make arise from forsaking my own station and trying to see the object from another person's point of view.

Ralph Waldo Emerson, 1803–1882
American essayist and poet
Journals

If the wrong fork in the road is taken, all the progress we have made over the years will be swept away.

Donald Ephlin
Vice President, United Auto Workers' Union
The Academy of Management Executive,
February 1988

In every affair consider what precedes and what follows, and then undertake it.

Epictetus, c. 60
Greek philosopher
That Everything be Undertaken Circumspectly

Second thoughts are invariably wiser.

Euripides, 480–405 B.C.
Greek playwright
Hippolytus

The opinion of the strongest is always the best.

Jean de La Fontaine, 1621–1695
French fabulist
The Wolf and the Lamb

Indecision is often worse than wrong action.

Gerald R. Ford
Thirty-eighth President of the United States
Harvard Business Review,
September/October 1987

[Explaining why each unit has a well equipped, problem solving room:] The decisions being made in the plants are at least as important as those being made in the boardroom—shouldn't the setting and amenities reflect that?

Gordon Foward
President, Chaparral Steel
Peters, *Thriving on Chaos* (Knopf, 1987)

Decision makers in the public and private sectors have been too quick to settle on a particular view of the future.... A surprising turn of events often results in havoc.

Jib Fowles
University of Houston
The New York Times, January 10, 1988

To do the contradictory is a tough problem.... You build a fireproof house and nevertheless take out fire insurance.

Felix Frankfurter, 1882–1965
U. S. Supreme Court Justice
Letters

When I have got them [the pros and cons] all together in one view, I endeavor to estimate their respective weights; and where I find two, one on each side, that seem equal, I strike them both out. If I find a reason pro equal to some two reasons con, I strike out the three. If I judge some two reasons con, equal to some three reasons pro, I strike out the five; and thus proceeding I find at length where the balance lies; and if, after a day or two of further consideration, nothing new that is of importance occurs on either side, I come to a decision accordingly.

Benjamin Franklin, 1706–1790
American printer and statesman
Letter to Joseph Priestley, 1772

The beginning of intelligence is discrimination between the probable and improbable, and acceptance of the inevitable.

Solomon ibn Gabirol, 1021–1069
Spanish poet and grammarian
The Choice of Pearls

The greater the uncertainty, the greater the amount of decision making and information processing. It is hypothesized that organizations have limited capacities to process information and adopt different organizing modes to deal with task uncertainty. Therefore, variations in organizing modes are actually variations in the capacity of organizations to process information and make decisions about events which cannot be anticipated in advance.

J. Galbraith
Organization Design (Addison-Wesley, 1977)

Numerous factors contribute to the acceptability of ideas. To a very large extent ... we associate truth with convenience—with what closely accords with self-interest and individual well-being or promises best to avoid awkward effort or unwelcome dislocation of life. We also find highly acceptable what contributes most to self-esteem.

John Kenneth Galbraith
Economist and diplomat
The Affluent Society (Houghton Mifflin, 1958)

Often you have to rely on your intuition.

William Gates
Chairman, Microsoft Corp.
Adam Smith's Moneyworld (PBS TV),
November 21, 1987

You cannot run a business, or anything else, on a theory.

Harold Geneen
CEO, IT&T
Managing (Doubleday, 1984)

Silence gives consent.

Oliver Goldsmith, 1728–1774
English poet and playwright
The Good Natured Man

The best Human Resources executives make decisions on the basis of what is fair and equitable, not what is popular—bearing in mind that not everyone will be pleased with these decisions. There are days when *no one seems* to be pleased, and that aspect of the job comes with the territory.

Priscilla Goss
Vice President for Human Resources,
American Management Association
Management Review, March 1987

[E]ven if today's veteran manager was once an outstanding engineer, he is not now the technical expert he was when he joined the company.... If Intel used people holding old-fashioned position power to make all its decisions, decisions would be made by people unfamiliar with the technology of the day.

Andrew S. Grove
CEO, Intel Corp.
High Output Management
(Random House, 1983)

The timid are easily drawn into hazardous resolutions by despair, as are the rash by recklessness.

Francesco Guicciardini, 1483–1540
Florentine historian and statesman
Istoria d'Italia

It's easy to make good decisions when there are no bad options.

Robert Half
President, Robert Half International
Robert Half on Hiring (Crown, 1985)

There is a point where we have to say that enough is enough and we have to start the implementation. That means we put fences around the consensus period.

Dennis Hayes
CEO, Hayes Microcomputer Products, Inc.
Continental Magazine, November 1987

We try to make management decisions that, if everything goes right, will preclude future problems. But everything does not always go right, and managers therefore must be problem solvers as well as decision makers.

James L. Hayes
President and CEO,
American Management Association
Memos for Management: Leadership
(AMACOM, 1983)

Amid the pressure of great events, a general principle gives no help [in decision making].

Georg Wilhelm Hegel, 1770–1831
German philosopher
Philosophy of History

I have but one lamp by which my feet are guided, and that is the lamp of experience. I know of no way of judging of the future but by the past.

Patrick Henry, 1736–1799
American patriot and orator
Speech to Virginia Convention, March 23, 1775

He thinks not well, that thinks not again.

George Herbert, 1593–1633
English clergyman and poet
Jacula Prudentum

He that thinks amiss, concludes worse.

George Herbert, 1593–1633
English clergyman and poet
Jacula Prudentum

Unless a variety of opinions are laid before us, we have no opportunity of selection, but are bound of necessity to adopt the particular view which may have been brought forward. The purity of gold cannot be ascertained by a single specimen; but when we have carefully compared it with others, we are able to fix upon the finest ore.

Herodotus, fifth century B.C.
Greek "Father of History"
History of the Persian War

I trust my instincts.

Amy Hirsch
Producer, ABC Circle Films
Working Woman, May 1988

How often have I said to you that when you have eliminated the impossible, whatever remains, however improbable, must be the truth.

Sherlock Holmes
(Arthur Conan Doyle), 1859–1930
English physician, writer, and sportsman
The Sign of Four

Ridicule often decides matters of importance more effectually, and in a better manner, than severity.

Horace, 65–8 B.C.
Roman poet
Ars Poetica

Whenever decisions are made strictly on the basis of bottom-line arithmetic, human beings get crunched along with the numbers.

Thomas R. Horton
President and CEO,
American Management Association
Management Review, January 1987

When in doubt, win the trick.

Edmond Hoyle, 1672–1769
English writer on games
Twenty-Four Rules for Learners

Untruth enters when we reason wrongly from our facts.

Elbert Hubbard, 1856–1915
American writer, printer, and editor
The Philosophy of Elbert Hubbard

There's few things as uncommon as common sense.

Frank McKinney ("Kin") Hubbard, 1868–1930
American caricaturist and humorist
Abe Martin Hoss Sense and Nonsense

Great blunders are often made, like large ropes, of a multitude of fibres.

Victor Hugo, 1802–1885
French Romantic writer and politician
Les Misérables

Irrationally held truths may be more harmful than reasoned errors.

Thomas Henry Huxley, 1825–1895
English biologist
Coming of Age of "The Origin of the Species"

Logical consequences are the scarecrows of fools and the beacons of wise men.

Thomas Henry Huxley, 1825–1895
English biologist
Animal Automatism

The superior man does not permit his thoughts to go beyond his situation.

I Ching: Book of Changes
China, c. 600 B.C.

I hold that man in the right who is most closely in league with the future.

Henrick Ibsen, 1828–1906
Norwegian playwright
An Enemy of the People

When you have to make a choice and don't make it, that is in itself a choice.

William James, 1842–1910
American psychologist and philosopher
Pragmatism

There is no more miserable human being than one in whom nothing is habitual but indecision.

William James, 1842–1910
American psychologist and philosopher
The Principles of Psychology

Delay is preferable to error.

Thomas Jefferson, 1743–1826
Third President of the United States
Letter to George Washington, May 16, 1792

Multitudes, multitudes in the valley of decision.

Old Testament, Joel 3:14

There may be times when the best decision is to do nothing.

Ray Josephs
President, Ray Josephs Associates, Inc.
Leadership in the Office (AMACOM, 1963)

The lack of realistic guidelines for entrepreneurial decision making ... is a major reason large corporations find the creation of new ventures vexing.

Rosabeth Moss Kantor
Harvard Business School
and William H. Fonville
Vice President, Goodmeasure, Inc.
Management Review, January 1987

Shakespeare's *Othello* is the story of a high-powered military officer betrayed by one of his subordinates, Iago, who is passed over for a promotion. To get back at Othello, Iago tries to convince him that his wife has been unfaithful. Othello's intuition tells him that his wife had been true and that he should not doubt her. But the vengeful Iago puts on a convincing show—so convincing that Othello, never questioning Iago's motives, kills his wife and then kills himself. If only Othello had listened to his heart instead of his head.

> Beverly Kempton
> Business writer
> *Working Woman*, October 1987

How long will you keep hopping between two opinions?

> Old Testament, I Kings 18:21

I could make dumb decisions every day for the short term, and it would look great this year or next year, but it sure as hell wouldn't look good for the long term.

> Lawrence Kichen
> Chairman, Lockheed
> *High Technology Business,* April 1988

It ain't nothin' till I call it.

> Bill Klem, 1874–1951
> Professional baseball umpire
> Frequent response to players and managers

We must never assume that which is incapable of proof.

> George Henry Lewes, 1817–1878
> English philosopher and literary critic
> *Physiology of Common Life*

When you have got an elephant by the hind leg, and he is trying to run away, it's best to let him run.

> Abraham Lincoln, 1809–1865
> Sixteenth President of the United States
> Remark at a Cabinet meeting, April 14, 1865

All men are liable to error; and most men are, in many points, by passion or interest, under temptation to it.

> John Locke, 1632–1704
> English philosopher
> *An Essay Concerning Human Understanding*

Men are never so likely to settle a question rightly as when they discuss it freely.

> Thomas Babington Macaulay, 1800–1859
> English statesman, historian, and biographer
> *Southey's Colloquies*

A boss's mere expression of an opinion can be interpreted as a decision—even a direct order—by a staff member caught in the clutches of risk avoidance.

> R. Alec Mackenzie
> Management consultant and author
> *The Time Trap* (McGraw-Hill, 1972)

Some people say a decision has to marinate before you can make it. Sometimes that's true. But the fact is, you'll never have all the information you need to make a decision—if you did, it would be a foregone conclusion, not a decision.

> David Mahoney
> Investment manager
> *Confessions of a Street-Smart Manager*
> (Simon & Schuster, 1987)

Men cling to the opinions of habit.

> Moses Maimonides, 1135–1204
> Egyptian physician and philosopher
> *Guide to the Perplexed*

No matter how deep a study you make, what you really have to rely on is your own intuition and when it comes down to it, you really don't know what's going to happen until you do it.

Konosuke Matsushita
Founder, Matsushita Electric Co. (Japan)
Cherry Blossoms and Robotics
(Young Presidents' Organization, 1983)

Leaders face the difficult decision of sacrificing to some degree their own personal agenda. There is not always enough time to specialize on issues dear to the heart.

Mary McClure
Vice Chairman, Council of State Governments
The Journal of State Government,
September/October 1987

Young people who really wanted a challenge went in and they looked around and found there was nothing they could decide, because everything had been decided for them. And a lot of young people would not tolerate that.... They simply left. And for those who stayed, they were trained not to make a decision. So when the time came that they moved up a bit and there was really something to be decided, they were lost, because they had never practiced on small decisions, and they had never made a mistake. So they figured out ways to continue not making decisions, to continue avoiding mistakes.

William G. McGowan
Chairman, MCI Communications Corp.
Inc. Magazine, August 1986

The decision which achieves organization objectives must be both (1) technologically sound and (2) carried out by people. If we lose sight of the second requirement or if we assume naively that people can be made to carry out whatever decisions are technically sound—we run the risk of decreasing rather than increasing the effectiveness of the organization.

Douglas McGregor
The Human Side of Enterprise
(McGraw-Hill, 1960)

People in general tend to assume that there is some "right" way of solving problems. Formal logic, for example, is regarded as a correct approach to thinking, but thinking is always a compromise between the demands of comprehensiveness, speed, and accuracy. There is no best way of thinking.

James L. McKenney
Harvard Business School
and Peter G. W. Keen
Massachusetts Institute of Technology
*Harvard Business Review on
Human Relations*, 1986

Managers exist to plan, direct and control the project. Part of the way they control is to listen to and weigh advice. Once a decision is made, that's the way things should proceed until a new decision is reached. Erosion of management decisions by [support] people who always "know better" undermines managers' credibility and can bring a project to grief.

Philip W. Metzger
Computer analyst and management writer
Managing Programming People
(Prentice-Hall, 1987)

Most managers are not capable of making decisions involving complex technological matters without help—lots of it.... The finest technical people on the job should have a dual role: doing technical work and advising management.

Philip W. Metzger
Computer analyst and management writer
Managing Programming People
(Prentice-Hall, 1987)

Among two people, only one is needed to make a decision. Among 2,000, only one is needed. Among 200,000, only one is needed. There is nothing democratic about decision making by sound leadership. It does not require votes, and when people insist on voting for an issue, it is a simple matter to stack the group with members who vote in favor of the leader's position.

Jinx Milea
University of Southern California
and Pauline Lyttle
President, Operational Politics, Inc.
Why Jenny Can't Lead, 1986

The manager faces the real danger of becoming a major obstruction in the flow of decisions and information.

Henry Mintzberg
McGill University School of Management
The Nature of Managerial Work
(Harper & Row, 1973)

The manager does not handle decisions one at a time; he juggles a host of them, dealing with each intermittently, all the while attempting to develop some integration among them.

Henry Mintzberg
McGill University School of Management
The Nature of Managerial Work
(Harper & Row, 1973)

One fallacy [in managerial reasoning] is that if you analyze the data carefully and thoughtfully enough, you will get the right answer. They look to the data, not the people.

Thomas Moore
Babson College
Mass High Tech, August 3–16, 1987

A leader is a man who makes decisions. Sometimes they turn out right and sometimes they turn out wrong; but either way, he makes them.

Mutual Benefit Life Insurance Co.
"Leaders are Made ... Not Born"
Leadership in the Office (AMACOM, 1963)

What the Japanese mean by "democracy" is a system that should take the side of, or give consideration to, the weaker or lower; in prac-

tice, any decision should be made on the basis of a consensus which includes those located lower in the hierarchy.

Chie Nakane
Japanese writer
Cherry Blossoms and Robotics
(Young Presidents' Organization, 1983)

We make more decisions in the hallways than most companies make behind closed doors.

John Oren
President, Eastway Delivery Service
Best of Business Quarterly, 1987

The primary value of differentiating between line and staff is in the area of decision making. The term line simply means that the final authority rests with positions in that structure.... Staff personnel have traditionally provided advice and service in support of the line. The line has authority to command. The staff ... has no authority to order the line manager to follow the suggestions.

R. Wayne Pace
Brigham Young University
Organizational Communication
(Prentice-Hall, 1983)

Those who judge by their feelings do not understand reasoning, for they wish to get an insight into a matter at a glance, and are not accustomed to look for principles. Contrarily, others, who are accustomed to argue from principles, do not understand the things of the heart, seeking for principles and not being able to see at a glance.

Blaise Pascal, 1623–1662
French scientist and philosopher
Meditations

If you put off everything till you're sure of it, you'll get nothing done.

Norman Vincent Peale
Clergyman and inspirational speaker
Reader's Digest, January 1972

He that won't hear *can't Judge*, and he that can't bear Contradiction, may, with all his Wit, miss the Mark.

William Penn, 1644–1718
Founder of Pennsylvania
Fruits of Solitude in Reflections and Maxims

Politics is the art of postponing decisions until they are no longer relevant.

Henri Queuille, 1884–1970
Premier of France
Carlucci, *The Bureaucrat*, Winter 1985-1986

Facts, as such, never settled everything. They are working tools only. It is the implications that can be drawn from facts that count, and to evaluate these requires wisdom and judgment that are unrelated to the computer approach to life.

Clarence B. Randall
Chairman, Inland Steel Corp.
Making Good in Management
(McGraw-Hill, 1964)

Teams are less likely [than individuals] to overlook key issues and problems or take the wrong actions.

Eugene Raudsepp
President, Creative Research, Inc.
MTS Digest, April/June 1987

Our theory of management is that the time to get a decision doubles for every two levels of management; thus, parallel instead of serial decisions are best solutions.

Eberhardt Rechtin
President, Aerospace Corp.
Speech, Washington D.C., September 26, 1978

Even with little ongoing change about them, managers sometimes find they need to have high flex in the apparently unchanging job they have. A manager supervising ten men might easily find that two work best when left

alone, two need continuous direction, three need to be motivated by objectives, and three others need a supportive climate. So, in the space of a day an effective manager may well use all four basic styles [of management] when dealing with such a variety as a dependent subordinate, an aggressive pair of coworkers, a secretary whose work has deteriorated, and his superior who is interested only in the immediate task at hand.... To the extent the organization and technology allow individual treatment, a high-flex and sensitive manager could satisfy the demands of all these different situations and so achieve maximum effectiveness.

W. J. Reddin
Managerial Effectiveness
(McGraw-Hill, 1970)

Everyone complains of his memory, and no one complains of his judgment.

François de La Rochefoucauld, 1613–1680
French politician, writer, and philanthropist
Reflections, or Sentences and Moral Maxims

Don't make decisions and commitments ahead of time that you don't have to make.

Milton J. Roedel
Manager of Exploratory Research, DuPont
Managers' Meeting, February 1963

A bad situation that drifts always gets worse.... A situation that cries out for authority ... cannot be allowed to degrade.

Felix Rohatyn
Chairman,
New York City Municipal Assistance Corp.
The New York Times, November 22, 1987

Too often the great decisions are originated and given form in bodies made up wholly of men, or so completely dominated by them that whatever of special value women have to offer is shunted aside without expression.

> Eleanor Roosevelt, 1884–1962
> American statesman and humanitarian
> Speech, United Nations, December 1952

Listening to both sides does not necessarily bring about a correct judgment.

> Dagobert D. Runes
> Editor, publisher, and philosopher
> *A Book of Contemplation*

In general, pride is at the bottom of all great mistakes.

> John Ruskin, 1819–1900
> English art critic and historian
> *The True and Beautiful*

A *Prince* who followeth his own Opinion too soon, is in danger of repenting it too late.

> George Savile (Lord Halifax), 1633–1695
> English politician and statesman
> *Maxims of State*

The most powerful factor in the decision making in an organization is precedent. The older the larger the organization, the more powerful the precedent.

> Lyle E. Schaller
> Yokefellow Institute
> *The Change Agent* (Abingdon, 1972)

Analysis is not a scientific procedure for reaching decisions which avoid intuitive elements, but rather a mechanism for sharpening the intuition of the decision maker.

> James R. Schlesinger
> U. S. Secretary of Defense
> Memorandum to Senate Committee on
> Government Operations, April 1968

Every man takes the limits of his own field of vision for the limits of the world.

> Arthur Schopenhauer, 1788–1860
> German philosopher
> *Studies on Pessimism*

The short-term and frequently shortsighted positions win out with disturbing regularity because American business is top-heavy with the ever expanding numbers of business school graduates who are trained advocates of the short-term profit.

> Michael P. Schulhof
> Executive Vice President, Sony of America
> *The New York Times*, February 1, 1981

Forced to choose among irrelevant alternatives, on the basis of misleading facts, and without the benefit of solid analysis, even the best judgement can do little but grope intuitively in the dark.

> Charles L. Schultze
> Director, U. S. Bureau of the Budget
> Senate testimony, August 23, 1967

No great marketing decisions have ever been made on quantitative data.

> John Sculley
> CEO, Apple Computer Co.
> Rowan, *The Intuitive Manager*
> (Little, Brown & Company, 1986)

People will make reasonable decisions if they are given proper information.

> Thom Serrani
> Mayor, Stamford, Connecticut
> *Management Review*, October 1986

The number of those who undergo the fatigue of judging for themselves is very small indeed.

> Richard Brinsley Sheridan, 1751–1816
> Irish playwright
> *The Critic*

As the decision-making function becomes more highly automated, corporate decision making will perhaps provide fewer outlets for creative drives than it now does.

Herbert A. Simon
Carnegie-Mellon University
Anshen and Bach, *Management and Corporations 1985* (McGraw Hill, 1960)

In the larger sense of the professional management of a large enterprise, this view of the whole, time and again, showed him [James Webb, first NASA Administrator] what was a management problem, and what was a policy decision.

George L. Simpson
Assistant Deputy Administrator, NASA
Haught, *Giants in Management*
(National Academy of
Public Administration, 1985)

Think not that thy word and thine alone must be right.

Sophocles, c. 496–406 B.C.
Greek tragic playwright
Antigone

News is what your city editor says it is.

John H. Sorrells
Executive Editor, Scripps Howard Newspapers
A Handbook of Scripps Howard, 1948

In many firms the technique is employed of having an executive-vice president rule on an issue [that is controversial], the president remaining uninvolved so that appeals to him are still possible. If no one screams, the decision is allowed to stand.

Ross Stagner
Michigan State University
Business Topics (MSU, Winter 1965)

There never were, since the creation of the world, two cases exactly parallel.

Philip Dormer Stanhope, 1694–1773
English Secretary of State
Letters of Lord Chesterfield to His Son

When a man of sense happens to be in that disagreeable situation, in which he is obliged to ask himself more than once, *"What shall I do?"* he will answer himself, Nothing. When his reason points out to him no good way, or at least no one way less bad than another, he will stop short, and wait for light. A little, busy mind runs on at all events, must be doing, and, like a blind horse, fears no dangers, because he sees none.

Philip Dormer Stanhope, 1694–1773
English Secretary of State
Maxims of the Earl of Chesterfield

A man's judgment cannot be better than the information on which he has based it. Give him no news, or present him only with distorted and incomplete data, with ignorant, sloppy, or biased reporting, with propaganda and deliberate falsehoods, and you destroy his whole reasoning process and make him somewhat less than a man.

Arthur Hays Sulzberger, 1891–1968
Publisher of *The New York Times*
Speech to the
New York State Publishers Association,
August 30, 1948

Decisions must be made at the lowest possible level for management at the top to retain its effectiveness.

Saxon Tate
Managing Director,
Canada and Dominion Sugar
Mackenzie, *The Time Trap*
(McGraw-Hill, 1972)

Any man more right than his neighbors, constitutes a majority of one.

> Henry David Thoreau, 1817–1862
> American naturalist and writer
> *The Duty of Civil Disobedience*

Get it right or let it alone.
The conclusion you jump to may be your own.

> James Thurber, 1894–1961
> American essayist and humorist
> *Further Fables for Our Time*

The most dominant decision type [that will have to be made in an organic organization] will be *decisions under uncertainty.*

> Henry L. Tosi
> University of Florida
> and Stephen J. Carroll
> University of Maryland
> *Management* (John Wiley & Sons, 1976)

Make every decision as if you owned the whole company.

> Robert Townsend
> Former CEO, Avis
> *Further Up the Organization* (Knopf, 1984)

The buck stops here.

> Harry S. Truman, 1884–1972
> Thirty-third President of the United States
> Sign on desk

I never sit on a fence. I am either on one side or another.

> Harry S. Truman, 1884–1972
> Thirty-second President of the United States
> Speech, October 30, 1948

It is generally recognized that an impartial decisionmaker is required by due process. This does not mean, however, that the decisionmaker must be completely indifferent. Rather, due process requires only that the decisionmaker not prejudge a specific case, or be so biased against a party as to be incapable of properly deciding his case according to the weight of the evidence. Courts have identified certain situations in which the risk of prejudice or bias on the part of the decisionmaker is so great that it is presumed to exist to an unconstitutional degree without requirting an actual showing of bias ... such as where the decisionmaker has a pecuniary interest, where he has acted as advocate for one of the parties involved in the controversy ... or where he has been the target of personal abuse from one of the parties. Beyond situations of this sort, courts have been reluctant to disqualify a decisionmaker on the mere possibility of bias.

> U. S. Supreme Court
> *Withrow* v. *Larkin* (1975)

To be guided in one's decisions by the present, and to prefer what is sure to what is uncertain (though more attractive), is an expedient, a narrow rule of policy. Not thus do states—nor even individual men—make their way to greatness.

> Marquis de Vauvenargues, 1715–1747
> French soldier and moralist
> *Reflections and Maxims*

I never varied from the managerial rule that the worst possible thing we could do was to lie dead in the water with any problem. Solve it. Solve it quickly, solve it right or wrong. If you solved it wrong, it would come back and slap you in the face and then you could solve it right. Lying dead in the water and doing nothing is a comfortable alternative because it is without risk, but it is an absolutely fatal way to manage a business.

> Thomas J. Watson, Jr.
> CEO, IBM, and U.S. Ambassador to Russia
> *Fortune*, 1987

Inconsistencies of opinion, arising from changes of circumstances, are often justifiable.

> Daniel Webster, 1782–1852
> American statesman and orator
> Speech, July 25, 1846

Computers can make judicial decisions, computers can make psychiatric judgments. They can flip coins in much more sophisticated ways than can the most patient human being. The point is that *they ought* not be given such tasks. They may even be able to arrive at "correct" decisions in some cases—but always and necessarily on bases no human being should be willing to accept.... [S]ince we do not now have any ways of making computers wise, we ought not now give to computers tasks that demand wisdom.

> Joseph Weizenbaum
> American computer scientist
> *Computer Power and Human Reason*
> (Penguin, 1984)

Two and two continue to make four, in spite of the whine of the amateur for three, or the cry of the critic for five.

> James Abbott McNeill Whistler, 1834–1903
> American-born painter, etcher, and writer
> *The Gentle Art of Making Enemies*

If you let decisions be made for you, you'll be trampled.

> Betsy White
> Citrus Division Manager, Ocean Spray
> *Working Woman,* April 1988

Somebody's got to be the guardian of the long term.

> Marina V. N. Whitman
> Vice President, General Motors
> *Forbes,* April 4, 1988

Experience is the name everyone gives to his mistakes.

> Oscar Wilde, 1854–1900
> Irish poet, wit, and dramatist
> *Lady Windermere's Fan*

There is such a choice of difficulties that I am myself at a loss how to determine.

> James Wolfe, 1726–1759
> English Major General
> Message to William Pitt, September 2, 1759

If I make the decision and I am right, you will never remember. If I make the decision and I am wrong, you will never forget.

> Robert Woolsey and Huntington Swanson
> *Operations Research for Immediate Application:*
> *A Quick and Dirty Manual* (Harper, 1975)

It is a lot easier to make decisions in a heterogeneous democratic society when the exact nature of the decisions are shrouded in generalities.

> Chester Wright
> Director, Financial Management Training
> Center, U. S. Civil Service Commission
> Hinrichs and Taylor, *Program Budgeting and*
> *Cost Benefit Analysis* (Goodyear, 1969)

When a wise man errs, he errs badly.

> Yiddish proverb

Don't be afraid when you have no other choice.

> Yiddish proverb

Managers often try to give others the feeling that they are participating in the decision process. When a manager involves people in a problem for which he has adequate information and clear criteria for making an acceptable decision, he is engaging in pseudoconsultation. When he involves others in lengthy discussions of trivial problems, he is engaging in pseudoparticipation. Most people recognize these ceremonies as a waste of time.

Dale E. Zand
New York University
Information, Organization, and Power
(McGraw-Hill, 1981)

11

Discipline

*When firmness is sufficient,
harshness is unnecessary.*

Justice discards party, friendship, kindred, and is therefore always represented as blind.

Joseph Addison, 1672–1719
English writer, critic, and statesman
The Guardian

Warning must precede punishment.

Babylonian Talmud, Yoma

Every organization has a Siberia.

Warren G. Bennis
President, University of Cincinnati
University of Maryland symposium,
January 21, 1988

The proper and only authority over the personal lives of employees, once they leave their place of employment, is the civil authority.

Jacob J. Blair
Labor arbitrator
Pioneer Gen-E-Motors Corp., 3 LA 486

If a person can't do something, go back to goal setting. If a person won't do something, reprimand.

Kenneth H. Blanchard
Chairman, Blanchard Training & Development
and Robert Lorber
President, R. L. Lorber & Associates, Inc.
Putting the One Minute Manager to Work
(William Morrow, 1984)

When firmness is sufficient, harshness is unnecessary.

Napoleon Bonaparte, 1769–1821
Emperor of France
Maxims

There is no class of men so difficult to be managed as those whose intentions are honest, but whose consciences are bewitched.

Napoleon Bonaparte, 1769–1821
Emperor of France
Maxims

A blow with a word strikes deeper than a blow with a sword.

> Robert Burton, 1577–1640
> Vicar of St. Thomas's, Oxford
> *The Anatomy of Melancholy*

The strategy of discipline is not simple. The maintenance of authority hinges upon a delicate complex of human factors.

> James Francis Byrnes, 1879–1972
> U. S. Supreme Court Justice
> *Southern S. S. Co. v. N.L.R.B.* (1941)

The best policy to follow in developing a reputation for severity is to make any decision that involves a conflict between the organization and an individual according to fixed principles announced in advance and applied so consistently that each application takes on a didactic character.... It does not matter so much whether the punishment is prosecution or expulsion or demotion or counseling, but it does matter that the full penalty be invoked in every case without regard to extenuating circumstances or to the possibility of reprisal by the offender's friends.

> Theodore Caplow
> *Managing an Organization*
> (CBS College Publishing, 1983)

Those who do not prevent crimes when they could, encourage them.

> Cato the Elder, 234–149 B.C.
> Roman soldier, administrator, and statesman
> Plutarch, *The Parallel Lives: Cato the Elder*

Let the punishment be equal with the offense.

> Cicero, 106–43 B.C.
> Roman orator and statesman
> *De Legibus*

The victim to too severe a law is considered as a martyr rather than a criminal.

> Charles Caleb Colton, c. 1780–1832
> English cleric, sportsman, and wine merchant
> *Lacon*

A great deal may be done by severity, more by love, but most by clear discernment and impartial justice.

> Johann Peter Eckerman, 1792–1854
> German scholar and author
> *Conversations with Goethe*

Generally, employees who file complaints of discrimination do so as a last resort.

> Rubye Fields
> President, Blacks in Government
> *Management Review*, December 1987

Managers must stress that excuses of company loyalty will not be accepted for acts that place its good name in jeopardy.... [S]uperiors must make it clear that employees who harm other people allegedly for the company's benefit will be fired.

> Saul W. Gellerman
> University of Dallas School of Management
> *Harvard Business Review*, July/August 1986

Little of value comes out of the common belief that discipline and punishment go hand in hand.

> Eric Harvey
> Executive Director,
> Performance Systems Corp.
> *Management*, March 1987

... the [American Society of Newspaper Editors] has never censured one of its own. This establishes a historical record of professional purity unmatched in human history. Presidents may be impeached, kings deposed and preachers defrocked. But editors are forever members in good standing.

Richard Harwood
Ombudsman, *The Washington Post*
The Washington Post, April 3, 1988

Kings must not use the axe for each offense;
Princes cure some faults by their patience.

Robert Herrick, 1591–1674
English poet
Hesperides

The superior man is clear-minded and cautious in imposing penalties.

I Ching: Book of Changes
China, c. 600 B.C.

The kings of former times made firm the laws through clearly defined penalties.

I Ching: Book of Changes
China, c. 600 B.C.

If it becomes necessary to discipline employees, they should be told "why" and be given every chance to be heard.

Johnson & Johnson Co.
The Employee Relations Manual, 1932

The sins committed by many pass un-punished.

Lucan, 39–65
Roman writer
Pharsalia

While a foolish ruler may squander his subjects' bread,
A corrupt minister will surely lose his head.

Malayan proverb

The object of punishment is, prevention from evil; it can never be made impulsive to good.

Horace Mann, 1796–1859
Educator, U. S. Congressman,
and President of Antioch College
Lectures and Reports on Education

People are rarely fired for incompetence. It's not getting along that's almost always the underlying reason for dismissal.

Stuart Margulies
Industrial psychologist
Speech, New York, April 13, 1988

If a company desires to put such a rule in effect, it has the responsibility of taking steps to insure that the employees know and understand it.

Whitley P. McCoy
Labor arbitrator
West Boylston Mfg. Co., 8 LA 54

He who refuses to remedy a wrong is guilty of a second wrong.

Mencius, c. 371–c. 288 B.C.
Chinese sage
The Real Man

The urge to save humanity is almost always a false-face for the urge to rule it.

Henry Louis Mencken, 1880–1956
Editor, author, and critic
Minority Report

The broad effects which can be obtained by punishment ... are the increase of fear, the sharpening of the sense of cunning, the mastery of desires; so it is that punishment tames man, but does not make him "better."

Georg Wilhelm Nietszche, 1844–1900
German philosopher
Genealogy of Morals

The key to effective reprimand is to fit the reprimand to the person's own self-image.

> George S. Odiorne
> University of Massachusetts
> *How Managers Make Things Happen*
> (Prentice-Hall, 1982)

The emphasis in sound discipline must be on *what's wrong*, rather than "*who's to blame.*"

> George S. Odiorne
> University of Massachusetts
> *How Managers Make Things Happen*
> (Prentice-Hall, 1982)

Do not lay on the multitude the blame that is due to a few.

> Ovid, 14 B.C.–A.D. c. 17
> Roman poet
> *Ars Amatoria*

The proper end of ... punishment is not the satisfaction of justice, but the prevention of crimes.

> William Paley, 1743–1805
> English theologian and philosopher
> *Principles of Moral and Political Philosophy*

You can get something done in a short time with fear, but in the long run it just doesn't pay off.

> Wendell Parsons
> CEO, Stamp-Rite
> *Nation's Business*, March 1988

It has long been recognized that the essential purpose of industrial discipline is not so much to punish workers as it is to correct their faults and behavior and thus make them better and more productive workers.

> Harry H. Platt
> Labor arbitrator
> *Republic Steel Corporation*, 25 LA 733

Philip being arbitrator between two wicked persons, he commanded one to fly out of Macedonia and the other to pursue him.

> Plutarch, c. 46–c. 120
> Greek biographer and philosopher
> *Apothegms of Kings and Great Commanders:*
> *Philip of Macedonia*

The great thieves punish the little ones.

> Barber, *The Book of 1000 Proverbs*, 1876

He who stiffens his neck against many reproofs will suddenly be broken beyond repair.

> Old Testament, Proverbs 29:2

Forgive others often, yourself never.

> Publilius Syrus, c. 42 B.C.
> Roman writer
> *Maxims*

Don't hit at all if it is honorably possible to avoid hitting; but *never* hit soft.

> Theodore Roosevelt, 1858–1919
> Twenty-sixth President of the United States
> Bishop, *Theodore Roosevelt*

The two proper reasons for imposing penalties on an employee who is guilty of infraction or neglect [are] *to reform the offender*, and the other is to *deter others* who may be influenced by what is happening.

> Aaron Q. Sartain and Alton W. Baker
> Southern Methodist University
> *The Supervisor and His Job*
> (McGraw-Hill, 1965)

The fact is that in connection with imposed discipline, the supervisor is playing for high stakes.

> Aaron Q. Sartain and Alton W. Baker
> Southern Methodist University
> *The Supervisor and His Job*
> (McGraw Hill, 1965)

Men are not hanged for stealing horses, but that horses may not be stolen.

> George Savile (Lord Halifax), 1633–1695
> English politician and statesman
> *Of Punishment*

The genius of impeachment lay in the fact that it could punish the man without punishing the office.

> Arthur M. Schlesinger, Jr.
> American historian and writer
> Rowes, *The Book of Quotes* (Dutton, 1979)

[I]mprovements in the quality of work-life ... often reduce dismissals and resignations.... [E]ven if the firm has an ethical discharge system, with just cause, due process, and mitigating mechanisms, the best solution to the problem is to structure the firm so that the dismissal issue seldom arises.

> Milton Snoeyenbos and John Wesley Roberts
> Georgia State University
> *Business Ethics* (Prometheus, 1983)

A worker fired for an industrial misdeed has sustained a loss that might effect his working life for a long time.

> Lawrence Stessin
> Hofstra University
> *Employee Discipline*
> (Bureau of National Affairs, 1960)

When men of talents are punished, authority is strengthened.... Every ... example of punishment has in it some injustice, but the suffering individual is compensated by the public good.

> Tacitus, c. 55–117
> Roman orator, politician, and historian
> *Annals of the Julian Emperors*

Although the emotional impact of being fired varies with the individual, studies show that the trauma associated with termination is so great that it can be compared in intensity to divorce or the death of a loved one. Shock, depression, anger, self-pity, confusion, and loss of identity are some common feelings and reactions. The person is filled with anxiety and self-doubt about the prospects of finding a new job, the reactions of family and peers, and finances. The individual may be extremely bitter and negative about the future to the point of seeking revenge. He or she may go to work for a customer or a competitor, file a lawsuit against the company, or spread malicious rumors. Since such negative actions can substantially damage a company's reputation and can have serious effect on its recruiting efforts, community image, and employee morale and loyalty, it is in a company's best interests to handle terminations as positively as possible.

> Angelo M. Triosi
> Management consultant
> *Supervisory Management*, June 1980

Proper warnings must be given by a supervisor before imposing discipline.

> Maurice S. Trotter
> New York University
> *Supervisor's Handbook on Insubordination*
> (Bureau of National Affairs, 1967)

It is better to risk saving a guilty person than to condemn an innocent man.

> François Marie Voltaire, 1694–1778
> French writer
> *Zadig*

Do you hava any idea why you were fired?—
I think ultimately because they didn't like me.
I think it's probably that simple. There are
still people in the company who are quasi alcoholics or who don't do any work. They're
still there. And people who don't make
waves. I had a lot of people working for me,
and I was under a lot of pressure. I'm probably the kind of person who under those circumstances is not invisible. Probably what it
came down to was simply that I was not liked.
But I don't really know.

Anonymous manager
Maurer, *Not Working*
(Holt, Rinehart and Winston, 1977)

12

Entrepreneurs

*A man must make his opportunity
as oft as find it.*

We also encourage entrepreneurship internally by a policy of transfer pricing. Transfer pricing means that each plant is responsible for putting a firm price on what it makes or does.... The plant has to deliver at that price and make a profit. If the price is too high, the receiver of that work is free to look elsewhere—either inside or outside the company—to obtain an alternate source. In other words, every step of our manufacturing process is compared to what is going on outside the business. Each step has to compete as a source of supply.

John Akers
CEO, IBM
Naisbett and Aburdene, *Re-inventing the Corporation* (Warner, 1985)

Being in your own business is working 80 hours a week so that you can avoid working 40 hours a week for someone else.

Ramona E. F. Arnett
President, Ramona Enterprises, Inc.
Speech, Boston 1973

[The reason why most economics textbooks do not treat entrepreneurship:] The majority of economics professors never learned anything about entrepreneurship (the topic is barely touched on in most graduate schools) and don't have the desire to learn about it at this late date.

Roger Arnold
University of Nevada
The Wall Street Journal, October 8, 1987

Entrepreneurship is a tough subject to teach. There is much in the discussion that is not immediately amenable to geometric and mathematical representations, and the majority of economics professors simply don't want to bother with a topic that is not easily handled by their tools.

Roger Arnold
University of Nevada
The Wall Street Journal, October 8, 1987

A man must make his opportunity, as oft as find it.

Francis Bacon, 1561–1626
Lord Chancellor of England
Advancement of Learning

[Starting a company is] ... like walking on a high wire. You can only make it if you concentrate all your attention on getting to the other side.

James Bernstein
Founder, General Health, Inc.
Inc. Magazine, February 1988

The first rule [of entrepreneurship] has to be that you do something you really love—you can't make it otherwise.

David Birch
Economist and author
U.S. News & World Report, December 21, 1987

Show me an entrepreneur without a vision and I'll show you an entrepreneur who needs a new PR firm. Just don't try and put your vision in the bank.

John Case
Senior Editor, *Inc. Magazine*
Inc. Magazine, December 1987

To open a business is very easy; to keep it open is very difficult.

Chinese proverb

Entrepreneurs are among the best examples of achievement and of maintaining an attitude of expectancy. These people who invest gargantuan amounts of time and energy—and often risk their life savings—to start a business, seldom contemplate failure. Virtually every moment they devote to their work is given over to mobilizing themselves and their people to sieze opportunities that they see abounding all around them.

Allen Cox
Management consultant
The Making of the Achiever
(Dodd Mead, 1985)

[Extrapolating from the current data showing women starting businesses at twice the rate of men:] By the end of the century there are likely to be as many businesses owned by women as by men.

Carol Crockett
Director,
Office of Women's Business Ownership,
U. S. Department of Commerce
The New York Times, April 17, 1988

Entrepreneur: a high-rolling risk-taker who would rather be a spectacular failure than a dismal success.

Jim Fisk and Robert Barron
The Official MBA Handbook of Great Business Quotations (Simon & Schuster, 1984)

What qualities ... characterize today's biz-kids?... [S]elf-confidence, ingeneuity, an interest in finding practical solutions to real problems—and a poet's belief that if the first effort doesn't pay off, the world won't end.

Peter Fuhrman
Business writer
Forbes, April 27, 1987

The entrepreneur, especially when starting out, knows that he is operating on the threshold of success or failure. A single mistake can ruin him.

Harold Geneen
CEO, IT&T
Managing (Doubleday, 1984)

Where are the corporate entrepreneurs? The answer is: There are none.

> Harold Geneen
> CEO, IT&T
> *Managing* (Doubleday, 1984)

The wave of the future in American business, it seems to me, is with the entrepreneurs!

> Harold Geneen
> CEO, IT&T
> *Managing* (Doubleday, 1984)

It is better to take over and build upon an existing business than to start a new one.

> Harold Geneen
> CEO, IT&T
> *Managing* (Doubleday, 1984)

As an entrepreneurial startup company you look at the business like a racer doing a sprint. But as a company gets successful, you've got to get your people to realize that it's a marathon they're in.

> Trip Hawkins
> President, Electronic Arts, Inc.
> *Computer & Software News*, November 9, 1987

Good management and entrepreneurship are not synonymous.

> James L. Hayes
> President, American Management Association
> *Memos for Management: Leadership*
> (AMACOM, 1983)

Endless meetings, sloppy communications, and red tape steal the entrepreneur's time.

> James L. Hayes
> President, American Management Association
> *Memos for Management: Leadership*
> (AMACOM, 1983)

The truly well-rounded consultant, and generally the most successful one, functions well in many professional capacities: Consultant, lecturer, writer, teacher, leader, and mentor. Consulting itself is only the beginning.

> Herman Holtz
> Government Operations consultant
> *How to Succeed as an Independent Consultant*
> (John Wiley & Sons, 1983)

If it's a good idea ... go ahead and do it. It is much easier to apologize than it is to get permission.

> Grace Murray Hopper
> Rear Admiral, U. S. Navy (retired)
> Speech, Washington, D.C., February 1987

[Referring to his entrepreneurial attempt to build an electronic mail business, having failed with a similar activity in the U.S. Postal Service:] We have the gift of hindsite and the advantage of new technology.

> Eugene C. Johnson
> Cofounder, TCOM
> *Venture,* April 1988

Raising venture capital is a full time job.

> Betty Kadis
> Cofounder, Wakefield Software Systems, Inc.
> *Working Woman*, February 1988

Everything looks like a failure in the middle.... Very few ventures look like winners throughout their entire development cycle. Most get bogged down in the middle of the project and encounter fierce resistance or come up against seemingly insurmountable technical problems. Thus the history of new ventures is full of stories about fundamentally sound ideas that were aborted prematurely when their "immune systems" were at their weakest.

> Rosabeth Moss Kantor
> Harvard Business School
> and William H. Fonville
> Vice President, Goodmeasure, Inc.
> *Management*, January 1987

If entrepreneurs are to be held in high esteem, it does not follow that managers should be denigrated.

> Roger Kaplan
> Associate Editor, *Reader's Digest*
> *Harvard Business Review*, May/June 1987

Point of view is worth 80 IQ points.

> Alan Kay
> Director of Research, Apple Computer Co.
> Hickman and Silva, *Creating Excellence*
> (New American Library, 1984)

If Enterprise is afoot, wealth accumulates whatever may be happening to Thrift; and if Enterprise is asleep, wealth decays whatever Thrift may be doing.

> John Maynard Keynes, 1883–1946
> English economist, writer, and diplomat
> *A Treatise on Money*, 1930

Entrepreneurs are simply those who understand that there is little difference between obstacle and opportunity and are able to turn both to their advantage.

> Victor Kiam
> CEO, Remington
> *Going For It!* (William Morrow, 1986)

An entrepreneur wakes up in the middle of the night in a cold sweat saying, "It's not gonna work." But ... if he succeeds, he can make millions. And when you win, you really win. It's euphoria.

> Dale Lang
> Magazine owner and entrepreneur
> *USA Today*, February 23, 1988

The entrepreneurial approach is not a sideline at 3M. It is the heart of our design for growth.

> Lewis Lehr
> Chairman, 3M Company
> Speech, University of Nebraska,
> April 2, 1983

Self employment has become a realistic possibility only for the exceptional, not for the average American whose work future is likely to be found in a large organization.

> Michael Maccoby
> JFK School of Government, Harvard University
> *The Leader* (Simon & Schuster, 1981)

Successful big corporations should devolve into becomming "confederations of entrepreneurs."

> Norman McCrae
> Associate Editor, *The Economist*
> *The Economist*, December 25, 1976

Entrepreneurship should not be the province only of those who have the organizational patience and ability to set up from scratch every bit of the infrastructure that a new business needs.

> Norman McCrae
> Associate Editor, *The Economist*
> *The Economist*, December 25, 1976

We're going to see a lot more young people entering entrepreneurial ventures.

> Fredric V. Malek
> President, Marriott Corp., Hotel Division
> *Business Week*, August 24, 1987

But they [the entrepreneurs] don't start a business for the money, they do it for the challenge. It's not unusual for them to start many different businesses. They have to; it's addictive.

> Doug Mellinger
> Director,
> Association of Collegiate Entrepreneurs
> *Nation's Business*, March 1988

We are shifting from a managerial society to an entrepreneurial society.

> John Naisbitt
> Chairman, Naisbitt Group
> *Megatrends* (Warner, 1984)

Steve Wozniak couldn't get Hewlett-Packard to take an interest in small computers. He very reluctantly left to join Steve Jobs, who couldn't sell a similar idea to Atari. They formed Apple Computers.

> Gifford Pinchot III
> The International Institute of Intrapreneurs
> *Intrapreneuring* (Harper & Row, 1986)

I'd rather have a Class A entrepreneur with a Class B idea than a Class B entrepreneur with a class A idea.

> Gifford Pinchot III
> The International Institute of Intrapreneurs
> *Intrapreneuring* (Harper & Row, 1986)

Since one of their [entrepreneurs'] basic tools is daydreaming, their natural inclination in any spare moment is to play over a new business opportunity in their mind's eye.

> Gifford Pinchot III
> The International Institute of Intrapreneurs
> *Intrapreneuring* (Harper & Row, 1986)

Many companies simply recognize the entrepreneurial orientation of professionals and, in general, allow these employees free rein to try new things, provided they stay within the business objectives of the enterprise.

> Joseph A. Raelin
> Boston College School of Management
> *Clash of Cultures: Managers and Professionals*
> (Harvard Business School, 1986)

Problems can become opportunities when the right people come together.

> Robert Redford
> Movie actor and entrepreneur
> *Harvard Business Review*, May/June 1987

Paper entrepreneurialism relies on financial and legal virtuosity. Through shrewd maneuvering, accounting and tax rules can be finessed, and the numbers on balance sheets and tax returns manipulated.... Assets can be rearranged on paper to improve cash flow or to defer payments. And threatened lawsuits or takeovers can be used to extract concessions from other players. Huge profits are generated by these ploys. They are the most imaginative and daring ventures in the American economy. But they do not enlarge the economic pie; they merely reassign the slices.

> Robert B. Reich
> JFK School of Government, Harvard University
> *The Next American Frontier*, 1983

If the United States is to compete effectively ... we must bring collective entrepreneurship to the forefront.... That will require us to change our attitudes, to downplay the myth of the entrepreneurial hero, and to celebrate our creative teams.

> Robert B. Reich
> JFK School of Government, Harvard University
> *Harvard Business Review*, May/June 1987

To be successful as an entrepreneur, you have to build a company around your whole life, not just the business aspect.

> Warren Rodgers
> CEO, Computer Specialists, Inc.
> *Inc. Magazine*, February 1988

Entrepreneurs are the lead players in the drama [of business]. In at least four specific settings their role is crucial. A new industry ... a new product in an existing industry ... the one who opens up new markets ... when, so to speak, the economic ground shifts.... The category of entrepreneur includes all the people who set out to change the corner of the business world in which they find themselves—all the people, in a word, who push the system along its restless path.

> Commentary by Eric Sevareid
> TV newsman and host
> *Enterprise: The Making of Business in America* (McGraw-Hill, 1983)

Many individuals ... become entrepreneurs even though they don't have the supposedly requisite characteristics or motives.... No test will assure you that an individual will become an entrepreneur before the fact.

> Albert Shapero
> Ohio State University
> *The Wharton Magazine*, Fall 1978

The people who get on in this world are the people who get up and look for the circumstances they want, and, if they can't find them, make them.

> George Bernard Shaw, 1856–1950
> Nobel laureate in literature
> *Mrs. Warren's Profession*

There's a vast ocean of frustrated middle managers out there, and we're helping them [with financing to] become entrepreneurs.

> Theodore Stolberg
> Partner, Weiss, Peck & Greer
> *Inc. Magazine*, November 1987

Vision is the art of seeing things invisible.

> Jonathan Swift, 1667–1775
> English cleric & satirist
> *Thoughts on Various Subjects*

Entrepreneurs are needed not only to start new business ventures ... but also to put life into existing companies, especially large ones.

> Anders Wall
> CEO, Beijerinvest (Sweden)
> Speech, New York City, April 23, 1980

[Political] Campaigning today is one of the purest forms of individual entrepreneurship available in an age of bureaucratized enterprises. A candidate enlists a small staff, raises capital, invests it in marketing his product (himself) and the market decides.

> George Will
> Syndicated columnist
> *Newsweek*, February 1, 1988

13
Ethics

When in doubt, don't.

Morality is a private and costly luxury.

Henry Brooks Adams, 1838–1918
American historian
The Education of Henry Adams

He that always gives way to others will end in having no principles of his own.

Aesop, c. 620–c. 560 B.C.
Greek fabulist
The Man and His Two Wives

A member [of the American Institute of Certified Public Accountants] may not knowingly misrepresent facts, and when engaged in the practice of public accounting ... shall not subordinate his judgment to others.

American Institute of
Certified Public Accountants
Code of Professional Ethics, Rule 102

Honesty is the cornerstone of all success, without which confidence and ability to perform shall cease to exist.

Mary Kay Ash
CEO, Mary Kay Cosmetics
Vital Speeches of the Day, April 1, 1988

During my eighty-seven years I have witnessed a whole succession of technological revolutions. But none of them has done away with the need for character in the individual or the ability to think.

Bernard Mannes Baruch, 1870–1965
Presidential advisor and financial analyst
My Own Story (Henry Holt, 1957)

It is not just a matter of a fear to be allayed by reassurances (concerning the possible misuse of secretly obtained information), but a resentment that anyone—even a thoroughly trustworthy official—should be able to satisfy any curiosity, without the knowledge let alone the consent of the subject. For since what others know about him can radically alter a man's view of himself, to treat the collation of personal information about him as if it raised purely technical problems of safeguards against abuse is to disregard his claim to consideration and respect as a person.

Stanley I. Benn
Management writer and consultant
Wasserstrom, *Today's Moral Problems*
(Macmillan, 1975)

[Referring to competitor's propietary information:] If you're willing to spend the money and criminality doesn't bother you, you can pretty much buy anything you want.

August Bequai
Attorney and expert in corporate espionage
Newsweek, May 2, 1988

True courage is the knowledge of right and the determination to do it. False courage is a willingness to do what is wrong because others say it is right.

Josh Billings
(Henry Wheeler Shaw), 1818–1885
American writer and auctioneer
Josh Billings: His Book

The world has achieved brilliance without conscience. Ours is a world of nuclear giants and ethical infants.

Omar Nelson Bradley, 1893–1981
Permanent Chairman, Joint Chiefs of Staff
Armistice Day speech, 1948

[S]ome of those legendary monsters [of American business]... whom Teddy Roosevelt called "malefactors of great wealth"—yes, they *were* monsters. But gee, they were interesting monsters.

Matthew Bruccoli
English professor and business biographer
M Magazine, September 1987

I think it's unethical to take money for poor quality performance.

Alvin Burger
Founder, "Bugs" Burger Bug Killers, Inc.
Inc. Magazine, June 1984

The greater the power, the more dangerous the abuse.

Edmund Burke, 1729–1797
English statesman, orator, and writer
Speech, Middlesex, 1771

Conducting your business in a socially responsible way is good business. It means that you can attract better employees and that customers will know what you stand for and like you for it.

M. Anthony Burns
CEO, Ryder Systems
The New York Times, January 3, 1988

Business leaders today can't shrink from their obligation to set a moral example.

Willard C. Butcher
Chairman, The Chase Manhattan Corp.
Speech, New Orleans, May 15, 1987

The possibility that ethical and commercial considerations will conflict has always faced those who run companies. It is not a new problem. The difference now is that a more widespread and critical interest is being taken in our decisions and in the ethical judgements which lie behind them.

Adrian Cadbury
Chairman, Cadbury Schweppes (England)
Harvard Business Review,
September/October 1987

An honest politician is one who, when he is bought, stays bought.

Simon Cameron, 1799–1889
American financier and politician
Attributed

Morality is not merely different in different communities. Its level is not the same for all the component groups within the same community.

> Benjamin Nathan Cardozo, 1870–1938
> U. S. Supreme Court Justice
> *Paradoxes of Legal Science*

Truth is the safest lie.

> Maxwell Carver
> Contributing Editor, *Discover*
> *Discover,* April 1988

An honest man's word is as good as his bond.

> Miguel de Cervantes, 1547–1616
> Spanish novelist
> *Don Quixote*

Honesty is the best policy.

> Miguel de Cervantes, 1547–1616
> Spanish novelist
> *Don Quixote*

It is a fine thing to be honest, but it is very important for a Prime Minister to be right.

> Winston Churchill, 1874–1965
> English Prime Minister, writer, and soldier
> Speech, Free Trade Hall, Manchester, 1923

Government is a trust, and the officers of the government are trustees, and both ... are created for the benefit of the people.

> Henry Clay, 1777–1852
> U. S. Secretary of State
> Speech at Lexington, Massachusetts,
> May 16, 1829

He who has gold makes and accomplishes whatever he wishes in the world and finally uses it to send souls into paradise.

> Christopher Columbus, 1451–1506
> Italian navigator and entrepreneur
> Thatcher, *Christopher Columbus*
> (G. P. Putnam's Sons, 1903)

Necessity makes an honest man a knave.

> Daniel Defoe, c. 1661–1731
> English writer and satirist
> *Serious Reflections of Robinson Crusoe*

In the ethics of interdependence there are only obligations, and all obligations are mutual obligations. Harmony and trust—that is, interdependence—require that each side be obligated to provide what the other side needs to achieve its goals and to fulfil itself.

> Peter F. Drucker
> Management consultant and writer
> *The Changing World of the Executive*
> (Quadrangle, 1982)

Property has its duties as well as its rights.

> Thomas Drummond, 1797–1840
> English engineer and public administrator
> Letter to the Earl of Donoughmore,
> May 22, 1838

I am proud of the fact that I never invented weapons to kill.

> Thomas Alva Edison, 1847–1931
> American inventor and entrepreneur
> *The New York Times,* June 8, 1915

The Code of Ethics of Government Service, passed by both the House and the Senate, starts with the principle that every employee of the government should put loyalty to the highest moral principles and to country above loyalty to persons, parties, or government department.... To believe that the government cannot run unless one puts the President above everything else is a formula for a dictatorship, and not for a republic.

Daniel Ellsberg
Former Rand Corp. analyst
Peters and Branch, *Blowing the Whistle*
(Praeger, 1972)

[To a salesman:] If it's such a good deal, why did they come looking for you?

Mark Fisher
Detective, Newport Beach Police Department
U.S. News & World Report, December 21, 1987

Assuredly, the most gifted man errs who, in dealing with humanity, depends upon his own insight and intelligence and discards the moral law of society, created by respect for the individual.

Ferdinand Foch, 1851–1929
French military leader and teacher
Speech at Napoleon's tomb, May 5, 1921

In a free society there is one and only one social responsibility to business—to use its resources and engage in activities designed to increase profits so long as it stays within the rules of the game, which is to say, engages in open and free competition without deception or fraud.

Milton Friedman
Nobel laureate in economics
Capitalism and Freedom

[Of Robin Hood:] The gentlest thief that ever was.

Thomas Fuller, 1608–1661
Chaplain in extraordinary to Charles II
The Worthies of England

In matters of conscience, the law of the majority has no place.

Mohandas K. Gandhi, 1869–1948
Indian religious and political leader
Reader's Digest, December 1987

When in doubt, don't.

Saul W. Gellerman
University of Dallas School of Management
Harvard Business Review, July/August 1986

The practice of declaring codes of ethics and teaching them to managers is not enough to deter unethical conduct.

Saul W. Gellerman
University of Dallas School of Management
Harvard Business Review, July/August 1986

Advancement often depends not on rightness of action, but on acceptable behavior and image, e.g. self-control, appearance and dress, perception as a team player, style and patron power. The result of all this is ethical erosion.

Robert W. Goddard
Publications Director,
Liberty Mutual Insurance Co.
Personnel Journal, March 1988

Everybody has a little bit of Watergate in him.

Billy Graham
American evangelist
Remark, February 3, 1974

The challenge ... is to find a socially responsible niche where you can effectively give back to the community in which you operate and in which you have prospered.

Earl G. Graves
Publisher and Editor, *Black Enterprise*
The New York Times, January 3, 1988

It may well be that corporations should drop all ideas about their supposed "social responsibilities," or at least confine their good works to community-chest drives, gifts to universities and playing fields for the Little League. Once companies begin to assume more grandiose and controversial obligations, they will inevitably be judged by standards they are ill-equipped to meet.

Andrew Hacker
Cornell University
The New York Times, November 17, 1963

[Describing the results of a survey of personnel executives:] There was little consensus about the reasons for unethical behavior and even less about what to do about it .... The one place nearly all respondents agreed they *didn't* have a problem [of ethics] was their own department.

Allan Halcrow
Managing Editor, *Personnel Journal*
Personnel Journal, November 1987

The most dangerous of all moral dilemmas: when we are obliged to conceal truth in order to help the truth to be victorious. If this should at any time become our duty in the role assigned us by fate, how straight must be our path at all times if we are not to perish.

Dag Hammerskjöld, 1905–1961
Secretary-General of the United Nations
Markings

The 1975 statement of principles [of the American Society of Newspaper Editors] ... exhorts the society's members to adhere to "the highest ethical and professional" standards, to avoid "impropriety" and, in general, to be upright citizens. But those standards are nowhere defined. Therefore, in a practical sense, they do not exist. If they do not exist, they can't be violated, and in that *Catch-22* situation there are no sinners among us.

Richard Harwood
Ombudsman, *The Washington Post*
The Washington Post, April 3, 1988

As a small business-person, you have no greater leverage than the truth.

Paul Hawken
Founder, Smith & Hawken
Inc. Magazine, August 1987

If managers are careless about basic things— telling the truth, respecting moral codes, proper professional conduct—who can believe them on other issues?

James L. Hayes
President, American Management Association
Memos for Management: Leadership
(AMACOM, 1983)

They [corporations] feel neither shame, remorse, gratitude or goodwill.

William Hazlitt, 1778–1830
English essayist and critic
Table Talk

Let us distinguish between the creation of wealth for the community and the extortion of wealth from the community.

William Randolph Hearst, 1863–1951
Newspaper publisher and U. S. Congressman
Signed editorial, March 28, 1918

The ethics of dissent are a very real issue in profit center management. Is the good of the corporation the overriding concern? Or is it personal [or divisional] survival?

Bruce Henderson
CEO, Boston Consulting Group, Inc.
Henderson on Corporate Strategy (Abt, 1979)

Ethics must begin at the top of an organization. It is a leadership issue and the chief executive must set the example.

Edward L. Hennessy, Jr.
CEO, Allied Signal, Inc.
The New York Times, January 3, 1988

Temptation is not always invitation.

Oliver Wendell Holmes, Jr., 1841–1935
U. S. Supreme Court Justice
Erie Railroad v. *Hilt* (1917)

First, there is the law. It must be obeyed. But the law is the minimum. You must act ethically.

IBM
Business Guidelines for Employees

A little sin is big when a big man commits it.

Abraham ibn Ezra, 1092–1167
Spanish poet, philosopher, and polemicist
Commentary to Genesis 32:9

An honest heart being the first blessing, a knowing head is the second.

Thomas Jefferson, 1743–1826
Third President of the United States
Letter to Peter Carr, August 19, 1785

If I accustom a servant to tell a lie for me, have I not reason to apprehend that he will tell many lies for himself?

Samuel Johnson, 1709–1784
English lexicographer and essayist
Boswell's Life of Dr. Johnson

There are some people for whom a love of the works of nature seems to engender a corresponding hatred of the works of man.

G. M. Keller
CEO, Chevron Corp.
Speech, San Francisco, October 30, 1987

The strength of our commitment to a high level of ethical [business] behavior ... has deteriorated almost in direct proportion to declining societal values.

Robert L. Koch
Vice President for Personnel,
Bally of Switzerland
Personnel Journal, November 1987

The Constitution prevents the government from spying on individuals, yet any company in the United States can wiretap to eavesdrop on its employees.

George Kohl
Director of Special Projects,
Communications Workers of America
Best of Business Quarterly, 1987

Executives have to start understanding that they have certain legal and ethical responsibilities for information under their control.

Jim Leeke
Computer Journalist
PC Week, August 11, 1987

You are not to do evil that good may come of it.
[*Non faciat malum, ut inde veniat bonum.*]

Legal maxim

Only if entrepreneurs offer constructive solutions to important societal problems in an ethically acceptable way will they enjoy freedom of action.

Klaus M. Leisinger
Department Director, Ciba-Geigy, Ltd.
The New York Times, February 21, 1988

I desire so to conduct the affairs of this administration that if at the end, when I come to lay down the reins of power, I have lost every other friend on earth, I shall at least have one friend left, and that friend shall be down inside of me.

> Abraham Lincoln, 1809–1865
> Sixteenth President of the United States
> Speech to the Missouri Committee
> of Seventy, 1864

I can remember senior officials without a smile on their faces saying, "Well, Minister, we have studied the contract with great care and we see no way in which we can get out of it." They do not grasp that in business a reputation for keeping absolutely to the letter and spirit of an agreement, even when it is unfavorable, is the most precious of assets, although it is not entered in the balance sheets.

> Oliver Lyttleton
> (Viscount Chandos), 1893–1980
> English banking and metals executive
> *Memoirs of Lord Chandos*
> (New American Library, 1963)

If the chief party, whether it be the people, or the army, or the nobility, which you think most useful and of most consequence to you for the conservation of your dignity be corrupt, you must follow their humor and indulge them, and in that case, honesty and virture are pernicious.

> Niccolò Machiavelli, 1469–1527
> Florentine statesman and philosopher
> *The Prince*

A wrong-doer is often a man that has left something undone, not always he that has done something.

> Marcus Aurelius, 121–180
> Roman Emperor and Stoic philosopher
> *Meditations*

If it is not seemly, do it not; if it is not true, speak it not.

> Marcus Aurelius, 121–180
> Roman Emperor and Stoic philosopher
> *Meditations*

We can't define ethics universally.

> Virginia K. McDermott
> Vice President, Allergan, Inc.
> *Personnel Journal*, November 1987

We had been a proud group who felt that people who knew nothing were telling us what to do. It took us a long time to realize that regulators, legislators, even environmentalists had a right to ask questions.

> Keith R. McKennon
> President, Dow Chemical USA
> *The New York Times*, November 22, 1987

Time is a great legalizer, even in the field of morals.

> Henry Louis Mencken, 1880–1956
> Editor, author, and critic
> *A Book of Prefaces*

Competition is as rife in the career of fraudulent practice as in that of real excellence.

> John Stuart Mill, 1806–1873
> English philosopher and economist
> *Endowments*

There's a tendency to think of conflicts of interest as an administrative problem: identifying potential or actual conflicts and then resolving them.... But often, resolving them requires a leadership decision, not an administrative one.

> Ira Millstein
> Managing Partner, Weil, Gotshal & Manges
> *Of Counsel*, October 5, 1987

Unless a man feels he has a good enough memory, he should never venture to lie.

> Michel Eyquem de Montaigne, 1533–1592
> French philosopher and essayist
> *Essays*

Deterioration of a government begins almost always by the decay of its principles.

> Charles de Secondat Montesquieu, 1689–1755
> French lawyer, writer, and philosopher
> *The Spirit of the Laws*

I owe the public nothing.

> John Pierpont (J. P.) Morgan, 1837–1913
> American financier
> Josephson, *The Robber Barons*
> (Harcourt Brace, 1934)

It is not enough to do good; one must do it the right way.

> John Morley, 1838–1923
> English statesman and man of letters
> *On Compromise*

The competitive urge is a fine, wholesome direction of energy. But ... the desire to win must be wedded to an ideal, an ethical way of life. It must never become so strong that it dwarfs every other aspect of the game of life.

> Edward R. Murrow, 1908–1965
> Radio journalist
> Holman, *This I Believe*

The market is full of hucksters, promoting quick-fix ethics programs.

> Mark J. Pastin
> Director, Lincoln Center For Ethics
> *Business Week*, February 15, 1988

Philanthropy is an important intelligence function in a business—a way of letting some light into the company.

> Robert L. Payton
> President, Exxon Education Foundation
> *The New York Times*, February 21, 1988

Dishonesty is never an accident. Good men, like good women, never see temptation when they meet it.

> John Peers
> President, Logical Machines Corp.
> *1,001 Logical Laws* (Doubleday, 1979)

For even wisdom is got the better by self-interest.

> Pindar, c. 522–443 B.C.
> Greek lyric poet
> *Odes*

Moral good is a practical stimulus; it is no sooner seen than it inspires an impulse to practice.

> Plutarch, c. 46–c. 120
> Greek biographer and philosopher
> *The Parallel Lives: Pericles*

Do everything you can to avoid the *appearance* of wrong doing.

> James H. A. Pooley
> Attorney
> *Venture,* April 1988

The ends must justify the means.

> Matthew Prior, 1664–1721
> English poet and diplomat
> *Hans Carvel*

Knaves imagine nothing can be done without knavery.

> Barber, *The Book of 1000 Proverbs*, 1876

Money is welcome though it comes in a dirty bag.

> Barber, *The Book of 1000 Proverbs*, 1876

He that lies down with the dogs will rise up with the fleas.

> Barber, *The Book of 1000 Proverbs*, 1876

False scales are an abomination to the Lord; But a just weight is his delight.

> Old Testament, Proverbs 11:1

We may with advantage at times forget what we know.

> Publilius Syrus, c. 42 B.C.
> Roman writer
> *Maxims*

No man is justified in doing evil on the grounds of expediency.

> Theodore Roosevelt, 1858–1919
> Twenty-sixth President of the United States
> *The Strenuous Life*

Life is nothing but a competition to be the criminal rather than the victim.

> Bertrand Russell, 1872–1970
> English mathematician and philosopher
> Cooke, *Six Men*

Laws that regulate the workplace or the environment ... set forth an ideology concerning the standards a civilized society ought to set for itself and respect. Laws of this kind do not correct, but replace, market mechanisms for collective choice.... Through these laws we get a normative purchase upon—we control—the moral character of our relations with one another.

> Mark Sagoff
> Center for Philosophy and Public Policy,
> University of Maryland
> *Maryland Law Review* (1982)

When you discuss the viability of a marketing strategy ... the question of whether it is ethically appropriate becomes part of the ... discussion.

> Anthony M. Santomero
> The Wharton School
> *Working Woman*, March 1988

Ethical pressures and decisions are viewed through the prism of one's own personal values. The distinction between personal and organizational values, however, often becomes blurred, especially the longer one stays with a particular organization and/or advances up the hierarchial ladder.

> Warren H. Schmidt
> University of Southern California
> and Barry Z. Posner
> Santa Clara University
> *Public Administration Review*,
> September/October 1986

A criminal is a person with predatory instincts who has not sufficient capital to form a corporation.

> Howard Scott
> Economist
> *The New Dictionary of Thoughts*, 1957

Organized crime inevitably gravitates to cash.

> Daniel Seligman
> Business reporter
> *Fortune*, March 2, 1987

Let me have no lying; it becomes none but tradesmen.

> William Shakespeare, 1564–1616
> English dramatist and poet
> *The Winter's Tale*

The critical issue in the Nuremberg trials was the question of responsibility. Men who ceded themselves to the organization had lost their moral being: they were willing to profit or suffer by the decisions of the organization, and they were willing to do anything. Once a totalitarian organization has destroyed the moral equilibrium of those it controls, the will of the organization becomes absolute.

Earl Shorris
Manager and writer
The Oppressed Middle
(Anchor/Doubleday, 1981)

Sitting up here in Stamford, there's no way I can effect what an employee is doing in Texas, Montana or Maine. Making speeches and sending letters just doesn't do it. You need a culture and peer pressure that spells out what is acceptable and isn't and why.

Andrew C. Sigler
Chairman, Champion International Corp.
Business Week, February 15, 1988

The corporate reformation will be enduring only if statements of ethical standards are matched by the building of institutions and procedures within the corporation to insure that the standards are enforced.

Leonard Silk
"Ethical Guidelines for Companies"
The New York Times, June 15, 1978

People of the same trade seldom meet together. But [when they do] the conversation ends in a conspiracy against the public, or in some diversion to raise prices.

Adam Smith, 1723–1790
Scottish political economist
Inquiry into the ... Wealth of Nations

As corporate [philanthropic] foundations try to increase their influence inside their companies, the foundation's executives could chose social causes that would work for the corporation but not really help society.

Craig Smith
Editor, *Corporate Philanthropy Report*
The New York Times, February 21, 1988

Greatness is not manifested by unlimited pragmatism, which places such a high premium on the end justifying *any* means and *any* methods.

Margaret Chase Smith
U. S. Senator
Address to National Republican Women,
April 16, 1962

Political corruption is not a matter of men or classes or education or character of any sort; it is a matter of pressure. Wherever the pressure is brought to bear, society and government cave in. The problem, then, is one of discovering and dealing with the cause or the source of the pressure to buy and corrupt.

Joseph Lincoln Steffens, 1866–1936
American journalist and editor
Autobiography

The art of ethical management lies in unmixing the "grey" areas to achieve clarity in resolution of ethical dilemmas.

Sheldon S. Steinberg
Senior Vice President,
University Research Corp.
Workshop on Ethical Practices, July 1987

We [women] are not more moral, we are only less corrupted by power.

Gloria Steinem
Author and feminist
The New York Times, August 26, 1971

There is no evil in the atom; only in men's souls.

Adlai Ewing Stevenson, 1900–1965
U. S. Ambassador to the United
Nations and Governor of Illinois
Speech, Hartford, Connecticut, 1952

The traitor was always hated because he was ... a person without honor of any kind ... unmoved by higher loyalty or human bond.... The whistle-blowers have actually reversed the operation of the classical traitor, as they have usually been the only people in their organizations taking a stand on some kind of ideal.

Charles Taylor and Peter Branch
Blowing the Whistle (Praeger, 1972)

I reject the idea that holding public men and women to a high standard of behavior means that no one will want to run for president. I think it means we can look forward to a better crop than we have had before.

Cal Thomas
Syndicated columnist
The Washington Times, October 2, 1987

It is not a man's duty, as a matter of course, to devote himself to the eradication of any, even the most enormous wrong; he may still properly have other concerns to engage him; but it is his duty, at least, to wash his hands of it.

Henry David Thoreau, 1817–1862
American naturalist and writer
On the Duty of Civil Disobedience

Did you ever expect a corporation to have a conscience when it has no soul to be damned and no body to be kicked?

Edward Thurlow, 1731–1806
Lord Chancellor of England
Wilberforce, *Life of Thurlow*

A person who is fundamentally honest doesn't need a code of ethics. The Ten Commandments and The Sermon on the Mount are all the ethical codes anybody needs.

Harry S. Truman, 1884–1972
Thirty-third President of the United States
Remark, July 10, 1958

What do I care about the law. H'aint I got the power?

Cornelius Vanderbilt, 1794–1877
American shipping and railroad magnate
Josephson, *The Robber Barons*
(Harcourt Brace, 1934)

I would sooner be esteemed an ignoramus than a liar.

Benedetto Varchi, c. 1502–1565
Italian poet and historian
L'Ercolano

Despite the codes of ethics, the ethics programs, and the special departments—*corporations* don't make the ultimate decisions about ethics. Ethical choices are made by *individuals*.

M. Euel Wade, Jr.
Senior Vice President,
Southern Company Services, Inc.
Speech, University of Georgia,
November 5, 1987

All those men have their price.

Robert Walpole, 1676–1745
English politician and writer
Coxe, *Memoirs of Walpole*

To me, one of the most vivid proofs that there is a moral governance in the universe is the fact that when men or governments work intelligently and far-sightedly for the good of others, they achieve their own prosperity too.

Barbara Ward, 1914–1981
English economist, writer, and educator
The Rich Nations and the Poor Nations

Few men have virtue to withstand the highest bidder.

George Washington, 1732–1799
First President of the United States
Letter to Robert Howe, August 17, 1779

I hate deception, even where the imagination only is concerned.

> George Washington, 1732–1799
> First President of the United States
> Letter to Dr. Cochran, August 16, 1779

There is a time when integrity should take the rudder from team loyalty.

> Thomas J. Watson, Jr.
> CEO, IBM, and U. S. Ambassador to Russia
> *Fortune*, 1977

Of all the abuses of law, the greatest and most pernicious ... is the setting up of the laws as a system of morality, and making them the guide of our conscience, which a law never can be.

> Richard Whatley, 1787–1863
> Archbishop of Dublin and Professor of
> Political Economy, Oxford University
> *Thoughts and Apothegms*

[Referring to the mounting toll of railroad accidents:] The public can take care of itself. It's as much as I can do to take care of the railroad [finances].

> Anonymous 19th Century railroad executive
> Josephson, *The Robber Barons*
> (Harcourt Brace, 1934)

Pressure to do it faster, better and cheaper ... puts people in positions in which they feel unethical behavior is the only alternative they have to get ahead.

> Anonymous respondent to survey on ethics
> *Personnel Journal*, November 1987

Do what you have to do. Just don't tell me about it.

> Anonymous manager
> *Personnel Journal*, November 1987

[Generalizing from the 1639 Boston criminal trial of Robert Keayne, a merchant who was convicted of making sixpence profit on a shilling of sales, some of the most unethical and morally false principles of trade were specified:]

That a man may might sell as dear [at as high a price] as he can and buy as cheap as he can.

If a man lose by casualty of sea, etc., in some of his commodities, he may raise the price of the rest.

That he may sell as he bought, though he paid too dear [too much].

> Anonymous Boston minister's sermon, 1639
> Quoted by John Winthrop (1588–1649)
> Governor of Massachusetts Bay Colony
> *Winthrop's Journal*
> (Charles Scribner's Sons, 1908)

14

Experience

Experience gives the test first,
the lesson afterwards

All experience is an arch, to build upon.

Henry Brooks Adams, 1838–1918
American writer and historian
The Louisville (Kentucky) *Journal*,
January 1, 1863

It is costly wisdom that is bought by experience. By experience we find out a shorter way by a long wandering. Learning teacheth more in one year than experience in twenty.

Roger Ascham, 1515–1568
English classicist, diplomat, and gambler
Scholemaster

Theories are always very thin and unsubstantial; experience only is tangible.

Hosea Ballou, 1771–1852
American clergyman
Universalist Expositor

True wisdom is plenty of experience, observation and reflection. False wisdom is plenty of ignorance, arrogance and impudence.

Josh Billings
(Henry Wheeler Shaw), 1818–1885
American writer and auctioneer
Josh Billings: His Book

The experience requirement creates problems for many professional service organizations. Firms with expertise in limited areas often have difficulty diversifying into new lines of work. And inexperienced professionals often find it difficult to find any work at all. "Newness" in the professions isn't nearly as favorable an attribute as it might be for a soft drink company or an airline.

Paul N. Bloom
University of Maryland
Harvard Business Review,
September/October 1984

Circumstances? I make circumstances!

> Napoleon Bonaparte, 1769–1821
> Emperor of France
> *Maxims*

In our own times, as well as in history, we may find examples, but never models.

> Napoleon Bonaparte, 1769–1821
> Emperor of France
> *Maxims*

I have lived long enough to be battered by the realities of life and not too long to be downed by them.

> John Mason Brown, 1900–1969
> American essayist, critic, and lecturer
> Speech, 1958

[T]hough discernment teaches us the folly of others, experience singly can teach us our own!

> Fanny Burney, 1752–1840
> English novelist
> *Cecilia*

You cannot create experience. You must undergo it.

> Albert Camus, 1913–1960
> French philosopher and writer
> *Notebooks, 1935-1942*

Often a liberal antidote of experience supplies a sovereign cure for a paralyzing abstraction built upon a theory.

> Benjamin Nathan Cardozo, 1870–1938
> U. S. Supreme Court Justice
> *Paradoxes of Legal Science*

What is all knowledge, too, but recorded Experience.

> Thomas Carlyle, 1795–1881
> Scottish essayist and historian
> *Essays*

"Tut, tut, child, " said the Dutchess. "Everything's got a moral if only you can find it."

> Lewis Carroll
> (Charles Lutwidge Dodgson), 1832–1898
> English mathematician and writer
> *Alice's Adventures in Wonderland*

"The horror of that moment," the King went on, "I shall never, *never* forget!"
"You will, though," the Queen said, "if you don't make a memorandum of it."

> Lewis Carroll
> (Charles Lutwidge Dodgson), 1832–1898
> English mathematician and writer
> *Alice's Adventures in Wonderland*

I am sure that the mistakes of that time [World War I] will not be repeated; we shall probably make another set of mistakes.

> Winston Churchill, 1874–1965
> English Prime Minister, writer, and soldier
> Speech in Parliament, June 8, 1944

Wisdom is not to be obtained from text-books, but must be coined out of human experience in the flame of life.

> Morris Raphael Cohen, 1880–1947
> American philosopher and educator
> *A Dreamer's Journey*

He went like one that hath been stunned,
And is of sense forlorn:
A sadder and wiser man,
He rose the morrow morn.

> Samuel Taylor Coleridge, 1772–1834
> English poet, editor, and critic
> *The Rime of the Ancient Mariner*

A youth without fire is followed by an old age without experience.

> Charles Caleb Colton, c. 1780–1832
> English cleric, sportsman, and wine merchant
> *Lacon*

Experience does not err; only your judgments err by expecting from her what is not in her power.

> Leonardo da Vinci, 1452–1519
> Italian artist, inventor, and scientist
> *Notebooks*

Information's pretty thin stuff, unless mixed with experience.

> Clarence Day, 1874–1935
> American essayist and humorist
> *The Crow's Nest*

Experience is the child of Thought, and Thought is the child of Action.

> Benjamin Disraeli, 1804–1881
> English Prime Minister and novelist
> *Vivian Grey*

Great things spring from casualties.

> Benjamin Disraeli, 1804–1881
> English Prime Minister and novelist
> *Sybil*

Man is not the creature of circumstances. Circumstances are the creatures of men.

> Benjamin Disraeli, 1805–1881
> English Prime Minister and novelist
> *Vivian Grey*

The one thing to do is to do nothing .... you survive humiliation and that's an experience of incalculable value.

> T. S. Eliot, 1888–1965
> English poet, critic, and playwright
> *The Cocktail Party*

Sensible people find nothing useless.

> Jean de La Fontaine, 1621–1695
> French fabulist and playwright
> *Fables*

Records of old wars mean nothing to me. History is more or less bunk. It's tradition.

> Henry Ford, 1863–1947
> Founder, Ford Motors, Inc.
> *The Chicago Tribune*, May 1916

Whoever lives is always learning.

> Giovanni Battista Gelli, 1498–1563
> Florentine writer
> *Capricci del Bottaio*

Talent is nurtured in solitude; character is formed in the stormy billows of the world.

> Johann Wolfgang von Goethe, 1749–1832
> German poet and dramatist
> *Torquato Tasso*

We know the mistake of doing nothing from our own experience.

> Mikhail Gorbachev
> Premier, USSR
> *Perestroika* (Harper & Row, 1987)

Experience joined with common sense,
To mortals is a providence.

> Matthew Green, 1696–1737
> English poet
> *The Spleen*

It is without doubt most dangerous to be guided by precedent, unless the circumstances are in exact agreement, not only generally, but in every particular.

> Francesco Guicciardini, 1483–1540
> Florentine historian and statesman
> *Istoria d'Italia*

We cannot afford to forget any experiences, even the most painful.

> Dag Hammerskjöld, 1905–1961
> Secretary-General of the United Nations
> *Markings*

What experience and history teach is this— that people and governments have never learned anything from history, or acted on principles deduced from it.

> Georg Wilhelm Hegel, 1770–1831
> German philosopher
> *Philosophy of History*

In the fell clutch of circumstance,
I have not winced nor cried aloud;
Under the bludgeonings of chance
My head is bloody, but unbowed.

> William Ernest Henley, 1849–1903
> English writer and editor
> *Echoes*

Remember that men are dependent on circumstances, and not circumstances on men.

> Herodotus, fifth century B.C.
> Greek "Father of History"
> *History of the Persian War*

Knowledge and timber shouldn't be much used till they are seasoned.

> Oliver Wendell Holmes, 1809–1894
> American physician and popular writer
> *The Autocrat of the Breakfast Table*

The life of the law has not been logic; it has been experience.

> Oliver Wendell Holmes, Jr., 1841–1935
> U. S. Supreme Court Justice
> *The Common Law*

Experience is not what happens to you; it is what you do with what happens to you.

> Aldous Huxley, 1894–1963
> English novelist and critic
> *Brave New World*

Nothing ever becomes real till it is experienced. Even a proverb is no proverb to you till your life has illustrated it.

> John Keats, 1795–1821
> English poet
> Letter to George and Georgiana Keats

I don't want men of experience working for me. The experienced man is always telling me why something can't be done. He is smart; he is intelligent; he thinks he knows the answers. The fellow who has not had any experience is so dumb he doesn't know a thing can't be done—and he goes ahead and does it.

> Charles F. Kettering, 1876–1958
> President, GM Research Corp.
> *How to Live With Life* (Reader's Digest, 1965)

Experience is a hard teacher because she gives the test first, the lesson afterwards.

> Vernon Law
> Former pitcher, Pittsburgh Pirates
> *This Week in Baseball*, August 14, 1960

No man's knowledge can go beyond his experience.

> John Locke, 1632–1704
> English philosopher
> *An Essay Concerning Human Understanding*

The difference between optimists and pessimists is that generally pessimists have had more experience.

> Clare Boothe Luce, 1903–1987
> Congresswoman, playwright, and diplomat
> Speech, National Press Club, 1977

There is no security on this earth; there is only opportunity.

> Douglas MacArthur, 1880–1964
> Five-star General of the U. S. Army
> Whitney, *MacArthur: His Rendezvous
> with History* (Knopf, 1955)

He who makes a study of times present and times past will have no difficulty in coming to the conclusion that in every city and in every nation are to be found the same desires and the same caprices, and that so it has always been.

> Niccolò Machiavelli, 1469–1527
> Florentine statesman and philosopher
> *Discourses*

In order to get experience you have to get knocked around. Getting knocked around is the norm. If somebody has not been knocked around by life, I get concerned, not only about his judgment but about his resiliency. Experience, if it doesn't kill you, teaches you how to bounce back.

> David Mahoney
> Chairman, Norton Smith, Inc.
> *Confessions of a Street-Smart Manager*
> (Simon & Schuster, 1987)

Men are too apt to reduce unknown Things to the Standard of what they know, and bring a Prejudice or Tincture from Things they have been conversant in, to judge thereby of Things in which they have not been conversant. I have known a Fidler gravely teach that the Soul was Harmony; a Geometrician very positive that the Soul must be extended; and a Physician, who having pickled half a Dozen Embryos and dissected as many Rats and Frogs, grew conceited and affirmed there was no Soul at all, and that it was a vulgar Error.

> Bernard Mandeville, c. 1670–1733
> English physician and satirist
> *The Fable of the Bees*

The most important wings on an airplane are on the pilot.

> T. Allen McArtor
> Administrator, FAA
> Speech, Aero Club of Washington,
> September 15, 1987

The gods cannot help one who loses opportunities.

> Mencius, c. 372–c. 289 B.C.
> Chinese philosopher
> *The Real Man*

It's too costly today to learn from your own experience. You not only learn much faster, but it is also much cheaper to learn from other people's experiences.

> Robert L. Montgomery
> President, R. L. Montgomery & Associates
> *How to Sell in the 1980's*
> (Prentice-Hall, 1980)

Not sense data or atoms or electrons or packets of energy, but purposes, interests, and meanings constitute the underlying facts of human experience.

> Lewis Mumford
> American author, editor, and critic
> *The Conduct of Life*

It is the weight, not numbers, of experiments that is to be regarded.

> Isaac Newton, 1642–1727
> English mathematician and philosopher
> *The Correspondence of Isaac Newton*

Each person standing at one part of the elephant can make his own limited, analytic assessment of the situation, but we do not obtain an elephant by adding "scaly," "long and soft," "massive and cylindrical" together in any conceivable proportion. Without the development of an overall perspective, we remain lost in our individual investigations.

Such a perspective is a province of another mode of knowledge, and cannot be achieved in the same way that individual parts are explored. It does not arise out of a linear sum of independent observations.

> Robert E. Ornstein
> Langley Porter Neuropsychiatric Institute
> *The Psychology of Consciousness* (Harcourt Brace Jovanovich, 1977)

I am I plus my circumstances and if I do not save it, I cannot save myself.

> José Ortéga y Gasset, 1883–1955
> Spanish essayist and philosopher
> *Meditations on Quixote*

... by chance you will say, but chance only favors the mind which is prepared.

> Louis Pasteur, 1822–1895
> French chemist and inventor of inoculation
> Address, University of Lille, 1854

Experience is good if not bought too dear.

> Barber, *The Book of 1000 Proverbs*, 1876

No one knows what he can do till he tries.

> Publilius Syrus, c. 42 B.C.
> Roman writer
> *Maxims*

The Japanese are regularly encouraged to reflect on their experience. Some executives even do Zen meditation with the purpose of clearing their minds so they may reflect on their experiences more deeply. Reflection may lead one to push harder, another to back off.

> Thomas P. Rohlen
> Consultant on Japanese organizations
> Pascale and Athos,
> *The Art of Japanese Management*
> (Simon & Schuster, 1981)

Perhaps the most important thing that has come out of my life is the discovery that if you prepare yourself at every point as well as you can, with whatever means you have, however meager they may seem, you will be able to grasp opportunity for broader expedrience when it appears. Without preparation you cannot do it.

> Eleanor Roosevelt, 1884–1962
> American humanitarian and author
> *The Autobiography of Eleanor Roosevelt*

Experience makes for shrewdness; it's the heart that makes for wisdom.

> Dagobert D. Runes
> Editor, publisher, and philosopher
> *A Book of Contemplation*

The brain is unlike any organ in the body in that its internal structure is always changing and developing as a result of experience. This gives it the unlimited capacity for learning.

> Peter Russell
> Psychologist and management consultant
> *The Brain Book* (Hawthorne, 1979)

The great difficulty in education is to get experience out of ideas.

> George Santayana, 1863–1952
> Spanish-born American poet and philosopher
> *The Life of Reason*

Men are wise, not in proportion to their experience, but to their capacity for experience.

> George Bernard Shaw, 1856–1950
> Nobel laureate in literature
> *Man and Superman*

The knowledge of the world is only to be acquired in the world, and not in a closet.

> Philip Dormer Stanhope, 1694–1773
> English Secretary of State
> *Letters of Lord Chesterfield to His Son*

Nothing succeeds like success, except the failure that reverses it.

> Leo Stein, 1872–1947
> American writer and editor
> *Journey into the Self*

In school, you get a theoretical eduction, but to really learn the business, you have to do it.

> Rosa Sugranes
> CEO, Iberia Tiles
> *Hispanic Business,* June 1987

A man should never be ashamed to own he has been in the wrong, which is but saying, in other words, that he is wiser to-day than he was yesterday.

> Jonathan Swift, 1667–1775
> English cleric and satirist
> *Thoughts on Various Subjects*

They have learned nothing and forgotten nothing.

> Charles Maurice Talleyrand, 1754–1838
> French statesman and diplomat
> Ascribed to him by Chevalier de Parat

And others' follies teach us not,
Nor much their wisdom teaches,
And most, of sterling worth, is what
Our own experience preaches.

> Alfred (Lord) Tennyson, 1809–1892
> English poet
> *Will Waterproof's Lyrical Monologue*

We should be careful to get out of an experience only the wisdom that is in it—and stop there; lest we be like the cat that sits down on the hot stove-lid. She will never sit down on a hot stove-lid again—and that is well; but also she will never sit down on a cold one anymore.

> Mark Twain
> (Samuel Langhorne Clemens), 1835–1910
> American author and riverboat captain
> *Following the Equator*

Any piece of knowledge I acquire today has a value at this moment exactly proportioned to my skill to deal with it. Tomorrow, when I know more, I recall that piece of knowledge and use it better.

> Mark Van Doren, 1894–1973
> American poet and critic
> *Liberal Education*

Believe one who has tried it.

> Virgil, 70–19 B.C.
> Roman Epic Poet
> *Aeneid*

The difference between ancients and moderns is that the ancients asked what have we experienced, and moderns asked what can we experience.

> Alfred North Whitehead, 1861–1947
> English philosopher and mathematician
> *Adventures in Ideas*

Does he have 17 years of experience or one year of experience 17 times?

> Paul R. Wiesenfeld
> Attorney, Rockville, Maryland
> Maryland Bar Association meeting,
> December 1987

Experience is the name everyone gives to their mistakes.

> Oscar Wilde, 1854–1900
> Irish poet, playwright, and novelist
> *Lady Windermere's Fan*

Experience is what enables you to recognize a mistake when you make it again.

Earl Wilson
Syndicated columnist
The Official MBA Handbook of Great Business Quotations (Simon & Schuster, 1984)

It is other people's experience that makes the older man wiser than the younger man.
[*Ogbon ologbon ni ki ijeki a pe agba ni were.*]

Yoruba proverb

You don't learn anything the second time you're kicked by a mule.

Anonymous (Texas)

Two men went into business together. One had all the money; the other, all the experience. At the end of the year the man with the experience had all the money, and the man who had started with money had a lot of experience.

Anonymous

Good judgment comes from experience, and experience comes from poor judgment.

Sign in a lumber yard
Wheaton, Maryland

15

Goals & Objectives

Wait till last year.

The unfinished is nothing.

> Henri Frédéric Amiel, 1821–1881
> Swiss journalist and critic
> *Journal intime*

We have set some clear long range objectives. If they are not met, then the company should find a president better than me who can meet them.

> Tatsuhiko Andoh
> President, Okatoku Securities Co. (Japan)
> *Cherry Blossoms and Robotics*
> (Young Presidents' Organization, 1983)

While we pursue the unattainable we make impossible the realizable.

> Robert Ardrey
> Writer
> *The Social Contract* (Atheneum, 1970)

Any company (or any organization for that matter) needs a strong, unifying sense of direction. But that need is particularly strong in an organization in which tasks are differentiated and responsibilities are dispersed.

> Christopher A. Bartlett
> Harvard Business School
> and Sumantra Ghoshal, Institute of Business
> Administration, Fontainebleau (France)
> *Harvard Business Review*,
> November/December 1986

Do not seek to follow in the footsteps of the men of old; seek what they sought.

> Matsuo Basho, 16th century
> Japanese poet
> *The Rustic Gate*

Whatsoever thou takest in hand, remember the end, and thou shalt never do amiss.

> Apocrypha, Wisdom of Ben Sira 7:36

It is the very essence of intelligence to coordinate means with a view to a remote end, and to undertake what it does not feel absolutely sure of carrying out.

> Henri Bergson, 1859–1941
> Nobel laureate in literature (France)
> *Two Sources of Morality and Religion*

Injustice, poverty, slavery, ignorance—these may be cured by reform or revolution. But men do not live only be fighting evils. They live by positive goals, individual and collective, a vast variety of them, seldom predictable, at times incompatible.

> Isaiah Berlin
> British philosopher and writer
> *Four Essays on Liberty*

You must call each thing by its proper name or that which must get done will not.

> A. Harvey Block
> President, Bokenon Systems
> Speech, Washington D.C., June 13, 1977

You cannot seek for the ideal outside the realm of reality.

> Léon Blum, 1872–1949
> Premier of France
> *New Conversations*

I don't want to do what's expected [of me]. It's no fun.

> Jimmy Breslin
> Columnist, *Newsday* (New York)
> National Public Radio, March 6, 1988

First, I believed it could be done. Second, I believed that it could be done within the time period that had been set. Third, I was consumed with accomplishing the task. Fourth, I told all with whom I came into contact of my goal and asked for their help.

> James E. Buerger
> Publisher, *Travelhost National*
> *Travelhost National*, January 22, 1984

I came, I saw, I conquered.
[*Veni, vidi, vici.*]

> Julius Caesar, 100–44 B.C.
> Roman general and statesman
> Quoted by Suetonius, *Lives of the Caesars*

If I understood too clearly what I was doing, where I was going, then I probably wasn't working on anything very interesting.

> Peter Carruthers
> Physicist
> *The New York Times*, May 6, 1984

[Referring to the Los Angeles Dodgers:] Wait till last year.

> Johnny Carson
> TV comedian and talk show host
> Monologue, August 2, 1979

We mean to hold our own. I have not become the King's First Minister in order to preside over the liquidation of the British Empire.

> Winston Churchill, 1874–1965
> English Prime Minister, writer, and soldier
> Speech, Mansion House, November 10, 1942

Telling a manager he's got to reach 25% growth isn't particularly relevant if his market isn't growing at all.

> Ian A. Cole
> Nomura Research Institute (England)
> *Business Week*, December 21, 1987

The business of America is business.

> Calvin Coolidge, 1872–1933
> Thirtieth President of the United States
> Speech to the
> Society of American Newspaper Editors,
> January 17, 1923

The achiever ... is a person who sets goals and meets them. He or she is someone we can count on to get the right things done in a su-

perior way and keep getting them done....
[T]oday's achiever—working in a highly collaborative setting—is someone who gets
things done through others.

> Allen Cox
> Management consultant and author
> *The Making of the Achiever*
> (Dodd Mead, 1985)

The secret of success is constancy to purpose.

> Benjamin Disraeli, 1804–1881
> English Prime Minister and novelist
> Speech, June 24, 1870

Criticism has few terrors for a man with a
great purpose.

> Benjamin Disraeli, 1804–1881
> English Prime Minister and novelist
> *Life of George Bentinck*

Objectives are not fate; they are direction.
They are not commands; they are commitments. They do not determine the future; they
are means to mobilize the resources and energies of the business for the making of the
future.

> Peter F. Drucker
> Management consultant and writer
> *People and Performance*
> (Harper & Row, 1977)

Goals should be specific, realistic and
measureable.

> William G. Dyer
> Brigham Young University
> *Strategies for Managing Change*
> (Addison-Wesley, 1984)

The published objectives of a company will
never reflect all the goals and values of the

corporation as an institution or its management as human beings.

> Richard Eells
> Columbia University School of Business
> *California Management Review*,
> Summer 1959

Perfection of means and confusion of goals ...
characterize our age.

> Albert Einstein, 1879–1955
> Nobel laureate in physics
> Hayes, *Memos for Management: Leadership*
> (AMACOM, 1983)

What makes life dreary is the want of a motive.

> George Eliot (Marian Evans), 1819–1880
> English novelist, essayist, and editor
> *Daniel Deronda*

How can you be in two places at once when
you're not anywhere at all?

> The Firesign Theatre
> *Don't Crush That Dwarf, Hand Me the Pliers*

A business that makes nothing but money is a
poor kind of business.

> Henry Ford, 1863–1947
> Founder, Ford Motors, Inc.
> *The Hawk Eye* (Burlington, Iowa),
> January 20, 1940

Good purposes should be the director of good
actions, not the apology for bad.

> Thomas Fuller, 1608–1661
> Chaplain in extraordinary to Charles II
> *Gnomologia*

An ability to tolerate ambiguity helps to avoid
overdetermining one's goals.... As they
proceed, peak performers can adjust goals....
What they are doing is balancing between

change and stasis, between innovation and consolidation.

Charles Garfield
President, Performance Sciences Corp.
Peak Performers (Avon, 1986)

There is something sick about a person whose only interest is money. And the same can be said, I think, for the company whose sole goal is profit.

Richard J. Haayen
CEO, Allstate Insurance Company
Nation's Business, March 1988

Setting goals can be the difference between success and failure.... Goals must not be defined so broadly that they cannot be quantified. Having quantifiable goals is an essential starting point if managers are to measure the results of their organization's activities.... Too often people mistake being busy for achieving goals.

Philip D. Harvey
Founder, Population Services International
and James D. Snyder
President, Snyder Associates, Inc.
Harvard Business Review,
January/February 1987

The world owes all its onward impulses to men who are ill at ease. The happy man inevitably confines himself within ancient limits.

Nathaniel Hawthorne, 1804–1864
American writer
The House of Seven Gables

Please realize that the first duty of newspaper men is to get the news and *print the news.*

William Randolph Hearst, 1863–1951
Newspaper publisher and U. S. Congressman
Editor & Publisher, August 12, 1944

Don't look for the secrets of Japanese management: look for Japan's use of Western methods to achieve Western-style objectives—and copy that.

Robert Heller
Editor, *Management Today*
The Supermanagers (Dutton, 1984)

Overly optimistic goals nearly always result in one of two extremes. If the goal is seen as a must, then the division manager must "go for broke." This can result in reckless risk taking. More commonly ... ultraconservative action. The reasoning is: "Why take any chances to achieve an unattainable goal."

Bruce Henderson
CEO, Boston Consulting Group, Inc.
Henderson on Corporate Strategy (Abt, 1979)

Who aimeth at the sky
Shoots higher much than he that means a tree.

George Herbert, 1593–1633
English clergyman and poet
Antiphon

If thou well hast begun, go on for right;
It is the End that crowns us, not the Fight.

Robert Herrick, 1591–1674
English poet
Hesperides

The productivity of a work group seems to depend on how the group members see their own goals in relation to the goals of the organization.

Paul Hersey
California American University
and Kenneth H. Blanchard
University of Massachusetts
Management of Organizational Behavior
(Prentice-Hall, 1972)

[M]anagement should emphasize the contributions to total goals rather than the accomplishments of subgroup goals.

Paul Hersey
California American University
and Kenneth H. Blanchard
University of Massachusetts
Management of Organizational Behavior
(Prentice-Hall, 1972)

[One] must not always assume that obscure and obfuscated objectives are totally lacking in function.

Harley H. Hinrichs
U. S. Naval Academy
Program Budgeting and Cost Benefit Analysis
(Goodyear, 1969)

When the world is not so simple as to see goals in terms of "maximizing goodies" or "minimizing baddies," when uncertainties and incommensurabilities may prevail, objectives and/or criteria may be quite different from the conventional sort.

Harley H. Hinrichs
U. S. Naval Academy
Program Budgeting and Cost Benefit Analysis
(Goodyear, 1969)

To have a grievance is to have a purpose in life.

Eric Hoffer, 1902–1983
American writer, longshoreman, and critic
The Passionate State of Mind

I find the great thing in this world is, not where we stand, as in what direction we are moving.

Oliver Wendell Holmes, 1809–1894
American physician and popular writer
The Autocrat of the Breakfast Table

A body of law is more rational and more civilized when every rule it contains is referred articulately and definitely to an end which it subserves and when the grounds for desiring that end are stated, or are ready to be stated in words.

Oliver Wendell Holmes, Jr., 1841–1935
U. S. Supreme Court Justice
Quoted in *Wigmore on Evidence*

[Management by objectives is] ... a process whereby the superior and the subordinate managers of an enterprise jointly identify its common goals, define each individual's major areas of responsibility in terms of the results expected of him, and use these measures as guides for operating the unit and assessing the contribution of each of its members.

Robert House
Management consultant
Administrative Science Quarterly, 1971

The great end of life is not knowledge but action.

Thomas Henry Huxley, 1825–1895
English biologist
Science and Culture

Great minds have purposes, others have wishes. Little minds are tamed and subdued by misfortune; but great minds rise above them.

Washington Irving, 1783–1859
American essayist and novelist
Elbert Hubbard's Scrap Book

No matter how high or how excellent technology may be and how much capital may be accumulated, unless the group of human beings which comprise the enterprise works together toward one unified goal, the enterprise is sure to go down the path of decline.

Takashi Ishihara
President, Nissan Motor Co. (Japan)
Cherry Blossoms and Robotics
(Young Presidents' Organization, 1983)

Goal setting has traditionally been based on past performance. This practice has tended to perpetuate the sins of the past.

J. M. Juran
Chairman, Juran Institute
Training, December 1986

I push in just one direction, not in every direction.

Rita Levi-Montalcini
Nobel laureate in physiology
and medicine (Italy)
Omni, March 1988

[Explaining why he climbed Mt. Everest:]
Because it's there!

G. H. L. Malory
English mountain climber
Hunt, *The Ascent of Everest*

Sighted sub. Sank same.

David Francis Miller
Pilot, U. S. Navy
Radio message, February 26, 1942

The greatest disservice that Harvard Business School has ever played on corporate America is management by objectives.

James McManus
Chairman, Marketing Corporation of America
Inc. Magazine, September 1986

Management by objectives is a philosophy of managing that is based on identifying purposes, objectives, and desired results, establishing a realistic program for obtaining these results, and evaluating performance in achieving them.

R. Henry Miglione
Oral Roberts University
An MBO Approach to Long-Range Planning
(Prentice-Hall, 1983)

By asking for the impossible we obtain the best possible.

Giovanni Battista Niccolini, 1782–1861
Italian dramatic poet
Vannucci

Superordinate goals—the goals above all others ... play a pragmatic role by influencing implementation at the operational level. Because an executive cannot be everywhere at once, many decisions are made without his knowledge. What superordinate goals do, in effect, is provide employees with a "compass" and point their footsteps in the right direction ... [to] independent decisions. For example, at IBM that translates into never sacrificing customer service; at Matsushita [Electric Company of Japan] it means never cheating a customer by knowingly producing or selling defective merchandise.

Richard T. Pascale
Stanford University School of Business
and Anthony G. Athos
Harvard Business School
The Art of Japanese Management
(Simon & Schuster, 1981)

To tend, unfailingly, unflinchingly, towards a goal, is the secret of success.

Anna Pavlova, 1881–1931
Russian ballerina
Franks, *Pavlova*

It is profitable Wisdom to know when we have done enough: Much Time and Pains are spared, in not flattering our selves against Probabilities.

William Penn, 1644–1718
Founder of Pennsylvania
Fruits of Solitude in Reflections and Maxims

M[anagement] B[y] O[bjectives] has become one more way to make organizations behave like machines.

> Julien Phillips
> Principal, McKinsey & Co.
> *Success*, February 1988

The harder you work, the luckier you get.

> Gary Player
> Professional golfer
> *The Official MBA Handbook of Great Business Quotations* (Simon & Schuster, 1984)

Where there is no vision, the people perish.

> Old Testament, Proverbs 29:18

Management has a responsibility to explain to the employee how the routine job contributes to the business's objectives. If management cannot explain the value of the job, then it should be eliminated and the employee reassigned.

> Douglas M. Reid
> Vice President, Xerox Corp.
> *Harvard Business Review*,
> November/December 1986

So little done, so much to do.

> Cecil Rhodes, 1853–1902
> English Colonial administrator, financier,
> and philanthropist
> Last words

The most important reason for our success is we set our objectives and make sure we follow through on them. Even if you're a self-taught executive like I am, that method works.

> Annette Beneteau Roux
> Chairman, Beneteau (France)
> *The New York Times*, August 30, 1987

Every goal and every change from the status quo has a price tag on it.

> Lyle E. Schaller
> Yokefellow Institute
> *The Change Agent* (Abingdon, 1972)

To climb steep hills
Requires slow pace at first.

> William Shakespeare, 1564–1616
> English dramatist and poet
> *Henry the Seventh*

If you don't know where you're going, any path will take you there.

> Sioux proverb

Every individual intends only his own gain, and he is in this, as in so many other cases, led by an invisible hand to promote an end which was no part of his intention.

> Adam Smith, 1723–1790
> Scottish political economist
> *Inquiry into ... the Wealth of Nations*

Whatever is worth doing at all, is worth doing well.

> Philip Dormer Stanhope, 1694–1773
> English Secretary of State
> *Letters of Lord Chesterfield to His Son*

They say you can't do it, but sometimes it doesn't always work.

> Casey Stengel, 1891–1975
> Professional baseball manager
> Koppet, *A Thinking Man's Guide to Baseball*

Before a man gives up his old gods, he should have something of value to replace them.

> Swahili proverb

It is not enough to be industrious; so are the ants. What are you industrious about?

> Henry David Thoreau, 1817–1862
> American naturalist and writer
> Hoffman, *The Public Speaker's Scrapbook*

You've got to think about "big things" while you're doing small things, so that all the small things go in the right direction.

> Alvin Toffler
> Futurist and writer
> *Newsweek*, April 4, 1988

He who determines the end, provides the means.

> Benedetto Varchi, c. 1502–1565
> Italian poet and historian
> *L'Ercolano*

He set his heart upon the goal, not on the prize.

> William Watson, 1858–1935
> English essayist and poet
> *Tribute to Matthew Arnold*

No experiment on programmer performance should be undertaken without clear, explicit and reasonable goals—unless that experiment is designed to measure the effect of unclear, implicit, or unreasonable goals.

> Gerald M. Weinberg and Edward L. Schulman
> Organizational consultants
> *Human Factors*, 1974

The slippage we have experienced is in the schedule of actual accomplishment versus plan. But our plan was exceedingly ambitious.

> B. Joseph White
> Vice President, Cummins Engine Co.
> *The Academy of Management Executive*,
> February 1988

There is one quality more important than "know-how" and we cannot accuse the United States of any undue amount of it. That is "know-what" by which we determine not only how to accomplish our purposes, but what our purposes are to be.

> Norbert Wiener, 1894–1964
> Pioneer computer scientist
> *The Human Use of Human Beings*

Targets set by individual managers are relevant to the company's goals because the entire management group is involved in the total planning process.

> Walter S. Wilkstrom
> *Managing by-and-with Objectives*
> (National Industrial Conference Board, 1968)

The "management by objectives" school ... suggests that detailed objectives be spelled out at all levels in the corporation. This method is feasible at lower levels of management, but it becomes unworkable at the upper levels. The top manager must think out objectives in detail, but ordinarily some of the objectives must be withheld, or at least communicated to the organization in modest doses. A conditioning process that may stretch over months or years is necessary in order to prepare the organization for radical departures from what it is currently striving to attain.

> H. Edward Wrapp
> University of Chicago
> *Harvard Business Review on
> Human Relations*, 1986

For Hispanics, the store is the end, the goal. For Koreans, it's entry level.

> Philip Young
> Pace University
> *The New York Times*, March 19, 1985

We set our own goals—way more than the company asks for.

Joe Zalman
Manager, Computer Center Store, Radio Shack
Computer & Software News, December 7, 1987

Ready! Fire! Aim!

Anonymous

On a country hike, two city kids met a grizzly bear. One kid sat down to put on a pair of sneakers and make ready to run. The other kid said, scoffing, "I've read all there is to read about grizzly bears, and no man alive can outrun a grizzly." The first kid looked up and said, "I don't care about outrunning the bear. I just want to outrun you!"

Anonymous (but probably from Brooklyn)

It doesn't matter if you're on the right track. If you're not moving fast enough, you'll still get run over.

Anonymous

16

Growth, Size, & Scale

Bigness has not delivered the goods, and this fact is no longer a secret

---

Bigness has not delivered the goods, and this fact is no longer a secret.

> Walter Adams
> President, Michigan State University
> and James Brock
> Economist
> *The Bigness Complex* (Pantheon, 1986)

Conclusion [with regard to downsizing by American companies in the 1980's:] The scalpel is in greater use than the meat ax. Far more force reductions are aimed at specific targets within a company than spread over the entire organization. Nearly half affect only one worksite. Only a fragment involve a total shutdown of a plant or office. And among both salaried workers and nonexempts, downsizing eliminates fewer than 10 jobs far more often than 50 or more.

> American Management Association
> *Responsible Reductions in Force*, 1987

Companies which get misled by their own success are sure to be blindsided.

> Warren G. Bennis
> President, University of Cincinnati
> University of Maryland symposium,
> January 21, 1988

The greater the rate of company expansion, the easier it is to find valuable new jobs for people.

> Ed Bersoff
> Founder, BTG, Inc.
> *Inc. Magazine*, December 1987

The restructuring going on in industries, companies, and countries is a way of dealing with global overcapacity.

> Joseph L. Bower
> Harvard Business School
> *Fortune*, March 2, 1987

As a company grows, the president tends to fade away into his office.

> Joseph Cherry
> President, Cherry Tire Service, Inc.
> *Inc. Magazine*, January 1988

The more common pattern [of business innovation] is that the ideas are developed by smaller companies that get to the point where they need more money, and they get bought by the larger companies. General Foods, for instance, has never created anything—they have simply bought up the Posts and the Jell-Os.

> Laurel Cutler
> Vice Chairman, FCB/Leber Katz Partners
> *Inc. Magazine*, November 1987

Size has lost its significance as it becomes increasingly clear that a company's rank in the *Fortune 500* is of limited importance.

> Martin Davis
> Chairman, Gulf & Western
> *Fortune*, December 1985

If it's not growing, it's going to die.

> Michael Eisner
> CEO, Walt Disney Productions
> *60 Minutes* (TV program), November 22, 1987

You're not going to grow if you run your company like the Soviet Union's economy.

> Lawrence Ellison
> CEO, Oracle Systems Corp.
> *The New York Times*, February 28, 1988

No great thing is created suddenly.

> Epictetus, c. 60–120
> Roman Stoic philosopher
> *Encheiridon*

We know we can make and sell tortillas, but it's something else to be accountable for how you grow.

> Anthony Estrada
> CEO, Candy's Tortilla Factory, Inc.
> *Hispanic Business,* June 1987

Everyone says a business should stick to its niche. Niches, however, are usually quite dark and very confining.

> Melvyn Estrin
> CEO, Human Service Group, Inc.
> Speech, Washington, D.C., February 1983

We were trying to get the company to critical size, so it could do something.

> Howard Gittis
> Vice Chairman, Compact Video, Inc.
> *Forbes,* April 4, 1988

A great deal of fat has been cut, and perhaps a little bone as well.... Downsizing was becoming a fad. Because everyone is doing it, a manager who isn't wonders why he's not and looks around at his staff to see who he can do without.

> Eric Rolfe Greenberg
> American Management Association
> *The New York Times*, August 23, 1987

Owner-run companies are often run in an arbitrary, dictatorial way. In fact, often that is what limits [their] growth.

> Andrew S. Grove
> CEO, Intel Corp.
> *One-On-One With Andy Grove*
> (G. P. Putnam's Sons, 1987)

A merchant that gains not, loseth.

> George Herbert, 1593–1633
> English clergyman and poet
> *Jacula Prudentum*

Growth is often a painful process.

> Elbert Hubbard, 1856–1915
> American writer, printer, and editor
> *The Philosophy of Elbert Hubbard*

The dinosaur's eloquent lesson is that if some bigness is good, an overabundance of bigness is not necessarily better.

> Eric Johnston
> President, U. S. Chamber of Commerce
> *Quote*, February 23, 1958

When you're green, you're growing. When you're ripe, you rot.

> Ray Kroc, 1902–1984
> Chairman, McDonald's
> Favorite saying

The entrepreneurial approach is not a sideline at 3M. It is the heart of our design for growth.

> Lewis Lehr
> Chairman, 3M Company
> Speech, University of Nebraska,
> April 2, 1983

Our experience shows that local people—both workers and managers—often have better ideas than executives from remote conglomerates about how to run their businesses. Conglomerate owners may abandon plants because they see more profitable opportunities elsewhere. Conglomerate owners may react too hurriedly to temporary losses, and pull out before making much effort to turn the business around. But employee and local community owners have too much to lose from such choices, and because of their personal stake in the firms, have every reason to try and make them viable.

> Stanley N. Lundine
> U. S. Congressman (New York)
> *Congressional Record*, March 1, 1978

Successful big corporations should devolve into becomming "confederations of entrepreneurs."

> Norman McCrae
> Associate Editor
> *The Economist*, December 25, 1976

You can grow very quickly if you bid too low, but that's when you come and go.

> Patricia De. L. Marvil
> CEO, Securigard, Inc.
> *Hispanic Business,* June 1987

There seem to be hardly any growth problems not summed up under the label of *qualified managerial personnel.*

> Sorrell M. Mathes
> Department Manager, The Conference Board
> *Handling Company Growth*
> (National Industrial Conference Board, 1967)

Growth stresses systems.

> Larry McFadin
> President, Philip Crosby Associates, Inc.
> *Inc. Magazine*, February 1988

The small [manufacturing] company must rely on outside "experts" for making the critical decisions [regarding environmental controls] involving sums that sometimes exceed the total valuation of the company's present plant.

> J. J. Obrzut
> *Iron Age*, July 1, 1971

What separates growing and adaptive organizations from dinosaurs is that the former accept the necessity of constantly working to overcome the inevitable temptations to play it the company way, and steadily work to create a culture that encourages positive and productive behavior.

> James O'Toole
> University of Southern California
> *Making America Work* (Continuum, 1981)

Put no more so many yrons in the fyre at once.

> William Paget, 1505–1563
> Lord Privy Seal of England
> Letter, 1549

Growth is directly proportionate to promises made; profit is inversely proportionate to promises kept.

> John Peers
> President, Logical Machine Corp.
> *1,001 Logical Laws* (Doubleday, 1979)

You can't get the CEO of a $5 billion company excited about a $100,000 market.... We don't want to go through the learning process in smaller markets.

> Lee Rivers
> Director, Corporate Planning, Allied Signal
> Peters, *Thriving on Chaos* (Knopf, 1987)

In practically all our activities we seem to suffer from the inertia resulting from our great size.... There are so many people involved and it requires such a tremendous effort to put something new into effect that a new idea is likely to be considered insignificant in comparison with the effort that it takes to put it across.

> Alfred P. Sloan, 1875–1966
> President and Chairman, General Motors
> Adams and Brock, *The Bigness Complex*
> (Pantheon, 1986)

Large organizations can't tolerate constant turmoil.

> Philip Smith
> Chairman, General Foods
> *Fortune,* September 28, 1987

Where is all this great stuff coming from? It's coming out of little two and three man companies, because they're finding out that forty guys can't do something that three people can do. It's just the law of human nature.

> Roger Smith
> Chairman, General Motors
> *Detroit Free Press*, March 1985

If I'm doing business with Marriott, I'd better be able to service Marriott all over the country. If I can't, somebody else is going to come in who can.

> Sandy Solomon
> Founder, Sweet Street Desserts, Inc.
> *The New York Times,* May 1, 1988

If you grow fast enough no one will ever notice that your management is as screwed up as the rest of the buisness world.

> Lyle Spencer
> Founder, Science Research Associates
> (Acquired by IBM)
> Planning meeting, June 1960

Rapid growth is not necessarily the best measure of success. Indeed, it is probably detrimental to most businesses.

> Mark H. Spohr
> President, Pacific Medsoft, Inc.
> *Inc. Magazine*, March 1988

Business could collapse if it rained during the key months and you can't use that as an excuse to your stockholders if you call yourself a growth company. So Black & Decker cut back sharply on outdoor products.

> Paul W. Sturm
> Business writer
> *Forbes*, February 5, 1979

As the company grows it must be more human—not less.

Swift & Co.
Employee Relations Manual, 1921

Corporate growth has been bought at terrible moral cost.

Alvin Toffler
Futurist and writer
Future Shock (Random House, 1970)

Big seems to breed bigger. As total employment increases, so does the number of management layers required to keep things under control.

Robert M. Tomasko
Principal, Temple, Barker & Sloane, Inc.
Downsizing (AMACOM, 1987)

Growth is a by-product of the pursuit of excellence and not itself a worthy goal.

Robert Townsend
Former CEO, Avis
Further Up the Organization (Knopf, 1984)

We all had the feeling we could do no wrong. We got carried away by our own growth.

William H. Wilson
Founder, Pioneer/Eclipse Corp.
Inc. Magazine, February 1988

17

Human Relations

Always avoid the acute angle.

Practical politics consists in ignoring facts.

Henry Brooks Adams, 1838–1918
American writer and historian
The Education of Henry Adams

Familiarity breeds contempt.

Aesop, c. 620–c. 560 B.C.
Greek fabulist
The Fox and the Lion

Changeable people are not easily satisfied.

Aesop, c. 620–c. 560 B.C.
Greek fabulist
The Moon and Her Mother

It is probably not love that makes the world go around, but rather those mutually supportive alliances through which partners recognize their dependance on each other for the achievement of shared and private goals.... Treat employees like partners, and they act like partners.

Fred Allen
Chairman, Pitney-Bowes Co.
Leaders Magazine, 1978

Nothing is more characteristic of a man than the manner in which he behaves toward fools.

Henri Frédéric Amiel, 1821–1881
Swiss journalist and critic
Journal intimé

Because the executives [trying to avoid interpersonal problems] don't say what they really mean or test the assumptions they really hold, their skills inhibit a resolution of the important intellectual issues.... Thus the meetings end with only lists and no decisions.... [P]eople's tendency to avoid conflict, to duck tough issues, becomes institutionalized and leads to a culture that can't tolerate straight talk.

Chris Argyris
Harvard Graduate School of Education
Harvard Business Review,
September/October 1986

Man is by nature a social animal, and an individual who is unsocial naturally and not accidentally is either beneath our notice or more than human. Society is something in nature that precedes the individual. Anyone who either cannot lead the common life or is so self-sufficient as not to need to, and therefore does not partake of society, is either a beast or he is a god.

> Aristotle, 384–322 B.C.
> Greek philosopher and teacher
> *Politics*

One who publicly shames another has done the same thing as shedding that person's blood.

> Babylonian Tamud, Bava Metziah

All the strategic planning, financial rejiggering and number crunching in the world won't help if it can't succeed in changing human behavior. And that it seems, is the hardest thing of all to do.

> Sarah Bartlett
> Business writer
> *Business Week*, August 24, 1987

Good humor makes all things tolerable.

> Henry Ward Beecher, 1813–1887
> American clergyman
> *Proverbs from Plymouth Pulpit*

It is a good deed to forget a poor joke.

> Brendan Behan, 1923–1964
> Irish playwright
> Pepper, *The Wit and Wisdom of the 20th Century* (Sphere, 1987)

It is a very delicate job to forgive a man, without lowering him in his own estimation, and yours too.

> Josh Billings
> (Henry Wheeler Shaw), 1818–1885
> American writer and auctioneer
> *Josh Billings: His Book*

One of the greatest diseases is to be nobody to anybody.

> Agnes Gonxha Bojaxhiu (Mother Teresa)
> Roman Catholic nun and humanitarian
> *Reader's Digest*, December 1987

Technicians do not respond well to human problems, which require flexibility, improvisation, listening, and patience. They prefer to stick to problems that don't talk back—determining a bid price, doing a financial analysis, designing a new scheduling system for loading the milling machines—and often do not notice when a subordinate could use coaching, wants support, or needs a push. Work is assigned to subordinates in terms of who is available and what tasks have to get done, rather than in order to maximize motivation by matching jobs with a subordinate's interests.

> David L. Bradford
> Stanford University School of Business
> and Allan R. Cohen
> Babson College
> *Managing for Excellence* (Wiley, 1984)

As a management consultant I have found that most of my clients spend more time talking about how to cope with problem employees, bosses, customers, and co-workers than about anything else.

> Robert M. Bramson
> Psychologist and management consultant
> *Coping With Difficult People*
> (Anchor Press/Doubleday, 1981)

No passion so effectually robs the mind of all its power of acting and reasoning as fear.

> Edmund Burke, 1729–1797
> English statesman, orator, and writer
> *On the Sublime and Beautiful*

It is a much better practice for you to measure the affection of your subordinates by their zeal to comply with your orders than by their eagerness to fraternize with you.

Theodore Caplow
Managing an Organization
(CBS College Publishing, 1983)

The greatest of faults, I should say, is to be conscious of none.

Thomas Carlyle, 1795–1881
Scottish essayist and historian
Of Heroes and Hero-Worship

Always avoid the acute angle.

Dale Carnegie, 1888–1955
American public speaking teacher
How to Win Friends and Influence People

Kindness is greater than law.

Chinese proverb

When your own tooth aches, you know how to sympathize with one who has a toothache.

Chinese proverb

Fools are more to be feared than the wicked.

Christina, 1626–1689
Queen of Sweden
Maxims

I believe that, generally speaking, given free institutions on a fair basis, the best side of men's nature will in the end surely come uppermost. But this doctrine has its limits.

Winston Churchill, 1874–1965
English Prime Minister, writer, and soldier
Speech, House of Commons,
February 22, 1906

A fanatic is one who can't change his mind and won't change the subject.

Winston Churchill, 1874–1965
English Prime Minister, writer, and soldier
Halle, *Irrepressible Churchill*

Any man can make mistakes, but only an idiot persists in his error.

Cicero, 106–43 B.C.
Roman orator and statesman
Philipics

No one limps because another is hurt.

Danish proverb

The ultimate goal is to be happy. I don't believe in happiness that isn't based on effort, pain, and work.

Carlo De Benedetti
CEO, Olivetti
Business Week, August 24, 1987

The strain and discouragement of frankly facing the complex tangle of motives at work in most human situations tempt everyone into the errors of oversimplification.

Henry S. Dennison, 1877–1952
Founder, Dennison Corp.
Organization and Management
(Harvard, 1948)

Immodest words admit of no defense,
For want of decency is want of sense.

Wentworth Dillon
(Earl of Roscommon), c. 1633–1685
English poet
Essay on Translated Verse

Wherever we have contributed only the economic factors of production, especially capital, we have not achieved development. In the few cases where we have been able to generate management energies we have generated rapid development. Development, in other words, is a matter of human energies rather than of economic wealth. And the generation and direction of human energies is the task of management. Management is the mover and development is a consequence.

> Peter F. Drucker
> Management consultant and writer
> *People and Performance*
> (Harper & Row, 1977)

Beware the fury of a patient man.

> John Dryden, 1631–1700
> English poet
> *Absalom and Achitophel*

Wisdom is not a product of schooling but of the lifelong attempt to acquire it.

> Albert Einstein, 1879–1955
> Nobel laureate in physics
> *Albert Einstein, The Human Side*
> (Princeton, 1979)

Life is not so short but that there is always time enough for courtesy.

> Ralph Waldo Emerson, 1803–1882
> American essayist and poet
> *Social Aims*

It is excellent advice both in writing and in action to avoid a too great elevation at first. Let one's beginnings be temperate and unpretending, and the more elevated parts will rise from these with a just and full effect. We were not made to breathe oxygen, or to talk poetry, or to be always wise.

> Ralph Waldo Emerson, 1803–1882
> American essayist and poet
> *Journals*

We boil at different degrees.

> Ralph Waldo Emerson, 1803–1882
> American essayist and poet
> *Literary Ethics*

Let your questions focus on the other person. Say, "What do you think?" rather than "Do you agree with me?"

> Barry Farber
> Radio interviewer
> *Making People Talk* (William Morrow, 1987)

The opinion of the strongest is always the best.

> Jean de La Fontaine, 1621–1695
> French fabulist
> *The Wolf and the Lamb*

Tact, respect, and generosity toward variant views will always commend themselves to those charged with the duties of legislation so as to achieve a maximum of good will and to require a minimum of unwilling submission to a general law.

> Felix Frankfurter, 1882–1965
> U. S. Supreme Court Justice
> *West Virginia State Board of Education*
> v. *Barnette* (1942)

This preservation of harmony within a [Japanese] firm by giving the illusion that nobody loses and everybody wins is difficult for outsiders [Americans] to understand.

> Joseph N. Froomkin
> Management consultant
> *Journal of the Academy of Management*,
> March 1964

Chagrin and mortification caused by their progressively self-discovered quadrillions of errors would long ago have given humanity such an inferiority complex that it would have become too discouraged to continue with the life experience. To avoid such a proclivity humans were designedly given pride, vanity and inventive memory, which, all together can and usually do incline us to self deception.

Buckminster Fuller
Inventor and designer
Critical Path (St. Martin's Press, 1981)

The naturally autocratic supervisor who is exposed to human relations training ... may [be] harder to work for than he was before being "enlightened."

Saul W. Gellerman
University of Dallas School of Management
Motivation and Productivity
(AMACOM, 1963)

What you manage in business is people.

Harold Geneen
CEO, IT&T
Managing (Doubleday, 1984)

Every day we [blacks] must work to break down the barriers of racism by showing that we can be the best whether we are making deals on Wall Street or delivering goods on Main Street.

Earl Graves
Publisher and Editor, *Black Enterprise*
Black Enterprise, April 1988

In human relations, kindness and lies are worth a thousand truths.

Graham Greene
English novelist
The Heart of the Matter

How much grief could be avoided if everyone at the workplace simply practiced a bit of consideration and courtesy! Current trends in management, including the idea of participatory management, are heading in this

direction, even if they often obscure things by making them seem too complex.

Andrew S. Grove
CEO, Intel Corp.
One-On-One With Andy Grove
(G. P. Putnam's Sons, 1987)

When it comes to people and their quirks, idiosyncracies, and personality flaws, the variety seems to be limitless. The manager's aim always remains the same: to keep these human beings from clogging up the workings of their group.

Andrew S. Grove
CEO, Intel Corp.
One-On-One With Andy Grove
(G. P. Putnam's Sons, 1987)

Treat others as ends, never as means.

Dag Hammerskjöld, 1905–1961
Secretary-General of the United Nations
Markings

Good words are worth much, and cost little.

George Herbert, 1593–1633
English clergyman and poet
Jacula Prudentum

Everyone thinks his sack heaviest.

George Herbert, 1593–1633
English clergyman and poet
Jacula Prudentum

Courtesy on one side only lasts not long.

George Herbert, 1593–1633
English clergyman and poet
Jacula Prudentum

If you don't know how, why pretend?

Huang O, 1498–1569
Chinese poet
A Farewell to A Southern Melody

Because of the prestige of science as a source of power, and because of the general neglect of philosophy, the popular Weltanschaung ["world view"] of our times contains a large element of what may be called "nothing-but" thinking. Human beings ... are nothing but bodies, animals, even machines.... Values are nothing but illusions that have somehow got themselves mixed up with our experience of the world; mental happenings are nothing but epiphenomena.... Spirituality is nothing but ... and so on.

> Aldous Huxley, 1894–1963
> English author and critic
> *Science, Liberty, and Peace*

If [a man] is brusque in his manner, others will not cooperate. If he is agitated in his words, they will awaken no echo in others. If he asks for something without having first established a [proper] relationship, it will not be given to him.

> *I Ching*: Book of Changes
> China, c. 600 B.C.

If you need a friend, get a dog.

> Carl Icahn
> CEO, Icahn & Co.
> *Institutional Investor*, May 1986

From listening comes wisdom; from speaking comes repentance.

> Italian proverb

Suffer fools gladly. They may be right.

> Holbrook Jackson, 1874–1948
> English writer and editor
> *Platitudes in the Making*

Dogmatism is puppyism come to its full growth.

> Douglas Jerrold, 1803–1857
> British humorist
> *Douglas Jerrold's Wit*

The wish to be independent of all men, and not to be under obligation to any one is the sure sign of a soul without tenderness.

> Joseph Joubert, 1754–1824
> French moralist and critic
> *Thoughts*

Civility is not a sign of weakness, and sincerity is always subject to proof.

> John Fitzgerald Kennedy, 1917–1963
> Thirty-fifth President of the United States
> Inaugural address, January 20, 1961

Opportunities are usually disguised as hard work, so most people don't recognize them.

> Ann Landers
> Syndicated advice columnist
> Rowes, *The Book of Quotes* (Dutton, 1979)

[Abrasive people] must be told *very early on* how their behavior undermines them. All too often afraid to do this, their bosses quickly become resentful and withdraw, leaving their subordinates uncomfortable but not knowing why. Feeling anxious, the abrasive subordinate then attempts to win back the regard and esteem of the boss in the only way he knows, by intensifying this behavior. That only makes things worse.

> Harry Levinson
> Psychologist, Harvard Medical School
> *Harvard Business Review on Human Relations*, 1986

Cranks live by theory, not by pure desire. They want votes, peace, nuts, liberty ... not because they love these things ... but because they think they ought to have them. That is one element which makes the crank.

> Rose Macaulay, 1881–1958
> English novelist and essayist
> *A Casual Commentary*

[A]nyone with a good memory and a decent ability to time the punchline can tell a joke. But a sense of humor runs deeper. It involves the ability to laugh at oneself and find the absurd in everyday life. Most jokes, on the other hand, make fun not of man's condition but of something or somebody else.

> Dyan Machan
> Writer, "Careers"
> *Forbes*, November 2, 1987

People influence people.

> Robert F. Mager
> Psychologist and educational technologist
> *Developing Attitude Toward Learning*
> (Fearon, 1968)

Consumers are statistics. Customers are people.

> Stanley Marcus
> Chairman emeritus, Neiman-Marcus
> Peters and Austin, *A Passion for Excellence*
> (Random House, 1985)

He who knows his own incapacity knows something, after all.

> Margaret of Anjoulême, c. 1492–1549
> Queen of Navarre
> *Heptameron*

Dreadful things are just as apt to happen when stupid people control a situation as when definitely ill-natured people are in charge.

> Don Marquis, 1878–1937
> American newspaperman and humorist
> *Chapters for the Orthodox*

An idea isn't responsible for the people who believe in it.

> Don Marquis, 1878–1937
> American newspaperman and humorist
> *Archy Does His Part*

These guys [purchasing executives] have great loyalty to their own business, but their number one loyalty is to their own tush.

> William G. McGowan
> Chairman, MCI Communications Corp.
> *Inc. Magazine*, August 1986

Our goal should be minimum standardization of human behavior.

> Douglas McGregor
> *The Human Side of Enterprise*
> (McGraw-Hill, 1960)

[A sense of humor] always withers in the presence of the messianic delusion, like justice and truth in front of patriotic passion.

> Henry Louis Mencken, 1880–1956
> Editor, author, and critic
> *Prejudices*

A network is not a team. Nor is it a support system, which many women mistake it for. A man's network is the sum total of all those people with whom he barters. It is ever expanding among those of mutual interest and goals, not necessarily of mutual values and likes. They are the people with whom he does business, people who may join his team for some purpose, and others who may not.

> Jinx Milea
> University of Southern California
> and Pauline Lyttle
> President, Operational Politics, Inc.
> *Why Jenny Can't Lead*, 1986

The most brilliant persons are not always the happiest or the most esteem'd; more rarely still the best beloved. Too much presumption in their excellencies, too little indulgence to the defects of others if it does not totally destroy our admiration certainly eliminates our affection.

Elizabeth Montagu, 1720–1800
English essayist
The Letters of Mrs. Elizabeth Montagu

Nothing is so firmly believed as what we least know.

Michel Eyquem de Montaigne, 1533–1592
French philosopher and essayist
Works

High-tech robots and high-touch quality circles are moving into our factories at the same time—and the more robots, the more circles.... The more high-tech around us, the more the need for human touch.

John Naisbitt
Chairman, Naisbitt Group
Megatrends (Warner, 1984)

By comparison [to American firms], human relations in European business still have a kind of rustic simplicity.

Otto Nowotny
Harvard Business Review, March/April 1964

If you know anything that will make a brother's heart glad, run quick and tell it; and if it is something that will only cause a sigh, *bottle it up, bottle it up.*

Old Farmer's Almanac (1854)

The Japanese employ open discussions with generalities that leave room for movement and compromise. They have *nineteen* ways of saying no—suggestive of the extrreme fi-

nesse with which their language navigates the shoals of conflict, avoiding it if possible.

Richard T. Pascale
Stanford University School of Business
and Anthony G. Athos
Harvard Business School
The Art of Japanese Management
(Simon & Schuster, 1981)

Return the Civilities thou receivest, and be *ever* grateful for Favours.

William Penn, 1644–1718
Founder of Pennsylvania
Fruits of Solitude in Reflections and Maxims

[The best people centered managers] model exorbitantly high standards. They demand a lot, but show by energetic example what they demand.... They delegate.... Workers are set out on their own to constantly innovate.... They clear hurdles from the employees path.... They're obsessive about trying things.... They motivate through an inspiring vision.... They may or may not pat people on the back often ... they do something much more important ... they unmistakably demonstrate belief in the talent of and concern for the dignity of each worker.

Tom Peters
Business writer
Washington Business Journal,
August 24, 1987

Now as to politeness ... I would venture to call it benevolence in trifles.

William Pitt ("the Elder"), 1708–1788
English Secretary of State
and virtual Prime Minister
Correspondence, 1838-1840

Cato used to say that wise men profited more by fools, than fools by wise men; for that wise men avoided the faults of fools, but that fools would not imitate the good examples of wise men.

> Plutarch, c. 46–c. 120
> Greek biographer and philosopher
> *The Parallel Lives: Marcus Cato*

We may with advantage at times forget what we know.

> Publilius Syrus, c. 42 B.C.
> Roman writer
> *Maxims*

One of our ironclad rules is "Never do business with anybody you don't like." If you don't like somebody, there's a reason. Chances are it's because you don't trust him, and you're probably right. I don't care who it is or what guarantees you get—cash in advance or whatever. If you do business with somebody you don't like, sooner or later you'll get screwed.

> Henry V. Quadracci
> President, Quad/Graphics, Inc.
> *Inc. Magazine*, August 1987

We all have sufficient strength to endure the misfortunes of others.

> François de La Rochefoucauld, 1613–1680
> French politician, writer, and philanthropist
> *Reflections, or Sentences and Moral Maxims*

The true way to be deceived is to think oneself more knowing than others.

> François de La Rochefoucauld, 1613–1680
> French politician, writer, and philanthropist
> *Reflections, or Sentences and Moral Maxims*

Don't hide your failures and mistakes. Bury them in full public view with due humility and contrition. Who has the heart to castigate a repentant sinner?

> Milton J. Roedel
> Manager of Exploratory Research, DuPont
> Managers' meeting, February 1963

No one can make you feel small without your consent.

> Eleanor Roosevelt, 1884–1962
> American statesman and humanitarian
> *This Is My Story*

Cleanliness is a consideration for others rather than oneself.

> Dagobert D. Runes
> Editor, publisher, and philosopher
> *A Book of Contemplation*

There is no animal more difficult to understand than man.

> Leonardo Salviati, 1540–1589
> Italian humanist
> *La Spina*

Humility is a virtue all preach, none practice; and yet everybody is content to hear.

> John Selden, 1584–1654
> English jurist, Orientalist, and statesman
> *Table Talk*

Condemn the fault, and not the actor of it!

> William Shakespeare, 1654–1616
> English dramatist and poet
> *Measure for Measure*

I have heard of some kind of men that put quarrels purposely on others to taste their valour.

> William Shakespeare, 1564–1616
> English dramatist and poet
> *Twelfth Night*

Press not a falling man too far!

> William Shakespeare, 1564–1616
> English dramatist and poet
> *King Henry VIII*

For I am nothing if not critical.

William Shakespeare, 1564–1616
English dramatist and poet
Othello

The hardest knife ill-used doth lose its edge.

William Shakespeare, 1564–1616
English dramatist and poet
Sonnet 95

Martyrdom is the only way in which a man can become famous without ability.

George Bernard Shaw, 1856–1950
Nobel laureate in literature
Essays in Fabian Socialism

Keep your friends close, but keep your enemies closer.

Sicilian proverb

You don't work with [people] for 30 years ... and then suddenly turn against their collective opinion.... When you come in from the outside, with no emotional ties to the business, you can do things a lot more ruthlessly.

Bruce Smart, Jr.
CEO, The Continental Group
Fortune, March 2, 1987

None love the messenger who brings bad news.

Sophocles, c. 496–406 B.C.
Ancient Greek dramatist
Antigone

Those whom you can make like themselves better will, I promise you, like you very well.

Philip Dormer Stanhope, 1694–1773
English Secretary of State
Letters of Lord Chesterfield to His Son

Mankind is made up of inconsistencies, and no man acts invariably up to his predominant character. The wisest man sometimes acts weakly, and the weakest sometimes wisely.

Philip Dormer Stanhope, 1694–1773
English Secretary of State
Letters of Lord Chesterfield to His Son

Good manners are the settled medium of social, as specie is of commercial, life; returns are equally expected for both.

Philip Dormer Stanhope, 1694–1773
English Secretary of State
Letters of Lord Chesterfield to His Son

It is always right to detect a fraud, and to perceive a folly; but it is often very wrong to expose either. A man of business should always have his eyes open; but must often seem to have them shut.

Philip Dormer Stanhope, 1694–1773
English Secretary of State
Maxims of the Earl of Chesterfield

People prefer theory to practice because it involves them in no more real responsibility than a game of checkers, while it permits them to feel they're doing something serious and important.

Leo Stein, 1872–1947
American writer and editor
Journey into the Self

Courage is resistance to fear, mastery of fear—not absence of fear.

Mark Twain
(Samuel Langhorne Clemens), 1835–1910
American author and riverboat captain
Pudd' nhead Wilson's Calendar

The folly of mistaking a paradox for a discovery, a metaphor for a proof, a torrent of verbiage for a spring of capital truths, and oneself for an oracle, is inborn in us.

> Paul Ambroise Valéry, 1871–1945
> French poet and philosopher
> *The Method of Leonardo da Vinci*

The best index to a person's character is (a) how he treats people who can't do him any good, and (b) how he treats people who can't fight back.

> Abigail Van Buren
> Advice columnist
> May 16, 1974

It is not true that equality is a law of nature. Nature knows no equality. Its sovereign law is subordination and dependence. Law has no power to equalize men in defiance of nature.

> Marquis de Vauvenargues, 1715–1747
> French soldier and moralist
> *Reflections and Maxims*

Optimism is the madness of maintaining that everything is right when it is wrong.

> François Marie Voltaire, 1694–1778
> French writer
> *Candide*

Let us work without disputing; it is the only way to render life tolerable.

> François Marie Voltaire, 1694–1778
> French writer
> *Candide*

Don't confuse being stimulating with being blunt.

> Barbara Walters
> TV reporter and commentator
> *How to Talk with Practically Anybody About Practically Anything* (Dell, 1971)

If you humiliate people publicly, they may support you publicly, but they will hate you privately.

> Vernon Walters
> U. S. Ambassador to the United Nations
> *American Interest* (TV program),
> August 22, 1987

There's no telling how far a person can go if he's willing to let other people take the credit.

> Robert Woodruff
> CEO, Coca Cola
> *Inc. Magazine*, August 1987

Observe people when they are angry, for it is then that their true nature is revealed.

> The Zohar

Working with people is difficult, but not impossible.

> Graffito on a copier
> The George Washington University,
> Washington, D.C.

18

Information Management

When all candles be out, all cats be gray.

Most MIS [Management Information Systems] designers "determine" what information is needed by asking managers what information they would like to have. This is based on the (often erroneous) assumption that managers know that information they need and want it.

Russell L. Ackoff
Management Information Systems scientist
Management Science, December 1967

When you are drowning in numbers you need a system to separate the wheat from the chaff.

Anthony Adams
Vice President, Campbell Soup Co.
The New York Times, April 24, 1988

Built into decentralization is the age old tug between autonomy and control: superiors want no surprises, subordinates want to be left alone. The subordinates push for autonomy; they assert that by leaving them alone, top management will show its trust from a distance. The superiors, on the other hand, try to keep control through information systems. The subordinates see the control devices as

confirming their suspicions—their superiors don't trust them.

Chris Argyris
Harvard Graduate School of Education
Harvard Business Review,
September/October 1986

Information may be accumulated in files, but it must be retrieved to be of use in decision making.

Kenneth J. Arrow
Nobel laureate in economics
The Limits of Organization (Norton, 1974)

Knowledge and human power are synonomous, since the ignorance of the first frustrates the effect.

Francis Bacon, 1561–1626
Lord Chancellor of England
Novum Organum

[Referring to the U. S. Department of State:] The inflow of information and intelligence ...

has long since passed the point of digestibility.

Stephan K. Bailey
President,
American Society of Public Administration
Agenda For the Nation
(The Brookings Institution, 1968)

I am not young enough to know everything.

James Matthew Barrie, 1860–1937
English novelist and dramatist
Peers, *1,001 Logical Laws* (Doubleday, 1979)

Every man has a right to his opinion, but no man has a right to be wrong in his facts.

Bernard Mannes Baruch, 1879–1965
Presidential advisor and financial analyst
Sign on desk

There is a profound difference between information and meaning.

Warren G. Bennis
President, University of Cincinnati
University of Maryland symposium,
January 21, 1988

There is no absolute knowledge. And those who claim it open the door to tragedy. All information is imperfect. We have to treat it with humility.

Jacob Bronowski
Mathematician and scientist
The Ascent of Man
BBC TV, 1973

An individual without information cannot take responsibility; an individual who is given information cannot help but take responsibility.

Jan Carlzon
CEO, SAS (Sweden)
Moments of Truth (Ballinger, 1987)

Knowledge is the only instrument of production that is not subject to diminishing returns.

John Maurice Clark, 1884–1971
Columbia University
Journal of Political Economy, October 1927

Telecommunications enables companies to move information rather than people.

Eric K. Clemons
The Wharton School
and F. Warren McFarlan
Harvard Business School
Harvard Business Review, July/August 1986

When you know a thing, to hold that you know it; and when you do not know a thing, to allow that you do not know it; this is knowledge.

Confucius, c. 551–c. 479 B.C.
Chinese philosopher and teacher
Analects

All observation must be for or against some view if it is to be of any service!

Charles Darwin, 1809–1882
English naturalist and writer
More Letters of Charles Darwin

Information's pretty thin stuff, unless mixed with experience.

Clarence Day, 1874–1935
American essayist and humorist
The Crow's Nest

When I want to know what France is thinking, I ask myself.

Charles De Gaulle, 1890–1970
Military leader and President of France
Attributed

He [Socrates] said that there was only one good, namely, knowledge; and only one evil, namely, ignorance.

> Diogenes Laertius, c. 200–250
> Greek historian and writer
> *Lives and Opinions of Eminent Philosophers:*
> *Socrates*

All business proceeds on beliefs, or judgments of probabilities, and not on certainties.

> Charles William Eliot, 1834–1926
> President of Harvard University
> *The New Dictionary of Thoughts*, 1957

There is no knowledge that is not power.

> Ralph Waldo Emerson, 1803–1882
> American essayist and poet
> *Old Age*

In a democracy, the public has a right to know not only what the government decides, but why and by what process.

> Gerald R. Ford
> Thirty-eighth President of the United States
> Speech, September 13, 1976

Knowledge is power they say. Knowledge is not only power it is good fun.

> E. M. Forster, 1879–1970
> English novelist
> *Commonplace Book*

[A]s the planning process proceeds to a specific financial or marketing state, it is usually discovered that a considerable body of "numbers" is missing, but needed—numbers for which there has been no regular system of collection and reporting; numbers that must be collected outside the firm in some cases. This serendipity usually pays off in a much better management information system in the form of reports which will be collected and reviewed routinely.

> William H. Franklin, Jr.
> Georgia State University
> *Financial Strategies*, Fall 1987

The greater the uncertainty, the greater the amount of decision making and information processing. It is hypothesised that organizations have limited capacities to process information and adopt different organizing modes to deal with task uncertainty. Therefore, variations in organizing modes are actually variations in the capacity of organizations to process information and make decisions about events which cannot be anticipated in advance.

> J. Galbraith
> *Organization Design* (Addison-Wesley, 1977)

One of the greatest pieces of economic wisdom is to know what you do not know.

> John Kenneth Galbraith
> Economist and diplomat
> *Time*, March 3, 1961

Ninety–nine percent of all surprises in business are negative.

> Harold Geneen
> CEO, IT&T
> *Managing* (Doubleday, 1984)

The highest art of professional management requires the literal ability to "smell" a "real fact" from all others.

> Harold Geneen
> CEO, IT&T
> *Managing* (Doubleday, 1984)

Public accounting taught me analytical approaches to business problems, objective reasoning, and the highest order of discipline in making factual presentations.

Harold Geneen
CEO, IT&T
Managing (Doubleday, 1984)

A real challenge for some organizations is to build more qualitative information into their formal systems. One method used in some companies is to request a written narrative with each submission of statistics from the field. Another method is to hold periodic, in-depth discussions involving several managers from different levels so that each can contribute whatever qualitative data are available to him.

Larry E. Greiner
University of Southern California
Paul D. Leitch
U. S. Army Food Engineering Directorate
and Louis D. Barnes
Harvard Business School
Harvard Business Review on Human Relations, 1986

Information gathering is the basis of all other managerial work, which is why I choose to spend so much of my day doing it.

Andrew S. Grove
CEO, Intel Corp.
High Output Management
(Random House, 1983)

There is an especially efficient way to get information, much neglected by most managers. That is to visit a particular place in the company and observe what's going on there.

Andrew S. Grove
CEO, Intel Corp.
High Output Management
(Random House, 1983)

Verbal sources [to acquire information] are the most valuable, but what they provide is

also sketchy, incomplete, and sometimes in-accurate like a newspaper headline.

Andrew S. Grove
CEO, Intel Corp.
High Output Management
(Random House, 1983)

Individual contributors who gather and disseminate know-how and information should also be seen as middle managers, because they exert great power within the organization.

Andrew S. Grove
CEO, Intel Corp.
High Output Management
(Random House, 1983)

The lack of needed information, and of adequately informed judgments on it, often betrays intelligent and sincere public leaders into making reckless and inconsistent promises to the public. Much of the "credibility gap" arises from this failure of governmental processes to produce needed current facts and information.

Luther H. Gulick
President and Chairman,
National Institute of Public Administration
Program Planning for National Goals
(National Planning Association, 1968)

No talent in management is worth more than the ability to master facts—not just any facts, but the ones that provide the best answers. Mastery thus involves knowing what facts you want; where to dig for them; how to dig; how to process the mined ore; and how to use the precious nuggets of information that are finally in your hand. The process can be laborious—which is why it is so often botched.

Robert Heller
Editor, *Management Today*
The Supermanagers (Dutton, 1984)

A dwarf on a giant's shoulder, sees further of the two.

> George Herbert, 1593–1633
> English clergyman and poet
> *Jacula Prudentum*

When all candles be out, all cats be grey.

> John Heywood, c. 1497–c. 1580
> English poet
> *Proverbes*

Desire to know why, and how, curiosity, which is a lust of the mind, that by a perseverance of delight is the continued and indefatigable generation of knowledge, exceedeth the short vehemence of any carnal pleasure.

> Thomas Hobbes, 1588–1679
> English philosopher
> *Leviathan*

Fresh news is got only by enterprise and expense.

> Oliver Wendell Holmes, Jr., 1841–1935
> U. S. Supreme Court Justice
> *International News Service* v.
> *Associated Press* (1918)

A man should keep his little brain attic stocked with all the furniture that he is likely to use, and the rest he can put away in the lumber-room of his library, where he can get it if he wants it.

> Sherlock Holmes
> (Arthur Conan Doyle), 1859–1930
> English physician, writer, and sportsman
> *The Five Orange Pips*

Practically all large corporations insure their data bases against loss or damage or against their inability to gain access to them. Some day, on the corporate balance sheet, there will be an entry which reads, "Information"; for in most cases, the information is more valuable than the hardware which processes it.

> Grace Murray Hopper
> Rear Admiral, U. S. Navy (retired)
> Speech, Washington, D.C., February 1987

Knowlege is of two kinds. We know a subject ourselves, or we know where we can find information upon it.

> Samuel Johnson, 1709–1784
> English lexicographer and essayist
> *Boswell's Life of Dr. Johnson*

In an information society, information is power.... For the future, government, business, and other consumers will seek, pay, and value people with information. Consultants are the people with information.... Effective handling of consultants will mark the successful decision maker.

> Robert E. Kelley
> Management consultant and author
> *Consulting* (Charles Scribner's Sons, 1981)

The facts speak for themselves.
[*Res ipsa loquitur.*]

> Latin proverb

Executives have to start understanding that they have certain legal and ethical responsibilities for information under their control.

> Jim Leeke
> Computer journalist
> *PC Week*, August 11, 1987

The broad availability and low cost of computer and telecommunications equipment provides both the *impetus* and the *means* to perform new record-keeping functions. These functions can bring the individual substantial benefits, but there are also disadvantages for the individual. On one hand, they can give him easier access to services that make his life more comfortable or convenient. On the other, they also tempt others to demand, and make it easier for them to get access to, information about him for purposes he does not expect and would not agree to if he were asked.

> David F. Linowes
> Chairman, Congressional Privacy Protection
> Study Commission
> *Personal Privacy in an Information Society*,
> Washington, D.C., 1977

The improvement of the understanding is for two ends: first, for our own increase of knowledge; secondly, to enable us to deliver and make out that knowledge in others.

> John Locke, 1632–1704
> English philosopher
> *Some Thoughts Concerning Reading and Study*

Given a multilevel organization having component groups which perform a variety of functions in order to accomplish a unified objective, an MIS [Management Information System] is an integrated structure of data bases and information flow over all levels and components, whereby information collection and transfer is optimized to meet the needs of the organization.

> Larry E. Long
> Management Information Systems consultant
> *Manager's Guide to Computers and
> Information Systems* (Prentice-Hall, 1983)

Every person seems to have a limited capacity to assimilate information, and if it is presented to him too rapidly and without adequate repetition, this capacity will be exceeded and communication will break down.

> R. Duncan Luce
> University of Pennsylvania
> *Developments in Mathematical Psychology*
> (The Free Press, 1960)

The modern scientist sometimes feels overwhelmed by the size and the growth rate of the technical literature.

> Michael Mahoney
> University of California
> *The New York Times*, February 16, 1988

[The majority of companies surveyed] say they occasionally, rarely or never share proprietary information with employees. Without being informed I don't see how those employees can make meaningful contributions to their companies.

> Jerry McAdams
> Vice President, Maritz, Inc.
> *CFO*, October 1987

We were so internally focused that we lost touch [with customers].

> Whitney McFarlin
> President, Everest & Jennings International
> *Forbes*, February 9, 1987

Facts are friendly. Facts that tend to reinforce what you are doing and give you a warm glow are nice, because they help in terms of psychic reward. Facts that raise alarms are equally friendly, because they give you clues about how to respond, how to change, where to spend the resources.

> Irwin Miller
> Former CEO, Cummins Engine Co.
> *The Renewal Factor* (Bantam, 1987)

Data are most valuable at their point of origin. The value of data is directly related to their timeliness.

> Lawrence M. Miller
> Business consultant
> *American Spirit* (William Morrow, 1984)

It is more important for the manager to get his information quickly and efficiently than to get it formally.

Henry Mintzberg
McGill University School of Management
The Nature of Managerial Work
(Harper & Row, 1973)

The manager faces the real danger of becoming a major obstruction in the flow of decisions and information.

Henry Mintzberg
McGill University School of Management
The Nature of Managerial Work
(Harper & Row, 1973)

Doubts are more cruel than the worst of truths.

Jean Baptiste Molière, 1622–1673
French playwright
Le Misanthrope

Nothing is so firmly believed as what we least know.

Michel Eyquem de Montaigne, 1533–1592
French philosopher and essayist
Works

It is much harder to ask the right question than it is to find the right answer to the wrong question.

E. E. Morison
Massachusetts Institute of Technology
Greenberger, *Management and the Computer of the Future* (M. I. T., 1962)

We are drowning in information but starved for knowledge.

John Naisbitt
Chairman, Naisbitt Group
Megatrends (Warner, 1984)

If you don't give people information, they'll make up something to fill the void.

Carla O'Dell
President, O'Dell & Associates
CFO, October 1987

However a survey is defined, it is essentially an investigation of social life in process; in a given area (as distinct from the study of an abstract subject); at a given time (as distinct from a historical review).

Howard W. Odum and Katherine Jocher
The Russell Sage Foundation
An Introduction to Social Research, 1929

[Referring to the job of the 1987 Presidential Task Force on Market Mechanisms:] We can't do this on the basis of anecdotes. Get us the data.

John R. Opel
Chairman, IBM
The New York Times, February 14, 1988

I am not afraid of facts, I welcome facts, *but a congeries of facts is not equivalent to an idea.* This is the essential fallacy of the so-called "scientific" mind. People who mistake facts for ideas are incomplete thinkers; they are gossips.

Cynthia Ozick
American writer and critic
We Are the Crazy Lady

The amount of data available to them [marketing managers] is increasing at a pace that will defy their capacity to assimilate it.... Methods will have to be developed to manage billions of numbers a day.

Andrew J. Parsons
Partner, McKinzie & Co.
The New York Times, April 24, 1988

The information we have is not what we want.
The information we want is not what we need.
The information we need is not available.

John Peers
President, Logical Machine Corp.
1,001 Logical Laws (Doubleday, 1979)

Refuse not to be informed: For that shews
Pride or Stupidity.

William Penn, 1644–1718
Founder of Pennsylvania
Fruits of Solitude in Reflections and Maxims

Doubt is the key to knowledge.

Persian proverb

Things are not always what they seem.

Phaedrus, A.D. first century
Roman writer & fabulist
Fables

Information respecting current events ... is not
the creation of the writer, but is a report of
matters that ordinarily are *publici juris*; it is
the history of the day.

Mahlon Pitney, 1858–1924
U. S. Supreme Court Justice
International News Service v.
Associated Press (1918)

Information, that is imperfectly acquired, is
generally as imperfectly retained.

William Playfair, 1759–1823
English graphical designer
The Commercial and Political Atlas

I never heard of any real authority for any such
proposition as that one owes full disclosure of
the truth to all men at all times.

Frederick Pollock, 1845–1937
English jurist and legal scholar
The Holmes-Pollock Letters, July 2, 1928

Be aware of the kind of information your
employer considers confidential.

James H. A. Pooley
Attorney
Venture, April 1988

All I know is what I read in the papers.

Will Rogers, 1879–1935
American actor and humorist
Recurring line

Immediate memory is limited to about seven
"chunks" of information. Most people can
remember about seven numbers in a row,
seven colors, seven shapes or seven of any
other item. So if you need to remember more
than seven items, it's better to organize them
into a smaller number of chunks.

Peter Russell
Psychologist and management consultant
The Brain Book (Hawthorne, 1979)

We can expect the revolution in communications to extend the power of our brains. Its
ultimate effect will be the transformation and
unification of all techniques for the exchange
of ideas and information, of culture and learning. It will not only generate new knowledge,
but will supply the means for its world-wide
dissemination and absorption.

David Sarnoff, 1891–1971
Founder and President, RCA
Wisdom of Sarnoff and the World of RCA

Where there is no knowledge there can be no
insight, and where there is no insight there can
be no knowledge.

The Mishna, Sayings of the Fathers

What one sees depends upon where one sits.

James R. Schlesinger
U. S. Secretary of Defense
Memorandum to Senate Committee on
Government Operations, April 1968

There was a time that we only worried about protecting basic research results during wartime. Now it is something that has crept into our peacetime, entrepreneurial society.

Alan Schriesheim
Director, Argonne National Laboratory
The New York Times, August 2, 1987

Some people scorn to be taught; others are ashamed of it, as they would be of going to school when they are old; but it is never too late to learn ... and ... no shame to learn as long as we are ignorant, that is to say, as long as we live.

Seneca, 4 B.C.–A.D. 65
Roman writer and rhetorician
Epistles to Lucilius

And seeing ignorance is the curse of God,
Knowledge the wing wherewith we fly to
Heaven.

William Shakespeare, 1564–1616
English dramatist and poet
Henry the Sixth

Whatever people think, is.

Otis Singletary
Chancellor, University of Kentucky,
and Director, U. S. Job Corps
Speech, Washington D.C., January 1966

The ultimate result of shielding men from the effects of folly is to fill the world with fools.

Herbert Spencer, 1829–1903
English philosopher and social scientist
State Tamperings with Money, 1893

You will find that the truth is often unpopular and the contest between agreeable fancy and disagreeable fact is unequal. For, in the vernacular, we Americans are suckers for good news.

Adlai Ewing Stevenson, 1900–1965
U. S. Ambassador to the United
Nations and Governor of Illinois
Prochnow, *The Toastmaster' Treasure Chest*
(Harper & Row, 1979)

A man's judgment cannot be better than the information on which he has based it. Give him no news, or present him only with distorted and incomplete data, with ignorant, sloppy, or biased reporting, with propaganda and deliberate falsehoods, and you destroy his whole reasoning process and make him somewhat less than a man.

Arthur Hays Sulzberger, 1891–1968
Publisher, *The New York Times*
Speech to the
New York State Publishers Association,
August 30, 1948

The system treats what is reported to it as real: the outside reality is immaterial.

Melvin J. Sykes
Attorney
Maryland Law Review, 1978

The tendency to hide unfavorable information often occurs in companies that are quick to reward success and equally quick to punish failure.

Robert M. Tomasko
Principal, Temple, Barker & Sloane, Inc.
Downsizing (AMACOM, 1987)

When information is centralized and controlled, those who have it are extremely influential. Since information is [usually] localized in control subsystems, these subsystems have a great deal of organization influence.

> Henry L. Tosi
> University of Florida
> and Stephen J. Carroll
> University of Maryland
> *Management* (John Wiley & Sons, 1976)

The fact of being reported multiplies the apparent extent of any deplorable development by five-to-tenfold.

> Barbara Tuchman
> English historian and journalist
> *A Distant Mirror*

In the case of news, we should always wait for the sacrament of confirmation.

> François Marie Voltaire, 1694–1778
> French satirist and historian
> Letter to Count d'Argental, August 28, 1760

The secret of business success is not *who* you know. It's *what* you know.

> *The Wall Street Journal*
> TV advertisement, 1987

You don't just wait for information to come to you.

> Robert H. Waterman
> Management consultant and writer
> *The Renewal Factor* (Bantam, 1987)

Intelligence from the source is much more useful than laundered reports.

> John R. Whitney
> Executive-in-Residence
> Columbia University Business School
> *Harvard Business Review,*
> September/October 1987

A group may have more group information or less group information than its members. A group of non-social animals, temporarily assembled, contains very little group information, even though its members may possess much information as individuals. This is because very little that one member does is noticed by the others and is acted on by them in a way that goes further in the group.

> Norbert Wiener, 1894–1964
> Pioneer computer scientist
> *Cybernetics* (M. I. T., 1961)

No company can be made completely leakproof. It's a futile effort.

> D. Otis Wolkins
> Vice President, GTE
> *Newsweek,* May 2, 1988

Everyone spoke of an information overload, but what there was in fact was a non-information overload.

> Richard Saul Wurman
> *What-If, Could-Be* (Philadelphia, 1976)

In management, there are few things as dangerous as a comprehensive, accurate answer to the wrong question. This is pseudoknowledge. It easily misleads management into erroneous actions. Pseudoknowledge has mushroomed with the advent of computers, which have made available masses of data that answer questions managers found too costly to ask before. In too many instances, however, the data are collected but not used because they answer irrelevant questions.

> Dale E. Zand
> New York University
> *Information, Organization, and Power*
> (McGraw-Hill, 1981)

19

Innovation & Creativity

... all progress depends on the unreasonable man.

Never kill an idea, just deflect it.

3M Company
Company saying

Small firms are far more efficient innovators than industrial giants ... small firms are more prolific inventors than giant companies; small firms exert significantly greater research and development effort than large ones; small firms devise and develop inventions at substantially lower costs than large firms.

Walter Adams
President, Michigan State University
and James Brock
Economist
The Bigness Complex (Pantheon, 1986)

The creative person wants to be a know-it-all. He wants to know about all kinds of things: ancient history, nineteenth century mathematics, current manufacturing techniques, flower arranging, and hog futures. Because he never knows when these ideas might come together to form a new idea. It may happen

six minutes later or six months or six years down the road. But he has faith that it will happen.

Carl Ally
Founder, Ally & Gargano Advertising Agency
Oech, *A Whack on the Side of the Head*
(Warner, 1983)

Few ideas are in themselves practical. It is for want of imagination in applying them, rather than in acquiring them that they fail. The creative process does not end with an idea–it only starts with an idea.

John Arnold
Massachusetts Institute of Technology
Business Week, December 29, 1956

We weren't forced to follow the old ideas.

J. Georg Bednorz
IBM researcher and Nobel laureate
Success, February 1988

185

We like to test things.... No matter how good an idea sounds, test it first.

Henry Block
CEO, H&R Block
Inc. Magazine, December 1987

The most creative ideas are those you can get the other guys to think up.

Lud Bock
Head Counselor, Camp Arcady
Staff meeting, August 1953

Imagination rules the world.

Napoleon Bonaparte, 1769–1821
Emperor of France
Maxims

In differentiation, not in uniformity, lies the path of progress.

Louis Dembitz Brandeis, 1856–1941
U. S. Supreme Court Justice
Business—A Profession

There is no adequate defense, except stupidity, against the impact of a new idea.

Percy Williams Bridgman, 1882–1961
American physicist
The Intelligent Individual and Society

To innovate is not to reform.

Edmund Burke, 1729–1797
English statesman, orator, and writer
A Letter to a Noble Lord

The ideas I stand for are not mine. I borrowed them from Socrates. I swiped them from Chesterfield. I stole them from Jesus. And I put them in a book. If you don't like their rules, whose would you use?

Dale Carnegie, 1888–1955
American writer and public speaking teacher
Newsweek, August 8, 1955

Nothing is more dangerous than an idea when it is the only one you have.

Émile Chartier (Alain), 1868–1951
French philosopher and essayist
Oech, *A Whack on the Side of the Head*
(Warner, 1983)

We must beware of needless innovations, especially when guided by logic.

Winston Churchill, 1874–1965
English Prime Minister, writer, and soldier
Reply in Parliament, December 17, 1942

We ought not to be over-anxious to encourage innovation, in cases of doubtful improvement, for an old system must ever have two advantages over a new one; it is established and it is understood.

Charles Caleb Colton, c. 1780–1832
English cleric, sportsman, and wine merchant
Lacon

Creative people have much more confidence in their imaginitive leaps, in their intuition.

Laurel Cutler
Vice Chairman, FCB/Leber Katz Partners
Inc. Magazine, November 1987

Innovation: The fuel of corporate longevity.

Decision Process International
Advertisement
Training, December 1986

Above all, innovation is not *invention*. It is a term of economics rather than of technology.... The measure of innovation is the impact on the environment.... To manage innovation, a manager has to be at least literate with respect to the dynamics of innovation.

Peter F. Drucker
Management consultant and writer
People and Performance
(Harper & Row, 1977)

Because its purpose is to create a customer, the business enterprise has two—and only these two—basic functions: marketing and innovation. Marketing and innovation produce results; all the rest are "costs."

Peter F. Drucker
Management consultant and writer
People and Performance
(Harper & Row, 1977)

Innovation ... endows resources with a new capacity to create wealth.

Peter F. Drucker
Management consultant and writer
Harvard Business Review, May/June 1986

Most managers are rewarded if their unit operates efficiently and effectively. A highly creative unit, in contrast, might appear inneffective and uneven, and rather crazy to an outside or inside observer.

William G. Dyer
Brigham Young University
Strategies for Managing Change
(Addison-Wesley, 1984)

The value of an idea lies in the using of it.

Thomas Alva Edison, 1847–1931
American inventor and entrepreneur
Quoted in *Government Executive*,
January 1987

I never did anything worth doing by accident, nor did any of my inventions come by accident; they came by work.

Thomas Alva Edison, 1847–1931
American inventor and entrepreneur
Hurd, *Treasury of Great American Quotations*

Yesterday's miracle is today's intolerable condition.

Lewis D. Eigen
Executive Vice President,
University Research Corp.
Microcomputers for Executive Decision-Making
(FAA, 1985)

Every man of genius sees the world at a different angle from his fellows.

Havelock Ellis, 1859–1939
English scientist and author
The Dance of Life

If a man can write a better book, preach a better sermon, or make a better mouse-trap, than his neighbor, though he builds his house in the woods, the world will make a beaten path to his door.

Ralph Waldo Emerson, 1803–1882
American essayist and poet
Lecture, San Francisco
(also attributed to Elbert Hubbard)

Invention breeds invention.

Ralph Waldo Emerson, 1803–1882
American essayist and poet
Works and Days

Creative activity is one of the few self rewarding activities. Being creative is like being in love!

Woody Flowers
Massachusetts Institute of Technology
Discover (PBS TV), February 2, 1988

Those who govern, having much business on their hands, do not generally like to take the trouble of considering and carrying into execution new projects. The best public measures are therefore seldom adopted from previous wisdom, but forced by the occasion.

> Benjamin Franklin, 1706–1790
> American printer and statesman
> *Autobiography*

Originality is the only thing that counts. But the originator uses material and ideas that occur round him and pass through him. And out of his experience comes the original creation.

> George Gershwin, 1899–1937
> American composer
> Sayler, *Revolt in the Arts*

[Very successful] projects that entrepreneurs initiated and carried through had one essential quality. All had been thoroughly contemplated by the regnant experts and dominant companies, with their large research staffs and financial resources, and had been judged too difficult, untimely, risky, expensive and unprofitable.

> George Gilder
> Economist
> *The Spirit of Enterprise*
> (Simon & Schuster, 1984)

A sort of credo has grown up, to the effect that organization charts inhibit creativity, that a full flowering of creative research can be attained only through an unorganized, individualistic approach. All I can say is that experience teaches me otherwise.

> Estill I. Green
> Vice President, Bell Telephone Laboratories
> *Effective Administration of Research Programs*
> (Cornell University Press, 1958)

Somebody said that it couldn't be done,
But he with a chuckle replied
That "maybe it couldn't" but he would be one
Who wouldn't say no till he'd tried.
So he buckled right in with the trace of a grin
On his face. If he worried he hid it.

He started to sing as he tackled the thing
That couldn't be done, and he did it.

> Edgar A. Guest, 1881–1959
> Journalist and syndicated columnist
> *It Couldn't Be Done*

The past is a foreign country; they do things differently there.

> Leslie Poles Hartley, 1895–1972
> English author
> *The Go-Between*

If you do not expect the unexpected, you will not find it.

> Heraclitus, 535?–475? B.C.
> Greek philosopher
> *Fragments*

It is the customary fate of new truths to begin as heresies and to end as superstitions.

> Thomas Henry Huxley, 1825–1925
> English biologist
> *Coming of Age of "The Origin of Species"*

The uncreative mind can spot wrong answers, but it takes a creative mind to spot wrong questions.

> Anthony Jay
> Watzlawick, Weakland & Fish
> *Change* (Norton, 1974)

Great innovations should not be forced on slender majorities.

> Thomas Jefferson, 1743–1826
> Third President of the United States
> Letter to General Thaddeus Kosciusko, 1808

True artists ship.

> Steven Jobs
> Cofounder, Apple Computer Co.
> *Newsweek*, January 30, 1984

To the strongest and quickest mind it is far easier to learn than to invent.

> Samuel Johnson, 1709–1784
> English lexicographer and critic
> *The Rambler*

He is no wise man that will quit a certainty for an uncertainty.

> Samuel Johnson, 1709–1784
> English lexicographer and critic
> *The Idler*

The pioneers got all the arrows.

> Burt Lance
> Director,
> U. S. Office of Management and Budget
> Attributed

Many of those who were ahead of their time had to wait for it in not too comfortable quarters.

> Stanislaw J. Lec
> Polish writer and aphorist
> *Unkempt Thoughts* (St. Martin's Press, 1962)

By far the greatest flow of newness is not innovation at all. Rather, it is imitation.

> Theodore Levitt
> Editor, *Harvard Business Review*
> *HBR*, September/October 1966

[B]etween the two extremes of guesswork and formula there is a middle ground on which most managers operate. Here they recognize occasions which demand situational leadership—appropriately autocratic or laissez-faire—and other occasions which permit the integration of human resources with conscious renewal processes. Organizational renewal can live quite comfortably in this middle ground.

> Gordon L. Lippitt
> Human Resource Consultant
> *Organizational Renewal*
> (Appleton-Century-Crofts, 1969)

New opinions are always suspected, and usually opposed, without any other reason but because they are not already common.

> John Locke, 1632–1704
> English philosopher
> *An Essay Concerning Human Understanding*

It will be nonsense to sit in hierarchical offices trying to arrange what people in the offices below do with their imaginations.

> Norman McCrae
> Journalist and editor
> *The Economist*, December 25, 1976

We could have come up with some of the ideas they [consultants] suggested, but we aren't very creative.

> John Madden
> Chairman,
> First National Bank of Lagrange (Illinois)
> *Forbes*, November 2, 1987

I used to think that anyone doing anything weird was weird. I suddenly realized that anyone doing anything weird wasn't weird at all and it was the people saying they were weird that were weird.

> Paul McCartney
> Songwriter and musician (The Beatles)
> Peters, *Thriving on Chaos* (Knopf, 1987)

If companies think only about sharing the markets, they will never get involved in emerging businesses. They'll take a look at the business, decide that the "pie" is too small, and move on to other possibilities.

> Regis McKenna
> Marketing consultant and writer
> *The Regis Touch* (Addison-Wesley, 1986)

My theology, briefly,
Is that the Universe
Was Dictated
But not signed.

> Christopher Morley, 1890–1957
> American writer and editor
> *Safe and Sane*

It first appeared like a crazy idea. It turned out he had a great idea.

> J. Richard Munro
> CEO, Time, Inc.
> *USA Today*, February 23, 1988

New ideas ... are not born in a conforming environment.

> Roger von Oech
> President, Creative Think
> *A Whack on the Side of the Head*
> (Warner, 1983)

The best leaders are apt to be found among those executives who have a strong component of orthodoxy in their character. Instead of resisting innovation, they symbolize it.

> David Ogilvy
> Founder, Ogilvy-Mather Advertising
> *Ogilvy on Advertising* (Crown, 1983)

Every act of creation is first of all an act of destruction.

> Pablo Picasso, 1881–1973
> Spanish artist
> Oech, *A Whack on the Side of the Head*
> (Warner, 1983)

Innovations never happen as planned.

> Gifford Pinchot III
> The International Institute of Intrapreneurs
> *Intrapreneuring* (Harper & Row, 1986)

Ignore people who say it can't be done.

> Elaine Rideout
> Federal Retirement Thrift Investment Board
> *Management*, 1987

The creativity ... that emerges from the company comes from the many ideas of the people who are here.

> John Rollwagen
> CEO, Cray Research
> Adams, *Transforming Work*
> (Miles River Press, 1984)

[Referring to IBM Nobel Prize laureates Alex Mueller and Georg Bednorz:] They disobeyed a superior and revolutionized an industry.

> Mark B. Roman
> Contributing Editor, *Success*
> *Success*, February 1988

Man is God's instrument for carrying out the ongoing creation.

> James Rouse
> Founder, Rouse Development Corp.
> *Fortune*, March 23, 1981

Rules, though unavoidable, always have weaknesses. Particularly so in advertising, where originality is a part of its primary force, and where a violation of "what others do" is often a way of success.

> Raymond Rubicam
> Founder, Young & Rubicam ad agency
> Mandell, *Advertising* (Prentice-Hall, 1984)

Progress, far from consisting in change, depends on retentiveness.... Those who cannot remember the past are condemned to fulfil it.

> George Santayana, 1863–1952
> Spanish-American poet and philosopher
> *The Life of Reason*

Only through adventurous thinkers can the search for new knowledge succeed. Without this knowledge, the world would stagnate as a pool without an inlet; neither would there be an outlet for its progress.

> David Sarnoff, 1891–1971
> Founder and President, RCA
> *Wisdom of Sarnoff and the World of RCA*

Marketers spend an unbelievable amount of money on new products with a very low success ratio. Companies have much too little interest in products under their noses that offer enormous potential if someone looks at them as a new opportunity.

> Neve Savage
> Director, Caldwell Davis Savage Agency
> *The Wall Street Journal on Marketing*
> (Dow Jones-Irwin, 1986)

The innovator is not an opponent of the old; he is a proponent of the new.

> Lyle E. Schaller
> Yokefellow Institute
> *The Change Agent* (Abingdon, 1972)

"Almost nothing new works" is a common expression among innovative persons. This phrase is not spoken, however, in a defeatest tone of voice, but rather in simple recognition of the fact that innovation is a high risk venture.

> Lyle E. Schaller
> Yokefellow Institute
> *The Change Agent* (Abingdon, 1972)

The reasonable man adapts himself to the world: the unreasonable one persists in trying to adapt the world to himself. Therefore all progress depends on the unreasonable man.

> George Bernard Shaw, 18856–1950
> Nobel laureate in literature
> *Man and Superman*

Do not do what is already done.

> Terence, c. 190–159 B.C.
> Roman playwright
> *Phormio*

There's no evidence that you can keep an organization creative, although I think it is possible with a lot of energy and time.

> Walter Ulmer
> President, Center for Creative Leadership
> *Fortune*, September 28, 1987

A recent study of product innovation in the scientific instruments and tool machinery industries indicates that 80 percent of all product innovations are initiated by the customer.

> Eric von Hippel
> Management consultant and computer analyst
> *Technology Review*, January 1978

[In 1927, considering the possibility of talking pictures:] Who the hell wants to hear actors talk?

> Harry Warner
> Founder, Warner Brothers Studio
> Cerf and Navasky, *The Experts Speak*
> (Pantheon, 1984)

There is a world market for about five computers. [Spoken in 1943]

> Thomas J. Watson, Sr., 1874–1956
> Founder and first President, IBM
> Cerf and Navasky, *The Experts Speak*
> (Pantheon, 1984)

There is always more chance of hitting upon something valuable when you aren't too sure what you want to hit upon.

Alfred North Whitehead, 1861–1947
English mathematician and philosopher
Dialogues

Legend has it that Elias Howe intently studied his mother sewing, then invented the sewing machine.... Howe did not try to duplicate with his invention precisely what his mother did. He merely tried to duplicate the result.

Daniel E. Whitney
American roboticist
Harvard Business Review, May/June 1986

As engineering technique becomes more and more able to achieve human purposes, it must become more and more accustomed to formulate human purposes. In the past, a partial and inadequate view of human purpose has been relatively innocuous only because it has been accompanied by technical limitations that made it difficult for us to perform operations involving a careful evaluation of human purpose. This is only one of the many places where human impotence has shielded us from the full destructive impact of human folly.

Norbert Wiener, 1894–1964
American computer pioneer
God and Golem, Inc. (M. I. T., 1964)

There has developed a substantial vested interest in past solutions. Although the United States has been a leading knowledge society, stimulating contention, imagination, and creative improvisation has become an increasingly serious problem in large organizations and in government agencies.

Dale E. Zand
New York University
Information, Organization, and Power
(McGraw-Hill, 1981)

When two divisions are competing to make the same new product, I often get involved. I listen to both and usually the facts favor one division or the other. We all try to get the facts out on the table and let reason speak for itself. We build "acceptance time" into these discussions. By that I mean that people need time to accustom themselves to new ways of thinking about things. We press—but we always try to allow people to come around to a point of view in their own way.

Anonymous group manager
Matsushita Electric Co. (Japan)
Pascale and Athos,
The Art of Japanese Management
(Simon & Schuster, 1981)

The majority of new ideas are not unusual; what is unusual is the experience of having new ideas.

Anonymous

The amount a person uses his imagination is inversely proportional to the amount of punishment he will receive for using it.

Anonymous workshop participant
Oech, *A Whack on the Side of the Head*
(Warner, 1983)

20

Labor Relations

My way or the highway.

Union gives strength.

Aesop, c. 620–c. 560 B.C.
Greek fabulist
The Bundle of Sticks

Treat employees like partners, and they act like partners.

Fred Allen
Chairman, Pitney-Bowes Co.
Leaders Magazine, 1979

Most important for us is a good spiritual relationship between employees and management.

Tatsuhiko Andoh
President, Okatoku Securities Co. (Japan)
Cherry Blossoms and Robotics
(Young Presidents' Organization, 1983)

Artisans are not required to stand up from their labor when a Sage passes by.

Babylonian Talmud, Nedarim

A work force is willing to go through many painful things if it believes in the long-term goals.

Richard Belous
Labor economist, The Conference Board
The New York Times, April 12, 1988

[Commenting on the possibility of participative management:] I'm not going to have the monkeys running the zoo.

Frank Borman
Astronaut and CEO, Eastern Airlines
The Washington Monthly, June 1986

You either take it [a pay cut proposed by management] or you don't have a job. It's that simple.

Anette Brooks
Mill Operator, General Electric Co.
The New York Times, March 13, 1988

Most of the collective bargaining since the 1940's has resulted in wage settlements in excess of productivity increases.

> Courtney C. Brown
> Columbia University School of Business
> *Dun's Review*, August 1979

The quality of employees will be directly proportional to the quality of life you maintain for them.

> Charles E. Bryan
> President, Local 100,
> International Association of Machinists
> and Aerospace Workers
> *The New York Times*, February 21, 1988

The worker cannot help himself alone. There is no limit to what must be done for a piece of bread. One must bite his lips till they bleed, and keep silent when he is alone. He must not remain silent. He must unite with his fellow workers and fight. To defend their honor as men, the workers must be well organized.

> Abraham Cahan, 1860–1951
> American journalist and newspaper editor
> *A Bintel Brief* (Doubleday, 1971)

There never has yet existed a wealthy and civilized society in which one portion of the community did not, in point of fact, live on the labour of the other.

> John C. Calhoun, 1782–1850
> American lawyer and statesman
> Speech on receiving Abolition Petition,
> February 1837

The one is master and depends on profits. The other is servant and depends on salary.

> Andrew Carnegie, 1835–1919
> American industrialist and philanthropist
> Quoted in *Harvard Business Review*,
> September/October 1987

Where we are dealing with organized labor, we are going to get about the type of leadership that we are ourselves.

> Cyrus S. Ching
> Vice President, Uniroyal
> *Journal of Business*, 1978

The labor of a human being is not a commodity or article of commerce.

> Clayton Anti-Trust Act, 1914

A truly American sentiment recognizes the dignity of labor and the fact that honor lies in honest toil.

> Grover Cleveland, 1837–1908
> Twenty-second and twenty-fourth
> President of the United States
> Letter accepting nomination for President,
> August 18, 1884

I have considered the pension list of the republic a roll of honour.

> Grover Cleveland, 1837–1908
> Twenty-second and twenty-fourth
> President of the United States
> Veto message, July 5, 1888

We're not nice to our people just at negotiating time or thirty days before; we try and be fair and honest and good and sweet 365 days a year.

> Izzy Cohen
> CEO, Giant Food
> Schatz, *Managing By Influence*
> (Prentice-Hall, 1986)

Technical management probably began in prehistoric times. A talented Neanderthal spear-sharpener discovered that in addition to his technical achievements, he could manage others of his tribe to accomplish superior spear-sharpening and was subsequently assigned these duties full time. He discovered that certain management skills helped considerably in getting the tribe's spears sharpened efficiently. A knock on the side of the head proved necessary for one of his technical people, while an approving grunt served to keep another on the right track.

> William A. Cohen
> American sociology professor
> *Principles of Technical Management*
> (AMACOM, 1980)

There is no right to strike against the public safety by anybody, anywhere, any time.

> Calvin Coolidge, 1872–1933
> Thirtieth President of the United States
> Telegram to Samuel Gompers,
> September 14, 1919

With all their faults, trade-unions have done more for humanity than any other organization of men that ever existed. They have done more for decency, for honesty, for education, for the betterment of the race, for the developing of character in man, than any other association of men.

> Clarence S. Darrow, 1857–1938
> American lawyer, reformer, and writer
> *The Railroad Trainman*, November, 1909

As a result of ... male supremacy in the unions, women remain essentially unorganized, despite the fact that they are becoming an even larger part of the labor force.

> Marlene Dixon
> Critic, activist, and writer
> *Ramparts Magazine*, December 1969

[T]he first criterion in identifying those people within an organization who have management responsibility is not command over people. It is responsibility for contribution. Function rather than power has to be the distinctive criterion and the organizing principle.

> Peter F. Drucker
> Management consultant and writer
> *People and Performance*
> (Harper & Row, 1977)

Direct production workers—machinists, bricklayers, farmers—are a steadily declining portion of the work force in a developed economy. The fastest growing group consists of "knowledge workers"—accountants, engineers, social workers, nurses, computer experts of all kinds, teachers and researchers. And the fastest growing group among knowledge workers themselves are managers.

> Peter F. Drucker
> Management consultant and writer
> *People and Performance*
> (Harper & Row, 1977)

Once 85 percent of national income goes to employees, the labor union has lost its original rationale: that of increasing the share of the national income that goes to the "wage fund." All one labor union can do is increase the share of its members at the expense of other employees.

> Peter F. Drucker
> Management consultant and writer
> *Management in Turbulent Times*
> (Harper & Row, 1980)

In his work the individual is at least securely attached to a part of reality, the human community.

> Sigmund Freud, 1856–1939
> Father of psychoanalysis
> *Civilization and its Discontents*

Workplace cooperation can work. But for it to work, employees and managers must abandon the adverserial relationship that has proved so destructive to American capitalism. We need to establish a new tradition in the workplace—a tradition of increased employee ownership and shared enterprise, in which management becomes accountable to workers and employees become ready to assume the increased responsibility that comes from power sharing.

Alex Gibney
Syndicated economics writer
The Washington Monthly, June 1986

Union officials cannot be looked upon as guarantors that the contract will not be violated. They are not subject to punishment in instances where the rank-and-file do not follow their advice. They are readily differentiated from Management executives who can exert persuasive authority through the threat of discharge.

Harry M. Gilden
Labor arbitrator
Amour & Co., 8 LA 758

Collective bargaining does not establish some hitherto non-existing rights; it provides the power to enforce rights of labor which the labor movement was dedicated to long before.

Arthur J. Goldberg
U. S. Supreme Court Justice
and Ambassador to the United Nations
Managements Rights and the Arbitration Process
(Bureau of National Affairs, 1956)

Ill fares the land, to hastening ills a prey, where wealth accumulates, and men decay.

Oliver Goldsmith, 1728–1774
English writer
The Traveller

The periods of unemployment accompanying depression in the business cycle ... present a challenge to all our claims to progress, humanity, and civilization.

Samuel Gompers, 1850–1924
President, American Federation of Labor
Seventy Years of Life and Labor

Dishonest people try to exploit [the system]; they know only their rights; but they do not want to know their duties. They work poorly, shirk and drink hard.

Mikhail Gorbachev
Premier, USSR
Perestroika (Harper & Row, 1987)

The labor union is an elemental response to the human instinct for group action in dealing with group problems.

William Green, 1873–1952
President, American Federation of Labor
Speech, 1925

Most workers don't trust management.

Chris Gunnell
Mechanic, Ford Motor Co. (Great Britain)
The New York Times, February 14, 1988

The real question is why employers and employees have such divergent perceptions of their goals.

Betty Hartzell
Publisher, *Personnel Journal*
Personnel Journal, March 1988

That lack of energy that distinguishes ... human beings who depend for subsistence on charity, monopolized labor, or anything else, but their own independent exertions.

Nathaniel Hawthorne, 1804–1864
American writer
The Scarlet Letter

The knife is in the meat, and the drink is in the horn, and there is revelry in [King] Arthur's Hall, and none may enter therein but the son of a king of a priveleged country, or a craftsman bringing his craft.

The Story of Kilhweh and Olewen
Fourteenth century Welsh epic
The Red Book of Hergest

The wealth of a country is its working people.

Theodor Herzl, 1860–1904
Austrian journalist and Zionist leader
Altneuland

What labor is demanding all over the world today is not a few material things like more dollars and fewer hours of work, but the right to a voice in the conduct of industry.

Sidney Hillman, 1887–1946
Vice President,
Congress of Industrial Organizations
Speech, 1918

Back in the 1930's, the unions were like a 21 year old woman. She was beautiful, had a gorgeous body, a sparkling personality, and she seduced a lot of people into the union movement. That's fine. The problem is that this 21 year old siren is now in her 60's and she's forty pounds overweight, needs a facelift, and has a terrible disposition.... The difficulty is that she still thinks she's 21.

Eric Hoffer, 1902–1983
Philosopher, writer, and longshoreman
Oech, *A Whack on the Side of the Head*
(Warner, 1983)

You are troubled, I perceive, that your servant is run away from you; but I do not hear yet that you are either robbed, or strangled, or poisoned, or betrayed, or accused, by him; so that you have escaped well in comparison with your fellows.

Horace, 65–8 B.C.
Roman poet and satirist
Epistles to Lucilius

The interesting prospect about an economy with fewer workers is that they will choose where they will work. Some will force companies to offer much higher salaries and wages. Others will challenge their companies

to manage them well, both to increase production and to keep them from leaving.

Bill Hunter
President, Hunter Associates
Business Week, October 5, 1987

Managers have an awareness that they are the direct representatives of the employees.

Takashi Ishihara
President, Nissan Motor Co. (Japan)
Cherry Blossoms and Robotics
(Young Presidents' Organization, 1983)

We need to energize our members.

John T. Joyce
President, National Bricklayers Union
The Wall Street Journal, August 24, 1987

Picket line violence by an employee may render him unfit for further employment by the antagonisms it arouses and the attitude it expresses toward management, toward other workers or toward plant and equipment.

Clark Kerr
Labor arbitrator
Cudahy Packing Co., 11 LA 1138

The Constitution prevents the government from spying on individuals, yet any company in the United States can wiretap to eavesdrop on its employees.

George Kohl
Director of Special Projects,
Communications Workers of America
Best of Business Quarterly, 1987

Labor is prior to, and independent of capital. Capital is only the fruit of labor, and could never have existed if labor had not first existed.

Abraham Lincoln, 1809–1865
Sixteenth President of the United States
Message to Congress, December 3, 1861

The strongest bond of human sympathy, outside of the family relation, should be one uniting all working people, of all nations, and tongues, and kindreds.

> Abraham Lincoln, 1809–1865
> Sixteenth President of the United States
> Letter to the New York Workingman's
> Association, March 21, 1864

I agree with you, Mr. Chairman, that the workingmen are the basis for all governments, for the plain reason that they are the more numerous.

> Abraham Lincoln, 1809–1865
> Sixteenth President of the United States
> Speech, Cincinnati, February 12, 1861

The greatest problem with unions is that they control the amount of productivity that workers will be allowed to achieve. Wages aren't really the problem.

> Royal Little
> Founder, Textron
> *Best of Business Quarterly*, 1987

The laborer is worthy of his hire.

> New Testament, Luke 10:7

Union leadership ... is no longer in the hands of the most highly skilled trade representatives; facile eloquence and a partisan hostility to all employers have become the appropriate qualifications.

> Elton Mayo, 1880–1949
> Harvard University
> *Democracy and Freedom* (Macmillan, 1919)

No society is civilized in which the many [work] in the interest of the few. When "work" signifies intelligent collaboration in the achievement of a social purpose, then "industrial unrest" will cease to be.

> Elton Mayo, 1880–1949
> Harvard University
> *Democracy and Freedom* (Macmillan, 1919)

[I]f you have lower than a 10% turnover, there is a problem. And if you have higher than, say 20%, there is a problem.

> William G. McGowan
> Chairman, MCI Communications Corp.
> *Inc. Magazine*, August 1986

It doesn't take a majority to make a rebellion; it takes only a few determined leaders and a sound cause.

> Henry Louis Mencken, 1880–1956
> Editor, author, and critic
> *Prejudices*

My way or the highway.

> Barry Minkow
> CEO, ZZZZ Best Co.
> *Inc. Magazine*, August 1987

We try for an interchange of ideas and principles—something more than a boss-employee relationship—in order to involve the worker.

> John Mollica
> Assistant Director for Labor Relations,
> General Motors Co.
> Tosi and Carroll, *Management* (Wiley, 1976)

John Morrow I was one time called. I was certainly born in Paris and had in keeping all mason work of St. Andrew's, the high church of Glasgow, Melrose and Paisley, of Nidderdale and of Galway. I pray to God and Mary both and to sweet St. John to keep this holy church free from injury due to witchcraft.

John Morrow, c. 1350
Master,
Paris stonecutters' and masons' guild
Inscription over doorway of Melrose Abbey,
Roxburghshire, Scotland

Employers generally get the kind of labor relations they ask for.

Philip Murray
Director, Congress of Industrial Organizations
Organized Labor and Production
(Harper, 1940)

There is a new minority in the American work force: white males.... In 1954, white males were in the majority, 62.5 percent of the work force. By June 1984, they had become the minority, 49.3 percent.... Increasingly, that "average worker" is a woman.

John Naisbett and Patricia Aburdene
Business writers and social researchers
Re-inventing the Corporation (Warner, 1985)

American workers have been conditioned by experience constantly to expect more from work—more money, more fringe benefits, better working conditions—while producing less and putting in less time and effort on the job.

James O'Toole
University of Southern California
Making America Work (Continuum, 1981)

[A]ffirmative action has worked so well for women, *particularly those in management and the professions*, that it is possible to forecast the day when these women will no longer need the special help of affirmative action to combat discrimination.

James O'Toole
University of Southern California
Making America Work (Continuum, 1981)

When a company has a layoff, it's most often the management's fault.

Kenneth Olsen
Founder and CEO, Digital Equipment Corp.
Speech, 1982

Observing the city to be filled with persons who flocked ... to Attica for the security of living, and that most of the country was barren and unfruitful, and that traders at sea import nothing to them who could give them nothing in exchange, he [Solon, c. 640–c. 558 B.C.] turned his citizens to trade, and made a law that no son be obliged to relieve a father who had not bred him up to any calling.

Plutarch, c. 46–c. 120
Greek biographer and philosopher
The Parallel Lives: Solon

But of all his measures the most commended was his distribution of the people [of Rome] by their trades into companies or guilds ... musicians, goldsmiths, carpenters, dyers, shoemakers, skinners, metal workers and potters.... In this manner all factions ... began for the first time to pass out of use, no person any longer being thought of or spoken of ... as a Sabine or a Roman, Romulan or a Tatian; and the new division became a source of general harmony and intermixture.

Plutarch, c. 46–c. 120
Greek biographer and philosopher
The Parallel Lives: Numa Pompilius

The guarantee of equal protection cannot mean one thing when applied to one individual and something else when applied to a person of another color. If both are not accorded the same protection, then it is not equal.

Lewis F. Powell, Jr.
U. S. Supreme Court Justice
University of California v. *Bakke* (1978)

It is significant that in Japan trade unions are among the most vocal advocates of long-term investment strategies that emphasize productivity and growth.

> Robert B. Reich
> JFK School of Government, Harvard University
> *The Next American Frontier*, 1983

I believe now, as I have all my life, in the right of workers to join unions and to protect their unions.

> Franklin Delano Roosevelt, 1882–1945
> Thirty-second President of the United States
> Radio address, May 2, 1943

It is one of the characteristics of a free and democratic nation that it have free and independent labor unions.

> Franklin Delano Roosevelt, 1882–1945
> Thirty-second President of the United States
> Speech, Teamsters' Union convention,
> Washington, D.C., September 11, 1940

It is essential that there should be organizations of labor. This is an era of organization. Capital organizes and therefore labor must organize.

> Theodore Roosevelt, 1858–1919
> Twenty-sixth President of the United States
> Speech, Milwaukee, October 14, 1912

I am a believer in unions. I am an honorary member in one union. But the union must obey the law, just as the corporation must obey the law.

> Theodore Roosevelt, 1858–1919
> Twenty-sixth President of the United States
> Remarks to striking Chicago teamsters,
> May 10, 1905

The nature of things continually tends to the destruction of equality.

> Jean Jacques Rousseau, 1712–1778
> French philosopher and writer
> *The Social Contract*

Changes are impossible to bring off when managers and unions are adversaries.

> Dean M. Ruwe
> Senior Vice President, Copeland Corp.
> and Wickham Skinner
> Harvard Business School
> *Harvard Business Review*, May/June 1987

If your employees know you are dependent on them, they'll walk out unless they get everything they want.

> Morris Sarna
> General Manager, Sutton Apartments, Inc.
> Speech, January 4, 1988

Unionized blue collar workers belong to the middle class, and they have middle-class values.

> Earl Shorris
> Manager and writer
> *The Oppressed Middle*
> (Anchor/Doubleday, 1981)

It was the general custom of the Incas to divide a newly conquered tribe into two approximately equal halves and to place a supervisor over each of them, but to give these two supervisors slightly different ranks. This was indeed the most suitable means for provoking rivalry between the two heads, which prevented any united action against the ruler.... One would doubtless have claimed unconditional prerogative because of his superiority, which, on the other hand, was not significant enough to suggest the same claim to the other.

Georg Simmel, 1858–1918
German philosopher and sociologist
The Sociology of Georg Simmel
(The Free Press, 1950)

[On labor unions:] Anything that you do to increase job security automatically does work for you. It makes your employees a closer part of the unit.

Roger B. Smith
CEO, General Motors Corp.
The Washington Post, October 11, 1987

We hire by the job, not by the hour.

Marlene Solomon
Publisher, *Magna Magazine*
Sales meeting, February 17, 1988

[The labor unions] are threatening my life; my job is my life.

Gregory A. Sprinkle
Wire Mill Worker, General Electric Co.
The New York Times, March 13, 1988

The sweat of a man's brows, and the exudations of a man's brains, are as much a man's own property as the breeches upon his backside.

Laurence Sterne, 1713–1768
English novelist
Tristram Shandy

Union organizers look for situations in which employees feel they have no control over issues that concern them.

Daniel C. Stone, Jr.
Vice President, Alpha Associates (Canada)
Personnel Journal, February 1986

Capitalism, in the sense of great individual undertakings, involving the control of large financial resources, and yielding riches to their masters as a result of speculation, money-lending, commercial enterprise, buccaneering, and war, is as old as history. Capitalism, as an economic system, resting on the organization of legally free wage-earners, for the purpose of pecuniary profit, by the owner of capital or his agents, and setting its stamp on every aspect of society, is a modern phenomenon.

Richard H. Tawney, 1880–1962
British economist
Religion and the Rise of Capitalism

The labor unions ... have rendered a great service in the past, not only to their members, but to the world, in shortening the hours of labor and in modifying the hardships and improving the conditions of wage-workers.

Frederick Winslow Taylor, 1856–1915
Pioneer management teacher
Harvard Business School lecture, 1912

[Referring to British labor unions:] By God, I'll confront them.

Margaret Thatcher
English Prime Minister
The New York Times, February 14, 1988

Labor unions have crippled American industry by narrowing job descriptions.

Robert Townsend
Former CEO, Avis
Further Up the Organization (Knopf, 1984)

Managers should realize the importance of each suggestion [from workers or groups of workers]. Try to find what it is in each suggestion that has worth. Each suggestion and the reaction to each suggestion can build trust.

Shoichiro Toyodo
President, Toyota Motor Co.
Cherry Blossoms and Robotics
(Young Presidents' Organization, 1983)

Mutual trust is the basis for labor-management relations.

Toyota Motor Co.
Joint declaration of management and labor
Cherry Blossoms and Robotics
(Young Presidents' Organization, 1983)

The facts show that politically independent unions do not exist anywhere. There have never been any. Experience and theory say that there never will be any.

Leon Trotsky, 1879–1940
Russian revolutionary and Communist theorist
Communism and Syndicalism

[In reaction to union demands in the early days:] I made a decision and announced it to the union. I would accept all their current demands and furthermore, put the union on notice that I was accepting in advance all of the union's future demands. Thus I entered into management based on full mutual trust.

Koichi Tsukamoto
President, Wacoal Corp. (Japan)
Cherry Blossoms and Robotics
(Young Presidents' Organization, 1983)

Long ago we stated the reason for labor organizations. We said that union was essential to give laborers opportunity to deal on an equality with their employer.

U. S. Supreme Court
National Labor Relations Board v.
Jones & Laughlin Steel Co. (1937)

Labor in this country is independent and proud. It has not to ask the patronage of capital, but capital solicits the aid of labor.

Daniel Webster, 1782–1852
American statesman and orator
Speech, April 2, 1824

Let us remember that the automatic machine is the precise economic equivalent for slave labor. Any labor that competes with slave labor must accept the economic conditions of slave labor.

Norbert Wiener, 1894–1964
Pioneer computer scientist
The Human Use of Human Beings
(Houghton Mifflin 1950)

An employee can enjoy the exclusive benefit of his pension fund only if he has a job secure enough and long enough to collect his deferred income pension. There is nothing that requires him to finance his own job loss [by investing union pension funds in corporations that act contrary to workers' perceived self-interests].

William W. Winpinsinger
President, International Association of
Machinists and Aerospace Workers
National Journal, January 27, 1979

The hardest work is to go idle.

Yiddish proverb

Unions cause many difficult problems for the management of companies. But can anyone who has been in the buisness world these last fifty years doubt that without the labor unions the standard of living in this country would be as high as it is? The prosperity of the nation itself—including the companies that the unions vex—is, in large part, due to the efforts of those same labor unions.

Phil Zahn, 1894–1985
Founder and CEO, Mamselle Dresses, Inc.
Annual shareholders' meeting, January 1978

Adam Smith was wrong. Individuals working for their own best interests are not good for the whole country. American management and labor are only hurting each other and themselves by adopting adversarial roles. While Americans are fighting with each other, the rest of the world will walk right by us economically.

Anonymous respondent
Competitiveness Survey
Harvard Business Review,
September/October 1987

Nobody except by them [the guild weavers] shall introduce himself, within the city [of London], into their mystery and nobody within Southwark or other places belonging to London except he be a member of their guild.

Charter granted to London's weavers by
King Henry I (1100–1135)

The union agrees that it will use its best efforts to cause the employees to individually and collectively perform and render efficient work in order to keep the company competitive and thus improve the job security of the employees.

Agreement between Dow Chemical Co. and
the United Steel Workers of America
The New York Times, October 7, 1979

21
Law

Agree, for the law is costly.

Law is order, and good law is good order.

> Aristotle, 384–322 B.C.
> Greek philosopher & teacher
> *Politics*

Bulls do not win bull fights;
People do.
People do not win people fights;
Lawyers do.

> Norman R. Augustine
> President and CEO, Martin Marietta Corp.
> *Augustine's Laws* (Penguin, 1987)

As fish die when they are out of water, so do people die when there is no law and order.

> Babylonian Talmud, Avodah Zarah

Judges must beware of hard constructions and strained inferences: for there is no worse torture than the torture of the laws.

> Francis Bacon, 1561–1624
> Lord Chancellor of England
> *Of Judicature*

Take all the robes of all the good judges that have ever lived on the face of the earth, and they would not be large enough to cover the iniquity of one corrupt judge.

> Henry Ward Beecher, 1813–1887
> American clergyman
> *Proverbs from Plymouth Pulpit*

When you have to pick a lawyer, look in his eyes for honesty.... These days when you pick a lawyer ... you never know what will happen.

> Larry Bird
> Professional basketball player
> *Adam Smith's Moneyworld* (PBS TV),
> February 20, 1988

The right to be let alone—the most comprehensive of rights and the most valued by civilized men.

> Louis Dembitz Brandeis, 1856–1941
> U. S. Supreme Court Justice
> *Olmstead* v. *the U.S.* (1928)

To say that "the law is an ass, an idiot" is not to impugn the character of those who must administer it.

>William Joseph Brennan
>U. S. Supreme Court Justice
>*In re Sawyer* (1958)

Corporations cannot commit treason, nor be outlawed nor excommunicated, for they have no souls.

>William Camden, 1551–1623
>English scholar and historian
>*Case of Sutton's Hospital*

What's the constitution between friends?

>Timothy John Campbell, 1840–1904
>U. S. Congressman
>Remark to President Grover Cleveland

We must distinguish between the sound certainty and the sham, between what is gold and what is tinsel; and then, when certainty is attained, we must remember that it is not the only good, that we can buy it at too high a price.

>Benjamin Nathan Cardozo, 1870–1938
>U. S. Supreme Court Justice
>*The Growth of the Law*

Sometimes even lawyers need lawyers.

>Billy Carter, 1937–1988
>President Jimmy Carter's brother
>*The Observer*, July 27, 1980

Never make a defence or apology before you be accused.
[The author of these words was later tried, condemned, and executed as a "tyrant and a traitor to the liberties of England."]

>Charles I, 1600–1649
>King of England
>Letter to Lord Wentworth, September 3, 1636

Settling a dispute through the law is like losing a cow for the sake of a cat.

>Chinese proverb

The good of the people is the chief law.
[*Salus populi suprema est lex.*]

>Cicero, 106–43 B.C.
>Roman orator and statesman
>*De Legibus*

No man has ever yet been hanged for breaking the spirit of the law.

>Grover Cleveland, 1837–1908
>Twenty-second and twenty-fourth
>President of the United States
>Hibben, *Peerless Leader*

It is unjust that any one should be judge in his own cause.
[*Iniquum est aliquem rei sui esse judicem.*]

>Edward Coke, 1552–1634
>English politician and jurist
>*Coke upon Littleton*

If you cannot avoid a quarrel with a blackguard, let your lawyer manage it, rather than yourself. No man sweeps his own chiminey, but employs a chiminey sweeper, who has no objection to dirty work, because it is his trade.

>Charles Caleb Colton, c. 1780–1832
>English cleric, sportsman, and wine merchant
>*Lacon*

The science of legislation is like that of medicine in one respect: that it is far more easy to point out what will do harm than what will do good.

>Charles Caleb Colton, c. 1780–1832
>English cleric, sportsman, and wine merchant
>*Lacon*

One with the law is a majority.

> Calvin Coolidge, 1872–1933
> Thirtieth President of the United States
> Speech, July 27, 1920

Arbitration can be done quickly ... it's far cheaper than litigation.

> J. Slater Davidson
> Arbitrator, American Arbitration Association
> *AARP News Bulletin*, December 1987

The simple answer is that in these courts ... the privelege [against self-incrimination] is not available to a corporation. It has no body to be kicked or soul to be damned.

> Lord Denning
> English jurist
> *British Steel Corporation*
> v. *Granada TV* (1981)

One witness shall not rise up against a man.... At the mouth of two or three witnesses shall a matter be established.

> Old Testament, Deuteronomy 19:15

"If the law supposes that," said Mr. Bumble, "the law is a ass, a idiot."

> Charles Dickens, 1812–1870
> English novelist and social reformer
> *Oliver Twist*

If there were no bad people there would be no good lawyers.

> Charles Dickens, 1812–1870
> English novelist and social reformer
> *The Old Curiosity Shop*

It is not a presumption of law that a hire-purchase finance company cannot be innocent.

> J. L. Diplock, 1907–1985
> English jurist
> *Snook* v. *London and West Riding Investments*
> (1967)

When men are pure, laws are useless; when men are corrupt, laws are broken.

> Benjamin Disraeli, 1804–1881
> English Prime Minister and novelist
> *Contarini Fleming*

Property has its duties as well as its rights.

> Thomas Drummond, 1797–1840
> English engineer and administrator
> Letter to the Earl of Donoughmore, May 1838

The good lawyer is not the man who has an eye to every side and angle of contingency, and qualifies all his qualifications, but who throws himself on your part so heartily, that he can get you out of a scrape.

> Ralph Waldo Emerson, 1803–1882
> American essayist and poet
> *Power*

To go to law is for two persons to kindle a fire, at their cost, to warm others and singe themselves to cinders.

> Owen Felltham, c. 1602–1668
> English writer
> *Resolves, Divine, Morall, Politicall*

Litigation is the pursuit of practical ends, not a game of chess.

> Felix Frankfurter, 1882–1965
> U. S. Supreme Court Justice
> *Indianapolis* v. *Chase National Bank* (1941)

If facts are changing, law cannot be static.

Felix Frankfurter, 1882–1965
U. S. Supreme Court Justice
Law and Politics

Laws *too gentle* are *seldom obeyed*; *too severe*, seldom *executed*.

Benjamin Franklin, 1706–1790
American printer and statesman
Poor Richard's Almanack

A countryman between two lawyers is like a fish between two cats.

Benjamin Franklin, 1706–1790
American printer and statesman
Poor Richard's Almanack

A jury consists of twelve persons chosen to decide who has the better lawyer.

Robert Frost, 1874–1963
American poet
Prochnow, *The Toastmaster's Treasure Chest*
(Harper & Row, 1979)

Agree, for the law is costly.

Thomas Fuller, 1608–1661
Chaplain in extraordinary to Charles II
Gnomologia

The more laws, the more offenders.

Thomas Fuller, 1608–1661
Chaplain in extraordinary to Charles II
Gnomologia

He declares himself guilty, who justifies himself before accusation.

Thomas Fuller, 1608–1661
Chaplain in extraordinary to Charles II
Gnomologia

The good advocate ... is the one that will not plead that cause wherein his tongue must be confuted by his conscience.... He is more careful to deserve, than greedy to take, fees.

Thomas Fuller, 1608–1661
Chaplain in extraordinary to Charles II
Holy and Profane States

For every law there is a loophole for he who would find it.

German proverb

Whenever the offence inspires less horror than the punishment, the rigour of penal law is obliged to give way to the common feelings of mankind.

Edward Gibbon, 1737–1794
English politician and historian
Decline and Fall of the Roman Empire

Two go to law; a third bears off the spoil.

Carlo Goldoni, 1707–1792
Italian dramatist
Le Nozze

Laws grind the poor, and rich men rule the law.

Oliver Goldsmith, 1728–1774
English poet, novelist, and dramatist
The Traveller

A verbal contract isn't worth the paper it's printed on.

Samuel Goldwyn, 1882–1974
American movie pioneer
Johnson, *The Great Goldwyn*

I know of no method to secure the repeal of bad or obnoxious laws so effectual as their strict construction.

> Ulysses S. Grant, 1822–1885
> Eighteenth President of the United States
> Inaugural address, March 4, 1869

Circumstances alter cases.

> Thomas Chandler Haliburton, 1796–1865
> Canadian jurist and humorist
> *The Old Judge*

There is something monstrous in commands couched in invented and unfamiliar language; an alien master is worst of all. The language of the law must not be foreign to those who are to obey it.

> Learned Hand, 1872–1961
> American jurist
> Speech, Washington, D.C., May 11, 1929

Our Constitution is color-blind, and neither knows nor tolerates classes among citizens. In respect of civil rights, all citizens are equal before the law. The humblest is the peer of the most powerful. The law regards man as man, and takes no account of his surroundings or of his color when his civil rights as guaranteed by the supreme law of the land are involved.

> John Marshall Harlan, 1833–1911
> U. S. Supreme Court Justice
> *Plessy* v. *Ferguson* (1896) [sole dissent]

Deceive not thy physician, confessor, nor lawyer.

> George Herbert, 1593–1633
> English clergyman and poet
> *Jacula Prudentum*

The worst of law is, that one suit breeds twenty.

> George Herbert, 1593–1633
> English clergyman and poet
> *Jacula Prudentum*

Lawsuits consume time, and money, and rest, and friends.

> George Herbert, 1593–1633
> English clergyman and poet
> *Jacula Prudentum*

Hard cases make bad law.

> William Searle Holdsworth, 1871–1944
> English legal historian
> *History of English Law*

Great cases like hard cases make bad law.

> Oliver Wendell Holmes, Jr., 1841–1935
> U. S. Supreme Court Justice
> *Northern Securities Company* v. *U.S.* (1904)

Like lawyers, we undertake a cause first and look for proof later.

> Elbert Hubbard, 1856–1915
> American writer, printer, and editor
> *The Philosophy of Elbert Hubbard*

[Referring to the dearth of litigation in Japanese businesses:] They've got about as many lawyers as we have *sumo* wrestlers.

> Lee Iacocca
> Chairman, Chrysler Corp.
> *Working Woman*, March 1988

A lean compromise is better than a fat lawsuit.

> Italian proverb

Never sue for assault or slander, settle them cases yourself.

Andrew Jackson, 1767–1845
Seventh President of the United States
Fredericks, *Wit and Wisdom of the Presidents*

The study of the law is useful in a variety of points of view. It qualifies a man to be useful to himself, to his neighbours, and to the public.

Thomas Jefferson, 1743–1826
Third President of the United States
Letter to T. M. Randolph, May 30, 1790

Johnson observed, that "he did not care to speak ill of any man behind his back, but he believed the gentleman to be an *attorney.*"

Samuel Johnson, 1709–1784
English lexicographer and essayist
Boswell's Life of Dr. Johnson

The law is the last result of human wisdom acting upon human experience for the benefit of the public.

Samuel Johnson, 1709–1784
English lexicographer and essayist
Johnsoniana

Morality cannot be legislated, but behavior can be regulated. Judicial decrees may not change the heart, but they can restrain the heartless.

Martin Luther King, Jr. 1929–1968
Clergyman and civil rights leader
Strength to Love

Now this is the Law of the jungle—as old and as true as the sky.

Rudyard Kipling, 1865–1936
English author
The Law of the Jungle

Impartiality is not neutrality—it is partiality for justice.

Stanislaw J. Lec
Polish writer and aphorist
Unkempt Thoughts (St. Martin's Press, 1962)

Executives have to start understanding that they have certain legal and ethical responsibilities for information under their control.

Jim Leeke
Computer Journalist
PC Week, August 11, 1987

Let the buyer beware, for he ought not to be ignorant of the nature of the property which he is buying from another party.
[*Caveat emptor quia ignorare non debuit quod jus alienum emit.*]

Legal maxim

Ignorance of the law is no excuse.
[*Ignorantia juris non excusat.*]

Legal maxim

Ancient custom has the force of law.
[*Vetustas pro lege semper habetur.*]

Legal maxim

Discourage litigation. Persuade your neighbor to compromise whenever you can.... As a peace-maker the lawyer has a superior opportunity of being a good man. There will still be business enough.

Abraham Lincoln, 1809–1865
Sixteenth President of the United States
Notes for a Law Lecture

The law is an inexhaustible reservoir of good stories because it deals with humanity between the hammer and the anvil.

Eliezer Lipsky
American attorney and critic
The New York Times, January 2, 1955

An employee is never presumed to engage his services permanently, thereby cutting himself off from all chances of improving his condition; indeed, in this land of opportunity it would be against public policy and the spirit of our institutions that any man should thus handicap himself.

Louisiana Supreme Court
Pitcher v. *United Oil & Gas Syndicate* (1932)

For as laws are necessary that good manners may be preserved, so there is need of good manners that laws may be maintained.

Niccolò Machiavelli, 1469–1527
Florentine statesman and philosopher
Discourses

You may never achieve zero defects. But if you want to avoid lawsuits, try to reach that goal.

Marisa Manley
Attorney, Ginsberg Organization
Harvard Business Review,
September/October 1987

A corporation is an artificial being, invisible, intangible, and existing only in contemplation of the law.

John Marshall, 1755–1835
Chief Justice of the United States
Trustees of Dartmouth College
v. *Woodward* (1819)

By your words will you be justified, and by your words you will be condemned.

New Testament, Matthew 12:37

We have in fact, spent a great deal of time appealing [government regulatory and administrative decisions] in court, and we've won our fair share. That gives us a lot of creditability in dealing with [the government agency] the next time around.

William G. McGowan
Chairman, MCI Communications Corp.
Inc. Magazine, August 1986

There's nothing wrong with our business. Lawsuits are the problem.

John A. McKinney
Chairman, Manville Corp. (asbestos producers)
The Official MBA Handbook of Great Business Quotations (Simon & Schuster, 1984)

He who knows only his own side of the case, knows little of that.

John Stuart Mill, 1806–1873
English philosopher and economist
On Liberty

Men of most renowned virtue have sometimes by transgressing most truly kept the law.

John Milton, 1608–1674
English poet
Tetrachordon

It would be better for us to have [no rules or laws] at all than to have them in so prodigious numbers as we have.

Michel Eyquem de Montaigne, 1533–1592
French philosopher and essayist
Works

The laws do not undertake to punish anything other than overt acts.

Charles de Secondat Montesquieu, 1689–1755
French lawyer, writer, and philosopher
The Spirit of the Laws

They have no lawyers among them, for they consider them a sort of people whose profession it is to disguise matters.

Thomas More, 1478–1535
English statesman and author
Utopia: Of Law and Magistrates

I don't know as I want a lawyer to tell me what I cannot do. I hire him to tell me how to do what I want to do.

John Pierpont (J. P.) Morgan, 1837–1913
American financier and philanthropist
Josephson, *The Robber Barons*
(Harcourt Brace, 1934)

Fighting [as opposed to settling] an unfounded charge to the best of your ability is honorable and shows good judgement.

Thomas C. Morrison
Partner, Patterson, Belknap, Webb & Tyler
Management Review, December 1987

Jury service is a duty as well as a privelege of citizenship; it is a duty that cannot be shirked on a plea of inconvenience or decreased earning power.

Frank Murphy, 1890–1949
U. S. Supreme Court Justice
Thiel v. *Southern Pacific Co.* (1945)

Lawyers are like beavers: They get in the main-stream and dam it up.

John Naisbitt
Chairman, Naisbitt Group
Megatrends (Warner, 1984)

It will not injure you to know enough of law to keep out of it.

Old Farmer's Almanac (1851)

Our Law says well, to delay Justice is Injustice.

William Penn, 1644–1718
Founder of Pennsylvania
Fruits of Solitude in Reflections and Maxims

Urge the lawyers or contracts department—none too gently—to experiment with handshake agreements or contracts of no more than two pages. It can be done.

Tom Peters
Business writer
Thriving on Chaos (Knopf, 1987)

The law follows custom.

Plautus, 254–184 B.C.
Roman playwright and carpenter
Trinummus

Rigorous law is often rigorous injustice.

Plautus, 254–184 B.C.
Roman playwright and carpenter
Heautontimoroumenos

I never heard of any real authority for any such proposition as that one owes full disclosure of the truth to all men at all times.

Frederick Pollock, 1845–1937
English jurist and legal scholar
The Holmes-Pollock Letters, July 2, 1928

Litigation is the basic legal right which guarantees every corporation its decade in court.

David Porter
The Official MBA Handbook of Great Business Quotations (Simon & Schuster, 1984)

Law is experience developed by reason and applied continually to further experience.

Roscoe Pound, 1870–1964
Dean, Harvard Law School
Christian Science Monitor, April 24, 1963

Let us consider the reasons of the case. For nothing is law that is not reason.

John Powell, 1633–1696
English jurist
Coggs v. *Bernard*

Fools and obstinate men make lawyers rich.

Barber, *The Book of 1000 Proverbs*, 1876

He hurts the good who spares the bad.
[*Bonis nocet quisquis pepercerit malis.*]

Publilius Syrus, c. 42 B.C.
Roman writer
Maxims

The judge is condemned when the guilty is acquitted.
[*Judex damnatur cum nocens absolvitur.*]

Publilius Syrus, c. 42 B.C.
Roman writer
Maxims

The profession of exploiting loopholes is eminently respectable. Some of the nation's must erudite and honorable people do it.

Robert B. Reich
JFK School of Government, Harvard University
Best of Business Quarterly, 1987

A lawyer's business is to keep his clients out of litigation.

Elihu Root, 1845–1937
Secretary of War and Nobel laureate in peace
Dictum

The first rule of advocacy. Never ask your witness a question unless you're quite sure of the answer.

John Rumpole
The Trials of Rumplole, 1979

A lawyer without history or literature is a mechanic, a mere working mason; if he possesses some knowledge of these, he may venture to call himself an architect.

Walter Scott, 1771–1832
Scottish poet, novelist, and biographer
Guy Mannering

Ignorance of the law excuses no man: not that all men know the law, but because 'tis an excuse every man will plead, and no man can tell how to confute him.

John Selden, 1584–1654
English jurist, Orientalist, and statesman
Table Talk

No man is bound to accuse himself.

John Selden, 1584–1654
English jurist, Orientalist, and statesman
Table Talk

If you judge, investigate; if you reign, command.
[*Si judicas, cognosce; si regnas, jube.*]

Seneca, c. 4–65
Roman philosopher and playwright
Medea

Good counselors lack no clients.

William Shakespeare, 1564–1616
English dramatist and poet
The Merry Wives of Windsor

The first thing we do, let's kill all the lawyers.

William Shakespeare, 1564–1616
English dramatist and poet
Henry the Sixth

A society which is based on the letter of the law and never reaches any higher is taking very scarce advantage of the high level of human possibilities. The letter of the law is too cold and formal to have a beneficial influence on society. Whenever the tissue of life is woven of legalistic relations, there is an atmosphere of moral mediocrity, paralyzing man's noblest impulses.

Aleksandr Solzhenitsyn
Russian writer and U. S. citizen
Commencement address,
Harvard University, 1978

Win your lawsuit, lose your money.

Spanish proverb

To the extent that ... trial by litigation really replaces the old notion of trial by battle, the system still succeeds in keeping the peace. Is this a small achievement?

Melvin J. Sykes
Attorney
Maryland Law Review, 1978

Corruption abounding in the commonwealth, the commonwealth abounded in laws.

Tacitus, c. 55–117
Roman orator, politician, and historian
Annals of the Julian Emperors

A man must not go to law because the musician keeps false time with his foot.

Jeremy Taylor, 1613–1667
English clergyman and writer
The Worthy Communicant

Advocates [attorneys] must deal plainly with their clients, and tell the true state of their case.

Jeremy Taylor, 1613–1667
English clergyman and writer
Rule and Exercise of Holy Living

No Law ... is a proper object of reverence. It is mere brute fact; and every living thing, still more every person exercising intelligent choice, is its superior.

William Temple, 1881–1944
Archbishop of Canterbury
Nature, Man and God

Some circumstantial evidence is very strong, as when you find a trout in the milk.

Henry David Thoreau, 1817–1862
American naturalist and writer
Journals

The law is good, if a man use it lawfully.

New Testament, I Timothy 1:8

Deals aren't usually blown by principals; they're blown by lawyers and accountants trying to prove how valuable they are.

Robert Townsend
Former CEO, Avis
Further Up the Organization (Knopf, 1984)

The Constitutional guarantees require, we think, a federal role that prohibits a public official from recovering damages for a defamatory falsehood relating to his official conduct unless he proves that the statement was made with "actual malice"—that is, with knowledge that it was false or with reckless disregard of whether it was false or not.

U. S. Supreme Court
New York Times Co. v. *Sullivan* (1964)

To Messrs. Morgan and Garrison: Gentlemen, you have undertaken to cheat me. I will not sue you. The law takes too long. I will ruin you.

> Cornelius Vanderbilt, 1794–1877
> American shipping magnate and philanthropist
> Letter to former business associates

Let the law never be contradictory to custom; for if the custom be good, the law is worthless.

> François Marie Voltaire, 1694–1778
> French philosopher and author
> *Philosophical Dictionary*

Liberty exists in proportion to wholesome restraint; the more restraint on others to keep off from us, the more liberty we have.

> Daniel Webster, 1782–1852
> American statesman and orator
> Speech at the Charleston Bar dinner,
> May 10, 1847

We have an expression in New York, when we meet a very difficult problem—"You will have to get a Philadelphia lawyer to solve that." Few people know that there is a basis in truth in the expression, for in 1735, when no New York lawyer could be obtained to defend John Peter Zenger, accused of criminal libel, because his two lawyers ... having challenged the jurisdisction of the court, had already been disbarred, the friends of Zenger came to Philadelphia and obtained the services of Andrew Hamilton, then eighty years of age, to go to New York without fee, and defend the action in the face of a hostile court.

> Harry Weinberger
> Speech, Independence Hall, Philadelphia,
> March 9, 1934

[A]bsent actual malice ... the First Amendment gives the press and the broadcast media a privilege to report and comment upon the official actions of public servants in full detail, with no requirement that the reputation or the privacy of an individual involved in or affected by the official action be spared from public view.

> Byron R. White
> U. S. Supreme Court Justice
> *Rosenbloom* v. *Metromedia, Inc.* (1971)

A judge sins if he looks not for merit in the accused.

> The Zohar

Rule of Judicial Avoidance: If a court can decide not to decide, that is the decision the court will make.

> Anonymous

A man who is his own lawyer has a fool for his client.

> Anonymous

It is illegal for an employer to:

A. Fail or refuse to hire or discharge an individual or otherwise to discriminate against any individual with respect to his compensation, terms, conditions, or privileges of employment, because of such individual's race, color, religion, sex, or national origin.

B. Limit, segregate, or classify his employees or applicants for employment in any way that would deprive or tend to deprive any individual of employment opportunities or otherwise adversely affect his status as an employee, because of such individual's race, color, religion, sex, or national origin.

> 1964 Civil Rights Act, Title VII, as amended
> by the Equal Opportunity Employment Act, 1972

The glorious uncertainty of law.

> Toast of Wilbraham at a dinner of English
> judges and council, Serjeants' Inn Hall,
> London, 1756

22

Leadership

Leadership cannot be taught ... only learned.

Management skills are only part of what it takes.... Managers must also be corporate *warriors* or leaders. These unique individuals are the problem identifiers. They possess a strong sense of vision; view firefighting as an opportunity to do things differently and smarter; and are business strategists who help identify key corporate growth issues. [The author is referring to Black managers, but the import is general.]

John W. Aldridge
President, Aldridge Associates
Management Review, December 1987

The productivity and competitive problems American manufacturers face result from ineffective top management, petrified in place, unwilling to accept change, failing to provide vision and leadership.

Philip H. Alspach
President, Intercon, Inc.
Harvard Business Review,
November/December 1986

We have set some clear long range objectives. If they are not met, then the company should find a president better than me who can meet them.

Tatsuhiko Andoh
President, Okatoku Securities Co. (Japan)
Cherry Blossoms and Robotics
(Young Presidents' Organization, 1983)

I am just the coach.

Luis Arzubi
Director, IBM R&D Laboratory, Essex Junction
New England Monthly, September 1987

Men in great places are thrice servants: servants of the sovereign or state, servants of fame, and servants of business.

Francis Bacon, 1561–1626
Lord Chancellor of England
Of Great Place

The actions of a responsible executive are contagious.

Joe D. Batton
Business writer
Hayes, *Memos for Management: Leadership*
(AMACOM, 1983)

[Referring to CEO Christopher Whittle:] It's great to work with somebody who wants to do things differently.

Keith Bellows
Vice President, Whittle Communications
USA Today, March 10, 1988

Failing organizations are usually over-managed and under-led.

Warren G. Bennis
President, University of Cincinnati
University of Maryland symposium,
January 21, 1988

The first job of a leader is to define a vision for the organization ... but without longevity of leadership you can have the "vision of the month club."

Warren G. Bennis
President, University of Cincinnati
University of Maryland symposium,
January 21, 1988

Leadership is the capacity to translate vision into reality.

Warren G. Bennis
President, University of Cincinnati
University of Maryland symposium,
January 21, 1988

Managers are people who do things right, and leaders are people who do the right thing.

Warren G. Bennis and Burt Nanus
Leaders (Harper & Row, 1985)

The key to successful leadership today is influence, not authority.

Kenneth H. Blanchard
University of Massachusetts
Schatz, *Managing By Influence*
(Prentice-Hall, 1986)

The source of good management is found in the imagination of leaders, persons who form new visions and manifest them with a high degree of craft. The blending of vision and craft communicates the purpose. In the arts, people who do that well are masters. In business, they are leaders.

Henry M. Boettinger
Director of Corporate Planning, AT&T
*Harvard Business Review on
Human Relations*, 1986

It is in times of difficulty that great nations, like great men, display the whole energy of their character and become an object of admiration to posterity.

Napoleon Bonaparte, 1769–1821
Emperor of France
Maxims

A leader is a dealer in hope.

Napoleon Bonaparte, 1769–1821
Emperor of France
Maxims

They love him, gentlemen, and they respect him, not only for himself, but for his character, for his integrity, and judgment and iron will; but they love him most for the enemies he has made.

General Edward Stuyvesant Bragg, 1827–1912
Speech nominating Grover Cleveland for
President of the United States, 1884

It is far safer to know too little than too much. People will condemn the one though they will resent being called upon to follow the other.

Samuel Butler, 1835–1902
English novelist and satirist
The Way of All Flesh

A leader has to *appear* consistent. That doesn't mean he has to *be* consistent.

> James Callaghan
> English Prime Minister
> *Harvard Business Review*,
> November/December 1986

Immense power is acquired by assuring yourself in your secret reveries that you were born to control affairs.

> Andrew Carnegie, 1837–1919
> American industrialist and philanthropist
> Ilich, *Power Negotiating*
> (Addison-Wesley, 1980)

We don't need any more leadership training; we need some followership training.

> Maureen Carroll
> Senior Vice President,
> University Research Corp.
> Management meeting, February 15, 1985

Yesterday's leaders may be tomorrow's goats—even though they're the same people with the same virtues.

> John Case
> Senior Editor, *Inc. Magazine*
> *Inc. Magazine*, December 1987

Remember General Custer.... An executive's judgement about the marketplace, people and a myriad of other variables are more important than abstract "leadership" qualities in determining a company's success or failure.

> John Case
> Senior Editor, *Inc. Magazine*
> *Inc. Magazine*, December 1987

I should rather men should ask why my statue is not set up, than why it is.

> Cato the Elder, 234–149 B.C.
> Roman politician
> Quoted by Plutarch, *Political Precepts*

Where we are dealing with organized labor, we are going to get about the type of leadership that we are ourselves.

> Cyrus S. Ching
> Vice President, Uniroyal
> *Journal of Business*, 1983

I am certainly not one of those who need to be prodded. In fact, if anything, I am a prod.

> Winston Churchill, 1874–1965
> English Prime Minister, writer, and soldier
> Speech in Parliament, November 11, 1942

The people are fashioned according to the example of their kings; and edicts are of less power than the life [example] of the ruler.

> Claudian, c. 365–c. 408
> Egyptian epic poet
> *De Quarto Consulatu Honorii
> Augustii Panegyris*

The Spartans were brutal when it came to cleaning house. Healthy children were carefully trained and then given a share of the enterprise. Weak ones were thrown off cliffs or left to die. It was called infanticide. Today we call it "outplacement." By any name it's still cruel. But nothing gets the message out about a ... leader's seriousness of purpose than a tough minded personnel policy.

> John K. Clemens
> Hartwick College
> *The New York Times*, August 16, 1987

Some types of authority exist by virtue of a person's expertise, or even his or her personality. Such a person may be in any organization and at any level.... The issue of whether an order has authority depends not necessarily on who gives the order but on whether it is accepted by those who receive it.

> William A. Cohen
> *Principles of Technical Management*
> (AMACOM, 1980)

Deliberate with caution, but act with decision, and yield with graciousness, or oppose with firmness.

> Charles Caleb Colton, c. 1780–1832
> English cleric, sportsman, and wine merchant
> *Lacon*

If you lead the people with correctness, who will dare not to be correct?

> Confucius, c. 551–c. 479 B.C.
> Chinese philosopher and teacher
> *Analects*

Very few natural-born leaders turn up in the work place.

> Milton S. Cotter
> President, Profiles, Inc.
> *Personnel Journal,* March 1988

A fool must now and then be right by chance.

> William Cowper, 1731–1800
> English poet
> *Conversation*

[Referring to his coach, John Robinson:] He makes you think you're invincible.

> Eric Dickerson
> Professional football player
> Peters, *Thriving on Chaos* (Knopf, 1987)
> (*see* Robinson, John)

We live in an age of prudence. The leaders of the people now generally follow.

> Benjamin Disraeli, 1804–1881
> English Prime Minister and novelist
> *Coningsby*

Charisma becomes the undoing of leaders. It makes them inflexible, convinced of their own infallibility, unable to change.

> Peter F. Drucker
> Management consultant and writer
> *The Wall Street Journal*, January 6, 1988

You do not lead by hitting people over the head—that's assault, not leadership.

> Dwight David Eisenhower, 1890–1969
> Thirty-fourth President of the United States
> Speech, Columbia University, 1949

To be a leader of men, one must turn one's back on men.

> Henry Havelock Ellis, 1859–1939
> English scientist and author
> Prochnow, *The Toastmaster's Treasure Chest*
> (Harper & Row, 1979)

To be great is to be misunderstood.

> Ralph Waldo Emerson, 1803–1882
> American poet and essayist
> *Self-Reliance*

Great men are more distinguished by range and extent, than by originality.

> Ralph Waldo Emerson, 1803–1882
> American essayist and poet
> *Shakespeare*

Wherever MacDonald sits, there is the head of the table.

> Ralph Waldo Emerson, 1803–1882
> American essayist and poet
> *The American Scholar*

People have been getting other people to do things ever since the Garden of Eden.

> Russell H. Ewing
> President, National Institute for Leadership
> *Leadership in the Office* (AMACOM, 1963)

To know is nothing at all. To imagine is everything.

Anatole France, 1844–1924
French novelist
The Daughter of Clemintine

Uncertainty will always be part of the taking-charge process.

John J. Gabarro
Harvard Business School
The Dynamics of Taking Charge
(Harvard Business School, 1987)

Leadership is the very heart and soul of business management.

Harold Geneen
CEO, IT&T
Managing (Doubleday, 1984)

Leadership cannot really be taught. It can only be learned.

Harold Geneen
CEO, IT&T
Managing (Doubleday, 1984)

Every time a chief executive takes an action for or against someone ... there is a reaction throughout the company.

Harold Geneen
CEO, IT&T
Managing (Doubleday, 1984)

Leadership is practiced not so much in words as in attitude and in actions.

Harold Geneen
CEO, IT&T
Managing (Doubleday, 1984)

He led his regiment from behind. He found it less exciting.

William Schwenck Gilbert, 1836–1911
English playwright and poet
The Gondoliers

Silence gives consent.

Oliver Goldsmith, 1728–1774
English poet and playwright
The Good Natured Man

Human beings are compounded of cognition and emotion and do not function well when treated as though they were merely cogs in motion.... The task of the administrator must be accomplished less by coercion and discipline, and more and more by persuasion.... Management of the future must look more to leadership and less to authority as the primary means of coordination.

Luther H. Gulick
President and Chairman,
National Institute of Public Administration
Papers on the Science of Administration (1937)

The humility which comes from others having faith in you.

Dag Hammerskjöld, 1905–1961
Secretary-General of the United Nations
Markings

No one knows for sure just what gives one leader inherent authority and causes another to have to depend on the authority vested in his position.

Patricia C. Haskell
Executive Editor, *Supervisory Management*
Leadership in the Office (AMACOM, 1963)

Jingshen is the Mandarin word for spirit and vivacity. It is an important word for those who would lead, because above all things, spirit and vivacity set effective organizations apart from those that will decline and die.

> James L. Hayes
> President and CEO,
> American Management Association
> *Memos for Management: Leadership*
> (AMACOM, 1983)

Leaders who are inarticulate ... make us all uneasy.

> James L. Hayes
> President and CEO,
> American Management Association
> *Memos for Management: Leadership*
> (AMACOM, 1983)

Before a leader must lead he must first belong.

> Bruce Henderson
> CEO, Boston Consulting Group, Inc.
> *Henderson on Corporate Strategy* (Abt, 1979)

'Twixt kings and tyrants there's this difference known: Kings seek their subjects' good, tyrants their own.

> Robert Herrick, 1591–1674
> English poet
> *Hesperides*

The successful organization has one major attribute that sets it apart from unsuccessful organizations: dynamic and effective leadership.

> Paul Hersey
> California American University
> and Kenneth H. Blanchard
> University of Massachusetts
> *Management of Organizational Behavior*
> (Prentice-Hall, 1982)

This shortage of effective leadership is not confined to business but is evident in the lack of able administrators in government, educa-tion, foundations, churches, and every other form of society.

> Paul Hersey
> California American University
> and Kenneth H. Blanchard
> University of Massachusetts
> *Management of Organizational Behavior*
> (Prentice-Hall, 1982)

Different leadership situations require different leader styles.

> Paul Hersey
> California American University
> and Kenneth H. Blanchard
> University of Massachusetts
> *Management of Organizational Behavior*
> (Prentice-Hall, 1982)

The very essence of leadership is [that] you have to have a vision. It's got to be a vision you articulate clearly and forcefully on every occasion. You can't blow an uncertain trumpet.

> Theodore Hesburgh
> President, Notre Dame University
> *Time*, May 1987

You stand in your own light.

> John Heywood, 1497–1580
> English author
> *Proverbes*

The leader of genius must have the ability to make different opponents appear as if they belonged to one category.

> Adolf Hitler, 1889–1945
> Führer of the Third German Reich
> *Mein Kampf*

The reward of the general is not a bigger tent, but command.

> Oliver Wendell Holmes, Jr., 1841–1935
> U. S. Supreme Court Justice
> Letter to Charles Bunn, 1917

Leadership is a two-way street, loyalty up and loyalty down. Respect for one's superiors; care for one's crew.

Grace Murray Hopper
Admiral, U. S. Navy (retired)
Speech, Washington, D.C., February 1987

You cannot manage men into battle. You manage things; you lead people.

Grace Murray Hopper
Admiral, U. S. Navy (retired)
Nova (PBS TV), 1986

[Leadership is] ... convincing people that however bad the news is, the end result is going to be better for them.

Robert B. Horton
CEO, British Petroleum America
The New York Times, January 10, 1988

[Business leaders] are like beads on a string—when one slips off, all the rest follow.

Henrick Ibsen, 1828–1906
Norwegian playwright
The League of Youth

A rotting fish begins to stink at the head.

Italian proverb

Leadership has a harder job to do than just choose sides. It must bring sides together.

Jesse Jackson
Clergyman, diplomat, and politician
Face the Nation, April 9, 1988

Management techniques are obviously essential, but what matters is leadership.... Leading the whole organization needs wisdom and flair and vision and they are another matter;

they cannot be reduced to a system and incorporated into a training manual.

Anthony Jay
Watzlawick, Weakland & Fish
Management and Machiavelli
(Holt, Rinehart, and Winston, 1967)

Great men are not always wise.

Old Testament, Job 32:7

[A new chief executive has to be] somebody who has effectively managed change. If you are looking outside for a new leader, you are saying things have to be altered.

John Johnson
President, Lamalie Associates
Fortune, February 3, 1986

[Asked why he would accept second place on the 1960 ticket with John Kennedy, with less power than as Senate majority leader:] Power is where power goes.

Lyndon Baines Johnson, 1908–1973
Thirty-sixth President of the United States
Remark to reporters, 1960

I'm the only President you've got.

Lyndon Baines Johnson, 1908–1973
Thirty-sixth President of the United States
Reminder to U. S. Senators, April 27, 1964

Those who are inclined to compromise can never make a revolution.

Kemal Atatürk, 1881–1938
Turkish general, statesman, and reformer
Speech in the National Assembly, 1920

It is much safer to be in a subordinate position than in one of authority.

Thomas à Kempis, c.1380–1471
German monk
Of the Imitation of Christ

I think I have a role to play which may be unpopular.

> Martin Luther King, Jr., 1929–1968
> Clergyman and civil rights leader
> Quoted in *The Washington Post*,
> April 3, 1988

A boss cannot obtain by decree the creativity, initiative, and dedication needed to do a job properly.

> Tony Kizilos and Roger P. Heinisch
> Systems and Research Center of Aerospace
> and Defense, Honeywell Corp.
> *Harvard Business Review*,
> September/October 1986

The conductor has the advantage of not seeing the audience.

> Andre Kostelanetz, 1901–1980
> Band leader and orchestra conductor
> Shapiro, *Encyclopedia of Quotations*
> *About Music*

You can delegate authority, but you can never delegate responsibility by delegating a task to someone else. If you picked the right man, fine, but if you picked the wrong man, the responsibility is yours—not his.

> Richard E. Krafve
> President, Raytheon
> *The Boston Sunday Globe*, May 22, 1960

As for the best leaders, the people do not notice their existence. The next best, the people honor and praise. The next, the people fear; and the next, the people hate.

> Lao-Tzu, 604–531 B.C.
> Chinese philosopher and founder of Taoism
> *Tao Te Ching*

When the best leader's work is done the people say, "We did it ourselves."

> Lao-Tzu, 604–531 B.C.
> Chinese philosopher and founder of Taoism
> *Tao Te Ching*

The superior leader gets things done with very little motion. He imparts instruction not through many words but through a few deeds. He keeps informed about everything but interferes hardly at all. He is a catalyst, and though things would not get done as well if he weren't there, when they succeed he takes no credit. And because he takes no credit, credit never leaves him.

> Lao-Tzu, 604–531 B.C.
> Chinese philosopher and founder of Taoism
> *Tao Te Ching*

Speak softly and carry a big carrot.

> Howard C. Lauer
> Assistant Executive Vice President,
> United Jewish Appeal Federation
> of Greater Washington, D.C.
> Notes for a book

It is best not to swap horses while crossing the river.

> Abraham Lincoln, 1809–1865
> Sixteenth President of the United States
> Speech accepting renomination,
> June 9, 1864

I've never seen a situation in which the guy who cuts a company down [manages the downsizing] is the one who brings it back.

> Richard Lindenmuth
> CEO, Robinson Nugent, Inc.
> *Newsweek*, April 25, 1988

The genius of a good leader is to leave behind him a situation which common sense, without the grace of genius, can deal with successfully.

Walter Lippmann, 1889–1974
Journalist and public philosopher
"Roosevelt Has Gone" (Column),
April 14, 1945

Feminine leadership style emphasizes cooperation over competition; intuition as well as rational thinking in problem solving; team structures where power and influence are shared within the group ... interpersonal competence; and participative decision making.

Marilyn Loden
Founder and president, Loden Associates
Management Review, December 1987

Contrary to the opinion of many people, leaders are not born. Leaders are made, and they are made by effort and hard work.

Vince Lombardi, 1913–1970
Professional football coach
Wiebusch, *Lombardy* (Follett, 1971)

It isn't necessary to have original ideas to be a successful leader.

Jonelle Long
President, Maid-To-Order, Inc.
Speech, Washington, D.C.,
November 14, 1987

A tale is told of a man in Paris during the upheaval in 1848, who saw a friend marching after a crowd toward the barricades. Warning him that these could not be held against the troops, that he had better keep away, he received the reply, "I must follow them. I am their leader."

A. Lawrence Lowell, 1856–1943
President of Harvard University
Conflicts of Principle

There is nothing more difficult to take in hand, more perilous to conduct, or more uncertain in its success, than to take the lead in the introduction of a new order of things.

Niccolò Machiavelli, 1469–1527
Florentine statesman and philosopher
Discourses

A boss's mere expression of an opinion can be interpreted as a decision—even a direct order—by a staff member caught in the clutches of risk avoidance.

R. Alec Mackenzie
Management consultant and author
The Time Trap (McGraw Hill, 1972)

All men of worship said it was merry to be under such a chieftain [King Arthur], that would put his person in adventure as other poor knights did.

Thomas Malory, d. 1470
English translator and compiler
Morte d'Arthur

Leadership is demonstrated when the ability to inflict pain is confirmed.

Robert Malott
Chairman, FMC Corp.
Fortune, August 6, 1984

He who can, commands, and he who will, obeys.

Alessandro Manzoni, 1785–1873
Italian novelist and poet
I Promessi Sposi

If the blind lead the blind, both shall fall into the ditch.

New Testament, Matthew 15:14

Leaders do not give up easily. Whether attributable to patience, perseverance of even

tenacity, effective leaders are not easily discouraged. They find successful courses of
action by refusing to acknowledge failure and
by continuing to work to resolve the problem.

Mary McClure
Vice Chairman, Council of State Governments
The Journal of State Government,
September/October 1987

There's a tendency to think of conflicts of interest as an administrative problem:
identifying potential or actual conflicts and
then resolving them.... But often, resolving
them requires a leadership decision, not an administrative one. When you turn down Client
X and instead agree to represent Client Y, you
may be making a significant decision about
the direction of the firm.

Ira Millstein
Managing Partner, Weil, Gotshal & Manges
Of Counsel, October 5, 1987

The prime occupational hazard of the
manager is superficiality.

Henry Mintzberg
McGill University School of Management
The Nature of Managerial Work
(Harper & Row, 1973)

Leadership, like swimming, cannot be learned
by reading about it.

Henry Mintzberg
McGill University School of Management
The Nature of Managerial Work
(Harper & Row, 1973)

That was the way things were done under Mr.
Misawa. He is now dead. Now, how shall we
proceed?
[Portion of memo sent to by Misawa to
employees resisting change.]

Chiyoshi Misawa
President, Misawa Homes (Japan)
The Renewal Factor (Bantam, 1987)

On the most exalted throne in the world, we
are still seated on nothing but our arse.

Michel Eyquem de Montaigne, 1533–1592
French philosopher and essayist
Essays

A man does not become celebrated in proportion to his general capacity, but because he
does or says something which happened to
need doing or saying at the moment.

John Morley, 1838–1923
English statesman and writer
On Compromise

When times get tough, old established businesses with managers but no leaders seek
help.

David J. Morris, Jr.
University of New Haven
Performance and Instruction Journal,
September 1986

Transitions of leadership are potential periods
of danger.

Fredrick C. Mosher
University of Virginia
Public Administration Review,
July/August 1985

A leader is a man who makes decisions.
Sometimes they turn out right and sometimes
they turn out wrong; but either way, he makes
them.

Mutual Benefit Life Insurance Co.
"Leaders are Made ... Not Born"
Leadership in the Office (AMACOM, 1963)

I start with the premise that the function of
leadership is to produce more leaders, not
more followers.

Ralph Nader
Consumer advocate
Time, November 8, 1976

Anonymity and withdrawal are part of the CEO's inventory of power. The reverse of anonymity is visibility, which brings with it an expectation of accountability. If you want to operate without accountability, you make yourself difficult to reach.

Ralph Nader
Consumer advocate
Best of Business Quarterly, Winter 1986

Leadership involves finding a parade and getting in front of it; what is happening ... is that those parades are getting smaller and smaller and there are many more of them.

John Naisbitt
Chairman, Naisbitt Group
Megatrends (Warner, 1984)

The new leader is a facilitator, not an order giver.

John Naisbitt
Chairman, Naisbitt Group
Megatrends (Warner, 1984)

One must have a good memory to be able to keep the promises one makes.

Georg Wilhelm Nietzsche, 1844–1900
German philosopher
Human, All Too Human

Life always gets harder toward the summit— the cold increases, responsibility increases.

Georg Wilhelm Nietzsche, 1844–1900
German philosopher
The Antichrist

The best leaders are apt to be found among those executives who have a strong component of orthodoxy in their character. Instead of resisting innovation, they symbolize it.

David Ogilvy
Founder, Ogilvy-Mather Advertising
Ogilvy on Advertising (Crown, 1983)

Hundreds of studies have been conducted in the United States into how the exercise of power affects leadership.... The consistent picture of the effective leader is one who adopts the style of a "superfollower," who serves with his followers' blessing and consent, and who is able to inspire because he is first able to respond to their needs and concerns. Power, in this context, means the ability to get things done, to mobilize resources, and to draw on what is necessary to accomplish goals. Power is thus more akin to "mastery" than to "domination" or "control...." People who use power best use it directly only as necessary to get the job done. They do not worry much about it as an end in itself.

Richard T. Pascale
Stanford University School of Business
and Anthony G. Athos
Harvard Business School
The Art of Japanese Management
(Simon & Schuster, 1981)

[It is bad for] a leader of anything to run around frazzled.

James B. Patterson
CEO, J. Walter Thompson USA
The New York Times, April 28, 1988

You can't lead a cavalry charge if you think you look funny on a horse.

John Peers
President, Logical Machine Corp.
1,001 Logical Laws (Doubleday, 1979)

Where Example *keeps pace* with Authority, Power hardly fails to be obey'd.

William Penn, 1644–1718
Founder of Pennsylvania
Fruits of Solitude in Reflections and Maxims

Mix *Kindness* with Authority: and rule more by *Discretion* than Rigour.

> William Penn, 1644–1718
> Founder of Pennsylvania
> *Fruits of Solitude in Reflections and Maxims*

[GM's] problems can't be solved with money. They have to be solved with leadership.

> H. Ross Perot
> Founder, Electronic Data Systems
> *Life*, February 1988

People sense weakness, and step in and try to take control.

> H. Ross Perot
> Founder, Electronic Data Systems
> *The Washington Post*, November 22, 1987

Good followers do not become good leaders.

> Laurence J. Peter
> University of Southern California
> *The Peter Principle* (William Morrow, 1969)

The brand of leadership we propose has a simple base of MBWA (Managing By Wandering Around). To "wander," with customers and vendors and our own people, is to be in touch with the first vibrations of the new.

> Tom Peters and Nancy Austin
> Business writers
> *A Passion for Excellence*
> (Random House, 1985)

The best leaders ... almost without exception and at every level, are master users of stories and symbols.

> Tom Peters
> Business Writer
> *Thriving on Chaos* (Knopf, 1987)

The pilot of a ship is worth as much as all the crew.

> Philo Judaeus, c. 20 B.C.–40 A.D.
> Alexandrian philosopher and polemicist
> *Virtues*

You know, Hannibal, how to gain a victory but not how to use it.

> Plutarch, c. 46–c. 120
> Greek biographer and philosopher
> *The Parallel Lives*

The pilot cannot mitigate the billows or calm the winds.

> Plutarch, c. 46–c. 120
> Greek biographer and philosopher
> *On the Tranquility of the Mind*

Impulse manages all affairs badly.

> Portugese proverb

The view only changes for the lead dog.

> *Sergeant Preston of the Yukon*
> Radio program, 1950s

Anyone can hold the helm when the sea is calm.

> Publilius Syrus, c. 42 B.C.
> Roman writer
> *Maxims*

The leader must know, must know that he knows, and must be able to make it abundantly clear to those about him that he knows.

> Clarence B. Randall
> Chairman, Inland Steel Co.
> *Making Good in Management*
> (McGraw-Hill, 1964)

You take people as far as they will go, not as far as you would like them to go.

Jeannette Rankin, 1880–1973
U. S. Congresswoman and suffragist
Josephson, *First Lady in Congress*

Leadership is a manager's ability to get subordinates to develop their capabilities by inspiring them to achieve.

John A. Reinecke
University of New Orleans
and William F. Schoell
University of Southern Mississippi
Introduction to Business
(Allyn and Bacon, 1983)

A project manager can delegate authority but not responsibility. Responsibility is indivisible. When something goes wrong and you cannot find the specific individual to put your finger on, then you have never really had the responsibility.

Hyman J. Rickover
Admiral, U. S. Navy (retired)
The New York Times, October 7, 1963

I never give them [the players] negative feedback.

John Robinson
College and professional football coach
Quoted by Bennis, January 21, 1988

The prospective chief executive has to be action-oriented. You find a lot of planners who can't act.

Gerard Roche
Chairman, Heidricks & Struggles
Fortune, February 3, 1986

We may give advice, but we cannot inspire the conduct.

François de La Rochefoucauld, 1613–1680
French politician, writer, and philanthropist
Reflections, or Sentences and Moral Maxims

A bad situation that drifts always gets worse.... A situation that cries out for authority ... cannot be allowed to degrade.

Felix Rohatyn
Chairman,
New York City Municipal Assistance Corp.
The New York Times, November 22, 1987

People ask the difference between a leader and a boss.... The leader leads, and the boss drives.

Theodore Roosevelt, 1858–1919
Twenty-sixth President of the United States
Speech, October 24, 1910

Speak softly and carry a big stick.

Theodore Roosevelt, 1858–1919
Twenty-sixth President of the United States
Speech at the Minnesota State Fair,
September 2, 1901

[Before David became king of Israel]... everyone who was in distress, and every one who was in debt, and every one who was discontented, gathered themselves unto him; and he became a captain over them.

Old Testament, I Samuel 22:2

A Prince who will not undergo the Difficulty of Understanding, must undergo the Danger of Trusting.

George Savile (Lord Halifax), 1633–1695
English politician and statesman
Political Thoughts and Reflections

In the old reality the expression "a new broom sweeps clean" frequently was a relavent descriptive term for what happens when new leadership came into an organization.... In the new reality "a new broom is soon worn out."

Lyle E. Schaller
Yokefellow Institute
The Change Agent (Abingdon, 1972)

Leadership is the total effect you have on the people and events around you. This effect is your influence. Effective leading is being consciously responsible for your organizational influence.... The essence of leadership is knowing that YOU CAN NEVER NOT LEAD. You lead by acts of commission and acts of omission.

> Kenneth and Linda Schatz
> Leadership and organizational consultants
> *Managing by Influence* (Prentice-Hall, 1986)

[L]eadership is best thought of as a function within the organization rather than the trait of an individual.

> Edgar H. Schein
> Massachusetts Institute of Technology
> *Organizational Psychology*
> (Prentice-Hall, 1980)

Example is leadership.

> Albert Schweitzer, 1875–1965
> Physician, music scholar, and philosopher
> Peters, *Thriving on Chaos* (Knopf, 1987)

When you say you'll meet someone at 11:00 AM, be there at 10:45. When you promise a check on the 30th, send it on the 28th. Whatever you agree to do, do a bit more. Start with your employees, then extend it to everyone you deal with. News will soon get around that you are a person of your word.

> Charles Scott
> CEO, Intermark
> *Inc. Magazine's Guide to*
> *Small Business Success*, 1987

The Hall was the place where the great Lord used to eat.... He ate not in private, except in time of sickness.... Nay, the King himself used to eat in the Hall, and his lords sat with him, and then he understood men.

> John Selden, 1584–1654
> English jurist, Orientalist, and statesman
> *Table Talk*

If you judge, investigate; if you reign, command.
[*Si judicas, cognosce; si regnas, jube.*]

> Seneca, c. 4–65
> Roman philosopher and playwright
> *Medea*

When the lion fawns upon the lamb, the lamb will never cease to follow him.

> William Shakespeare, 1564–1616
> English dramatist and poet
> *King Henry VI*

The force of his own merit makes his way.

> William Shakespeare
> English dramatist and poet, 1564–1616
> *King Richard III*

Fortune brings in some boats that are not steered.

> William Shakespeare, 1564–1616
> English dramatist and poet
> *Cymbeline*

Leadership is not manifested by coercion, even against the resented.

> Margaret Chase Smith
> U. S. Senator
> Address to National Republican Women,
> April 16, 1962

It is the merit of a general to impart good news and conceal the bad.

> Sophocles, 496?–406 B.C.
> Greek dramatist
> *Oedipus Coloneus*

He whose honor depends on the opinion of the mob must day by day strive with the greatest anxiety, act and scheme in order to retain his reputation.

> Benedict Spinoza, 1632–1677
> Dutch philosopher and oculist
> *Ethics*

Be wiser than other men, but do not tell them so.

> Philip Dormer Stanhope, 1694–1773
> English Secretary of State
> *Letters of Lord Chesterfield to His Son*

The shepherd always tries to persuade the sheep that their interests and his own are the same.

> Stendhal (Marie Henri Beyle), 1783–1842
> French novelist and biographer
> Prochnow, *The Toastmaster's Treasure Chest*
> (Harper & Row. 1979)

The pattern of personal characteristics of the leader must bear some relevant relationship to the characteristics, activities, and goals of the followers.... It becomes clear that an adequate analysis of leadership involves not only a study of leadership but also of situations.

> R. M. Stodgill
> *Journal of Psychology*, 1948

You should never compromise with regard to the type of people you have in leadership roles.... It's not that people are good or bad. It's that they either have the qualities that are suited for the job or not.

> Jim Swiggett
> CEO, Kollmorgen Corp.
> *Inc. Magazine*, February 1987

The proper arts of a general are judgment and prudence.

> Tacitus, c. 55–117
> Roman orator, politician, and historian
> *Annals of the Julian Emperors*

It is highly important for managers to be honest and clear in describing what authority they are keeping and what role they are asking their subordinates to assume.

> Robert Tannenbaum
> UCLA School of Management
> and Warren H. Schmidt
> UCLA School of Public Administration
> *Harvard Business Review*, March/April 1958

They who are in the highest places, and have the most power, have the least liberty, because they are most observed.

> John Tillotson, 1630–1694
> English clergyman
> *Reflections*

A leader is not an administrator who loves to run others, but someone who carries water for his people so that they can get on with their jobs.

> Robert Townsend
> Former CEO, Avis
> *The Tarrytown Letter*, August 1984

My definition of a leader ... is a man who can persuade people to do what they don't want to do, or do what they're too lazy to do, and like it.

> Harry S. Truman, 1884–1972
> Thirty-third President of the United States
> Miller, *More Plain Speaking*

If you can't stand the heat, stay out of the kitchen.

> Harry S. Truman, 1884–1972
> Thirty-third President of the United States
> *Mr. Citizen*

Clear-water rivers with gravel bottoms change their channels very gradually, and therefore one needs to learn them but once; but piloting becomes another matter when you apply it to vast streams like the Mississippi and the Missouri, whose alluvial banks cave and change constantly, whose snags are always hunting up new quarters, whose sandbars are never at rest, whose channels are forever dodging and shirking, and whose obstructions must be confronted in all nights and all weathers without the aid of a single lighthouse or buoy; for there is neither light nor buoy to be found anywhere in all this three or four thousand miles of villainous river.

Mark Twain
(Samuel Langhorne Clemens), 1835–1910
American author and riverboat captain
Life on the Mississippi

Character is power.

Booker T. Washington, 1856–1915
Principal, Tuskegee Institute
Quoted on *Tony Brown's Journal* (PBS TV),
August 22, 1987

The only basis of legitimacy for [charismatic authority] is personal charisma, so long as it is proved; that is, as long as it receives recognition and is able to satisfy the followers or disciples. But this lasts only so long as the belief in its charismatic inspiration remains.

Max Weber, 1864–1920
German sociologist
Max Weber (Crowell, 1963)

We follow, close order behind you,
Where you have pointed the way.

"The Corps"
Traditional song of West Point

Of the devoted priests of power, there are many who regard with impatience the limitations of mankind, and in particular the limitations consisting in man's undependability and unpredictability. You may know a mastermind of this type by the subordinates whom he chooses. They are meek, self-effacing, and wholly at his disposal; and on account of this, are generally ineffective when they

once cease to be limbs at the disposal of his brain. They are capable of great industry but of little independent initiative—the chamberlains of the harem of ideas to which their Sultan is wedded.

Norbert Wiener, 1894–1964
American computer scientist
God and Golem, Inc. (M. I. T., 1964)

Whom God would sorely vex, He endows with abundant good sense.

Yiddish proverb

In three ways is a wise man known: By his dealings with his fellow man, by his quickness in granting pardon, and his love of all people. The fool is known in three ways: By his quickness to answer, his volubility, and his faith in all people.

Joseph ibn Zabara, c. 1150
Spanish physician and writer
The Book of Delight

The king [Sigismund III] reigns, but he does not govern.

Jan Zamoyski, 1541–1605
Polish statesman, general, and author
Speech in Polish Parliament, 1605

Leaders focus on emotional issues that connect them with their followers.

John H. Zenger
President, Zenger-Miller, Inc.
Training, December 1985

Among the CEO's I know, the most successful ones have a very positive outlook. Every CEO has to be a cheerleader. At times you feel that you can list a series of disaster scenarios for your company.... Still, you have to be a cheerleader at least part of the time.

Richard A. Zimmerman
CEO, Hershey Foods
Chief Executive, Winter 1986/87

Lead, follow or get out of the way!

Anonymous

What many leaders need today is a bunch of dumb guys who are willing to follow.

Anonymous

Managerial achievement in human organization is not dependent on mechanical devices nor routine methods.... We are leading men, not handling robots.

Anonymous manager
Quoted in *American Management Review*,
November 1923

23

Management Style

Control freaks don't grow good companies.

[Referring to his incoming successor, John Foster Dulles:] He told me that he was not going to work as I had done, but would free himself from involvement with what he referred to as personnel and administrative problems, in order to have more time to think. I wondered how it would turn out.... For it had been my experience that thought was not of much use without knowledge and guidance, and that who should give me both and how competent they would be must depend on who chose, dealt with, assigned and promoted these people and established the organization within which they worked.

Dean Acheson, 1893–1971
U. S. Secretary of State
Sayles, *Managerial Behavior:*
Administration in Complex Organizations
(McGraw-Hill, 1964)

There is a certain blend of courage, integrity, character and principle which has no satisfactory dictionary name but has been called

different things at different times in different countries. Our American name for it is "guts."

Louis Adamic, 1899–1951
American writer
A Study in Courage

Hire the best.
Pay them fairly.
Communicate frequently.
Provide challenges and rewards.
Believe in them.
Get out of their way—
they'll knock your socks off.

Mary Ann Allison
Vice President, CitiCorp
and Eric Anderson
Financial writer
Managing Up, Managing Down
(Simon & Schuster, 1984)

Most good managers inspire loyalty.

Mary Ann Allison
Vice President, CitiCorp
and Eric Anderson
Financial writer
Managing Up, Managing Down
(Simon & Schuster, 1984)

Managers who are skilled communicators may also be good at covering up real problems.

Chris Argyris
Harvard Graduate School of Education
Harvard Business Review,
September/October 1986

People are the key to success in any undertaking, including business. The foremost distinguishing feature of effective managers seems to be their ability to recognize talent and to surround themselves with able colleagues.

Norman R. Augustine
President and CEO, Martin Marietta Corp.
Augustine's Laws (Penguin, 1987)

How to educate broad-gauged professionals for the public service; how to keep professional specialists accountable to politically responsible generalists within the executive and legislative branches; these are at present and prospectively among the most important unresolved issues of public management.

Stephan K. Bailey
President,
American Society of Public Administration
Agenda For the Nation
(The Brookings Institution, 1968)

[Referring to Tandy Chairman John Roach:] After hearing the caller's problem Roach ends 99% of his conversations with the line: "What would you like for me to do?"

David Beckerman
Vice President, Tandy Corp.
Computer & Software News, December 7, 1987

Whether your troops are behind you is the key.

Richard Belous
Labor Economist, Conference Board
The New York Times, April 12, 1988

Most companies spend all their time looking for another management concept and very little time following up the one they have just taught their managers.

Kenneth H. Blanchard
Chairman, Blanchard Training & Development
and Robert Lorber
President, R. L. Lorber & Associates
Putting the One Minute Manager to Work
(William Morrow, 1984)

The art of governing consists in not allowing men to grow old in their jobs.

Napoleon Bonaparte, 1769–1821
Emperor of France
Maxims

He who governs should possess energy without fanaticism, principles without demagogy, severity without cruelty. He must be neither weak nor vacillating, nor must he be ashamed to do his duty.

Napoleon Bonaparte, 1769–1821
Emperor of France
Maxims

The greater the man, the less he is opinionated; he depends on events and circumstances.

Napoleon Bonaparte, 1769–1821
Emperor of France
Maxims

[Commenting on the possibility of participative management:] I'm not going to have the monkeys running the zoo.

Frank Borman
Astronaut and CEO, Eastern Airlines
The Washington Monthly, June 1986

Organizational politics of the most petty and unsavory kind flourish only when only the head feels overall responsibility for the unit. Traditional leaders, who bear such great responsibility for coordinating all activities, by their very existence decrease the responsibility felt by subordinates.

David L. Bradford
Stanford University School of Business
and Allan R. Cohen
Babson College
Managing for Excellence (Wiley, 1984)

It's important if you're successful that you set an example for the people who work for you in the way you conduct your life. You know, jumping on a train rather than jumping in a limousine or going second class rather than first class. Little things are quite important.

Richard Branson
Chairman, Virgin Group (England)
Inc. Magazine, November 1987

I don't say "never" to anything.

Richard M. Bressler
CEO, Burlington Northern Railroad
Business Week, August 3, 1987

[Referring to AT&T Chairman Robert Allen:] He does not hover over you every step of the way.

Hal Burlington
Senior Vice President, AT&T
The New York Times, April 24, 1988

I see myself as a doer. I'm sure that other people have had ideas that were similar to mine. The difference is that I have carried mine into action, and they have not.

Nolan Bushnell
Founder, Atari Computer Co.
Oech, *A Whack on the Side of the Head*
(Warner, 1983)

Try to centralize budget and policy and decentralize operations.

Frank C. Carlucci
U. S. Secretary of Defense
Frank Carlucci on Management in Government
(Center for Excellence in Government, 1987)

Problems are solved on the spot, as soon as they arise. No frontline employee has to wait for a supervisor's permission.

Jan Carlzon
CEO, SAS (Sweden)
Moments of Truth (Ballinger, 1987)

Those who would administer wisely must, indeed, be wise, for one of the serious obstacles to the improvement of our race is indiscriminate charity.

Andrew Carnegie, 1835–1919
American industrialist and philanthropist
The Gospel of Wealth

I praise loudly, I blame softly.

Catherine II ("The Great"), 1729–1796
Empress of Russia
The Complete Works of Catherine II

A man without a smiling face ought not to open a shop.

Chinese proverb

It is absolutely necessary at a time like this that every Minister [of the Cabinet] who tries each day to do his duty shall be respected and their subordinates must know that their chiefs are not threatened men who are here today and gone tomorrow.

Winston Churchill, 1874–1965
English Prime Minister, writer, and soldier
Speech, House of Commons, June 18, 1940

To err is human. To forgive is not my policy.

Joseph Clark
High school principal, Paterson, New Jersey
Nightline (ABC TV), January 4, 1988

Traditional organization theory assumes that human beings always act rationally.... In this view, one issues a directive, it proceeds down through the chain of command, and it is followed.... But ... the directive put in at one end of the system does not always result in the desired action coming out the other end. Varying alliances and informal organizations grow within a formal organization and must be dealt with in some way. Managers may be wasting their time if they keep trying to achieve the impossible: make their people fit into the "rational" world as they see it.

William A. Cohen
Principles of Technical Management
(AMACOM, 1980)

I'm not afraid of being wrong. And I don't take credit for other people's work. So people use me. They use my brain, they use my personality, they use my position.

Deborah A. Coleman
Vice President and CFO, Apple Computer Co.
Working Woman, December 1987

Whenever we find ourselves more inclined to persecute than to persuade, we may then be certain that our zeal has more of pride in it than charity.

Charles Caleb Colton, c. 1780–1832
English cleric, sportsman, and wine merchant
Lacon

[Well-managed, innovative organizations] ... give their people the right to be wrong.

Laurel Cutler
Vice Chairman, FCB/Leber Katz Partners
Inc. Magazine, November 1987

Flexibility is the most requisite qualification for the management of great affairs.

Cardinal de Retz, 1614–1679
French ecclesiastic and politician
Political Maxims

Too impatient to follow the tangled skein through, everyone at one time or another ... finds rest and comfort in making believe that things are not so mixed up as in reality they are, and in deducing some embracing theory from a starched and ironed cosmos.

Henry S. Dennison, 1877–1952
Founder, Dennison Corp.
Organization and Management
(Harvard, 1948)

Little things affect little minds.

Benjamin Disraeli, 1804–1881
English Prime Minister and novelist
Sybil

Professional management may be competent, responsible and performing. But it still faces a severe crisis of legitimacy because it is no longer grounded in yesterday's economic power, that of the capitalistic owner, and is not grounded in anything else so far.

Peter F. Drucker
Management consultant and writer
Management in Turbulent Times
(Harper & Row, 1980)

A manager ... sets objectives ... organizes ... motivates and communicates ... measure[s]... [and] develops people. Every manager does these things—knowingly or not. A manager may do them well, or may do them wretchedly, but always does them.

Peter F. Drucker
Management consultant and writer
People and Performance
(Harper & Row, 1977)

[Advice for lobbyists:] Don't threaten; don't beg; and don't always believe you're right.

Richard Durbin
U. S. Congressman
Speech, Silver Spring, Maryland,
April 19, 1988

The key mission of contemporary management is to transcend the old models which limited the manager's role to that of controller, expert or morale booster. These roles do not produce the desired result of aligning the goals of the employees and the corporation.... These older models, vestiges of a bygone era, have served their function and must be replaced with a model of the manager as a developer of human resources.

Michael Durst
President, Training Systems, Inc.
Small Systems World, August 1985

I cannot do what most of my employees can do, and I'm pleased to let them know it by showing respect for the jobs they do. If I do know how to do their job, I keep that to myself. I want them to feel I'm dependent on them.

Judith Ann Eigen
President, Judith Ann Creations, Inc.
Speech, New York City, January 4, 1988

Self-trust is the first secret of success.

Ralph Waldo Emerson, 1803–1882
American essayist and poet
Success

The fox has many tricks, the hedgehog only one.
[*Multa novit vulpes, verum echinus unum magnum.*]

Desiderius Erasmus, c. 1466–1536
Dutch scholar and theologian
Adagia

I'm not a screamer or a fighter. I just try to work things out.

Jane Evans
Partner, Montgomery Securities Fund
Management Review, December 1987

There is nothing absolute in management affairs.

Henri Fayol, 1841–1925
Pioneer French management scientist
French Trade Association Bulletin, 1916

[The most successful companies at maintaining a competitive edge are] close to ruthless in cannibalizing their current products and processes just when they are the most lucrative and begin the search again, over and over. The best abandon the skills and products that have bought them success.

Dick Foster
Director, McKinsey & Co.
Peters, *Thriving on Chaos* (Knopf, 1987)

"We" rather than "I."

Charles Garfield
President, Performance Sciences Corp.
Peak Performers (Avon, 1986)

The man who delegates responsibilities for running the company, without knowing the intimate details of what is involved, runs the enormous risk of rendering himself superfluous.

Harold Geneen
CEO, IT&T
Managing (Doubleday, 1984)

Management must manage!

Harold Geneen
CEO, IT&T
Managing (Doubleday, 1984)

What you manage in business is people.

Harold Geneen
CEO, IT&T
Managing (Doubleday, 1984)

Management is direct: you don't manage through a memo or committee; it is hands on.

Hazel Frank Gluck
Commissioner,
New Jersey Department of Transportation
The Journal of State Government,
September/October 1987

The aim is [a] transition from an excessively centralized management system relying on orders to a democratic one based on the combination of democratic centralism and self-management.

Mikhail Gorbachev
Premier, USSR
Perestroika (Harper & Row, 1987)

It is commitment, not authority, that produces results.

William L. Gore
Founder and CEO, W. L. Gore & Associates
Naisbett and Aburdene, *Re-inventing the Corporation* (Warner, 1985)

You have to do many things yourself. Things that you cannot delegate.

Nadine Gramling
CEO, Southeastern Metals Manufacturing Co.
Nation's Business, February 1988

The more you want people to have creative ideas and solve difficult problems, the less you can afford to manage them with terror.

Daniel Greenberg
Chairman, Electro Rent Corp.
Newsweek, April 25, 1988

It would be difficult, if not impossible, to provide a highly structured environment that enhances a knowledge worker's method of functioning.

Ira B Gregerman
President, Productivity Associates
Knowledge Worker Productivity
(AMACOM, 1981)

Human beings are compounded of cognition and emotion and do not function well when treated as though they were merely cogs in motion.... The task of the administrator must be accomplished less by coercion and discipline, and more and more by persuasion.... Management of the future must look more to leadership and less to authority as the primary means of coordination.

Luther H. Gulick
President and Chairman,
National Institute of Public Administration
Papers on the Science of Administration, 1937

No one can be right all of the time, but it helps to be right most of the time.

Robert Half
President, Robert Half International
Robert Half on Hiring (Crown, 1985)

American management in the past has been singularly blind to the needs of human beings. Management wants to eliminate the human equation from business.

Edward T. Hall
Anthropologist and social researcher
Science, July 1985

[Manufacturing] excellence results from dedication to daily progress. Making something a little bit better every day.

Robert Hall
Indiana University
Peters, *Thriving on Chaos* (Knopf, 1987)

[Explaining her program of having she and other company officers lunch with other employees:] It's vital ... to assure them that they're not considered "kitchen help."

Lore Harp
Former President, Vector
Deal and Kennedy, *Corporate Cultures*
(Addison-Wesley, 1982)

You can't manage employees any more than you can manage customers. But there are things that you can do to keep them satisfied.

Paul Hawken
Founder, Smith & Hawken
Growing A Business (Simon & Schuster, 1987)

Many people equate good management with perfection. This is a fallacy. If perfection could be achieved, there would be no need for management.

James L. Hayes
President and CEO,
American Management Association
Memos for Management: Leadership
(AMACOM, 1983)

Effective managers live in the present—but concentrate on the future.

James L. Hayes
President and CEO,
American Management Association
Memos for Management: Leadership
(AMACOM, 1983)

American management, especially in the two decades after World War II, was universally admired for its strikingly effective performance. But times change. An approach shaped and refined during stable decades may be ill suited to a world characterized by rapid and unpredictable change, scarce energy, global competition for markets, and a constant need for innovation. This is the world of the 1980's and, probably, the rest of this century.

Robert H. Hayes and William J. Abernathy
Harvard Business Review, July/August 1980

If necessary [when a critical deadline is not met], we all go down to that department and help the manager meet the deadline.

Leonard V. Haynes
Chief of Operations,
Shearson Lehman Brothers
The New York Times, January 10, 1988

The executive must choose between using his power to strengthen the organization and using his power to strengthen his personal power base.

Bruce Henderson
CEO, Boston Consulting Group, Inc.
Henderson on Corporate Strategy (Abt, 1979)

Pardon all but thyself.

George Herbert, 1593–1633
English clergyman and poet
Jacula Prudentum

Every measure taken with temerity is liable to be perplexed with error, and punished by misfortune.

Herodotus, fifth century B.C.
Greek "Father of History"
History of the Persian War

'Twixt kings and tyrants there's this difference known:
Kings seek their subjects' good, tyrants their own.

Robert Herrick, 1591–1674
English poet
Hesperides

We manage with a mission. We don't strive for superior or excellent management. We strive to manage *for* the mission. We never lose sight of the fact that we are in this business to help girls grow.

Frances Hesselbein
Executive Director, Girl Scouts U.S.A.
Management Review, April 1987

I don't mean to sound arrogant, but it's my ass that's on the line.

Robert S. Hillman
CEO, The Eyecare Co.
Inc. Magazine, November 1987

I have always had an operating style of having things piled on my desk within arm's reach—to save time.... Piles are arranged for urgency—one stack for things to do as soon as possible; another for semi-urgent matters; another for "can wait till you get around to it;" another for leisure reading. This does make for a messy-looking shop...

K. R. Hinkley
President, Houston Light & Power Co.
Mackenzie, *The Time Trap*
(McGraw-Hill, 1972)

It has long been an axiom of mine that the little things are infinitely the most important.

Sherlock Holmes
(Arthur Conan Doyle), 1859–1930
English physician, writer, and sportsman
A Case of Identity

I just couldn't just sit in an office and issue orders.

Robert B. Horton
CEO, British Petroleum America
The New York Times, January 10, 1988

The superior man encourages people to approach him, by his readiness to receive them.

I Ching: Book of Changes
China, c. 600 B.C.

The triumph of hope over experience.

Samuel Johnson, 1709–1784
English lexicographer and critic
Boswell's Life of Dr. Johnson

Moderation is power.

George W. Keeton
Harris's Hints on Advocacy, 1943

Hemingway's *For Whom the Bell Tolls* takes place during the Spanish Civil War. It contrasts the accomplishments of Robert Jordan, an American who fights for the Loyalists, with the failure of a Fascist captain. Jordan, who listens and learns from the guerillas, accomplishes his goal. But the captain relies on his pistols and threats and is abandoned.

Beverly Kempton
Business writer
Working Woman, October 1987

Our restraint is not inexhaustible.

John Fitzgerald Kennedy, 1917–1963
Thirty-fifth President of the United States
Speech to the
American Society of Newspaper Editors,
Washington, D.C., April 20, 1961

The CEO ... must be constantly dissatisfied with something. But you must be careful, because people who are constantly dissatisfied, such as George Steinbrenner, are not fun to work for.

Robert Kennedy
CEO, Union Carbide
Financial World, April 5, 1988

The time to be toughest is when things are going the best.

> Donald E. Keogh
> President, Coca Cola
> *Working Woman*, March 1988

It seems to me that we too often focus on the inside aspects of the job of management, failing to give proper attention to the requirement for a good manager to maintain those relationships between his organization and the enviornment in which it must operate which permits it to move ahead and get the job done.

> Breene Kerr
> Manager, NASA
> Haught, *Giants in Management*
> (National Academy of
> Public Administration, 1985)

Management's ability to get the best from people increases when it chooses to share its power.

> Tony Kizilos and Roger P. Heinisch
> Systems and Research Center of Aerospace
> and Defense, Honeywell Corp.
> *Harvard Business Review*,
> September/October 1986

To lead the people, walk behind them.

> Lao-Tzu, c. 604–c. 531 B.C.
> Chinese philosopher and founder of Taoism
> *Tao Te Ching*

Things refuse to be mismanaged for long.
[*Res nollunt diu male administrari.*]

> Latin proverb

We're opportunistic ... we will seize the moment.

> Reginald Lewis
> Partner, TLC Group
> *USA Today*, December 23, 1987

I shall try to correct errors where shown to be errors, and I shall adopt new views as fast as they shall appear to be true views.

> Abraham Lincoln, 1809–1865
> Sixteenth President of the United States
> Letter to Horace Greeley,
> August 22, 1862

Managers can easily become too absorbed by form and insufficiently concerned with substance.

> Peter Lorange
> The Wharton School
> and Robert T. Nelson
> Management consultant
> *Sloan Management Review*, Spring 1987

Discussing novels, plays and short stories is a nonthreatening way for people in responsible positions to consider what is important and not important .... They can ask fundamental questions about themselves and the ways in which they operate.

> Sanford Lotter
> Brandeis University
> *Working Woman*, October 1987

Be not careless in deeds, nor confused in words, nor rambling in thought.

> Marcus Aurelius, 121–180
> Roman Emperor and Stoic philosopher
> *Meditations*

I favor a very democratic, open, egalitarian atmosphere combined with a slightly mysterious, benevolent authority.

> Fritz Maytag
> President, Anchor Brewing Co.
> *Harvard Business Review*, July/August 1986

I want candor, but I don't want anyone to ask me for patience.

> T. Allen McArtor
> Administrator, FAA
> Speech, Washington, D.C., July 27, 1987

I'm naturally a delegator. I guess I realized early in life that, unless you're going to be a violinist or something, your success will probably depend on other people.

> William G. McGowan
> Chairman, MCI Communications Corp.
> *Inc. Magazine*, August 1986

[When asked how he could be so familiar with the details of the Defense budget:] I do my own work.

> Robert S. McNamara
> President, Ford Motor Co., U. S. Secretary of
> Defense, and President of the The World Bank
> Haught, *Giants in Management*
> (National Academy of
> Public Administration, 1985)

Decide whether you are facing a managed or an unmanaged crisis; determine where you are on the pain curve and in the crisis sequence. Size up your company's standing in terms of the four major crisis factors: *dimension*, *control*, *time*, and *options* ... and if you are in the jaws of a crisis, face up to the fact.

> Gerald C. Meyers
> Chairman, American Motors
> *When It Hits the Fan* (Houghton Mifflin, 1986)

[In a crisis:] Resist the pressure to take premature action. Talk to your people individually to find the crisis heroes, the handful of managers who have a clear understanding of the situation, see it the way you do, and can deal with any ambiguity involved. After you find them, tell them what you expect and lean on them hard.

> Gerald C. Meyers
> Chairman, American Motors
> *When It Hits the Fan* (Houghton Mifflin, 1986)

Success depends on three things: who says it, what he says, how he says it; and of these three things, what he says is the least important.

> John Morley, 1838–1923
> English statesman and man of letters
> *Recollections*

It's not that I don't have opinions, rather that I'm paid not to think aloud.

> Yitzchak Navon
> President of Israel
> Face the Nation (TV program), 1978

Use your own best judgement at all times.

> Nordstrom Corp.
> Entire contents of $1.9 billion company's
> *Policy Manual*

One quality that has brought many executives up to their present positions is their ability to handle emergencies and to work under pressure. But an executive, in order to grow and endure, will soon find it imperative to concentrate on the elimination of emergencies.

> E. B. Osborn
> President, Economics Laboratory, Inc.
> *Executive Development Manual* (ELI, 1959)

I tell division managers if they have a profit problem, I give them about two years to fix it. But if they have a people problem, I give them about two weeks.

> Bill Parzybok
> Vice President, Hewlitt-Packard
> Naisbett and Aburdene, *Re-inventing the Corporation* (Warner, 1985)

Managing upward relies on informal relationships, timing, exploiting ambiguity, and implicit communication. And the irony of it all is that these most subtle skills must be learned and mastered by younger managers who not only lack education and directed experience in benign guerilla warfare but are further misguided by management myths which contribute to false expectations and a misleading perception of reality.

> Richard T. Pascale
> Stanford University School of Business
> and Anthony G. Athos
> Harvard Business School
> *The Art of Japanese Management*
> (Simon & Schuster, 1981)

Don't duck the most difficult problems. That just insures that the hardest part will be left when you're most tired. Get the big one done—it's downhill from then on.

> Norman Vincent Peale
> Clergyman and inspirational speaker
> *Reader's Digest*, January 1972

[Franklin Roosevelt] didn't like concentrated responsibility. Agreement with other people who he thought were good, right-minded, and trying to do the right thing by the world was almost as necessary to him as air to breathe.

> Frances Perkins, 1882–1965
> U. S. Secretary of Labor
> *The Roosevelt I Knew*

The first EDSer to see a snake kills it. At GM, the first thing you do is organize a committee on snakes. Then you bring in a consultant who knows a lot about snakes. Third thing you do is talk about it for a year.

> H. Ross Perot
> Founder, Electronic Data Systems
> Peters, *Thriving on Chaos* (Knopf, 1987)

Give a lot, expect a lot, and if you don't get it, prune.

> Tom Peters
> Business Writer
> *Thriving on Chaos* (Knopf, 1987)

[The best people-centered managers] model exorbitantly high standards. They demand a lot, but show by energetic example what they demand.... They delegate.... Workers are set out on their own to constantly innovate.... They clear hurdles from the employees path.... They're obsessive about trying things.... They motivate through an inspiring vision.... They may or may not pat people on the back often ... they do something much more important.... They unmistakably demonstrate belief in the talent of and concern for the dignity of each worker.

> Tom Peters
> Business Writer
> *Washington Business Journal*,
> August 24, 1987

Perseverance is more prevailing than violence; and many things which cannot be overcome together, yield themselves when taken little by little.

> Plutarch, c. 46–c. 120
> Greek biographer and philosopher
> *The Parallel Lives: Sertorius*

Impulse manages all affairs badly.

> Portugese proverb

Reprove your friends in secret, praise them in public.

> Publilius Syrus, c. 42 B.C.
> Roman writer
> *Maxims*

Never promise more than you can perform.

Publilius Syrus, c. 42 B.C.
Roman writer
Maxims

The style of participative management is at its best when the supervisor can draw out the best in his people, allow decisions to be made at the point of influence and contribution, and create a spirit that everyone is in it together and that if something is unknown, they'll learn it together.

Joseph A. Raelin
Boston College School of Management
Clash of Cultures: Managers and Professionals
(Harvard Business School, 1986)

Even with little ongoing change about them, managers sometimes find they need to have high flex in the apparently unchanging job they have. A manager supervising ten men might easily find that two work best when left alone, two need continuous direction, three need to be motivated by objectives, and three others need a supportive climate. So, in the space of a day an effective manager may well use all four basic styles [of management] when dealing with such a variety as a dependent subordinate, an aggressive pair of coworkers, a secretary whose work has deteriorated, and his superior who is interested only in the immediate task at hand.... To the extent the organization and technology allow individual treatment, a high-flex and sensitive manager could satisfy the demands of all these different situations and so achieve maximum effectiveness.

W. J. Reddin
Managerial Effectiveness
(McGraw-Hill, 1970)

He is an incorrigible believer. He believes in everything that works.

James Reston
Syndicated columnist, *The New York Times*
Prochnow, *The Toastmaster's Treasure Chest*
(Harper & Row 1979)

I never give them [the players] negative feedback.

John Robinson
College and professional football coach
Quoted by Bennis, January 21, 1988

Mismanagement openly acknowledged is a sign of democracy; in tyrannies there *seems* to be always perfection.

Dagobert D. Runes
Editor, publisher, and philosopher
A Book of Contemplation

Most managers, most of the time, treat the happenings of the past as if they were the permanent or given nature of things, rather than simply things that occurred in the past.

Kenneth and Linda Schatz
Leadership and management consultants
Management By Influence (Prentice-Hall, 1986)

The successful manager must be a good diagnostician and must value a spirit of inquiry.

Edgar H. Schein
Massachusetts Institute of Technology
Organizational Psychology
(Prentice-Hall, 1965)

Self confidence is important. Confidence in others is essential.

William A. Schreyer
CEO, Merrill Lynch & Co., Inc.
American Heritage, April 1988

You don't fool around and worry about whether you have white drapes or yellow drapes in your office. You worry about how to make the payroll.

Peter L. Scott
Chairman, Emhart Corp.
Sky, August 1, 1987

In the industrial age, the CEO sat on the top of the hierarchy and didn't really have to listen to anybody.... In the information age, you have to listen to the ideas of people regardless of where they are in the organization.

John Sculley
CEO, Apple Computer Co.
Nation's Business Today (TV program), 1987

Give every man thine ear, but few thy voice; Take each man's censure, but reserve thy judgment.

William Shakespeare, 1564–1616
English dramatist and poet
Hamlet

The reasonable man adapts himself to the world; the unreasonable one persists in trying to adapt the world to himself. Therefore, all progress depends on the unreasonable man.

George Bernard Shaw, 1856–1950
Nobel laureate in literature
Man and Superman

Power does not kill; it permits suicide.

Earl Shorris
Manager and writer
Power Sits at Another Table (Fireside, 1986)

Executives spend too much time analyzing and too little time acting.

Philip Smith
Chairman, General Foods
Fortune, September 28, 1987

I don't put up with foolishness.

Melvin Smoak
Principal, Orangeburg-Wilkinson High School
Newsweek, May 2, 1988

[Some] high-level executives ... maintain their *own power* or the *power of their divisions* with some disregard for profit implications.

Ross Stagner
Michigan State University
Business Topics (MSU, Winter 1965)

They that live in a trading street are not disturbed at the passage of carts.

Richard Steele, 1672–1729
English writer
The Spectator

[Referring to lawyers, accountants, and consultants:] Manage them before they manage you.

Howard H. Stevenson and William A. Sahlman
Harvard Business School
Harvard Business Review, March/April 1988

Endeavor to emulate the laser. Scan the landscape and manscape; eclectically collect observations and reflections; enlighten and illuminate; inform and educate; cut and sculpt with precision.

William C. Stwalley
Director, Center for Laser Science,
University of Iowa
Speech, Iowa City, April 23, 1988

Hire the best people and then delegate.

Carol A. Taber
Publisher, *Working Woman*
Management, October 1986

It is highly important for managers to be honest and clear in describing what authority they are keeping and what role they are asking their subordinates to assume.

Robert Tannenbaum
UCLA School of Management
and Warren H. Schmidt
UCLA School of Public Administration
Harvard Business Review, March/April 1978

What short term CEO will take a long-term view when it lowers his own income? Only a saint, and there aren't very many saints.

Lester C. Thurow
Dean, Sloan School of Management, M. I. T.
Newsweek, December 7, 1981

Control freaks don't grow good companies.

Jeffery A. Timmons
Babson College
Inc. Magazine, April 1986

People in organizations are different—and the differences create the major problem for managers.

Henry L. Tosi
University of Florida
and Stephen J. Carroll
University of Maryland
Management (John Wiley & Sons, 1976)

[Referring to President Zachary Taylor:] He became expert at doing nothing.

Harry S. Truman, 1884–1972
Thirty-third President of the United States
Miller, *More Plain Speaking*

The office is a fine place for day to day activity. But it's not the best place for big thinking.

W. E. Uzzell
President, Royal Crown Cola Co.
Mackenzie, *The Time Trap*
(McGraw-Hill, 1972)

Style is knowing who you are, what you want to say, and not giving a damn.

Gore Vidal
American writer
Daily Express

There are truths which are not for all men, nor for all times.

François Marie Voltaire, 1694–1778
French writer
Letter to Cardinal de Bernis

When you're right you take the bows, and when you're wrong you make the apologies.

Benjamin Ward
Police Commissioner, New York City
The New York Times, April 27, 1988

I don't like a lot of paper.... I rely on my memory and telephone contacts.

Ralph E. Ward
CEO, Chesebrough-Pond, Inc.
Management, January 1987

[T]he opinion and advice of my friends I receive at all times as a proof of their friendship and am thankful when they are offered.

George Washington, 1732–1799
First President of the United States
Letter to Robert R. Livingston, June 29, 1780

Isolation of top management is accepted in some quarters as a regrettable but inevitable result of doing business on a large scale. Not so at the better companies. They have made curiosity an institutional attribute. They listen to their customers of course. They also listen to competitors, first-line employees, suppliers, consultants, outside directors, politicians, and just about anyone else.

Robert H. Waterman
Management consultant and writer
The Renewal Factor (Bantam, 1987)

[Well-managed modern organizations] treat everyone as a source of creative input. What's most interesting is that they cannot be described as either democratically or autocratically managed. Their managers define the boundaries, and their people figure out the best way to do the job within those boundaries. The management style is an astonishing combination of direction and empowerment. They give up tight control in order to gain control over what counts: results.

Robert H. Waterman
Management consultant and writer
The Renewal Factor (Bantam, 1987)

One of the challenges was not to overreact [to threats and competitors].

Thomas J. Watson, Jr.
CEO, IBM, and U. S. Ambassador to Russia
Fortune, 1977

The lack of the alternatives to the establishment's management style makes it difficult for minorities to progress.

Patti Watts
Assistant Editor, *Management Review*
Management Review, December 1987

We [managers] must be willing to prove that we know what we're doing.

Patricia A. Weir
President, Encyclopedia Britannica
Speech, Houston, July 14, 1987

Seek simplicity, and distrust it.

Alfred North Whitehead, 1861–1947
English mathematician and philosopher
Science and the Modern World

The management practices that can cure a troubled company could have kept it well.

John R. Whitney
Executive-in-Residence,
Columbia University Business School
Harvard Business Review,
September/October 1987

Put your personnel work first because it is the most important.

Robert E. Wood, 1879–1969
President and Chairman, Sears Roebuck & Co.
Memo to territorial officers, December, 1931

While systems are important, our main reliance must always be put on men rather than on systems.

Robert E. Wood, 1879–1969
President and Chairman, Sears Roebuck & Co.
Memo to officers and Retail Policy Committee,
October 27, 1938

You must be able to work systematically, to be able to distinguish the main tasks from the routine.

Lev Zaikov
Chief, Moscow Communist Party,
and Politburo member
Newsweek, April 4, 1988

Among the CEO's I know, the most successful ones have a very positive outlook. Every CEO has to be a cheerleader. At times you feel that you can list a series of disaster scenarios for your company ... still, you have to be a cheerleader at least part of the time.

Richard A. Zimmerman
CEO, Hershey Foods
Chief Executive, Winter 1986-1987

A businessman is aggressive; a businesswoman is pushy. He's good on details; she's fussy. He loses his temper because he's so involved in his job; she's bitchy.

He follows through; she doesn't know when to give up. His judgments are her prejudices. He is a man of the world; she's been around. He climbed the ladder to success; she slept her way to the top. He's a stern taskmaster; she's hard to work for.

Anonymous

The lion tamer school of management: Keep them well fed and never let them know that all you've got is a chair and a whip.

Anonymous

24

Marketing

Treat the customer as an appreciating asset.

The worm lures the fish, not the fisherman and his tackle.

> Angler's maxim

To the place where green vegetables are brought in abundance, bring thine also to sell.

> Babylonian Talmud, Menahot

While the dust is still on your feet, sell what you have brought to the market.

> Babylonian Talmud, Pesahim

Every crowd has a silver lining.

> Phineas Taylor (P. T.) Barnum, 1810–1891
> American circus owner and showman
> Favorite saying

Not very many years ago, professionals could count on their reputations and country club contacts to obtain a steady stream of clients or patients. Today, though, lawyers, accountants, management consultants, architects, engineers, dentists, doctors, and other profes-sionals must do extensive marketing to maintain and build their practices.... Two increasingly popular choices for educating and "comforting" buyers are seminars and newsletters.

> Paul N. Bloom
> University of Maryland
> *Harvard Business Review*,
> September/October 1984

There is no such thing as "soft sell" or "hard sell." There is only "smart sell" and "stupid sell."

> Charles Brower
> President, Batton, Barton, Durstine & Osborn
> *Editor & Publisher*, December 7, 1957

Who borrows to build, builds to sell.

> Chinese proverb

I don't set trends. I just find out what they are and I exploit them.

> Dick Clark
> Disk jockey and studio executive
> Rowes, *The Book of Quotes* (Dutton, 1979)

Too often, we view foreign markets as dumping grounds for our surplus products.

> Philip Cotler
> Kellogg School of Management,
> Northwestern University
> *The New York Times,* February 21, 1988

Today, if you try to appeal to everybody by being bland and inoffensive, somebody is going to come in and begin to pick off significant chunks of your market.

> Laurel Cutler
> Vice Chairman, FCB/Leber Katz Partners
> *Inc. Magazine*, November 1987

The marketer is too often caught up in research, which is oriented more to the past than the future.

> Laurel Cutler
> Vice Chairman, FCB/Leber Katz Partners
> *Inc. Magazine*, November 1987

Most market research is a crock of ...

> Laurel Cutler
> Vice Chairman, FCB/Leber Katz Partners
> *Inc. Magazine*, November 1987

In many ways, marketing is like life. It seems that those who get ahead in life are natural born marketers. Elected politicians, your company's president, and all those whom society respects mastered the ability to successfully and visibly serve a constituency, shareholders or other target market.

> Jeffrey P. Davidson
> Marketing consultant
> *Management World*, September/October 1987

The average sale is made after the prospect has said "no" six times.

> Jeffrey P. Davidson
> Marketing consultant
> *The Washington Post*, May 20, 1985

It takes an accountant to sell accounting services.

> Robert Denney
> *Practical Accountant*, July 1981

[F]oreign managers take marketing seriously. In most American companies marketing still means no more than systematic selling. Foreigners today have absorbed more fully the true meaning of marketing: knowing what is value for the customer.

> Peter F. Drucker
> Management consultant and writer
> *The Changing World of the Executive*
> (Quadrangle, 1982)

Marketing ... is the whole business seen from the point of view of its final result, that is, from the customer's point of view. Concern and responsibility for marketing must, therefore, permeate all areas of the enterprise.

> Peter F. Drucker
> Management consultant and writer
> *People and Performance*
> (Harper & Row, 1977)

Because its purpose is to create a customer, the business enterprise has two—and only these two—basic functions: marketing and innovation. Marketing and innovation produce results; all the rest are "costs."

> Peter Drucker
> Management consultant & writer
> *People and Performance*
> (Harper and Row, 1977)

When goods multiply, so do their consumers.

> Old Testament, Ecclesiastes (Qoheleth) 5:10

Tomorrow, not one single thing of significance will occur in this nation—not one law will be passed, not one product purchased, not one management decision made, not one couple would get married—but that somebody had not sold a product, an idea or a concept to someone else. Marketing enables all other sophisticated human activity.

Lewis D. Eigen
Executive Vice President,
University Research Corp.
Marketing memorandum, February 17, 1980

In analysing history do not be too profound, for often the causes are quite superficial.

Ralph Waldo Emerson, 1803–1882
American essayist and poet
Journals

The craft of the merchant is this bringing a thing where it abounds to where it is costly.

Ralph Waldo Emerson, 1803–1882
American essayist and poet
Wealth

No living being is held by anything so strongly as its own needs.

Epictetus, c. 60–120
Roman Stoic philosopher
Encheiridon

Presenting a professional, upbeat face to the public does wonders for the way people perceive your business.

Steve Estridge
CEO, Temps & Co.
Inc. Magazine, February 1988

In *mass marketing*, a company seeks to appeal to a broad range of consumers by utilizing a single basic marketing program. In *market segmentation*, a company seeks to appeal to one well-defined consumer group by one marketing plan. In *multiple segmentation*, a company seeks to appeal to two or more well-defined consumer groups by different marketing plans.

Joel R. Evans and Barry Berman
Hofstra University
Essentials of Marketing (Macmillan, 1984)

The importance of marketing in a firm is evident when marketing is given line (decision-making) authority, the rank of the chief marketing officer is equal to that of others (usually vice-president), and adequate resources are provided. Marketing is not considered important by a firm that gives marketing staff advisory status, places marketing in a subordinate position (such as reporting to the production vice-president), equates marketing with sales, and withholds the resources needed to research, advertise, and conduct other marketing activities.... The smaller the role of marketing, the greater the possibility that the firm operates its marketing activities on a project, crisis, and fragmented basis.

Joel R. Evans and Barry Berman
Hofstra University
Essentials of Marketing (Macmillan, 1984)

Salesmanship is intuitive; it's a personality kind of thing, with maybe a bit of hocus pocus.

Manny Feris
National Sales Manager, Rambusch Lighting
Inc. Magazine, January 1988

Would you persuade, speak of interest, not of reason.

Benjamin Franklin, 1706–1790
American printer and statesman
Poor Richard's Almanack

No trend lasts forever. Every market is maturing. Growth and decay is as natural a process in business as it is biologically. This means that there are trends underway today, however imperceptible, that will affect the way you do business in the future—or determine whether you will be in business many years from now.

William H. Franklin, Jr.
Georgia State University
Financial Strategies, Fall 1987

Salespeople are idiosyncratic.

Richard P. Fried
President, Kanon Bloch Carre & Co.
Inc. Magazine, January 1988

In the affluent society no useful distinction can be made between luxuries and necessities.

John Kenneth Galbraith
Economist and diplomat
The Affluent Society (Houghton Mifflin, 1958)

The Dependence Effect: As a society becomes increasingly affluent, wants are increasingly created by the process by which they are satisfied.

John Kenneth Galbraith
Economist and diplomat
The Affluent Society (Houghton Mifflin, 1958)

Who would make money must begin by spending.

Carlo Goldoni, 1707–1792
Italian dramatist
La Bella Verita

When you design a product that flies off the shelves, it's just a matter of time before someone copies it.

Francis Goldwyn
President, Manhattan Toy Co., Ltd.
Working Woman, February 1988

We distinguished ourselves through our marketing.

Elizabeth Gould
Vice President, National Graphics
Nation's Business, January 1988

Marketing is very closely related to the art of *selling*. In fact, that's the reason for its existence. So I think it would be extremely useful for you to work in *sales*—of any kind. There's a lot in the sales process that's independent of the goods and services being sold, and much of it you can only learn through experience.

Andrew S. Grove
CEO, Intel Corp.
One-On-One With Andy Grove
(G. P. Putnam's Sons, 1987)

MEDAL OF DEFIANCE. *Awarded in recognition of extraordinary contempt and defiance beyond the normal call of engineering duty.* In total defiance of adverse market studies and surveys concluding the existence of no more than 50 large-screen electrostatic displays, Charles H. House, using all means available —principally pen, tongue, and airplane—to extol an unrecognized technical contribution, planted the seeds of a new market resulting in the shipment of 17,769 large screen displays to date.

Hewlett-Packard
Award presented to Charles House
April 1, 1982

Too many of my products seemed to be competing with each other.

Winston R. Hindle, Jr.
Senior Vice President,
General Electric Plastics
The New York Times, February 21, 1988

[Question asked of Albert Einstein while cutting his hair:] Tom [Edison] had the light bulb, the phonograph and motion pictures....

Did very well for himself. How's the relativity selling?

Miller Hocht
Barber
Omni, March 1988

Consulting is a business as well as a profession, and you must never lose sight of that. If being businesslike ever costs you a client or a sale, it is almost certain that the client or sale would not have been worth having.

Herman Holtz
Government Operations consultant
How to Succeed as an Independent Consultant
(John Wiley & Sons, 1983)

Sadly we are not moving toward a service economy, but a no-service economy.

Thomas R. Horton
President and CEO,
American Management Association
Speech to the Commonwealth Club,
San Francisco, January 11, 1988

Serve and sell.

Early IBM slogan

Merchants have no country.

Thomas Jefferson, 1743–1826
Third President of the United States
Letter to Horatio G. Spafford, March 17, 1814

A salesman guards his Rolodex more than anything else. It's his meal ticket.

Richard Jennings
Sales Manager, CardioData Corp.
Inc. Magazine, January 1988

Inexperienced salespeople ... will benefit from the professionalism, anticipation of questions and objections, and other fail-safe mechanisms that are often inherent in a company-prepared memorized audiovisual, or flip chart presentation. Consequently, this method should be considered when qualified new salespeople are scarce and when brevity of training is essential.

Marvin A. Jolson
Journal of Marketing, January 1975

You can hype a questionable product for a little while, but you'll never build an enduring business.

Victor Kiam
CEO, Remington
United Magazine, January 1984

[In selling:] Don't settle into a routine. It may seem easy to learn one approach or one set of "rules" ... but this can lead you into a standard dialogue that can put your customers to sleep.

Bernie Latt
Director of Retail Systems Management,
Distribution Plus, Inc.
Distribution Plus Dealer's Guide, 1987

Sell solutions, not just products.

Klaus M. Leisinger
Department Director, Ciba-Geigy, Ltd.
The New York Times, February 21, 1988

The real issue is value, not price.

Robert T. Lindgren
Cross & Trecker Corp.
Harvard Business Review, March/April 1988

Once you're face to face with a prospect, the key to selling is the ability to listen—not the ability to talk.

Phillip Matlick
Sales trainer and motivation consultant
Speech, New York, June 1976

If companies think only about sharing the markets, they will never get involved in emerging businesses. They'll take a look at the business, decide that the "pie" is too small, and move on to other possibilities.

Regis McKenna
Marketing consultant and writer
The Regis Touch (Addison-Wesley, 1986)

Marketing is the logical extension of quality client service. A [law] firm that takes the time and effort to find out what their existing clients like or dislike about their service, and in what areas these clients require additional legal service, already is doing a competent job of marketing.

Steve Nelson
Business writer
Of Counsel, October 5, 1987

You can [have] professionals do market research, make arrangements for seminars, and the like, but the task of marketing [legal services] ultimately has to be performed by the lawyer.

Howard Nemerovski
Managing Partner, Howard, Rice, Nemerovski,
Canady, Robertson, & Falk
Of Counsel, October 5, 1987

[Referring to retail merchandising programs such as galleries:] You have to let the customer know that you stand behind it.

Mary Ninos
Buyer, Marshall Field
Gift Reporter, April 1988

There is always a way to maneuver so that you can find success in the market place.

Nick Nishiwaki
President, Ranmaru Corp.
Gift Reporter, April 1988

As marketers, we have to bring our vision down to a useful level.

William Olsten
CEO, Olsten Services Corp.
Success, February 1988

Don't forget that it [your product or service] is not differentiated until the customer understands the difference.

Tom Peters
Business writer
Thriving on Chaos (Knopf, 1987)

Treat the customer as an appreciating asset.

Tom Peters
Business writer
Thriving on Chaos (Knopf, 1987)

The heart and soul of competing is knowing how to appeal to your customers.

Don Peterson
Chairman, Ford Motor Co.
Speech, San Francisco, July 1, 1987

Cutting prices is usually insanity if the competition can go as low as you can.

Michael Porter
Harvard Business School
Newsweek, April 25, 1988

They that buy an office must sell something.

Barber, *The Book of 1000 Proverbs*, 1876

It is an economic fact of life that in a competitive marketplace, the effectiveness of marketing is the primary determinant of business success.

Sonia Rappaport
Principal, Rappaport & Associates
The Washington Lawyer,
January/February 1987

Create demand.

Charles Revson
Founder, Revlon
Watchwords to Managers

We sell everything.

Giorgio Ronchi
President, Memorex Telex (Netherlands)
Forbes, April 4, 1988

People come here [her store] to brighten up....
We want people to feel the electricity.

Nancy Schrag
Owner, Seasons
Gift Reporter, April 1988

He that would live by traffic must hold himself at the disposal of everyone claiming business with him.

Walter Scott, 1771–1832
Scottish poet, novelist, and biographer
Ivanhoe

No great marketing decisions have ever been made on quantitative data.

John Sculley
CEO, Apple Computer
Rowan, *The Intuitive Manager*
(Little, Brown & Company, 1986)

Take a straw and throw it up into the air, you shall see by that which way the wind is.

John Selden, 1584–1654
English jurist, Orientalist, and statesman
Table Talk

The name of the game is new products.

Michael Shrimi
CFO, Bortz Chocolate Novelties, Inc.
The New York Times, May 1, 1988

If trade shows work for you, you have to work for the trade shows.

Jonathan P. Siegel
Information Communications Associates
Communications, October 1987

Objectives for sales promotion programs are rarely established and, when they are established, are not likely to be in quantitative terms. This shortcoming applies to the plan as a whole and to individual programs. Promotions may be scheduled simply because "there was one last year," or because competitors have them, or because of demands from the sales force for something to be done in their region.

Roger A. Strang
Harvard Business Review, July/August 1976

Fifty percent of Japanese companies do not have a marketing department, and ninety percent have no special section for marketing research. The reason is that everyone is considered to be a marketing specialist.

Hirotaka Takeuchi
Harvard Business School
Cherry Blossoms and Robotics
(Young Presidents' Organization, 1983)

Most of our competitors were manufacturing-oriented, generations of fine pickle makers and proud of it. We came in exactly the opposite, as marketers who manufactured [in order] to have something to sell.

Robert S. Vlasic
President, Vlasic Foods
Sevareid, *Enterprise: The Making of Business in America* (McGraw-Hill, 1983)

In the past you could enter markets at your own pace. Today you have to learn what customers want, make it and sell it, or someone else will.

E. Kirby Warren
Columbia University School of Business
The New York Times, February 21, 1988

Now they've hit a flat market or a down market and they aren't equipped for that, emotionally or otherwise.

Q. T. Wiles
Turnaround Operations consultant
Inc. Magazine, February 1988

[Referring to sales:] When it's good, you think it'll never get bad. When it's bad, you think it'll never get good.

Paul H. Young, Jr.
CEO, Paul Young Auto Mall
Hispanic Business, June 1987

When formulating policies or solving problems that cut across all functional departments, the marketer brings assumptions, concepts, and patterns of behavior that differ significantly from those of other managers.... The marketing manager often appears especially provocative and perplexing.... Relationships with other managers are valuable to the marketer only to the extent that they contribute to more effective marketing relationships with the important others outside the firm.

Dale E. Zand
New York University
Information, Organization, and Power
(McGraw-Hill, 1981)

What our industries lack ... what they lack more and more, is markets.

Anonymous French Government Minister, 1885
Heilbroner, *The Worldly Philosophers*
(Simon & Schuster, 1956)

25

Meetings, Committees, & Task Forces

A camel is a horse designed by a committee.

Interpersonal competence [is] ... the individual's ability to produce intended effects in such a way that he can continue to do so.

Chris Argyis
Harvard Graduate School of Education
Interrpersonal Competence and Organizational Effectiveness (Irwin, 1962)

Because the executives [trying to avoid interpersonal problems] don't say what they really mean or test the assumptions they really hold, their skills inhibit a resolution of the important intellectual issues.... Thus the meetings end with only lists and no decisions.... People's tendency to avoid conflict, to duck tough issues, becomes institutionalized and leads to a culture that can't tolerate straight talk.

Chris Argyris
Harvard Graduate School of Education
Harvard Business Review,
September/October 1986

A sudden, bold, and unexpected question doth many times surprise a man and lay him open.

Francis Bacon, 1561–1624
Lord Chancellor of England
Of Cunning

A long table and a square table, or seats about the walls, seem things of form, but are things of substance; for at a long table a few at the upper end sway all the business; but in the other form there is more use of the counselors' opinions that sit lower.

Francis Bacon, 1561–1626
Lord Chancellor of England
Of Counsel

Groupthink ... happens when a discussion results in convergence on invalid conclusions.... The problem itself may be incorrectly identified and the quality of inquiry of group discussion may not be good enough to challenge it. Or options for solving the problem... may not be fully identified....

When thinking is shallow, convergence may appear prematurely and may not be subject to challenge....[Poor quality decisions were often] made by a highly cohesive group that was relatively isolated.

Robert J. Blake and Jane S. Mouton
Scientific Methods, Inc.
Productivity: The Human Side
(AMACOM, 1981)

If a problem causes many meetings, the meetings eventually become more important than the problem.

Arthur Bloch
Writer and humorist
Murphy's Law (Price/Stern/Sloan, 1977)

The ideas that come out of most brainstorming sessions are usually superficial, trivial, and not very original. The are rarely useful. The process, however, seems to make uncreative people feel that they are making innovative contributions and that others are listening to them.

A. Harvey Block
CEO, Bokenon Systems Inc.
Debate, American Psychological Association,
Annual meeting, 1973

Feeling that you have to attend every meeting may mean that you don't trust someone on your staff to cover them well enough.

Harriet Braiker
Psychologist and management consultant
Working Woman, April 1988

Visuals act as punctuation points in your presentation. They offer relief to the audience and make the audience's commitment a series of short decisions to stay tuned instead of one long, unattractive obligation.

Ed Brenner
Photographer and publisher
Photo Lab Management, 1987

Meetings of this kind were generally conducted in the nature of seminars rather than for use in the laying down of pronounced policy. In other words, the aim always was to avoid cramming down the throats of those depended upon to carry out policy when defined, something that had not come to be digested and genuinely understood.

Donaldson Brown
Director, General Motors
Memo to then-CEO Alfred P. Sloan, 1922

Why doth one man's yawning make another yawn?

Robert Burton, 1577–1640
Vicar of St. Thomas's, Oxford
The Anatomy of Melancholy

[C]ommittees with with organizational tasks work best under a strong chairman who poses many questions, speaks more to the whole groupup than to individuals, defines the issues, keeps the discussion on its track, relates the amount of discussion to the available time, and attempts to arrive at group decisions.

Theodore Caplow
Managing an Organization
(CBS College Publishing, 1983)

The output of a multitude of minds must be expected to contain its proportion of vagaries.

Benjamin Nathan Cardozo, 1870–1938
U. S. Supreme Court Justice
The Growth of the Law

"Speak when you're spoken to!" the Red Queen sharply interrupted her.

Lewis Carroll
(Charles Lutwidge Dodgson), 1832–1898
English mathematician and writer
Through the Looking-Glass

I cannot divine how it happens that the man who knows the least is the most argumentative.

> Giovanni della Casa, 1503–1556
> Papal Secretary of State
> *Galateo*

Think twice—and say nothing.

> Chinese proverb

All the years that I have been in the House of Commons I have always said to myself one thing: "Do not interrupt", and I have never been able to keep to that resolution.

> Winston Churchill, 1874–1965
> English Prime Minister, writer, and soldier
> Speech in Parliament, July 10, 1935

[To a persistent interrupter:] The Honorable Gentleman ... has abrogated to himself a function which did not belong to him, namely, to make my speech instead of letting me make it.

> Winston Churchill, 1874–1965
> English Prime Minister, writer, and soldier
> Halle, *Irrepressible Churchill*

[Socialist William Graham] ... spoke without a note and almost without a point.

> Winston Churchill, 1874–1965
> English Prime Minister, writer, and soldier
> Remark, House of Commons, 1931

The supervisor [conducting a meeting] must be able to use the staff specialist [or outside expert] without letting the specialist take control of the meeting.

> William F. Cone
> Manager of Professional Development,
> Hughes Aircraft
> *Supervising Employees Effectively*
> (Addison-Wesley, 1974)

Groups convened to improve working methods and productivity should, at the very beginning, establish a time when they will go out of business.

> William F. Cone
> Manager of Professional Development,
> Hughes Aircraft
> *Supervising Employees Effectively*
> (Addison-Wesley, 1974)

He who wants to persuade should put his trust not in the right argument, but in the right word. The power of sound has always been greater than the power of sense.

> Joseph Conrad, 1857–1924
> Polish-born English novelist
> *A Personal Record*

Task forces have become necessary because the typical pyramidal hierarchy of the corporation with its man-in-box, departmentalized outlook—while well-equipped to handle daily operations—is not adaptable and quick enough to deal effectively with unanticipated challenges that are often interdepartmental or interdisciplinary in nature. Accordingly, the hierarchy often cannot meet such unanticipated problems with relish or clarity of purpose.

> Allen Cox
> Management consultant and author
> *The Making of the Achiever*
> (Dodd Mead, 1985)

Certian questions brought before Parliament are treated as "open" questions; that is, questions on which [Cabinet] Ministers in Parliament are allowed to take opposite sides without resigning.

> Homersham Cox
> English parliamentarian and historian
> *The Institutions of the English Government*

Even in a highly controlled meeting, there is a lot ... going on—bonding, rituals, glances, innuendos, and so forth. The real process of making decisions, of gathering support, of developing opinions, happens before the meeting—or after.

Terrence E. Deal
Harvard Business School
and Allan A. Kennedy
McKinsey & Co.
Corporate Cultures (Addison-Wesley, 1982)

The form of the meeting is simply a reflection of the culture.

Terrence E. Deal
Harvard Business School
and Allan A. Kennedy
McKinsey & Co.
Corporate Cultures (Addison-Wesley, 1982)

[I]n the exercise of sound leadership and initiative, the presiding officer is within his rights to shed light on a motion, to inform the members of the status or effect of a question, or to enlighten the assembly on facts within his knowledge to spur the assembly to action; and if such liberty is not abused by him the practice is not only tolerated but frequently welcomed. But the chair's comments and remarks commending or condemning speeches or opinions of members expressed in debate are unwise and unparliamentary. Judicious and efficient presiding officers avoid it; they are expected to be outwardly impartial and nonpartisan.

George Demeter
Parliamentarian,
U. S. House of Representatives
*Demeter's Manual of Parliamentary Law
and Procedure* (Little, Brown, 1969)

Let thy speech be better than silence, or be silent.

Dionysius the Elder, c. 430–367 B.C.
Tyrant of Syracuse
Fragment

Whenever executives, except at the very top level, spend more than a fairly small fraction of their time—maybe a quarter or less—in meetings, there is evidence of a case of malorganization. An excess of meetings indicates that jobs have not been defined clearly, have not been structured big enough, have not been made truly responsible. Also the need for meetings indicates that the decisions and relations analyses have not been made or have not been applied. The rule should be to minimize the need for people to get together to accomplish anything.

Peter F. Drucker
Management consultant and writer
People and Performance
(Harper & Row, 1977)

Learn to receive blows, and forgive those who insult you.

Mishna, The Fathers According to R. Nathan

No grand idea was ever born in a conference, but a lot of foolish ideas have died there.

F. Scott Fitzgerald, 1896–1940
American novelist
Prochnow, *The Toastmaster's Treasure Chest*
(Harper & Row, 1979)

Would you persuade, speak of interest, not of reason.

Benjamin Franklin, 1706–1790
American printer and statesman
Poor Richard's Almanack

Insofar as it represents a genuine reconciliation of differences, a consensus is a fine thing; insofar as it represents the concealment of differences, it is a miscarriage of democratic procedure. I think we Americans tend to put too high a price on unanimity ... as if there were something dangerous and illegitimate about honest differences of opinion honestly expressed by honest men.

> J. William Fulbright
> U. S. Senator
> Speech in the Senate, October 22, 1965

Contradiction should awaken Attention, not Passion.

> Thomas Fuller, 1608–1661
> Chaplain in extraordinary to Charles II
> *Gnomologia*

Once somebody asked me to identify the single most useful management technique that I learned through my years of managing. My answer was: the practice of regularly scheduled *one-on-one* meetings.

> Andrew S. Grove
> CEO, Intel Corp.
> *One-On-One With Andy Grove*
> (G. P. Putnam's Sons, 1987)

When a mission-oriented meeting fails to accomplish the purpose for which it was called, the blame belongs to the chairman.

> Andrew S. Grove
> CEO, Intel Corp.
> *High Output Management*
> (Random House, 1983)

Endless meetings, sloppy communications, and red tape steal the entrepreneur's time.

> James L. Hayes
> President,
> American Management Association
> *Memos for Management: Leadership*
> (AMACOM, 1983)

A good sign that either the meeting or some of the people are superfluous is when they try to get out of coming.

> Robert Heller
> Editor, *Management Today*
> *The Supermanagers* (Dutton, 1984)

Plain spoken people get most of the recognition because folks are afraid of them.

> Frank McKinney ("Kin") Hubbard, 1868–1930
> American caricaturist and humorist
> *Abe Martin Hoss Sense and Nonesense*

The one that listens is the one that understands.

> Jabo proverb

If a member finds that it is not the inclination of the House to hear him, and that by conversation or any other noise they endeavor to drown his voice, it is his most prudent way to submit to the pleasure of the House, and sit dowm.

> Thomas Jefferson, 1743–1826
> Third President of the United States
> Quoted in Hinds' *Precedents of the U. S. House of Representatives*

[Committees] never do anything completely wrong, but they never do anything brilliant either.

> Kelly Johnson
> Design Chief, Lockheed
> *Time*, December 1, 1975

If we must disagree, let's disagree without being disagreeable.

> Lyndon Baines Johnson, 1908–1973
> Thirty-sixth President of the United States
> Remark to U. S. Senators, 1965

Most of my meetings are held in bars, and most of my phone work gets done in the car. When people ask me why I don't even have an office, I tell them it's really very simple: I can't sell beer to a desk.

> James Koch
> CEO, The Boston Beer Co.
> *Inc. Magazine*, March 1988

While the staff meeting may not be the best place to solve complex problems, it surely is a place to express opinions.

Harry D. Kolb
Head of Personnel Development,
Humble Oil & Refining Co.
Leadership in the Office (AMACOM, 1963)

[Our] meetings force you to do your job. You'll find that there are issues that you don't think of and someone else will.

Edward Kopczynski
Senior VP, Shearson Lehman Brothers
The New York Times, January 10, 1988

There is something in the word "meeting" which arouses an instinctive and profound distrust in the bosoms of British people at this late hour in their history.

Doris Lessing
English writer and playwright
A Proper Marriage

He can compress the most words into the smallest ideas of any man I have ever met.

Abraham Lincoln, 1809–1865
Sixteenth President of the United States
Lincoln's Own Stories

Many meetings should not be called at all. Among them are those a manager calls because he is unable or unwilling to make a decision.

R. Alec Mackenzie
Management consultant and author
The Time Trap (McGraw-Hill, 1972)

Opinions cannot survive if one has no chance to fight for them.

Thomas Mann, 1875–1955
German novelist and essayist
The Magic Mountain

The purpose of a meeting is to bring depth and breadth of discussion to a problem that merits the attention and effort of every member present.

Alfred J. Marrow
Chairman, Harwood Manufacturing Corp.
Leadership in the Office (AMACOM, 1963)

Most men who chair meetings—unintentionally and often without knowing it—talk too much.

Alfred J. Marrow
Chairman, Harwood Manufacturing Corp.
Leadership in the Office (AMACOM, 1963)

Voluntary cooperation in the pursuit of an idea is one thing. But compulsory cooperation iseven more effective.

Charles Merz
Journalist and publicist
The Great American Band Wagon
(The John Day Company, 1928)

Where there is much desire to learn, there of necessity will be much arguing, much writing, many opinions; for opinion in good men is but knowledge in the making.

John Milton, 1608–1674
English poet and essayist
Areopagitica

When the result of a meeting is to schedule more meetings, it usually signals trouble.

Kevin J. Murphy
Management writer
Effective Listening (Bantam, 1987)

Teleconferencing is so rational, it will never succeed.

John Naisbitt
Chairman, Naisbitt Group
Megatrends (Warner, 1984)

It is most important that a [Japanese] meeting should reach a unanimous conclusion; it should leave no one frustrated or dissatisfied, for this weakens ... unity and solidarity.

Chie Nakane
Japanese Writer
Cherry Blossoms and Robotics
(Young Presidents' Organization, 1983)

There's a law of administration which I'd suggest holds true in almost every situation. That is, if the boss presents his solution first and asks for opinions about it, a vote of approval will follow almost every time.

George S. Odiorne
University of Massachusetts
How Managers Make Things Happen
(Prentice-Hall, 1982)

In one company, all committee meetings are scheduled one hour before lunch or before quitting time, in order that the chairman will not let things wander and the groups won't tend to drag things out. It's been found in this company that few meetings run overtime when they're scheduled this way.

George S. Odiorne
University of Massachusetts
How Managers Make Things Happen
(Prentice-Hall, 1982)

When any organizational entity expands beyond twenty-one members, the real power will be in some smaller body.

C. Northcote Parkinson
University of Malaya
*Parkinson's Law and Other Studies
in Administration*, 1957

The shape and size of a conference table will be crucial to the behavior of the group that will sit around it.

C. Northcote Parkinson
University of Malaya
*Parkinson's Law and Other Studies
in Administration*, 1957

Committees ... fall broadly into two categories, those (a) from which the individual member has something to gain; and those (b) to which the individual member merely has something to contribute.

C. Northcote Parkinson
University of Malaya
*Parkinson's Law and Other Studies
in Administration*, 1957

Individuals who are *repeatedly* persuasive in meetings are rarely those who come armed with with prepared speeches. Rather, they are individuals who can see other points of view and create compromises or new solutions, who can hold their views in suspension while permitting themselves to remain a part of the process—then intervene at the right point to guide the discussion to shore. They tend to choose words and images that *integrate* concerns in the group's thinking. The key is to find common ground and take others' points and use them creatively.

Richard T. Pascale
Stanford University School of Business
and Anthony G. Athos
Harvard Business School
The Art of Japanese Management
(Simon & Schuster, 1981)

Altogether, [Harold] Geneen [former CEO of International Telephone & Telegraph Company] and his top executives spent over three months each year in meetings. Why so many? Might not the same results have been achieved by reports? Not in Geneen's view—for it was the pressure-cooker atmosphere of the face-to-face sessions that sifted out the unshakeable facts and distilled them into sound and implementable decisions.

Richard T. Pascale
Stanford University School of Business
and Anthony G. Athos
Harvard Business School
The Art of Japanese Management
(Simon & Schuster, 1981)

Avoid *Company* where it is not *profitable* or necessary; and in those Occasions speak *little*, and *last*.

William Penn, 1644–1718
Founder of Pennsylvania
Fruits of Solitude in Reflections and Maxims

No committee could ever come up with anything as revolutionary as a camel—anything as practical and as perfectly designed to perform effectively under such difficult conditions.

Laurence J. Peter
University of Southern California
Peter's Quotations (Bantam, 1979)

When all men speak, no man hears.

Barber, *The Book of 1000 Proverbs*, 1876

Be a leader in meetings. Even those you don't chair.

Thomas L. Quick
Managing People at Work Desk Guide
(Executive Enterprise, Inc., 1983)

Some argue to prove a point, others to prove themselves.

Dagobert D. Runes
Editor, publisher, and philosopher
A Book of Contemplation

Most meetings are held to discuss a given situation or to monitor the task. Seldom do people meet to monitor the process, that is, the way we do the work and how we are working together. Little time is spent planning, monitoring, and creating the climate of the organization itself.

Kenneth and Linda Schatz
Leadership and organizational consultants
Managing by Influence (Prentice-Hall, 1986)

A multitude, from whatever cause assembled, seldom remains long silent.

Walter Scott, 1771–1832
Scottish poet, novelist, and biographer
Count Robert of Paris

In a typical freewheeling discussion in most companies, everybody throws out a certain number of thoughts and suggestions. A good boss will keep track of which idea came from which person, and then in his summary he'll compliment the various workers who made significant contributions.

Donald Seibert
Former CEO, J. C. Penney Co.
The Ethical Executive

When I first came into Parliament, Mr. Tierney, a great Whig authority, used always to say that the duty of an Opposition was very simple—it was, to oppose everything, and propose nothing.

Edward Stanley, 1799–1869
English Prime Minister and classical scholar
Speech, House of Commons, June 4, 1841

Perhaps Hell is nothing more than an enormous conference of those who, with little or nothing to say, take an eternity to say it.

Dudley C. Stone
Journal of Systems Management, 1987

Hardly anybody writes because you can't really write down all you know. And even if you do write it, nobody will read it. So there are meetings, and meetings about meetings, and meetings to plan reports, and meetings to review the status of reports. And what these meetings are about is people just trying to figure out what they are doing.

Paul Strassmann
Former Vice President, Xerox Corp.
Inc. Magazine, March 1988

The managers and the president are not arrogant within the company.... The boardroom is always open for the use of employees. Executive meetings are not held very often.... So when we are not using the room, our employees may be holding other meetings and an ordinary employee would be sitting in my chair.

> Setsuya Tabuchi
> President, Nomura Securities Co. (Japan)
> *Cherry Blossoms and Robotics*
> (Young Presidents' Organization, 1983)

Power is more safely retained by cautious than by severe councils.

> Tacitus, c. 55–117
> Roman orator, politician, and historian
> *Annals of the Julian Emperors*

Generally speaking, the fewer the better. As to both the number of meetings and the number of participants.

> Robert Townsend
> Former CEO, Avis
> *Further Up the Organization* (Knopf, 1984)

I don't like bipartisans. Whenever a fellow tells me he's bipartisan, I know he's going to vote against me.

> Harry S. Truman, 1884–1972
> Thirty-third President of the United States
> Goodman, *Give'em Hell, Harry* (Award, 1974)

It were not best that we should all think alike; it is difference of opinion that makes horseraces.

> Mark Twain
> (Samuel Langhorne Clemens), 1835–1910
> American author and riverboat captain
> *Pudd'nhead Wilson*

You can't get four people to agree on too many things.

> Charles T. Vaughn, Jr.
> CEO, L. Vaughn Co.
> *Inc. Magazine*, March 1988

One cool judgment is worth a thousand hasty councils. The thing to do is to supply light and not heat.

> Woodrow Wilson, 1856–1924
> Twenty-eighth President of the United States
> Speech, Pittsburgh, January 29, 1916

The length of the meeting increases in direct proportion to the square of the number of people present and awake.

> Anonymous

A camel is a horse that was designed by a committee.

> Anonymous (Washington, D. C.)

A meeting is a gathering of people seeking refuge from the dreariness of labor and the loneliness of thought.

> Anonymous

"Committee" is a noun of multitude, signifying many, but not signifying much.

> Anonymous

26

Motivation

When the going gets tough,
the tough get going.

'Tis not in mortals to command success;
But we'll do more, Sempronius—we'll
deserve it.

> Joseph Addison, 1672–1719
> English writer, critic, and statesman
> *Cato*

Accurate information is a key part of motivation.

> Mary Ann Allison
> Vice President, CitiCorp.
> and Eric Allison
> Financial writer
> *Managing Up, Managing Down*
> (Simon & Schuster, 1984)

Influence belongs to men of action, and for
purposes of action nothing is more useful than
narrowness of thought combined with energy
of will.

> Henri Frédéric Amiel, 1821–1881
> Swiss journalist and critic
> *Journal intimé*

Men, in general, desire what is good.

> Aristotle, 384–322 B.C.
> Greek philosopher and teacher
> *Politics*

In a barnyard, in front of a small shanty in
Haiti, three drummers would pour their souls
into a trepidous beat, sending a message of
hope to nowhere.

> Jean-Claude Aubin
> Haitian-American poet and businessman
> Speech, Washington, D.C., 1987

Motivation will almost always beat mere
talent.

> Norman R. Augustine
> President and CEO, Martin Marietta Corp.
> *Augustine's Laws* (Penguin, 1987)

Nothing creates more self-respect among employees than being included in the process of making decisions.

> Judith M. Bardwick
> University of California at San Diego
> *The Plateauing Trap* (AMACOM, 1986)

To say ... that the American worker is not really or primarily interested in money contradicts, in a deep sense, the very motive power of the economic system. Why else would people submit themselves to such a work environment?

> Daniel Bell
> Harvard University
> *Work and Its Discontents*

If the people don't want to come out to the park, nobody's going to stop them.

> Lawrence Peter "Yogi" Berra
> Professional baseball player, manager, coach
> Attributed

Only positive consequences encourage good future performance.

> Kenneth H. Blanchard
> Chairman, Blanchard Training & Development
> and Robert Lorber
> President, R. L. Lorber & Associates
> *Putting the One Minute Manager to Work*
> (William Morrow, 1984)

Studies ... document that today's young work force is motivated not just by dollar compensation but by the opportunity to make decisions on the job and to grow. But in many cases, the young support staffer's sense of direction is clouded by unrealisitc expectations of rapid career advancement coupled with the frustrating perception that the present job holds no opportunities for improvement.

> Paul Blessing
> Founder and Partner, Blessing/White, Inc.
> *Training and Development Journal*,
> November 1986

The margin between that which men naturally do, and that which they can do, is so great that a system which urges men on to action and develops individual enterprise and initiative is preferable, in spite of the wastes that necessarily attend their process.

> Louis Dembitz Brandeis, 1856–1941
> U. S. Supreme Court Justice
> *Efficiency and Trusts*

I have a lot of faith in what employees can do if they are treated right and properly motivated. But when I worked for other people, I saw colleagues work their buns off and get nothing out of it. I saw Wall Street rape employees.

> Warren Braun
> CEO, ComSonics, Inc.
> *Best of Business Quarterly*, 1987

If anything goes bad, I did it.

If anything goes semi-good, then we did it.

If anything goes real good then you did it.

That's all it takes to get people to win football games.

> Paul "Bear" Bryant, 1913–1983
> Football coach, University of Alabama
> Quoted in *Bits & Pieces* 1, 1987

No passion so effectually robs the mind of all its power of acting and reasoning as fear.

> Edmund Burke, 1729–1797
> English statesman, orator, and writer
> *On the Sublime and Beautiful*

Ambition can creep as well as soar.

> Edmund Burke, 1729–1797
> English statesman, orator, and writer
> *Letters on a Regicide Peace*

We're not money hungry. We're good at what we do, and we enjoy what we're doing. We feel that we're making a big difference in people's lives, and that turns us on.

Carlton Caldwell
President, Caldwell Laboratories
Best of Business Quarterly, 1987

Method is much, technique is much, but inspiration is even more.

Benjamin Nathan Cardozo, 1870–1938
U. S. Supreme Court Justice
Law and Literature

Big projects give people something to identify with and work toward.

Frank C. Carlucci
U. S. National Security Advisor
Frank Carlucci on Management in Government
(Center for Excellence in Government, 1987)

The fearful Unbelief is unbelief in yourself.

Thomas Carlyle, 1795–1881
Scottish essayist and historian
Sartor Resartus

The only way I can get you to do anything is by giving you what you want.

Dale Carnegie, 1888–1955
American writer and public speaking teacher
How to Win Friends and Influence People

We have to get people excited about using their talents or we'll all end up going down the tube together.

Patricia M. Carrigan
Plant Manager, General Motors Corp.
MTS Digest, April/June 1987

[P]rofessional dissatisfaction ... results because the specialized abilities of registered nurses are ... not fully utilized. Under current management practices ... nurses are often inhibited in their ability to provide high-quality, cost-effective care because they are required to perform nonclinical, nonnursing-related tasks.

Lawton Chiles
U. S. Senator
Remarks in the Senate, February 16, 1988

He that would thrive
Must rise at five;
He that hath thriven
May lie till seven.

John Clarke, 1609–1676
Physician and founder of Rhode Island
Paroemiologia Anglo-Latina

I don't think you should ever manage anything that you don't care passionately about.

Deborah A. Coleman
Vice President and CFO, Apple Computer Corp.
Peters, *Thriving on Chaos* (Knopf, 1987)

Applause is the spur of noble minds, the end and aim of weak ones.

Charles Caleb Colton, c. 1780–1832
English cleric, sportsman, and wine merchant
Lacon

We are perplexed, but not in despair.

New Testament, II Corinthians 4:8

The gladiators, for a long time past,
Seem to have lost their appetite for dying.

Pietro Cossa, 1833–1881
Italian painter and writer
Messalina

If you've got them by the balls, their hearts and minds will soon follow.

Charles Colson
Special Assistant to President Nixon
The Watergate tapes, 1974

I'm just not motivated to sell any [of my own] stock.... My personal motivation is to build the best software company in the world.

Richard Covey
President, System Software Associates
Venture, April 1988

We don't feel that wages are the primary motivator. The real motivation is when the worker feels he's making a contribution.

Russell Culomb
Plant Manager, General Electric Co.
Tosi and Carroll, *Management* (Wiley, 1976)

It is better to wear out than to rust out.

Richard Cumberland, 1632–1718
Bishop of Peterborough
Attributed

What we want to do in the workplace is facilitate commitment to doing a good job. Control and negative feedback undermine people's commitment and involvement.

Edward L. Deci
University of Rochester
Nation's Business, March 1988

To be truly motivated, one must make personal committments.

William G. Dyer
Brigham Young University
Strategies for Managing Change
(Addison-Wesley, 1984)

In the final choice a soldier's pack is not so heavy a burden as a prisoner's chains.

Dwight David Eisenhower, 1890–1969
Thirty-fourth President of the United States
Inaugural address, January 20, 1953

Success in your work, the finding a better method, the better understanding that insures the better performing is hat and coat, is food and wine, is fire and horse and health and holiday. At least, I find that any success in my work has the effect on my spirits of all these.

Ralph Waldo Emerson, 1803–1882
American essayist and poet
Journals

Nothing great was ever achieved without enthusiasm.

Ralph Waldo Emerson, 1803–1882
American essayist and poet
Heroism

Remember, a dead fish can float downstream, but it takes a live one to swim upstream.

William Claude (W. C.) Fields, 1880–1946
American comedian and film star
Mason, *Never Trust A Man Who Doesn't Drink*
(Montcalm, 1971)

Delegating means letting others become the experts and hence the best.

Timothy W. Firnstahl
CEO, Restaurant Services, Inc.
Harvard Business Review,
September/October 1986

Forty thousand wishes won't fill your bucket with fishes.

Fisherman's saying

When we see the ads for our own products, we know that we were the ones to do it. That's the thrill that makes it all worthwhile.

> George Freedman
> Director, New Products Center, Raytheon
> *Personnel*, January 1987

Everyone has noted the astonishing sources of energy that seem available to those who enjoy what they are doing or find meaning in what they are doing.

> Charles Garfield
> President, Performance Sciences Corp.
> *Peak Performers* (Avon, 1986)

They [her partners] were just terminally discouraged.

> Mary Garvey
> Partner, Grocery Express
> *Forbes,* April 4, 1988

The best way to inspire people to superior performance is to convince them by everything you do and by your everyday attitude that you are wholeheartedly supporting them.

> Harold Geneen
> CEO, IT&T
> *Managing* (Doubleday, 1984)

We all need to believe in what we are doing.

> Allan D. Gilmour
> Executive Vice President, Ford Motor Co.
> *The Academy of Management Executive,*
> February 1988

Successfully to accomplish any task it is necessary not only that you should give it the best there is in you, but that you should obtain for it the best there is in those under your guidance.

> George Washington Goethals, 1858–1928
> Chief Engineer, Panama Canal
> National Association of Corporation
> Schools *Bulletin*, February 1918

You must keep people scared every day.

> Peter Grace
> CEO, W. R. Grace Co.
> *Financial World,* April 5, 1988

Mediocrity obtains more with application than superiority without it.

> Baltasar Gracián, 1601–1658
> Spanish priest and popular writer
> *Oraculo Manual*

No task will be evaded merely because it is impossible.

> Richard R. Green
> Chancellor, New York City Public Schools
> Sign in office

Traditional workers who find their work interesting view the situation as a happy coincidence; for contemporary employees, interesting work is a *primary concern.*

> Ira B. Gregerman
> President, Productivity Associates
> *Knowledge Worker Productivity*
> (AMACOM, 1981)

Setting and communicating the right expectations is the most important tool a manager has for imparting that elusive drive to the people he supervises.

> Andrew S. Grove
> CEO, Intel Corp.
> *One-On-One With Andy Grove*
> (G. P. Putnam's Sons, 1987)

If a man goes into business with only the idea of making money, the chances are he won't.

> Joyce Clyde Hall, 1891–1982
> Founder, Hallmark Cards, Inc.
> Favorite saying

If a thing isn't worth doing, it isn't worth doing well.

> Sydney J. Harris
> Syndicated columnmist
> Advice

We want to be a place where people feel good about coming to work. When they work in a place that cares about them, they contribute a lot more than "duty."

> Dennis Hayes
> CEO, Hayes Microcomputer Products, Inc.
> *Continental Magazine*, November 1987

Money does motivate ... but only for a short time and only as long as it serves as a measure of worth or of power or of victory.

> James L. Hayes
> President and CEO,
> American Management Association
> *Memos for Management: Leadership*
> (AMACOM, 1983)

You have to be consistent, fair and encouraging with your people. They need a "thank you" now and then.

> Lonear Heard
> President, James T. Heard Management Corp.
> (McDonald's franchisee)
> *Black Enterprise*, September 1987

We may affirm absolutely that nothing great in the world has ever been accomplished without passion.

> Georg Wilhelm Hegel, 1770–1831
> German philosopher
> *The Philosophy of History*

Favors are used to reward. Favors also are used to punish by reducing the initiative available to others. Giving or withholding favors is the lever of organizational power.

> Bruce Henderson
> CEO, Boston Consulting Group, Inc.
> *Henderson on Corporate Strategy* (Abt, 1979)

The fox, when he cannot reach the grapes, says they are not ripe.

> George Herbert, 1593–1632
> English clergyman and poet
> *Jacula Prudentum*

Good words are worth much, and cost little.

> George Herbert, 1593–1632
> English clergyman and poet
> *Jacula Prudentum*

To him that will, ways are not wanting.

> George Herbert, 1593–1633
> English clergyman and poet
> *Jacula Prudentum*

The readiness of doing doth express
No other but the doer's willingness.

> Robert Herrick, 1591–1674
> English poet
> *Hesperides*

Achievement-motivated people are not gamblers. They prefer to work on a problem rather than leave the outcome to chance.

> Paul Hersey
> California American University
> and Kenneth H. Blanchard
> University of Massachusetts
> *Management of Organizational Behavior*
> (Prentice-Hall, 1982)

People differ not only in their ability to do but also in their "will to do."

Paul Hersey
California American University
and Kenneth H. Blanchard
University of Massachusetts
Management of Organizational Behavior
(Prentice-Hall, 1982)

Another characteristic of the achievement motivated person is that he seems to be more concerned with personal achievement than with the rewards of success.... He normally does not seek money for status or economic security.

Paul Hersey
California American University
and Kenneth H. Blanchard
University of Massachusetts
Management of Organizational Behavior
(Prentice-Hall, 1982)

Managements have always looked at man as an animal to be manipulated with a carrot and a stick. They found that when a man hurts, he will move to avoid pain—and they say, "We're motivating the employees." Hell, you're not motivating them, you're moving them.

Frederick Herzberg
University of Utah
The Managerial Choice
(Dow Jones-Irwin, 1976)

Whoever would change men must change the conditions of their lives.

Theodor Herzl, 1860–1904
Austrian journalist and Zionist leader
Diaries

Confidence circle: Accomplishment influences confidence, and confidence influences accomplishment.

Harold S. Hook
Chairman and CEO, American General Corp.
Forbes, October 19, 1987

Those who believe that they are exclusively in the right are generally those who achieve something.

Aldous Huxley, 1894–1963
English novelist and critic
Proper Studies

Genius is initiative on fire.

Holbrook Jackson, 1874–1948
English writer and editor
Platitudes in the Making

Dreams can be realized if you work hard.

Warren G. Jackson
President, Circulation Expertise, Ltd.
Black Enterprise, April 1988

I never trust a man 'till I've got his pecker in my pocket.

Lyndon Baines Johnson, 1908–1973
Thirty-sixth President of the United States
Attributed

Few things are impossible to diligence and skill.

Samuel Johnson, 1709–1784
English lexicographer and poet
A Dissertation on the Art of Flying

Everything that enlarges the sphere of human powers, that shows man he can do what he thought he could not do, is valuable.

Samuel Johnson, 1709–1784
English lexicographer and poet
Boswell's Life of Dr. Johnson

Where there is no hope there can be no endeavour.

Samuel Johnson, 1709–1784
English lexicographer and critic
The Rambler

Depend upon it, Sir, when a man knows he is to be hanged in a fortnight, it concentrates his mind wonderfully.

> Samuel Johnson, 1709–1784
> English lexicographer and critic
> *Boswell's Life of Dr. Johnson*

When the going gets tough, the tough get going.

> Kennedy family motto
> *The New York Times*, August 22, 1965

We were at an age when our beliefs influenced our behaviour, a characteristic of the young which it is easy for the middle aged to forget.

> John Maynard Keynes, 1883–1946
> English economist, writer, and diplomat
> Speech to the Bloomsbury "Memoir Club,"
> September 9, 1938
> Quoted in E. M. Forster's *Commonplace Book*

I liked the shaver so much that I bought the company.

> Victor Kiam
> CEO, Remington
> TV ad for Remington Electric Shavers

Sure I have muffed a few [calls] in my time. But I never called one wrong in my heart.

> Bill Klem, 1874–1951
> Professional baseball umpire
> Bohle, *American Quotations* (Gramercy, 1986)

The members [of the team] were dissatisfied with the authoritarian leading; they reacted either aggressively against the leader and toward each other or with apathetic submission. In the case of strong control the performance was a little higher than with the "democratic" leading style. Then soon a decrease followed. The members who reacted apathetically did not show any

motivation for performance and soon the decrease of motivation began.

> Hans Lenk
> German sports sociologist and writer
> *Team Dynamics*

If I knew what brand of whiskey he [General Ulysses S. Grant] drinks, I would send a barrel or so to some other generals.

> Abraham Lincoln, 1809–1865
> Sixteenth President of the United States
> Remark at a Cabinet meeting, 1864

If you aren't fired with enthusiasm, you will be fired with enthusiasm.

> Vince Lombardi, 1913–1970
> Professional football coach
> Rowes, *The Book of Quotes* (Dutton, 1979)

There are no hopeless situations; there are only men who have grown hopeless about them.

> Clare Boothe Luce, 1903–1987
> Congresswoman, playwright, and diplomat
> *Europe in the Spring*

It is fatal to enter any war without the will to win it.

> Douglas MacArthur, 1880–1964
> Five-star General of the U. S. Army
> Speech to the Republican National Convention,
> July 7, 1952

Where the willingness is great, the difficulties cannot be great.

> Niccolò Machiavelli, 1469–1527
> Florentine statesman and philosopher
> *The Prince*

People influence people.

> Robert F. Mager
> Psychologist and educational technologist
> *Developing Attitude Toward Learning*
> (Fearon, 1968)

Man never exerts himself but when he is rous'd by his Desires: While they lie dormant, and there is nothing to raise them, his Excellence and Abilities will be for ever undiscover'd, and the lumpish Machine, without Influence of his Passions, may be justly compared to a huge Wind-mill without a breath of Air.

> Bernard Mandeville, 1670–1733
> English physician and fabulist
> *The Fable of the Bees*

Do not think that what is hard for thee to master is impossible for man; but if a thing is possible and proper to man, deem it attainable by thee.

> Marcus Aurelius, 121–180
> Roman Emperor and Stoic philosopher
> *Meditations*

Constant labor of one uniform kind destroys the intensity and flow of a man's animal spirits, which find recreation and delight in mere change of activity.

> Karl Marx, 1818–1883
> German political philosopher
> *Capital*

If you ask people confidentially what they want most in their job—if they're paid anything decent at all—they will say that they want a greater sense of self worth.... And I think this giving of responsibility and respect and authority is one of the things that motivates people.

> Fritz Maytag
> President, Anchor Brewing Co.
> *Harvard Business Review*, July/August 1986

Most Americans say they want more money. Yet non-cash awards appear to be more effective motivators.

> Jerry McAdams
> Vice President, Maritz Information Resources
> *Management*, April 1987

Very few factors help produce economies of scale. Technology may be one, but not people. When it comes to motivating people and using their brainpower, you hit diseconomies of scale early. At that point, bigger isn't better.

> Alonzo L. McDonald
> CEO, Bendix, and White House Staff Director
> *Harvard Business Review*,
> November/December 1986

I go on working for the same reason that a hen goes on laying eggs.

> Henry Louis Mencken, 1880–1956
> Editor, author, and critic
> *Home Book of Quotations*, 1932

It's a company's responsibility to allow each individual to be as good as he or she is capable of being. People basically want to do a good job. I have never heard anybody walk out of this building and say, "Boy, I feel great! I did a lousy job today."

> Harvey Miller
> Co-owner, Quill Corp.
> *Nation's Business*, March 1988

Most corporations do serve a worthy purpose. Individuals seek to identify with it. The competitive leader will make the connection between our souls and our work, and will benefit from the energies released.

> Lawrence M. Miller
> Business consultant
> *American Spirit* (William Morrow, 1984)

We give a bonus for the employees to give them a sense of participation and to feel that they are members of the company because we are always saying our company has one fate. If the company goes well, everybody can enjoy. If the company goes wrong or goes bankrupt, people lose jobs.

> Akio Morita
> CEO, Sony Corp. (Japan)
> *Cherry Blossoms and Robotics*
> (Young Presidents' Organization, 1983)

It is absolutely necessary that they [your subordinates] want to do the job—not that you want to do the job.

> James Morton
> CEO, John Hancock Insurance Co.
> *Pinnacle* (CNN TV), January 1988

Nothing ever succeeds which exuberant spirits have not helped to produce.

> Georg Wilhelm Nietzsche, 1844–1900
> German philosopher
> *The Twilight of the Idols*

One does not know—cannot know —the best that is in one.

> Georg Wilhelm Nietzsche, 1844–1900
> German philosopher
> *Beyond Good and Evil*

There is no finish line.

> Nike Corporation motto

As a rule, initiative in an organization should be pushed down to the lowest possible level where decision can be made, through instilling a desire to excel at every level.

> George S. Odiorne
> University of Massachusetts
> *How Managers Make Things Happen*
> (Prentice-Hall, 1982)

You have to have people free to act, or they become dependent. They don't have to be told, they have to be allowed.

> John R. Opel
> Former Chairman, IBM
> Heller, *The Supermanagers* (Dutton, 1984)

We like the freedom to make a successful decision, or even an unsuccessful one, without having to explain it to some analyst.

> John Oren
> President, Eastway Delivery Service
> *Best of Business Quarterly*, 1987

The mere act of showing people you're concerned about them spurs them to better job performance.

> Jerome Peloquin
> President, Performance Control Corp.
> *Training*, November 1986

Celebrate what you want to see more of.

> Tom Peters
> Business writer
> *Thriving on Chaos* (Knopf, 1987)

How many things are looked upon as quite impossible until they have been actually effected?

> Pliny the Elder, 23–79
> Roman writer
> *Natural History*

Respect the man and he will do the more.

> Barber, *The Book of 1000 Proverbs*, 1876

We are more mindful of injuries than benefits.

> Barber, *The Book of 1000 Proverbs*, 1876

Where there is no vision, the people perish.

Old Testament, Proverbs 29:18

Of all the motivators of performance for professionals, job challenge stands at the top of the list, precisely because of its association with professionalism itself.

Joseph A. Raelin
Boston College School of Management
Clash of Cultures: Managers and Professionals
(Harvard Business School, 1986)

A systematic effort must be made to emphasize the group instead of the individual.... Group goals and responsibilities can usually overcome any negative reactions to the individual and enforce a standard of cooperation that is attainable by persuasion or exhortation.

Eugene Raudsepp
President, Creative Research, Inc.
MTS Digest, April/June 1987

It is easier to motivate workers to outproduce coworkers than to motivate them to operate at the pace dictated by machine.

John A. Reinecke
University of New Orleans
and William F. Schoell
University of Southern Mississippi
Introduction to Business
(Allyn and Bacon, 1983)

If you have great talents, industry will improve them. If you have but moderate abilities, industry will supply their deficiency.

Joshua Reynolds, 1723–1792
English portrait painter
Discourse to Students of the Royal Academy

I want to see you shoot the way you shout.

Theodore Roosevelt, 1858–1919
Twenty-sixth President of the United States
Speech at Madison Square, October 1917

When one is intensely interested in a certain cause, the tendency is to associate particularly with those who take the same view.

Theodore Roosevelt, 1858–1919
Twenty-sixth President of the United States
The Rough Riders

When men are rightly occupied, their amusement grows out of their work, as the color petals out of a fruitful flower.

John Ruskin, 1819–1900
English essayist
Sesame and Lilies

In order that people be happy in their work, these three things are needed: They must be fit for it: They must not do too much of it: And they must have a sense of success in it.

John Ruskin, 1819–1900
English essayist
Pre-Raphaelitism

Skilled work, of no matter what kind, is only done well by those who take a certain pleasure in it, quite apart from its utility, either to themselves in earning a living or to the world through its outcome.

Bertrand Russell, 1872–1970
English mathematician and philosopher
How to Become a Mathematician

The will to persevere is often the difference between failure and success.

David Sarnoff, 1891–1971
Founder and President, RCA
Wisdom of Sarnoff and the World of RCA

Unexpressed commitment appears much the same as noncommitment. Leaders can defend against the lack of commitment or can recognize that it lies just below the surface, unexpressed, until the climate is right for its expression. Whether you can see it or not, your people are committed. Even if you can't see it in any given instance, the only useful point of view is to assume they are committed.

> Kenneth and Linda Schatz
> Leadership and organizational consultants
> *Managing by Influence* (Prentice-Hall, 1986)

From time to time, life as a leader can look hopeless. After taking a hard look in the mirror at your leadership, you may be overwhelmed by the focus on what's needed. To help you, consider a man who lived through this:

Failed in business in '31
Defeated for the legislature in '32
Again failed in business in '34
Sweetheart died in '35
Had a nervous breakdown in '36
Defeated in election in '38
Defeated for Congress in '43
Defeated for Congress in '46
Defeated for Congress in '48
Defeated for Senate in '55
Defeated for Vice-President in '56
Defeated for Senate in '58
Elected President in '60

This man was Abraham Lincoln.

> Kenneth and Linda Schatz
> Leadership and organizational consultants
> *Management by Influence* (Prentice-Hall, 1986)

Three people were at work on a construction site. All were doing the same job, but when each was asked what his job was, the answers varied. "Breaking rocks," the first replied. "Earning my living," the second said. "Helping to build a cathedral," said the third.

> Peter Schultz
> CEO, Porsche
> *Waterman, The Renewal Factor*
> (Bantam, 1987)

I think that you learn to motivate people in a small company, because you can really see what happens. I just wish every executive

could have either started or worked in a small company.

> Peter L. Scott
> Chairman, Emhart Corp.
> *Sky*, August 1, 1987

To perform effectively, groups also need at least a minimal belief in their own efficacy.... Believing both that a job is important and that it can be done can easily lead group members to behave more aggressively.

> Gregory P. Shea
> The Wharton School
> and Richard A. Guzzo
> New York University
> *Sloan Management Review*, Spring 1987

Is it not strange that desire should so many years outlive performance.

> William Shakespeare, 1564–1616
> English dramatist and poet
> *King Henry IV*

Men prize the thing ungained more than it is.

> William Shakespeare, 1564–1616
> English dramatist and poet
> *King Henry VIII*

To business that we love, we rise betimes,
And go to it with delight.

> William Shakespeare, 1564–1616
> English dramatist and poet
> *Antony and Cleopatra*

Most salesmen try to take the horse to water and make him drink. Your job is to make the horse thirsty.

> Gabriel M. Siegel
> President, MediCab of New York, Inc.
> Speech to sales reps, August 1984

Reinforcements continue to be important, of course, long after an organism has learned *how* to do something, long after it has acquired behavior. They are necessary to maintain the behavior in strength.

> B. F. Skinner
> Harvard University
> *Harvard Educational Review*, 1954

It is not from the benevolence of the butcher, the brewer, or the baker that we expect our dinner, but from regard to their self-interest. We address ourselves, not to their humanity, but to their self-love.

> Adam Smith, 1723–1790
> Scottish political economist
> *Inquiry into ... the Wealth of Nations*

Sadness diminishes or hinders a man's power of action.

> Benedict Spinoza, 1632–1677
> Dutch philosopher and oculist
> *Ethics*

Whatever is worth doing at all, is worth doing well.

> Philip Dormer Stanhope, 1694–1773
> English Secretary of State
> *Letters of Lord Chesterfield to His Son*

The chief lesson I have learned in a long life is that the only way you can make a man trustworthy is by trusting him; and the surest way to make him untrustworthy is to distrust him and show your distrust.

> Henry L. Stimpson, 1867–1950
> U. S. Secretary of State and Secretary of War
> Memo to President Franklin Delano Roosevelt,
> September 1945

Money may be the way I keep score, but I started the business for other reasons.

> Betsy Tabac
> President, Tabac and Associates
> *Inc. Magazine*, February 1987

It's always the challenge of the future, this feeling of excitement, that drives me.

> Yoshihisa Tabuchi
> CEO, Nomura Securities (Japan)
> *Best of Business Quarterly*, Summer 1987

It's crazy to work this hard, but I love it.

> Joe Tanner
> Division Manager, DuPont
> Pinchot, *Intrapreneuring*
> (Harper & Row, 1986)

People don't change their behavior unless it makes a difference for them to do so.

> Fran Tarkenton
> Professional football player
> and management consultant
> *How to Motivate People: Team Strategy*
> *for Success* (Harper & Row, 1986)

While industrial psychologists have insisted for years that motivation must lie in positive things, not in the threat of firing, somehow that idea has never really caught on with some bosses.

> John Tarrant
> Business consultant and writer
> *Perks and Parachutes*
> (Simon & Schuster, 1985)

Why should we be in such desperate haste to succeed, and in such desperate enterprise? If a man does not keep pace with his companions, perhaps it is because he hears a different drummer. Let him step to the music which he hears, however measured or far away.

> Henry David Thoreau, 1817–1862
> American naturalist and writer
> *Walden*

Skill is nil without will.

> Judah ibn Tibbon, c. 1120–c. 1190
> Spanish physician and translator
> *A Father's Admonition to His Son*

When you're on the top of the heap, you really don't think about some of the things that you used to. I think the Greeks call it the sin of hubris.

> John R. Torell III
> President, Manufacturers Hanover Trust
> *Business Week*, August 24, 1987

It is not the martinets that make an army work; it's the morale that the leaders put into the men that makes an army work.

> Harry S. Truman, 1884–1972
> Thirty-third President of the United States
> Speech, October 24, 1950

For many there is hardly concealed discontent.... "I'm a machine," says the spot welder. "I'm caged," says the bank teller, and echoes the hotel clerk. "I'm a mule," says the steel worker. "A monkey can do what I do," says the receptionist. "I'm less than a farm implement," says the migrant worker. "I'm an object," says the high fashion model. Blue collar and white collar call upon the identical phrase: "I'm a robot."

> Studs Terkel
> American journalist
> *Working*, 1974

I love my work so much it doesn't seem like work.

> Terry Van Der Tuuk
> Owner, Graphic Technology, Inc.
> *Inc. Magazine*, April 1986

People want to be part of a winner.

> Albert Verderosa
> Divisional President, Grumman Corp.
> *Government Executive*, January 1987

The absence of a marked or consistent correlation between job satisfaction and performance casts some doubt on the generality or intensity of either effects of satisfaction on performance or performance on satisfaction.

> Victor H. Vroom
> Management researcher
> *Work and Motivation* (John Wiley & Sons, 1964)

If you do things by the job, you are perpetually driven; the hours are scourges. If you work by the hour, you gently sail on a stream of Time, which is always bearing you on to the heaven of Pay, whether you make any effort or not.

> Charles Dudley Warner, 1829–1903
> American editor and writer
> *My Summer in a Garden*

When people are treated as the main engine rather than interchangeable parts of a corporate machine, motivation, creativity, quality, and commitment to implementation well up.

> Robert H. Waterman
> Management consultant and writer
> *The Renewal Factor* (Bantam, 1987)

People don't resist their own ideas.

> William Werther
> University of Miami
> *Nation's Business*, March 1988

We decided to create an open and dialogue-intensive corporate culture. This generates creativity and motivation and brings out entrepreneurs at all levels. This is the true power and success of Bertelsmann.

> Mark Woessner
> CEO, Bertelsmann Group (West Germany)
> *The Washington Post*, November 22, 1987

If we cannot do what we will, we must will what we can.

Yiddish proverb

All you need is to tell a man he is no good ten times a day, and very soon he begins to believe it himself.

Lin Yutang, 1895–1976
Chinese philosopher and author
Prochnow, *The Toastmaster's Treasure Chest*
(Harper & Row, 1979)

Among the CEO's I know, the most successful ones have a very positive outlook. Every CEO has to be a cheerleader. At times you feel that you can list a series of disaster scenarios for your company.... Still, you have to be a cheerleader at least part of the time.

Richard A. Zimmerman
CEO, Hershey Foods
Chief Executive, Winter 1986–1987

[Referring to his managerial counterparts in local government:] How would you like to run a business where your top management can change every two years, your revenue can depend on the whims and fancies of state and national government, and you have to convince more than half a million people that you can collect garbage, control crime, enhance safety, and brighten the future better than anyone else?

Anonymous executive
Chief Executive, Winter 1982–1983

27
Negotiation

There's a difference between bending over backward and bending over forward.

It is not the oath that makes us believe the man, but the man the oath.

> Aeschylus, 525–456 B.C.
> Greek tragedian and poet
> *Fragments*

John, why do you not speak for yourself?

> Priscilla Alden, c. 1602–1687
> American pilgrim
> Longfellow, *The Courtship of Miles Standish*

Things look better merely by being divided into their parts, since they then seem to surpass a greater number of things than before. The same effect is produced by piling up facts.

> Aristotle, 384–322 B.C.
> Greek philosopher and teacher
> *Works*

It is generally better to deal by speech than by letter.

> Francis Bacon, 1561–1626
> Lord Chancellor of England
> *Of Negotiating*

It is a point of cunning, to wait upon him with whom you speak, with your eyes; as the Jesuits give it in precept: for there be many wise men that have secret hearts and transparent countenances.

> Francis Bacon, 1561–1626
> Lord Chancellor of England
> *Of Cunning*

Negotiators with a "fixed-pie" bias assume that for them to win something, the other side must lose it.

> Max H. Bazerman
> Kellogg School of Management,
> Northwestern University
> *Psychology Today*, June 1986

Government is the art of the momentarily feasible, of the least bad attainable, and not of the rationally most desirable.

> Bernard Berenson, 1865–1959
> Art critic and writer
> *Rumor and Reflection*

If it takes two to make a bargain, it ought to take two to break it.

> Josh Billings
> (Henry Wheeler Shaw), 1818–1885
> American writer and auctioneer
> *Josh Billings: His Book*

Politics is the art of the possible, the attainable ... the art of the next best.

> Otto von Bismarck, 1815–1898
> First Chancellor of the German Empire
> Remark to Prince Meyer von Waldeck,
> August 11, 1867

I am disquieted to see how hazy and vague our ideas are. We are going up against the wiliest politicians in Europe. There will be nothing hazy or vague about their ideas.

> Tasker Howard Bliss, 1853–1930
> Chief of Staff, U. S. Army,
> and peace negotiator at Versailles
> Diary, December 18, 1918

Either Caesar or nothing.
[*Aut Caesar aut nihil.*]

> Cesare Borgia, c. 1476–1507
> Italian cleric, diplomat, and general
> Motto

The old idea of a good bargain was a transaction in which one man got the better of another. The new idea of a good contract is a transaction which is good for both parties to it.

> Louis Dembitz Brandeis, 1856–1941
> U. S. Supreme Court Justice
> *Business—A Profession*

Nothing is settled until it is settled right.

> Louis Dembitz Brandeis, 1856–1941
> U. S. Supreme Court Justice
> Mason, *Brandeis: A Free Man's Life*

All government,—indeed, every human benefit and enjoyment, every virtue and every prudent act,—is founded on compromise and barter.

> Edmund Burke, 1729–1797
> English statesman, orator, and writer
> *On Conciliation with the American Colonies*

The concessions of the weak are the concessions of fear.

> Edmund Burke, 1729–1797
> English statesman, orator, and writer
> *On Conciliation with the American Colonies*

A man whose *word* will not inform you at all what he means or will do, is not a man you can bargain with. You must get out of that man's way, or put him out of yours!

> Thomas Carlyle, 1795–1881
> Scottish essayist and historian
> *On Heroes and Hero-Worship*

[All legislation] ... is founded upon the principle of mutual concession—an agreement in which there are reciprocal stipulations— ... a measure of mutual concession—a measure of mutual sacrifice.... Let him who elevates himself above humanity, above its weaknesses, its infirmities, its wants, its necessities, say, if he pleases, "I will never compromise"; but let no one who is not above the frailties of our common nature disdain compromise.

> Henry Clay, 1777–1852
> American statesman and political orator
> Speech in the U. S. Senate, April 8, 1850

We never take an adverserial position at the bargaining table, and we try to be fair.

> Izzy Cohen
> CEO, Giant Food
> Schatz, *Managing By Influence*
> (Prentice-Hall, 1986)

I'll make him an offer he can't refuse.

> Don Corleone
> Community leader and negotiator
> *The Godfather*

Never get angry. Never make a threat. Reason with people.

> Don Corleone
> Community leader and negotiator
> *The Godfather*

He who will not reason, is a bigot; he who cannot is a fool; and he who dares not is a slave.

> William Drummond, 1553–1610
> Scottish poet
> *Academical Questions*

Compromise is but the sacrifice of one right or good in the hope of retaining another, too often ending in the loss of both.

> Tryon Edwards, 1809–1894
> American theologian
> *The New Dictionary Of Thoughts*, 1957

Perfectionists make poor negotiators. If you hold out for the perfect deal, you'll likely never close. If you close, you'll almost always leave something on the table.

> Lewis D. Eigen
> Executive Vice President,
> University Research Corp.
> Training seminar, June 1985

Nothing astonishes men so much as commonsense and plain dealing.

> Ralph Waldo Emerson, 1803–1882
> American essayist and poet
> *Art*

First learn the meaning of what you say, and only then speak.

> Epictetus, c. 60–120
> Roman Stoic philosopher
> *Discourses*

Know how to ask. There is nothing more difficult for some people. Nor for others, easier.

> Baltasar Gracián, 1601–1658
> Spanish priest and popular writer
> *The Art of Worldly Wisdom*

A miser and a liar bargain quickly.

> Greek proverb

Probabilities are always a rational ground of contract.

> Alexander Hamilton, 1755–1804
> First U. S. Secretary of the Treasury
> *First Report on Public Credit*, 1790

The style of conduct which carries weight calls for stubbornness even in an act of concession: you have to be severe with yourself in order to have the right to be gentle to others.

> Dag Hammerskjöld, 1905–1961
> Secretary-General of the United Nations
> *Markings*

True luck consists not in holding the best of
    the cards at the table;
Luckiest he who knows just when to rise and
    go home.

> John Hay, 1838–1905
> American Secretary of State
> *Distichs*

Basic salesmanship lays down that you should seek, at all times, to make the other side show its cards before you do.

Robert Heller
Editor, *Management Today*
The Supermanagers (Dutton, 1984)

The more arbitrary your demands are, the better your relative ... position—provided you do not arouse an emotional reaction.

Bruce Henderson
CEO, Boston Consulting Group, Inc.
Henderson on Corporate Strategy (Abt, 1979)

Many things are lost for want of asking.

George Herbert, 1593–1633
English clergyman and poet
Jacula Prudentum

Be calm in arguing; for fierceness makes
Error a fault and truth discourtesy.

George Herbert, 1593–1633
English clergyman and poet
Antiphon

Care keeps the conquest; 'tis no less renown
To keep a city than to win a town.

Robert Herrick, 1591–1674
English poet
Hesperides

At any given moment, there is always a line representing what your boss will believe. If you step over it, you will not get your budget. Go as close to that line as you can.

Grace Murray Hopper
Rear Admiral, U. S. Navy (retired)
Speech, Washington, D.C., February 1987

Once you consent to some concession, you can never cancel it and put things back the way they are.

Howard R. Hughes, 1905–1976
Founder, Hughes Tool Co.
Drosnin, *Citizen Hughes*
(Holt, Rinehart & Winston, 1985)

You should not convey to an opponent, either by word or action, that you want whatever the opponent has.

John Ilich
Professional negotiator
Power Negotiating (Addison-Wesley, 1980)

In its purest form, it [a negotiation] is mind pitted against mind.

John Ilich
Professional negotiator
Power Negotiating (Addison-Wesley, 1980)

It is better to give away the wool than the sheep.

Italian proverb

Nothing gives one person so much advantage over another as to remain cool and unruffled under all circumstances.

Thomas Jefferson, 1743–1946
Third President of the United States
Ilich, *Power Negotiating*
(Addison-Wesley, 1980)

I'm a compromiser and a maneuverer. I try to get *something*. That's the way our system works.

Lyndon Baines Johnson, 1908–1973
Thirty-sixth President of the United States
The New York Times, December 8, 1963

Okay, Frank, next time you need a dam in Idaho, ask Walter Lippmann for one.

> Lyndon Baines Johnson, 1908–1973
> Thirty-sixth President of the United States
> Remark to Senator Frank Church of Idaho,
> *Esquire*, August 1967

When Studebaker introduced a new assembly line ... there was conflict between union and management over what the new rates should be. The problem was handled by simply rotating all the foremen and stewards on the new line until they got a foreman-steward combination that could agree on the rates that should be set.

> Daniel Katz
> Labor economist
> Kahan and Boulding, *Power and Conflict in Organizations* (Basic Books, 1964)

Let us never negotiate out of fear. But let us never fear to negotiate.

> John Fitzgerald Kennedy, 1917–1963
> Thirty-fifth President of the United States
> Inaugural address, January 20, 1961

The opposition may ask Questions for Clarification. Questions of this variety are permitted: "What exactly is your procedure again?" "You said ... ; did you mean this?" This process is supposed to forestall the impulse to disagreement until there is an effort at understanding.... It is also a way to emphasize the belief that a proponent is entitled to every consideration in making his position clear, and that it will not be argued down before it is adequately stated. If listeners can be encouraged to wonder about what speakers mean, that may open rather than freeze the disputed position.

> Irving I. Lee
> *Harvard Business Review*,
> January/February 1954

Pacts ought to be observed.
[*Pacta sunt servanda*.]

> Legal maxim

Where the two sides are too evenly matched to offer a reasonable chance of early success to either, the statesman is wise who can learn something from the psychology of strategy. If you find your opponent in a strong position costly to force, you should leave him a line of retreat—as the quickest way of loosening his resistance.

> Basil Henry Liddell-Hart, 1895–1970
> English military historian and strategist
> *Strategy*

To obtain a just compromise, concession must not only be mutual—it must be equal also.... There can be no hope that either will yield more than it gets in return.

> John Marshall, 1755–1835
> U. S. Supreme Court Justice
> Beveridge, *The Life of John Marshall*

Generally speaking, women can negotiate better than they can fight. Our role is not as a warrior, but as peacemaker; not in the Army but in the State Department; not on the battlefield but at the treaty conference table.

> Jinx Milea
> University of Southern California
> and Pauline Lyttle
> President, Operational Politics, Inc.
> *Why Jenny Can't Lead*, 1986

Negotiation is clearly not just a man's game for we women negotiate all the time. It's just that once again successful men do it with different insights, goals, and consequences.

> Jinx Milea
> University of Southern California
> and Pauline Lyttle
> Operational Politics, Inc.
> *Why Jenny Can't Lead*, 1986

Negotiate or lose the business.

Bruce Moore
CEO, H. R. Krueger Machine Tool, Inc.
Harvard Business Review, March/April 1988

Concentrate on the issues that are most important to you and minimize or ignore the nonessentials.

James C. Nunan
Vice President for Systems Control, SICON
and Thomas J. Hutton
Partner, Pierce/Hutton Associates
Personnel Journal, November 1987

He is a fool who lets slip a bird in the hand for a bird in the bush.

Plutarch, c. 46–c. 120
Greek biographer and philosopher
Of Garrulity

The greatest strength [of the negotiator] lies in thinking up new proposals as soon as strong objections are made.

Walther Rathenau, 1867–1922
CEO, AEG (General Electric of Germany)
Reflexionen, 1908

We hardly find any persons of good sense save those who agree with us.

François de La Rochefoucauld, 1613–1680
French politician, writer, and philanthropist
Reflections, or Sentences and Moral Maxims

Keep your cards on top of the table. You can get away with a lot more freedom when people know what you are up to even if they don't like it or have reservations.

Milton J. Roedel
Manager of Exploratory Research, DuPont
Managers' meeting, February 1963

Lady Kent articled with Sir Edward Herbert, that he should come to her when she sent for him, and stay with her as long as she would have him, to which he set his hand; then he articled with her, that he should go away when he pleased, and stay away as long as he pleased, to which she set her hand. This is the epitome of all the contracts in the world.

John Selden, 1584–1654
English jurist, Orientalist, and statesman
Table Talk

Have more than thou showest,
Speak less than thou knowest.

William Shakespeare, 1564–1616
English dramatist and poet
King Lear

Don't negotiate with yourself. Have the patience to wait for the other fellow to make a counter-offer after you've made one.

Richard Smith
Partner, Smith, McWorter & Pachter
Speech, Washington D.C., February 12, 1988

A skillful negotiator will most carefully distinguish between the little and the great objects of his business, and will be as frank and open in the former, as he will be secret and pertinacious in the latter.

Philip Dormer Stanhope, 1694–1773
English Secretary of State
Maxims of the Earl of Chesterfield

Mr. G. Paton Smith wished to ask whether the six members ... constituted the "stone wall" which was to oppose all progress?

Hansard's House of Commons' Journals, 1876

No man can lose what he never had.

Izaak Walton, 1593–1683
English biographer and businessman
The Compleat Angler

Compromise may be man's best friend.

George Will
Syndicated columnist
The Washington Post, February 28, 1988

If they give you, take; if they take from you—
yell!

Anonymous

There's a difference between bending over
backward and bending over forward.

Anonymous (New York)

28
Office Politics

You lose a lot of time hating people.

A memorandum is written not to inform the reader but to protect the writer.

> Dean Acheson, 1893–1971
> U. S. Secretary of State
> Attributed

A friend in power is a friend lost.

> Henry Brooks Adams, 1838–1918
> American writer and historian
> *The Education of Henry Adams*

Better a certain enemy than a doubtful friend.

> Aesop, c. 620–c. 560 B.C.
> Greek fabulist
> *The Hound and the Hare*

The fury of my companions destroys me.

> Akkadian proverb

The manager who supports the boss—the manager whom the boss can rely on and

trust—is the one who will be given the most freedom and the least supervision.

> Mary Ann Allison
> Vice President, CitiCorp.
> and Eric Allison
> Financial writer
> *Managing Up, Managing Down*
> (Simon & Schuster, 1984)

You lose a lot of time hating people.

> Marian Anderson
> American opera singer
> *The New York Times*, April 18, 1965

He who attends to his own business does not soil his hands.

> Pietro Aretino, 1492–1556
> Italian satirist
> *Lo Ipocrito*

In dealing with cunning persons, we must ever consider their ends, to interpret their speeches; and it is good to say little to them, and that which they least look for.

Francis Bacon, 1561–1626
Lord Chancellor of England
Of Negotiating

People need the protection of promotion and evaluation procedures that diminish the importance of internal politics.

Judith M. Bardwick
University of California at San Diego
The Plateauing Trap (AMACOM, 1986)

The more one knows about a person, the greater one's power to destroy him.

Stanley I. Benn
Management writer and consultant
Wasserstrom, *Today's Moral Problems*
(Macmillan, 1975)

Don't have any more secrets that you can keep yourself.

Josh Billings
(Henry Wheeler Shaw), 1818–1885
American writer and auctioneer
Josh Billings: His Book

Neither yield to nor deal with agitators.

Napoleon Bonaparte, 1769–1821
Emperor of France
Maxims

By assuming sole responsibility for their departments, managers produce the very narrowness and self-interest they deplore in subordinates. When subordinates are relegated to their narrow specialities, they tend to promote their own practical interests, which then forces other subordinates into counteradvocacy. The manager is thereby thrust into the roles of arbitrator, judge, and referee. Not only do priorities become distorted, but decisions become loaded with win/lose dynamics. So, try as the manager

might, decisions inevitably lead to disgruntlement and plotting for the next battle.

David L. Bradford
Stanford University School of Business
and Allan R. Cohen
Babson College
Managing for Excellence (Wiley, 1984)

Politics is the art of the possible.

Richard Austen Butler, 1902–1984
English politician
Epigraph, *The Art of the Possible*

There is no use for any man's taking up his abode in a house built of glass. A man always is to be himself the judge how much of his mind he will show to other men; even to those he would have work along with him. There are impertinent inquiries made; your rule is, to leave the inquirer uninformed on that matter; not, if you can help it, misinformed, but precisely as dark as he was!

Thomas Carlyle, 1795–1881
Scottish essayist and historian
Of Heroes and Hero-Worship

It is not praise that does me good, but when men speak ill of me, then, with a noble assurance I say to myself, as I smile at them, "Let us be revenged by proving them to be liars."

Catherine II ("The Great"), 1729–1796
Empress of Russia
Correspondence avec le Baron F. M. Grimm

Beware the man whose stomach moves not when he laughs.

Chinese proverb

Craft is common both to skill and deceit.

Winston Churchill, 1874–1965
English Prime Minister, writer, and soldier
Halle, *Irrepressible Churchill*

We often injure our cause by calling in that which is weak, to support that which is strong.

Charles Caleb Colton, c. 1780–1832
English cleric, sportsman, and wine merchant
Lacon

The Wheel of Fortune turns round incessantly, and who can say to himself, "I shall today be uppermost" ?

Confucius, c. 551–c. 479 B.C.
Chinese philosopher and teacher
Analects

The people you want to reach, whether they're your coworkers, your boss or an organizational president, should be viewed as distinct target audiences that require different approaches and strategies.

Jeffrey P. Davidson
Marketing consultant
Management World, September/October 1987

Forewarned, forearmed; who threats his enemy lends him a sword to guard himself with.

Louis de Dorfort, c. 1640–1709
French-born English statesman and general
Arden of Feversham

It is never allowable, in an inferior, to equal himself in words to a superior, although he may rival him in actions.

Cardinal de Retz, 1614–1679
French ecclesiastic and politician
Political Maxims

If one cannot keep silent about one's own affairs, still less can one expect others to do so.

Anton Francesco Doni, c 1513–1574
Italian writer, editor, and bibilographer
I Marmi

Don't jump on a man unless he's down.

Finley Peter Dunne, 1867–1936
American humorist
Prochnow, *The Toastmaster's Treasure Chest*
(Harper & Row, 1979)

In politics, loyalty is everything.

James Eastland
U. S. Senator
Speakes, *Speaking Out* (Scribners, 1988)

Managing in some large organizations is akin to a horseman trying to escape a Western posse that's chasing him. He could sit backwards in the saddle, guarding his rump and have a good angle to fire at the pursuers. He'll nail a lot of them but will rarely get away. The alternative tactic is to face forward, eyes ahead on where you want to go. Ride like hell, and just occasionally fire over your shoulder to keep the bastards at bay.

Lewis D. Eigen
Executive Vice President,
University Research Corp.
Management seminar,
U. S. Job Corps, June 1965

Most of the trouble in the world is caused by people wanting to be important.

T. S. Eliot, 1888–1965
American-born English poet
The Cocktail Party

Nothing is so dangerous as an ignorant friend; a wise enemy is better.

Jean de La Fontaine, 1621–1695
French fabulist
Fables

It is a double pleasure to deceive the deceiver.

Jean de La Fontaine, 1621–1695
French fabulist
The Cock and the Fox

Three may keep a secret, if two of them are dead.

> Benjamin Franklin, 1706–1790
> American printer and statesman
> *Poor Richard's Almanack*

If you are unable to bite, refrain from showing your teeth.

> French proverb

Good fences make good neighbors.

> Robert Frost, 1874–1963
> American poet
> *Mending Wall*

Personal maneuvering spreads most malignantly in stagnant companies.... We were expanding so fast that there was plenty of room ... to advance and grow with the company.

> Harold Geneen
> CEO, IT&T
> *Managing* (Doubleday, 1984)

The eyes believe themselves; the ears believe other people.

> German proverb

All victories breed hate.

> Baltasar Gracián, 1601–1658
> Spanish priest and popular writer
> *The Art of Worldly Wisdom*

People busy covering their rears are wasting energy and time that ought to be devoted to challenging competitors.

> Daniel Greenberg
> Chairman, Electro Rent Corp.
> *Newsweek,* April 25, 1988

The great secret of life is never to be in the way of others.

> Thomas Chandler Haliburton, 1796–1865
> Canadian jurist and humorist
> *Sam Slick*

Never ennoble anybody in such a way that he may harm you; and never trust anybody so exclusively that you lose the capital and the state to him.

> Han Tzu, 280–233 B.C.
> Chinese philosopher and teacher
> In Mousheng, *Men and Ideas*

The president of a railroad forces his associates to attend meetings, shivering at dawn, in an old circus tent. In another frame of mind, he will suddenly present a browbeaten underling with a new Lincoln Continental or a two-week vacation in Hawaii.... The ambition to rise out of his species and attain a higher form of being—not only after death, like most people, but now, today—cuts him off, sometimes intolerably, and when this happens he lunges in the direction of humanity. For him, sudden gifts are the coin of brotherhood. They perform a dual service, at once binding and unsettling to the recipient, and at the same time allowing the imitation-diety an illusion of having reached someone.

> Alan Harrington
> Advertising executive and manager
> *The Immortalist* (Celestial Arts, 1977)

More trouble is caused in the world by indiscreet answers than by indiscreet questions.

> Sydney J. Harris
> American journalist
> *Chicago Daily News*, March 27, 1958

Power is the ability to initiate activity for others and to disregard others' initiative. Power can be used to strengthen power....

The first use of power is to preserve and compound it.

> Bruce Henderson
> CEO, Boston Consulting Group, Inc.
> *Henderson on Corporate Strategy* (Abt, 1979)

The corporation without an explicit strategy will fall into the hands of politicians.

> Bruce Henderson
> CEO, Boston Consulting Group, Inc.
> *Henderson on Corporate Strategy* (Abt, 1979)

It is good to have some friends both in heaven and hell.

> George Herbert, 1593–1633
> English clergyman and poet
> *Jacula Prudentum*

No rumour wholly dies, once bruited wide,
But deathless like a goddess doth abide.

> Hesiod, eighth century B.C.
> Greek poet
> *Works and Days*

If I am not for myself, who will be for me?
If I am only for myself, what am I?
If not now—when?

> Hillel the Elder, c. 30 B.C.–c. A.D. 25
> Jewish sage and teacher
> *Sayings of the Fathers*

An ounce of loyalty is worth a pound of cleverness.

> Elbert Hubbard, 1856–1915
> American writer, printer, and editor
> *Elbert Hubbard's Note Book*

Play off everyone against each other so that you have more avenues of action open to you.

> Howard R. Hughes, 1905–1976
> Founder, Hughes Tool Co.
> *The Hughes Legacy: Scramble for the Billion*
> (Time, 1976)

He [John Hampden] had a head to contrive, a tongue to persuade, and a hand to execute any mischief.

> Edward Hyde, 1609–1674
> English politician, statesman, and historian
> *History of the Rebellion*

The show of their countenance doth witness against them.

> Old Testament, Isaiah 3:9

The president has to live alone and like it. If he indulges in the luxury of thinking out loud, he sets off a chain reaction of rumors throughout the organization. He is the final, focal point of all the competitive pressures of men in the organization who are ambitious. If he confides in one and not in the others, he immediately lowers the morale of his executive staff.

> J. Elliott Janney
> *Harvard Business Review*, May/June 1952

Fish die by their mouth.

> Japanese proverb

A single zealot may commence persecutor, and better men be his victims.

> Thomas Jefferson, 1743–1826
> Third President of the United States
> *Notes on the State of Virginia*

What it takes to operate inside the structure of an authoritarian business organization may initially go against your democratic American grain.

Robert Jelinek
Executive Vice President,
Young & Rubicam, Inc.
Working Woman, March 1988

Powerlessness corrupts. Absolute powerlessness corrupts absolutely.

Rosabeth Moss Kantor
Harvard Business School
Peters, *Thriving on Chaos* (Knopf, 1987)

[Office] politics is the process of getting along with the querulous, the garrulous and the congenitally unlovable.

Marilyn Moats Kennedy
Managing Partner, Career Strategies, Inc.
Newsweek, September 16, 1985

Trust not him with your secrets, who, when left alone in your room, turns over your papers.

Johann Kaspar Lavater, 1741–1801
Swiss theologian
Aphorisms on Man

Even a flounder takes sides.

Stanislaw J. Lec
Polish writer and aphorist
Unkempt Thoughts (St. Martin's Press, 1962)

Abrasive persons can make significant contributions to an organization, but managers need to steer them again and again into taking those political steps that will enable them to experience success rather than rejection. Rather than corral such people, who tend to figuratively butt their heads against restrictions, mangagers do better to act like sheepdogs, gently nudging them back into position when they stray.

Harry Levinson
Psychologist, Harvard Medical School
*Harvard Business Review on
Human Relations*, 1986

If the chief party, whether it be the people, or the army, or the nobility, which you think most useful and of most consequence to you for the conservation of your dignity be corrupt, you must follow their humor and indulge them, and in that case, honesty and virture are pernicious.

Niccolò Machiavelli, 1469–1527
Florentine statesman and philosopher
The Prince

It is necessary for a prince who desires to maintain his position, to acquire the power of not being good, and to use that power, or not, according to circumstances.

Niccolò Machiavelli, 1469–1527
Florentine statesman and philosopher
The Prince

The employee, whether he is civil service or a political appointee, has not only the right but the obligation to make his views known in the most strenuous way possible to his superiors, and through them, to their superiors. He should try like hell to get his views across and adopted within the organization—but not publicly, and only until a decision is reached by those superiors. Once the decision is made, he must do the best he can to live with it and put it into practice. If he finds that he cannot do it, then he ought not to stay with the organization.

Frederick Malek
Secretary, U. S. Department of Health,
Education, and Welfare
Peters and Branch, *Blowing the Whistle*
(Praeger, 1972)

Beyond salaries, plenty of companies offer special bonuses or achievement awards. The people who receive such awards generally have an excellent manager pulling for them.

Philip W. Metzger
Computer analyst and management writer
Managing Programming People
(Prentice-Hall, 1987)

Who has no friends nor enemies is without talents or energy.

Old Farmer's Almanac (1836)

It's not whether you win or lose, but how you place the blame.

John Peers
President, Logical Machine Corp.
1,001 Logical Laws (Doubleday, 1979)

[Referring to General Motors, of which he had been a Director:] Too much energy is being used up in corporate in-fighting. The corporation ought to be devoting its energies to making the finest cars in the world, and not get tied up in Machiavellian intrigues.

H. Ross Perot
Founder, Electronic Data Systems
The Washington Post, November 22, 1987

People sense weakness, and step in and try to take control.

H. Ross Perot
Founder, Electronic Data Systems
The Washington Post, November 22, 1987

Who naught suspects is easily deceived.

Petrarch (Francesco Petrarca), 1304–1374
Italian poet
Sonnets

There wasn't any of the empire-building and political infighting. Everybody was trying to focus on the problems.

Thomas G. Plaskett
President, Pan American World Airways
The New York Times, April 12, 1988

Zeno first started the doctrine that knavery is the best defense against a knave.

Plutarch, 46–120
Greek biographer and philosopher
Of Bashfulness

Drink nothing without sniffing it; sign nothing without reading it.

Portugese proverb

High places have their precipices.

Barber, *The Book of 1000 Proverbs*, 1876

If you have no enemies, it is a sign Fortune has forgot you.

Barber, *The Book of 1000 Proverbs*, 1876

Reprove thy friend privately; commend him publicly.

Barber, *The Book of 1000 Proverbs*, 1876

The wise man avoids evil by anticipating it.

Publilius Syrus, c. 42 B.C.
Roman writer
Maxims

Treat your friend as if he might become an enemy.

Publilius Syrus, c. 42 B.C.
Roman writer
Maxims

Let no man's word or deed seduce thee
To do or say what is not to thy best good.
Think first, then act; lest thy deed foolish be.

> Pythagoras, c. 500 B.C.
> Greek philosopher and mathematician
> Quoted in *Ethical Sentences from Stoboeus*

What cannot be cured must be endured.

> François Rabelais, 1494–1547
> French physician, humorist, and satirist
> *Works*

To get along, go along.

> Sam Rayburn, 1882–1961
> Speaker of the House of Representatives
> Advice to freshman Congressman
> Lyndon Baines Johnson, 1937

As hard as it might be and as unrealistic as it might seem, in my experience it is always better to act, to work and to perform as if there were no such thing as racial discrimination.

> Emmett Rice
> *Black Enterprise*, October 1979

It is sometimes necessary to play the fool to avoid being deceived by cunning men.

> François de La Rochefoucauld, 1613–1680
> French politician, writer, and philanthropist
> *Reflections, or Sentences and Moral Maxims*

There is great ability in knowing how to conceal one's ability.

> François de La Rochefoucauld, 1613–1680
> French politician, writer, and philanthropist
> *Reflections, or Sentences and Moral Maxims*

There is no better friend than a frank enemy.

> Dagobert D. Runes
> Editor, publisher, and philosopher
> *A Book of Contemplation*

Life is too short for the indulgence of animosity.

> Walter Scott, 1771–1832
> Scottish poet, novelist, and biographer
> Lockhart, *Life of Sir Walter Scott*

It was a maxim of Queen Caroline to bear herself towards her political friends with such caution, as if there was a possiblity of their one day being her enemies, and toward political opponents with the same degree of circumspection, as if they might again become friendly to her measures.

> Walter Scott, 1771–1832
> Scottish poet, novelist, and biographer
> *The Heart of Midlothian*

When people won't let you alone, it's because you haven't learned to make them do it.

> David Seabury
> American psychologist
> *The Art of Selfishness*
> (Simon & Schuster, 1964)

Every one that flatters thee,
Is no friend in misery.

> William Shakespeare, 1564–1616
> English dramatist and poet
> *Poems*

Take note, take note, O world,
To be direct and honest is not safe.

> William Shakespeare, 1564–1616
> English dramatist and poet
> *Othello*

O mischief! Thou art swift
To enter in the thoughts of desperate men!

> William Shakespeare, 1564–1616
> English dramatist and poet
> *Romeo and Juliet*

Let your own discretion be your tutor:
Suit the action to the word,
The word to the action.

> William Shakespeare, 1564–1616
> English dramatist and poet
> *Hamlet*

'Tis better playing with a lion's whelp
Than with an old one dying.

> William Shakespeare, 1564–1616
> English dramatist and poet
> *Antony and Cleopatra*

Power does not corrupt men; fools, however,
if they get into a position of power, corrupt
power.

> George Bernard Shaw, 1856–1950
> Nobel laureate in literature
> Winsten, *Days with Bernard Shaw*

Keep your friends close, but keep your
enemies closer.

> Sicilian proverb

Liars ought to have good memories.

> Algernon Sidney, 1622–1683
> English statesman
> *Discourses on Government*

In your friendships, and in your enmities, let
your confidence and your hostilities have certain bounds; make not the former dangerous,
nor the latter irreconcileable. There are
strange vicissitudes in business.

> Philip Dormer Stanhope, 1694–1773
> English Secretary of State
> *Maxims of the Earl of Chesterfield*

A lot of talented people get politically
strangled in a large company.

> Paul Stevens
> CEO, Trio
> *Business Age,* April 1988

What some invent the rest enlarge [i.e.
rumor].

> Jonathan Swift, 1667–1775
> English cleric and satirist
> *Journal of a Modern Lady*

Walls have tongues, and hedges ears.

> Jonathan Swift, 1667–1775
> English cleric and satirist
> *Pastoral Dialogue*

Lord Northcliffe ... aspired to power instead
of influence, and as a result forfeited both.

> A. J. P. Taylor
> English historian and writer
> *English History, 1914-1945*

It does not do to leave a live dragon out of your
calculations, if you live near him.

> J. R. R. Tolkein
> English professor and popular novelist
> *Reader's Digest*, September 1978

There is a difference between attacking a
decision and attacking the man who made the
decision.

> Maurice S. Trotter
> New York University
> *Supervisor's Handbook on Insubordination*
> (Bureau of National Affairs, 1967)

Carry the battle to them. Don't let them bring it to you. Put *them* on the defensive. And don't ever apologize for anything.

> Harry S. Truman, 1884–1972
> Thirty-third President of the United States
> Advice to Senator Hubert Humphrey,
> *The New York Times*, September 20, 1964

As long as I count the votes what are you going to do about it?

> William Marcy ("Boss") Tweed, 1823–1878
> Tammany Hall grand sachem
> Remark during the New York City
> mayorality election, 1871

A snake lurks in the grass.
[*Latet anguis in herba.*]

> Virgil, 70–19 B.C.
> Roman poet
> *Eclogue*

Capture inner-office supporters by involving them in developmental goals and programs. It gives others a vested interest in speeding up the approval process.

> Terry Ware
> Special Assistant,
> U. S. Government Printing Office
> *Management*, 1987

Be courteous to all, but intimate with few; and let those few be well tried before you give them your confidence.

> George Washington, 1732–1799
> First President of the United States
> Letter to Bushrod Washington,
> January 15, 1783

Politics can be good or bad. Few things get done without a power base. Hence many of our finest managers are closet politicians.... Those that make things happen are politically skilled and understand the use of power.

> Robert H. Waterman
> Management consultant and writer
> *The Renewal Factor* (Bantam, 1987)

A man cannot be too careful in the choice of his enemies.

> Oscar Wilde, 1854–1900
> Irish poet, playwright, and novelist
> *The Picture of Dorian Gray*

The eyes and ears of man are not always dependent upon his will, but a man's tongue is always dependent upon his will.

> The Zohar

[On hearsay:] One man's word is no man's word.

> Anonymous

It is easy to acquire an enemy, but difficult to acquire a friend.

> Anonymous

29

Organization

Structure is not organization.

Chaos often breeds life, when order breeds habit.

Henry Brooks Adams, 1838–1919
American writer and historian
The Education of Henry Adams

Too many cooks spoil the brothel.

Polly Adler, 1900–1962
American madam and management writer
A House is Not a Home
(Rinehart, 1953)

Never reorganize except for a good business reason. But if you haven't reorganized in a while, that's a good business reason.

John Akers
CEO, IBM
Waterman, *The Renewal Factor*
(Bantam, 1987)

[D]ownsizing has become an organizational activity, often independent of economic growth or contraction.

American Management Association
Responsible Reductions in Force, 1987

Equality ... is the result of human organization.... We are not born equal.

Hannah Arendt, 1906–1975
German-American philosopher and critic
The Origins of Totalitarianism

Built into decentralization is the age old tug between autonomy and control: superiors want no surprises, subordinates want to be left alone. The subordinates push for autonomy; they assert that by leaving them alone, top management will show its trust from a distance. The superiors, on the other hand, try to keep control through information systems. The subordinates see the control devices as confirming their suspicions—their superiors don't trust them.

Chris Argyris
Harvard Graduate School of Education
Harvard Business Review,
September/October 1986

The purpose of organizations is to exploit the fact that many decisions require the participation of many individuals for their effectiveness.

Kenneth J. Arrow
Nobel laureate in economics
The Limits of Organization (Norton, 1974)

If a sufficient number of management layers are superimposed on top of each other, it can be assured that disaster is not left to chance.

Norman R. Augustine
President and CEO, Martin Marietta Corp.
Augustine's Laws (Penguin, 1987)

It is better to be the reorganizer than the reorganizee.

Norman R. Augustine
President and CEO, Martin Marietta Corp.
Augustine's Laws (Penguin, 1987)

The whole object of the organization is to get cooperation, to get to each individual the benefit of all the knowledge and all the experience of all individuals.

Hamilton McFarland Barksdale
Management Executive Committee, Dupont
Committee meeting minutes, October 11, 1909

Executive work is not that *of* the organization, but the specialized work of *maintaining* the organization.

Chester I. Barnard, 1886–1961
President, U. S. O.
The Functions of the Executive (Harvard, 1938)

Organizations are a system of cooperative activities—and their coordination requires something intangible and personal that is largely a matter of relationships.

Chester I. Bernard, 1886–1961
President, U. S. O.
The Functions of the Executive (Harvard, 1938)

If we view organizations as adaptive, problem-solving structures, then inferences about effectiveness have to be made, not from static measures of output, but on the basis of the processes through which the organization approaches problems. In other words, no single measurement of organizational efficiency or satisfaction—no single time-slice of organizational performance—can provide valid indicators of organizational health.

Warren G. Bennis
President, University of Cincinnati
General Systems Yearbook, 1962

Organizations facing complexity and change must hire competent, educated people at the managerial level ... many with MBA's and other advanced or technical degrees. Try as the managers might, they will rarely be able to keep technically ahead of their new subordinates in all areas.... The most specific knowledge of the task must be left to the highly trained subordinates who now often have their own areas of expertise.

David L. Bradford
Stanford School of Business
and Allan R. Cohen
Babson College
Managing for Excellence (Wiley, 1984)

Organization can never be a substitute for initiative and for judgment.

Louis Dembitz Brandeis, 1856–1941
U. S. Supreme Court Justice
Business—A Profession

[Explaining why company offices are dispersed in many buildings with less than 80 employees in each:] People always want to deal with the top person in the building. So somebody besides me takes complete responsibility.

Richard Branson
Chairman, Virgin Group (England)
Inc. Magazine, November 1987

With the finest of personnel, an illogical organization structure makes waste through internal friction and lost motion; it fails to retain and develop good men and to invite into its membership new men of high quality.

Henry S. Dennison, 1877–1952
Founder, Dennison Corp.
Organization and Management
(Harvard, 1948)

Modern organization makes demands on the individual to learn something he has never been able to do before: to use organization intelligently, purposefully, deliberately, responsibly ... to manage organization ... to make ... his job in it serve his ends, his values, his desire to achieve.

Peter F. Drucker
Management consultant and writer
The Age of Discontinuity
(Harper & Row, 1968)

Both the businessman and the civil servant tend to underrate the difficulty of managing service institutions. The businessman thinks it's all a matter of being efficient, the civil servant thinks it's all a matter of having the right procedures and controls. Both are wrong—service institutions are more complex than either business or government agencies—as we are painfully finding out in our attempts to make the hospital a little more manageable.... [D]efining what its task is and what it should not be is the most essential step in making the institutions of the Third Sector manageable, managed, and performing.

Peter F. Drucker
Management consultant and writer
The Changing World of the Executive
(Quadrangle, 1982)

We want to give every individual influence in every job, and the old organization structure just won't do.

Karl Johan Edstrom
Personnel Director, Grangesberg (Sweden)
Jenkins, *Job Power, Blue and White Collar Democracy* (Doubleday, 1973)

An institution is the lengthened shadow of one man.

Ralph Waldo Emerson, 1803–1882
American essayist and poet
Self Reliance

You want [only] one person to be in charge.

Donald Engen
Former Administrator, FAA
Newsweek, May 2, 1988

Government ... is neither business, nor technology, nor applied science. It is the art of making men live together in peace and with reasonable happiness.

Felix Frankfurter, 1882–1965
U. S. Supreme Court Justice
The New Republic, October 31, 1928

True freedom is not the absence of structure—letting the employees go off and do whatever they want—but rather a clear structure that enables people to work within established boundaries in an autonomous and creative way.

Erich Fromm
Psychologist, philosopher, and writer
Escape from Freedom (Rinehart, 1941)

A box in the organization chart is not sufficient to get [an] operation going; it must have the backing of an important leader.

Joseph N. Froomkin
Management consultant
Journal of the Academy of Management,
March 1964

In most large Japanese firms many employees have titles.... These titles are usually devoid of power; they have been created to accommodate the psychological needs of employees with many years of seniority. An American can only admire this relatively painless way of keeping peace within a company.

Joseph N. Froomkin
Management consultant
Journal of the Academy of Management,
March 1964

The greater the uncertainty, the greater the amount of decision making and information processing. It is hypothesised that organizations have limited capacities to process information and adopt different organizing modes to deal with task uncertainty. Therefore, variations in organizing modes are actually variations in the capacity of organizations to process information and make decisions about events which cannot be anticipated in advance.

J. Galbraith
Organization Design
(Addison-Wesley, 1977)

Every company has two organizational structures: the formal one is written on the charts; the other is the living relationship of the men and women in the organization.

Harold Geneen
CEO, IT&T
Managing (Doubleday, 1984)

A sort of credo has grown up, to the effect that organization charts inhibit creativity, that a full flowering of creative research can be attained only through an unorganized, individualistic approach. All I can say is that experience teaches me otherwise.

Estill I. Green
Vice President, Bell Telephone Laboratories
Effective Administration of Research Programs
(Cornell University Press, 1958)

[Referring to managers after a reorganization:] If they end up having to share [secretaries], people feel as if they've been demoted.

David Hackney
Campbell Soup Co.
The New York Times, April 27, 1988

[These days, secretaries] ... handle more bosses but less coffee.

Trish Hall
Journalist
The New York Times, April 27, 1988

Where there is no specific advantage to the divisions [of an organization] being associated with one another, there is no justification for them to march under the same corporate banner.

Bruce Henderson
CEO, Boston Consulting Group, Inc.
Henderson on Corporate Strategy (Abt, 1979)

Many institutions are quite effective, even though they seem to break all the rules of organization structure—universities, for example. Japanese companies can be extremely effective competitors even though their internal structure seems incomprehensible to the Westerner.

Bruce Henderson
CEO, Boston Consulting Group, Inc.
Henderson on Corporate Strategy (Abt, 1979)

It is a paradox that the greater the decentralization, the greater the need for both leadership and explicit policies from the top management.

Bruce Henderson
CEO, Boston Consulting Group, Inc.
Henderson on Corporate Strategy (Abt, 1979)

The successful organization has one major attribute that sets it apart from unsuccessful organizations: dynamic and effective leader-ship.

Paul Hersey
California American University
and Kenneth H. Blanchard
University of Massachusetts
Management of Organizational Behavior
(Prentice-Hall, 1982)

An organization with an indispensable man is guilty of management failure.

Harold S. Hook
Chairman and CEO, American General Corp.
Forbes, October 19, 1987

Weak character coupled with honored place, meager knowledge with large plans, limited powers with heavy responsibility, will seldom escape disaster.

I Ching: Book of Changes
China, c. 600 B.C.

The most important thing ... is to reduce the number of management layers.

F. Kenneth ("Ken") Iverson
CEO, Nucor Corp.
Inc. Magazine, April 1986

Very small groups of highly skilled generalists show a remarkable propensity to succeed.

Ramchandran Jaikumar
Harvard Business School
Harvard Business Review,
November/December 1986

Authority and responsibility are rarely balanced.

Joe Kelly
Concordia University (Montreal)
How Managers Manage (Prentice-Hall, 1980)

The idea that an executive should have only one boss has to be discarded.

Joe Kelly
Concordia University (Montreal)
How Managers Manage (Prentice-Hall, 1980)

Don't agonize. Organize.

Florynce R. Kennedy
Writer and feminist
Ms. Magazine, March 1973

As organizational researchers, we have wondered why certain decisions are made and particular strategies chosen. Why does an organization end up with a particular kind of structure? Why is a certain individual selected for a particular job?.... [T]he problems of many troubled companies are deeply ingrained, based on the deep-seated neurotic styles and fantasies of top executives.

Manfred F. R. Kets de Vries and Danny Miller
McGill University School of Management
The Neurotic Organization
(Jossey-Bass, 1984)

What has always frustrated me about staff is that the people you want solving problems end up administering.

Charles Knight
Chairman, Emerson Electric
Tomasko, *Downsizing* (AMACOM, 1987)

One of the misconceptions in our cultural heritage is that organizations exist purely to get things done. This is only one of their purposes; it is their work purpose. But every organization is also a social system that serves as an instrumentality for helping people meet human needs and achieve human goals. In fact, this is the primary purpose for which people take part in organizations—to meet their needs and achieve their goals—and when an organization does not serve this purpose for them they tend to withdraw from it.

Malcolm Knowles
North Carolina State University
The Adult Learner (Gulf, 1978)

The facts with which a highly centralized institution deals tend to be the men and women of that institution itself, and their ideas and ambitions. To maintain perspective and human understanding in the atmosphere of centralization is a task that many able and conscientious people have found well-nigh impossible.

David Eli Lilienthal, 1899–1981
American public official
T. V. A.—Democracy on the March
(Harper & Row, 1944)

Educated workers in rich countries do not like to be organized from the top.... It will be nonsense to sit in hierarchical offices trying to arrange what people in the offices below do with their imaginations.

Norman McCrae
Associate Editor
The Economist, December 25, 1976

Large organizations ... divorce themselves from their economic reason for being. They become independent political units.

Alonzo L. McDonald
CEO, Bendix, and White House Staff Director
Harvard Business Review,
November/December, 1986

Most organizations, left to their own devices, are going to atrophy, to get so institutional, so bureaucratic, that they get to the point where their original reason for existence has been lost, and they stagnate. So you have to have change, and by that I mean dramatic change.

William G. McGowan
Chairman, MCI Communications Corp.
Inc. Magazine, August 1986

Organizations may fantasize that parts of themselves do not exist. An organization may disown, alienate, or dissociate itself from and repress parts of itself.

Uri Merry and George I. Brown
The Neurotic Behavior of Organizations
(Gestalt Institute of Cleveland, 1987)

The whittling away of middle management is further reinforcing the trend for companies to smash the hierarchical pyramid and adopt new people structures such as networks, intrapreneurs, and small teams.

John Naisbett and Patricia Aburdene
Business writers and social researchers
Re-inventing the Corporation (Warner, 1985)

[Former Secretary of Defense Robert S. McNamara] ... believed that any large organization was characterized by inertia. It needed to be kicked, and kicked hard, if that inertia was to be overcome. He developed list upon list of new initiatives which would have the effect of kicking the organization.

Paul Nitze
American arms control negotiator
Haught, *Giants in Management*
(National Academy of
Public Administration, 1985)

One of the vices of the virtue of decentralization is that people don't share ideas.

Anthony J. F. O'Reilly
CEO, Heinz Foods
The New York Times, May 8, 1988

Organizations are social beings and their success depends on trust, subtlety and intimacy.

William Ouchi
UCLA School of Management
Theory Z (Addison-Wesley, 1981)

We trained hard ... but every time we were beginning to form up into teams, we would be reorganized. I was to learn later in life that we tend to meet new situations by reorganizing .... and a wonderful method it can be for creating the illusion of progress while producing confusion, inefficiency, and demoralization.

Petronius Arbiter, d. A.D. 65
Roman governor and advisor (*arbiter*) to Nero
Satyricon

It is becoming clear that America's economic future depends less on lonely geniuses and backyard inventors than on versatile organizations. Our abundance of Nobel laureates attests to American cleverness. Technical advances originate disproportionately in America—semiconductors, videocassette recorders, and automobile stamping technologies, to name only a few. Our problem is that we are not consolidating this technological leadership into enduring commercial leadership because our industrial organization is not adaptable enough.

Robert B. Reich
JFK School of Government, Harvard University
The Next American Frontier, 1983

How machines are related to each other often determines the organizational structure [of the people].

John A. Reinecke
University of New Orleans
and William F. Schoell
University of Southern Mississippi
Introduction to Business
(Allyn and Bacon, 1983)

You cannot have divided authority.

Felix Rohatyn
Chairman,
New York City Municipal Assistance Corp.
The New York Times, November 22, 1987

[A]n examination of cultural issues at the organizational level is absolutely essential to a basic understanding of what goes on in or-

ganizations, how to run them, and how to improve them.

Edgar H. Schein
Massachusetts Institute of Technology
Organizational Culture and Leadership
(Jossey-Bass, 1985)

Within a complicated bureaucratic structure distortions inevitably creep into the process of acquiring and organizing evidence.

James R. Schlesinger
U. S. Secretary of Defense
Memorandum to Senate Committee on
Government Operations, April 1968

Middle managers make nothing but the organization ...

Earl Shorris
Manager and writer
The Oppressed Middle
(Anchor/Doubleday, 1981)

All organizations engage in the three basic activities of strategy, tactics, and logistics. Strategy defines the job. Tactics does the job. Logistics provides the resources to get the job done—not only material resources, but also manpower, funds, and data.

Robert L. Siegel
Branch Manager, McLaughlin Research Corp.
Speech, Arlington, Virginia,
November 18, 1987

The Dying Organization is characterized by vaguely defined outputs existing in a state of confused authority distribution emanating from a placid centralization of non-direction, converging into disjointed efforts toward crisis fire-fighting reacted to by "on-the-job retired" employees.

Mark B. Silber
Organizational psychologist
Privately circulated communication

The difference between "structure" and "stricture" is "I."

> Marlene Solomon
> Publisher, *Magna Magazine*
> Sales meeting, February 17, 1988

In many firms the technique is employed of having an executive vice president rule on an issue [that is controversial], the president remaining uninvolved so that appeals to him are still possible. If no one screams, the decision is allowed to stand.

> Ross Stagner
> Michigan State University
> *Business Topics* (MSU, Winter 1965)

The man who goes alone can start today; but he who travels with another must wait till that other is ready.

> Henry David Thoreau, 1817–1862
> American naturalist and writer
> *Walden*

Napoleon felt that 5 reports was the greatest desirable span; Karl von Clausewitz maintained that 10 was more appropriate. Henri Fayol ... was more flexible.... He suggests 15 for lower level supervisors but only 4 for senior executives.... Sears Roebuck & Company, in either ignorance or disregard of these theoreticians, managed the post World War II growth spurt with its headquarters merchandising vice president having 44 senior managers reporting directly to him. Their store managers each also coped, somehow, with supervising about 40 department heads.

> Robert M. Tomasko
> Principal, Temple, Barker & Sloane, Inc.
> *Downsizing* (AMACOM, 1987)

Draw them [organization charts] in pencil. Never formalize, print and circulate them.

> Robert Townsend
> Former CEO, Avis
> *Further Up the Organization* (Knopf, 1984)

Most people in big companies are administered, not led. They are treated as personnel, not as people.

> Robert Townsend
> Former CEO, Avis
> *Further Up the Organization* (Knopf, 1984)

Organizations exist for only one purpose: to help people reach ends together that they could not achieve individually.

> Robert H. Waterman
> Management consultant and writer
> *The Renewal Factor* (Bantam, 1987)

Structure is not organization.

> Robert H. Waterman
> Management consultant and writer
> *Business Horizons*, June 1980

Every management layer you can strip away makes you more responsive.

> John R. Whitney
> Executive-in-Residence
> Columbia University Business School
> *Harvard Business Review*,
> September/October 1987

The only way for a large organization to function is to decentralize, to delegate real authority and responsibility to the man on the job. But be certain you have the right man on the job.

> Robert E. Wood, 1879–1969
> President and Chairman, Sears Roebuck & Co.
> *Ordnance*, July/August 1951

Think of the sequence. You create something. You grow it. You look for a competitive advantage. Then you really tie it down tight, making it as efficient as possible. Those are very different jobs.

Alan Zakon
Computer scientist and entrepreneur
Hickman and Silva, *Creating Excellence*
(New American Library, 1984)

30

Performance Measurement & Evaluation

If you can't measure it, you can't manage it.

No longer is organizational or individual performance measured by reality. It is, these days, assessed by the difference between expectation and reality. Good managers must manage the expectations as well as the reality.

Clark Abt
Founder, Abt Associates, Inc.
Staff meeting, 1974

Much outcry. Little outcome.

Aesop, c. 560 B.C.
Greek fabulist
The Mountains in Labour

Another day, another zero.

Alfalfa (Carl Switzer), 1926–1959
Our Gang comedy series star

The medicine man who is praised for the rain will also be blamed for the drought.

American Indian proverb

Finding the "competitive value added" by staff employees and department gives downsizers a means of determining which functions it can do without with the least detriment to operations.

American Management Association
Responsible Reductions in Force, 1987

To do easily what is difficult for others is the mark of talent. To do what is impossible for talent is the mark of genius.

Henri Frédéric Amiel, 1821–1881
Swiss journalist and critic
Journal intime

Whoever receiving a statement in confidence proceeds to repeat it, is a scoundrel, or very leaky. If he does it for personal gain, he is a scoundrel; and if he does so without a personal object he is leaky; both characters are equally bad.

Anaxandrides, c. 376 B.C.
Greek dramatist and satirist
Fragments

[In monitoring performance:] So long as the results are satisfactory, nothing is done; but when deterioration occurs there is a thorough investigation of its causes.... The sinking of the *Titanic* led to iceberg patrols.

Kenneth J. Arrow
Nobel laureate in economics
The Limits of Organization (Norton, 1974)

There is not anything so excellent, but some will carp at it.

Mary Astel, c. 1666–1731
English pamphleteer
Quoted in *Letters of Lady Montagu*

People need the protection of promotion and evaluation procedures that diminish the importance of internal politics.

Judith M. Bardwick
University of California at San Diego
The Plateauing Trap (AMACOM, 1986)

If we view organizations as adaptive, problem-solving structures, then inferences about effectiveness have to be made, not from static measures of output, but on the basis of the processes through which the organization approaches problems. In other words, no single measurement of organizational efficiency or satisfaction—no single time-slice of organizational performance—can provide valid indicators of organizational health.

Warren G. Bennis
President, University of Cincinnati
General Systems Yearbook, 1962

The most successful managers are those that can quickly grasp how their bosses think.

Amy Bermar
Business and computer writer
PC Week, August 11, 1987

You can't think and hit the ball at the same time.

Lawrence Peter "Yogi" Berra
Professional baseball player, manager, coach
Attributed

Everyone who does the best he can do is a hero.

Josh Billings
(Henry Wheeler Shaw), 1818–1885
American writer and auctioneer
Josh Billings: His Book

The man who never makes any blunders is a very nice piece of machinery—that's all.

Josh Billings
(Henry Wheeler Shaw), 1818–1885
American writer and auctioneer
Josh Billings: His Book

As in a game of cards, so in the game of life we must play what is dealt to us; and the glory consists, not so much in winning, as in playing a poor hand well.

Josh Billings
(Henry Wheeler Shaw), 1818–1885
American writer and auctioneer
Josh Billings: His Book

Achieving good performance is a journey, not a destination.

Kenneth H. Blanchard
Chairman, Blanchard Training and Development
and Robert Lorber
President, R. L. Lorber & Associates
Putting the One Minute Manager to Work
(William Morrow, 1984)

Many firms have developed weighted-sum formulas to judge the performance of professionals. The businesses give credit for billable hours that a person has sold (for a year or two after the client has been brought in) and for billable hours worked. They then assign weights based on the desirability of each client, the value the firm places on selling versus performing professional tasks, and other factors.

Paul N. Bloom
University of Maryland
Harvard Business Review,
September/October 1984

People in the corporate world play to a higher audience that equates action with results. The constant pressure is to demonstrate that you are a tough manager capable of making tough decisions.

Charles J. Bodenstab
CEO, Battery & Tire Warehouse, Inc.
Inc. Magazine, August 1987

The greatest general is he who makes the fewest mistakes.

Napoleon Bonaparte, 1769–1821
Emperor of France
Maxims

We have to earn our wings *every* day.

Frank Borman
Astronaut and CEO, Eastern Airlines
TV commercial, 1986

No one ever won a chess game by betting on each move. Sometimes you have to move backward to get a step forward.

Amar Bose
CEO, Bose Corp.
Best of Business Quarterly, 1987

Understanding should precede judging.

Louis Dembitz Brandeis, 1856–1941
U. S. Supreme Court Justice
Burns Bakery Co. v. *Bryan* (1923)

When your work speaks for itself, get out of the way.

Thomas "Wayne" Brazell
U. S. Army Materiel Command
Training session, McLean, Virginia,
February 18, 1988

Your audience gives you everything you need. They tell you. There is no director who can direct you like an audience.

Fanny Brice, 1891–1951
American comedienne and singer
Katkov, *The Fabulous Fanny*

They use [how much] money they've spent as a measure of success because there's very little else to measure.

David Brinkley
Broadcast journalist
This Week (TV program), March 16, 1988

It is the nature of all greatness not to be exact.

Edmund Burke, 1729–1797
English statesman, orator, and writer
On American Taxation

Comparisons are odious.

Robert Burton, 1577–1640
Vicar of St. Thomas's, Oxford
The Anatomy of Melancholy

An expert is one who knows more and more about less and less.

Nicholas Murray Butler, 1862–1947
Nobel laureate in peace
Commencement address, Columbia University

God was satisfied with his own work, and that is fatal.

> Samuel Butler, 1835–1902
> English novelist and translator
> *Note-Books of Samuel Butler*

Skill and luck play equal parts in the management of crisis. The skill can be practiced, but not the luck.... If you, as a manager, perceive your role as "putting out fires," then you are a poor manager and ought to be replaced by someone who attached more importance to fire prevention. The fundamental procedures for preventing organizational crises are early detection and the rehersal of drills that transform crises into routine problems.

> Theodore Caplow
> *Managing an Organization*
> (CBS College Publishing, 1983)

By a small sample we may judge the whole piece.

> Miguel De Cervantes, 1547–1616
> Spanish novelist
> *Don Quixote*

When a conflict in schedule occurs between interviewing [and evaluating] subordinates and hobnobbing with the boss, the appraisal session is sure to lose every time.... So it goes throughout the entire organization, with bosses at every level spending as little time on appraisal as possible in order to have time for "more important" things.

> William F. Cone
> Manager of Professional Development,
> Hughes Aircraft
> *Supervising Employees Effectively*
> (Addison-Wesley, 1974)

Extremes of fortune are true wisdom's test, And he's of men most wise, who bears them best.

> Richard Cumberland, 1732–1811
> English diplomat and popular writer
> *Philemon*

Thou art weighed in the balances, and art found wanting.

> Old Testament, Daniel 5:27

How you measure the performance of your managers directly affects the way they act.

> John Dearden
> Harvard Business School
> *Harvard Business Review*,
> September/October 1987

80 percent of American managers cannot answer with any measure of confidence these seemingly simple questions: What is my job? What in it really counts? How well am I doing?

> W. Edwards Deming
> Management consultant and author
> Tomasko, *Downsizing* (AMACOM, 1987)

It doesn't matter if a cat is black or white, so long as it catches mice.

> Deng Xiaoping
> Premier of China
> *Time*, January 6, 1986

We know that the key to the productivity of the knowledge worker and his achievement is to demand responsibility from him or her. All knowledge workers, from the lowliest and youngest to the company's chief executive officer, should be asked at least once a year, "What do you *contribute* that justifies your being on the payroll? What should this company, this hospital, this government agency, this university hold you accountable for, by way of contribution and results? Do you know what your goals and objectives are? And what do you plan to do to attain them?

Peter F. Drucker
Management consultant and writer
The Changing World of the Executive
(Quadrangle, 1982)

To make service institutions perform does not require "great people." It requires instead a system. The essentials of this system may not be too different from the essentials of performance in a business enterprise, as the present "management boom" in the service institution assumes. But the application will be different. For the service institutions are not +businesses; "performance" means something quite different for them.

Peter F. Drucker
Management consultant and writer
People and Performance
(Harper & Row, 1977)

Even the most competent management probably bats, at best 0.300 in the innovation area, with one real success for every three tries.

Peter F. Drucker
Management consultant and writer
Management in Turbulent Times
(Harper & Row, 1980)

[W]hen a variety of tasks have all to be performed in cooperation, syncronization, and communication, a business needs managers and a management. Otherwise, things go out of control; plans fail to turn into action; or, worse, different parts of the plans get going at different speeds, different times, and with different objectives and goals, and the favor of the "boss" becomes more important than performance.

Peter F. Drucker
Management consultant and writer
People and Performance
(Harper & Row, 1977)

Prior to the October [1987 stock market] crash, too many market players were looking at numbers and stock prices rather than at the realities of management quality. They were doing their looking in the easy place rather than in the right place.

Esther Dyson
Editor and publisher, *Release 1.0*
Forbes, November 30, 1987

Genius is one percent inspiration and ninety-nine percent perspiration.

Thomas Alva Edison, 1847–1931
American inventor and entrepreneur
Quoted in *Life*, 1932

We judge others according to results; how else?—not knowing the process by which results are arrived at.

George Eliot (Marian Evans), 1819–1880
English novelist, essayist, and editor
The Mill on the Floss

Nothing great was ever achieved without enthusiasm.

Ralph Waldo Emerson, 1803–1882
American essayist and poet
Circles

Difficulties show what men are.

Epictetus, c. 60–120
Roman Stoic philosopher
Encheiridon

The greater the difficulty, the more glory in surmounting it. Skillful pilots gain their reputation from storms and tempests.

Epicurus, 341–270 B.C.
Greek philosopher
Sovran Maxims

If the nation has incompetent teachers, it is because it hired them in the first place, then not only tolerated them but protected them. The way to get rid of incompetents in teaching should be no different than it is in any other workplace—provide them assistance for improvement, and if that fails, replace them with competent people.

C. Emily Feistritzer
Director,
National Center for Education Research
The Washington Post, December 16, 1987

Business leaders often get credit for the successful decisions that were forced on them.

Oliver A. Fick
Environmental Services Manager,
International Paper Co.
Harvard Business Review, July/August 1986

The praising of people for [what] they don't deserve is the surest way of making them contemptible, and leading others into the thinking of their faults.

Sarah Fielding, 1710–1768
English author
David Simple

By the work one knows the workman.

Jean de La Fontaine, 1621–1695
French writer and fabulist
The Hornets and the Bees

[T]he planning process invariably begins with what must be an honest appraisal of past failures and accomplishments. Moreover, planning identifies and seeks input from key parts of the organization, forcing discussion, argument, consensus and communication of issues important to the firm. Almost always this leads to new opportunities which would

not have been considered if a forum for healthy debate had not been provided.

William H. Franklin, Jr.
Georgia State University
Financial Strategies, Fall 1987

Young managers [in the United States in contrast to Japan] often sink or swim because of fortuitous circumstances since they are judged on results rather than methods.

Joseph N. Froomkin
Management consultant
Journal of the Academy of Management,
March, 1964

Good is not good where better is expected.

Thomas Fuller, 1608–1661
Chaplain in extraordinary to Charles II
Gnomologia

It is much more difficult to measure non-performance than performance. Performance stands out like a ton of diamonds. Non-performance can almost always be explained away.

Harold Geneen
CEO, IT&T
Managing (Doubleday, 1984)

If your desk isn't cluttered, you probably aren't doing your job.

Harold Geneen
CEO, IT&T
Managing (Doubleday, 1984)

The best carpenters make the fewest chips.

German proverb

Evaluating programmers has been sort of like judging paintings—"I may not know much about art, but I know what I like." The result may be personally aesthetically satisfying in the art world—and then again, it may not—but in the programming world it leads to a kind of educated cronyism.

> Robert L. Glass
> Software developer and project manager
> *Computerworld*, February 4, 1980

[Michigan's] Department of Commerce has begun surveying clients of seven programs providing direct services to businesses to find out how satisfied they are with the state's efforts. "We have consciously thought of ourselves as the Michigan Development Corporation.... We've tried to think of ourselves in private sector terms, as being in business to provide a service to Michigan businesses."

> Lou Glazer
> Deputy Director, Michigan Dept. of Commerce
> *Governing the States and Localities*,
> February 1988

The deed is everything, its repute nothing.

> Johann Wolfgang von Goethe, 1749–1832
> German poet and dramatist
> *Grosser Verhof*

Tell me, how did you love my picture?

> Samuel Goldwyn, 1882–1974
> American movie mogul
> Johnson, *The Great Goldwyn*

Most things depend on the satisfaction of others.

> Baltasar Gracián, 1601–1658
> Spanish priest and popular writer
> *Oraculo Manual*

If you build a house over a crack in the earth, it's your own fault.

> Albert A. Grant
> President, American Society of Civil Engineers
> Speech, Washington, D. C., May 30, 1988

My failures have been errors of judgment, not of intent.

> Ulysses S. Grant, 1822–1885
> Eighteenth President of the United States
> Message to Congress, December 5, 1876

Lack of a raise budget should *not* be used as a reason to withhold performance evaluations.... When ... Intel found it had to delay its merit-raise program ... we decided that it was important to go ahead with the performance reviews—despite the lack of raises. One reason was that our employees needed to be told how they were doing, where they stood, and how they could improve, as much or more than ever.

> Andrew S. Grove
> CEO, Intel Corp.
> *One-On-One With Andy Grove*
> (G. P. Putnam's Sons, 1987)

The output of a manager is the output of the organizational units under his supervision or influence.

> Andrew S. Grove
> CEO, Intel Corp.
> *High Output Management*
> (Random House, 1983)

One cannot describe or measure job performance before it occurs.

> Robert M. Guion
> Industrial psychologist
> Dunnette, *Handbook of Industrial and Organizational Psychology*
> (Rand-McNally, 1976)

Unexpressed competence appears much the same as incompetence.

> Jay Hall
> Management trainer and writer
> *The Competence Process* (Telometrics, 1980)

Setting goals can be the difference between success and failure.... Goals must not be defined so broadly that they cannot be quantified. Having quantifiable goals is an essential starting point if managers are to measure the results of their organization's activities.... Too often people mistake being busy for achieving goals.

Philip D. Harvey
Founder, Population Services International
and James D. Snyder
President, Snyder Associates, Inc.
Harvard Business Review,
January/February 1987

The men who create productivity, opportunity, employment, wealth and wages for a community are public benefactors and should be recognized as such.

William Randolph Hearst, 1863–1951
Newspaper publisher and U. S. Congressman
Signed editorial, March 28, 1918

It is easier to discover a deficiency in individuals, in states and in Providence, than to see their real import and value.

Georg Wilhelm Hegel, 1770–1831
German philosopher
Philosophy of History

Some men are born mediocre, some men achieve mediocrity, and some men have mediocrity thrust upon them. With Major Major it had been all three.

Joseph Heller
American novelist
Catch-22

Effective management always means asking the right question.

Robert Heller
Editor, *Management Today*
The Supermanagers (Dutton, 1984)

The performance of profit center managers is [usually] measured over a moderate time span. The penalty for unsatisfactory absolute performance over the short-term is severe. The proper balance between known performance and potential future benefits is never clear.

Bruce Henderson
CEO, Boston Consulting Group, Inc.
Henderson on Corporate Strategy (Abt, 1979)

It is not fit the public trust should be lodged in the hands of any, till they are first proved and found fit for the business they are to be entrusted with.

Matthew Henry, 1662–1714
English clergyman and writer
Commentaries

Our own actions are our security, not others' judgments.

George Herbert, 1593–1633
English clergyman and poet
Jacula Prudentum

Neither snow nor rain nor heat nor gloom of night stays these couriers [Persian postriders] from the swift accomplishment of their appointed rounds.

Herodotus, fifth century B.C.
Greek "Father of History"
History of the Persian War

Competence implies control over enviornmental factors—both physical and social. People with this motive do not wish to wait passively for things to happen; they want to be able to manipulate their enviornment and make things happen.

Paul Hersey
California American University
and Kenneth H. Blanchard
University of Massachusetts
Management of Organizational Behavior
(Prentice-Hall, 1982)

We expect more of ourselves than we have any right to, in virtue of our endowments.

Oliver Wendell Holmes, 1809–1894
American physician and popular writer
Over the Teacups

"I [Sherlock Holmes] followed you."
"I [Dr. Watson] saw no one."
"That is what you may expect to see when I follow you."

Sherlock Holmes
(Arthur Conan Doyle), 1859–1930
English physician, writer, and sportsman
The Devil's Foot

As a rule, adversity reveals genius and prosperity conceals it.

Horace, 65–8 B.C.
Roman poet and satirist
Odes

He has half the deed done, who has made a beginning.

Horace, 65–8 B.C.
Roman poet and satirist
Epistles

Don't make excuses—make good.

Elbert Hubbard, 1856–1915
American writer, printer, and editor
Epigrams

[In response to a heckler who shouted "From a tailor up!":] Some gentleman says I have been a tailor. That does not disconcert me in the least; for when I was a tailor I had the reputation of being a good one, and making close fits; I was always punctual with my customers, and always did good work.

Andrew Johnson, 1805–1875
Seventeenth President of the United States
Quoted by Smiles, *Self-Help*

He who praises everybody praises nobody.

Samuel Johnson, 1709–1784
English lexicographer and critic
Letter to Thomas Boswell, September 21, 1777

Good public administration implies far more than organizational and management techniques.... Public administration must be directly associated with development of efficacious solutions to the vexing problems of our era.

Jong S. Jun
*Public Administration: Understanding
Management, Politics, and Law in the
Public Sector* (Random House, 1986)

I do not give you to posterity as a pattern to imitate, but as an example to deter.

Junius (Pseudonym), 1768–1772
English Whig author
Letter to the Duke of Grafton

It is common ... to see supervisors trying to give all their employees high ratings so that they can buy employee cooperation and "look good" as managers.

Rosabeth Moss Kantor
Harvard Business School
Personnel, January 1987

Keep it simple. The purpose of performance evaluation should be to draw a line between above and below average performers.

Joe Kelly
Concordia University (Montreal)
How Managers Manage (Prentice-Hall, 1980)

The evaluation is the driving force for promotions and raises. What is said about you in your evaluation determines where you go.

James Kennedy
Chairman, Pro-Minority Action Coalition
Black Enterprise, April 1988

Evaluation is a time for accounting; for comparing actions with consequences; for detecting flaws and making improvements; for planting the seeds of future challenge.

> Don Koberg and Jim Bagnall
> *The Universal Traveler: A Soft-Systems Guidebook to Creativity, Problem Solving, and the Process of Design*
> (William Kaufmann, 1974)

Corporate performance is an uncertain measure of executive success. Sometimes a good manager makes what seems to be the right choice at the time but is undermined by unpredictable events.

> Edward Lazear
> University of Chicago Business School
> *The New York Times,* April 27, 1988

Every skilled person is to be believed with reference to his own art.
[*Cuilibet in arte sua perito est credendum.*]

> Legal maxim

We are convinced that the major reason for his failure to produce rests in his lack of understanding of what his duties are, of what is expected of him, ... and in the hopelessness which must inevitably grow out of such a situation.

> Paul N. Lehoczky
> Labor arbitrator
> *Texas Electric Steel Castings Co.*, 27 LA 55

The common remark of top managers, "It's up to you here" or "You can't keep a good man down" is often a cloak for the fact that promotion is completely chancy and that merit plays a subordinate role simply because no system for assessing performance by men in junior and middle management exists.

> Roy Lewis and Rosemary Stewart
> *The Boss* (Phoenix, 1958)

It is possible to be a sage in some things and a child in others, to be at once ferocious and retarded, shrewd and foolish, serene and irritable.

> Walter Lippmann, 1889–1974
> Journalist and public philosopher
> *A Preface to Morals*

Too many executives try to sweep their mistakes under the rug.

> Royal Little
> Founder, Textron
> *Best of Business Quarterly*, 1987

The finest eloquence is that which gets things done; the worst is that which delays them.

> David Lloyd George, 1863–1945
> English Prime Minister
> Speech at the Conference of Paris, 1919

We judge ourselves by what we feel capable of doing, while others judge us by what we have already done.

> Henry Wadsworth Longfellow, 1807–1882
> American poet
> *Kavanaugh*

Much of the success of the administrator in carrying out a program depends upon how far it is his sole object overshadowing everything else, or how far he is thinking of himself; for this last is an obstruction that has caused many a good man to stumble and a good cause to fall. The two aims are inconsistent, often enough for us to state as a general rule that one cannot both do things and get the credit for them.

> A. Lawrence Lowell, 1856–1943
> President of Harvard University
> *What a University President Has Learned*

Whether or not one should give credence to a prophet depends on the character of his doctrines, not his race.

> Moses Maimonides, 1135–1204
> Egyptian physician and philosopher
> *Letter to Yemen*

A wrong-doer is often a man who has left something undone, not always he that has done something.

> Marcus Aurelius, 121–180
> Roman Emperor and Stoic philosopher
> *Meditations*

Don't let the performance appraisal be a one-sided lecture. Give your employee a chance to talk.

> Margie Markham
> Contributing Editor, *Meeting News*
> *Meeting News*, December 1987

Formal performance appraisal plans are designed to meet three needs, one for the organization and two for the individual:

1. They provide systematic judgments to back up salary increases, promotions, transfers, and sometimes demotions or terminations;

2. They are a means of telling a subordinate how he is doing, and suggesting needing changes in his behavior, attitudes, skills, or job knowledge; they also let him know "where he stands" with the boss.

3. They are being increasingly used as a basis for the coaching and counseling of the individual by the superior.

> Douglas McGregor, 1879–1964
> Professor of Management, M. I. T.,
> and President of Antioch College
> *Harvard Business Review*, May/June 1957

There is no grade of "perfect" in crisis management—it is a matter of reducing pain and damage—but the results are measurable in big dollar savings and protection of human resources.

> Gerald C. Meyers
> Chairman, American Motors
> *When It Hits the Fan* (Houghton Mifflin, 1986)

The most reliable predictor of future human behavior is past human behavior.

> George Mitchel
> U. S. Senator
> *This Week* (TV program), August 16, 1987

Any plant growing in the wrong place is a "weed."

> *Old Farmer's Almanac* (1947)

If I miss one day's practice, I notice it. If I miss two days, the critics notice it. If I miss three days, the audience notices it.

> Ignace Paderewski, 1860–1941
> Polish concert pianist and patriot
> Sign over practice-room, with attribution
> Juilliard School of Music, New York

A man like a *Watch*, is to be valued for his *Goings*.

> William Penn, 1644–1718
> Founder of Pennsylvania
> *Fruits of Solitude in Reflections and Maxims*

The Peter Principle: In a hierarchy, every employee tends to rise to the level of his own incompetence.

> Laurence J. Peter
> University of Southern California
> *The Peter Principle* (William Morrow, 1969)

Only a mediocre person is always at his best.

> Laurence J. Peter
> University of Southern California
> *The Peter Principle* (William Morrow, 1969)

Applaud the new, rough-cut or not, and yawn at even good performance that involves no bold moves and no fast-paced experiments.

> Tom Peters
> Business writer
> *Thriving on Chaos* (Knopf, 1987)

Our fixation with financial measures leads us to downplay or ignore less tangible non-financial measures such as product quality, customer satisfaction, order lead time, factory flexibility, the time it takes to launch a new product, and the accumulation of skills by labor over time. Yet these are increasingly the real drivers of corporate success over the middle to long term.

> Tom Peters
> Business writer
> *The Washington Post*, October 4, 1987

It is not sufficient for people to do their assigned jobs.

> Al Pietrasanta
> Program manager, IBM
> Metzger, *Managing Programming People*
> (Prentice-Hall, 1987)

A worker may be negligent on a specific occasion and be subject to discipline, therefore, without its necessarily compelling the conclusion that he is incompetent.

> Harry H. Platt
> Labor arbitrator
> *Copco Steel and Engineering Co.*, 13 LA 586

All seems infected to the infected spy,
As all looks yellow to the jaundiced eye.

> Alexander Pope, 1688–1744
> English poet
> *Essay on Criticism*

Order is Heav'ns first law; and this confest,
Some are, and must be, greater than the rest.

> Alexander Pope, 1688–1744
> English poet
> *An Essay on Man*

Judge not of men and things at first sight.

> Barber, *The Book of 1000 Proverbs*, 1876

Reputation is often got without merit and lost without fault.

> Barber, *The Book of 1000 Proverbs*, 1876

He may find fault, but let him mend it if he can.

> Barber, *The Book of 1000 Proverbs*, 1876

Both good and evil are the work of our own hands.

> Apocrypha, Psalms of Solomon 9:4

There is no great genius without some touch of madness.

> Publilius Syrus, c. 42 B.C.
> Roman writer
> *Maxims*

We will take the good will for the deed.

> François Rabelais, 1494–1547
> French physician, humorist, and satirist
> *Works*

Regardless of how "efficient" the management operation [of a law firm] is, it is not "effective" unless it keeps clients happy.

Sonia Rappaport
Principal, Rappaport & Associates
The Washington Lawyer,
January/February 1987

Professional education in America is putting progressively more emphasis on the manipulation of symbols to the exclusion of other sorts of skills—how to collaborate with others, to work in teams, to speak foreign languages, to solve concrete problems—which are more relevant to the new competitive enviornment. And more and more, America's best students have turned to professions that allow them to continue attending to symbols, from quiet offices equipped with a telephone, telex, and a good secretary. The world of truly productive people, engaged in the untidy and difficult struggle with real production problems, is becoming alien to America's best and brightest.

Robert B. Reich
JFK School of Government, Harvard University
The Next American Frontier, 1983

Post-mortems on defeats are never very useful unless they say something about the future.

James Reston
Syndicated columnist
The New York Times

Never mind;
If some of us were not so far behind,
The rest of us were not so far ahead.

Edwin Arlington Robinson, 1869–1935
American poet
Inferentia

We should not judge a man's merits by his qualities, but by the use he makes of them.

François de La Rochefoucauld, 1613–1680
French politician, writer, and philanthropist
Reflections, or Sentences and Moral Maxims

When I say I believe in a square deal I do not mean to give every man the best hand. If the cards come do not come to any man, or if they do come, and he has not got the power to play them, that is his affair. All I mean is that there shall be no crookedness in the dealing.

Theodore Roosevelt, 1858–1919
Twenty-sixth President of the United States
Speech, Dallas, Texas, April 5, 1905

It is by the quality of his mistakes that you recognize the amateur.

Dagobert D. Runes
Editor, publisher, and philosopher
A Book of Contemplation

That it is safer for a *Prince* to Judge of *Men* by what they do to one another, than what they do to him.

George Savile (Lord Halifax), 1633–1695
English politician and statesman
Maxims of State

It is the north wind that made the Vikings.

Scandinavian proverb

It is not good to be better than the very worst.

Seneca, c. 4 B.C.–A.D. 65
Roman orator and rhetorician
Epistles to Lucilius

We are not the first,
Who, with best meaning, have incurr'd the worst.

> William Shakespeare, 1564–1616
> English dramatist and poet
> *King Lear*

He hath indeed better bettered expectation.

> William Shakespeare, 1564–1616
> English dramatist and poet
> *Much Ado About Nothing*

Some are born great, some achieve greatness, and some have greatness thrust upon 'em.

> William Shakespeare, 1564–1616
> English dramatist and poet
> *Twelfth Night*

The opportunity for candor in the performance appraisal process is frequently lost because of the management's unwillingness to deal with the unpleasant.

> Donald T. Shire
> Vice President, Air Products & Chemicals Co.
> *Harvard Business Review*,
> November/December 1986

Initiative is doing the right thing without being told.

> William J. Siegel, 1910–1966
> Vice President and Comptroller,
> Printz-Biederman Manufacturing Co.
> Sign in office

We can judge a man faithful or unfaithful only by his works.

> Benedict Spinoza, 1632–1677
> Dutch philosopher and oculist
> *Theologico-Political Treatise*

Forget return on assets. What is most important is how a company is leveraging its scarcest resource, its management.

> Paul Strassmann
> Former Vice President, Xerox
> *Inc. Magazine*, March 1988

In complex systems, malfunctions and even total nonfunction may not be detectable for long periods, if ever.

> Melvin J. Sykes
> Attorney
> *Maryland Law Review*, 1978

To endure is greater than to dare; to tire out hostile fortune; to be daunted by no difficulty; to keep heart when all have lost it; to go through intrigue spotless; to forego even ambition when the end is gained—who can say this is not greatness?

> William Makepeace Thackeray, 1811–1863
> English novelist, journalist, and editor
> *The Virginians*

Often, the most significant feature of good ... work is that it has kept something bad from happening to the company. How can we measure bad things that do not happen?

> Robert M. Tomasko
> Principal, Temple, Barker & Sloane, Inc.
> *Downsizing* (AMACOM, 1987)

Nobody knows what is the best he can do.

> Arturo Toscanini, 1867–1957
> Italian symphonic and operatic conductor
> *Wisdom of Sarnoff and the World of RCA*

About the meanest thing you can say about a man is that he means well.

> Harry S. Truman, 1884–1972
> Thirty-third President of the United States
> Speech, May 10, 1950

The brightest flashes in the world of thought are incomplete until they have been proved to have their counterparts in the world of fact.

> John Tyndall, 1820–1893
> English physicist
> *Scientific Materialism*

It's only the companies that you're unfamiliar with that are well managed.

> Fred Vanderschmidt
> Director, Abt Associates, Inc.
> Managers' conference, June 1974

I come from a state that raises corn and cotton and cockleburs and Democrats, and frothy eloquence neither convinces nor satisfies me. I'm from Missouri, you've got to show me.

> Willard Duncan Vandiver, 1852–1932
> U. S. Congressman
> Speech at the Five O'Clock Club,
> Philadelphia, 1902

The absence of a marked or consistent correlation between job satisfaction and performance casts some doubt on the generality or intensity of either effects of satisfaction on performance or performance on satisfaction.

> Victor H. Vroom
> Management researcher
> *Work and Motivation* (Wiley, 1964)

A farmer was asked what sort of year he had just had. "Medium" came the reply. "What do you mean by 'medium'?" "Worse than last year but better than next."

> Peter Walker
> Pepper, *The Wit and Wisdom of the 20th Century* (Sphere, 1987)

You don't hear things that are bad about your company unless you ask. It is easy to hear good tidings, but you have to scratch to get the bad news.

> Thomas J. Watson, Jr.
> CEO, IBM, and U. S. Ambassador to Russia
> *Fortune*, 1979

No experiment on programmer performance should be undertaken without clear, explicit and reasonable goals—unless that experiment is designed to measure the effect of unclear, implicit, or unreasonable goals.

> Gerald M. Weiberg and Edward L. Schulman
> Organizational consultants
> *Human Factors*, 1974

That department has the gentlest learning curve I've ever seen.

> Burton Weinstein
> Attorney
> *The Washington Post*, February 28, 1988

Buyers are graded not only on their successes, but also on their failures. Too many hits means the buyer isn't taking enough chances.

> Les Wexner
> Founder, The Limited
> *Forbes*, April 1987

Things difficult to quantify are inconvenient for analysts to credit.

> George Will
> Syndicated columnist
> *The Washington Post*, February 28, 1988

Here lies our sovereign lord the king,
Whose word no man relies on;
He never says a foolish thing,
Nor ever does a wise one.

> John Wilmot, c. 1612–1658
> Epitaph for Charles II
> (written before the latter's death)

I'm a very good man. I'm just a very bad wizard.

The Wizard of Oz

The essence of the knowledge organization is that work is done in the head. This means that knowledge work can't be seen. It does not fit into discrete, tangible units, and it is difficult to measure. Generally, managers with a traditional production, marketing, or accounting orientation find this difficult to comprehend.

Dale E. Zand
New York University
Information, Organization, and Power
(McGraw-Hill, 1981)

Who sees leadership more clearly than subordinates?

John H. Zenger
President, Zenger-Miller, Inc.
Training, December 1985

If you can't measure output, then measure input.

Anonymous (Washington, D.C.)

If you can't measure it, you can't manage it.

Anonymous (Washington, D.C.)

She is efficient in doing things right, and effective in doing the right thing.

Anonymous (U.S. Army)

31

Personnel Selection

Here lies a man who knew how to enlist
... people better than himself.

That combination of delightful things, a French cook on board an English ship.

Francisco Algarotti, 1712–1764
Italian philosopher and critic
Lettere sulla Russia

A good secretary is worth killing for.

Mary Ann Allison
Vice President, CitiCorp.
and Eric Allison
Financial writer
Managing Up, Managing Down
(Simon & Schuster, 1984)

In hiring we almost never look at intrinsic motivation.

Teresa M. Amabile
Brandeis University
Journal of Personality and
Social Psychology, 1985

1. The individual test taker has the right to the confidentiality of the test results and the right to informed consent regarding the use of those test results.

2. The individual has the right to expect that only people qualified to interpret the scores will have access to those scores, or that sufficient information will accompany the test scores to ensure their appropriate interpretation.

3. The individual has the right to expect that the test is equally fair to all test takers in the sense of being equally familiar or unfamiliar, so that the test results reflect the test taker's true abilities.

Policy on employment tests and testing
American Psychological Association, 1980

It is well known that certain foreign peoples are naturally adapted to certain kinds of work. For instance, Finns, Croatians, and Austrians make good miners; Italians and Swedes are good railroad builders; Russians, Lithuanians, and Poles are good foundry and steel mill workers; Jews, French, and Irish do not take well to monotonous or repetitive work but are particularly adapted to any work requiring action, artistry, and enthusiasm. For all-round rough work, Norwegians, Greeks, Russians, and German Poles are generally recommended.

American School of Correspondence
Employment Management and Safety Engineering, 1919

I have never been able to select quality employees in advance. I have learned, however, how to get rid of the poor and mediocre ones.

Ramona E. F. Arnett
President, Ramona Enterprises, Inc.
Speech, New York City, June 8, 1979

Young men are fitter to invent than to judge, fitter for execution than for counsel, and fitter for new projects than for settled business.

Francis Bacon, 1561–1626
Lord Chancellor of England
Of Youth and Age

There are people who interview extremely well and perform poorly. But the reverse is also true. There are lots of people who interview terribly but have done a great job.

Paul W. Barada
President, Barada Associates, Inc.
Insight, February 1, 1988

People need the protection of promotion and evaluation procedures that diminish the importance of internal politics.

Judith M. Bardwick
University of California at San Diego
The Plateauing Trap (AMACOM, 1986)

We hired the wrong people ... because we were in such a hurry to fill those positions.

Lynn Tendler Bignell
Founder, Gilbert Tweed Associates
Inc. Magazine, November 1987

I yield to no one in my earnest hope that the time will come when an "affirmative action" program is unnecessary and is ... only a relic of the past.... Then persons will be regarded as persons, and discrimination of the type we address today will be an ugly feature of history that is instructive but that is behind us.... In order to get beyond racism, we must first take account of race.... And in order to treat some persons equally, we must treat them differently.

Harry A. Blackmun
U. S. Supreme Court Justice
University of California v. *Bakke* (1978)

The secretary you hire this year will need a higher level of computer competency than a mid-level manager needed seven or eight years ago.

Buck Blessing
Founding partner, Blessing/White, Inc.
Training and Development Journal,
November 1986

[At the end of pre-service training:] We give a test and offer employment to those who score the best.

Henry Block
CEO, H&R Block
Inc. Magazine, December 1987

I'm not hiring for where I am; I'm hiring for where I'll be.

Fred Bramante, Jr.
CEO, Daddy's Junky Music Shops, Inc.
Inc. Magazine, February 1987

Discrimination is the act of treating differently two persons ... under like circumstances.

Louis Dembitz Brandeis, 1856–1941
U. S. Supreme Court Justice
National Life Insurance Co. v. *U.S.* (1927)

It would be going against the entire intent and spirit of seniority clauses were we to hold that the failure of long term employees ultimately because of age, to meet production standards is a proper cause for discharge.

Joseph Brandschain
Labor arbitrator
Dodge Corp., 8 LA 250

A state government may adopt race-conscious programs if the purpose of such programs is to remove the disparate racial impact its actions might otherwise have and if there is reason to believe that the disparate impact is itself the product of past discrimination, whether its own or that of society at large.

William Joseph Brennan
U. S. Supreme Court Justice
University of California v. *Bakke* (1978)

[Humanities graduates] achieved the best overall performance, and were most suited for change, which is the leading feature of the high-speed, high-pressure, high-tech world we now occupy.

Chales L. Brown
Chairman, AT&T
Personnel Journal, February 1986

Some people, however long their experience or strong their intellect, are temperamentally incapable of reaching firm decisions.

James Callaghan
English Prime Minister
Harvard Business Review,
November/December 1986

The company with the second best organization ends up second place in the market

D. Wayne Calloway
CEO, PepsiCo, Inc.
Harvard Business Review,
September/October 1987

We won't promote anyone until he has trained a capable replacement. Otherwise, the promotion would leave us too vulnerable.

Robert Campion
Chairman, Lear Siegler
Garfield, *Peak Performers* (Avon, 1986)

Not the coveting of the place alone, but the fitness of the man for the place withal: that is the question.

Thomas Carlyle, 1795–1881
Scottish essayist and historian
Of Heroes and Hero-Worship

Here lies a man who knew how to enlist into his service people better than himself.

Andrew Carnegie, 1835–1919
American industrialist and philanthropist
Epitaph

For out and out he is the worthiest ...

Geoffrey Chaucer, c. 1340–1400
English poet and diplomat
Troilus and Criseyde

Some types of authority exist by virtue of a person's expertise, or even his or her personality. Such a person may be in any organization and at any level.... The issue of whether an order has authority depends not necessarily on who gives the order but on whether it is accepted by those who receive it.

William A. Cohen
Principles of Technical Management
(AMACOM, 1980)

You put together the best team that you can with the players you've got, and replace those who aren't good enough.

Robert L. Crandall
President, American Airlines
Management, January 1987

A few honest men are better than numbers. If you choose godly, honest men to be captains of horse, honest men will follow them.

Oliver Cromwell, 1599–1658
Lord Protector of England
Reorganization of the Army

Selection by means other than tests is subject to the same challenges as a testing program.

Lee J. Cronbach
Industrial psychologist
Public Personnel Management,
January/February 1980

Personnel selection is a political act and a proper concern for national policy.

Lee J. Cronbach
Industrial psychologist
Public Personnel Management,
January/February 1980

You will not be able to tell that they are capable of greatness until you provide them with a packed house, a 3-and-2 count and the game is on the line.

Mario Cuomo
Governor of New York
Newsweek, April 4, 1988

For me, the best CEO's come out of R&D. They're articulate, creative, inventive—but they're also rigorous.

Laurel Cutler
Vice Chairman, FCB/Leber Katz Partners
Inc. Magazine, November 1987

It takes a wise man to discover a wise man.

Diogenes Laertius, c. 200–250
Greek historian and writer
*Lives and Opinions of Eminent Philosophers:
Xenophanes*

Obviously, the [employment] interviewer learns little or nothing when he is talking.

John D. Drake
President, Behavioral Sciences Technology
Interviewing for Managers (AMACOM, 1972)

It is safest to employ honest men, even though they may not be the cleverest.

Ekken Kaibara, 1630–1714
Japanese scholar and writer
The Way of Contentment

The mandate for equal opportunity doesn't dictate disregard for the differences in candidates' qualities and skills. There is no constitutional right to play ball. All there is is a right to compete for it on equal terms.

Tim Ellis III
Judge, U. S. District Court,
Alexandria, Virginia
Croteau v. *Osbourn Park High School* (1988)

In politics and in trade, bruisers and pirates are of better promise than talkers and clerks.

Ralph Waldo Emerson, 1803–1882
American essayist and poet
Manners

No change of circumstances can repair a defect of character.

Ralph Waldo Emerson, 1803–1882
American essayist and poet
Character

We cannot, in the universal imbecility, indecision, and indolence of man, sufficiently congratulate ourselves on this strong and ready actor, who took occasion by the beard, and showed us how much may be accomplished by the mere force of such virtues as all men possess in less degrees; namely, by punctuality, by personal attention, by courage, and by thoroughness.

Ralph Waldo Emerson, 1803–1882
American essayist and poet
Napoleon

The fact that a test was prepared by an individual or organization claiming expertise in test preparation does not, without more, justify its use.

U. S. Equal Employment
Opportunity Commission
Cited in *Griggs* v. *Duke Power Co.* (1971)

[Adverse impact of hiring procedures is:] [A] substantially different rate of selection in hiring, promotion, or other employment decision which works to the disadvantage of members of a race, sex, or ethnic group. A selection procedure which has no adverse impact generally does not violate Title VII [of the 1964 Civil Rights Act, as amended by the Equal Opportunity Employment Act of 1972].... This means that an employer may usually avoid the application of the guidelines by use of procedures which have no adverse impact. [The employer must show job-relatedness or otherwise establish] ... a clear relation between performance on the selection procedure and performance on the job.

U. S. Equal Employment
Opportunity Commission,
U. S. Civil Service Commission,
U. S. Department of Labor,
U. S. Department of Justice,
"Uniform Guidelines on Employee Selection"
43 *Federal Register* 38290, August 25, 1978

We wanted people from big companies that had already been through what we were going through. We assumed that we were going to succeed extraordinarily, and we needed men who had been through all the plateaus before.

Kenneth G. Fisher
President, Prime Computer, Inc.
Tosi and Carroll *Management* (Wiley, 1976)

To protect their [weak] self-esteem, some managers hire people who are technically or interpersonally less skilled than themselves.

Eric G. Flamholtz
University of California, Los Angeles
and Yvonne Randal
Director, Management Systems Consulting
The Inner Game of Management
(AMACOM, 1987)

Our supervisors do their own hiring. The two people we have in personnel [for a work force of 1,000] do some initial screening and look after group health insurance and a few other things.

Gordon Foward
President, Chaparral Steel
Harvard Business Review, May/June 1987

I didn't want to work for someone else, and my brothers had the same sentiment. I happen to be president because I'm the oldest.

Jaime Fullana, Jr.
CEO, F&R Construction Co. (Puerto Rico)
Hispanic Business, June 1987

The society which scorns excellence in plumbing because plumbing is a humble activity, and tolerates shoddiness in philosophy because philosophy is an exalted activity, will have neither good plumbing nor good philosophy. Neither its pipes nor its theories will hold water.

John W. Gardner
President of the Carnegie Foundation
for the Advancement of Teaching
Excellence (Harper & Row, 1961)

A man is not always what he appears to be, but what he appears to be is always a significant part of what he is.

Willard Gaylin
Psychiatrist, Columbia University,
College of Physicians and Surgeons
The New York Times, October 7, 1977

I wanted men about me who shared my enthusiasm for work.

> Harold Geneen
> CEO, IT&T
> *Managing* (Doubleday, 1984)

[He] ... was a manager before he even reached business school. Instinctively, he had grasped the essentials of good business management ... because when one action failed, he tried another, and then another, until he achieved his goal. That's managing.

> Harold Geneen
> CEO, IT&T
> *Managing* (Doubleday, 1984)

White men tend to see other white men with the same characteristics for promotion.

> Martin Gibson
> Group President, Corning Glass Works
> *The Washington Post*, March 8, 1988

Never let that bastard back in here—unless we need him!

> Samuel Goldwyn, 1882–1974
> American movie mogul
> Johnson, *The Great Goldwyn*

We have no difficulty finding the leaders: They have people following them.

> William L. Gore
> Founder and CEO, W. L. Gore & Associates
> Pinchot, *Intrapreneuring*
> (Harper & Row, 1986)

A personnel officer should possess a sensitive ear, a caring heart and the skin of a rhinocerous.

> Priscilla Goss
> Vice President for Human Resources,
> American Management Association
> *Management Review*, March 1987

If the new manager doesn't fit the culture, the buisness, or you, chances are the replacements [new employees] he brings in won't either.

> Richard Gould
> Vice President for Human Resources,
> General Host Corp.
> *Management Review*, March 1987

The use of personal history in [employee] selection is based on the concept that a person's past behavior is predictive of his or her future behavior.... Selecting people poses many problems and raises many issues, some of which are either highly technical or impinge on human rights.

> Donald Grant
> University of Georgia
> *Professional Psychology*, June 1980

The technical supervisor, if he is to be successful, must possess two distinct abilities. He must have a high degree of technical competence and at the same time he needs skill in handling people. Such a combination is by no means easy to find. Every so often some misguided soul, conceiving these two abilities to be antithetical suggests that individuals be selected ... on the basis of knowledge of people with no regard for technical competence. I shudder to think how disastrous this would be in my own organization.

> Estill I. Green
> Vice President, Bell Telephone Laboratories
> *Effective Administration of Research Programs*
> (Cornell University Press, 1958)

[Remarking on his hiring a man who had been responsible for a $377 million loss at his previous job:] We believe in second chances.

> Alan C. Greenberg
> Chairman, Bear Stearns
> *Business Week*, February 15, 1988

One cannot describe or measure job performance before it occurs.

> Robert M. Guion
> Industrial psychologist
> Dunnette, *Handbook of Industrial and Organizational Psychology*
> (Rand McNally, 1976)

The acceptance of tests [as employment selection devices]... reflected the widespread conviction that men—and sometimes women—were to be judged on their individual skills and ability ... rather than on appearance, class, heritage, or personal connections.

> Matthew Hale
> Consultant in employment testing and training
> *Ability Testing: Uses, Consequences, and Controversies*
> (National Academy Press, 1982)

[By 1965] Interest in personality testing had already peaked ... in part because validation studies generally showed them to be poor predictors of success, and in part because ... they violated the right to privacy of those tested.

> Matthew Hale
> Consultant in employment testing and training
> *Ability Testing: Uses, Consequences, and Controversies*
> (National Academy Press, 1982)

Credentials are not the same as accomplishments.

> Robert Half
> President, Robert Half International
> *Robert Half on Hiring* (Crown, 1985)

The world owes all its onward impulses to men who are ill at ease. The happy man inevitably confines himself within ancient limits.

> Nathaniel Hawthorne, 1804–1864
> American author
> *The House of Seven Gables*

Employ men of brains, breeding and acquaintance.

> William Randolph Hearst, 1863–1951
> Newspaper publisher and U. S. Congressman
> Letter to Hearst publishers, 1932

It is not fit the public trust should be lodged in the hands of any, till they are first proved and found fit for the business they are to be entrusted with.

> Mathew Henry, 1662–1714
> English clergyman and writer
> *Commentaries*

People differ not only in their ability to do but also in their "will to do."

> Paul Hersey
> California American University
> and Kenneth H. Blanchard
> University of Massachusetts
> *Management of Organizational Behavior*
> (Prentice-Hall, 1972)

Ideologues are consistent in their beliefs, but they are terrible managers.

> Frederick Herzberg
> University of Utah
> *The Managerial Choice*
> (Dow Jones-Irwin, 1976)

If a guy has a really good success pattern, I'll go along with him if he says he can go to the moon on Scotch tape.

> Raymond Herzog
> Former CEO, 3M Company
> Deal and Kennedy, *Corporate Cultures*
> (Addison-Wesley, 1982)

There's no such thing as almost qualified. There's only qualified.

> Bruce Hicks
> Spokesman, Continental Airlines
> *The Washington Post*, November 22, 1987

The world's great men have not commonly been great scholars, nor its great scholars great men.

> Oliver Wendell Holmes, 1809–1894
> American physician and popular writer
> *The Autocrat of the Breakfast Table*

Mediocrity knows nothing higher than itself, but talent instantly recognizes genius.

> Sherlock Holmes
> (Arthur Conan Doyle), 1859–1930
> English physician, writer, and sportsman
> *The Valley of Fear*

We believe in keeping the units small and recruiting the best people we can find, giving them as much responsibility as early as we can, moving them up rapidly, and keeping track of them.

> Irwin Holtzman
> Vice President, Johnson & Johnson
> *Fortune,* September 28, 1987

It is a fine thing to have ability, but the ability to discover ability in others is the true test.

> Elbert Hubbard, 1856–1915
> American writer, printer, and editor
> *The Philosophy of Elbert Hubbard*

Inferior people should not be employed.

> *I Ching*: Book of Changes
> China, c. 600 B.C.

Among those who aspire to power he is the best who is naturally intelligent and discerning; who has acquired a knowledge of what happens in the world of changing times and tumbling empires; who is adroit at negotiating with the enemy and who can keep a secret.

> Ibn Al-Tiqtaqa, c. 1250
> Arab writer and philosopher
> *Al Fakhri*

One of the key advantages of testing is its help in the selection of leaders and supervisors, men with the capacity to get along well with those under them, command their respect, and co-operate to get the job done thoroughly and pleasantly.

> R. R. Irwin
> Personnel Director, Lockheed Aircraft Corp.
> *Personnel Journal,* 1942

To seek out the best [persons to serve in the government] through the whole Union, we must resort to the information which from the best of men, acting disinterestedly and with ther purest motives, is sometimes incorrect.... No duty the Executive had to perform was so trying as to put the right man in the right place.

> Thomas Jefferson, 1743–1826
> Third President of the United States
> Letter to Elias Shipman of New Haven,
> July 12, 1801

If workers are carefully selected, the problems of discipline will be negligible.

> Johnson & Johnson Co.
> *The Employee Relations Manual,* 1932

[A new chief executive has to be] somebody who has effectively managed change. If you are looking outside for a new leader, you are saying things have to be altered.

> John Johnson
> President, Lamalie Associates
> *Fortune,* February 3, 1986

A man used to vicissitudes is not easily dejected.

> Samuel Johnson, 1709–1784
> English lexicographer and critic
> *A Dissertation on the Art of Flying*

Chaucer's *Canterbury Tales* looks at a handful of pilgrims about to embark on a religious journey. The seemingly simple bunch in-

cludes a friar, a cook, a monk and a wife....
The friar is money-hungry, the cook diseased,
and the monk jolly. And the fat, middle-aged
wife of Bath is as lusty as a new bride.
Together they prove that you shouldn't judge
a book by its cover.

> Beverly Kempton
> Business writer
> *Working Woman*, October 1987

The first requirement for efficiency and
economy ... is highly competent personnel.

> John Fitzgerald Kennedy, 1917–1963
> Thirty-fifth President of the United States
> Quoted in *Management*, 1987

There's an old saying, "Never send a boy to
do a man's job, send a lady."

> John Fitzgerald Kennedy, 1917–1963
> Thirty-fifth President of the United States
> Speech to Democratic women, New York,
> November 5, 1960

The greatest risk in choosing managers by
team is that top management may reject the
decision.

> Tony Kizilos and Roger P. Heinisch
> Systems and Research Center of Aerospace
> and Defense, Honeywell Corp.
> *Harvard Business Review*,
> September/October 1986

I have always believed that success would be
the inevitable result ... if we sent the right man
to fill the right place.

> Austen Henry Layard, 1817–1894
> English archaeologist and diplomat
> Speech in Parliament, January 15, 1855

I can't spare this man [General Ulysses
Grant]; *he fights*.

> Abraham Lincoln, 1809–1865
> Sixteenth President of the United States
> Remark to A. K. McClure

Never let an inventor run a company. You can
never get him to stop tinkering and bring
something to market.

> Royal Little
> Founder, Textron
> *Best of Business Quarterly*, 1987

A survey last year by Hodge-Cronin & Associates found that 98% of 737 chief
executives would hire a candidate with a good
sense of humor over a humorless type.

> Dyan Machan
> Career counselor and writer
> *Forbes*, November 2, 1987

Measured against technical standards or
against standards of acceptability, present
personality tests and inventories do not justify
use as selection methods.

> John W. Macy, Jr.
> Chairman, U. S. Civil Service Commission
> Senate testimony, June 7-10, 1965

At MCI we have a policy that 40% of the job
openings at every level have to be filled from
the outside. You're constantly having new
blood coming in.

> William G. McGowan
> Chairman, MCI Communications Corp.
> *Inc. Magazine*, August 1986

We don't start out with the assumption that
our company is for everybody.

> William G. McGowan
> Chairman, MCI Communications Corp.
> *Inc. Magazine*, August 1986

Get the brightest people and train them well.

> Charles Merrill
> Founder, Merrill Lynch
> TV ad, 1988

Practically every secretary is a typist, but not every typist is a secretary.

Philip W. Metzger
Computer analyst and management writer
Managing Programming People
(Prentice-Hall, 1987)

The successful conduct of an industrial enterprise requires two quite distinct qualifications: fidelity and zeal.

John Stuart Mill, 1806–1873
English philosopher and economist
Principles of Political Economy

The prime occupational hazard of the manager is superficiality.

Henry Mintzberg
McGill University School of Management
The Nature of Managerial Work
(Harper & Row, 1973)

We must recognize that although the management school gives students M.B.A. and M.P.A. degrees, it does not in fact teach them how to manage. Hence, these degrees can hardly be considered prerequisites for managing, and the world is full of highly competent managers who have never spent a day in a management course.

Henry Mintzberg
McGill University School of Management
The Nature of Managerial Work
(Harper & Row, 1973)

Every man shall have an equal chance throughout the land ...

The Book of Mormon, Mosiah 29: 38

I need people around me with a sense of humor.

Robert J. Morrill
Owner, Microwave Radio Corp.
Inc. Magazine, November 1987

Generally, corporations recruit their entry-level workers—practically everyone from file clerks to accountants and junior executives—from the eighteen-to-twenty-four age group. In the 1970s, the number of people in that age group increased 22 percent. Companies could afford to be very choosy. In the 1980s, that group will decline by 15 percent. Figured in real numbers, it is even more dramatic: By 1990, there will be 4.5 million fewer entry-level workers than in 1980, according to the Census Bureau.

John Naisbett and Patricia Aburdene
Business writers and social researchers
Re-inventing the Corporation (Warner, 1985)

Distrust all in whom the impulse to punish is powerful.

Georg Wilhelm Nietzsche, 1844–1900
German philosopher
Thus Spake Zarathustra

Who heeds not experience, trust him not.

John Boyle O'Reilly, 1844–1890
English poet and newspaper editor
Rules of the Road

A company in need of a messiah is also a company in a hurry. Eager to find a hero, the search committee often puts more energy into persuading the candidate to take the job than into considering how well he will mesh with the company.

Patricia O'Toole
Management consultant and business writer
Corporate Messiah (William Morrow, 1984)

If each of us [other executives in the firm] hires people smaller than we are, we shall become a company of dwarfs.

David Ogilvy
Founder, Ogilvy & Mather Advertising
Ogilvy on Advertising (Vintage Books, 1985)

You definitely don't pick the next leader before you need him—he never survives.

> Kenneth Olsen
> Founder and CEO, Digital Equipment Corp.
> *Chief Executive*, Winter 1986-87

No particular method of selecting officials will produce officers who are best suited for the job.

> C. Northcote Parkinson
> University of Malaya
> *Parkinson's Law and Other Studies in Administration*, 1957

If your cow doesn't give milk, sell him.

> John Peers
> President, Logical Machine Corp.
> *1,001 Logical Laws* (Doubleday, 1979)

He that has more Knowledge than Judgment, is made for *another Man's* use more than his own.

> William Penn, 1644–1718
> Founder of Pennsylvania
> *Fruits of Solitude in Reflections and Maxims*

[S]tockholders don't often elect directors [of a corporation]. Unfortunately, there are no Republican and Democratic slates to choose from. The directors are recommended by management [from among] ... the boss's buddies. And that's the flaw right there because it flies in the face of accountability. If I'm going to pick people to oversee me, I'm going to choose those who are compatible.

> H. Ross Perot
> Founder, Electronic Data Systems
> *Life*, February 1988

Promote people who love people, who cherish their subordinates' accomplishments, and who create excitement.... Promote into leadershop positions those who perform like leaders.

> Tom Peters
> Business writer
> *Thriving on Chaos* (Knopf, 1987)

We need impassioned champions by the thousands. Yet the impassioned champion is anathema to everything that civil, organized corporate endeavor stands for. But we must hire him, even though he will alienate some good people, irritate almost everyone, and in the end fail anyway more often than not.

> Tom Peters
> Business writer
> *Thriving on Chaos* (Knopf, 1987)

There is no great genius without some touch of madness.

> Publilius Syrus, c. 42 B.C.
> Roman writer
> *Maxims*

Problems can become opportunities when the right people come together.

> Robert Redford
> Actor and entrepreneur
> *Harvard Business Review*, May/June 1987

They [his headhunting clients] want tough-minded, battle scarred veterans of competitive wars.

> Gerard Roche
> Chairman, Heidrick & Struggles
> *Fortune*, September 28, 1987

We're committed to promoting managers solely from within. That way they have the requisite background, and we have the confidence they know how to react—correct that, *proact*—in a crisis mode.

> Warren Rodgers
> CEO, Computer Specialists, Inc.
> *Inc. Magazine*, February 1988

High achievers are magnets for work.

> Leah Rosch
> Associate Editor, *Working Woman*
> *Working Woman,* April 1988

Good people attract other good people.

> Roberto Ruiz
> CEO, Maya Construction Co.
> *Hispanic Business,* June 1987

In order that people be happy in their work, these three things are needed: They must be fit for it: They must not do too much of it: And they must have a sense of success in it.

> John Ruskin, 1819–1900
> English art critic and historian
> *Pre-Raphaelitism*

Trust the man who hesitates in his speech and is quick and steady in action, but beware of long arguments and long beards.

> George Santayana, 1863–1952
> Spanish-born American philosopher and writer
> *Soliloquies in England*

I don't want workaholics working for me.

> George A. Schaefer
> CEO, Caterpillar Corp.
> *Business Week,* August 31, 1987

[T]he successful manager must be a good diagnostician and must value a spirit of inquiry.

> Edgar H. Schein
> Massachusetts Institute of Technology
> *Organizational Psychology*
> (Prentice-Hall, 1965)

There is not much in the research of the last half dozen years to bolster the confidence of a personnel interviewer concerned with the reliability and validity of his decisions.

> N. Schmitt
> Industrial psychologist
> *Personnel Psychologist,* 1976

What ambitious people want is to get ahead, which means they would do their best even at jobs they loathed.

> Robert J. Schoenberg
> Business author
> *The Art of Being a Boss* (Harper & Row, 1978)

Eagles come in all shapes and sizes, but you will recognize them chiefly by their attitudes. With things crumbling around them, they still will have some optimism. They haven't given up. They have ideas, plans and solutions to problems.... Remember, eagles don't flock.

> Charles Scott
> CEO, Intermark
> *Inc. Magazine's Guide to*
> *Small Business Success,* 1987

The happy combination of fortuitous circumstances.

> Walter Scott, 1771–1832
> Scottish poet, novelist, and biographer
> *The Monastery*

Simple tests have been devised and applied in certain typical economic situations and that there is a positive correlation between the standing in the tests and the standing in the practical work cannot be doubted.

> Walter Dill Scott, 1869–1955
> Early testing and efficiency expert
> and President of Northwestern University
> *Psychological Bulletin,* 1913

There's small choice in rotten apples.

> William Shakespeare, 1564–1616
> English dramatist and poet
> *The Taming of the Shrew*

Let me have men about me that are fat,
Sleek-headed men, and such as sleep o'
nights:
Yon Cassius has a lean and hungry look;
He thinks too much: such men are dangerous.

> William Shakespeare, 1564–1616
> English dramatist and poet
> *Julius Caesar*

Many individuals ... become entrepreneurs
even though they don't have the supposedly
requisite characteristics or motives.... No test
will assure you that an individual will become
an entrepreneur before the fact.

> Albert Shapero
> Ohio State University
> *The Wharton Magazine*, Fall 1978

In any organization men should move up from
the bottom to the top. That develops loyalty,
ambition and talent, because there is a chance
for promotion. Never inject a man into the
top, if it can be avoided. In a big organization,
to have to do that, I think, is a reflection on
management. Of course there are always exceptional cases.

> Alfred P. Sloan, 1875–1966
> President and Chairman, General Motors
> *Adventures of a White Collar Man*

You don't work with [people] for 30 years ...
and then suddenly turn against their collective
opinion.... When you come in from the outside, with no emotional ties to the business,
you can do things a lot more ruthlessly.

> Bruce Smart, Jr.
> CEO, The Continental Group
> *Fortune*, March 2, 1987

Those who look into practical life will find
that fortune is usually on the side of the industrious, as the winds and waves are on the
side of the best navigators. In the pursuit of
even the highest branches of human inquiry,
the commoner qualities are found the most
useful—such as common sense, attention, application, and perseverance.

> Samuel Smiles, 1812–1904
> Scottish physician and biographer
> *Self-Help*

The merit concept is not a simple one. Once
it may have consisted solely of the ability to
perform the job; but, today, there are additional criteria to be considered.

> James P. Springer
> City Personnel Director, Milwaukee
> *Readings in Professional Personnel Assessment*
> (International Personnel
> Management Association, 1984)

This company took off with a great team of
class A players. Now if we want class A
people, we have to hire class C's and make
them into class A's.

> Edward Staley, Jr.
> CEO, Commonwealth
> *Inc. Magazine*, December 1987

Distrust all those who love you extremely
upon a very slight acquaintance, and without
any visible reason. Be upon your guard too
against those who confess, as their weaknesses, all the cardinal virtues.

> Philip Dormer Stanhope, 1694–1773
> English Secretary of State
> *Maxims of the Earl of Chesterfield*

You must look into people as well as at them.

> Philip Dormer Stanhope, 1694–1773
> English Secretary of State
> *Letters of Lord Chesterfield to His Son*

There are really not many jobs that actually require a penis or a vagina, and all other occupations should be open to everyone.

Gloria Steinem
Editor and publisher, *Ms. Magazine*
The Official MBA Handbook of Great Business Quotations (Simon & Schuster, 1984)

[A] major factor in separations may be under-hiring and overhiring ... a great deal of the agony of separation could be eliminated by working harder at the front end—the selection process. Making sure not only that the candidates *can* do the job, which is the easy part of the procedure, but that they *will* do the job.

Donald H. Sweet
Personnel Journal, October 1979

You should never compromise with regard to the type of people you have in leadership roles.... It's not that people are good or bad. It's that they either have the qualities that are suited for the job or not.

Jim Swiggett
CEO, Kollmorgen Corp.
Inc. Magazine, February 1987

Forethought and prudence are the proper qualities of a leader.

Tacitus, c. 55–117
Roman orator, politician, and historian
Annals of the Julian Emperors

Tests do not discriminate against various groups; people do.... The same test may be used in a biased way in one situation and in an unbiased way in another situation.

Mary L. Tenopyr
Industrial psychologist
American Psychologist, October 1981

Despite the compelling evidence that valid and otherwise suitable alternatives to tests will not be found and that the ... combination of other data with test results weakens overall validity, employers will probably still continue to seek alternatives. The legal and regulatory pressures to do so can be expected to continue despite the scientific facts involved.

Mary L. Tenopyr
Industrial psychologist
American Psychologist, October 1981

In 1985 the average U.S. corporate manager stayed put for only 4.5 years.... Personnel selection often depends as much on interpersonal chemistry as on track record.

Robert M. Tomasko
Principal, Temple, Barker & Sloane, Inc.
Downsizing (AMACOM, 1987)

In selection the emphasis is on rejection. The purpose is to select from a large group of applicants the person best suited for a particular role. In placement, however, the emphasis is on how a particular individual can best be used.

Henry L. Tosi
University of Florida
and Stephen J. Carroll
University of Maryland
Management (John Wiley & Sons, 1976)

I don't care if his skills are weak and he's got no experience. Look at that enthusiasm and energy level. He's going to be terrific!

Edgar Trenner
Director, Camp Arcady
Staff meeting, July 1954

[Pre-employment tests must be] predictive or significantly correlated with important elements of work behavior which comprise or are relevant to the job or jobs for which candidates are being evaluated.

U. S. Supreme Court
Albemarle Paper Co. v. *Moody* (1975)

Congress has placed on the employer the burden of showing that any given requirement must have a manifest relationship to the employment in question.... Nothing in the [Civil Rights] Act [of 1964] precludes the use of testing or measuring procedures; obviously they are useful. What Congress has forbidden is giving these devices and mechanisms controlling force unless they are demonstrably a reasonable measure of job performance.

> U. S. Supreme Court
> *Griggs* v. *Duke Power Co.* (1971)

[Title VII of the 1964 Civil Rights Act] does not command that any person be hired simply because he was formerly the subject of discrimination, or because he is a member of a minority group. Discriminatory preference for any group, minority or majority, is precisely and only what Congress proscribed ...

> U. S. Supreme Court
> *Griggs* v. *Duke Power Co.* (1971)

When you've got an old company, you have to ask: how long can a company [continue to] find talented people among its own relatives?

> Charles T. Vaughn, Jr.
> CEO, L. Vaughn Co.
> *Inc. Magazine*, March 1988

Men are not to be judged by what they do not know, but by what they know, and by the manner in which they know it.

> Marquis de Vauvenargues, 1715–1747
> French soldier and moralist
> *Reflections and Maxims*

We are not all capable of everything.
[*Non omnia possumus omnes.*]

> Virgil, 70–19 B.C.
> Roman poet
> *Eclogue*

Judge a man by his questions rather than by his answers.

> François Marie Voltaire, 1694–1778
> French writer
> *Candide*

I never hesitated to promote someone I didn't like. The comfortable assistant—the nice guy you like to go on fishing trips with—is a great pitfall. Instead, I looked for those sharp, scratchy, harsh, almost unpleasant guys who see and tell you about things as they really are. If you can get enough of them around you, and have patience enough to hear them out, there is no limit to where you can go.

> Thomas J. Watson, Jr.
> CEO, IBM, and U. S. Ambassador to Russia
> *Fortune*, 1977

If you proved ineffectual at a job, you were not put out on the street; you were reassigned to a level where you were known to perform well. In doing this we would sometimes strip a man of a fair amount of dignity, but we would then make a great effort to rebuild his self-respect.

> Thomas J. Watson, Jr.
> CEO, IBM, and U. S. Ambassador to Russia
> *Fortune*, 1977

The most important man in the room is the one who knows what to do next.

> James L. Webb
> First Administrator of NASA
> Favorite maxim

Let's face it, we're all superb interviewees. No matter what the job, for one hour we can convince ourselves and almost any interviewer that we can do it and like it.

> Alan Weiss
> President, Summit Consulting Group Inc.
> *Success*, February 1988

Hiring and training are costly—but it is infinitely more costly to have a marginal or barely average man on the company rolls for 30 years.

Gordon W. Wheeling
Personnel Manager, Beckman & Whitley
Leadership in the Office (AMACOM, 1963)

Intelligence is quickness to apprehend, as distinct from ability, which is capacity to act wisely on the thing apprehended.

Alfred North Whitehead, 1861–1947
English philosopher and mathematician
Dialogues

If the [employment] tests were rigorously applied across the board today, half of the most dynamic men in business would be out walking the streets for a job.

Walter H. Whyte, Jr.
Social critic and writer
Fortune, 1954

I look for young people with a sense of being in the world.

Selma Williams
Editor-in-Chief, *North Shore Weeklies*
New England Monthly, September 1987

There is no indispensable man.

Woodrow Wilson, 1856–1924
Twenty-eighth President of the United States
Speech accepting the Democratic nomination,
August 7, 1912

[Referring to the paucity of females in many scientific and technical areas:] The world cannot afford the loss of the talents of half its people if we are to solve the many problems that beset us.

Rosalyn S. Yalow
Nobel laureate in medicine & physiology
Address, Stockholm, December 10, 1977

A cork will do for a king, if you need him that badly.

Yiddish proverb

Anyone who thinks there is some good in everyone hasn't interviewed enough people.

Anonymous personnel director,
Eastman Kodak Co.
Peers, *1,001 Logical Laws* (Doubleday, 1979)

When I sat on one of those selection boards I had as much clout as a referee in a professional wrestling match.

Anonymous executive
Quoted in *Management*, 1987

The best parachute folders are the ones who jump themselves.

Anonymous

32

Planning

You can never plan the future by the past.

═══════════════════════════════════════

The seeds of every company's demise are contained in its business plan.

Fred Adler
CEO, Adler and Co.
Inc. Magazine, February 1987

Think before you act.

Aesop, c. 620–c. 560 B.C.
Greek fabulist
The Fox and the Goat

One study of 58 business organizations with identifiable formal planning functions (not necessarily planning departments) found that the individuals responsible for formal planning spend half their time working alone, reading, and writing reports. The study suggests that the formal planners' relative isolation from meetings with managers and other organization members may be one factor contributing to a lack of planning effectiveness. The danger of such isolation can be reduced if planning is not separated from the implementation of plans.

Robert Albanese
Texas A&M University
Aguilar, Howell, and Vancil,
Formal Planning Systems
(Harvard Business School, 1970)

I'm able to perceive what the issues are before they become issues.

Stewart Alsop III
Editor, *PC Letter*
The New York Times, February 28, 1988

It is impossible for all things to be precisely set down in writing; for rules must be universal, but actions are concerned with particulars.

Aristotle, 384–322 B.C.
Greek philosopher and teacher
Politics

The notion that big business and big labor and big government can sit down around a table somewhere and work out the direction of the American economy is at complete variance with the reality of where the American economy is headed. I mean, it's like dinosaurs gathering to talk about the evolution of a new generation of mammals.

> Bruce Babbitt
> Governor of Arizona
> *Inc. Magazine*, August 1987

"Intelligent" means a person who can see implications and draw conclusions.

> Babylonian Talmud, Hagiga

For many years it had been the [Soviet] practice to take the livestock census on January 1, a rather harmless date; presumably it was selected by an innocent planner with the primary objective of facilitating schedules. However, the collective farms have targets of livestock holdings which they are required to meet, as well as targets of meat deliveries to the State. Ordinarily the peasants would bring their stock for slaughter in the early fall, when they are fattest from the summer grazing. But in order to meet their livestock targets on January 1, they kept their stock through the cold early winter months so that they could be counted in the census. The consequence was a disastrous loss of weight.

> Joseph Berliner
> Grusky and Miller, *The Sociology of Organizations* (The Free Press, 1970)

Prediction is very difficult, especially about the future.

> Neils Bohr, 1885–1962
> Nobel laureate in physics
> Favorite saying

When all looks fair about, and thou seest not a cloud so big as a Hand to threaten thee, forget not the Wheel of things: think of sullen vicissitudes, but beat not thy brains to foreknow them. Be armed against such obscurities rather by submission than foreknowledge.

> Thomas Browne, 1605–1682
> English writer and physician
> *Christian Morals*

You can never plan the future by the past.

> Edmund Burke, 1729–1797
> English statesman, orator, and writer
> *Letter to a Member of the National Assembly*

'Tis best to build no castles in the air.

> Fanny Burney, 1752–1840
> English novelist
> *Diary and Letters of Madame D'Arblay*

The best-laid schemes o' mice an' men,
Gang aft a-gley,
And leave us naught but grief and pain,
For promised joy.

> Robert Burns, 1759–1796
> Scottish national poet
> *To A Mouse*

Coming events cast their shadows before.

> Thomas Campbell, 1777–1844
> English attorney and poet
> *Lochiel's Warning*

"It's a poor sort of memory, that only works backwards," the Queen remarked.

> Lewis Carroll
> (Charles Lutwidge Dodgson), 1832–1898
> English mathematician and writer
> *Alice's Adventures in Wonderland*

It is a mistake to look too far ahead. Only one link of the chain of destiny can be handled at a time.

> Winston Churchill, 1874–1965
> English Prime Minister, writer, and soldier
> Speech in Parliament, February 27, 1945

Do not let your plans for a new world divert your energies from saving what is left of the old.

> Winston Churchill, 1874–1965
> English Prime Minister, writer, and soldier
> Memorandum to the Minister of Public
> Works and Buildings, January 6, 1941

[Organizational] change is intervention, and intervention even with good intentions can lead to negative results in both the short and long run. For example, a change in structure in going from application of one theory to another might cause the unwanted resignation of a key executive, or the loss of an important customer.... [T]he factor of change, acts as an overriding check against continual organizational alterations. It means that regardless of how well meant a change is, or how much logic dictates this change, its possible negative effects must be carefully weighed against the hoped-for benefits.

> William A. Cohen
> *Principles of Technical Management*
> (AMACOM, 1980)

As the dimensions of the tree are not always regulated by the size of the seed, so the consequences of things are not always proportionate to the apparent magnitude of those events that have produced them.

> Charles Caleb Colton, c. 1780–1832
> English cleric, sportsman, and wine merchant
> *Lacon*

Happy is that city which in time of peace thinks of war.

> Inscription on armoury, Venice
> Sixteenth century

The cautious seldom err.

> Confucius, c. 551–c. 479 B.C.
> Chinese philosopher and teacher
> *Analects*

A fool must now and then be right by chance.

> William Cowper, 1731–1800
> English poet
> *Conversation*

There is no data on the future.

> Laurel Cutler
> Vice Chairman, FCB/Leber Katz Partners
> *Inc. Magazine*, November 1987

Any plan is bad which is not susceptible to change.

> Bartolommeo de San Concordio, 1475–1517
> Florentine painter and writer
> *Giunta agli Ammaestramenti degli Antichi*

Extreme views are never just; something always turns up which disturbs the calculations founded on their data.

> Benjamin Disraeli, 1804–1881
> English Prime Minister and novelist
> *Tancred*

What we anticipate seldom occurs; what we least expect generally happens.

> Benjamin Disraeli, 1804–1881
> English Prime Minister and novelist
> *Henrietta Temple*

When nothing is sure, everything is possible.

> Margaret Drabble
> English novelist
> *The Middle Ground*

Predicting the future is easy. It's trying to figure out what's going on now that's hard.

> Fritz R. S. Dressler
> President, FRS Dressler Associates
> *The New York Times*, August 30, 1987

The only thing we know about the future is that it is going to be different.

> Peter F. Drucker
> Management consultant and writer
> *People and Performance*
> (Harper & Row, 1977)

In complex situations, we may rely too heavily on planning and forecasting and underestimate the importance of random factors in the environment. That reliance can also lead to delusions of control.

> Hillel J. Einhorn and Robin M. Hogarth
> Center for Decision Research,
> University of Chicago Business School
> *Harvard Business Review*,
> January/February 1987

All business proceeds on beliefs, or judgments of probabilities, and not on certainties.

> Charles William Eliot, 1834–1926
> President of Harvard University
> *The New Dictionary of Thoughts*, 1957

Take nothing for granted.

> Ralph Waldo Emerson, 1803–1882
> American essayist and poet
> *Journals*

It is a lesson which all history teaches wise men to put trust in ideas, and not in circumstances.

> Ralph Waldo Emerson, 1803–1882
> American essayist and poet
> *War*

Unless to Thought is added Will,
Apollo is an imbecile.

> Ralph Waldo Emerson, 1803–1882
> American essayist and poet
> *Fragments on the Poetic Gift*

In every affair consider what precedes and what follows, and then undertake it.

> Epictetus, c. 60
> Greek philosopher
> *That Everything Be Done with Circumspection*

If our original plan had had a lower goal, we would have achieved less.

> William E. Foster
> CEO, Stratus
> *Inc. Magazine*, February 1987

It is important not to ignore forecasts that are uncongenial.

> Jib Fowles
> University of Houston
> *The New York Times*, January 10, 1988

Understanding product life cycles can help companies plan their market segmentation strategy.

> William H. Franklin, Jr.
> Georgia State University
> *Financial Strategies*, Fall 1987

There are two classes of people who tell what is going to happen in the future: Those who don't know, and those who don't know they don't know.

John Kenneth Galbraith
Economist and diplomat
The Washington Post, February 28, 1988

A competent manager can usually explain necessary planning changes in terms of specific facts which have contributed to the change. The existing fear, or attitude of failure, which results from missed completion dates should be replaced by a more constructive fear of failing to keep a plan updated.

Philip F. Gehring Jr.
Texas Education Agency
and Udo W. Pooch
Texas A&M University
Rullo, *Advances in Computer Programming Management* (Hayden, 1980)

We were spending so much time planning for the next year and the next five years that our units were not making their current quarterly earnings.

Harold Geneen
CEO, IT&T
Managing (Doubleday, 1984)

There will be no more long-range planning.

Memo to executives from Harold Geneen
CEO, IT&T
Managing (Doubleday, 1984)

You read a book from the beginning to the end. You run a business the opposite way. You start with the end, and then you do everything you must to reach it.

Harold Geneen
CEO, IT&T
Managing (Doubleday, 1984)

If you plan ahead more than two years, you lose your flexibility and run the risk of locking yourself into approaches that will lag behind new developments. So I dream far ahead, but I don't plan far ahead.

Fred M. Gibbons
President, Software Publishing Corp.
Inc. Magazine, February 1987

If we can't figure something out in three weeks, we probably shouldn't bother.

Steven Gilbert
Managing partner, Chemical Ventures, Inc.
Venture, April 1988

Every moment spent planning saves three or four in execution.

Crawford Greenwalt
President, Du Pont
Mackenzie, *The Time Trap*
(McGraw-Hill, 1972)

Everything someone does on a daily basis should be traceable back to an annual or quarterly plan.

Richard E. Griggs
Founder, MANFIT
Black Enterprise, April 1988

The *preparation* of an annual plan is in itself the end, not the resulting bound volume... To prepare and justify [a plan], people go through a lot of soul-searching analysis and juggling, and it is this mental exercise that is valuable.

Andrew S. Grove
CEO, Intel Corp.
High Output Management
(Random House, 1983)

Planning and competition can be combined only by planning for competition, but not by planning against competition.

Friedrich A. Hayek
Nobel laureate in economics
The Road to Serfdom
(University of Chicago, 1944)

I have but one lamp by which my feet are guided, and that is the lamp of experience. I know of no way of judging of the future but by the past.

> Patrick Henry, 1736–1799
> American patriot and orator
> Speech to Virginia Convention, March 23, 1775

For want of a nail the shoe is lost, for want of a shoe the horse is lost, for want of a horse the rider is lost.

> George Herbert, 1593–1632
> English clergyman and poet
> *Jacula Prudentum*

The mouse that hath but one hole is quickly taken.

> George Herbert, 1593–1632
> English clergyman and poet
> *Jacula Prudentum*

It is a capital mistake to theorize before one has data.

> Sherlock Holmes
> (Arthur Conan Doyle), 1859–1930
> English physician, writer, and sportsman
> *Scandal in Bohemia*

He has half the deed done, who has made a beginning.

> Horace, 65–8 B.C.
> Roman poet
> *Epistles to Lucilius*

Everybody knows the future is not as certain as it once was.

> William J. Janawitz
> Manager, Manufacturing Equipment, Kodak
> *The New York Times*, March 6, 1988

Good results without good planning come from good luck, not good management.

> David Jaquith
> President, Vega Industries, Inc.
> Mackenzie, *The Time Trap* (McGraw-Hill, 1972)

It is always much easier to design than to perform. A man proposes his schemes of life in a state of abstraction and disengagement, exempt from the enticements of hope, the solicitations of affection, the importunities of appetite, or the depressions of fear, and is in the same state with him that teaches upon land the art of navigation, to whom the sea is always smooth, and the wind always prosperous.

> Samuel Johnson, 1709–1784
> English lexicographer and critic
> *Boswell's Life of Dr. Johnson*

The secret of the Kennedy success in politics was not money but meticulous planning and organization.

> Rose Fitzgerald Kennedy
> Kennedy family matriarch
> *Times to Remember* (Doubleday, 1974)

In the long run we are all dead.

> John Maynard Keynes, 1883–1946
> English economist, writer, and diplomat
> Quoted on *MacNeil-Lehrer News Hour* (TV)
> February 2, 1988

Business plans may be great for bankers and investors, but if companies really followed them, you might never have heard of Compaq, Lotus or Ben & Jerry's.

> Erik Larson
> Business writer
> *Inc. Magazine*, February 1987

When everything has to be right, something isn't.

Stanislaw J. Lec
Polish writer and aphorist
Unkempt Thoughts (St. Martin's Press, 1962)

Occassionally we see a company with all these visible success characteristics—but it still isn't going anywhere. Plans are carefully prepared by a competent staff; product possibilities of real potential are staked out; the company's record of service is outstanding; and yet progress is disappointing. When this occurs, the usual missing ingredients are management leadership and moral courage. In the final analysis, planning cannot be meaningful without management foresight, management support, management decision, and management follow-through.

P. J. Lovewell
Director of Research, Stanford University
Odiorne, *How Managers Make Things Happen*
(Prentice-Hall, 1982)

Which of you, intending to build a tower, sitteth not down first and counteth the cost, whether he have sufficient to finsh it?

New Testament, Luke 14:28

There is no security on this earth; there is only opportunity.

Douglas MacArthur, 1880–1964
Five-star General of the U. S. Army
Whitney, *MacArthur: His Rendezvous with History* (Knopf, 1955)

Relatively few [executives responding to a survey] believe that planning has made a significant contribution to their recent growth. The majority view—even among firms that have formal planning procedures—[credits]

good business conditions rather than deliberate planning.

Sorrell M. Mathes
Department Manager, The Conference Board
Handling Company Growth
(National Industrial Conference Board, 1967)

No matter how deep a study you make, what you really have to rely on is your own intuition and when it comes down to it, you really don't know what's going to happen until you do it.

Konosuke Matsushita
Founder, Matsushita Electric Co. (Japan)
Cherry Blossoms and Robotics
(Young Presidents' Organization, 1983)

If I had given this speech forty years ago, I should have told you that transistors had recently been developed, and that they would one day make vacuum-tube technology obsolete.... I don't know what the 1987 equivalent of the 1947 transistor is, but I'm confident that we have to bring it into operation in less than forty years. People simply need technological acceleration to achieve the service levels we've already promised.

T. Allen McArtor
Administrator, FAA
Speech, Washington, D.C., August 18, 1987

[In a startup company] you basically throw out all assumptions every three weeks.

Scott McNealy
CEO, Sun Microsystems, Inc.
Inc. Magazine, February 1987

[Referring to his own original buisness plan:] You look at a plan like this, and you can see that the people who made it didn't appreciate some of the basics of business.

Robert M. Metcalfe
Chairman, 3Com Corp.
Inc. Magazine, February 1987

... which erring men call chance.

John Milton, 1608–1674
English poet
Comus

If anything can go wrong, it will, and at the most inopportune time.

Murphy's Law

The one thing I'm sure of is that whatever we're now planning for next year will be changed by next year.

William Newman
Director,
Center for Management Development, FAA
Meeting, February 24, 1988

[L]ong-range plans are most valuable when they are revised and adjusted and set anew at shorter periods. The five-year plan is reconstructed each year in turn for the following five years. The soundest basis for this change is accurate measurement of the results of the first year's experience with the plan against the target of the plan.

George S. Odiorne
University of Massachusetts
Management by Objectives (Pitman, 1965)

Cromwell was about to ravage all Christendom; the royal family was undone, and his own forever established, save for a little grain of sand which formed in his ureter. Rome itself was trembling under him; but this small piece of gravel having formed there, he is dead, his family cast down, all is peaceful, and the king is restored.

Blaise Pascal, 1623–1662
French scientist and philosopher
Meditations

Method goes far to prevent Trouble in Business: For it makes the Task easy, hinders Confusion, saves abundance of Time, and in-

structs those that have Business depending, both on what to do and what to hope.

William Penn, 1644–1718
Founder of Pennsylvania
Fruits of Solitude in Reflections and Maxims

Unpredictability cannot be removed, or perhaps even substantially reduced, by excessive planning.

Tom Peters
Business writer
Thriving on Chaos (Knopf, 1987)

Consider the little mouse, how sagacious an animal it is which never entrusts its life to one hole only.

Plautus, 254–184 B.C.
Roman playwright and carpenter
Truculentus

How many things are looked upon as quite impossible until they have been actually effected.

Pliny the Elder, 23–79
Roman writer
Natural History

The pilot cannot mitigate the billows or calm the winds.

Plutarch, c. 46–c. 120
Greek biographer and philosopher
On the Tranquility of the Mind

Perseverance is more prevailing than violence; and many things which cannot be overcome together, yield themselves when taken little by little.

Plutarch, c. 46–c. 120
Greek biographer and philosopher
The Parallel Lives: Sertorius

Provide for the worst; the best will save itself.

Barber, *The Book of 1000 Proverbs*, 1876

Amid a multitude of projects, no plan is devised.

Publilius Syrus, c. 42 B.C.
Roman writer
Maxims

It is a bad plan that admits of no modification.

Publilius Syrus, c. 42 B.C.
Roman writer
Maxims

In every enterprise consider where you would come out.

Publilius Syrus, c. 42 B.C.
Roman writer
Maxims

Problems can be reduced by allowing employees to help plan changes rather than directing them to execute a plan made by others.

Eugene Raudsepp
President, Creative Research, Inc.
MTS Digest, April/June 1987

Because of the high mobility of capital and management, those who have the strongest stake in the long-term health of an enterprise are apt to be its lowest-level employees, whose mobility is most limited. Because they cannot merely hop to another job, such employees must live with the consequences of declining long-term productivity within an industry and a region. Investors and managers are generally better placed to reverse the decline, but they have less incentive—they can simply withdraw. (It is significant that in Japan trade unions are among the most vocal advocates of long-term investment strategies that emphasize productivity and growth.)

Robert B. Reich
JFK School of Government, Harvard University
The Next American Frontier, 1983

The prospective chief executive has to be action-oriented. You find a lot of planners who can't act.

Gerard Roche
Chairman, Heidricks & Struggles
Fortune, February 3, 1986

We planned it that way.

Franklin Delano Roosevelt, 1882–1945
Thirty-second President of the United States
Speech, Charleston, South Carolina,
October 23, 1935

The prophet knows no more than ordinary man but he knows it earlier.

Dagobert D. Runes
Editor, publisher, and philosopher
A Book of Contemplation

He who considers too much will perform little.

Johann von Schiller, 1759–1805
German poet and playwright
William Tell

They [Wall Street] aren't thinking five or 10 years down the road, and they don't really care if the Japanese have a 30 year plan or not.

Charles E. Schumer
U. S. Congressman
Best of Business Quarterly, Summer 1987

Were everything to happen in the ordinary chain of events, the future would be subject to the rules of arithmetic.... But extraordinary events, and wonderful runs of luck, defy the calculations of mankind, and throw impenetrable darkness on future contingencies.

> Walter Scott, 1771–1832
> Scottish poet, novelist, and biographer
> *Guy Mannering*

To fear the worst oft cures the worse.

> William Shakespeare, 1564–1616
> English dramatist and poet
> *Troilus and Cressida*

Too swift arrives as tardy as too slow.

> William Shakespeare, 1564–1616
> English dramatist and poet
> *Romeo and Juliet*

Fortune brings in some boats that are not steered.

> William Shakespeare, 1564–1616
> English dramatist and poet
> *Cymbeline*

Striving to better, oft we mar what's well.

> William Shakespeare, 1564–1616
> English dramatist and poet
> *Hamlet*

Good people can fix a lot of flaws in poor planning, but it's never the other way around.

> Roland Shmitt
> Senior VP, General Electric Co.
> *Government Executive*, January 1987

Men don't plan to fail—they fail to plan.

> William J. Siegel, 1910–1966
> Vice President and Comptroller,
> Printz-Biederman Manufacturing Co.
> Sign on desk

The ability to predict market changes doesn't come about by careful communication with customers and sales organizations. It comes about from an ability to look at the fundamentals of the economy.

> Jim Swiggett
> CEO, Kollmorgen Corp.
> *Inc. Magazine*, February 1987

I was a great admirer of old D. H. Burnham of Chicago, who organized the Chicago regional planning, and he had a motto over his mantel on which was written, "MAKE NO LITTLE PLANS." You can always amend a big plan, but you can never expand a little one. I don't believe in little plans. I believe in plans big enough to meet a situation which we can't possible foresee now.

> Harry S. Truman, 1884–1972
> Thirty-third President of the United States
> Speech, November 2, 1949

To look forward you have to look back a little bit.... One of the problems with forecasting is that you can't see the future very well.

> Sherman Uchill
> President, Sherman Howe Computer Stores
> *The New York Times*, August 30, 1987

Our planning system was dynamite when we first put it in. The thinking was fresh; the form mattered little.... It was idea-oriented. We then hired a head of planning, and he hired two vice presidents, and then he hired a planner; and the books got thicker, and the printing more sophisticated, and the covers got harder, and the drawings got better.

> John Welch
> CEO, General Electric Co.
> Tomasko, *Downsizing* (AMACOM, 1987)

The more frequent shifts in technology, consumer preferences, resource availability, foreign exchange rates, and so forth trim the time available to recoup investments. Consequently, better forecasting and faster responses to external changes have to be built into the planning process.

Boris Yavitz
Director, Federal Reserve Bank of New York
and William H. Newman
Columbia University Business School
Strategy in Action (The Free Press, 1982)

Even a cat can cross your plans.

Yiddish proverb

If you don't look far enough ahead, you may not get good enough insights.

Jason Yoon
Founder, PriVac, Inc.
The Washington Post, April 25, 1988

Don't cross the bridge until you come to it, and then be sure there's a bridge.

Anonymous

33

Problem Solving

It is much easier to be critical than to be correct.

In most management problems there are too many possibilities to expect experience, judgement, or intuition to provide good guesses, even with perfect information.

> Russell L. Ackoff
> Management Information Systems scientist
> *Management Science*, December 1967

They were not just intelligent, but prided themselves on being "rational".... They were eager to find formulas, preferably expressed in a pseudo-mathematical language, that would unify the most disparate phenomena with which reality presented them; that is, they were eager to discover *laws* by which to explain and predict political and historical facts as though they were as necessary, and thus as reliable, as the physicists once believed natural phenomena to be.... [T]hey did not *judge*, they calculated.... [A]n utterly irrational confidence in the calculability of

reality [became] the leitmotif of the decision making.

> Hannah Arendt, 1909–1975
> German-American philospher and critic
> *Crises of the Republic*
> (Harcourt Brace Jovanovich, 1972)

The perception of a problem is always relative. Your headache feels terrific to the druggist.

> Ramona E. F. Arnett
> President, Ramona Enterprises, Inc.
> Staff meeting, January 1986

If a man will begin with certainties, he shall end in doubts; but if he will be content to begin with doubts, he shall end in certainties.

> Francis Bacon, 1561–1626
> Lord Chancellor of England
> *Advancement of Learning*

The remedy is worse than the disease.

Francis Bacon, 1561–1626
Lord Chancellor of England
Of Seditions

... hypothetical questions get hypothetical answers.

Joan Baez
Folk-singer, writer, and peace activist
Daybreak

Every organizational policy solves certain problems and generates others.

Judith M. Bardwick
University of California at San Diego
The Plateauing Trap (AMACOM, 1986)

Management and medicine have one thing in common. They can both cause problems as well as solve them.

Warren G. Bennis
President, University of Cincinnati
University of Maryland symposium,
January 21, 1988

The problem of crossing the sea
Troubled Moses less than it would me;
Neither aircraft nor ship
Was required for the trip,
Which he'd booked through the best Agency.

D. R. Bensen
Biblical Limericks (Ballantine, 1986)

Put the policy manual back on the shelf when common sense points to a better way.

Thomas V. Bonoma
Harvard Business School
Harvard Business Review,
November/December 1986

One thing has become increasingly clear in pursuing the nature of knowing. It is that the conventional apparatus of the psychologist—both his instruments of investigation and the conceptual tools he uses in the interpretation of his data—leaves one approach unexplored. It is an approach whose medium of exchange seems to be the metaphor paid out by the left hand. It is a way that grows happy hunches and "lucky" guesses, that is stirred into connective activity by the poet and the necromancer looking sidewise rather than directly. Their hunches and intuitions generate a grammar of their own—searching out connections, suggesting similarities, weaving ideas loosely in a trial web.

Jerome Bruner
American psychologist
On Knowing (Atheneum, 1973)

Like him in Aesop, that, when his cart was stalled, lay flat on his back, and cryed, aloud, "Help, Hercules!" but that was to little purpose.... [So] he whipt his horses withal, and put his shoulder to the wheel.

Robert Burton, 1577–1640
Vicar of St. Thomas's, Oxford
The Anatomy of Melancholy

A problem that is located and identified is already half solved!

Bror R. Carlson
Director of Accounting,
International Minerals & Chemicals Co.
Managing for Profit (IM&C, 1961)

Problems are solved on the spot, as soon as they arise. No frontline employee has to wait for a supervisor's permission.

Jan Carlzon
CEO, SAS (Sweden)
Moments of Truth (Ballinger, 1987)

Dealing with people is the biggest problem you face, especially if you are a business man.

> Dale Carnegie, 1888–1955
> American public speaking teacher
> *How to Win Friends and Influence People*

At this point they came in sight of thirty or forty windmills... [A]s soon as Don Quixote saw them he said to his squire, "Fortune is arranging matters for us better than we could have shaped our desires ourselves, for look there, friend Sancho Panza, where thirty or more monstrous giants present themselves, all of whom I mean to engage in battle and, and with whose spoils we shall begin to make our fortunes."

> Miguel de Cervantes, 1547–1616
> Spanish novelist
> *Don Quixote*

Out of intense complexities intense simplicities emerge.

> Winston Churchill, 1874–1965
> English Prime Minister, writer, and soldier
> *The World Crisis*

Trying to paint a picture is like trying to fight a battle. It is, if anything, more exciting than fighting it successfully. But the principle is the same. It is the same kind of problem as unfolding a long, sustained, interlocked argument.

> Winston Churchill, 1874–1965
> English Prime Minister, writer, and soldier
> *Thoughts and Adventures*

The problems of victory are more agreeable than those of defeat, but they are no less difficult.

> Winston Churchill, 1874–1965
> English Prime Minister, writer, and soldier
> Speech, November 11, 1942

It is a condition which confronts us—not a theory.

> Grover Cleveland, 1837–1908
> Twenty-second and twenty-fourth
> President of the United States
> Message to Congress, December 6, 1887

Doctors are like everyone else; once they understand what some of the underlying problems are, they can mange them more effectively.

> Norman J. Cowen
> Hand surgeon, Washington, D.C.
> *Washington-Baltimore Theatre Guide*,
> May 1988

It is much easier to be critical than to be correct.

> Benjamin Disraeli, 1804–1881
> English Prime Minister and novelist
> Speech, January 24, 1860

The originality of a subject is in its treatment.

> Benjamin Disraeli, 1804–1881
> English Prime Minister and novelist
> *Lothair*

Desperate cures must be to desperate ills applied.

> John Dryden, 1631–1700
> English poet
> *The Hind and the Panther*

[Writing to a student:] Do not worry about your difficulties in mathematics; I can assure you that mine are still greater.

> Albert Einstein, 1879–1955
> Nobel laureate in physics
> *Albert Einstein, The Human Side*
> (Princeton, 1979)

We should hold to the usage until we are clear it is wrong.

> Ralph Waldo Emerson, 1803–1882
> American essayist and poet
> *Journals*

I like people who can do things. When Edward and I struggled in vain to drag our big calf into the barn, the Irish girl put her finger into the calf's mouth and led her in directly.

> Ralph Waldo Emerson, 1803–1882
> American essayist and poet
> *Journals*

Who shall forbid a wise skepticism, seeing that there is no practical question on which anything more than an approximate solution can be had?

> Ralph Waldo Emerson, 1803–1882
> American essayist and poet
> *Representative Men*

The cause of all human evils is not being able to apply general principles to special cases.

> Epictetus, c. 60–120
> Roman Stoic philosopher
> *Dissertations*

Q. E. D.
[*Quod erat demonstrandum.*]
Thus is it demonstrated (proven).

> Euclid, c. 300 B.C.
> Greek geometer
> *Elements*

There comes a time in the affairs of man when he must take the bull by the tail and face the situation.

> William Claude (W. C.) Fields, 1880–1946
> American comedian and film star
> Mason, *Never Trust A Man Who Doesn't Drink*
> (Montcalm, 1971)

View thinking as a strategy. Thinking is the best way to resolve difficulties. Maintain faith in your ability to think your way out of problems. Recognize the difference between worrying and thinking. The former is repeated, needless problem analysis while the latter is solution generation.

> Timothy W. Firnstahl
> CEO, Restaurant Services, Inc.
> *Harvard Business Review*,
> September/October 1986

[Explaining why each unit has a well equipped, problem solving room:] The decisions being made in the plants are at least as important as those being made in the boardroom—shouldn't the setting and amenities reflect that?

> Gordon Foward
> President, Chaparral Steel
> Peters, *Thriving on Chaos* (Knopf, 1987)

The meek is known in anger, a hero in war, and a friend in time of need.

> Solomon ibn Gabirol, 1021–1069
> Spanish poet and grammarian
> *The Choice of Pearls*

The enemy of conventional wisdom is not ideas but the march of events.

> John Kenneth Galbraith
> Economist and diplomat
> *The Affluent Society* (Houghton Mifflin, 1958)

Peak performers concentrate on solving problems rather than placing blame for them.

> Charles Garfield
> President, Performance Sciences Corp.
> *Peak Performers* (Avon, 1986)

This is not a cure, but a calamity.

> Germanicus, 15 B.C.–A.D. 19
> Roman general and writer
> Quoted by Tacitus,
> *Annals of the Julian Emperors*

There is no situation that cannot be made more difficult with a just a little bit of effort.

> David Gerrold
> Author
> *The Galactic Whirlpool* (Bantam, 1980)

All problems present themselves to the mind as threats of failure.

> J. J. Gordon
> Founder of the "Brainstorming" process
> *Creative Computing*, October 1983

It is better to solve problems than crises.

> John Guinther
> American writer and humorist
> *The Malpractitioners* (Doubleday, 1978)

Someone who gets no help makes no progress.

> Robert Half
> President, Robert Half International
> *Robert Half on Hiring* (Crown, 1985)

We will either find a way or make one.

> Hannibal, 247–183 B.C.
> Carthaginian general
> Attributed

[Describing Indian mathematician Srinivasa Ramanujan, 1887–1920:] With his memory, his patience, and his power of calculation, he combined a power of generalization, a feeling for form, and a capacity for rapid modification of his hypotheses, that were often really startling, and made him, in his own field, without a rival in his day.

> G. H. Hardy
> *An Introduction to the Theory of Numbers*
> (Oxford, 1960)

We try to make management decisions that, if everything goes right, will preclude future problems. But everything does not always go right, and managers therefore must be problem solvers as well as decision makers.

> James L. Hayes
> President and CEO,
> American Management Association
> *Memos for Management: Leadership*
> (AMACOM, 1983)

It's hard to solve a problem when you don't even know it exists.

> Fred Heiser
> Chairman, Heiser-Egan, Inc.
> Remark at meeting, June 1987

If you don't expect the unexpected, you will not find it.

> Heraclitus, 535?–475? B.C.
> Greek philosopher
> Attributed

Having settled on some set of objectives ... the next logical step is to see what limits its achievement.

> Harley H. Hinrichs
> United States Naval Academy
> *Program Budgeting and Cost Benefit Analysis*
> (Goodyear, 1969)

(General propositions do not decide concrete cases. The decision will depend on a judgment or intuition more subtle than any articulate major premise.

> Oliver Wendell Holmes, Jr., 1841–1935
> U. S. Supreme Court Justice
> *Lochner* v. *New York* (1905)

It is quite a three-pipe problem.

> Sherlock Holmes
> (Arthur Conan Doyle), 1859–1930
> English physician, writer, and sportsman
> *The Red-Headed League*

How often have I said to you that when you have eliminated the impossible, whatever remains, *however improbable*, must be the truth?

> Sherlock Holmes
> (Arthur Conan Doyle), 1859–1930
> English physician, writer, and sportsman
> *The Sign of Four*

Aspirin doctor: A manager who tries to solve every problem the same way, like a doctor who prescribes aspirin for every unknown illness.

> Harold S. Hook
> Chairman and CEO, American General Corp.
> *Forbes*, October 19, 1987

Irrationally held truths may be more harmful than reasoned errors.

> Thomas Henry Huxley, 1825–1895
> English biologist
> *Coming of Age of the "Origin of Species"*

Try several solutions at once. Maybe none of them, alone, would solve the problem, but in combination they do the job.

> Ray Josephs
> President, Ray Josephs Associates, Inc.
> *Leadership in the Office* (AMACOM, 1963)

Good public administration implies far more than organizational and management techniques.... Public administration must be directly associated with development of efficacious solutions to the vexing problems of our era.

> Jong S. Jun
> *Public Administration: Understanding Management, Politics, and Law in the Public Sector* (Random House, 1986)

When Studebaker introduced a new assembly line ... there was conflict between union and management over what the new rates should be. The problem was handled by simply rotating all the foremen and stewards on the new line until they got a foreman-steward combination that could agree on the rates that should be set.

> Daniel Katz
> Labor economist
> Kahan and Boulding, *Power and Conflict in Organizations* (Basic Books, 1964)

Our problems are man-made; therefore they can be solved by men. And man can be as big as he wants. No problem of human destiny is beyond human beings.

> John Fitzgerald Kennedy, 1917–1963
> Thirty-fifth President of the United States
> Commencement address,
> The American University,
> Washington, D.C., June 10, 1963

The great enemy of the truth is very often not the lie—deliberate, contrived, and dishonest—but the myth—persistent, persuasive and unrealistic.

> John Fitzgerald Kennedy, 1917–1963
> Thirty-fifth President of the United States
> Commencement address,
> Yale University, June 11, 1962

I find that the three administrative problems on a campus are sex for the students, athletics for the alumni, and parking for the faculty.

> Clark Kerr
> President, University of Washington
> *Time*, November 17, 1958

Reserarchers have found a connection between a well-developed sense of humor and problem-solving.... [H]umorous people are usually wiser and have broader perspectives. And they are often better workers.

> Dyan Machan
> Career counselor and writer
> *Forbes*, November 2, 1987

Nine times out of ten, in the arts as in life, there is actually no truth to be discovered; there is only error to be exposed.

> Henry Louis Mencken, 1880–1956
> American editor, author, and critic
> *Prejudices*

An optimist is the kind of person who believes a housefly is looking for a way to get out.

> George Jean Nathan, 1882–1958
> American editor and critic
> *The Theater in the Fifties*

Sometimes the answer [which may be apparent to some] is not always obvious to everybody.

> Charles Osgood
> Journalist
> *CBS Morning News*, December 29, 1987

Some people have a notion, that, when things come to their worst, they will mend. Why should they?

> C. Northcote Parkinson
> University of Malaya
> *The Law and the Profits*, 1960

[T]he process of problem analysis consists of determining the *difference* between what you have and what you would like to have.

> Bobby R. Patton and Kim Griffin
> *Problem-Solving Group Interraction*
> (Harper & Row, 1973)

The best hypothesis, in the sense of the one most recommending itself to the inquirer, is the one which can be the most readily refuted if it is false. This far outweighs the trifling merit of being likely. For after all, what is a *likely* hypothesis? It is one which falls in with our preconceived ideas. But these may be wrong. Their errors are just what the scientific man is gunning for more particularly. But if a hypothesis can quickly and easily be cleared away so as to go toward leaving the field free for the main struggle, this is an immense advantage.

> Charles Sanders Peirce, 1839–1914
> American philosopher
> *Collected Papers*

A patient mind is the best remedy for trouble.

> Plautus, 254–184 B.C.
> Roman playwright and carpenter
> *Asinaria*

Perseverance is more prevailing than violence; many things which cannot be overcome when they are together, yield themselves up when taken little by little.

> Plutarch, c. 46–c. 120
> Greek biographer and philosopher
> *The Parallel Lives: Sertorius*

The conscious self is narrowly limited, and as far as the subliminal self we know not its limitations.... [C]alculations must be made in the ... period of conscious work, that which follows the inspiration, that in which one verifies the results of this inspiration and deduces their consequences. The rules of these calculations are strict and complicated. They require discipline, attention, will, and therefore consciousness. In the subliminal self, on the contrary, reigns what I should call liberty ... the priveleged unconscious phenomena, those susceptible of becoming conscious, are those which, directly or indirectly, affect most profoundly our emotional sensibility.... The role of this unconscious work in mathematical invention appears to me incontestable, and traces of it would be found in other cases where it is less evident.

Jules Henri Poincaré, 1854–1912
French mathematician
Mathematical Creation

Success in solving the problem depends on choosing the right aspect, on attacking the fortress from its accessible side.

George Polya
Hungarian mathematician
How to Solve It

My focus is not on selling. It's more on making sure that people who become clients are willing and able to pay for my services. Then I concentrate on providing service—I simply help clients buy what they need. I'm always in a problem-solving mode, and that puts me on the client's side of the table.

Don Ray
Financial planner and management consultant,
FSC Securities Corp.
Financial Strategies, Fall 1987

The problem-solving approach allows for mental double-clutching. It does not require a direct switch from one point of view to another. It provides a period "in neutural" where there is an openness to facts and, therefore, a willingness to consider alternative views.

William Reddin
Management consultant
Managerial Effectiveness
(McGraw-Hill, 1970)

Once we've figured this out we won't have this problem again—if we can remember how we did it.

Ward Rinehart
Population Information Program,
The Johns Hopkins University
Poplac News, Spring 1988

Listen and learn.

Franklin Delano Roosevelt, 1882–1945
Thirty-second President of the United States
Favorite motto during his first 100 days

[The] problem mostly isn't "them" but "us."

Hobart Rowan
Syndicated columnist
The Washington Post, February 28, 1988

I never was satisfied with a problem that I understood only partly. I wanted to understand it as completely as I could.

David Sarnoff, 1891–1971
Founder and President, RCA
Wisdom of Sarnoff and the World of RCA

In this day of labor-saving devices and robot machinery, we have electronic computers which solve quickly and accurately the most complex scientific and mathematical problems. But such instruments provide no substitute for thinking. The human brain must continue to frame the problems for the electronic machine to solve.

David Sarnoff, 1891–1971
Founder and President, RCA
Wisdom of Sarnoff and the World of RCA

Managers don't have problems. Managers solve problems.

Bernard Schulman
President, Hot Pink Party Services, Inc.
Favorite saying

In desperate circumstances men look to strange and unusual remedies.

> Walter Scott, 1771–1832
> Scottish poet, novelist, and biographer
> *Peveril of the Peak*

The number of those who undergo the fatigue of judging for themselves is very small indeed.

> Richard Brinsley Sheridan, 1751–1816
> Irish playwright
> *The Critic*

Solid good sense is often nonsense solidified.

> Leo Stein, 1872–1947
> American writer and editor
> *Journey into the Self*

Systems represent someone's attempt at solution to problems, but they do not solve problems; they produce complicated responses.

> Melvin J. Sykes
> Attorney
> *Maryland Law Review*, 1978

Discovery [of a solution] consists of looking at the same thing as everyone else and thinking something different.

> Albert Szent-Gyorgyi
> Nobel laureate in medicine and physiology
> Oech, *A Whack on the Side of the Head*
> (Warner, 1983)

Management science [operations research] also involves the philosophy of approaching a problem in a logical manner (i.e., a scientific approach). The logical, consistent, and systematic approach to problem solving can be as useful (and valuable) as the knowledge of the mechanics of the mathematical techniques themselves.

> Bernard W. Taylor III
> Virginia Polytechnical Institute
> *Introduction to Management Science*
> (William C. Brown, 1986)

It is a characteristic of wisdom not to do desperate things.

> Henry David Thoreau, 1817–1862
> American naturalist and writer
> *Walden*

Most people first search for ready-made solutions, a solution designed by others, or, perhaps, by oneself in the past.

> Henry L. Tosi
> University of Florida
> and Stephan J. Carroll
> University of Maryland
> *Management* (John Wiley & Sons, 1976)

No matter how complicated a problem is, it usually can be reduced to a simple, comprehensible form which is often the best solution.

> Dr. An Wang
> CEO, Wang Laboratories
> *Nation's Business*, December 1987

Human thought is the process by which human ends are ultimately answered.

> Daniel Webster, 1782–1852
> American statesman and orator
> Oration at Bunker Hill,
> June 17, 1825

The correct solution to any problem depends principally on a true understanding of what the problem is.

> Arthur Mellen Wellington, 1847–1895
> American civil engineer, manager,
> and pioneer Operations Research scientist
> *The Economic Theory of Railway Location*, 1887

357

There is a technique, a knack, for thinking, just as there is for doing other things. You are not wholly at the mercy of your thoughts, any more than they are you. They are a machine you can learn to operate.

Alfred North Whitehead, 1861–1947
English mathematician and philosopher
Symbolism

We cannot think first and act afterwards. From the moment of birth we are immersed in action, and can only fitfully guide it by taking thought.

Alfred North Whitehead, 1861–1947
English mathematician and philosopher
Science and the Modern World

The mind of Caesar ... rejoices in commiting itself.... [Caesar] felt his mind to be operating only when it is interlocking itself with significant consequences.

Thornton Wilder, 1897–1975
American novelist and playwright
The Ides of March

Most people would rush ahead and implement a solution before they know what the problem is.

Q. T. Wiles
Turnaround Operations consultant
Inc. Magazine, February 1988

Define the problem before you pursue a solution.

John Williams
CEO, Spence Corp.
*Inc. Magazine's Guide to
Small Business Success*, 1987

People would rather live with a problem they cannot solve than accept a solution they cannot understand.

Robert Woolsey and Huntington Swanson
*Operations Research for Immediate Application:
A Quick and Dirty Manual* (Harper, 1975)

How can I get from here to there by a route that doesn't seem possible?

Steven Wozniak
Cofounder, Apple Computer and Chairman, CL 9
Omni, April 1988

Knowledge-based organizations require managers to be problem-centered rather than territory-centered.

Dale E. Zand
New York University
Information, Organization, and Power
(McGraw-Hill, 1981)

The scientist takes off from the manifold observatioons of predecessors, and shows his intelligence, if any, by his ability to to discriminate between the important and the negligible, by selecting here and there the significant stepping-stones that will lead across the difficulties to new understanding. The one who places the last stone and steps across to the *terra firma* of accomplished discovery gets all the credit. Only the initiated know and honor those whose patient integrity and devotion to exact observation have made the last step possible.

Hans Zinsser, 1878–1940
American bacteriologist
As I Remember Him

34
Productivity

The productivity of work is the responsibility of the manager.

It is probably not love that makes the world go around, but rather those mutually supportive alliances through which partners recognize their dependence on each other for the achievement of shared and private goals.

Fred Allen
Chairman, Pitney-Bowes Co.
Leaders, 1979

The productivity and competitive problems American manufacturers face result from ineffective top management, petrified in place, unwilling to accept change, failing to provide vision and leadership.

Philip H. Alspach
President, Intercon, Inc.
Harvard Business Review,
November/December 1986

The phrase "improved staff utilization" covers a wide territory, but in essence it means fewer people working more productively. On the shop floor, if often means that machines perform tasks previously done by human hands. This would include robotics and "expert" computer systems for quality control. But time and motion studies, better training systems, and financial remuneration based on product output rather than hours worked can and do improve blue collar productivity on the same old machines.

American Management Association
Responsible Reductions in Force, 1987

Industry can do anything which genius can do, and very many things which it cannot.

Henry Ward Beecher, 1813–1887
American clergyman
Proverbs from Plymouth Pulpit

[T]hrough the sound management of attitudes toward productivity, it is possible to create an orientation that results in more productivity while retaining quality.... [A]ttitudes precede action, and if attitudes toward work are adverse to the wanted action, they will have a negative effect on the outcome.

> Robert J. Blake and Jane S. Mouton
> Scientific Methods, Inc.
> *Productivity: The Human Side*
> (AMACOM, 1981)

People who produce good results feel good about themselves.

> Kenneth H. Blanchard
> Chairman, Blanchard Training and Development
> and Robert Lorber
> President, R. L. Lorber & Associates
> *Putting the One Minute Manager to Work*
> (William Morrow, 1984)

[Recalling early nonfunctional attempts at productivity improvement:] One "productivity initiative" from those days (long since reversed) was the removal of bathroom stall doors to discourage reading on company time.

> Richard J. Boyle
> Vice President, Honeywell Corp.
> *Harvard Business Review*,
> January/February 1984

Efficiency and economy imply employment of the right instrument and material as well as their right use in the right manner.

> Louis Dembitz Brandeis, 1856–1941
> U. S. Supreme Court Justice
> *St. Louis & Ohio Railway* v. *U.S.* (1928)

Most of the collective bargaining since the 1940's has resulted in wage settlements in excess of productivity increases.

> Courtney C. Brown
> Columbia University School of Business
> *Dun's Review*, August 1979

Away with the cant of "Measures not men!".... Men are everything, measures comparatively nothing.

> George Canning, 1770–1827
> English Prime Minister
> and Chancellor of the Exchequer
> Speech, House of Commons, 1801

Now I want you gentlemen on the other side of the House [the Democrats] to fish or cut bait [by voting for a bill that would make the silver dollar legal tender]. Gentlemen of the other side, do something positive for once during this session.

> Joseph Gurney Cannon, 1836–1926
> Speaker of the U. S. House of Representatives
> *Congressional Record*, 1876

[T]he basic principles of managing an organization successfully happen to be rather simple and straightforward. These principles, which have to do with the coordination of other people's efforts, do not vary appreciably from one type of organization to another or even, I would insist, from one culture to another. The right way to run an organization is the same in Patagonia and in Minnesota, whatever the differences in appearance.

> Theodore Caplow
> *Managing an Organization*
> (CBS College Publishing, 1983)

"Genius" (which means transcendent capacity of taking trouble, first of all).

> Thomas Carlyle, 1795–1881
> Scottish essayist and historian
> *Of Heroes and Hero-Worship*

Unskilled fools quarrel with their tools.

> Chinese proverb

To obtain the most from a man's energy it is necessary to increase the effect without increasing the fatigue.

> Charles Augustin Coulomb, 1736–1806
> French behavioral scientist
> *Observations*, 1791

Cutting costs without improvements in quality is futile.

> W. Edwards Deming
> Management consultant
> *Forbes,* April 4, 1988

The secret of success is constancy to purpose.

> Benjamin Disraeli, 1804–1881
> English Prime Minister and novelist
> Speech, June 24, 1870

Knowledge work, unlike manual work, cannot be replaced by capital investment. On the contrary, capital investment creates the need for more knowledge work.

> Peter F. Drucker
> Management consultant and writer
> *Management in Turbulent Times*
> (Harper & Row, 1980)

The productivity of work is not the responsibility of the worker but of the manager.

> Peter F. Drucker
> Management consultant and writer
> *Management in Turbulent Times*
> (Harper & Row, 1980)

The service institution has performance trouble precisely because it is not a business. What "businesslike" usually means in a service instiutution is little more than control of cost. What characterizes a business, however, is focus on results—return on capital, share of market, and so on.... The basic problem of service insitiutions is not high cost but lack of effectiveness.

> Peter F. Drucker
> Management consultant and writer
> *Management in Turbulent Times*
> (Harper & Row, 1980)

If you want to utilize your people to a maximum degree, it is definitely cheaper to have an existing guy work overtime than to add another person.

> Josef Ehrengruber
> President, Virginia Crews Coal Co.
> *Regardies*, June 1986

Our productivity [is] the wonder of the world.

> Dwight David Eisenhower, 1890–1969
> Thirty-fourth President of the United States
> Inaugural address, January 20, 1953

Because we don't have as many people pounding out manufactured things as we once did, many fallaciously conclude our productivity has withered.

> Malcom S. Forbes
> Editor-in-Chief, *Forbes Magazine*
> *Forbes*, April 4, 1988

All things are easy to industry, all things difficult to sloth.

> Benjamin Franklin, 1706–1790
> American printer and statesman
> *Poor Richard's Almanack*

It is seldom in the individual's interest to be as productive as he could be. Most people function far below their capacity mainly because of the essentially dependent relationship of any individual to the organization that employees. When a man is financially dependent upon the continuity of his paychecks, he will be more interested in preserving that continuity than in inflating the next check.

> Saul Gellerman
> University of Dallas School of Management
> *Fortune*, March 1968

Let us read with method, and propose to ourselves an end to what our studies may point. The use of reading is to aid us in thinking.

> Edward Gibbon, 1737–1794
> English politician and historian
> *Autobiography*

Usually, the faster the motions, the more output.

> Frank B. Gilbreth
> Pioneer management scientist
> *Motion Study* (Van Nostrand, 1911)

Where several years ago we saw training used as a form of personal growth, in recent years we've seen an increasing emphasis on training activities designed to meet corporate objectives that not uncommonly revolve around the issue of productivity.

> Jack Gordon
> Editor, *Training*
> *Training*, November 1986

Opportunities abound for linking productivity to business strategy.

> John L. Grahn
> Productivity Director, General Mills, Inc.
> *Harvard Business Review*,
> November/December 1986

[Y]ou can improve your own and your groups' productivity, whether or not the rest of the company follows suit.

> Andrew S. Grove
> CEO, Intel Corp.
> *High Output Management*
> (Random House, 1983)

Forecasting future work demands and then adjusting the output ... represents a very important way in which productivity can be improved.

> Andrew S. Grove
> CEO, Intel Corp.
> *High Output Management*
> (Random House, 1983)

One way to increase productivity is to do whatever we are doing now, but *faster*.... There is a second way. We can change the *nature* of the work we do, not how fast we do it.

> Andrew S. Grove
> CEO, Intel Corp.
> *High Output Management*
> (Random House, 1983)

Automation is certainly one way to improve the leverage of all types of work. Having machines to help them, human beings can create more output.

> Andrew S. Grove
> CEO, Intel Corp.
> *High Output Management*
> (Random House, 1983)

In the first round of work simplification ... you can reasonably expect a 30 to 50 percent reduction.... To implement the actual simplification, you must question why each step is performed. Typically, you will find that many steps exist in your work flow for no good reason. Often they are there by tradition or because formal procedure ordains it, and nothing practical ordains it.

> Andrew S. Grove
> CEO, Intel Corp.
> *High Output Management*
> (Random House, 1983)

Stressing output is the key to improving productivity, while looking to increase activity can result in just the opposite.

> Andrew S. Grove
> CEO, Intel Corp.
> *High Output Management*
> (Random House, 1983)

If little labour, little are our gaines:
Man's fortunes are according to his paines.

> Robert Herrick, 1591–1674
> English poet
> *Hesperides*

The productivity of a work group seems to depend on how the group members see their own goals in relation to the goals of the organization.

> Paul Hersey
> California American University
> and Kenneth H. Blanchard
> University of Massachusetts
> *Management of Organizational Behavior*
> (Prentice Hall, 1972)

Productivity is the name of the game, and gains in productivity will only come when better understanding and better relationships exist between management and the work force.... Managers have traditionally developed the skills in finance, planning, marketing and production techniques. Too often the relationships with their people have been assigned a secondary role. *This is too important a subject not to receive first-line attention.*

> William Hewlitt
> Founder and CEO, Hewlitt-Packard Co.
> Speech, "The Human Side of Management"

Productivity is closely tied to morale, and morale is a reflection of how people see themselves. If you can improve your employees'

perceptions of themselves, you can improve their morale—and thereby boost productivity.

> Howard Hurst
> President, Memphis Personnel Association
> *Personnel Journal*, March 1986

It is good not to have too many trades: "Many trades, few blessings."

> Jewish proverb

Cost accounting is the number one enemy of productivity.

> H. Thomas Johnson and Robert S. Kaplan
> *Relevance Lost: The Rise and Fall of*
> *Management Accounting*
> (Harvard Business School, 1987)

Controlling waste is like bailing a boat—you have to keep at it.

> Lyndon Baines Johnson, 1908–1974
> Thirty-sixth President of the United States
> Speech, December 4, 1964

If we make improvements in our productivity, it gets taken into account when we negotiate.... You cannot negotiate at the same old price.

> Lawrence Kichen
> Chairman, Lockheed
> *High Technology Business,* April 1988

The three most important things ... right now are costs, costs and costs. And costs can be summed up in one word: productivity.

> Ann Knight
> Financial analyst, Paine Webber
> *The New York Times*, September 20, 1987

Contrary to what you may think, your company will be a lot more productive if you refuse to tolerate competition among your employees.

Alfie Kohn
Management lecturer and author
No Contest: The Case Against Competition
(Houghton Mifflin, 1987)

Management that is destructively critical when mistakes are made kills initiative and it's essential that we have many people with initiative if we're to continue to grow.

Lewis Lehr
President, 3M Company
McGregor, *The Human Side of Enterprise*
(McGraw-Hill, 1960)

The greatest problem with unions is that they control the amount of productivity that workers will be allowed to achieve. Wages aren't really the problem.

Royal Little
Founder, Textron
Best of Business Quarterly, 1987

[Productivity is]...being able to do things that you were never able to do before.

Jim Manzi
President, Lotus Development Corp.
Fortune, March 2, 1987

Dull people always write dull copy, but bright people write bright copy only when they work hard at it.

William M. Marsteller
Advertising executive
Mandell, *Advertising* (Prentice-Hall, 1984)

Looking for differences between the more productive and less productive organizations, we found that the most striking difference is the number of people who are involved and feel responsibility for solving problems.

Michael McTague
Management and training consultant
Personnel Journal, March 1986

The entire Industrial Revolution increased productivity by a factor of about 100. The micro-electronic revolution has already enhanced productivity by a factor of more than a million—and the end isn't in sight yet.

Carver Mead
California Institute of Technology
Lecture, Manhattan Institute, November 1988

The hand that follows intellect can achieve.

Michelangelo Bounarroti, 1475–1564
Sculptor, painter, architect, inventor
The Artist

The greatest gains in productivity for production workers in the first part of this century can be associated with the application of the principles of scientific management to rank-and-file job design. Productivity gains through task specialization and work simplification techniques seem to have reached the point of diminshing returns. We may have reached a stage in industrial management where the greatest gains in productivity are now to be realized through the cooperative efforts of a motivated work force.

R. Henry Miglione
Oral Roberts University
Human Resource Management,
Summer 1970

People are more likely to be productive if they feel they are fairly treated.

Louis A. Mischkind
Director, Executive Development Program, IBM
Personnel Journal, February 1986

Investment depends on expected returns but if such returns cannot be reliably estimated, management cannot reliably invest in research and development or for increased productivity.

Akio Morita
CEO, Sony Corp. (Japan)
Cherry Blossoms and Robotics
(Young Presidents' Organization, 1983)

Government enterprise is the most inefficient and costly way of producing jobs.

Richard Milhous Nixon
Thirty-seventh President of the United States
The Memoirs of Richard Nixon

When work is organized in traditional ways, many workers are quite willing to slide along, producing at low levels, producing at low levels, watching the clock, and waiting to collect their paychecks. But when managers organize work appropriately, worker effort and output are high.... [P]roductivity increases when workers are given full responsibility for the quantity and quality of their work.

James O'Toole
University of Southern California
Making America Work (Continuum, 1981)

["Pareto's Optimum," also known as the 20/80 Rule:] Twenty percent of the participants are responsible for eighty percent of the activity.

Vilfredo Pareto, 1848–1923
Italian economist and sociologist
Mind and Society

[R]egardless of society or culture, mankind has discovered only a limited number of tools for making organizations work. Of these, some tend to be overused and others underemployed. Given the magnitude of the task

of running large organizations, we need to get all the use we can out of all the tools available.

Richard T. Pascale
Stanford University School of Business
and Anthony G. Athos
Harvard Business School
The Art of Japanese Management
(Simon & Schuster, 1981)

The best way to have a good idea is to have a lot of ideas.

Linus Pauling
Nobel laureate in chemistry and peace
Peers, *1,001 Logical Laws* (Doubleday, 1979)

Internal inconsistency is more highly valued than efficiency.

John Peers
President, Logical Machine Corp.
1,001 Logical Laws (Doubleday, 1979)

It takes five years to develop a new car in this country. Heck, we won World War II in four years.

H. Ross Perot
Founder, Electronic Data Systems
Peters, *Thriving on Chaos* (Knopf, 1987)

Luck is infatuated with the efficient.

Persian proverb

Under the influence either of poverty or wealth, workmen and their work are equally liable to deteriorate.

Plato, 427–347 B.C.
Greek philosopher and teacher
The Republic

Some are always busy and never do anything.

Barber, *The Book of 1000 Proverbs*, 1876

The outcome of any professional's effort depends on the ability to control working conditions.

Joseph A. Raelin
Boston College School of Management
Clash of Cultures: Managers and Professionals
(Harvard Business School Press, 1986)

[P]aper entrepreneurialism is supplanting product entrepreneurialism as the most dynamic and innovative business in the American economy. Paper entrepreneurs provide nothing of tangible use. For an economy to maintain its health, entrepreneurial rewards should flow primarily to products, not to paper.

Robert B. Reich
JFK School of Government, Harvard University
The Next American Frontier, 1983

Computer technology has, quite simply, not delivered its long awaited productivity payback.

Stephen S. Roach
Senior economist, Morgan Stanley
PC Week, December 8, 1987

We have always found that people are most productive in small teams with tight budgets, time lines and the freedom to solve their own problems.

John Rollwagen
CEO, Cray Research
Adams, *Transforming Work*
(Miles River Press, 1984)

When companies see their productivity drop, they should ask how they can improve jobs, and not merely by setting up new productivity targets but also by sharing gains with workers and responding to their needs.

Jerome M. Rosow
President, Work in America Institute, Inc.
Tosi and Carroll, *Management* (Wiley, 1976)

In order that people be happy in their work, these three things are needed: They must be fit for it: They must not do too much of it: And they must have a sense of success in it.

John Ruskin, 1819–1900
English art critic and historian
Pre-Raphaelitism

The divorce of income from effort, and the success of producing goods for which the market will pay money, does gradually take a toll from productivity growth and even from the level of productivity.

Paul A. Samuelson
Nobel laureate in economics
The New York Times, August 30, 1987

Operating managers should in no way ignore short-term performance imperatives [when implementing productivity improvement programs.] The pressures arise from many sources and must be dealt with. Moreover, unless managers know that the day-to-day job is under control and improvements are being made, they will not have the time, the perspective, the self-confidence, or the good working relationships that are essential for creative, realistic strategic thinking and decision making.

Robert H. Schaefer
Founder, Robert H. Schaefer & Associates
Harvard Business Review,
November/December 1986

It is not entirely coincidence that the same years that have seen industry increasingly, almost exclusively, run by financially oriented business school graduates have also seen the worst productivity performance since the Depression.

Michael P. Schulhof
Executive Vice President, Sony of America
The New York Times, February 1, 1981

Never to be doing nothing.

Walter Scott, 1771–1832
Scottish poet, novelist, and biographer
Motto

It's in changing the way people work that I think the answers to productivity are going to be found.

John Sculley
CEO, Apple Computer Co.
Fortune, March 2, 1987

Recent studies have found greater absenteeism and lower productivity among working parents of unsupervised children.

Michelle Seligson
Director, School Age Child Care Project,
Wellesley College
*National Association of Bank
Women's Journal*, 1984

The very way managers define productivity improvement and the tools they use to achieve it push their goal further out of reach.... Most of the productivity-focused programs I have seen blithely assume that competitive position lost on grounds of higher cost is best recovered by cost-reduction programs. This logic is tempting but wrong. These programs cannot succeed. They have the wrong targets and misconstrue the nature of the competitive challenge they are supposed to address. Worse, they incur huge opportunity costs. By tying managers at all levels to short-term considerations, they short-circuit the development of an aggressive manufacturing strategy. But they also do harm. These programs, for example, hinder innovation.

Wickham Skinner
Harvard Business School
Harvard Business Review, July/August 1986

The labor of some of the most respectable orders in the society is, like that of menial servants, unproductive of any value.

Adam Smith, 1723–1790
Scottish political economist
Inquiry into ... the Wealth of Nations

[To make a price change:] Everybody had to be consulted—the marketing, accounting, and systems people, and the lawyers—and then all of their input had to be assimilated, the conflicts had to be ironed out, and the whole thing glued together. The actual ... change was less than 1% of the effort and could have been done in an hour. The rest took 100 days and cost $100,000.

Paul Strassmann
Former Vice President, Xerox
Inc. Magazine, March 1988

Two centuries ago 85% of the world's people were needed just to produce enough food. Now, in America, fewer that 4% are producing food, yet they produce such a surplus that they don't know what to do with it.

John Templeton
Investment counselor and market analyst
Forbes, January 25, 1988

We can no longer plunk a machine [computer] in front of a guy and make him more productive. Those days are over.

Paul Trotter
Information Systems manager, Chemical Bank
PC Week, December 8, 1987

If you do things by the job, you are perpetually driven; the hours are scourges. If you work by the hour, you gently sail on a stream of Time, which is always bearing you on to the heaven of Pay, whether you make any effort or not.

Charles Dudley Warner, 1829–1903
American editor and writer
My Summer in a Garden

[Well managed modern organizations] treat everyone as a source of creative input. What's most interesting is that they cannot be described as either democratically or autocratically managed. Their managers define the boundaries, and their people figure out the best way to do the job within those boundaries. The management style is an astonishing combination of direction and empowerment. They give up tight control in order to gain control over what counts: results.

Robert H. Waterman
Management consultant & writer
The Renewal Factor (Bantam, 1987)

There was a time when people were "factors of production" managed little differently from machines or capital. No more. The best people will not tolerate it. And if that way of managing ever generated productivity, it has the reverse effect today. While capital and machines either are or can be managed toward sameness, people are individuals. They must be managed that way.

Robert H. Waterman
Management consultant and writer
The Renewal Factor (Bantam, 1987)

Double your rate of failure.... Failure is a teacher—a harsh one, perhaps, but the best.... That's what I have to do when an idea backfires or a sales program fails. You've got to put failure to work for you.... You can be discouraged by failure or you can learn from it.

So go ahead and make mistakes. Make all you can. Because that's where you will find success. On the far side of failure.

Thomas J. Watson, Sr., 1874–1956
Founder and first President, IBM
Quoted in *How to Live With Life*
(Reader's Digest, 1965)

Engineering is the ability to do for $1 what any damn fool can do for $5.

Arthur Mellen Wellington, 1847-1895
American civil engineer, manager,
and pioneer Operations Research scientist
Quoted in *Washington Business Journal*,
September 7, 1987

The way to get higher productivity is to train better managers and have fewer of them.

William Woodside
Chairman, Primerica
Peters, *Thriving on Chaos* (Knopf, 1987)

When two men in business always agree, one of them is unnecessary.

William Wrigley, Jr., 1861–1932
Founder and President, Wrigley & Co.
Favorite saying

Productivity is only productivity if it's measurable.

Anonymous

35

Public Relations &
Advertising

Great companies make meaning.

The effect of power and publicity on all men is the aggravation of self, a sort of tumor that ends by killing the victim's sympathies.

Henry Brooks Adams, 1838–1910
American writer and historian
The Education of Henry Adams

Six months' oblivion amounts to newspaper-death, and ... resurrection is rare.

Henry Brooks Adams, 1838–1918
American writer and historian
The Education of Henry Adams

A good name is like a precious ointment; it filleth all around about, and will not easily away; for the odors of ointments are more durable than those of flowers.

Francis Bacon, 1561–1626
Lord Chancellor of England
Of Praise

We try to anticipate some of your questions so that I can respond "no comment" with some degree of knowledge.

William Baker
Spokesman, CIA
Newsweek, May 2, 1988

Advertising made me.
[Remark to President Ulysses Grant who said, "You are better known than I am."]

Phineas Taylor (P. T.) Barnum, 1810–1891
American circus owner and showman
Quoted in *Editor & Publisher*, July 31, 1934

Private opinion is weak, but public opinion is almost omnipotent.

Henry Ward Beecher, 1813–1887
American clergyman
Proverbs from Plymouth Pulpit

Public relations is the attempt, by information, persuasion, and adjustment, to engineer public support for an activity, cause, move-ment, or institution.

Edward L. Bernays
Pioneer American publicist
The Engineering of Consent, 1938

The wheel that squeaks the loudest
Is the one that gets the grease.

Josh Billings
(Henry Wheeler Shaw), 1818–1885
American writer and auctioneer
Josh Billings: His Book

Black people aren't dark-skinned white people. We have different preferences and customs and we require a special effort.

Thomas Burrell
President, Burrell Advertising, Inc.
The Wall Street Journal, March 23, 1988

Make a virtue out of necessity.

Robert Burton, 1577–1640
Vicar of St. Thomas's, Oxford
The Anatomy of Melancholy

We have a deep respect for public opinion but we do not let our course be influenced from day to day by Gallup polls, favorable though they may be.... I have heard it said that a Government should keep its ear to the ground, but they should also remember that this is not a very dignified attitude.

Winston Churchill, 1874–1965
English Prime Minister, writer, and soldier
Speech to Conservative Party, October 10, 1953

They [professionals] are just like any other business. The more advertising they see from their competitors, the more they are going to advertise.

Fred D. Crisp, Jr.
Director of Sales and Marketing
The News & Observer (Raleigh, North Carolina)
Presstime, March 1988

If you've done it, it ain't braggin'.

Dizzy Dean
Former professional baseball player
Attributed

What we call public opinion is generally public sentiment.

Benjamin Disraeli, 1804–1881
English Prime Minister and novelist
Speech, House of Commons, August 3, 1880

"Party" is organized opinion.

Benjamin Disraeli, 1804–1881
English Prime Minister and novelist
Speech, Oxford University, November 25, 1864

The good time users among managers spend many more hours on their communications up than on their communications down. They tend to have good communications down, but they seem to obtain these as an effortless by-product. They do not talk to their subordinates about their problems, but they know how to make the subordinates talk about theirs.

Peter F. Drucker
Management consultant and writer
People and Performance
(Harper & Row, 1977)

And Shakespeare, or Franklin, or Aesop, coming to Illinois, would say, I must give my wisdom a comic form, instead of tragics or elegiacs ... and he is no master who cannot vary his forms.

Ralph Waldo Emerson, 1803–1882
American essayist and poet
Journals

Eloquence is the power to translate a truth into language perfectly intelligible to the person to whom you speak.

> Ralph Waldo Emerson, 1803–1882
> American essayist and poet
> *Eloquence*

It is a good part of wisdom to have known the foolish desires of the crowd and their unreasonable notions.

> Desiderius Erasmus, c. 1466–1536
> Dutch scholar and theologian
> *De Utilitate Colloquiorum*

Most business leaders should do things that will convince the public that their interests go beyond just making a buck.

> Gerald R. Ford
> Thirty-eighth President of the United States
> *Harvard Business Review*,
> September/October 1987

The mob does not deserve to be enlightened.

> Frederick III ("The Great"), 1712–1784
> King of Prussia
> Letter to Voltaire, August 6, 1776

To get an audience, create a disturbance.

> Gaelic maxim

[T]here is a persistent and never—ending competition between what is relevant and what is merely acceptable. In this competition, while a strategic advantage lies with what exists, all tactical advantage is with the acceptable. Audiences of all kinds most applaud what they like best.

> John Kenneth Galbraith
> Economist and diplomat
> *The Affluent Society* (Houghton Mifflin, 1958)

[B]usiness managers must stay sensitive to shifts in public policy.... At Exxon we make frequent use of opinion research surveys to identify social concerns and to gauge their importance in the public mind.

> C. C. Garvin
> Chairman of the Board, Exxon Corp.
> Address to shareholders, 1981 Annual Meeting

If thou givest a benefit, keep it close; but if thou receivest one, publish it, for that invites another.

> Elizabeth Grymeston, c. 1563–1603
> English writer
> *Miscelanea*

The only question here is what techniques the advertiser may use to convey essential truth to the television viewer. If the claim is true and valid, then the technique for projecting that claim, within broad boundaries, falls purely within the advertiser's art. The warrant of the Federal Trade Commission is to police the verity of the claim itself.

> John Marshall Harlan, 1899–1971
> U. S. Supreme Court Justice
> *Federal Trade Commission* v.
> *Colgate-Palmolive Co.* (1965)

I have found it to be the craft of arranging truths so that people will like you. Public-relations specialists make flower arrangements of the facts, placing them so that the wilted and less attractive petals are hidden by sturdy blooms.

> Alan Harrington
> Advertising executive and manager
> *Life in the Crystal Palace* (Knopf, 1959)

Nothing is more unjust or capricious than public opinion.

> William Hazlitt, 1778–1830
> English essayist and critic
> *Characteristics*

If you make a product good enough even though you live in the depths of the forest, the public will make a path to your door, says the philosopher. But if you want the public in sufficient numbers, you would better construct a highway. Advertising is that highway.

> William Randolph Hearst, 1863–1951
> Newspaper publisher and U. S. Congressman
> Mandell, *Advertising* (Prentice-Hall, 1984)

Character counts in advertising as in all other things. Only men of intelligence and initiative can fully comprehend that advertising is the science of human service.

> William Randolph Hearst, 1863–1951
> Newspaper publisher and U. S. Congressman
> Letter to Hearst Publishers, 1932

Successful public relations isn't just a matter of the power of the idea—it's the combined effect of the idea and its application, and you exploit that effect, not just for the short run, but for the long.

> Robert Heller
> Editor, *Management Today*
> *The Supermanagers* (Dutton, 1984)

Fine words dress ill deeds.

> George Herbert, 1593–1633
> English clergyman and poet
> *Jacula Prudentum*

The broad mass of a nation ... will more easily fall victim to a big lie than to a small one.

> Adolf Hitler, 1889–1945
> Führer of the Third German Reich
> *Mein Kampf*

Be it true or false, what is said about men often has as much influence upon their lives, and especially upon their destinies, as what they do.

> Victor Hugo, 1802–1885
> French Romantic writer and politician
> *Les Misérables*

It is far easier to write ten passably effective sonnets, good enough to take in the not too inquiring critic, than one effective advertisement that will take in a few thousand of the uncritical buying public.

> Aldous Huxley, 1894–1963
> English novelist and critic
> Mandell, *Advertising* (Prentice-Hall, 1984)

If you have a singer, your fame increases.

> Jabo proverb

The opinions of men are not the object of civil government, nor under its jurisdiction.

> Thomas Jefferson, 1743–1826
> Third President of the United States
> *Virginia Statute of Religious Freedom*

One might think that a man of genius could browse in the greatness of his own thoughts and dispense with the cheap applause of the mob which he despises. But actually he falls a victim to the more mighty herd instinct; his searching, his findings, and his call are inexorably meant for the crowd and must be heard.

> Carl Gustav Jung, 1875–1961
> Swiss psychologist and psychiatrist
> *Transformations and Symbolisms of the Libido*

One fifth of the people are against everything all the time.

> Robert Francis Kennedy, 1925–1968
> Attorney General of the United
> States and U. S. Senator
> Remark to campaign workers,
> New York, November 1964

Nothing succeeds like the appearance of success.

> Christopher Lasch
> University of Rochester
> *The Culture of Narcissism*, 1979

Some like to understand what they believe in. Others like to believe in what they understand.

> Stanislaw J. Lec
> Polish writer and aphorist
> *Unkempt Thought* (St. Martin's Press, 1962)

A publicist without a passion cannot make a place for himself.

> Shemarya Levin, 1867–1935
> Russian writer and polemicist
> *The Arena*

Public opinion in this country is everything.

> Abraham Lincoln, 1809–1865
> Sixteenth President of the United States
> Speech, Cincinatti, Ohio, 1859

What we face today is not a crisis of safety brought on by deregulation, but a crisis of public confidence.

> T. Allen McArtor
> Administrator, FAA
> Speech, U. S. Senate, October 15, 1987

"The medium is the message" because it is the medium that shapes and controls the scale and form of human association and action.

> Marshall McLuhan, 1911–1980
> University of Toronto
> *Understanding Media: The Extensions of Man*,
> 1964

Opinion which is never organized is never heard.

> Charles Merz
> Journalist and publicist
> *The Great American Band Wagon*
> (The John Day Company, 1928)

[I]nternal public relations may be more important than external efforts.

> William Nickels
> University of Maryland
> *Marketing Communication and Promotion*
> (John Wiley & Sons, 1984)

The first essential is to know what one wishes to say; the second is to decide to whom one wishes to say it.

> Harold Nicolson, 1886–1961
> English biographer and diplomat
> *The Atlantic Monthly*, January 1946

If your lip would keep from slips.
Five things observe with care:
To whom you speak, of whom you speak,
And how, and when, and where.

> William E. Norris, 1847–1925
> English novelist
> *Thirlby Hall*

Advertising in the final analysis should be news. If it's not news it's worthless.

> Adolph S. Ochs, 1858–1935
> American newspaper publisher
> Quoted in *The New York Times*,
> March 9, 1958

The most important word in the vocabulary of advertising is TEST. If you pretest your product with consumers, and pretest your advertising, you will do well in the marketplace.

> David Ogilvy
> Founder, Ogilvy-Mather Advertising
> *Confessions of an Advertising Man*
> (Atheneum, 1963)

Great companies make meaning.

> Richard T. Pascale
> Stanford University School of Business
> and Anthony G. Athos
> Harvard Business School
> *The Art of Japanese Management*
> (Simon & Schuster, 1981)

The important thing in staging any kind of [public relations] event is to have something for everyone. You have to have the right mix of legitimacy, charity and entertainment.... You have to make sure that there's no reason not to come.

> Glen Paul
> President, Clancy-Paul
> *Computer & Software News*, January 11, 1988

The peculiar value of news is in the spreading of it while it is fresh.

> Mahlon Pitney, 1858–1924
> U. S. Supreme Court Justice
> *International News Service*
> v. *Associated Press* (1918)

Crafty evasions save not veracity.

> Barber, *The Book of 1000 Proverbs*, 1876

Let another man praise thee, and not thine own mouth.

> Old Testament, Proverbs 27:2

Publicity, *publicity*, PUBLICITY is the greatest moral factor and force in our public life.

> Joseph Pulitzer, 1847–1911
> Newspaper publisher and businessman
> Speech to editors of *The New York World*,
> December 29, 1895

You have lost your subject when you have lost his inclination; you are to preside over the minds, not the bodies of men. The soul is the essence of a man; and you cannot have the true man against his inclination.

> Walter Raleigh, 1552–1618
> English statesman and writer
> *To a Young Prince*

A successfully executed public relations program can expand a [law] firm's visibility and broaden opportunities with particular audiences. In developing this visibility the law firm will have the opportunity of representing more clients in more geographic areas as well as retention of existing clients.

> Sonia Rappaport
> Principal, Rappaport & Associates
> *The Washington Lawyer*,
> January/February 1987

The more complicated life becomes, the more people are attracted by simple solutions; the more irrational the world seems, the more they long for rational answers; and the more diverse everything is, the more they want it all reduced to identity.

> James Reston
> Syndicated columnist, *The New York Times*

We had to combine organizational efficiency with the excitement and entertainment of a circus.

> Nikki Rickett
> Associate Director of Public Affairs,
> The White House
> *Management*, 1987

People's minds are changed through observation and not through argument.

> Will Rogers, 1879–1935
> American actor and humorist
> *Will Rogers* (Hallmark, 1969)

That essential American strategy: publicity.

Richard H. Rovere
American historian and political writer
Senator Joe McCarthy (Farrar, 1965)

Industrial laboratories have always had to balance proprietary discoveries against the value of publishing results.

Roland Schmitt
Chief Scientist and Vice President,
General Electric Co.
The New York Times, August 2, 1987

[Of the need for "corrective disclosure" when the press releases prepared by the management were inaccurate:] In general, outside directors should be expected to maintain a general familiarity with their company's communications with the public.... [W]hen important events central to the survival of the company are involved, directors have a responsibility affirmatively to keep themselves informed of developments within the company and to seek out the nature of corporate disclosures to determine if adequate disclosures are being made.

Securities & Exchange Commission
In re. National Telephone Co.,
January 16, 1978

Be not thy tongue thy own shame's orator.

William Shakespeare, 1564–1616
English dramatist and poet
The Comedy of Errors

I would to God thou and I knew where a commodity of good names were to be bought.

William Shakespeare, 1564–1616
English dramatist and poet
King Richard II

More matter, with less art.

William Shakespeare, 1564–1616
English dramatist and poet
Hamlet

Assume a virtue, if you have it not.

William Shakespeare, 1564–1616
English dramatist and poet
Hamlet

Reputation is an idle and most false imposition; oft got without merit, and lost without deserving.

William Shakespeare, 1564–1616
English dramatist and poet
Othello

Ill deeds are doubled with an evil word.

William Shakespeare, 1564–1616
English dramatist and poet
The Comedy of Errors

Advertising enriches life by quickening the imagination, arousing interest and enlarging the taste.

Ralph W. Sockman, 1889–1970
American clergyman
Mandell, *Advertising* (Prentice-Hall, 1984)

It is the merit of a general to impart good news and conceal the bad.

Sophocles, c. 496–406 B.C.
Greek dramatist
Oedipus Coloneus

To please people is a great step towards persuading them.

Philip Dormer Stanhope, 1694–1773
English Secretary of State
Letters of Lord Chesterfield to His Son

Censure is the tax a man pays to the public for being eminent.

Jonathan Swift, 1667–1775
English cleric and satirist
Thoughts on Various Subjects

Proper words in proper places, make the true definition of style.

Jonathan Swift, 1667–1775
English cleric and satirist
Letter to a Young Clergyman, January 9, 1720

Without ... advertising, information ... would take years to reach all of us who might benefit by it and progress would be delayed.

Harry S. Truman, 1884–1972
Thirty-third President of the United States
Mandell, *Advertising* (Prentice-Hall, 1984)

[A] profound national commitment to the principle that debate on public issues should be uninhibited, robust, and wide-open, and that it may well include vehement, caustic, and sometimes unpleasantly sharp attacks on government and public officials.

U. S. Supreme Court
New York Times Co. v. *Sullivan* (1964)

[To a journalist who interrupted his dinner:]
The public be damned; you get out of here!

William Henry Vanderbilt, 1821–1885
President, New York Central Railroad
Stone, *Fifty Years A Journalist* (Ryer, 1921)

One must be prepared to stick like a barnacle on a boat's bottom. He should know before he begins that he must spend money—lots of it.... He cannot hope to reap results commensurate with his expenditure early in the game.

John Wanamaker, 1838–1922
Founder, Wanamaker's Department Stores
Mandell, *Advertising* (Prentice-Hall 1984)

The masses are no asses.

Yiddish proverb

You can't take a thought and theory in English and put it into Spanish. You must be able to direct the advertisement to the Spanish idiosyncrasy.

Terre Zubizaretta
President, Zubi Advertising, Inc.
Hispanic Business, June 1987

We're not paying you to make us look like a bunch of idiots. We're paying you so others won't find out we're a bunch of idiots.

Anonymous executive to PR firm president

36

Quality Control

Quality is everyone's responsibility.

The [quality control] issue has more to do with people and motivation and less to do with capital and equipment than one would think. It involves a cultural change.

> Michael Beer
> Harvard Business School
> *The Washington Post*, October 11, 1987

If you're going to put your name on all your products, you should never produce a bad product. If you make a mistake, you'll hurt your whole company.

> Bruno Bich
> Vice President of Sales and Marketing,
> Bic Pen Co.
> Alsop and Abrams, *The Wall Street Journal on Marketing* (Dow Jones-Irwin, 1986)

Good wares make good markets.

> Nicholas Breton, c. 1555–c. 1625
> English poet and satirist
> *Crossing of Proverbs*

We love quality.

> Robert Campeau
> CEO, Campeau Corp. (Canada)
> *The New York Times,* April 4, 1988

By a small sample we may judge the whole piece.

> Miguel De Cervantes, 1547–1616
> Spanish author
> *Don Quixote*

I am easily satisfied with the best.

> Winston Churchill, 1874–1965
> English Prime Minister, writer, and soldier
> Favorite saying

The maxim, "Nothing prevails but perfection" may be spelled, PARALYSIS.

> Winston Churchill, 1874–1965
> English Prime Minister, writer, and soldier
> Halle, *Irrepressible Churchill*

Quality is a matter of faith. You set your standards, and you have to stick by them no matter what. That's easy when you've got plenty of product on hand, but it's another thing when the freezer is empty and you've got a truck at the door waiting for the next shipment to come off the production line. That's when you really earn your reputation for quality.

> Ben Cohen
> President, Ben & Jerry's Homemade, Inc.
> *Inc. Magazine*, November 1987

The best [automobiles] of ours are [now] about as good as the worst of theirs [the Japanese], and that is a tremendous achievement.

> Robert E. Cole
> University of Michigan
> *Fortune*, February 1987

Nothing done in haste is thorough, and an eye for small things leaves big things undone.

> Confucius, c. 551–c. 479 B.C.
> Chinese philosopher and teacher
> *Analects*

Mr. Lely, I desire you would use all your skill to paint my picture truly like me, and not flatter me at all; but remark all these roughness, pimples, warts, and everything as you see me, otherwise I will never pay a farthing for it.

> Oliver Cromwell, 1599–1658
> Lord Protector of England
> Quoted by Walpole, *Anecdotes of Painting*

If the fibre of the hemp is rotten, you will never make a good rope of it.

> Massimo Taparelli D'Azeglio, 1798–1866
> Italian statesman and author
> *I Miei Ricordi*

It is a wretched taste to be gratified with mediocrity when the excellent lies before us.

> Isaac D'Israeli, 1766–1848
> English man of letters
> *Curiosities of Literature: Quotation*

The value of a man's life is in direct proportion to his commitment to excellence.

> Dallas Cowboys professional football team
> Sign in locker room, 1986

Quality is *everyone's* responsibility.

> W. Edwards Deming
> Quality Control scientist
> *Inc. Magazine*, February 1987

Henry Ford made great contributions, but his Model T was not a quality car.

> W. Edwards Deming
> Quality Control scientist
> San Jose *Mercury-News*, April 17, 1987

All, as they say, that glitters is not gold.

> John Dryden, 1631–1700
> English poet
> *The Hind and the Panther*

[R]unning numbers on a computer [is] easier than trying to judge quality.

> Esther Dyson
> Editor and publisher, *Release 1.0*
> *Forbes*, November 30, 1987

Good, better, best
Never let it rest
Until the good becomes the better
And the better becomes the best.

> Elementary school rhyme

The concern about the quality of teachers seems to be paying off.... [N]early a third of teachers with less than five years experience graduated from college *summa*, *magna*, or *cum laude* and 41 percent had been on the Dean's List while in college.

C. Emily Feistritzer
Director,
National Center for Education Research
The Washington Post, December 16, 1987

Our people ... are responsible for their own product and its quality. We expect them to act like owners.

Gordon Foward
President, Chaparral Steel
Peters, *Thriving on Chaos* (Knopf, 1987)

Carelessness is worse than theft.

Gaelic proverb

We, the senior managers, are the biggest problem [in improving productivity]. We assume too much; like our powers too much.

Robert Galvin
CEO, Motorola Corp.
Government Executive, January 1987

It was just 10 years ago that ... Honeywell Corp. and Lockheed ... started what are believed to be the first quality circles in this country. Both have scrapped their programs.

Beverly Geber
Associate Editor, *Training*
Training, December 1986

In high-technology products, it is far less expensive to install production-line controls than to maintain a huge maintenance staff to make costly repairs on defective products in the field.

Harold Geneen
CEO, IT&T
Managing (Doubleday, 1984)

In quality control, you are controlling the down side.

Harold Geneen
CEO, IT&T
Managing (Doubleday, 1984)

Customers don't want to hear that [they're buying a perfect product] anymore. What they want to know is that the company is prepared to stand by its product.

John Goodman
Marketing consultant
Alsop and Abrams, *The Wall Street Journal on Marketing* (Dow Jones-Irwin, 1986)

Detect and fix any problem in a production process at the *lowest-value* stage possible.

Andrew S. Grove
CEO, Intel Corp.
High Output Management
(Random House, 1983)

Make no mistake: realizing significant improvements in the quality of a product or service ... is *hard, hard work* involving a serious amount of grunting and sweating and heavy lifting on the part of *all employees*. It will mean "doing things better," but it will also mean "doing things differently"—which is to say, it will mean *change*.

John Guaspari
Management writer
Management, March 1987

When a product is manufactured by workers who find their work meaningful, it will inevitably be a product of high quality.

Pehr G. Gyllenhammar
Managing Director, Volvo (Sweden)
Tosi & Carroll, *Management* (Wiley, 1976)

379

Quality is very simple. So simple, in fact, that it is difficult for people to understand.

> Roger Hale
> CEO, Tennant Co.
> *Quest for Quality* (Tennant, 1987)

[Manufacturing] ... excellence results from dedication to daily progress. Making something a little bit better every day.

> Robert Hall
> Indiana University
> Peters, *Thriving on Chaos* (Knopf, 1987)

Try to be conspicuously accurate in everything, pictures as well as text. Truth is not only stranger than fiction, it is more interesting.

> William Randolph Hearst, 1863–1951
> Newspaper publisher and U. S. Congressman
> Letter of Instruction to Hearst Publishers,
> September 25, 1929

Of a pigs tail you can never make a good shaft.

> George Herbert, 1593–1633
> English clergyman and poet
> *Jacula Prudentum*

Ill ware is never cheap.

> George Herbert, 1593–1633
> English clergyman and poet
> *Jacula Prudentum*

Good and quickly seldom meet.

> George Herbert, 1593–1633
> English clergyman and poet
> *Jacula Prudentum*

You can spend a lifetime, and, if you're honest with yourself, never once was your work perfect.

> Charlton Heston
> Actor
> *Reader's Digest,* December 1987

It takes constant follow-up to make sure that when you say something is going to happen, it does.

> Judy T. Hofmann
> Assistant Secretary, U. S. Department of
> Housing and Urban Development
> *Management,* 1987

Anybody can cut prices, but it takes brains to make a better article.

> Alice Hubbard, 1861–1915
> American author and lecturer
> *The New Dictionary of Thoughts*, 1957

From a dog you don't make salami.

> Hungarian proverb

My experience of the world is that things left to themselves don't get right.

> Thomas Henry Huxley, 1894–1963
> English biologist
> *Aphorisms and Reflections*

In the average ... plant 20 to 25 percent of the cost of goods sold is spent on finding and correcting errors. And many of the workers do not actually produce anything—they just correct mistakes.

> Henry J. Johansson
> Head, Manufacturing Practice,
> Coopers & Lybrand
> *The New York Times*, January 17, 1988

We're not trying to attach blame, just get it right.

> Don Kelly
> Production Manager, General Electric Co.
> *The Renewal Factor* (Bantam, 1987)

You don't have to preach honesty to men with a creative purpose.... A genuine craftsman will not adulterate his product. The reason isn't because duty says he shouldn't, but because passion says he couldn't.

> Walter Lippmann, 1889–1974
> Journalist and public philosopher
> Quoted in *Elbert Hubbard's Scrap Book*

In Japan, statistical methods are commonly known not only by quality control engineers, but by all company personnel.... One means of public recognition of a company's quality control activities is the Deming Prize for Application, given on the basis of "the degree of disseminationm, state of application of statistical quality control, and future promise." This award is the most distinguished quality control prize in Japan, and many companies make it a prime goal in their efforts to promote quality.

> Keith Lockyer and John Oakland
> Heller, *The Supermanagers* (Dutton, 1984)

You may never achieve zero defects. But if you want to avoid lawsuits, try to reach that goal.

> Marisa Manley
> Attorney, Ginsberg Organization
> *Harvard Business Review*,
> September/October 1987

In testing, simulate the toughest conditions your product is likely to encounter.

> Marisa Manley
> Attorney, Ginsberg Organization
> *Harvard Business Review*,
> September/October 1987

Look beneath the surface; let not the quality nor its worth escape thee.

> Marcus Aurelius, 121–180
> Roman Emperor and Stoic philosopher
> *Meditations*

Let no act be done at haphazard, nor otherwise than according to the finished rules that govern its kind.

> Marcus Aurelius, 121–180
> Roman Emperor and Stoic philosopher
> *Meditations*

As great as computers are, they cannot tell you about the quality of your product. The profitability, yes, but not the quality. The human eye, the human experience, is the one thing that can make quality better—or poorer.

> Stanley Marcus
> Chairman emeritus, Neiman-Marcus
> Peters and Austin, *A Passion for Excellence*
> (Random House, 1985)

If you refuse to accept anything but the best, you very often get it.

> W. Somerset Maugham, 1874–1965
> English novelist and playwright
> *The Mixture as Before*

Intolerance of mediocrity has been the main prop of my independence.

> Elsa Maxwell, 1883–1963
> American hostess and writer
> *R. S. V. P.*

My program starts with people. Too often, we focus on numbers—of controllers, pilots, technicians, maintenance inspectors—rather than on quality.

> T. Allen McArtor
> Administrator, FAA
> Speech, U. S. Senate, October 15, 1987

[Q]uality assurance is the job of the managers responsible for the product. A separate group can't "assure" much if the responsible managers have not done their jobs properly.... Managers should be held responsible for quality and not allowed to slough off part of their responsibility to a group whose name sounds right but which cannot be guaranteed quality if the responsible managers have not been able to do so.

> Philip W. Metzger
> Computer analyst and management writer
> *Managing Programming People*
> (Prentice-Hall, 1987)

What the [early] fast food chains offered— and it was an entirely new thing—was a predictable level of sanitation, service and quality.

> Joseph Monninger
> Business writer
> *American Heritage,* April 1988

A watch might be designed in Switzerland, have its electronic parts manufactured in Japan, have its timekeeping module assembled in Hong Kong, its watch case produced in the U.S., its face produced in Japan, and its final assembly completed in the Virgin Islands before being sold in the U. S..... A brand name which formerly represented the perceived excellence of Swiss or American craftsmanship now stands for managerial excellence in coordinating labor and logistics in many nations to assure high standards of quality and service.

> Russell M. Moore
> *Marketing News,* October 17, 1980

As the American economy becomes more labor-intensive as a result of the shift toward service, clerical and knowledge work, the *attitudes* of workers become central factors in national productivity. In our mature, postindustrial economy the success or failure of the national enterprise rests on the willingness of individual workers to take responsibility for the quality and quantity of their work, to take initiative in those increasingly frequent work situations that cannot be routinely handled, to show a real interest in the welfare of customers, suppliers, and fellow workers—in short, to *care* about their work.

> James O'Toole
> University of Southern California
> *Making America Work* (Continuum, 1981)

The engineering is secondary to the vision.

> Cynthia Ozick
> American writer and critic
> *The Hole/Birth Catalog*

If you put off everything till you're sure of it, you'll get nothing done.

> Normal Vincent Peale
> Clergyman and inspirational speaker
> *Reader's Digest*, January 1972

Starting this afternoon, don't walk past a shoddy product or service without comment or action—ever again.

> Tom Peters
> Business writer
> *Thriving on Chaos* (Knopf, 1987)

Almost all quality improvement comes via simplification of design, manufacturing, layout, processes and procedures.

> Tom Peters
> Business writer
> *Thriving on Chaos* (Knopf, 1987)

Most of the professors appreciated it when you washed off the blackboard but not Dr. [Albert] Einstein. Every morning he'd burst into tears. Way I see it, I had a job to do, and I was bound and determined to do it right. He wasn't the only perfectionist in the university business.

> Garth Peterson
> Former janitor, Princeton University
> Quoted in *Omni*, March 1988

Under the influence either of poverty or wealth, workmen and their work are equally liable to deteriorate.

> Plato, 427–347 B.C.
> Greek philosopher and teacher
> *The Republic*

Ease and speed in doing a thing do not give the work lasting solidity or exactness of beauty. For ease and quickness of execution are not fitted to give those enduring qualities that are necessary in a work for all time; while, on the other hand, the time that is laid out on labor is amply repaid in the permanence it gives to the performance.

> Plutarch, c. 46–c. 120
> Greek biographer and philosopher
> *The Parallel Lives: Pericles*

For when the ancients said that a work begun was half done, they meant that we ought to take the utmost pains in every undertaking to make a good beginning.

> Polybius, c. 202–120 B.C.
> Greek historian
> *History*

Nothing can be done at once hastily and prudently.

> Publilius Syrus, c. 42 B.C.
> Roman writer
> *Maxims*

It is quality rather than quantity that matters.

> Publilius Syrus, c. 42 B.C.
> Roman writer
> *Maxims*

[Referring to the early movie producers he had worked for:] They didn't want it good. They wanted it Thursday.

> Ronald Wilson Reagan
> Fortieth President of the United States
> TV interview, 1982

Professional organizations had believed that by hiring well qualified, technically capable people, quality control would take care of itself.... Managers rationalized that quality control lapses could not be helped and were simply another cost of doing business. Now it is clear that quality control issues affect virtually all professions from medicine and accounting to law and insurance brokerage.

> Henry A. Revzan
> Senior VP, Rollins Burdick Hunter Co.
> *Management*, October 1986

Our policy is "Nothing is no good."

> Will Rogers, 1879–1935
> American actor and humorist
> *The Illiterate Digest*

There is hardly anything in the world that some man cannot make a little worse and sell a little cheaper.

> John Ruskin, 1819–1900
> English art critic and historian
> *The Seven Lamps of Architecture*

Not only is there but one way of doing things rightly, but there is one way of seeing them, and that is, seeing the whole of them.

> John Ruskin, 1819–1900
> English art critic and historian
> *The Two Paths*

Quality is never an accident; it is always the result of intelligent effort.

> John Ruskin, 1819–1900
> English art critic and historian
> *Seven Lamps of Architecture*

Mathematics takes us into the region of absolute necessity, to which not only the actual world, but every possible world, must conform.

Bertrand Russell, 1872–1970
English mathematician and philosopher
The Study of Mathematics

We don't settle for the norm or even a little bit above average. It's what we call Class 4, or the best in the world—not *one* of the best in the world.

Ralph R. Russo
Vice President, Apple Computer Co.
Working Woman, December 1987

[When asked how long a film should be:] How long is it good?

Nick Schenck
American entertainer
Wilk, *The Wit and Wisdom of Hollywood*
(Atheneum, 1971)

My attitude has long been one of two-and-a-half cheers for [programmatic] systems analysis. I recognize—and have emphasized—its limitations. I will make no excuses for offences committed in its name. But despite the limitations and distortions, I remain an unabashed, if qualified, defender of the value of analysis.... [It is] "quantified common sense."

James R. Schlesinger
U. S. Secretary of Defense
Memorandum to Senate Committee on
Government Operations, April, 1968

Realistically, we cannot yet expect that every choice be backed up by a full analytic approach.

Charles L. Schultze
Director, U. S. Bureau of the Budget
U.S. Senate Testimony, August 23, 1967

It is quality rather than quantity that matters.

Seneca, c. 3 B.C.–A.D. 65
Roman orator and rhetorician
Epistles

When you bought their [Japanese] television set, it didn't mean taking the repairman into the family.

Irving G. Snyder
Vice President, Dow Chemical USA
Peters, *Thriving on Chaos* (Knopf, 1987)

All things excellent are as difficult as they are rare.

Benedict Spinoza, 1632–1677
Dutch philosopher and oculist
Ethics

Whatever is worth doing at all, is worth doing well.

Philip Dormer Stanhope, 1694–1773
English Secretary of State
Letters of Lord Chesterfield to His Son

We have to grant quality its moral dimension .... It should be recognized as a virtue—something to be sought for its own sake—not just a profitable strategy.

Edward Tenner
Quality, Winter 1987

When people are treated as the main engine rather than interchangeable parts of a corporate machine, motivation, creativity, quality, and commitment to implementation well up.

Robert H. Waterman
Management consultant and writer
The Renewal Factor (Bantam, 1987)

[T]he basic philosophy, spirit, and drive of an organization have far more to do with its relative achievements than do technological or economic resources, organizational structure, innovation, and timing. But they are, I think, transcended by how strongly the people in the organization believe in its basic precepts and how faithfully they carry them out.

> Thomas J. Watson, Jr.
> CEO, IBM, and U. S. Embassador to Russia
> McKinsey Lecture, Columbia University, 1962

Industry in Art is a necessity—not a virtue—and any evidence of [industry] in the production is a blemish, not a quality; a proof, not of achievement, but of absolutely insufficient work, for work alone will efface the footsteps of work.

> James Abbott McNeill Whistler, 1834–1903
> American-born painter, etcher and writer
> *The Gentle Art of Making Enemies*

Don't, Sir, you'll spoil it! [Comment made to his drawing instructor at the West Point Military Academy who was attempting to "improve" one of Whistler's drawings.]

> James Abbott McNeill Whistler, 1834–1903
> American-born painter, etcher and writer
> Quoted in *American Heritage,* April 1988

You cannot make, my Lord, I fear, a velvet purse of a sow's ear.

> John Wolcot, 1738–1819
> English poet and physician
> *Lord B. and His Notions*

It's important to begin by acknowledging that the Japanese tend to be extremely literate with numbers—far more so than most American businessmen I've met. Too much has been made of the vagueness of our verbal language. We compensate for this with a facility at the "numbers language." To be sure, it's a rigorous system. But because I believe, and my seniors believe, that I should be running my division, I treat the control system process like some people treat their morning jog. It's rigorous exercise but it makes me stronger.

> Anonymous Division Manager
> Matsushita Industries, Ltd. (Japan)
> *Business Horizons,* June 1980

[It is a function of the executive] to reflect sadly that one could have done it right in 20 minutes, and now one has to spend two days to find out why it has taken three weeks for someone else to do it wrong.

> Anonymous Document
> "Functions of the Executive"
> Mackenzie, *The Time Trap*
> (McGraw-Hill, 1972)

37

Quantitative Techniques & Analysis

*If two lines on a graph cross,
it must be important.*

The less we understand a phenomenon, the
more variables we require to explain it.

Russell L. Ackoff
Management Information Systems scientist
Management Science, December 1967

Figures are not always facts.

Aesop, c. 620–c. 560 B.C.
Greek fabulist
The Widow and the Hen

They were not just intelligent, but prided
themselves on being "rational".... They were
eager to find formulas, preferably expressed
in a pseudo-mathematical language, that
would unify the most disparate phenomena
with which reality presented them; that is,
they were eager to discover *laws* by which to
explain and predict political and historical
facts as though they were as necessary, and
thus as reliable, as the physicists once
believed natural phenomena to be.... [T]hey

did not *judge*, they calculated.... [A]n utterly
irrational confidence in the calculability of
reality [became] the leitmotif of the decision
making.

Hannah Arendt, 1906–1975
German-American philospher and critic
Crises of the Republic
(Harcourt Brace Jovanovich, 1972)

Whenever parameters can be quantified, it is
usually desirable to do so.

Norman R. Augustine
President and CEO, Martin Marietta Corp.
Augustine's Laws (Penguin, 1987)

In short, the scientific account of affairs involved the formalization of interactions

between men, machines, materials and money, all spread over [a] complex system.

Stafford Beer
Director of Operations Research,
United Steel (Britain)
Decision and Control (Wiley, 1966)

The most valuable use of such [mathematical] models usually lies less in turning out the answer in an uncertain world than in shedding light on how much difference an alteration in the assumptions and/or variables used would make in the answer yielded by the models.

Edward G. Bennion
Stanford University School of Business
Bursk and Chapman,
New Decision-Making Tools for Managers
(New American Library, 1963)

The more we have, the more we want, and the more we want, the less we have.

Josh Billings
(Henry Wheeler Shaw), 1818–1885
American writer and auctioneer
Josh Billings: His Book

[Operations] research workers must ... guard against the temptation for the executive machine to stop while they think.

P. M. S. Blackett, 1897–1974
Nobel laureate in physics
Boulding and Spivey, *Linear Programming and the Theory of the Firm* (Macmillan, 1960)

Figures—a language implying certitude.

Louis Dembitz Brandeis, 1856–1941
U. S. Supreme Court Justice
Lief, *Brandeis: The Personal History of an American Ideal*

Arithmetic is the first of the sciences and the mother of safety.

Louis Dembitz Brandeis, 1856–1941
U. S. Supreme Court Justice
Letter to Norman Hapgood,
September 25, 1911

I do not mind lying, but I hate inaccuracy.

Samuel Butler, 1835–1902
English novelist and translator
Note-Books of Samuel Butler

Nothing is so fallacious as facts, except figures.

George Canning, 1770–1827
English Prime Minister and
Chancellor of the Exchequer
Attributed

A witty statesman [Benjamin Disraeli?] said, you might prove anything by figures.

Thomas Carlyle, 1795–1881
Scottish essayist and historian
Chartism

Conclusive facts are inseparable from inconclusive [facts] except by a head that already understands and knows.

Thomas Carlyle, 1795–1881
Scottish essayist and historian
Chartism

"Take some more tea," the March Hare said to Alice, very earnestly. "I've had nothing yet," Alice replied in an offended tone, "so I can't take more." "You mean you can't take *less*," said the Hatter: "It's very easy to take *more* than nothing.

Lewis Carroll
(Charles Lutwidge Dodgson), 1832–1898
English mathematician and writer
Alice's Adventures in Wonderland

Statistics are no substitute for judgment.

> Henry Clay, 1777–1852
> U. S. Secretary of State
> *The New Dictionary of Thoughts*, 1957

If two lines on a graph cross, it must be important.

> Ernest F. Cooke
> University of Baltimore
> Remark to a student, February 1985

I am surprised that Doctor Johnson did not perceive that these round numbers were no falser than abstractions. They are, indeed, abstractions. For they differ from numbers that are less round only in their neglect of an irrelevant precision, a degree of precision that was not needed for the purpose in hand, and that might be confusing or even misleading.

> Charles P. Curtis
> Attorney and Member,
> The Harvard Corporation
> *A Commonplace Book*
> (Simon & Schuster, 1957)

The concept of number is the obvious distinction between the beast and man. Thanks to number, the cry becomes song, noise acquired rhythm, the spring is transformed into a dance, force becomes dynamic, and outlines [become] figures.

> Joseph Marie de Maistre, 1753–1821
> French philosopher and statesman
> Auden and Kronenberger,
> *The Viking Book of Aphorisms*

There are three kinds of lies: lies, damned lies, and statistics.

> Benjamin Disraeli, 1804–1881
> English Prime Minister and novelist
> Quoted in *The Autobiography of Mark Twain*

It has been said that figures rule the world. Maybe. But I am sure that figures show us whether it is being ruled well or badly.

> Johann Peter Eckerman, 1792–1854
> German scholar and author
> *Conversations with Goethe*

Sophisticated mathematical techniques are terrific for helping *you* decide what to strive and fight for. But let it go there. No congressman was ever convinced to introduce legislation by linear programming, and you can't sell a product or service with a regression analysis. Instead of logic, you need examples, anecdotes, principles and, above all, passion.

> Lewis D. Eigen
> Executive Vice President,
> University Research Corp.
> *Microcomputers for Executive Decision-Making*
> (Federal Aviation Administration, 1985)

I am convinced that a completely new and enlightening inspiration is needed [to understand electricity]. I also believe, on the other hand, that the flight into statistics is to be regarded only as a temporary expedient that bypasses the fundamentals.

> Albert Einstein, 1879–1955
> Nobel laureate in physics
> *Albert Einstein, The Human Side*
> (Princeton, 1979)

As far as the laws of mathematics refer to reality, they are not certain; and as far as they are certain, they do not refer to reality.

> Albert Einstein, 1879–1955
> Nobel laureate in physics
> Quoted in *Omni*, April 1988

The methods of statistics are so variable and uncertain, so apt to be influenced by circumstance, that is never to be sure that one is operating with figures of equal weight.

> Havelock Ellis, 1859–1939
> British scientist and writer
> *The Dance of Life*

Who shall forbid a wise skepticism, seeing that there is no practical question on which anything more than an approximate solution can be had?

> Ralph Waldo Emerson, 1803–1882
> American essayist and poet
> *Montaigne*

There is no royal road to geometry.

> Euclid, c. 300 B.C.
> Greek mathematician
> Quoted by Proclus, *Commentaria in Euclidem*

The only relevant test of the validity of a hypothesis is comparison of prediction with experience.

> Milton Friedman
> Nobel laureate in economics
> *Essays in Positive Economics*
> (University of Chicago Press, 1953)

The professional's grasp of the numbers is a measure of the control he has over the events that the figures represent.

> Harold Geneen
> CEO, IT&T
> *Managing* (Doubleday, 1984)

The drudgery of the numbers will make you free.

> Harold Geneen
> CEO, IT&T
> *Managing* (Doubleday, 1984)

When you have mastered the numbers, you will in fact no longer be reading numbers, any more than you read words when reading books. You will be reading meanings.

> Harold Geneen
> CEO, IT&T
> *Managing* (Doubleday, 1984)

Top managers are currently inundated with reams of information concerning the organizational units under their supervision. Behind this information explosion lies a seemingly logical assumption made by information specialists and frequently accepted by line managers: if top management can be supplied with more "objective" and "accurate" *quantified* information, they will make "better" judgments about the performance of their operating units.... A research study we have recently completed indicates that quantified performance information may have a more limited role than is currently assumed or invisioned; in fact, managers rely more on subjective information than they do on so-called "objective" statistics in assessing the overall performance of lower-level units.

> Larry E. Greiner
> University of Southern California
> Paul D. Leitch
> U. S. Army Food Engineering Directorate
> and Louis D. Barnes
> Harvard Business School
> *Harvard Business Review on Human Relations*, 1986

Analysts are short sighted; all they want is profits.

> Robert Hahn
> Vice President, Continental Resources
> *PC World*, April 1988

The use of [a] model or any of the mathematical techniques of the operations researcher does not imply management by computer.

> James C. Hetrick
> Operations Researcher, Arthur D. Little Co.
> Bursk and Chapman,
> *New Decision-Making Tools for Managers*
> (New American Library, 1963)

Probability is the very guide of life.

> Thomas Hobbes, 1588–1679
> English philosopher
> *Leviathan*

I ought to know by this time that when a fact appears to be opposed to a long train of deductions it invariably proves to be capable of bearing some other interpretation.

> Sherlock Holmes
> (Arthur Conan Doyle), 1859–1930
> English physician, writer, and sportsman
> *The Sign of Four*

One accurate measurement is worth a thousand expert opinions.

> Grace Murray Hopper
> Rear Admiral, U. S. Navy (retired)
> Frequent remark

Extrapolations are useful, particularly in the form of soothsaying called forecasting trends. But in looking at the figures or the charts made from them, it is necessary to remember one thing constantly: The trend to now may be a fact, but the future trend represents no more than an educated guess. Implicit in it is "everything else being equal" and "present trends continuing." And somehow everything else refuses to remain equal.

> Darell Huff
> *How to Lie with Statistics*
> (Norton, 1954)

Round numbers are always false.

> Samuel Johnson, 1709–1784
> English lexicographer and critic
> Letter to Thomas Boswell, March 30, 1778

Twice nothing is still nothing.

> Cyrano Jones
> "The Trouble With Tribbles"
> *Star Trek*

Human decisions affecting the future ... cannot depend on strict mathematical expectation.

> John Maynard Keynes, 1883–1946
> English economist, writer, and diplomat
> *The General Theory of Employment,*
> *Interest and Money*

Anecdotes may be more useful than equations in understanding the problem.

> Robert Kuttner
> Economics correspondent, *The New Republic*
> *The New York Times*, January 17, 1988

He uses statistics as a drunken man uses lampposts—for support rather than illumination.

> Andrew Lang, 1844–1912
> Scottish scholar and writer
> Attributed

[It is] an attempt to clothe unreality in the garb of mathematical reality.

> James Ramsay MacDonald, 1866–1937
> English Prime Minister
> Greenberger, *Management and the Computer*
> *of the Future* (M. I. T., 1962)

Exactitude is not truth.

> Henri Matisse, 1869–1954
> French post-impressionist painter
> Favorite saying

To measure is to know.

> James Clerk Maxwell, 1831–1879
> Scottish physicist
> *Treatise on Electricity and Magnetism*

The numbers of accidents and fatalities are so small that one cannot logically construct any statistically valid relationship between airline deregulation and the number of fatalities, near misses, or safe travel. Debates over numbers miss the heart of the issue.

T. Allen McArtor
Administrator, FAA
Speech, U. S. Senate, October 15, 1987

[Management science techniques] have had little impact on areas of decision-making where the management problems do not lend themselves to explicit formulation, where there are ambiguous or overlapping criteria for action, and where the manager operates through intuition.

James L. McKenney
Harvard Business School
and Peter G. W. Keen
Massachusetts Institute of Technology
Harvard Business Review on Human Relations, 1986

The peculiarity of the evidence of mathematical truths is that all the argument is on one side.

John Stuart Mill, 1806–1873
English philosopher and economist
On Liberty

In his search for elegance the management scientist has hindered his ability to participate in solving policy problems.... The management scientist must be prepared to forego elegance, to adjust his technique to the problem rather than searching for problems that fit the technique.

Henry Mintzberg
McGill University School of Management
The Nature of Managerial Work
(Harper & Row, 1973)

There are in the field of economic events no constant relations, and consequently no measurement is possible.

Ludwig von Mises 1881–1973
American economist
Human Action

[T]he knowledge of numbers is one of the chief distinctions between us and the brutes.

Mary Wortley Montagu, 1689–1762
English poet and essayist
Letter to the Countess of Bute,
January 28, 1753

[There is a] persistent human temptation to make life more explicable by making it more calculable; to put experience in some logical scheme that, by its order and niceness, will make what happens seem more understandable, analysis more bearable, decision simpler.

E. E. Morison
Massachusetts Institute of Technology
Greenberger, *Management and the Computer of the Future* (M. I. T., 1962)

We lose all intelligence by averaging.

John Naisbitt
Chairman, Naisbitt Group
Megatrends (Warner, 1984)

Constants aren't.

John Peers
President, Logical Machine Corp.
1,001 Logical Laws (Doubleday, 1979)

Accuracy is the sum total of your compensating mistakes.

John Peers
President, Logical Machine Corp.
1,001 Logical Laws (Doubleday, 1979)

I've made it a point never to learn my Social Security number because I'm a person, not a number.

H. Ross Perot
Founder, Electronic Data Systems
Life, February 1988

People, including managers, do not live by pie charts alone—or by bar graphs or three inch statistical appendices to 300 page reports. People live, reason, and are moved by symbols and stories.

Tom Peters
Business Writer
Thriving on Chaos (Knopf, 1987)

Ability in Mathematics Required.

Inscription over door of Plato's Academy

The systemic [mathematical] approach to decision analysis has its merits and demerits, and vivid testimony appears on both sides of the ledger. Also, what is a merit to some is a dismerit to others. Someone might wax eloquent and say, "Decision analysis is great because it encourages the introduction of subjective judgements and preferences into the formal analysis." But others might retort, "That's a disadvantage as I see it. Managers can now legitimatize their prejudices and misconceptions".... Obviously, my tally comes out in favor of decision analysis.

Howard Raiffa
Harvard University
*Decision Analysis:
Lectures on Choices under Uncertainty*

All the ... computer models and fancy forms will quickly lose their appeal (if they had any to begin with) unless top management pays a lot of attention to the results they generate.

Bernard C. Reimann
Cleveland State University
The Planning Forum, 1987

Financial planning models do not always ask the right questions.... We think that financial planning models are necessary, but we also think they should carry the label: Let the user beware!

Stephen A. Ross
Yale University
and Randolph W. Westerfield
The Wharton School
Corporate Finance
(Times-Mirror/Mosby College, 1988)

Mathematics takes us into the region of absolute necessity, to which not only the actual world, but every possible world, must conform.

Bertrand Russell, 1872–1970
English mathematician and philosopher
The Study of Mathematics

A little inaccuracy sometimes saves tons of explanation.

Saki (H. H. Munro), 1879–1916
English humorist and novelist
The Comments of Moung Ka

In economics and finance, nothing can be measured with the great accuracy of the physical sciences. But approximate measurement will suffice, so long as the method of measurement remains roughly the same over time.

Paul A. Samuelson
Nobel laureate in economics
Economics (McGraw-Hill)

Just enough of a good thing is always too little.

George Savile (Lord Halifax), 1633–1695
English politician and statesman
Miscellaneous Thoughts and Reflections

No great marketing decisions have ever been made on quantitative data.

John Sculley
CEO, Apple Computer Co.
Rowan, *The Intuitive Manager*
(Little, Brown, and Company, 1986)

The numbers tell you *how* your business is going, not *why*.

Jonathan P. Siegel
Information Communications Associates
Speech, McLean, Virginia, September 12, 1987

A single death is a tragedy, a million deaths is a statistic.

Joseph Stalin, 1879–1953
Russian political leader
Attributed

There are two kinds of statistics, the kind you look up and the kind you make up.

Rex Stout, 1886–1975
American detective writer
Death of a Doxy

Management science [Operations Research] also involves the philosophy of approaching a problem in a logical manner (i.e., a scientific approach). The logical, consistent, and systematic approach to problem solving can be as useful (and valuable) as the knowledge of the mechanics of the mathematical techniques themselves.

Bernard W. Taylor III
Virginia Polytechnic Institute
Introduction to Management Science
(Brown, 1986)

Mathematical models are more precise and less ambiguous than quantitative models and are therefore of greater value in obtaining specific answers to certain managerial questions.

Henry L. Tosi
University of Florida
and Stephen J. Carrol
University of Maryland
Management (John Wiley & Sons, 1976)

Companies were collapsing because of their bias for numeracy over action. Analysis paralysis.

Robert H. Waterman
Management consultant and writer
The Renewal Factor (Bantam, 1987)

The recent history of the behavioral sciences has shown us how deeply the success of mathematics as used in physics has affected disciplines quite far removed from physics. Many psychologists and sociologists have for generations discussed their subject matter in terms of differential equations and statistics, for example. They may have begun by believing that the calculi they adopted were merely a convenient shorthand for describing the phenomena with which they deal. But, as they construct ever larger conceptual frameworks out of elementary components originally borrowed from foreign contexts, and as they give these frameworks names and manipulate them as elements of still more elaborate systems of thought, these frameworks cease to serve as mere modes of description and become ... determinants of their own view of the world.

Joseph Weizenbaum
American computer scientist
Computer Power and Human Reason
(Penguin, 1984)

Difficult as it is to collect good physical data, it is far more difficult to collect long runs of economic or social data so that the whole of the run shall have a uniform significance. The data on the production of steel, for instance, change their significance not only with every invention that changes the technique of the steelmaker but with every social and economic change affecting business and industry at large, and in particular, with every technique changing the demand for steel or the supply and nature of the competing materials.

Norbert Wiener, 1894–1964
American computer scientist
God and Golem, Inc., (M. I. T., 1964)

393

Knowledge specialists may ascribe a degree of certainty to their models of the world that baffles and offends managers. Often the complexity of the world cannot be reduced to mathematical abstractions that make sense to a manager. Managers who expect complete, one-to-one correspondence between the real world and each element in a model are disappointed and skeptical.

> Dale E. Zand
> New York University
> *Information, Organization, and Power*
> (McGraw-Hill, 1981)

Let us use true scientific method as an aid to human judgement—not as a hindrance. Science is human experience; it is not an alternative to judgement, and it is certainly not something that can operate outside human experience.

> Solly Zuckerman
> English Operations Research scientist
> *Foreign Affairs*, January 1962

It's important to begin by acknowledging that the Japanese tend to be extremely literate with numbers—far more so than most American businessmen I've met. Too much has been made of the vagueness of our verbal language.

We compensate for this with a facility at the "numbers language." To be sure, it's a rigorous system. But because I believe, and my seniors believe, that I should be running my division, I treat the control system process like some people treat their morning jog. It's rigorous exercise but it makes me stronger.

> Anonymous division manager
> Matsushita Industries, Ltd. (Japan)
> *Business Horizons*, June 1980

A new study reveals that sexually transmitted diseases are a leading cause of statistics.

> Anonymous

Torture the data long enough and they will confess to anything.

> Anonymous

If you can't measure it, you can't manage it.

> Anonymous

If you don't measure it, it won't happen.

> Anonymous

38

Remuneration & Perks

That's the Latin word for three farthings.

Everyone wants a new and more equitable compensation plan provided he will then get more than he does now.

> Charles Abod
> CFO, Human Service Group
> Staff Meeting, December 1984

[On leaving office:] I will happily have to seek what is known as gainful employment, which does not describe holding public office.

> Dean Acheson, 1893–1971
> U. S. Secretary of State
> *Time*, December 22, 1952

You may share the labors of the great, but you will not share the spoils.

> Aesop, c. 620–c. 560 B.C.
> Greek fabulist
> *The Lion's Share*

Making a living is only part of life.

> Cecil Andrus
> Governor of Idaho
> *The Wall Street Journal*, April 7, 1988

Inferiors revolt in order that they may be equal, and equals revolt in order that they may be superior.

> Aristotle, 384–322 B.C.
> Greek philosopher and teacher
> *Politics*

Troubles arise, not only over inequalities of property, but over inequalities of honor.

> Aristotle, 384–322 B.C.
> Greek philosopher and teacher
> *Politics*

A wage hike is very hard to take away, but bonuses and profit-sharing can disappear very quickly in hard times.... More people are realizing that bonuses look like raises, but really aren't.

> Al Bauman
> Economist, U. S. Bureau of Labor Statistics
> *The New York Times*, May 1, 1988

To say ... that the American worker is not really or primarily interested in money contradicts, in a deep sense, the very motive power of the economic system. Why else would people submit themselves to such a work environment?

Daniel Bell
Harvard University
Work and Its Discontents

First, I charge a retainer; then I charge a reminder; next I charge a refresher; and then I charge a finisher.

Judah P. Benjamin, 1811–1844
Confederate Secretary of State
Clark, *Great Sayings by Great Lawyers*

I am accustomed to pay men back in their own coin.

Otto von Bismarck, 1815–1898
First Chancellor of the German Empire
To the Ultramontanes

We are so culturally wedded to the notion of individual achievement that many companies have to pay big bonuses to outstanding individual performers at the same time that the company as a whole is going down the tubes and has no cash to pay the bills.

A. Harvey Block
CEO, Bokenon Systems Inc.
Lecture, Cambridge, Massachusetts,
September 1977

The best of wages will not compensate for excessively long working hours which undermine health.

Louis Dembitz Brandeis, 1856–1941
U. S. Supreme Court Justice
Lief, *Brandeis: The Personal History of
an American Ideal*

Value has been defined as the ability to command the price.

Louis Dembitz Brandeis, 1856–1941
U. S. Supreme Court Justice
St. Louis & Ohio Railroad v. *U. S.* (1928)

I have a lot of faith in what employees can do if they are treated right and properly motivated. But when I worked for other people, I saw colleagues work their buns off and get nothing out of it. I saw Wall Street rape employees.

Warren Braun
CEO, ComSonics
Best of Business Quarterly, 1987

Most of the collective bargaining since the 1940's has resulted in wage settlements in excess of productivity increases.

Courtney C. Brown
Columbia University School of Business
Dun's Review, August 1979

We can improve our service by paying more attention, and more money, to the people we hire.

Alvin Burger
Founder, "Bugs" Burger Bug Killers, Inc.
Inc. Magazine, June 1984

Poverty begets sedition and villainy.

Robert Burton, 1577–1640
Vicar of St. Thomas's, Oxford
The Anatomy of Melancholy

All progress is based upon the universal innate desire on the part of every organism to live beyond its income.

Samuel Butler, 1835–1902
English novelist and satirist
Note-Books of Samuel Butler

When a supervisor proves that he has done a good job, he doesn't get just a kind word or a pat on the back. He gets something that rings the cash register—something he can take home and show his wife.

Bror R. Carlson
Director of Accounting,
International Minerals and Chemicals Co.
Managing for Profit (IM&C, 1961)

The progress of human society consists ... in ... the better and better apportioning of wages to work.

Thomas Carlyle, 1795–1881
Scottish essayist and historian
Past and Present

The one is master and depends on profits. The other is servant and depends on salary.

Andrew Carnegie, 1835–1919
American industrialist and philanthropist
Quoted in *Harvard Business Review*,
September/October 1987

They can expect nothing but their labour for their pains.

Miguel de Cervantes, 1547–1616
Spanish novelist
Don Quixote (Preface)

Though the people support the government, the government should not support the people.

Grover Cleveland, 1837–1908
Twenty-second and twenty-fourth
President of the United States
Veto, Texas Seed Bill, February 16, 1887

The field of Public Relations is now becoming dominated by women. Unfortunately, in our society, when any profession has become dominated by women, pay scales have declined.

John B. Cox
Director of Communications,
National Association of College
and University Business Officers
PR Strategies U. S. A., April 1, 1988

If you treat your employees right, they won't steal from you.

Philip Crosby
Founder, Philip Crosby Associates, Inc.
Inc. Magazine, February 1988

An ordinary employer can grant wage increases by reducing profits, raising prices and cutting down his work force. But the state can not use these methods.

Charles De Gaulle, 1890–1970
Military leader and President of France
Memoirs of Hope (Simon & Schuster, 1970)

We use rewards sometimes to try to force people to do what they don't want to do but what *we* want them to do.... When subordinates are experiencing the reward structure as one that's pushing them around or controlling them, even rewards can be demotivating.

Edward L. Deci
University of Rochester
Nation's Business, March 1988

Managers need to realize that they are being paid for enabling people to do the work for which those people are being paid.

Peter F. Drucker
Management consultant and writer
Management in Turbulent Times
(Harper & Row, 1980)

Attribution of credit for bonus purposes is always sticky. If you take any team that has recently had a major success and ask each team member to honestly and confidentially estimate his personal percentage of contribution to the success, the sum always seems to exceed three hundred percent.

Lewis D. Eigen
Executive Vice President,
University Research Corp.
Management meeting, September 1984

No man can be wise on an empty stomach.

> George Eliot (Marian Evans), 1819–1880
> English novelist, essayist, and editor
> *Adam Bede*

Some employees would rather quit than ask for a raise.

> Edgar S. Elman
> Management consultant
> *Inc. Magazine's Guide to*
> *Small Business Success*, 1987

The reward of a thing well done, is to have done it.

> Ralph Waldo Emerson, 1803–1882
> American essayist and poet
> *New England Reformers*

Nothing is to be had for nothing.

> Epictetus, c. 60–120
> Roman Stoic philosopher
> *Encheiridon*

[R]ewards should be proportionate to risk. Few executives would change companies if it entailed a large risk.

> Oliver A. Fick
> Environmental Services Manager,
> International Paper Co.
> *Harvard Business Review*, July/August 1986

My idea was then and still is that if a man did his work well, the price he could get for that work, the profits, and all financial matters would care for themselves.

> Henry Ford, 1863–1947
> American industrialist
> *My Life and Work*

[Commenting on his firm's recent change from piecework to salary compensation:] It has enabled us to cross–train people on dif-ferent jobs.... I think people are working a lot harder than they were before."

> John Gantner
> Operations Manager, Edmonds Shoe Corp.
> *Inc. Magazine*, January 1988

There are forty-seven [development] team members signatures inside the mold for the plastic case of the [Apple] Macintosh [computer].

> Charles Garfield
> President, Performance Sciences Corp.
> *Peak Performers* (Avon, 1986)

I offer neither pay, nor quarters, nor provisions; I offer hunger, thirst, forced marches, battles and death.

> Giuseppe Garibaldi, 1807–1882
> Italian patriot and military leader
> Trevelyan, *Garibaldi's Defense*
> *of the Roman Republic*

The motivational effects of expected [pay] increases are very small indeed. Psychologically, the raise is already incorporated into what [the worker] regards as his earnings base; it is not "something extra."

> Saul Gellerman
> University of Dallas School of Management
> *Fortune*, March 1968

It is seldom in the individual's interest to be as productive as he could be. Most people function far below their capacity mainly because of the essentially dependent relationship of any individual to the organization that employees. When a man is financially dependent upon the continuity of his paychecks, he will be more interested in preserving that continuity than in inflating the next check.

> Saul Gellerman
> University of Dallas School of Management
> *Fortune*, March 1968

In the business world, everyone is paid in two coins: cash and experience. Take the experience first; the cash will come later.

> Harold Geneen
> CEO, IT&T
> *Managing* (Doubleday, 1984)

The name of political economy has been constantly invoked against every effort of the working classes to increase their wages.

> Henry George, 1839–1897
> American economist, writer, and lecturer
> *The Life of Henry George*
> (National Single Tax League, 1900)

Empty heads love long titles.

> German proverb

We're overpaying him, but he's worth it.

> Samuel Goldwyn, 1882–1974
> American movie mogul
> Johnson, *The Great Goldwyn*

A reward cannot be valued if it is not understood.

> Phillip C. Grant
> Husson College
> *Personnel Journal,* March 1988

By work you get money, by talk you get knowledge.

> Thomas Chandler Haliburton, 1796–1865
> Canadian jurist and humorist
> *The Old Judge, or Life in a Colony*

Money does motivate ... but only for a short time and only as long as it serves as a measure of worth or of power or of victory.

> James L. Hayes
> President and CEO,
> American Management Association
> *Memos for Management: Leadership*
> (AMACOM, 1983)

There is no economy for a community in inadequate compensation either for leaders or laborers. Let every man be compensated liberally in proportion to the benefit he confers upon the community.... Do not seek to eliminate wealth that is a reward for beneficial effort.

> William Randolph Hearst, 1863–1951
> Newspaper publisher and U. S. Congressman
> Signed editorial, March 28, 1918

Service without reward is punishment.

> George Herbert, 1593–1633
> English clergyman and poet
> *Jacula Prudentum*

Money, to achievement-oriented people, is valuable primarily as a measurement of their performance. It provides them with a means of assessing their progress and comparing their achievements with those of other people. They normally do not seek money for status or economic security.

> Paul Hersey
> California American University
> and Kenneth H. Blanchard
> University of Massachusetts
> *Management of Organizational Behavior*
> (Prentice-Hall, 1982)

Another characteristic of the achievement motivated person is that he seems to be more concerned with personal achievement than with the rewards of success.... He normally does not seek money for status or economic security.

Paul Hersey
California American University
and Kenneth H. Blanchard
University of Massachusetts
Management of Organizational Behavior
(Prentice-Hall, 1982)

I know of no salary plan that will guarantee against eventual employee dissatisfaction with pay.

Frederick Herzberg
University of Utah
The Managerial Choice
(Dow Jones-Irwin, 1976)

Money is life to us wretched mortals.

Hesiod, eighth century B.C.
Greek poet
Works and Days

The bad and good alike in honor share.

Homer, c. 700 B.C.
Greek poet
The Iliad

Fame is delightful, but as collateral it does not rank high.

Elbert Hubbard, 1856–1915
American writer, printer, and editor
Epigrams

Happiness is not a reward—it is a consequence. Suffering is not a punishment—it is a result.

Robert G. Ingersoll, 1833–1899
American lawyer and agnostic
The Christian Religion

[Commenting on his 1986 $20.6 million total remuneration:] That's the American way. If

little kids don't aspire to make money like I did, what the hell good is this country?

Lee Iacocca
CEO, Chrysler
Fortune, May 25, 1987

The journey is the reward.

Steven Jobs
Cofounder, Apple Computer Corp.
Macintosh computer development team,
Slogan

No man but a blockhead ever wrote except for money.

Samuel Johnson, 1709–1784
English lexicographer and critic
Boswell's Life of Dr. Johnson

Needing everyone's cooperation, they [managers] tend to treat everyone alike [with respect to remuneration] in order to avoid the discomfort of defending differential treatment.

Rosabeth Moss Kantor
Harvard Business School
Personnel, January 1987

High pay does not equal good service, and, as McDonald's has shown, low pay need not result in poor service .... High-quality service depends on high-quality management. If U.S. providers fail to learn this lesson, they should not be surprised if Americans have accounts at Japanese banks, fly Singapore Airlines or eat in French-owned restaurants.

Robert E. Kelley
Carnegie-Mellon University
The Wall Street Journal, October 12, 1987

I love the competitive environment. Money becomes part of the scorecard.

Donald P. Kelly
Chairman, Beatrice. Co.
Business Week, February 15, 1988

[Why he eliminated first-class air travel in the firm:] The front of the plane arrives at the same time as the rear.

> Victor Kiam
> CEO, Remington
> *United Magazine*, January 1984

Get more for those under you and those over you, and your raise is almost inevitable.

> Michael Korda
> Business and management writer
> *Power! How to Get It, How to Use It*
> (Random House, 1975)

The laborer who fails to ask for his wages must endure any delay.

> Korean proverb

The most common and durable source of faction has been the various and unequal distribution of property.

> James Madison, 1751–1836
> Fourth President of the United States
> *The Federalist Papers*

Nothing can have value without being an object of utility.

> Karl Marx, 1818–1833
> German political philosopher
> *Capital*

There is a Japanese saying that if you are going to endow power to a person, you have to give that person a monetary remuneration commensurate with that responsibility.

> Konosuke Matsushita
> Founder, Matsushita Electric Co. (Japan)
> *Cherry Blossoms and Robotics*
> (Young Presidents' Organization, 1983)

We used to have bonuses. We still give them occasionally. You know, the thing about a bonus is that if you pay it two years in a row, it's built in and the wives or husbands have already spent it. Then if you don't pay it, every one gets upset.

> Fritz Maytag
> President, Anchor Brewing Co.
> *Harvard Business Review*, July/August 1986

Most Americans say they want more money. Yet non-cash awards appear to be more effective motivators.

> Jerry McAdams
> Vice President,
> Maritz Information Resources
> *Management*, April 1987

The bad workmen who form the majority of the operatives in many branches of industry are decidedly of opinion that bad workmen ought to receive the same wages as good.

> John Stuart Mill, 1806–1873
> English philosopher and economist
> *On Liberty*

The distribution of wealth depends on the laws and customs of society.

> John Stuart Mill, 1806–1873
> English philosopher and economist
> *Principles of Political Economy*

Sometimes American companies use employees to make money for the management. That's why management gets a great bonus.... In Japan we don't pay bonus [only] to the managers. We pay bonus to the employees because if we make a profit, we want to have them enjoy it together with us.

> Akio Morita
> CEO, Sony Corp. (Japan)
> *Cherry Blossoms and Robotics*
> (Young Presidents' Organization, 1983)

We give a bonus for the employees to give them a sense of participation and to feel that they are members of the company because we are always saying our company has one fate. If the company goes well, everybody can enjoy. If the company goes wrong or goes bankrupt, people lose jobs.

> Akio Morita
> CEO, Sony Corp. (Japan)
> *Cherry Blossoms and Robotics*
> (Young Presidents' Organization, 1983)

What drove me was not the money, but the psychic income of seeing a possibility out there in the market and watching it grow—of watching the people grow with it.

> Dick Nadeau
> Project Director, DuPont
> Pinchot, *Intrapreneuring*
> (Harper & Row, 1986)

People who work sitting down get paid more than people who work standing up.

> Ogden Nash, 1902–1971
> American writer & humorist
> Byrne, *The Other 637 Best Things
> Anybody Ever Said*

First, abandon executive perks.

> J. S. Ninomiya
> Safety Planning Manager, Ford Motor Co.
> *Harvard Business Review*, March/April 1988

[Referring to the presidential yacht *Sequoia*:] They pay you nickels and dimes, but this is what makes it worth it.

> Richard Milhous Nixon
> Thirty-seventh President of the United States
> Remark to attorney James D. St. Clair
> Woodward and Bernstein, *The Final Days*
> (Simon & Schuster, 1976)

The widespread use of custom-tailored titles to compensate for a lack of job satisfaction is

a short range expedient which merely starts a vicious circle.

> Otto Nowotny
> *Harvard Business Review*,
> March/April 1964

These guys don't write you a check just for wearing the right tie.

> Joseph R. Parella
> Partner, Wasserstein, Parella & Co.
> *The New York Times*, February 28, 1988

The highest salary that EDS ever paid me was $68,000, because I tied my fate to the stockholders' fate. Today many companies pay their chief executives obscene salaries and treat customers and stockholders as a nuisance.

> H. Ross Perot
> Founder, Electronic Data Systems
> *Life*, February 1988

Reward workers while the sweat's still on their brow.

> H. Ross Perot
> Founder, Electronic Data Systems
> *Life*, February 1988

You can't look the troops in the eye and say, "It's been a bad year; we can't do anything for you," but then say, "By the way, we're going to pay ourselves a $1 million bonus."

> H. Ross Perot
> Founder, Electronic Data Systems
> Peters, *Thriving on Chaos* (Knopf, 1987)

Far too many executives have become more concerned with the "four P's"—*pay, perks, power and prestige*—rather than making profits for shareholders.

> T. Boone Pickens, Jr.
> Founder, United Shareholders Association
> Fund raising letter, March 1988

Under the influence either of poverty or wealth, workmen and their work are equally liable to deteriorate.

Plato, 427–347 B.C.
Greek philosopher and teacher
The Republic

The last benefit is the one remembered.

Barber, *The Book of 1000 Proverbs*, 1876

The ability to deal with people is as purchasable a commodity as sugar or coffee. And I will pay more for that ability than for any other under the sun.

John Davidson Rockefeller, 1839–1937
American industrialist and philanthropist
Quoted by Dale Carnegie,
How to Win Friends and Influence People

Far and away the best prize that life offers is the chance to work hard at work worth doing.

Theodore Roosevelt, 1858–1919
Twenty-sixth President of the United States
Labor Day speech, Syracuse, 1903

The highest reward for a man's toil is not what he gets for it, but what he becomes by it.

John Ruskin, 1819–1900
English art critic and historian
Sesame and Lilies

[T]he divorce of income from effort, and the success of producing goods for which the market will pay money, does gradually take a toll from productivity growth and even from the level of productivity.

Paul A. Samuelson
Nobel laureate in economics
The New York Times, August 30, 1987

It looks like only the top 10% will be rewarded under the new [compensation] system. That's enough to scare me.

Donald Savage
President, Local 1869, United Auto Workers
Black Enterprise, April 1988

Fine words butter no parsnips.

Walter Scott, 1771–1832
Scottish poet, novelist, and biographer
The Legend of Montrose

Remuneration! O! That's the Latin word for three farthings.

William Shakespeare, 1564–1616
English dramatist and poet
Love's Labour's Lost

He is well paid that is well satisfied.

William Shakespeare, 1564–1616
English dramatist and poet
The Merchant of Venice

The manager must decide what type of group is wanted. If cooperation, teamwork, and synergy really matter, then one aims for high task interdependence. One structures the jobs of group members so that they have to interact frequently ... to get their jobs done. Important outcomes are made dependent on group performance. The outcomes are distributed equally. If frenzied, independent activity is the goal, then one aims for low task interdependence and large rewards are distributed competitively and unequally.

Gregory P. Shea
The Wharton School
and Richard A. Guzzo
New York University
Sloan Management Review, Spring 1987

[Referring to Tandy, his previous employer:] The thing that's always made it go is an attempt to compensate everybody on their results.... You learn to read a profit and loss.... If it's not good your compensation is going to suffer, and if it's great, you're going to do very well.

John Shirley
President, Microsoft Corp.
Computer & Software News, December 7, 1987

The challenge of the eighties is to keep your key people.

Alan Shugart
President, Seagate Technology
Business Week, February 6, 1984

Using money as a motivator leads to a progressive degradation in the quality of everything produced.

Philip Slater
American sociologist and writer
Wealth Addiction

Tax-free benefits ... are of considerably more value to an executive in a high bracket than to a line worker in a low to middle bracket. Thus it's not surprising that tax-free benefits accrue disproportionately to those with higher incomes.

Fortney H. Stark
U. S. Congressman
The New York Times, September 18, 1983

Equality is equity.

Noah Hayes Swayne, 1804–1884
U. S. Supreme Court Justice
Pacific Insurance Co. v. Soule (1868)

Care should be taken to make sure that the deferred amounts [in a company-sponsored deferred compensation or salary reduction plan] are not subtracted from the amount on which your pension, insurance, and health benefits are calculated. The manager whose

pension base is diminished by the amount deferred may lose more than he gains.

John Tarrant
Business consultant and writer
Perks and Parachutes
(Simon & Schuster, 1985)

To motivate top employee performance, you must compensate your superstars: Provide them with competitive pay without boosting salaries for mediocre or poor performers.

Clarence Thomas
Chairman,
Equal Employment Opportunity Commission
Management, 1987

If I don't get present-day satisfaction, I won't stay. I won't work for the future. Nobody is going to guarantee its arrival.

Terrence Thompson
Senior Financial Representative, Bechtel Co.
Time, March 6, 1978

What short term CEO will take a long-term view when it lowers his own income? Only a saint, and there aren't very many saints.

Lester C. Thurow
Dean, Sloan School of Management, M. I. T.
Newsweek, December 7, 1981

A person who has a good boss and congenial fellow workers will not change jobs for a few dollars more.

Maurice S. Trotter
New York University
Supervisor's Handbook on Insubordination
(Bureau of National Affairs, 1967)

It isn't the sum you get, it's how much you can buy with it that's the important thing; and it's that that tells whether your wages are high in fact or only high in name.

> Mark Twain
> (Samuel Langhorne Clemens), 1835–1910
> American author and riverboat captain
> *A Connnecticut Yankee at King Arthur's Court*

Simple thankes is a slender recompens ...

> Frances Walsingham, c. 1560–1603
> English poet
> Letter to Robert Cecil, December 1599

The best part [of Wal-mart's Buy American program], as important as any other, is to try to get our manufacturers to create a partnership with their workers the way we've tried to do with our people, and share the profits with them.

> Sam Walton
> Founder, Wal-Mart
> *Nation's Business,* April 1988

If you do things by the job, you are perpetually driven; the hours are scourges. If you work by the hour, you gently sail on a stream of Time, which is always bearing you on to the heaven of Pay, whether you make any effort or not.

> Charles Dudley Warner, 1829–1903
> American editor and writer
> *My Summer in a Garden*

As to pay, Sir, I beg leave to assure the Congress that as no pecuniary consideration could have tempted me to accept this arduous employment at the expense of my domestic ease and happiness, I do not wish to make any profit from it.

> George Washington, 1732–1799
> First President of the United States
> Speech to the Continental Congress,
> accepting appointment as Commander-in-Chief
> June 16, 1775

It is not that pearls fetch a high price *because* men have dived for them; but on the contrary, men dive for them because they fetch a high price.

> Richard Whatley, 1787–1863
> Archbishop of Dublin and Professor of
> Political Economy, Oxford University
> *Introductory Lectures on Political Economy*

[To the question, "For two days' labour, you ask two hundred guineas?" Whistler replied:] No, I ask it for the knowledge of a lifetime.

> James Abbott McNeill Whistler, 1834–1903
> American-born painter, etcher and writer
> Seitz, *Whistler Stories*

It's no disgrace to be poor, but it's no great honor either.

> Yiddish proverb

If you pay peanuts, you get monkeys.

> Anonymous

39

Research & Development

*If you're going to make rubber tires...
go see the damn rubber trees.*

Small firms are far more efficient innovators than industrial giants.... Small firms are more prolific inventors than giant companies; small firms exert significantly greater research and development effort than large ones; small firms devise and develop inventions at substantially lower costs than large firms.

Walter Adams
President, Michigan State University
and James Brock
Economist
The Bigness Complex (Pantheon, 1986)

Intelligence is the faculty of making artificial objects, especially tools, to make tools.

Henri Bergson, 1859–1941
Nobel laureate in literature
Creative Evolution

They [the Japanese] will get a lot of payoff [from their 5th generation computer R&D effort] even if they don't reach all their targets.

David H. Brandin
Vice President, SRI International
The New York Times, July 8, 1984

At its heart, research is a profoundly social process based on written discourse among scientists in widely separated laboratories.

William J. Broad
Journalist
The New York Times, February 16, 1988

Significant advances rarely come through to commercialization in less than five years—usually the range is 10 to 15 years.

Theodore L. Cairns
Director, Central Research, DuPont
Speech, San Francisco, May 8, 1974

Some of the problems society deems most important, and on which industry's technical ingenuity might be very helpful, turn out to be among the poorest risks for industrial R&D.

Theodore L. Cairns
Director, Central Research, DuPont
Speech, San Francisco, May 8, 1974

The concept of stride is very important in developing computers. If you take a stride that is too large, you get bruised. If you take a step in one dimension, you better be careful about taking a step in another, or the step may get too long.

Seymour Cray
Founder, Cray Research, Inc.
Time, March 28, 1988

The presence of a body of well-instructed men, who do not have to labor for their daily bread, is important to a degree which cannot be overestimated; as all high intellectual work is carried on by them, and on such work material progress of all kinds mainly depends.

Charles Darwin, 1809–1882
English naturalist
The Descent of Man

Physiological experiments on animals is justifiable for real investigation, but not for mere damnable and detestable curiosity.

Charles Darwin, 1809–1882
English naturalist
Letter to E. Ray Lankester

Ignorance never settles a question.

Benjamin Disraeli, 1804–1881
English Prime Minister & novelist
Speech, House of Commons, May 14, 1866

The U.S. Government, primarily the Department of Defense, has been the principal financier and stimulus behind electronic digital computer development in the U. S.

Hugh P. Donaghue
Assistant to the Chairman, Control Data Corp.
U. S. Senate testimony, July 1974

He who would search for pearls must dive below.

John Dryden, 1631–1700
English poet
Prologue to Lee's Sophonisba

Imagination is more important than knowledge.

Albert Einstein, 1879–1955
Nobel laureate in physics
Hurd, *Treasury of Great American Quotations*

The more one chases after quanta, the better they hide themselves.

Albert Einstein, 1879–1955
Nobel laureate in physics
Albert Einstein, The Human Side
(Princeton, 1979)

Research is a crock!

Michael Eisner
CEO, Walt Disney Productions
60 Minutes (TV program), November 22, 1987

Men love to wonder, and that is the seed of our science.

Ralph Waldo Emerson, 1803–1882
American essayist and poet
Works and Days

No great thing is created suddenly, any more than a bunch of grapes or a fig. If you tell me that you desire a fig, I answer that there must be time. Let it first blossom, then bear fruit, then ripen.

> Epictetus, c. 60–120
> Roman Stoic philosopher
> *Discourses*

[To design or develop anything:] You never have enough information, and you never have enough time.

> Woody Flowers
> Massachusetts Institute of Technology
> *Discover* (PBS TV), February 2, 1988

Our largest challenge is to cut the time it takes to get technology out of the lab and into operations.

> Gordon Foward
> President, Chaparral Steel
> *Washington Business Journal*,
> September 7, 1987

Art imitates nature, and necessity is the mother of invention.

> Richard Franck, 1624–1708
> English writer
> *Northern Memoirs*

Closely related to basic research, indeed frequently indistinguishable from it, is the refinement and synthesis of the results of basic research, with a slant toward practical application but without firm schedules for completion.... What we call this ... depends a good deal on where it is done.

> Estill I. Green
> Vice President, Bell Telephone Laboratories
> *Effective Administration of Research Programs*
> (Cornell University Press, 1958)

Our technological standing will continue to decline without the discoveries that come only from basic research.

> Phillip A. Griffiths
> Provost, Duke University
> *High Technology*, August 1987

Reverse engineering is permitted as long as you spend enough time and energy to do it.

> Allen R. Grogan
> Editor, *The Computer Lawyer*
> *Business Week*, August 31, 1987

Defending against raiders hurts investment in new research.

> Edward L. Hennessy, Jr.
> Chairman, Allied Signal, Inc.
> *The New York Times*, March 13, 1988

Desire to know why, and how, curiosity, which is a lust of the mind, that by a perseverance of delight is the continued and indefatigable generation of knowledge, exceedeth the short vehemence of any carnal pleasure.

> Thomas Hobbes, 1588–1679
> English philosopher
> *Leviathan*

Academic freedom is simply a way of saying that we get the best results in education and research if we leave their management to people who know something about them.

> Robert Maynard Hutchins, 1899–1977
> President and Chancellor,
> University of Chicago
> *The Higher Learning in America*

We have tried to restore the dying art of going out and capturing what is perceived as a possible technology.

> James Ionson
> Team Leader, Strategic Defense Initiative
> *Management*, 1987

Many things difficult to design prove easy to performance.

> Samuel Johnson, 1709–1784
> English lexicographer and critic
> *A Dissertation on the Art of Flying*

A corporation cannot afford to nurse its capital by not spending on R&D; if you do, the world will pass you by.

> Lawrence Kichen
> Chairman, Lockheed Corp.
> *High Technology Business,* April 1988

The most beautiful thing in the world is, precisely, the conjunction of learning and inspiration. Oh, the passion for research and the joy of discovery.

> Wanda Landowska, 1879–1959
> Polish harpsichordist and music critic
> Resout, *Landowska on Music*

It's ... most profitable to work in teams where different investigators offer their particular expertise.

> Rita Levi-Montalcini
> Nobel laureate in physiology
> and medicine (Italy)
> *Omni*, March 1988

Never let an inventor run a company. You can never get him to stop tinkering and bring something to market.

> Royal Little
> Founder, Textron
> *Best of Business Quarterly*, 1987

Those who have read of everything are thought to understand everything too; but it is not always so—reading furnishes the mind only with materials of knowledge; it is thinking that makes what is read ours. We are of the ruminating kind, and it is not enough to cram ourselves with a great load of collections; unless we chew them over again, they will not give us strength and nourishment.

> John Locke, 1632–1704
> English philosopher
> *Some Thoughts Concerning Education*

If you're going to make rubber tires, you should go to Malaya and see the damn rubber trees.

> Fritz Maytag
> President, Anchor Brewing Co.
> *Harvard Business Review*, July/August 1986

The study being presented today [on the tiltrotor] reflects the enormous work involved in bringing tomorrow's technology from potential to performance.

> T. Allen McArtor
> Administrator, FAA
> Speech, Washington, D. C., July 30, 1987

Investment depends on expected returns but if such returns cannot be reliably estimated, management cannot reliably invest in research and development or for increased productivity.

> Akio Morita
> CEO, Sony Corp. (Japan)
> *Cherry Blossoms and Robotics*
> (Young Presidents' Organization, 1983)

I do not know what I may appear to the world; but to myself I seem to have been only like a boy playing on the seashore, and diverting myself in now and then finding a smoother pebble or a prettier shell than ordinary, whilst the great ocean of truth lay all undiscovered before me.

> Isaac Newton, 1642–1727
> English scientist and mathematician
> *Brewster's Memoirs of Newton*

Laziness, rather than necessity, is often the mother of invention.

> Robert Noyce
> Vice Chairman, Intel Corp.
> *Silicon Valley* (PBS TV), August 25, 1987

Firstly, gradualness. About this most important condition of fruitful scientific work I can never speak without emotion. Gradualness, gradualness, gradualness.

> Ivan Petrovich Pavlov, 1849–1936
> Nobel laureate in physiology and medicine
> Speech to Russian students,
> February 27, 1936

Although G[eneral] M[otors] spends $3 billion a year on research and development, it isn't first or best in anything. Not one penny of that money should be spent on things that won't help make GM No. 1 in innovation, design and quality.

> H. Ross Perot
> Founder, Electronic Data Systems
> *Life*, February 1988

Successful researchers do not typically plod through their scientific careers stumbling on things accidentally. Powerful innate curiosity comnbined with many other exceptional aptitudes is surely involved; but one cannot avoid the conclusion that the careful sorting out of trivia and the selection of important objectives play critical roles in influencing the results of a successful basic research program.

> Joseph A. Raelin
> Boston College School of Management
> *Clash of Cultures: Managers and Professionals*
> (Harvard Business School Press, 1986)

Why should we subsidize intellectual curiosity?

> Ronald Wilson Reagan
> Fortieth President of the United States
> *Omni*, March 1988

I like to think of research as the distance we must travel between the problem and the answer. In my own field, I have seen this distance traveled many times against many obstacles—both natural and man-made—which at the time, seemed insurmountable.

> David Sarnoff, 1891–1971
> Founder and President, RCA
> *Wisdom of Sarnoff and the World of RCA*

Friend, let this be enough.
If thou wouldst go on reading,
Go and thyself become the writing and the meaning.

> Johann Scheffler, 1624–1677
> German physician and poet
> Quoted in Weizsäcker, *The History of Nature*

Industrial laboratories have always had to balance proprietary discoveries against the value of publishing results.

> Roland Schmitt
> Chief Scientist and Vice President,
> General Electric Co.
> *The New York Times*, August 2, 1987

By treating everything as a research problem, we tend to devise elegant, inventive solutions without adequate attention to cost, manufacturability, and quality.

> Roland Schmitt
> Chief Scientist and Vice President,
> General Electric Co.
> *Washington Business Journal*,
> September 7, 1987

One so inclined may lament the decline of the free-ranging independent [researcher] and his replacement by the captive inventor of the corporate laboratory. Yet in the face of team research, expensive equipment, and lengthy projects needed to exploit the potentialities of modern science, such a shift was inevitable.

> Jacob Schmookler
> University of Minnesota
> *Technological Progress and the Modern American Corporation* (Harvard, 1960)

There was a time that we only worried about protecting basic research results during wartime. Now it is something that has crept into our peacetime, entrepreneurial society.

> Alan Schriesheim
> Director, Argonne National Laboratory
> *The New York Times*, August 2, 1987

Habits of firm and assiduous application, of gaining the art of controlling, directing, and concentrating the powers of his mind for earnest investigation,—an art far more essential than even that acquaintance with classical learning, which is the primary object of study.

> Walter Scott, 1771–1832
> Scottish poet, novelist, and biographer
> *Waverly*

We try to picture what the products will be and then say, what technology should we be working on today to help us get there?

> John Sculley
> CEO, Apple Computer Co.
> *Inc. Magazine*, January 1988

[In scientific research:] Political savvy, physical endurance, money, and maybe guts, can be as important as scientific insight.

> Gary Taubes
> Science writer
> *Nobel Dreams: Power, Deceit, and the Ultimate Experiment* (Random House, 1987)

The brightest flashes in the world of thought are incomplete until they have been proved to have their counterparts in the world of fact.

> John Tyndall, 1820–1893
> English physicist
> *Scientific Materialism*

A recent study of product innovation in the scientific instruments and tool machinery industries indicates that 80 percent of all product innovations are initiated by the customer.

> Eric von Hippel
> Management consultant & computer analyst
> *Technology Review*, January 1978

They [the firm's R&D unit] are not held accountable for reaching specific goals. They are not told how to carry out their responsibilities.

> Ben Watkins
> New England Sales Manager, Cole & Wiley
> Tosi and Carroll, *Management* (Wiley, 1976)

Developing products is an art, not a science.... Firms that try to improve product development by codifying it in a manual don't really learn. The book always gets too complicated, so they end up scrapping it and starting from scratch.

> Steven Wheelwright
> Stanford University School of Business
> *Fortune*, March 2, 1987

[Commenting upon one of the early experiments with a precursor to the Kitty Hawk airplane:] We were greatly pleased with the results excepting a few little accidents to the machine.

> Orville Wright, 1871–1948
> Pioneer aviator
> Quoted in *American Heritage*, April 1988

Necessity, mother of invention.

William Wycherly, 1640–1716
English playwright
Love in a Wood

Definition of R&D: Indoor recreation for the over-educated.

Anonymous

40

Risk

Fortune aids the brave.

===

It is easy to be brave when far away from danger.

> Aesop, c. 620–c. 560 B.C.
> Greek fabulist
> *The Kid and the Wolf*

Most companies are risk aversive. They don't like to say so, but they are.

> Warren G. Bennis
> President, University of Cincinnati
> University of Maryland symposium,
> January 21, 1988

Management and medicine have one thing in common. They can both cause problems as well as solve them.

> Warren G. Bennis
> President, University of Cincinnati
> University of Maryland symposium,
> January 21, 1988

I have a propensity for taking risks. I'd rather get in on the ground floor of something chan-cy than into something safe that's been around for 50 years.

> Cathleen Black
> Publisher, USA Today
> *Eastern Review,* April 1988

Our whole way of life today is dedicated to the removal of risk. Cradle to grave we are supported, insulated, and isolated from the risks of life—and if we fall, our government stands ready with Bandaids of every size.

> Shirley Temple Black
> American actress and diplomat
> Speech, Kiwanis International Convention,
> Texas, June 1967

There is no such thing as an innocent purchaser of stocks.

> Louis Dembitz Brandeis, 1856–1941
> U. S. Supreme Court Justice
> Testimony, Senate Committee on
> Interstate Commerce, December 14, 1911

Fate laughs at probabilities.

> Edward George Bulwer-Lytton, 1803–1873
> English novelist and playwright
> *Eugene Aram*

He that is down needs fear no fall.

> John Bunyan, 1628–1688
> English preacher and writer
> *The Pilgrim's Progress*

There is no less likely way of winning a war than to adhere pedantically to the maxim of "safety first."

> Winston Churchill, 1874–1965
> English Prime Minister, writer, and soldier
> Speech in Parliament, April 10, 1941

They [the Navy] can't risk a failure [of an experiment with new techniques] because even if they learn something from the failure, everybody's going to say they were fools for trying it. It enforces a kind of conservatism that is fundamentally unhealthy.

> Tom Clancy
> Novelist, military expert,
> and insurance executive
> *U.S. News & World Report*, June 15, 1987

Behold the turtle: He only makes progress when he sticks his neck out.

> James Bryant Conant, 1893–1978
> President of Harvard University
> Quoted in *Success*, February 1988

I want to work with the top people, because only they have the courage and the confidence and the risk-seeking profile that you need.

> Laurel Cutler
> Vice Chairman, FCB/Leber Katz Partners
> *Inc. Magazine*, November 1987

The individual in the large organization ... like the uncalculating animals, is also a defenseless creature who calculatingly practices deception for safety's sake against the invisible threats around him.

> Melville Dalton
> Sociologist
> *Men Who Manage* (John Wiley & Sons, 1959)

The best way to compel weak-minded people to adopt our opinion, is to terrify them from all others, by magnifying their danger.

> Cardinal de Retz, 1614–1679
> French ecclesiastic and politician
> *Political Maxims*

Success is the child of Audacity.

> Benjamin Disraeli, 1804–1881
> English Prime Minister and novelist
> *The Rise of Iskander*

By eleven o'clock, there remain at the roulette table only those desperate players, the real gamblers, for whom there exists but the roulette table ... who know nothing of what is going on around them and take no interest in any matters outside the roulette saloon, but only play and play from morning till night, and would gladly play all round the clock if it were permitted. These people are always annoyed when midnight comes, and they must go home, because the roulette bank is closed. And when the chief croupier, about 12 o'clock, just before the close calls out, 'The last three turns, gentlemen!', these men are ready to stake all they have in their pockets on those last three turns, and it is certain that it is just then that these people lose most.

> Fyodor Dostoyevski, 1821–1881
> Russian novelist
> *The Gambler*

He must realize that his control can never be complete, that he must be prepared to take a risk, and this is because all action takes place in time and future time is necessarily unknown to us.

> A. R. C. Duncan
> Queens University (Canada)
> Lecture, Executive Development Group,
> June 1964

No great deed is done
By falterers who ask for certainty.

> George Eliot (Marian Evans), 1819–1880
> English novelist, essayist, and editor
> *The Spanish Gypsy*

It was a high counsel that I once heard given to a young person, "Always do what you are afraid to do."

> Ralph Waldo Emerson, 1803–1882
> American essayist and poet
> *Heroism*

[R]ewards should be proportionate to risk. Few executives would change companies if it entailed a large risk.

> Oliver A. Fick
> Environmental Services manager,
> International Paper Co.
> *Harvard Business Review*, July/August 1986

Lady Godiva put everything she had on a horse.

> William Claude (W. C.) Fields, 1880–1946
> American comedian and film star
> Mason, *Never Trust A Man Who Doesn't Drink*
> (Montcalm, 1971)

My center is giving way, my right is in retreat; situation excellent. I will attack.

> Ferdinand Foch, 1851–1929
> French soldier and military leader
> Statement at Battle of the Marne, 1918
> Ashton, *Biography of the Late Marshall Foch*

People would rather die in the consensus than survive out on a limb.

> Richard Fontaine
> Fund manager, T. Rowe Price
> *The Washington Post*, March 14, 1988

You've got to have an atmosphere where people can make mistakes. If we're not making mistakes we're not going anywhere.

> Gordon Foward
> President, Chaparral Steel
> Peters, *Thriving on Chaos* (Knopf, 1987)

Aversion to risk may be the cause of all [managerial] shortcomings, as a top manager has no time to manage, but spends his time checking his new ideas with everybody who can possibly be affected by them.

> Joseph N. Froomkin
> Management consultant
> *Journal of the Academy of Management*,
> March 1964

He that will not sail till all dangers are over must never put to sea.

> Thomas Fuller, 1608–1661
> Chaplain in extraordinary to Charles II
> *Gnomologia*

In both R & D and software development, heavy expenditures of resources are required in order to produce future benefits of uncertain magnitude

> Philip F. Gehring, Jr.
> Texas Education Agency
> and Udo W. Pooch
> Texas A&M University
> Rullo, *Advances in Computer Programming
> Management* (Hayden, 1980)

Nothing noble is done without risk.

> André Gide, 1869–1951
> French novelist, critic, and essayist
> *Journal*

It is more important to minimize risk than to maximize profit.

> Bernard S. Glassman
> Builder and real estate developer
> Speech, Bethesda, Maryland, October 1, 1987

Man errs so long as he strives.

> Johann Wolfgang von Goethe, 1749–1832
> German poet and dramatist
> *Faust*

[Addressing his staff after a series of setbacks:] I want you to tell me exactly what's wrong with me and MGM even if it means losing your job.

> Samuel Goldwyn, 1882–1974
> Founder, MGM Studios
> Quoted by Bennis, January 21, 1988

A mistake is simply another way of doing things.

> Katherine Graham
> Publisher, *The Washington Post*
> Quoted by Bennis, January 21, 1988

Without danger you cannot get beyond danger.

> George Herbert, 1593–1633
> English clergyman and poet
> *Jacula Prudentum*

I don't mean to sound arrogant, but it's my ass that's on the line.

> Robert S. Hillman
> CEO, The Eyecare Co.
> *Inc. Magazine*, November 1987

Try new things and always be ready to lay yourself on the line.

> Judy T. Hofmann
> Assistant Secretary, U. S. Department
> of Housing and Urban Development
> *Management,* 1987

All life is an experiment.

> Oliver Wendell Holmes, Jr., 1841–1935
> U. S. Supreme Court Justice
> Dissent, *Abrams* v. *U. S.* (1919)

A long shot, Watson; a very long shot!

> Sherlock Holmes
> (Arthur Conan Doyle), 1859–1930
> English physician, writer, and sportsman
> *Silver Blaze*

The greatest mistake you can make in life is to be continually fearing you will make one.

> Elbert Hubbard, 1856–1915
> American writer, printer, and editor
> *The Philosophy of Elbert Hubbard*

Every business and every product has risks. You can't get around it.

> Lee Iacocca
> Chairman, Chrysler Corp.
> Speech, San Francisco, August 10, 1987

One of the rules of caution is not to be too cautious.

> Bahya ibn Paquda, c. 1050–1120
> Spanish religious philosopher
> *Duties of the Heart*

Unless you enter the tiger's den, you cannot take her cubs.

> Japanese proverb

Accidental success is a temptation to providence.

> Flavius Josephus, c. 37–100
> Graeco-Roman historian
> *History of the Jewish War*

Great successes never come without risks.

> Flavius Josephus, c. 37–100
> Graeco-Roman historian
> *History of the Jewish War*

Entrepreneurs are risk takers, willing to roll the dice with their money or reputations on the line in support of an idea or enterprise. They willingly assume responsibility for the success or failure of a venture and are answerable for all its facets. The buck not only stops at their desks, it starts there too.

> Victor Kiam
> CEO, Remington
> *Going For It!* (William Morrow, 1986)

As befits a company that was founded on a mistake, we have continued to accept mistakes as a normal part of running a business.... However, we expect our mistakes to have originality. We can afford almost any mistake *once.*

> Lewis Lehr
> Chairman, 3M Company
> Speech, Philadelphia, April 26, 1979

Write on your doors the saying wise and old,
"Be bold! be bold!" and everywhere, "Be bold;
Be not too bold!" Yet better the excess
Than the defect; better the more than less;
Better like Hector in the field to die,
Than like a perfumed Paris turn and fly.

> Henry Wadsworth Longfellow, 1807–1882
> American poet
> *Morituri Salutamus*

There are so many ways you can fail.

> David Lubrano
> CFO, Appolo Computer Co.
> *CFO,* August 1985

Business more than any other occupation is a continual dealing with the future; it is a continual calculation, an instinctive exercise in foresight.

> Henry Robinson Luce, 1898–1967
> American publisher and founder of *Time*
> *Fortune*, October 1960

Wisdom consists in being able to distinguish among dangers and make a choice of the least harmful.

> Niccolò Machiavelli, 1469–1527
> Florentine statesman and philosopher
> *The Prince*

A boss's mere expression of an opinion can be interpreted as a decision—even a direct order—by a staff member caught in the clutches of risk avoidance.

> R. Alec Mackenzie
> Management consultant and author
> *The Time Trap* (McGraw-Hill, 1972)

The man who makes no mistake does not usually make anything.

> William Connor Magee, 1821–1891
> Orator and Prelate of the Church of England
> Speech at Mansion House, London,
> January 24, 1889

All men of worship said it was merry to be under such a chieftain [King Arthur], that would put his person in adventure as other poor knights did.

> Thomas Malory, d. 1470
> English translator and compiler
> *Morte d'Arthur*

Risk! Risk anything! Care no more for the opinion of others, for those voices. Do the hardest thing on earth for you. Act for yourself. Face the truth.

> Katherine Mansfield,
> (Kathleen Beauchamp Murry), 1888–1923
> English poet and short-story writer
> Prochnow, *The Toastmaster's Treasure Chest*
> (Harper & Row, 1979)

If at first you don't succeed, you may not be encouraged to try again.

> Edwin McDowell
> Journalist
> *The New York Times,* April 25, 1988

Young people who really wanted a challenge went in and they looked around and found there was nothing they could decide, because everything had been decided for them. And a lot of young people would not tolerate that.... They simply left. And for those who stayed, they were trained not to make a decision. So when the time came that they moved up a bit and there was really something to be decided, they were lost, because they had never practiced on small decisions, and they had never made a mistake. So they figured out ways to continue not making decisions, to continue avoiding mistakes.

> William G. McGowan
> Chairman, MCI Communications Corp.
> *Inc. Magazine,* August 1986

How far high failure overleaps the bound of low successes.

> Lewis Morris, 1835–1907
> Welsh poet
> *Epic of Hades*

After I came to work here I failed the first actuarial examination I took. I had never failed anything before.

> James Morton
> CEO, John Hancock Insurance Co.
> Quoted on *Pinnacle* (CNN TV), January 1988

Life shrinks or expands in proportion to one's courage.

> Anaïs Nin, 1903–1977
> French-born American novelist and dancer
> *Diaries of Anaïs Nin*

[A]ffirmative action can be viewed as the ultimate in risk reduction because it provides insurance against the "bad luck" of having been born black or female.

> James O'Toole
> University of Southern California
> *Making America Work* (Continuum, 1981)

Educated risks are the key to success.

> William Olsten
> CEO, Olsten Services Corp.
> *Success,* February 1988

Where the probability of Advantage *exceeds not* that of Loss, Wisdom *never* Adventures.

> William Penn, 1644–1718
> Founder of Pennsylvania
> *Fruits of Solitude in Reflections and Maxims*

One has the right to be wrong.

> Claude Pepper
> U. S. Congressman
> *Reader's Digest,* December 1987

He that will not sail till all dangers are over must never put to sea.

> Barber, *The Book of 1000 Proverbs,* 1876

[With reference to the stock market "meltdown" of October 1987:] Nobody who has been on a falling elevator and survived ever again approaches such a conveyance without a fundamentally reduced degree of confidence.

Robert Reno
Investment analyst and financial writer
Time, November 2, 1987

If you aren't making mistakes in a new venture you are the wrong man for the job. A good warrior doesn't win every battle. He wins the war.

Milton J. Roedel
Manager of Exploratory Research, DuPont
Managers' meeting, February 1963

Power invariably means both responsibility and danger.

Theodore Roosevelt, 1858–1919
Twenty-sixth President of the United States
Quoted in *The New York Times Magazine*,
October 27, 1957

If men would think more, they would act less.

George Savile (Lord Halifax), 1633–1695
English politician and statesman
Miscellaneous Thoughts and Reflections

"Almost nothing new works" is a common expression among innovative persons. This phrase is not spoken, however, in a defeatest tone of voice, but rather in simple recognition of the fact that innovation is a high risk venture.

Lyle E. Schaller
Yokefellow Institute
The Change Agent (Abingdon, 1972)

He that is overcautious will accomplish little.

Johann von Schiller, 1759–1805
German poet and dramatist
William Tell

Our doubts are traitors,
And make us lose the good we oft might win,
By fearing to attempt.

William Shakespeare, 1564–1616
English dramatist and poet
Measure for Measure

There is a tide in the affairs of men,
Which, taken at the flood, leads on to fortune.
Omitted, all the voyages of their life
Is bound in shallows, and in miseries.

William Shakespeare, 1564–1616
English dramatist and poet
Julius Caesar

The better part of valour is discretion.

William Shakespeare, 1564–1616
English dramatist and poet
King Henry IV

If you do it right 51 percent of the time you will end up a hero.

Alfred P. Sloan, 1875–1966
President and Chairman, General Motors
Deal & Kennedy, *Corporate Cultures*
(Addison-Wesley, 1982)

Everything is sweetened by risk.

Alexander Smith, 1830–1867
Scottish poet
Of Death and the Fear of Dying

Fortune is not on the side of the faint-hearted.

Sophocles, c. 496–406 B.C.
Greek tragic playwright
Fragments

[Referring to *in vitro* fertilization procedures:] You can't know all the possibilities, and therefore you take some risks. You try to minimize them as much as possible, but there are potentials for people to have outcomes that they will not be pleased about.

> Robert Stillman
> The George Washington University Hospital
> *The Washington Post*, April 12, 1988

Bold if you will, but circumspectly bold.

> Torquato Tasso, 1544–1595
> Italian astronomer and poet
> *Gerusalemme Liberata*

Fortune aids the brave.
[*Audentis fortuna juvat.*]

> Terence, c. 190–159 B.C.
> Roman comedy writer
> *Phormio*

[Referring to technological risk taking:] The competition has to make the first move before anyone else will follow.

> Lester C. Thurow
> Dean, Sloan School of Management, M. I. T.
> *Working Woman*, March 1988

The fear of being considered stupid may make a new or timid employee reluctant to ask questions or to admit that he does not understand.

> Maurice S. Trotter
> New York University
> *Supervisor's Handbook on Insubordination*
> (Bureau of National Affairs, 1967)

October. This is one of the peculiarly dangerous months to speculate in stocks in. The others are July, January, September, April, November, May, March, June. December, August, and February.

> Mark Twain
> (Samuel Langhorne Clemens), 1835–1910
> American author and riverboat captain
> *Pudd' nhead Wilson's Calendar*

Behold, the fool saith, "Put not thine eggs in the one basket—which is but a manner of saying, "Scatter your money and your attention"; but the wise man saith, "Put all your eggs in the one basket and—*watch that basket.*"

> Mark Twain
> (Samuel Langhorne Clemens), 1835–1910
> American author and riverboat captain
> *Pudd' nhead Wilson's Calendar*

Courage is resistance to fear, mastery of fear—not absence of fear.

> Mark Twain
> (Samuel Langhorne Clemens), 1835–1910
> American author and riverboat captain
> *Pudd' nhead Wilson's Calendar*

Activity makes more men's fortunes than caution.

> Marquis de Vauvenargues, 1715–1747
> French soldier and moralist
> *Reflections and Maxims*

Avoid Gaming. This is a vice which is productive of every possible evil; equally injurious to the morals and health of its votaries. It is the child of avarice, the brother of iniquity, and the father of mischief.

> George Washington, 1732–1799
> First President of the United States
> Letter to Bushrod Washington,
> January 15, 1783

I never varied from the managerial rule that the worst possible thing we could do was to lie dead in the water with any problem. Solve it. Solve it quickly, solve it right or wrong. If you solved it wrong, it would come back and slap you in the face and then you could solve it right. Lying dead in the water and doing nothing is a comfortable alternative because it is without risk, but it is an absolutely fatal way to manage a business.

Thomas J. Watson, Jr.
CEO, IBM, and U. S. Ambassador to Russia
Fortune, 1977

Buyers are graded not only on their successes, but also on their failures. Too many hits means the buyer isn't taking enough chances.

Les Wexner
Founder, The Limited
Forbes, April 1987

A good manager must be willing take a stand even at the risk of offending people.

Betsy White
Citrus Division Manager, Ocean Spray
Working Woman, April 1988

The time you save in not making changes and taking risks can be used to perfect current practices. Your employees will be grateful to you for letting them know exactly where they stand—and will reward you by being unimaginative, uninspired and unhappy.

Donald C. Whitham
Supervisory Special Agent, FBI Academy
The National Sheriff, August/September 1986

When luck joins the game, cleverness scores double.

Yiddish proverb

41

Rules, Red Tape, & Bureaucracy

Any fool can make a rule.

[To improve communications practices of computer departments] you have to break the back of the bureaucracy you've established.

Michael Albrecht, Jr.
Principal, Nolan, Norton & Co.
PC Week, December 8, 1987

Against the egalitarian order of persuasion stands the authoritarian order, which is always hierarchical. If authority is to be defined at all, then, it must be in contradistinction to both coercion by force and persuasion through argument.

Hannah Arendt, 1906–1975
German-American philosopher and critic
Friedrich, *Authority*

Good laws, if they are not obeyed, do not constitute good government.

Aristotle, 384–322 B.C.
Greek philosopher and teacher
Politics

It is impossible for all things to be precisely set down in writing; for rules must be universal, but actions are concerned with particulars.

Aristotle, 384–322 B.C.
Greek philosopher and teacher
Politics

The perfect bureaucrat everywhere is the man who manages to make no decisions and escape all responsibility.

Brooks Atkinson
American drama critic and essayist
Once Around the Sun

The number of units reporting to a single administrator is not the essential factor in determining topside control. Ten units is too many if each has its own power base in the legislature or in clientele groups of significant political influence. A hundred units are manageable if most of them lack an independent base of power, and if their mission is precise and low voltage.

Stephan K. Bailey
President,
American Society of Public Administration
Agenda For the Nation
(The Brookings Institution, 1968)

I have dubbed many things as red tape which I would not have considered as such if I had taken the broad view. I was performing my duties as well as I knew how. I was at them every working hour my strength would permit. Yet I was being called upon for information and data that seemed to me quite unnecessary.

Hamilton McFarland Barksdale
Management Executive Committee, Dupont
Committee meeting minutes, October 11, 1909

Government is not an exact science.

Louis Dembitz Brandeis, 1856–1941
U. S. Supreme Court Justice
Truax v. *Corrigan* (1921)

The U. S. government entered the [Second World] war owning $650,000 worth of printing and reproducing equipment. After less than a year, it had $50 million worth.

David Brinkley
Broadcast journalist
Washington Goes to War (Knopf, 1988)

No rule is so general, which admits not some exception.

Robert Burton, 1577–1640
Vicar of St. Thomas's, Oxford
The Anatomy of Melancholy

"Whate'er is best administered is best," may truly be said of a juridicial system, and the due distribution of justice depends much more upon the rules by which suits are to be con-

ducted, than on the perfection of the code by which rights are defined.

John Campbell, 1779–1861
English jurist and statesman
Lives of the Lord Chancellors: Somers

Few formulas are so absolute as not to bend before the blast of extraordinary circumstances.

Benjamin Nathan Cardozo, 1870–1938
U. S. Supreme Court Justice
Evangelical Lutheran Church
v. *Sahlem* (1934)

[New units and layers of organization] frequently obscure accountability and authority.

Frank C. Carlucci
U. S. National Security Advisor
Frank Carlucci on Management in Government
(Center for Excellence in Government, 1987)

After an existence of nearly twenty years of almost innocuous desueutude these laws are brought forth.

Grover Cleveland, 1837–1908
Twenty-second and twenty-fourth
President of the United States
Message to Congress, March 1, 1886

Men cling to sanctified phrases not only because of the insights they contain but even more because, through ritual and repetition, they have become redolent with the wine of human experience.

Morris Raphael Cohen, 1880–1947
American philosopher and educator
A Dreamer's Journey

Let all things be done decently and in order.

New Testament, I Corinthians 14:40

I consider this concept [tradeoff] one of the most important considerations that any management claiming to do strategic thinking and planning can impose upon itself.... A tradeoff for size is the necessity for additional controls and an increase in formal communication accompanied by slower movement and decision making.... Successful growth companies *manage* bureaucracy by reducing it wherever possible, but they do not deny its existence and expect their people to do the same.

Allen Cox
Management consultant and author
The Making of the Achiever (Dodd Mead, 1985)

If the copying machines that came along later had been here during the [Second World] war, I'm not sure the allies would have won. We'd all have drowned in paper.

Alan Dickey
World War II Pentagon architect
Brinkley, *Washington Goes to War*
(Knopf, 1988)

Anyone who takes it on himself, on his own authority, to break a bad law, thereby authorizes everybody else to break the good ones.

Denis Diderot, 1713–1784
French encyclopedist and philosopher
Supplement to the Voyage of Bougainville

The greatest of all evils is a weak government.

Benjamin Disraeli, 1804–1881
English Prime Minister and novelist
Coningsby

It is not enough to know that the men applying the standard are honorable and devoted men. This is a government of *laws*, not of *men*.... It is not without significance that most of the provisions of the Bill of Rights are procedural. It is procedure that spells much of the difference between rule by law and rule by whim or caprice.

William O. Douglas, 1898–1980
U. S. Supreme Court Justice
Anti-Fascist Refugee Committee v. *McGrath*
(1951)

Trust men, and they will be true to you; treat them greatly, and they will shew themselves great, though make an exception in your favour to all their rules of trade.

Ralph Waldo Emerson, 1803–1882
American essayist and poet
Prudence

Order, Hierarchy, Discipline.

Motto of the Italian Fascist Party

A lot of top businesspeople become totally frustrated when they move into a cabinet position or as head of a department. They're used to much more power in business.... In government, they must suddenly follow strict procedures and regulations. It's a difficult adjustment.

Gerald R. Ford
Thirty-eighth President of the United States
Harvard Business Review,
September/October 1987

The history of American freedom is, in no small measure, the history of procedure.

Felix Frankfurter, 1882–1965
U. S. Supreme Court Justice
Malinski v. *New York* (1945)

To rely on a tidy formula for the easy determination of what is a fundamental right for purposes of legal enforcement may satisfy a longing for certainty but ignores the movements of a free society.

Felix Frankfurter, 1882–1965
U. S. Supreme Court Justice
Wolf v. *Colorado* (1948-1949)

In two words: im—possible.

> Samuel Goldwyn, 1882–1974
> American movie mogul
> Johnson, *The Great Goldwyn*

Once standing rules have been installed, there are fewer things that a supervisor has to direct a worker to do; thus the frequency of worker-foreman interaction is somewhat lessened.

> Alvin W. Gouldner
> Columbia University School of Business
> *Patterns of Industrial Bureaucracy*
> (The Free Press, 1954)

By a strange paradox, *formal* rules gave supervisors something with which they could "bargain" in order to secure *informal* cooperation from workers.

> Alvin W. Gouldner
> Columbia University School of Business
> *Patterns of Industrial Bureaucracy*
> (The Free Press, 1954)

I've had it up to here with organizations which are afraid to let their people do things.

> Al Grey
> Commandant, U. S. Marine Corps
> *60 Minutes* (TV program), March 27, 1988

Wherever there is authority, there is a natural inclination to disobedience.

> Thomas Chandler Haliburton, 1796–1865
> Canadian jurist and humorist
> *Nature and Human Nature*

Large companies have too much at stake to let a herd of racehorses loose in the fields. They need people who are comfortable with rules, regulations, and corporate manuals; who will be willing to take orders and play by the rules; who thrive in a structured enviornment. I call them "mules".... If you want to destroy a small company, just hire a mule driver to manage a bunch of racehorses.

> Wilson Harrell
> CEO, Formula 409, Inc.
> *Inc. Magazine*, September 1986

Policies and procedures governing every turn will restrict the growth of managerial judgement.

> James L. Hayes
> President and CEO,
> American Management Association
> *Memos for Management: Leadership*
> (AMACOM, 1983)

To rest upon a formula is a slumber that prolonged, means death.

> Oliver Wendell Holmes, Jr., 1841–1935
> U. S. Supreme Court Justice
> *Ideals and Doubts*

If employees understand the reasons behind the rules and regulations, the chances are excellent that they will respect them.

> Johnson and Johnson Co.
> *The Employee Relations Manual*, 1932

If you're going to play the game properly you'd better know every rule.

> Barbara Jordan
> U. S. Congresswoman
> *Ebony*, February 1975

No important institution is ever merely what the law makes it. It accumulates about itself traditions, conventions, ways of behavior, which ... are not less formidable in their influence.

> Harold J. Laski, 1893–1950
> English political scientist
> *The American Presidency*

When the rules of the game prove unsuitable for victory, the gentlemen of England change the rules of the game.

> Harold J. Laski, 1893–1950
> English political scientist
> Speech to Communist Pary leadership,
> Moscow, July 1934

Important principles may and must be flexible.

> Abraham Lincoln, 1809–1865
> Sixteenth President of the United States
> Last public address, April 11, 1865

[When you are going to break company rules:] Announce what you are going to do but don't wait for permission.

> Bernie Loomis
> Division Manager, General Mills
> Pinchot, *Intrapreneuring*
> (Harper & Row, 1986)

When considering regulations half of what is published is probably 50 percent incorrect. The rest is 75 percent wrong.

> Norman Mailer
> American novelist and criminologist
> Quoted in *Management*, 1987

[Congressman Maverick coined the word "gobbledygook" during World War II, after quoting the following lines written by the head of a government agency:] ... maladjustments co-extensive with problem areas ... alternative but nevertheless meaningful minimae ... utilization of factors which in a dynamic democracy can be channelized into both quantitative phases ...

> Maury Maverick, 1895–1954
> U. S. Congressman
> Brinkley, *Washington Goes to War*
> (Knopf, 1988)

[B]ureaucracy, the rule of no one, has become the modern form of despotism.

> Mary McCarthy
> American writer
> *The New Yorker*, 1958

Much benevolence of the passive order may be traced to a disinclination to inflict pain upon oneself.

> George Meredith, 1828–1909
> English novelist and poet
> *The Ordeal of Richard Feverel*

[Referring to the 20 tons of paper and file cabinets found aboard the Navy's latest frigates:] I find it mind-boggling. We do not shoot paper at the enemy.

> Joseph Metcalf
> Admiral, U. S. Navy
> *Newsweek*, May 1987

Hierarchies remain; our belief in their efficacy does not.

> John Naisbitt
> Chairman, Naisbitt Group
> *Megatrends* (Warner, 1984)

Use your own best judgement at all times.

> Nordstrom Corp.
> Entire contents of $1.9 billion company's
> *Policy Manual*

Everyone gets trapped in routines, but being a good manager of routine business doesn't make you a good manager.

> George S. Odiorne
> University of Massachusetts
> *How Managers Make Things Happen*
> (Prentice-Hall, 1982)

[Owens had asked the Quartermaster for assistance in ridding his office of an ant infestation. He had been told that the Quarter-master could help only if the ants had not come from nests outside the building in which case he should direct his request to Engineering.] It is rather difficult to determine which ant comes from within and which from without ... and this could result in a Quarter-master ant being exterminated by Engineering poison ... and lead to lengthy letters of explanation.

Frank C. Owens
Captain, U. S. Army Medical Corps
World War II memorandum
Brinkley, *Washington Goes to War*
(Knopf, 1988)

[When dealing with organizations:] The first rule, clearly, is to persist.

C. Northcote Parkinson
University of Malaya
The Law and the Profits, 1960

Our customer's paper work is profit. Our own paper work is loss.

John Peers
President, Logical Machine Corp.
1,001 Logical Laws (Doubleday, 1979)

Computers (and other electronic office equipment) seem to confound the problem of [paper] buildup rather than solve it.

Jon Pepper
Computer writer
Working Woman, April 1988

At first, with [Max Weber's] celebration of the efficiency of bureaucracy, he was received with only reluctant respect, and even with hostility. But it turned out, surprisingly, that managers were not. When asked, they acknowledged that they preferred clear lines of communication, clear specifications of authority and responsibility, and clear knowledge of whom they were responsible to.... Gradually, studies began to show that

bureaucratic organizations could change faster than nonbureaucratic ones, and that morale could be higher where there was clear evidence of bureaucracy.

Charles Perrow
Industrial sociologist
Organizational Dynamics, Summer 1973

You won't reduce the paperwork in a lasting fashion until you remove the underlying cause for it—mistrust and adversarial relations.

Tom Peters
Business writer
Thriving on Chaos (Knopf, 1987)

I beg each and every one of you to develop a passionate and public hatred for bureaucracy. Become a nuisance!

Tom Peters
Business writer
Commencement speech, U. S. Navy
Civil Engineer Corps Officer School,
December 1986

Rather than deal with forms, massive rules and regulations, we just slap some dough down, put some sauce on top of it and try to keep the customer happy.

Louis Piancone
Pizza entrepreneur
The Washington Post, April 17, 1988

Everyone does whatever is necessary ... without moaning, "It's not in my job description."

Johna Pierce
Public Affairs Director,
U. S. Human Nutrition Information Service
Management, 1987

To be sure, the promulgation and endorsement of reasonable work and conduct rules governing employees is within the permissible limits of managerial discretion.

> Harry H. Platt
> Labor arbitrator
> Arbitration Decision, *Riley Stoker Corp.*
> 7 LA 764

Practice what you preach.
[*Facias ipse quod faciamus suades.*]

> Plautus, 254–184 B.C.
> Roman playwright and carpenter
> *Asinaria*

Order is Heaven's first law.

> Alexander Pope, 1688–1744
> English poet and translator
> *An Essay on Man*

Large organizations do not automatically signify difficulties for professionals. Some managements, aware of the interest in autonomy among the professional staff, will purposely flatten the organizational hierarchy or decentralize by spinning off divisions which are then allowed to function rather autonomously. They may allow certain professional units to function very independently not only from other operational units but also from top management.

> Joseph A. Raelin
> Boston College School of Management
> *Clash of Cultures: Managers and Professionals*
> (Harvard Business School, 1986)

Bureaucracy is the layer, or layers, of management that lie between the person who has decision-making authority on a project and the highest level person who is working on it full time.

> Herbert Rees
> President, Eastman Technology, Inc.
> *Inc. Magazine*, August 1987

I think one may fairly generalize that a government employee ... is seriously restricted in his freedom of speech with respect to any matter for which he has been assigned responsibility.

> William Rehnquist
> U. S. Supreme Court Justice
> Peters and Branch, *Blowing the Whistle*
> (Praeger, 1972)

We are forced to participate in the games of life before we can possibly learn how to use the options in the rules governing them.

> Philip Reiff
> University of Pennsylvania
> *Freud: The Mind of the Moralist*
> (Doubleday, 1961)

They trashed the rules and found new ways to win.

> Mark B. Roman
> Contributing Editor, *Success*
> *Success*, February 1988

No man is above the law and no man is below it; nor do we ask any man's permission when we require him to obey it.

> Theodore Roosevelt, 1858–1919
> Twenty-sixth President of the United States
> Speech, January 1905

We thumbed our noses at rules and procedures.

> Perry Rosenthal
> Chairman, Polymer Technology
> *Nation's Business*, December 1987

Rules, though unavoidable, always have weaknesses. Particularly so in advertising, where originality is a part of its primary force, and where a violation of "what others do" is often a way of success.

Raymond Rubicam
Founder, Young & Rubicam Advertising
Mandell, *Advertising* (Prentice Hall, 1984)

Those who bow to the man above will always step on the man below.

Dagobert D. Runes
Editor, publisher, and philosopher
A Book of Contemplation

Public bureaucracy breeds private bureaucracy.... The more government expands, the more it stimulates a vast suppoprting apparatus of trade associations, lawyers, lobbyists, research groups, economists, and consultants—all trying to shape the direction of new federal regulations and spending programs.

Paul A. Samuelson
Nobel laureate in economics
The Washington Post, June 6, 1978

[Referring to the fact that the lack of any company policy manuals distresses the lawyers:] So be it.

Betsy Sanders
Vice President, Nordstrom
Peters, *Thriving on Chaos* (Knopf, 1987)

As it becomes bigger, the tendency of a corporation is to create pockets of bureaucracy that love to write memorandums. I'm just not a memo writer. I like to look someone in the eye and say "Let's talk."

Peter L. Scott
Chairman, Emhart Corp.
Sky, August 1, 1987

When I hear any man talk of an unalterable law, the only effect it produces on me is to convince me that he is an unalterable fool.

Sydney Smith, 1771–1845
English clergyman, essayist, and wit
Peter Plymley's Letters

Bad administration ... can destroy good policy; but good administration can never save bad policy.

Adlai Ewing Stevenson, 1900–1968
U. S. Ambassador to the United
Nations and Governor of Illinois
Speech, Los Angeles, September 11, 1952

Bigger organizations spend too much time and overhead on internal communications.

Jim Swiggett
CEO, Kollmorgen Corp.
Inc. Magazine, February 1987

Systems tend to persist and grow.

Melvin J. Sykes
Attorney
Maryland Law Review, 1978

Any fool can make a rule.

Henry David Thoreau, 1817–1862
American naturalist and writer
Journal

Most managers were trained to be the thing they most despise—bureaucrats.

Alvin Toffler
Futurist and writer
Newsweek, April 4, 1988

When information is centralized and controlled, those who have it are extremely influential. Since information is [usually] localized in control subsystems, these subsystems have a great deal of organization influence.

Henry L. Tosi
University of Florida
and Stephen J. Carroll
University of Maryland
Management (John Wiley & Sons, 1976)

If you have to have a policy manual, publish the Ten Commandments.

Robert Townsend
Former CEO, Avis
Further Up the Organization (Knopf, 1984)

It is best to reduce all important rules to writing and make sure that all employees have actual knowledge of them. Merely posting them may not be sufficient.

Maurice S. Trotter
New York University
Supervisor's Handbook on Insubordination
(Bureau of National Affairs, 1967)

Whenever you have an efficient government you have a dictatorship.

Harry S. Truman, 1884–1972
Thirty-third President of the United States
Speech, Columbia University, 1959

We cannot always oblige, but we can always speak obligingly.

François Marie Voltaire, 1694–1778
French philosopher and author
Philosophical Dictionary

We can overcome gravity, but sometimes the paper work is overwhelming.

Werhner Von Braun
Pioneer rocket scientist
Attributed, early 1960's

The wider the inter-departmental consultation on a problem, the less will any agency accept responsibility for the final report.

Editorial
The Washington Star, February 18, 1979

The control system [of General Electrics's then unprofitable appliance business] had become so complex that nobody could make any sense of it. The turnaround began by throwing out the monstrous controls process and simplifying the matrix organization it fed upon.

Robert H. Waterman
Management consultant and writer
The Renewal Factor (Bantam, 1987)

The tedium of the bureaucracy does get to me.

James Webb
Secretary of the Navy
McNeil-Lehrer Report (PBS TV),
February 23, 1988

Things should not be multiplied unnecessarily.
[*Entia non sunt multiplicanda praeter necessitatem.*]

William of Ockham, c. 1300–c. 1349
English philosopher and monk
Quodlibeta

If we devise too elaborate a system of checks and balances, and have too many inspectors going out as representatives of the parent organization, it will be only a matter of time before the self-reliance and initiative of our managers will be destroyed and our organization will be gradually converted into a huge bureaucracy.

Robert E. Wood, 1879–1969
President and Chairman, Sears Roebuck & Co.
Memo to officers and Retail Policy Committee,
October 27, 1938

Managers are being confronted by a *wider range of external pressures* that must be taken into account in their major decisions ... includ[ing] environmental protection, employment opportunities for minorities and all sorts of disadvantaged, shielding the consumer, and conforming to increasing government regulations.

> Boris Yavitz
> Director,
> Federal Reserve Bank of New York
> and William H. Newman
> Columbia University School of Business
> *Strategy in Action* (The Free Press, 1982)

One important function of strategy is to counteract a tendency of professional managers to become too conservative and bureaucratic.

> Boris Yavitz
> Director,
> Federal Reserve Bank of New York
> and William H. Newman
> Columbia University School of Business
> *Strategy in Action* (The Free Press, 1982)

It takes 25 girls behind a typewriter to put one man behind a trigger in this war!

Send your typewriter to war!

An idle typewriter is a help to Hitler!

> World War II clerical recruiting slogans
> Brinkley, *Washington Goes to War*
> (Knopf, 1988)

The proverbial wisdom of the populace in the streets, on the roads, and in the markets, instructs the ear of him who studies man more fully than a thousand rules ostentatiously arranged.

> From title page of anonymous book
> *Proverbs, or the Manual of Wisdom*
> (London, 1804)

Regulation is the substitution of error for chance.

> Anonymous (Washington, D.C.)

In this organization no one signs what he writes or writes what he signs.

> Anonymous (Washington, D.C.)

There's no particular reason for it. It's just company policy.

> Anonymous

The Golden Rule. He who has the gold makes the rules.

> Anonymous

42

Strategic Thinking

Without competitors there would be no need for strategy.

World trade means competition from anywhere; advancing technology encourages cross-industry competition. Consequently, strategic planning must consider who our *future* competitors will be, not only who is here today.

Mary Ann Allison
Vice President, CitiCorp.
and Eric Allison
Financial writer
Managing Up, Managing Down
(Simon & Schuster, 1984)

If you can't beat them, join them.

American political maxim

Sir Walter [Raleigh], being strangely surprised and put out of his countenance at so great a table, gives his son a damned blow over the face. His son, as rude as he was, would not strike his father, but strikes over the face the gentleman that sat next to him and said "Box about: 'twill come to my father anon."

John Aubrey, 1626–1697
English antiquarian
Lives of Eminent Men

Organization is not neutral in its effect upon policy, and those who hold power do not lightly relinquish is.

Stephan K. Bailey
President,
American Society of Public Administration
Agenda For the Nation
(The Brookings Institution, 1968)

I believe in making strategic acquisitions when they lead to better products, lower production and distribution costs and increased sales.... I'm against the takeover artists who buy companies, sell off the pieces, pocket the cash and then walk away.

Karl D. Bays
CEO, IC Industries
Speech, Financial Executives Institute,
Chicago, April 1988

432

It is always good
When a man has two irons in the fire.

> Francis Beaumont, 1584–1616
> and John Fletcher, 1579–1625
> English dramatists
> *The Faithful Friends*

High profits stem largely from superior ex-ecution or forceful opportunism, not structural competitive barriers.

> Amer Bhide
> *Harvard Business Review*,
> September/October 1986

When you sit down to argue out a strategy, you have to stick with it.

> Edward Brennan
> CEO, Montgomery Ward
> *USA Today*, March 9, 1988

High premiums are being paid today not par-ticularly for quality service or long-term building of a business but rather for making money quickly, getting rich, and getting out. And that's wrong.

> Willard C. Butcher
> Chairman, The Chase Manhattan Corp.
> Speech, New Orleans, May 15, 1987

Councillors of state sit plotting and playing their high chess-game whereof the pawns are men.

> Thomas Carlyle, 1795–1881
> Scottish essayist and historian
> *Sartor Resartus*

Never do what you wouldn't have known.

> Chinese proverb

If we open a quarrel between the past and the present, we shall find we have lost the future.

> Winston Churchill, 1874–1965
> English Prime Minister, writer, and soldier
> Speech, House of Commons, 1940

A hopeful disposition is not the sole qualifica-tion to be a prophet.

> Winston Churchill, 1874–1965
> English Prime Minister, writer, and soldier
> Speech in Parliament, April 30, 1927

There's no one grand stroke that does it. It's a lot of little steps.

> Peter A. Cohen
> Chairman, Shearson Lehman Brothers
> *The New York Times*, January 10, 1988

If you design a really great product, then you don't need service and support.

> Deborah A. Coleman
> Vice President and CFO, Apple Computer Co.
> *Working Woman*, December 1987

You need to have enough immediate profits that you can finance the long-range growth without diluting the stock.

> Paul Cook
> CEO, Raychem Corp.
> *Forbes*, November 2, 1987

We must run all hazards, where we think our-selves in a situation to reap some advantage, even from the want of success.

> Cardinal de Retz, 1614–1679
> French ecclesiastic and politician
> *Political Maxims*

Never take anything for granted.

> Benjamin Disraeli, 1804–1881
> English Prime Minister and novelist
> Speech, October 5, 1864

Negative expectation thwarts realization, and self-congratulation guarantees disaster. (Or, simply put: if you think of it, it won't happen quite that way.)

> Michael Donner
> Editor, *Games Magazine*
> *Games Magazine*, September/October 1979

Managers are the basic and scarcest resource of any business enterprise.

> Peter F. Drucker
> Management consultant and writer
> *The Practice of Management*
> (Harper & Row, 1954)

He who attempts too much seldom succeeds.

> Dutch proverb

Good thoughts are no better than good dreams, unless they be executed!

> Ralph Waldo Emerson, 1803–1882
> American essayist and poet
> *Nature*

[W]hen you strike at a king, you must kill him.

> Ralph Waldo Emerson, 1803–1882
> American essayist and poet
> Advice to Oliver Wendell Holmes, Jr.
> *Felix Frankfurter Reminiscences*, 1960

I am better able to retract what I did not say than what I did say.

> Solomon ibn Gabirol, 1021–1069
> Spanish poet and grammarian
> *The Choice of Pearls*

The only salvation ... is for a company to produce several different products, so that when the demand for one goes down, the company can deploy its assets to the products for which there is a demand.

> Harold Geneen
> CEO, IT&T
> *Managing* (Doubleday, 1984)

They [Japanese firms] are big believers in continuity and stability, and don't react to slumps in business.

> Charles Gifford
> Executive Vice President, Noritake, Inc.
> *Gift Reporter,* April 1988

Asking the right questions takes as much skill as giving the right answers.

> Robert Half
> President, Robert Half International
> *Robert Half on Hiring* (Crown, 1985)

Any approach to strategy quickly encounters a conflict between corporate objectives and corporate capabilities. Attempting the impossible is not good strategy; it is just a waste of resources.

> Bruce Henderson
> CEO, Boston Consulting Group, Inc.
> *Henderson on Corporate Strategy* (Abt, 1979)

"Induce your competition not to invest in those products, markets, and services where you expect to invest the most." That is the fundamental rule of strategy.

> Bruce Henderson
> CEO, Boston Consulting Group, Inc.
> *Henderson on Corporate Strategy* (Abt, 1979)

If it isn't bolted down, bring it home.

> Grace Murray Hopper
> Rear Admiral, U. S. Navy (retired)
> Speech, Washington, D.C., February 1987

The trouble ... is that we constantly put second things first.

> Lyndon Baines Johnson, 1908–1973
> Thirty-sixth President of the United States
> Mackenzie, *The Time Trap*
> (McGraw Hill, 1972)

The best way to predict the future is to invent it.

> Alan Kay
> Director of Research, Apple Computer Co.
> Hickman and Silva, *Creating Excellence*
> (New American Library, 1984)

The ideas of economists and political philosophers, both when they are right and when they are wrong, are more powerful than is commonly understood.... Practical men, who believe themselves to be quite exempt from any intellectual influences, are usually the slaves of some defunct economist. Madmen in authority, who hear voices in the air, are distilling their frenzy from some academic scribbler of a few years back.

> John Maynard Keynes, 1883–1946
> English economist, writer, and diplomat
> *The General Theory of Employment, Interest,
> and Money* (Harcourt, Brace, and World, 1936)

I became a good pitcher when I stopped trying to make them miss the ball and started trying to make them hit it.

> Sandy Koufax
> Former professional baseball player
> Koppet, *A Thinking Man's Guide to Baseball*

Peace through stalemate based on a coincident recognition by each side of the opponent's strength is at least preferable to peace through common exhaustion—and has often provided a better foundation for lasting peace.

> Basil Henry Liddell-Hart, 1895–1970
> English military historian and strategist
> *Strategy*

There is no security on this earth; there is only opportunity.

> Douglas MacArthur, 1880–1964
> Five-star General of the U. S. Army
> Whitney, *MacArthur: His Rendezvous
> with History* (Knopf, 1955)

Although it be detestable in every thing to employ fraud, nevertheless in the conduct of war it is praiseworthy and admirable, and he is commended who overcomes the foe by strategem, equally with him who overcomes by force.

> Niccolò Machiavelli, 1469–1527
> Florentine statesman and philosopher
> *Discourses*

I have never seen synergy or cross-selling work.

> David H. Maister
> Management consultant
> *Business Week*, December 21, 1987

Speed has become an important element of strategy.

> Regis McKenna
> Marketing consultant and writer
> *The Regis Touch* (Addison-Wesley, 1986)

Be selective. Keep your mind available for critical information, on which you will be required to act.

> Rosemary McMahon, *et al*
> *On Being in Charge*
> (World Health Organization, 1980)

[S]trategic planning and crisis management are complimentary. They coexist comfortably because both deal with the management of change. Crisis management concentrates on those brief moments of instability that must be dealt with first in order to get on with the larger and less time-sensitive job of reaching strategic objectives.

Gerald C. Meyers
Former chairman, American Motors
When It Hits the Fan (Houghton Mifflin, 1986)

Managing in accordance with a strategic plan is a learned art. The longer you use the tool, the better you are able to manage with it.

R. Henry Miglione
Oral Roberts University
An MBO Approach to Long-Range Planning
(Prentice-Hall, 1983)

A good way to outline a strategy is to ask yourself: "How and where am I going to commit my resources?" Your answer constitutes your strategy.

R. Henry Miglione
Oral Roberts University
An MBO Approach to Long-Range Planning
(Prentice-Hall, 1983)

The success of most things depends upon knowing how long it would take to succeed.

Charles de Secondat Montesquieu, 1689–1755
French lawyer, writer, and philosopher
Pensée

Now and into the 1990s, three powerful trends are transforming the business environment and compelling companies to re-invent themselves ....

1. The shift in strategic resource from financial capital in the industrial society to human capital in the information society.

2. The whittling away of middle management.

3. The labor shortages and coming seller's market of the booming 1980s and 1990s.

John Naisbett and Patricia Aburdene
Business writers & social researchers
Re-inventing the Corporation (Warner, 1985)

One expression of the importance of human capital is the new corporate preoccupation with health and fitness. Corporations are treating their human assets with new concern, encouraging their people to stop smoking, lose weight, exercise, and learn to manage stress. What might have been considered an intrusion into one's personal life in the past is fair game when people are a company's strategic resource.

John Naisbett and Patricia Aburdene
Business writers and social researchers
Re-inventing the Corporation (Warner, 1985)

It is not possible to succeed with a brilliant idea and superb execution of the wrong strategy, but it is possible to attain some success with no idea and a dull execution of the right strategy. This becomes painfully apparent almost every time you turn on your television set.

John O'Tool
Advertising executive
Mandell, *Advertising* (Prentice Hall, 1984)

Coaching subordinates is a business strategy and one of the vital ways a manager makes things happen; not just in this accounting period, but over the long haul.

George S. Odiorne
University of Massachusetts
How Managers Make Things Happen
(Prentice-Hall, 1982)

Without competitors there would be no need for strategy.

Kenichi Ohmae
The Mind of the Strategist
(McGraw-Hill, 1982)

Either do not attempt at all, or go through with it.

> Ovid, 14 B.C.–c. A.D. 17
> Roman poet
> *Ars Amatoria*

Matushita [Electric Company of Japan]'s strategic assumption is that profits are linked to growth and that investments which promote growth will eventually pay off in profits *over the long term.*

> Richard T. Pascale
> Stanford University School of Business
> and Anthony G. Athos
> Harvard Business School
> *The Art of Japanese Management*
> (Simon & Schuster, 1981)

The majority of our strategic successes were ideas that we borrowed from the marketplace, usually from a small regional or local competitor. In each case what we did was spot a promising new idea, improve on it, and then out-execute our competitor.

> Andrew Pearson
> Former President, PepsiCo
> *The Renewal Factor* (Bantam, 1987)

[T]he most important strategic marketing issues ... are the achievement of superior quality ... the attainment of enough corporate flexibility to permit lightning-fast market creation as soon as the slightest opportunity is sensed, the capacity to listen constantly to customers and the constant improvement of every product and procedure that involves the customers.

> Tom Peters
> Business writer
> *Washington Business Journal*,
> October 19, 1987

George W. Plunkitt. He Seen His Opportunities, and He Took 'Em.

> George Washington Plunkitt, 1842–1924
> Tammany Hall leader
> Epitaph

For the part of a consummate general is not only to see the way leading to victory, but also when he must give up all hope of victory.

> Polybius, c. 202–120 B.C.
> Greek historian
> *History*

Always choose the way that seems the best, however rough it may be. Custom will render it easy and agreeable.

> Pythagoras, c. 500 B.C.
> Greek philosopher and mathematician
> Quoted in *Ethical Sentences from Stoboeus*

In today's competitive legal market, a firm needs a marketing strategy, perhaps not to survive but to prosper.

> Sonia Rappaport
> Principal, Rappaport & Associates
> *The Washington Lawyer*,
> January/February 1987

Always assume your opponent to be smarter than you.

> Walther Rathenau, 1867–1922
> CEO, AEG (General Electric of Germany)
> *Reflexionen*, 1908

The best Qualification of a Prophet is to have a good memory.

> George Savile (Lord Halifax), 1633–1695
> English politician and statesman
> *Miscellaneous Thoughts and Reflections*

Fortune turns on her wheel the fate of kings. [*Praecipites regum casus fortuna rotat.*]

Seneca, 4 B.C.–A.D. 65
Roman writer and rhetorician
Agamemnon

Advantage is a better soldier than rashness.

William Shakespeare, 1564–1616
English dramatist and poet
King Henry the Fifth

We will not anticipate the past; so mind, young people,—our retrospection will be all to the future.

Richard Brinsley Sheridan, 1751–1816
Irish dramatist and parliamentary orator
The Rivals

Belief in experts' infallibility is one of the least likely to succeed strategies in the new business world.

Howard H. Stevenson and William A. Sahlman
Harvard Business School
Harvard Business Review, March/April 1988

We have no eternal allies and we have no perpetual enemies. Our interests are eternal and perpetual, and these interests it is our duty to follow.

Henry John Temple
(Lord Palmerston), 1784–1865
English Prime Minsiter
Speech on the Polish Question,
March 1, 1848

If you can't beat 'em, confuse 'em.

Harry S. Truman, 1884–1972
Thirty-third President of the United States
Attributed

The office is a fine place for day to day activity. But it's not the best place for big thinking.

W. E. Uzzell
President, Royal Crown Cola Co.
Mackenzie, *The Time Trap*
(McGraw-Hill, 1972)

War is not as onerous as servitude.

Marquis de Vauvenargues, 1715–1747
French soldier and moralist
Reflections and Maxims

[Successful organizations] comprehend uncertainty. They set direction, not detailed strategy. They are the best strategists precisely because they are suspicious of forecasts and open to surprise. They think strategic planning is great—as long as no one takes the plans too seriously.

Robert H. Waterman
Management consultant and writer
The Renewal Factor (Bantam, 1987)

[B]old objectives require conservative engineering.

James E. Webb
First Administrator of NASA
*Space Age Management:
The Large-Scale Approach* (McGraw Hill, 1969)

He who hesitates is a damn fool.

Mae West, 1892–1980
American actress
Lieberman, *3,500 Good Quotes for Speakers*

[Referring to the growth of Japanese companies in the last 40 years:] To achieve this growth, a short term orientation and dividend policy was bypassed in favor of an environment that supported a long term corporate strategy.

Tamotsu Yamaguchi
Resident Managing Director, Bank of Tokyo
The Academy of Management Executive,
February 1988

[S]trategic change is likely to call for different management techniques than continuous running of well-established business-units.... If effectively done, strategic management can have even greater payoffs in rough seas than in clear sailing.

Boris Yavitz
Director,
Federal Reserve Bank of New York
and William H. Newman
Columbia University School of Business
Strategy in Action (The Free Press, 1982)

Jet travel, photo-phones, television via satellite, electronic computers, worldwide news services all increase the range of factors to be considered and the speed of responses to events everywhere. And they add to the information explosion. One result is that

strategic shifts must be more discerning and more frequent.

Boris Yavitz
Director,
Federal Reserve Bank of New York
and William H. Newman
Columbia University School of Business
Strategy in Action (The Free Press, 1982)

If you can't tell me something about your business I don't already know, you probably aren't going to surprise our competitors either.

Anonymous CEO to division heads
Hickman and Silva, *Creating Excellence*
(New American Library, 1984)

Be careful, but not full of care.

Anonymous

If the journey is long, take only the necessities. This leaves room to acquire luxuries along the way.

Anonymous

43

Stress & Stress Management

Learn calm to face what's pressing.

In business, paranoia is not a psychosis, it's reality; it's probably survival.

Fred Adler
CEO, Adler & Co.
Inc. Magazine, February 1987

It is better to bend than to break.

Aesop, c. 620–c. 560 B.C.
Greek fabulist
The Oak and the Reeds

[Referring to his refusal to attend meetings prior to 8:00 A.M.:] I need some peace and quiet at home.

Bernard Appel
President, Radio Shack
Computer & Software News, December 7, 1987

Whenever you have a tight situation and there's a close pitch, the umpire gets a squawk no matter how he calls it. You wonder why men want to take a job in which they get so much abuse.

Red Barber
Sports announcer and commentator
World Series radio broadcast,
October 6, 1952

It is not work that kills men; it is worry. Work is healthy; you can hardly put more upon a man than he can bear. Worry is rust upon the blade. It is not the revolution that destroys the machinery, but the friction.

Henry Ward Beecher, 1813–1887
American clergyman
Proverbs from Plymouth Pulpit

Anxiety will make a man old before his time.

Apocrypha, Wisdom of Ben Sira 30:24

Lawyers and psychiatrists collect almost as much money from industrial stress cases as do the stressed workers themselves.

> John Blackstone
> Broadcast journalist
> CBS news, December 25, 1987

It is in times of difficulty that great nations, like great men, display the whole energy of their character and become an object of admiration to posterity.

> Napoleon Bonaparte, 1769–1821
> Emperor of France
> *Maxims*

I started my company more than a year ago. Company growth has been incredible. But with it came lots of headaches and problems, chief of which was my impending burnout.

> Leo H. Bradman
> Executive Director,
> Bradman Therapy Centers, Inc.
> *Inc. Magazine*, February 1988

People react defensively to situations in which they feel both threatened and under pressure. The threat is usually not physical.... In the workaday world, the blows we receive most frequently are psychological, and the deepest wounds we get from them are to our motivation and our feelings of self-worth.

> Robert M. Bramson
> Psychologist and management consultant
> *Coping With Difficult People*
> (Anchor Press/Doubleday, 1981)

Humor is just another defense against the universe.

> Mel Brooks
> Comedian, writer, and director
> Rowes, *The Book of Quotes* (Dutton, 1979)

The trouble with Archie is, he don't know how to worry without getting upset.

> Edith Bunker
> Television sitcom character, 1970's
> *All in the Family*

No passion so effectually robs the mind of all its power of acting and reasoning as fear.

> Edmund Burke, 1729–1797
> English statesman, orator, and writer
> *On the Sublime and Beautiful*

Melancholy [clinical depression] ... this thunder and lightening of perturbation ... disturbing the soul, and all the faculties of it ... with fear, sorrow, &c. which are the ordinary symptoms of this disease.

> Robert Burton, 1577–1640
> Vicar of St. Thomas's, Oxford
> *The Anatomy of Melancholy*

Leaders make mistakes when they're too tired and overwhelmed with paper.

> James Callaghan
> English Prime Minister
> *Harvard Business Review,*
> November/December 1986

In my position you have to read when you want to write and to talk when you would like to read; you have to laugh when you feel like crying; twenty things interfere with twenty others; you have not time for a moment's thought, and nevertheless you have to be constantly ready to act without allowing yourself to feel lassitude, either body or spirit; ill or well, it makes no difference, everything at once demands that you should attend to it on the spot.

> Catherine II ("The Great"), 1729–1796
> Empress of Russia
> *Correspondence avec le Baron F. M. Grimm*

Many remedies are suggested for the avoidance of worry and mental overstrain by persons who, over prolonged periods, have to bear exceptional responsibilities and discharge duties upon a very large scale. Some advise exercise, and others, repose. Some counsel travel, and others, retreat. Some praise solitude, and others, gaiety. No doubt all these may play their part according to the individual temperament. But the element which is constant and common in all of them is Change.

Winston Churchill, 1874–1965
English Prime Minister, writer, and soldier
Painting as a Pastime

I don't have ulcers; I give them.

Harry Cohen, 1891–1958
American film producer
Ringo, *Nobody Said It Better*
(Rand McNally, 1980)

Human nature decrees that every business executive shall believe his business to be surrounded by more difficulties and intricacies than could possibly exist in any other enterprise.

Howard Coonley
Harvard Business Review,
September/October 1987

Worry is a form of fear. It is a realization of inadequacy, which in turn is the byproduct lack of time to think through confidently to sound objectives and good plans.... The vicious spiral of worry and the emotional strains [produced thereby] ... can only end in physical disaster.

Ralph J. Cordiner
President, General Electric Co.
Professional Management in General Electric
(General Electric Company, 1954)

Every man has his measure, and any overstraining of them is unsound business.

Massimo Taparelli D'Azeglio, 1798–1866
Italian statesman and author
I Miei Ricordi

You can have the best systems in the world, but if your people aren't fresh, if they're burned out, it won't matter. They won't provide the kind of service that customers expect.

Bob Daniels
Owner, Copperfield Chimney Supply, Inc.
Inc. Magazine, November 1987

For me, it [a particular policy] offered ... the strain of an onerous responsibility. But what else was I there for?

Charles De Gaulle, 1890–1970
Military leader and President of France
Memoirs of Hope (Simon & Schuster, 1970)

As a cure for worrying, work is better than whiskey.

Thomas Alva Edison, 1847–1931
American inventor
Radio interview, 1931

Don't ever become a general. If you become a general, you just plain have too much to worry about.

Dwight David Eisenhower, 1890–1969
Thirty-fourth President of the United States
Prochnow, *The Toastmaster's Treasure Chest*
(Harper & Row, 1979)

Things are in the saddle,
And ride mankind.

Ralph Waldo Emerson, 1803–1882
American essayist and poet
Ode (inscribed to W. H. Channing)

Let not the sun go down upon thy wrath.

New Testament, Book of Ephesians 4:26

No man is free who is not master of himself.

Epictetus, c. 60–120
Roman Stoic philosopher
Encheiridon

Next day, Moses sat as a magistrate among the people, while the people stood about Moses from morning until evening. But when Moses' father-in-law [Jethro] saw how much he had to do for the people, he said, ... "Why do you act alone?.... The thing you are doing is not right; you will surely wear yourself out, you as well as this people. For the task is too heavy for you; you cannot do it alone. Now listen to me.... Seek out among all the people capable men who fear God, trustworthy men who spurn ill-gotten gain; and set these over them as chiefs of thousands, hundreds, fifties and tens. Let them exercise authority over the people at all times; let them bring every major dispute to you, but decide every minor dispute themselves. Make it easier for yourself, and let them share the burden with you. If you do this—and God so commands you—you will be able to bear up, and all these people will go home content.

Old Testament, Exodus 18:13-23

Time deals gently only with those who take it gently.

Anatole France, 1844–1944
French writer
The Crime of Sylvestre Bonnard

Drive thy business; let it not drive thee.

Benjamin Franklin, 1706–1790
American printer and statesman
Poor Richard's Almanack

[Responding to the question of whether he has ever had a nervous breakdown:] No, but I'm a carrier.

Fred Friendly
President, CBS News
Quoted by Bennis, University of Maryland
symposium, January 21, 1988

Recreation is a second creation, when weariness hath almost annihilated one's spirits. It is the breathing of the soul, which otherwise would be stifled with continual business.

Thomas Fuller, 1608–1661
Chaplain in extraordinary to Charles II
Holy and Profane States

The worst disease which can afflict ... executives in their work is not, as popularly supposed, alcoholism; it's egotism.

Harold Geneen
CEO, IT&T
Managing (Doubleday, 1984)

[Referring to the firm's founder, Sam Walton:] Sam's only hobby besides bird hunting is working.

David D. Glass
CEO, Wal-Mart
Business Week, February 15, 1988

Every manager knows the problem of battling the daily, even hourly, barrage of operating data that assaults his mind. The realization that I could not track every detail of my business came as my days got longer, my nights got shorter, and my leaden briefcase seemed increasingly likely to unhinge my right shoulder.

Axel L. Grabowsky
CEO, Harte & Co.
*Inc. Magazine's Guide to
Small Business Success*, 1987

The worst situation is when the boss says one thing and does another. The employee then has to decide whether to follow the explicitly stated rules of the workplace or to emulate the boss — with the two choices contradictory! This poses a real no-win situation and puts the worst kind of stress on the employee, one from which he or she should escape as soon as possible.

> Andrew S. Grove
> CEO, Intel Corporation
> *One-On-One With Andy Grove*
> (G. P. Putnam's Sons, 1987)

Burnout is one of the costliest factors.... We're beating guys up so hard for results, that all the human resource guidelines just go to hell in a handbasket.

> Robert Guerra
> Executive, Federal Data Systems
> *Computer & Software News*, November 9, 1987

Cheerfulness is health; the opposite, melancholy, is disease.

> Thomas Chandler Haliburton, 1796–1865
> Canadian jurist and humorist
> *Sam Slick's Wise Saws*

The world breaks everyone, and afterward many are strong at the broken places.

> Ernest Hemingway, 1899–1961
> American novelist
> *A Farewell to Arms*

Executive stress is difficult to overstate when there is a conflict among policy restrictions, near-term performance, long-term good of the company, and personal survival.

> Bruce Henderson
> CEO, Boston Consulting Group, Inc.
> *Henderson on Corporate Strategy* (Abt, 1979)

Those who are skilled in archery bend their bow only when they are preparing to use it; when they do not require it, they allow it to remain unbent, for otherwise it would be unserviceable when the time for using it arrived. So it is with man. If he were to devote himself unceasingly to a dull round of business, without breaking the monotony by cheerful amusements, he would fall imperceptibly into idiocy, or be struck by paralysis. It is the conviction of this truth that leads to the proper division of my time.

> Herodotus, fifth century B.C.
> Greek "Father of History"
> *History of the Persian War*

[Responding to a reporter's observation that his team looked very tired and stressed out after a losing playoff effort:] If they had won, they wouldn't look so tired and stressed.

> Nat "Red" Holtzman
> Professional basketball coach
> *Madison Square Garden Productions*
> (TV program), 1969

Anger is momentary madness, so control your passion or it will control you.

> Horace, 65–8 B.C.
> Roman poet and satirist
> *Epistles*

Learn calm to face what's pressing.

> Horace, 65–8 B.C.
> Roman poet and satirist
> *Odes*

The average human being can deal with just about anything except uncertainty.

> Robert B. Horton
> CEO, British Petroleum America
> *The New York Times*, January 10, 1988

It is better to lose the saddle than the horse.

> Italian proverb

When I hear a man talk about how hard he works, and how he hasn't taken a vacation in five years, and how seldom he sees his family I am certain that this man will not succeed in the creative aspects of business ... and most of the important things that have to be done are the result of creative acts.

Herman C. Krannert
Chairman, Inland Container Corp.
The Forum, Spring 1969

Sure I'm nervous. But I've been nervous for 15 years.

Jeffrey Lane
President, Shearson Lehmann Brothers
Business Week, December 21, 1987

There is an old proverb about the pace that kills.... Sir Harry was killing himself by work at high pressure.

Stanley Edward Lane-Poole, 1854–1931
English Orientalist and archaeologist
Sir Harry Parkes in China

Illegitimi non carborundum.
[Don't let the bastards wear you down.]

Latin proverb

He who has lost his head has many headaches.

Stanislaw J. Lec
Polish writer and aphorist
Unkempt Thoughts (St. Martin's Press, 1962)

The moment you stop working, you are dead.

Rita Levi-Montalcini
Nobel laureate in physiology
and medicine (Italy)
Omni, March 1988

Haste is self-defeating because of the anxieties it creates. There is no substitute for ample time to enable the members of an or-

ganization to reach the level of skillful and easy, habitual use of the new leadership.

Rensis Likert
University of Michigan
New Patterns of Management
(McGraw-Hill, 1961)

Being away from the office is very therapeutic.

Royal Little
Founder, Textron
Best of Business Quarterly, 1987

The Nature of twentieth-century man is anxiety.

Norman Mailer
American novelist and criminologist
Prochnow, *The Toastmaster's Treasure Chest*
(Harper & Row, 1979)

Just as the body becomes exhausted by hard labor and is reinvigorated by rest, so the mind needs its weariness relieved by rest.

Moses Maimonides, 1135–1204
Egyptian physician and philosopher
The Eight Chapters on Ethics

If someone insults you,
Endure him lightheartedly;
And if all slander you,
Give no heed to them:
'Tis nothing new
To hear such frequent talk:
It will all vanish into thin air
[*Autant en emporte le vent*].

Margaret of Anjoulême, 1492–1549
Queen of Navarre
Heptameron

445

[In scientific research:] The pressure to produce results and publish data before competitors take the lead makes for a manic world.

> Laurence A. Marshall
> Gettysburg College
> *The Sciences*, November/December 1987

I enjoy not having to work for somebody else. An outside investor would give me a lot of stress.

> Patricia De. L. Marvil
> CEO, Securigard, Inc.
> *Hispanic Business,* June 1987

Constant labor of one uniform kind destroys the intensity and flow of a man's animal spirits, which find recreation and delight in mere change of activity.

> Karl Marx, 1818–1833
> German political philosopher
> *Capital*

Some people respond to stress by becoming compulsive workaholics. The "workaholic" is a person who is trying to improve his or her importance. The workaholic is running very hard to avoid failure. You can examine your workaholic tendencies by answering the following questions:

Do you take work home with you regularly?

Do you accept phone calls even when trying to complete an important job or when you are taking a break?

Do you fear delegating important work to others?

Do you have a cluttered, disorganized work area?

Are you reluctant to take vacations because you fear that things will go wrong at work?

> Michael T. Matteson and John M. Ivanovitch
> University of Houston
> *Managing Job Stress and Health*
> (The Free Press, 1982)

Hard work never killed anybody, but why take a chance?

> Charlie McCarthy (Edgar Bergen), 1903–1978
> Radio personality & ventriloquist
> Frequent line

There's a burnout problem among programmers just as there is in any group. You can't expect a programmer to sit for weeks, months, years, doing the same type of programming, and not slack off.... Preventing stagnation is the manager's job.... Get them totally away from their current jobs.

> Philip W. Metzger
> Computer analyst and management writer
> *Managing Programming People*
> (Prentice-Hall, 1987)

Just as the body can be trained to tolerate psysiological stress, so presumably can the mind be trained to tolerate psychological stress.

> Henry Mintzberg
> McGill University School of Management
> *The Nature of Managerial Work*
> (Harper & Row, 1973)

[Burnout] is one of the greatest dangers facing us. If you lose your sense of humor and the ability to step back, you will go nuts.

> Sam Missimer
> Vice President, Clancy-Paul Associates
> *Computer & Software News*, April 17, 1987

I endeavor ... to be wise when I cannot be merry, easy when I cannot be glad, content with what cannot be memded and patient when there is no redress.

Elizabeth Montagu, 1720–1800
English essayist
The Letters of Mrs. Elizabeth Montagu

Life is easier to take than you'd think; all that is necessary is to accept the impossible, do without the indispensable and bear the intolerable.

Kathleen Norris, 1880–1966
American writer
Prochnow, *The Toastmaster's Treasure Chest*
(Harper & Row, 1979)

If a man cannot find ease in himself, it is vain to seek elsewhere.

Old Farmer's Almanac (1836)

A police agency's reaction to personal stress is critical to success or failure of the entire police mission.

Don Omodt
President, National Sheriffs' Association
The National Sheriff, October/November 1986

Razors pain you;
Rivers are damp;
Acids stain you;
And drugs cause cramp.
Guns aren't lawful;
Nooses give;
Gas smells awful;
You might as well live.

Dorothy Parker, 1893–1967
American writer and poet
Résumé

One of the most reliable findings of behavioral science is that persons who are in failure situations experience heightened tension and anxiety and are most likely to revert to past success behavior.... Organizations that

provoke fear tend to exacerbate these tendencies.

Richard T. Pascale
Stanford University School of Business
and Anthony G. Athos
Harvard Business School
The Art of Japanese Management
(Simon & Schuster, 1981)

The attention of senior management is being stolen by combat for survival.... Top managment is suffering a work-place equivalent of post-traumatic stress disorder. It believes it must focus its full attention in the financial, legal and defensive manipulation areas or it'll lose the rest of the game.

Mark Pasten
Arizona State University
The Washington Post, January 5, 1988

All work and no play means you make money hand over fist.

John Peers
President, Logical Machine Corp.
1,001 Logical Laws (Doubleday, 1979)

It is therefore as great an Instance of Wisdom as a Man in Business can give, to be *Patient under the Impertinencies and Contradictions that attend it.*

William Penn, 1644–1718
Founder of Pennsylvania
Fruits of Solitude in Reflections and Maxims

You can't take yourself too seriously. You should try to have fun.

Pete Peterson
Executive Vice President, WordPerfect
Computer & Software News, 1987

We human beings are resilient. We can handle a lot without falling apart. In fact, that's the positive function of our stress reaction. It helps us to rise to the occasion and get ourselves safely through even the roughest times—at least temporarily. Stress exhaustion and the debilitating effects of stress are usually the result of a high-risk life style, lived month after month, year after year. It is the long-term drain that wears us out, not the one "bad" month or even one "bad" year. No one stressor defeats us.

Marty Pipp
Program Specialist, University Research Corp.
New URC Times, January 1988

Good fortune will elevate even petty minds, and give them the appearance of a certain greatness and stateliness, as from their high place they look down upon the world; but the truly noble and resolved spirit raises itself, and becomes more conspicuous in times of disaster and ill fortune.

Plutarch, c. 46–c. 120
Greek biographer and philosopher
The Parallel Lives: Eumenes

We are confronted with insurmountable opportunities.

Pogo

Know, all the good that individuals find,
Or God and Nature meant to mere Mankind,
Reason's whole pleasured, all the joys of Sense,
Lie in three words, Health, Peace, Competence.

Alexander Pope, 1688–1744
English poet
An Essay on Man

Anyone can hold the helm when the sea is calm.

Publilius Syrus, c. 42 B.C.
Roman writer
Maxims

How happy the life unembarrassed by the cares of business.

Publilius Syrus, c. 42 B.C.
Roman writer
Maxims

I have a great objection to seeing anyone, particularly anyone whom I care about, lose his self-control.

Eleanor Roosevelt, 1884–1962
American statesman and humanitarian
My Day, February 3, 1958

Twenty-five years ago, we had more intermittent stress. We had a chance to bounce back before we encountered another crisis. Today, we have chronic, unremitting stress.

Geneva Rowe
Psychotherapist
Newsweek, April 25, 1988

All violent feelings ... produce in us a falseness in all our impressions of external things.

John Ruskin, 1819–1900
English art critic and historian
Modern Painters

In the old reality the expression "a new broom sweeps clean" frequently was a relevant descriptive term for what happens when new leadership came into an organization.... In the new reality "a new broom is soon worn out."

Lyle E. Schaller
Yokefellow Institute
The Change Agent (Abingdon, 1972)

A company in trouble is like an army fighting a losing battle. The grandest plans of its generals have been abandoned, bravery turns to panic, and the organization crumbles as the casualties mount.

> Charles Scott
> CEO, Intermark
> *Inc. Magazine Guide to*
> *Small Business Success*, 1987

The frequent habit of late hours is always detrimental to health, and sometimes has consequences which last for life.

> Walter Scott, 1771–1832
> Scottish poet, novelist, and biographer
> Lockhart, *Life of Sir Walter Scott*

The cheerfulness and the joy that come from one's own nature are not easily affected by external matters.

> Magdeleine de Scudéry, 1607–1701
> French poet, novelist, and *salon* leader
> *Ibrahim or the Illustrious Bassa*

Nature likes variety. Remember this, not only in planning your day, but in planning your life. Our civilization tends to force people into highly specialized occupations which may become monotonously repetitive. Remember that stress is the great equalizer of biologic activities and if you use the same parts of your body or mind over and over again, the only means Nature has to force you out of the groove is general (systemic) stress.

> Hans Selye
> University of Montreal
> *The Stress of Life* (McGraw-Hill, 1976)

What fates inmpose, that men must needs abide,
It boots not to resist both wind and tide.

> William Shakespeare, 1564–1616
> English dramatist and poet
> *Henry the Fourth*

He that is proud eats up himself.

> William Shakespeare, 1564–1616
> English dramatist and poet
> *Troilus and Cressida*

White collar workers and, to a far greater extent, middle managers suffer fear rather than boredom; and the diseases of stress have more than replaced the dangers of working with heavy equipment or toxic chemicals.

> Earl Shorris
> Manager and writer
> *The Oppressed Middle*
> (Anchor/Doubleday, 1981)

He whose honor depends on the opinion of the mob must day by day strive with the greatest anxiety, act and scheme in order to retain his reputation.

> Benedict Spinoza, 1632–1677
> Dutch philosopher and oculist
> *Ethics*

Hasten slowly.
[*Festina lente.*]

> Suetonius, c. 120
> Roman biographer and historian
> *Lives of the Caesars: Divas Augustus*

When the mind is in a state of uncertainty the smallest impulse directs it to either side.

> Terence, 185–159 B.C.
> Roman playwright
> *Andria*

If you can't stand the heat, stay out of the kitchen.

> Harry S. Truman, 1884–1972
> Thirty-third President of the United States
> *Mr. Citizen*

Courage has more resources against misfortune than has reason.

> Marquis de Vauvenargues, 1715–1747
> French soldier and moralist
> *Reflections and Maxims*

He who can endure all things may venture all things.

> Marquis de Vauvenargues, 1715–1747
> French soldier and moralist
> *Reflections and Maxims*

For me, walking the tightrope is living. Everything else is waiting.

> Carl Wallenda
> Tightrope walker
> Quoted by Bennis, January 21, 1988

If you do things by the job, you are perpetually driven; the hours are scourges. If you work by the hour, you gently sail on a stream of Time, which is always bearing you on to the heaven of Pay, whether you make any effort or not.

> Charles Dudley Warner, 1829–1903
> American editor and writer
> *My Summer in a Garden*

All of our senior executives, including me, knew what it felt like to be thrown into deep water not knowing if you could swim.

> Thomas J. Watson, Jr.
> CEO, IBM, and U. S. Ambassador to Russia
> *Fortune*, 1977

There is no refuge from confession but suicide; and suicide is confession.

> Daniel Webster, 1782–1846
> American statesman and orator
> *Argument on the murder of Captain White*

Out of the strain of the doing,
Into the peace of the done.

> Julia Louise Matilda Woodruff, 1833–1909
> English Poet
> *Gone*

I've been working 15 or 16 hours a day trying to shorten working hours.

> Toshio Yamaguchi
> Japanese Labor Minister
> *Management*, 1987

Your health comes first—you can always hang yourself later.

> Yiddish proverb

New Moon was no longer a mom and pop operation and Mom and Pop were getting stretched a little thin.

> Michael Young and Randi Freundlich Young
> Founders, New Moon, Inc.
> *Inc. Magazine*, November 1987

In the production organization, stress occurs as physical fatigue from boredom, monotony, and exertion. The production organization uses workers' muscles and ignores their minds.... In the knowledge organization stress occurs as mental and emotional fatigue from excessive variety in tasks, constantly changing relationships, and demand for unrelenting alertness and concentration. The [knowledge] organization uses the manager's and the specialist's minds and ignores their muscles.

> Dale E. Zand
> New York University
> *Information, Organization, and Power*
> (McGraw-Hill, 1981)

[Reporting on a survey of the effects of downsizing:] Managers perceived as stressed and under more pressure to produce ... are perceived as being more concerned with the well-being of their employees.

Ron Zemke
President, Performance Research Associates
Training, November 1986

Anger is an acid that can do more harm to the vessel in which it's stored than to anything on which it's poured.

Anonymous
How to Live With Life
(Reader's Digest, 1965)

44

Supervision

Eyes are more exact witnesses than ears.

First and foremost as a manager or supervisor ... your job is to get things done through other people.... You are paid to manage, not perform every task.

> Mary Ann Allison
> Vice President, CitiCorp.
> and Eric Allison
> Financial writer
> *Managing Up, Managing Down*
> (Simon & Schuster, 1984)

Men might be better if we better deemed
Of them.
The worst way to improve the world
Is to condemn it.

> Philip James Bailey, 1816–1902
> English poet
> *A Mountain Sunrise*

Suspicion is far more apt to be wrong than right; oftener unjust than just. It is no friend to virtue, and always an enemy to happiness.

> Hosea Ballou, 1771–1852
> American clergyman
> *Universalist Expositor*

Most bosses know instinctively that their power depends more on employees' compliance than on threats or sanctions.

> Fernando Bartolome
> Bentley College
> and Andre Laurent
> Institute of Business Administration,
> Fontainebleau, France
> *Harvard Business Review*,
> November/December 1986

We do not expect you to follow us all the time, but if you would have the goodness to keep in touch with us occasionally ...

> Thomas Beecham
> Conductor, The London Philharmonic Orchestra
> Quoted by David Lipsey, Manager of Sales,
> Data Sciences, Inc., June 2, 1988

Don't over-react to the trouble makers.

> Warren G. Bennis
> President, University of Cincinnati
> University of Maryland symposium,
> January 21, 1988

Feedback is the breakfast of champions.

> Kenneth H. Blanchard
> Chairman, Blanchard Training & Development
> and Robert Lorber
> President, R. L. Lorber & Associates
> *Putting the One Minute Manager to Work*
> (William Morrow, 1984)

As a manager the important thing is not what happens when you are there, but what happens when you are not there.

> Kenneth H. Blanchard
> Chairman, Blanchard Training & Development
> and Robert Lorber
> President, R. L. Lorber & Associates
> *Putting the One Minute Manager to Work*
> (William Morrow, 1984)

A man is known by his conduct to his wife, to his family, and to those under him.

> Napoleon Bonaparte, 1769–1821
> Emperor of France
> *Maxims*

Most managers are reluctant to comment on ineffective or inappropriate interpersonal behavior. But these areas are often crucial for professional task success. This hesitancy is doubly felt when there is a poor relationship between the two.... Too few managers have any experience in how to confront others effectively; generally they can more easily give feedback on inadequate task performance than on issues dealing with another's personal style.

> David L. Bradford
> Stanford University School of Business
> and Allan R. Cohen
> Babson College
> *Managing for Excellence* (Wiley, 1984)

You and I know that there is a correlation between the creative and the screwball. So we must suffer the screwball gladly.

> Kingman Brewster, Jr.
> President, Yale University
> Speech, Hartford, Connecticut, 1964

Most managers cannot resist the temptation to exercise their authority over [technical] processes.

> Bill Brickley
> The Type Works/Star Maker Machine Works
> *Personal Computing,* March 1988

Any fool can write a bad ad—but it takes a real genius to keep his hands off a good one.

> Leo Burnett
> Advertising executive
> Mandell, *Advertising* (Prentice-Hall, 1984)

A good manager is a man who isn't worried about his own career but rather the careers of those who work for him.

> H. M. S. Burns
> President, Shell Oil Co.
> Elliott, *Men at the Top*
> (Harper & Row, 1959)

Authority intoxicates.

> Samuel Butler, 1612–1680
> English poet
> *Miscellaneous Thoughts*

Why kick the man downstream who can't put the parts together because the parts really weren't designed properly?

> Philip Caldwell
> Former CEO, Ford Motor Co.
> *Sky,* August 1, 1984

When they [managers] can't manage because of too much oversight, it permeates the entire organization.

Frank C. Carlucci
U. S. National Security Advisor
Frank Carlucci on Management in Government
(Center for Excellence in Government, 1987)

Problems are solved on the spot, as soon as they arise. No frontline employee has to wait for a supervisor's permission.

Jan Carlzon
CEO, SAS (Sweden)
Moments of Truth (Ballinger, 1987)

There's no substitute for personal contact.... People want to be recognized as people.

Patricia M. Carrigan
Plant Manager, General Motors Corp.
MTS Digest, April/June 1987

Be a pattern to others and then all will go well.

Cicero, 106–43 B.C.
Roman orator and statesman
Works

Busy supervisors will not do things [additional activities like training follow-up] without a push.

Ruth Colvin Clark
Manager, Training and Information Services,
California Edison Co.
Training, November 1986

Men are born with two eyes, but with one tongue, in order that they should see twice as much as they say.

Charles Caleb Colton, c. 1780–1832
English cleric, sportsman, and wine merchant
Lacon

You [the new supervisor] will need to be fully aware of your dependence on your boss and on the employees working under your supervision, as well as the good will and support of other supervisors at your level.

William F. Cone
Manager of Professional Development,
Hughes Aircraft
Supervising Employees Effectively
(Addison-Wesley, 1974)

While you may rightfully feel a human concern for the employee and his welfare, your primary concern is the employee's effectiveness at work.

William F. Cone
Manager of Professional Development,
Hughes Aircraft
Supervising Employees Effectively
(Addison-Wesley, 1974)

The superior man seeks to perfect the admirable qualities of [other] men, and does not seek to mention their bad qualities.

Confucius, c. 551–c. 479 B.C.
Chinese philosopher and teacher
Analects

A master sees more than four servants.

Danish proverb

Rather than allowing them [subordinates] the autonomy to get involved and do the work in their own ways, what happens all too often is the manager wants the workers to do it the manager's way.

Edward L. Deci
University of Rochester
Nation's Business, March 1988

Take nothing on its looks; take everything on evidence. There's no better rule.

Charles Dickens, 1812–1870
English novelist
Great Expectations

It is much easier to be critical than to be correct.

> Benjamin Disraeli, 1804–1881
> English Prime Minister and novelist
> Speech, January 24, 1860

Little things affect little minds.

> Benjamin Disraeli, 1804–1881
> English Prime Minister and novelist
> *Sybil*

The mature woman ... after having raised her children has been a "chief executive officer" at home for ten years or more. No one told her whether to dust first or make the beds first—and both chores got done. Yet when she starts working, she is put under a "supervisor" who treats her as a moron who has never done anything on her own before when what she needs is a teacher and an assistant.

> Peter F. Drucker
> Management consultant and writer
> *Management in Turbulent Times*
> (Harper & Row, 1980)

It makes little sense to subject all employees to training programs, to personnel policies, and to supervision designed for one group of employees, and in particular designed, as so many of the policies are, for yesterday's typical entrant into the labor force—the fifteen or sixteen year old without any experience. More and more we will have to have personnel policies that fit the person rather than bureaucratic convenience or tradition.

> Peter F. Drucker
> Management consultant and writer
> *Management in Turbulent Times*
> (Harper & Row, 1980)

In order for me to look good, everybody around me has to look good.

> Doris Drury
> Chair, Federal Reserve Bank, Kansas City
> *Frontier*, June 1984

That man may err was never yet denied.

> John Dryden, 1631–1700
> English poet
> *The Hind and the Panther*

What loneliness is more lonely than distrust?

> George Eliot (Marion Evans), 1819–1880
> English novelist, essayist, and editor
> *Middlemarch*

A foolish consistency is the hobgoblin of little minds, adored by little statesmen and philosophers and divines.

> Ralph Waldo Emerson, 1803–1882
> American essayist and poet
> *Self-Reliance*

The hearing ear is always found close to the speaking tongue.

> Ralph Waldo Emerson, 1803–1882
> American essayist and poet
> *English Traits*

The eagle does not catch flies.
[*Aquila non captat muscas.*]

> Desiderius Erasmus, c. 1466–1536
> Dutch scholar and theologian
> *Adages*

Their [your subordinates'] jobs are just as important to them as yours is to you. Each employee looks to you to help him obtain the income, security, standing and opportunity he wants to earn through his work.

> Waldo E. Fisher
> The Wharton School
> *Employee Appraisal:*
> *What the Supervisor Should Know*
> (California Institute of Technology, 1957)

To be effective, a manager must accept a decreasing degree of direct control.

> Eric G. Flamholtz
> University of California at Los Angeles
> and Yvonne Randal
> Consultant, Management Systems Consulting
> *The Inner Game of Management*
> (AMACOM, 1987)

Give up control even if it means the employees have to make some mistakes.

> Frank Flores
> CEO, Marsden Reproductions
> *Hispanic Business,* June 1987

It thou art be a master, be sometimes blind; if a servant, sometimes deaf.

> Thomas Fuller, 1608–1661
> Chaplain in extraordinary to Charles II
> *Gnomologia*

The lowest morale in the plant was found among those men whose supervisors were rated *between* the democratic and authoritarian extremes.... [T]hese foremen may have varied inconsistently in their tactics, permissive at one moment and hardfisted the next, in a way that left their men frustrated and unable to anticipate how they would be treated.

> Saul W. Gellerman
> University of Dallas School of Management
> *Motivation and Productivity*
> (AMACOM, 1963)

Managers in all too many American companies do not achieve the desired results because nobody makes them do it.

> Harold Geneen
> CEO, IT&T
> *Managing* (Doubleday, 1984)

A programmer or analyst can only perform to the best abilities of the manager.

> Fred A. Gluckson
> Advanced Systems, Inc.
> Rullo, *Advances in Computer Programming Management* (Heyden, 1980)

Once standing rules have been installed, there are fewer things that a supervisor has to direct a worker to do; thus the frequency of worker-foreman interaction is somewhat lessened.

> Alvin W. Gouldner
> Columbia University School of Business
> *Patterns of Industrial Bureaucracy*
> (The Free Press, 1954)

By a strange paradox, *formal* rules gave supervisors something with which they could "bargain" in order to secure *informal* cooperation from workers.

> Alvin W. Gouldner
> Columbia University School of Business
> *Patterns of Industrial Bureaucracy*
> (The Free Press, 1954)

Many know how to flatter; few understand how to give praise.

> Greek proverb

The technical supervisor faces an almost unique problem, how to divide his all too precious time between technical and administrative work.

> Estill I. Green
> Vice President, Bell Telephone Laboratories
> *Effective Administration of Research Programs*
> (Cornell University Press, 1958)

Even the frankest and bravest of subordinates do not talk with their boss the same way they talk with colleagues.

Robert Greanleaf
Director of Management Research, AT&T
Servant Leadership: A Journey into the Nature of Legitimate Power and Greatness
(Paulist Press, 1977)

[Y]our job [as a supervisor or manager] is not to *criticize* your employees but to *critique* their work.

Andrew S. Grove
CEO, Intel Corp.
One-On-One With Andy Grove
(G. P. Putnam's Sons, 1987)

There is an especially efficient way to get information, much neglected by most managers. That is to visit a particular place in the company and observe what's going on there.

Andrew S. Grove
CEO, Intel Corp.
High Output Management
(Random House, 1983)

Bricks and mortar don't need explanations. Capital equipment never asks why. But people do, and people need answers.

John Guaspari
Management writer
Management, March 1987

The dog that trots about finds a bone.

Gypsy proverb

All employees ... deserve to be treated as responsible adults, if that is the behavior we expect of them.

Eric Harvey
Executive Director,
Performance Systems Corp.
Management Review, March 1987

Eyes are more exact witnesses than ears.

Heraclitus, 535?–475? B.C.
Greek philosopher
Fragments

Benefits please like flowers when they are fresh.

George Herbert, 1593–1633
English clergyman and poet
Jacula Prudentum

A good judge conceives quickly, judges slowly.

George Herbert, 1593–1633
English clergyman and poet
Jacula Prudentum

Who must account for himself and others, must know both.

George Herbert, 1593–1633
English clergyman and poet
Jacula Prudentum

When you have a supervisor checking a man on a job, he's not a supervisor. He's a checker.

Frederick Herzberg
University of Utah
The Managerial Choice
(Dow Jones-Irwin, 1976)

When a subordinate does only what he is told to do, that employee's effectiveness is likely to be low, because the boss can't possibly tell him everything.

Harold S. Hook
Chairman and CEO, American General Corp.
Forbes, October 19, 1987

Tomato plant problem: Don't overload an individual with duties. Based on the maxim

"Don't plant more tomato plants than you can carry water to."

Harold S. Hook
Chairman and CEO, American General Corp.
Forbes, October 19, 1987

Ridicule often decides matters of importance more effectually, and in a better manner, than severity.

Horace, 65–8 B.C.
Roman poet
Ars Poetica

[Commenting on "management by walking around":] The theory is that the captain needs to get away from the bridge and roam the ship. But somebody's got to be steering the ship. Good managers don't wander aimlessly; their visits are planned and purposeful.

Thomas R. Horton
President and CEO,
American Management Association
Detroit News, January 12, 1987

Facts do not cease to exist because they are ignored.

Aldous Huxley, 1894–1963
English novelist and critic
A Note on Dogma

[M]anagers have an awareness that they are the direct representatives of the employees.

Takashi Ishihara
President, Nissan Motor Co. (Japan)
Cherry Blossoms and Robotics
(Young Presidents' Organization, 1983)

We criticize him, he appears, we change our words.

Jabo proverb

Be swift to hear, slow to speak, and slow to wrath.

New Testament, James 1:19

Praise, like gold and diamonds, owes its value only to its scarcity.

Samuel Johnson, 1709–1784
English lexicographer and critic
Boswell's Life of Dr. Johnson

Example is always more efficacious than precept.

Samuel Johnson, 1709–1784
English lexicographer and critic
Rasselas

The use of travelling is to regulate imagination by reality, and instead of thinking how things may be, to see them as they are.

Samuel Johnson, 1709–1784
English lexicographer and critic
Johnsoniana

I'm still waiting for an employee to complain that he or she has received too much feedback from his supervisor.

Gary F. Jonas
Chairman, University Research Corp.
Staff meeting, March 1984

[Successive memos reacting to a subordinate's three drafts of a position paper:]

This is awful. Do it again.

This is worse than the first version. Can't you do better?

I'll read it now.

Henry Kissinger
U. S. Secretary of State
Deal and Kennedy, *Corporate Cultures*
(Addison-Wesley, 1982)

A problem worker is usually a worker with a problem.

> Samuel B. Kutash
> Rutgers University
> *Leadership in the Office* (AMACOM, 1963)

He who has no faith in others shall find no faith in them.

> Lao-Tzu, c. 604–c. 531 B.C.
> Chinese philosopher and founder of Taoism
> *Tao Teh King*

You can close your eyes to reality but not to memories.

> Stanislaw J. Lec
> Polish writer and aphorist
> *Unkempt Thoughts* (St. Martin's Press, 1962)

Crews under authoritarian guidance ... were often observed to start reserving their forces whenever the coach did not look. They did not really exhaust themselves if the coach was absent; they were not able to conduct a really full-scale training by themselves, without immediate guidance and control.

> Hans Lenk
> German sports sociologist and writer
> *Team Building*

Some people are so good at learning the tricks of the trade that they never get to learn the trade.

> Sam Levenson, 1911–1980
> Teacher and comedian
> *You Don't Have to be in Who's Who to Know What's What* (Simon & Schuster, 1979)

Some managers always treat their subordinates in a way that tends to superior performance. But most managers, like Professor Higgins, unintentionally treat their subordinates in a way that leads to lower performance than they are capable of achieving. The way managers treat their subordinates is subtly influenced by what they expect of them. If a manager's expectations are high, productivity is likely to be excellent. If his expectations are low, productivity is likely to be poor. It is as though there were a law that caused a subordinate's performance to rise or fall to meet his manager's expectations.

> J. Sterling Livingston
> *Harvard Business Review*, July/August 1969

For some must follow, and some command
Though all are made of clay!

> Henry Wadsworth Longfellow, 1807–1882
> American poet
> *Keramos*

Employees are most apt to deal with their problems when they believe that they will be helped in good faith.

> Paul V. Lyons
> Partner, Foley, Hoag & Eliot
> *Management*, March 1987

The myth of efficiency lies in the assumption that the most efficient manager is ipso facto the most effective; actually the most efficient manager working on the wrong task will not be effective.

> R. Alec Mackenzie
> Management consultant and author
> *The Time Trap*
> (McGraw-Hill, 1972)

A supervisor has to be able to talk sufficiently well at the level of those with whom he deals that they can understand him.

> Milton M. Mandell
> *Leadership in the Office* (AMACOM, 1963)

If you make an honest mistake, the company will be very forgiving. Treat it as a training expense and learn from it.

> Konosuke Matsushita
> Founder, Matsushita Electric Co. (Japan)
> *Cherry Blossoms and Robotics*
> (Young Presidents' Organization, 1983)

We're counting on you [employees]. We trust you. And if you screw up, just tell us about it; don't worry about it. We're not encouraging you to screw up, but for heaven's sake, if you do, don't worry. We're all in this together, and we don't know what we're doing either, so come on and join in.

> Fritz Maytag
> President, Anchor Brewing Co.
> *Harvard Business Review*,
> July/August 1986

If you want people to understand, you've got to explain.

> Joe J. McKay
> CEO, Blackfeet Indian Writing Co.
> *Success*, February 1988

Until we believe that the expert in any job is the person performing it, we shall forever limit the potential of that person.

> Rene McPherson
> CEO, Dana Corp.
> Deal and Kennedy *Corporate Cultures*
> (Addison-Wesley, 1982)

The front-line supervisor is probably the strongest motivating or demotivating element of all.

> Harvey L. Miller
> Co-owner, Quill Corp.
> *Nation's Business*, March 1988

Compliment before you correct. Try to find something on which to compliment a man before you correct him. He will be more receptive to your correction.

> James C. Miller
> Personnel Development Manager,
> Standard Brands, Inc.
> *Leadership in the Office* (AMACOM, 1963)

Doing what you were good at ... is not the job ... [H]elping other people improve their performance—not doing their job for them—is what management is.

> Susan H. Miller
> Director of Editorial Development,
> Scripps Howard Newspapers
> *Presstime*, March 1988

It is extremely important that I know the other person is extremely receptive to what I'm saying. If he is not, then I will become a cause of the error if something goes wrong. I'm as much to blame as him.

> Raymond Miyashiro
> CEO, Trans Hawaiian
> *Nation's Business*, March 1988

In general, American workers appear to be over supervised.

> James O'Toole
> University of Southern California
> Peters, *Thriving on Chaos* (Knopf, 1987)

The key to effective reprimand is to fit the reprimand to the person's own self image.

> George S. Odiorne
> University of Massachusetts
> *How Managers Make Things Happen*
> (Prentice-Hall, 1982)

Coaching subordinates isn't an addition to a manager's job; it's an integral part of it.

> George S. Odiorne
> University of Massachusetts
> *How Managers Make Things Happen*
> (Prentice-Hall, 1982)

Oversee your workmen. No man will work for his brother as for himself. If they be boys, separate them; for it is true: one boy is a boy; two boys are a half of a boy; but three boys are no boy at all.

Old Farmer's Almanac (1804)

We like the freedom to make a successful decision, or even an unsuccessful one, without having to explain it to some analyst.

John Oren
President, Eastway Delivery Service
Best of Business Quarterly, 1987

Beside the task of acquiring the ability to organize a day's work, all you will ever learn about management is child's play.

E. B. Osborn
President, Economics Laboratory, Inc.
Executive Development Manual (ELI, 1959)

The spirited horse, which will of itself strive to win the race, will run still more swiftly if encouraged.

Ovid, 14 B.C.–c. A.D. 17
Roman poet
Epistolae ex Ponto

[Sexual] Harassment can be different things to different people.... [W]e tell people: It's harassment when something starts bothering somebody.

George Palmer
Du Pont Co. spokesman
The Wall Street Journal, February 10, 1988

A man has a right to pass through this world, if he wills, without having his picture published, his business enterprises discussed, his successful experiments written up for the benefit of others, or his eccentricities com-mented upon, whether in handbills, circulars, catalogues, newspapers or periodicals.

Alton Brooks Parker, 1852–1926
Chief Justice, New York Court of Appeals
Roberson v. *Rochester Folding Box Co.*
(1902)

Believe nothing against another, but upon *good* authority: Nor report what may hurt another, unless it be a *greater* hurt to others to conceal it.

William Penn, 1644–1718
Founder of Pennsylvania
Fruits of Solitude in Reflections and Maxims

Rarely promise: But, if Lawful, *constantly* perform.

William Penn, 1644–1718
Founder of Pennsylvania
Fruits of Solitude in Reflections and Maxims

Celebrate what you want to see more of.

Tom Peters
Business writer
Thriving on Chaos (Knopf, 1987)

A man who is always ready to believe what is told him will never do well, especially a businessman.

Petronius Arbiter, d. A.D. 65
Roman governor and advisor (*arbiter*) to Nero
Satyricon

Servants won't be diligent when the master's careless.

Barber, *The Book of 1000 Proverbs*, 1876

Suspicion may be no fault; showing it is a great one.

Barber, *The Book of 1000 Proverbs*, 1876

They who seek only for faults see nothing else.

> Barber, *The Book of 1000 Proverbs*, 1876

He who reproves men will get more thanks in the end than he who flatters them.

> Old Testament, Proverbs 28:23

There is no great genius without some touch of madness.

> Publilius Syrus, c. 42 B.C.
> Roman writer
> *Maxims*

We will take the good will for the deed.

> François Rabelais, 1494–1547
> French physician, humorist, and satirist
> *Works*

You [the supervisor] must have an immediate subordinate to whom you can delegate authority. If you don't, train someone.

> Homer T. Rosenberger
> Branch Chief, U. S. Department of Commerce
> *Leadership in the Office* (AMACOM, 1963)

Discretion is the tact not to see what can't be helped.

> Dagobert D. Runes
> Editor, publisher, and philosopher
> *A Book of Contemplation*

Work is of two kinds: first, altering the position of matter at or near the earth's surface relative to other matter; second, telling other people to do so.

> Bertrand Russell, 1872–1970
> English mathematician and philosopher
> *The Conquest of Happiness*

The supervisor's attendance is seen by employees as the accepted standard.

> Paul Sandwith
> Senior Consultant, Alpha Association (Canada)
> *Personnel Journal*, November 1987

Workers cannot be expected to perform regularly and consistently at full capacity.

> Wilbert E. Scheer
> Director of Personnel,
> Illinois Blue Cross/Blue Shield
> *Leadership in the Office* (AMACOM, 1963)

The painful anxiety natural to a proud mind, when it deems its slightest action subject for a moment to the watchful construction of others.

> Walter Scott, 1771–1832
> Scottish poet, novelist, and biographer
> *Guy Mannering*

He, who has committed a fault, is to be corrected both by advice and by force, kindly and harshly, and to be made better for himself and for others, not without chastisement, but without passion.

> Seneca, c. 4 B.C.–A.D. 65
> Roman philosopher and playwright
> *De Ira*

You see, really and truly, apart from the things anyone can pick up (the dressing and the proper way of speaking, and so on), the difference between a lady and a flower girl is not how she behaves but how she's treated. I shall always be a flower girl to Professor Higgins, and always will; but I know I can be a lady to you, because you always treat me as a lady, and always will.

> George Bernard Shaw, 1856–1950
> Nobel laureate in literature
> *Pygmalion*

Behavior is determined by its consequences.

B. F. Skinner
Harvard University
Beyond Freedom and Dignity (Knopf, 1971)

You have to be an adult to work here.

Marlene Solomon
Publisher, *Magna Magazine*
Advice to an employee, December 14, 1987

The ultimate result of shielding men from the effects of folly is to fill the world with fools.

Herbert Spencer, 1829–1903
English philosopher
State Tamperings with Money

What is the function of a manager if it is not to judge and to weed out the incompetents in his workforce?

Lawrence Stessin
Hofstra College
Employee Discipline
(Bureau of National Affairs, 1960)

"Who will guard the guards?" says a Latin verse, —*Quis custodiet ipsos custodes*?" I answer, "The enemy." It is the enemy who keeps the sentinel watchful.

Anne Sophie Swetchine, 1782–1857
Russian-French writer
Old Age

People in systems do not do what the system says they are doing.

Melvin J. Sykes
Attorney
Maryland Law Review, 1978

The managers of the company try not to sit at their desks.... We stroll around the corridors looking here and there.

Setsuya Tabuchi
President, Nomura Securities Co. (Japan)
Cherry Blossoms and Robotics
(Young Presidents' Organization, 1983)

Men would far rather even be blamed by their bosses ... than be passed by day after day without a word, and with no more notice than if they were a part of the machinery.

Frederick Winslow Taylor, 1856–1915
Pioneer management teacher
Harvard Business School lecture, 1912

[Referring to people who can harm an organization:] These are the people who think they are doing what is right when they aren't, and they do it with sustained gusto and enthusiasm.

J. D. Taylor
Rear Admiral, U. S. Navy
Government Executive, January 1987

Cleave ever to the sunnier side of doubt.

Alfred (Lord) Tennyson, 1809–1892
English poet
The Ancient Sage

To be a good shepherd is to shear the flock, not skin it!

Tiberius, 42 B.C.–A.D. 37
Roman emperor
Quoted in Suetonius, *Lives of the Caesars*

One of the most important tasks of a manager is to eliminate his people's excuses for failure.

Robert Townsend
Former CEO, Avis
Further Up the Organization (Knopf, 1984)

Managers should realize the importance of each suggestion [from workers or groups of workers]. Try to find what it is in each suggestion that has worth. Each suggestion and the reaction to each suggestion can build trust.

> Shoichiro Toyodo
> President, Toyota Motor Co. (Japan)
> *Cherry Blossoms and Robotics*
> (Young Presidents' Organization, 1983)

The employee's interpretation of an order may be different from that intended by the foreman.

> Maurice S. Trotter
> New York University
> *Supervisor's Handbook on Insubordination*
> (Bureau of National Affairs, 1967)

A supervisor should control his emotions; he should not allow a recalcitrant employee to upset him.

> Maurice S. Trotter
> New York University
> *Supervisor's Handbook on Insubordination*
> (Bureau of National Affairs, 1967)

Some foremen have, unfortunately, developed the idea that a supervisor must exercise his authority with a heavy hand, because this is the way *their* supervisor acted.

> Maurice S. Trotter
> New York University
> *Supervisor's Handbook on Insubordination*
> (Bureau of National Affairs, 1967)

Few things are harder to put up with than the annoyance of a good example.

> Mark Twain
> (Samuel Langhorne Clemens), 1835–1910
> American author and riverboat captain
> *Pudd'nhead Wilson's Calendar*

Place a group with strong independence drives under a supervisor who needs to keep his men under his thumb, and the result is very likely to be trouble. Similarly, if you take docile men who are accustomed to obedience and respect for their supervisors and place them under a supervisor who tries to make them manage their own work, they are likely to wonder uneasily whether he really knows what he is doing.

> Victor H. Vroom
> Management researcher
> *Some Personality Determinants of the Effects of Participation*
> (Prentice-Hall, 1960)

The duck who is tamed will never go anywhere anymore. We are convinced that business needs its wild ducks. And in IBM we try not to tame them.

> Thomas J. Watson, Sr., 1874–1956
> Founder and first President, IBM
> Deal and Kennedy, *Corporate Cultures*
> (Addison-Wesley, 1982)

Criticism comes much easier than craftsmanship.

> Zuexis, c. 400 B.C.
> Greek writer
> Quoted by Pliny, *Natural History*

When we do right you forget. When we do wrong you remember.

> Anonymous Hell's Angel
> Thompson, *The Hell's Angels*
> (Random House, 1967)

A good memory forgets the right thing at the proper time.

> Anonymous

You know where you are. The people you are with know where you are. God knows where you are. But does your secretary know where you are?

Anonymous secretary's note to her boss
Cone, *Supervising Employees Effectively*
(Addison-Wesley, 1974)

In life—as in bridge—one peek is worth two finesses.

Anonymous

Today I bent the truth to be kind, and I have no regret, for I am far surer of what is kind than I am of what is true.

Anonymous
Reader's Digest, December 1987

Good supervision is the art of getting average people to do superior work.

Anonymous

45

Team Building & Teamwork

Every team needs a coach.

Some management groups are not good at problem solving and decision making precisely because the participants have weak egos and are uncomfortable with competition.

Chris Argyris
Harvard Graduate School of Education
Harvard Business Review,
September/October 1986

Soloists are inspiring in opera and perhaps even in small entrepreneurial ventures, but there is no place for them in large corporations.

Norman R. Augustine
President and CEO, Martin Marietta Corp.
Augustine's Laws (Penguin, 1987)

The whole object of the organization is to get cooperation, to get to each individual the benefit of all the knowledge and all the experience of all individuals.

Hamilton McFarland Barksdale
Management Executive Committee, Dupont
Committee meeting minutes, October 11, 1909

[I]f the conventional approach of training individuals [in an organization] one-by-one were applied in developing a baseball or a football team, each of the team members would be trained at the hands of specialists, also one-by-one, away from the organization and isolated.... Then, all members would be returned to the organization and thrown together on the assumption that since all had learned individually, they automatically would be able to work together effectively.... [These] examples point to the fallacy in logic of a conventional approach to training when the goal of organizational health is successful team action.

Robert R. Blake and Jane S. Mouton
*American Society for Training and
Development Journal*, 1962

Teamwork is consciously espoused but unwittingly shunned by most people in business because they are deathly afraid of it. They think it will render them anonymous, invisible.

> Srully Blotnick
> Management consultant
> *The Corporate Steeplechase*
> (Facts On File, 1984)

At the same time that the manager works to develop management responsibility in subordinates, he or she must help develop the subordinates' abilities to share management of the unit's performance.... [N]either willingness to accept overall responsibility nor ability to do so are automatic and instant.

> David L. Bradford
> Stanford University School of Business
> and Allan R. Cohen
> Babson College
> *Managing for Excellence* (Wiley, 1984)

I don't like to work in a group. I don't get along well with other people.

> Jimmy Breslin
> Columnist, *Newsday* (New York)
> National Public Radio, March 6, 1988

Managing requires setting aside one's ego to encourage and develop the work of others. It requires a "big picture" and team perspective rather than an individual-achiever perspective.

> Sara M. Brown
> President, Sara Brown & Associates
> *Presstime*, March 1988

The hammers must be swung in cadence, when more than one is hammering the iron.

> Giordano Bruno, c. 1548–1600
> Italian philosopher and astronomer
> *Candelaio*

Work teams and group leaders are a way of setting worker against worker.

> Eddie Chapman
> Union Shop Steward, Ford Motor Co. (Britain)
> *The New York Times*, February 14, 1988

Behind an able man there are always other able men.

> Chinese proverb

You put together the best team that you can with the players you've got, and replace those who aren't good enough.

> Robert L. Crandall
> President, American Airlines
> *Management*, January 1987

A few honest men are better than numbers.

> Oliver Cromwell, 1599–1658
> Lord Protector of England
> Letter to William Spring, September 1643

We know we need better teamwork; the question is how to achieve it. Very few people defend the adversarial relationship, but no one has a clear idea of how to do away with it. The usual method is exhortation. But this approach has failed us time and time again.

> Robert F. Daniell
> CEO, United Technologies Corp.
> *Harvard Business Review*,
> September/October 1987

Top management work is work for a team rather than one man.

> Peter F. Drucker
> Management consultant
> Hayes, *Memos for Management: Leadership*
> (AMACOM, 1983)

All for one, one for all.
[*Tous pour un, un pour tous.*]

> Alexandre Dumas [Dumas *fils*], 1824–1895
> French playwright and novelist
> *Les Trois Mousquetiers*

The ratio of We's to I's is the best indicator of the development of a team.

> Lewis D. Eigen
> Executive Vice President,
> University Research Corp.
> Lecture, "Developing Cooperative Behavior,"
> Columbia University, September 6, 1959

We are by nature a tribal people.

> Linda Ellerbee
> Broadcast journalist
> *Omni*, April 1988

The country that has been leading the way to an entirely new conception of teamwork is the United States.

> Charles Garfield
> President, Performance Sciences Corp.
> *Peak Performers* (Avon, 1986)

Make it clear that everyone is on the same team. Avoid practices that make it clear that some ... are on the first team and others are part of another.

> Paul S. George
> University of Florida
> *Personnel Journal*, November 1987

Team building and attrition work against each other.... Organize individuals so they see themselves spending the foreseeable future together as a team, which usually leads to greater degrees of interpersonal commitment.

> Paul S. George
> University of Florida
> *Personnel Journal*, November 1987

The path to greatness is along with others.

> Baltasar Gracián, 1601–1658
> Spanish priest and popular writer
> *Oraculo Manual*

Those who are not team players will have to go.

> Jeanne Greenberg
> CEO, Caliper
> *Nation's Business,* April 1988

[T]he work of a business, of a government bureaucracy, of most forms of human activity, is something pursued not by individuals but by teams.

> Andrew S. Grove
> CEO, Intel Corp.
> *High Output Management*
> (Random House, 1983)

The modern working man feels the need of belonging to a team.

> Pehr G. Gyllenhammar
> Managing Director, Volvo (Sweden)
> Volvo press release, January 5, 1973

Although we may not say goodbye entirely to individual job specifications, groups will eventual'ᵥ be the work unit.

> James L. Hayes
> President and CEO,
> American Management Association
> *Memos for Management: Leadership*
> (AMACOM, 1983)

The productivity of a work group seems to depend on how the group members see their own goals in relation to the goals of the organization.

Paul Hersey
California American University
and Kenneth H. Blanchard
University of Massachusetts
Management of Organizational Behavior
(Prentice-Hall, 1972)

[M]anagement should emphasize the contributions to total goals rather than the accomplishments of subgroup goals.

Paul Hersey
California American University
and Kenneth H. Blanchard
University of Massachusetts
Management of Organizational Behavior
(Prentice-Hall, 1972)

The superior man encourages the people at their work, and exhorts them to help one another.

I Ching: Book of Changes
China, c. 600 B.C.

A community is like a ship; every one ought to be prepared to take the helm.

Henrik Ibsen, 1828–1906
Norwegian playwright
An Enemy of the People

No matter how high or how excellent technology may be and how much capital may be accumulated, unless the group of human beings which comprise the enterprise works together toward one unified goal, the enterprise is sure to go down the path of decline.

Takashi Ishihara
President, Nissan Motor Co.
Cherry Blossoms and Robotics
(Young Presidents' Organization, 1983)

Most people want to be part of a team.

Candice Kaspers
President, Kaspers & Associates
Nation's Business, April 1988

Homer's *Iliad* tells the story of Agamemnon, Greek king, and Achilles, his best warrior, who nearly lose the Trojan War because they cannot get along. Agamemnon cares more about proving how powerful he is than motivating Achilles to capture Troy. After the king takes Achilles' war prize, the warrior moves his army out. It takes years to finally win the war.

Beverly Kempton
Business writer
Working Woman, October 1987

The greatest risk in choosing managers by team is that top management may reject the decision.

Tony Kizilos and Roger P. Heinisch
Systems and Research Center of Aerospace
and Defense, Honeywell Corp.
Harvard Business Review,
September/October 1986

Teams left to run their own shows often lacked direction. Team members didn't have the skills to solve many of the technical problems that arose and found it hard to get functional support. Many team members also balked at evaluating and disciplining their peers. At first the problems were ascribed to inexperience. But as time went on and teams matured, managers and workers had to admit that the old adage still holds, "Every team needs a coach."

Janice A. Klein
Harvard Business School
and Pamela A. Posey
University of Vermont
Harvard Business Review,
November/December 1986

Getting everybody to agree on stuff never did seem to work for me.

> Milt Kuolt
> Founder, Horizon Air Industries, Inc.
> *Inc. Magazine*, March 1988

People seem to be utterly unaware that they are slacking off [when working] in groups.

> Bibb Latane
> University of North Carolina
> *Omni*, March 1988

The members [of the team] were dissatisfied with the authoritarian leading; they reacted either aggressively against the leader and toward each other or with apathetic submission. In the case of strong control the performance was a little higher than with the "democratic" leading style. Then soon a decrease followed. The members who reacted apathetically did not show any motivation for performance and soon the decrease of motivation began.

> Hans Lenk
> German sports sociologist and writer
> *Team Dynamics*

No one person can accomplish much if they don't work with others.

> Daniel Levinson
> Chief Justice,
> U. S. Merit Systems Protection Board
> *Management*, 1987

There are only two kinds of coaches—those who have been fired and those who will be fired.

> Ken Loeffler
> Professional basketball coach
> *St. Louis Post-Dispatch*, December 29, 1964

A management team should not be a fraternity.

> David Mahoney
> Investment manager
> *Confessions of a Street-Smart Manager*
> (Simon & Schuster, 1987)

If a house be divided against itself, that house cannot stand.

> New Testament, Mark 3:25

The most important attribute of team playing is the concept of team roles, which is often difficult to accept from a female point of view.... We are so used to taking turns, we rarely understand the quarterback always plays his position with fame and fortune—while the tight end labors unceremoniously for half the salary and twice the bruises. But both depend upon the respective skills of the other to get into the Super Bowl.

> Jinx Milea
> University of Southern California
> and Pauline Lyttle
> President, Operational Politics, Inc.
> *Why Jenny Can't Lead*, 1986

Society is the union of men and not the men themselves.

> Charles de Secondat Montesquieu, 1689–1755
> French lawyer, writer, and philosopher
> *The Spirit of the Laws*

We give a bonus for the employees to give them a sense of participation and to feel that they are members of the company because we are always saying our company has one fate. If the company goes well, everybody can enjoy. If the company goes wrong or goes bankrupt, people lose jobs.

> Akio Morita
> CEO, Sony Corp. (Japan)
> *Cherry Blossoms and Robotics*
> (Young Presidents' Organization, 1983)

It is most important that a [Japanese] meeting should reach a unanimous conclusion; it should leave no one frustrated or dissatisfied, for this weakens ... unity and solidarity.

> Chie Nakane
> Japanese writer
> *Cherry Blossoms and Robotics*
> (Young Presidents' Organization, 1983)

I'm not one who easily trusts others to get the job done. When we got into teamwork I found it particularly difficult to do my part.

> John Newman
> Controller, Liberty Furniture
> *Nation's Business,* April 1988

Intellectuals incline to be individualists, or even independents, are not team conscious and tend to regard obedience as a surrender of personality.

> Harold Nicolson, 1886–1961
> English biographer and diplomat
> Rowes, *The Book of Quotes* (Dutton, 1979)

No manager is an island.

> William Oncken, Jr.
> Management writer
> *Success,* February 1988

When a team outgrows individual performance and learns team confidence, excellence becomes a reality.

> Joe Paterno
> Football coach, Penn State University
> *American Heritage,* April 1988

Don't let your vision get diluted, but don't be afraid of teamwork.

> James B. Patterson
> CEO, J. Walter Thompson USA
> *The New York Times,* April 28, 1988

[S]uccessful coaches instinctively vary their approaches to meet the needs of this person at this time, or that group at that time. They perform five distinctly different roles: they educate, sponsor, coach, counsel and confront. Each approach is executed ... to facilitate learning and elicit creative contributions from all hands to the organization's overarching purpose.

> Tom Peters and Nancy Austin
> Management consultants and writers
> *A Passion for Excellence*
> (Random House, 1985)

Rewards should go to teams as a whole.

> Tom Peters
> Business writer
> *Thriving on Chaos* (Knopf, 1987)

"Great people" don't equal "great teams."

> Tom Peters
> Business writer
> *Thriving on Chaos* (Knopf, 1987)

A systematic effort must be made to emphasize the group instead of the individual.... Group goals and responsibilities can usually overcome any negative reactions to the individual and enforce a standard of cooperation that is not attainable by persuasion or exhortation.

> Eugene Raudsepp
> President, Creative Research, Inc.
> *MTS Digest,* April/June 1987

If the United States is to compete effectively ... we must bring collective entrepreneurship to the forefront.... That will require us to change our attitudes, to downplay the myth of the entrepreneurial hero, and to celebrate our creative teams.

> Robert B. Reich
> JFK School of Government, Harvard University
> *Harvard Business Review*, May/June 1987

This new [compensation] system will ... reward individuals [as well as] the team. But we're trying to make sure that we get as much teamwork as possible.

Roy S. Roberts
Vice President, General Motors Corp.
Black Enterprise, April 1988

It was my good fortune to help bring together the efficient men who are the controlling forces of the organization [Standard Oil]... but it is they who have done the hard tasks.

John Davidson Rockefeller, 1839–1937
American industrialist and phianthropist
Quoted in *American Heritage,* April 1988

No star playing, just football.

Knute K. Rockne, 1888–1931
Captain and coach,
Notre Dame University football team
Frequent admonition to players

Advanced technology required the collaboration of diverse professions and organizations, often with ambiguous or highly interdependent jurisdictions. In such situations, many of our highly touted rational management techniques break down; and new non-engineering approaches are necessary for the solution of these "systems" problems.

Leonard R. Sayles and Margaret K. Chandler
*Managing Large Systems: The Large-Scale
Approach* (Harper & Row, 1971)

Society is no comfort
To one not sociable.

William Shakespeare, 1564–1616
English dramatist and poet
Cymbeline

The manager must decide what type of group is wanted. If cooperation, teamwork, and synergy really matter, then one aims for high task interdependence. One structures the jobs of group members so that they have to interact frequently... to get their jobs done. Important outcomes are made dependent on group performance. The outcomes are distributed equally. If frenzied, independent activity is the goal, then one aims for low task interdependence and large rewards are distributed competitively and unequally.

Gregory P. Shea
The Wharton School
and Richard A. Guzzo
New York University
Sloan Management Review, Spring 1987

Cooperation can be set up, perhaps more easily than competition.

B. F. Skinner
Harvard University
Harvard Educational Review, 1954

Men will find that they can prepare with mutual aid far more easily what they need, and avoid more easily the perils which beset them on all sides, by united forces.

Benedict Spinoza, 1632–1677
Dutch philosopher and oculist
Ethics

Fortunately, it appears that most people are more cooperative than the standard economic model suggests.

Richard Thaler
Cornell University
The Washington Post, April 11, 1988

We're all in this alone.

Lily Tomlin
Comedienne and actress
Gross, *The Oxford Book of Aphorisms*

One step by 100 persons is better than 100 steps by one person.

> Koichi Tsukamoto
> President, Wacoal Corp. (Japan)
> *Cherry Blossoms and Robotics*
> (Young Presidents' Organization, 1983)

Essential to teamwork is trust.

> Robert H. Waterman
> Management consultant and writer
> *The Renewal Factor* (Bantam, 1987)

My most important contribution to IBM was my ability to pick strong and intelligent men and then hold the team together by persuasion, by apologies, by financial incentives, by speeches, by chatting with their wives, by thoughtfulness when they were sick or involved in an accident, and by using every tool at my command to make that team think that I was a decent guy. I knew I couldn't match all of them intellectually, but I thought that if I fully used every capability that I had, I could stay even with them.

> Thomas J. Watson, Jr.,
> CEO, IBM, and U. S. Ambassador to Russia
> *Fortune*, 1977

There is a time when integrity should take the rudder from team loyalty.

> Thomas J. Watson, Jr.
> CEO, IBM, and U. S. Ambassador to Russia
> *Fortune*, 1977

Confidence [in others] is a thing not to be produced by compulsion. Men cannot be forced into trust.

> Daniel Webster, 1782–1852
> American statesman and orator
> Speech, U. S. Senate, 1833

Sports constantly make demands on the participant for performance, and they develop integrity, self-reliance and initiative. They teach you a lot about working in groups, without being duly submerged in the group.

> Byron R. White
> U. S. Supreme Court Justice
> and college football All-American
> *Sports Illustrated*, December 10, 1962

A group may have more group information or less group information than its members. A group of non-social animals, temporarily assembled, contains very little group information, even though its members may possess much information as individuals. This is because very little that one member does is noticed by the others and is acted on by them in a way that goes further in the group.

> Norbert Wiener, 1894–1964
> Pioneer computer scientist
> *Cybernetics* (M. I. T., 1961)

[According to John De Lorean:] Charlie Chayne, vice-president of Engineering ... took a very strong stand against the Corvair as an unsafe car long before it went on sale in 1959. He was not listened to but instead told, in effect, "You're not a member of the team. Shut up or go looking for another job."

> J. Patrick Wright
> *On a Clear Day You Can See General Motors*
> (Wright, 1979)

We [the Politburo] never vote, because after we have all worked together to arrive at an opinion, there are no objectors left. And if there is still someone with his own opinion, we discuss it and work out some kind of convergence so that there will be unity.

> Lev Zaikov
> Chief, Moscow Communist Party,
> and Politburo member
> *Newsweek*, April 4, 1988

473

46

Time Management

Without haste, but without rest.

Time is money, and the way we spend it is the principal thing of interest about it.

> Accountants' maxim

There is nothing more requisite in business than dispatch.

> Joseph Addison, 1672–1719
> English writer, critic, and statesman
> *Ancient Medals*

Slow and steady wins the race.

> Aesop, c. 620–c. 560 B.C.
> Greek fabulist
> *The Hare and the Tortise*

He slept beneath the moon,
He basked beneath the sun;
He lived a life of going-to-do,
And died with nothing done.

> James Albery, 1838–1889
> English playwright
> Epitaph for himself

Showing up is 80 percent of life.

> Woody Allen
> Actor, comedian, writer, director
> Rowes, *The Book of Quotes* (Dutton, 1979)

A wage earner goes home when it's "quitting time." A manager leaves when the work is done—or takes it home.

> Mary Ann Allison
> Vice President, CitiCorp.
> and Eric Allison
> Financial writer
> *Managing Up, Managing Down*
> (Simon & Schuster, 1984)

Time is my biggest enemy.

> Bernard Appel
> President, Radio Shack
> *Computer & Software News*, December 7, 1987

Whoever admits that he is too busy to improve his methods has acknowledged himself to be at the end of his rope.

> J. Ogden Armour, 1863–1927
> President, Armour Meat Packing Co.
> *Conversations and Reflections*

Measure not dispatch by the time of sitting, but by the advancement of the business.

> Francis Bacon, 1561–1626
> Lord Chancellor of England
> *Of Dispatch*

To choose time is to save time.

> Francis Bacon, 1561–1626
> Lord Chancellor of England
> *Of Expense*

Always do one thing less than you think you can do.

> Bernard Mannes Baruch, 1870–1965
> Presidential advisor and financial analyst
> Quoted by Peter, *The Peter Principle*
> (William Morrow, 1969)

I would I could stand on a busy corner, hat in hand, and beg people to throw me all their wasted hours.

> Bernhard Berenson, 1865–1959
> Art critic and historian
> Prochnow, *The Toastmaster's Treasure Chest*
> (Harper & Row, 1979)

There's never enough time to do it right, but there's always time to do it over.

> Jack Bergman
> Vice President, Jordache Enterprises, Inc.
> Speech, Brooklyn, New York,
> November 25, 1987

After you have made up your mind just what you are going to do, is a good time to do it.

> Josh Billings
> (Henry Wheeler Shaw), 1818–1885
> American writer and auctioneer
> *Josh Billings: His Book*

The Ninety-Ninety Rule of Project Schedules: The first ninety percent of the task takes ninety percent of the time, and the last ten percent takes the other ninety percent.

> Arthur Bloch
> Writer and humorist
> *Murphy's Law* (Price/Stern/Sloan, 1977)

Murphy's Law holds no more than 80 percent of the time; unfortunately, it is impossible to predict when.

> Wayne Boucher
> Management author and motivational speaker
> *MBA Magazine*, August/September 1978

I learned how to get things done on time, because you had to get the papers delivered.

> Paul Brayton
> President, Brayton International
> *The Hawk Eye* (Burlington, Iowa),
> July 10, 1987

Monday is a bad way to spend one-seventh of your life.

> Thomas "Wayne" Brazell
> U. S. Army Materiel Command
> Training session, McLean, Virginia,
> February 18, 1988

How does a project get to be a year behind schedule? One day at a time.

> Fred Brooks
> System 360 Chief Designer, IBM
> Peters, *Thriving on Chaos* (Knopf, 1987)

Business dispatched is business well done, but business hurried is business ill done.

> Edward George Bulwer-Lytton, 1803–1873
> English novelist and playwright
> *Readers and Writer*

Nae man can tether time or tide.

> Robert Burns, 1759–1796
> Scottish national poet
> *Tam o' Shanter*

There is a maxim, "Never put off till tomorrow what you can do today." It is a maxim for sluggards. A better reading of it is, "Never do today what you can as well do tomorrow" because something may occur to make you regret your premature action.

> Aaron Burr, 1756–1836
> U. S. Senator
> Parton, *Life of Aaron Burr*

The ultimate inspiration is the deadline.

> Nolan Bushnell
> Founder, Atari
> Oech, *A Whack on the Side of the Head*
> (Warner, 1983)

I have not found out why we humans think of time as a line going from backwards, forwards, while it must be in all directions like everything else in the system of the world.

> Ferruccio Benvenuto Busoni, 1866–1924
> Italian composer and pianist
> *Busoni's Letters To His Wife*

Don't wait for the last judgment—it takes place every day.

> Albert Camus, 1913–1960
> Nobel laureate in literature (France)
> *The Fall*

Delay always breeds danger.

> Miguel de Cervantes, 1547–1616
> Spanish novelist
> *Don Quixote*

By the street of By-and-By, one arrives at the House-of-Never.

> Miguel de Cervantes, 1547–1616
> Spanish novelist
> *Don Quixote*

Do today. Finish today.

> Donald Chen
> General Manager, Lan Lir Ltd. (Taiwan)
> Instructions to staff, November 21, 1984

Do not anxiously hope for what is not yet come; do not vainly regret what is already past.

> Chinese proverb

If we open a quarrel between the past and the present, we shall find we have lost the future.

> Winston Churchill, 1874–1965
> English Prime Minister, writer, and soldier
> Speech, House of Commons, 1940

Unpunctuality is a vile habit.

> Winston Churchill, 1874–1965
> English Prime Minister, writer, and soldier
> *My Early Life*

I found I could add nearly two hours to my working day by going to bed for an hour after luncheon.

> Winston Churchill, 1874–1965
> English Prime Minister, writer, and soldier
> *My Early Life*

Worry is a form of fear. It is a realization of inadequacy, which in turn is the byproduct of lack of time to think through confidently to sound objectives and good plans.

> Ralph J. Cordiner
> President, General Electric Co.
> *Professional Management in General Electric*
> (General Electric Company, 1954)

A man who dares to waste one hour of time has not discovered the value of life.

> Charles Darwin, 1809–1882
> English biologist
> Prochnow, *The Toastmaster's Treasure Chest*
> (Harper & Row, 1979)

To know *how to wait* is the great secret of success.

> Joseph Marie de Maistre, 1753–1821
> French philosopher and statesman
> Quoted by Smiles, *Self-Help*

Every thing in this world has its critical moment; and the height of good conduct consists in knowing and siezing it.

> Cardinal de Retz, 1614–1679
> French ecclesiastic and politician
> *Political Maxims*

Once someone understands you respect his time, he will be more willing to speak with you.

> James Dennis
> Director of Marketing Communications,
> Hewlett-Packard
> *Black Enterprise,* April 1988

It was a favorite expression of Theophrastus that time was the most valuable thing a man could spend.

> Diogenes Laertius, c. 200–250
> Greek historian and writer
> *Lives and Opinions of Eminent Philosophers:*
> *Theophrastus*

Events are sometimes the best calendar.

> Benjamin Disraeli, 1804–1881
> English Prime Minister and novelist
> *Venetia*

Time goes, you say? Ah no!
Alas, time stays, *we* go.

> Austin Dobson, 1840–1921
> English poet and essayist
> *The Paradox of Time*

Time ... is nothing absolute; its duration depends on the rate of thought and feeling.

> John William Draper, 1811–1882
> English scientist
> *The Intellectual Development*
> *of Europe*

The good time users among managers spend many more hours on their communications up than on their communications down. They tend to have good communications down, but they seem to obtain these as an effortless by-product. They do not talk to their subordinates about their problems, but they know how to make the subordinates talk about theirs.

> Peter F. Drucker
> Management consultant and writer
> *People and Performance*
> (Harper & Row, 1977)

Time is the scarcest resource, and unless it is managed nothing else can be managed.

> Peter F. Drucker
> Management consultant and writer
> *Nation's Business*, April 1961

No man who is in a hurry is quite civilized.

> Will Durant, 1885–1981
> American philosopher and historian
> *What Is Civilization?*

I am long on ideas, but short on time. I expect to live to be only about a hundred.

> Thomas Alva Edison, 1847–1931
> American inventor
> Prochnow, *The Toastmaster's Treasure Chest*
> (Harper & Row, 1979)

Avoid anything that is unnecessary. Also avoid anything that your subordinates can do even though you might be able to do it better. Spend your time only on those critical tasks that no one else seems to be able to handle.

> Lewis D. Eigen
> Executive Vice President,
> University Research Corp.
> Lecture, Young Presidents' Organization,
> New York City, March 1969

When a man sits with a pretty girl for an hour, it seems like a minute. But let him sit on a hot stove for a minute—and it's longer than any hour. That's relativity.

> Albert Einstein, 1879–1955
> Nobel laureate in physics
> Prochnow, *The Toastmaster's Treasure Chest*
> (Harper & Row, 1979)

We must be very suspicious of the deceptions of the element of time. It takes a good deal of time to eat or to sleep, or to earn a hundred dollars, and a very little time to entertain hope and an insight which becomes the light of our lives.

> Ralph Waldo Emerson, 1803–1882
> American essayist and poet
> *Experience*

[Napoleon] directed Bourrienne to leave all his letters unopened for three weeks, and then observed with satisfaction how large a part of the correspondence had thus been disposed of itself, and no longer required an answer.

> Ralph Waldo Emerson, 1803–1882
> American essayist and poet
> *The Man of the World*

This time, like all times, is a very good one, if we but know what to do with it.

> Ralph Waldo Emerson, 1803–1882
> American essayist amd poet
> *The American Scholar*

No great thing is created suddenly, any more than a bunch of grapes or a fig. If you desire a fig, I answer you that there must be time. Let it first blossom, then bear fruit, then ripen.

> Epictetus, c. 60–120
> Roman Stoic philosopher
> *Discourses*

Procrastination brings loss, delay danger.
[*Dilatio damnum habet mora periculum.*]

> Desiderius Erasmus, c. 1466–1536
> Dutch scholar and theologian
> *Adolescens*

To win a race, the swiftness of a dart
Availeth not without a timely start.

> Jean de La Fontaine, 1621–1695
> French fabulist
> *Fables*

Time deals gently only with those who take it gently.

> Anatole France, 1844–1944
> French writer
> *The Crime of Sylvestre Bonnard*

Remember that time is money.

> Benjamin Franklin, 1706–1790
> American printer and statesman
> *Advice to a Young Tradesman*

Never leave that till tomorrow which you can do today.

> Benjamin Franklin, 1706–1790
> American printer and statesman
> *Poor Richard's Almanack*

The man who has nothing to do is always the busiest.

> French proverb

Without haste, but without rest.

> Johann Wolfgang von Goethe, 1749–1832
> German poet and dramatist
> Motto

Every year a year goes by.

> Carlo Goldoni, 1707–1792
> Italian dramatist
> *La Bella Verita*

Every moment spent planning saves three or four in execution.

> Crawford Greenwalt
> President, Du Pont
> Mackenzie, *The Time Trap*
> (McGraw-Hill, 1972)

Selectivity—the determination to choose what we will attempt to get done and what we won't—is the only way out of the panic that excessive demands on our time can create.

> Andrew S. Grove
> CEO, Intel Corp.
> *One-On-One With Andy Grove*
> (G. P. Putnam's Sons, 1987)

Just as you would not permit a fellow employee to steal a piece of office equipment ... you shouldn't let anyone walk away with the time of his fellow managers.

> Andrew S. Grove
> CEO, Intel Corp.
> *High Output Management*
> (Random House, 1983)

Time spent on hiring is time well spent.

> Robert Half
> President, Robert Half International
> *Robert Half on Hiring* (Crown, 1985)

We reckon hours and minutes to be dollars and cents.

> Thomas Chandler Haliburton, 1796–1865
> Canadian jurist and humorist
> *The Clockmaker*

The worst mistake you can make in trading abroad is to assume that other people operate on your timetable.

> Wilson Harrell
> International marketing consultant
> *Inc. Magazine*, August 1987

Urgency emphasizes timeliness.

> James L. Hayes
> President and CEO,
> American Management Association
> *Memos for Management: Leadership*
> (AMACOM, 1983)

If you're not wasting other people's time, the least you can ask is that they shouldn't waste yours.

> Robert Heller
> Editor, *Management Today*
> *The Supermanagers* (Dutton, 1984)

The mill cannot grind with water that's past.

> George Herbert, 1593–1633
> English clergyman and poet
> *Jacula Prudentum*

The summer day
Endures not forever: toil ye while ye may.

> Hesiod, eighth century B.C.
> Greek poet
> *Theognis*

479

It always takes longer than you expect, even when you take Hofstader's Law into account.

Douglas R. Hofstader
American computer scientist
Omni, May 1979

We haven't the time to take our time.

Eugene Ionesco
French author and playwright
Exit the King

Time—rather than cost or quality—is the overarching management objective which subsumes the others.

Rudyard Istvan
Vice President, The Boston Consulting Group
Newsweek, April 4, 1988

Tolstoy's *The Death of Ivan Ilyich* details the power-driven life of Ilyich, a Russian judge. At the height of his success Ilyich contracts a fatal disease. On his deathbed he takes a long look at his life only to realize that the last time he knew happiness was in his childhood. He received no fulfillment from his years at work. But Ilyich makes this discovery too late.

Beverly Kempton
Business writer
Working Woman, October 1987

The biggest sin is sitting on your ass.

Florynce R. Kennedy
Writer and feminist
Ms. Magazine, March 1973

There never has been any thirty-hour week for men who had anything to do.

Charles Franklin Kettering, 1876–1958
President and General Manager,
GM Research Corp.
Prochnow, *The Toastmaster's Treasure Chest*
(Harper & Row, 1979)

There cannot be a crisis next week. My schedule is already full.

Henry Kissinger
U. S. Secretary of State
Time, January 24, 1977

Better late than never.
[*Potius sero quam nunquam.*]

Latin proverb

The present is big with the future.

Gottfried Wilhelm von Leibniz, 1646–1716
German philosopher and mathematician
Theodiced

I'm going to stop putting off things starting tomorrow.

Sam Levenson, 1911–1980
Teacher and comedian
*You Don't Have to be in Who's Who to Know
What's What* (Simon & Schuster, 1979)

There are many things waiting to be done.

Li Peng
Chinese Prime Minister
The New York Times, November 25, 1987

Delay is ever fatal to those who are prepared.

Lucan, 39–65
Roman writer
The Civil War

Procrastination is the art of keeping up with yesterday.

Don Marquis, 1878–1937
American newspaperman and humorist
certain maxims of archy

Isn't it nice that no one cares which twenty-three hours of the day I work?

> Thurgood Marshall
> U. S. Supreme Court Justice
> *The New York Times*, August 22, 1965

Leaders face the difficult decision of sacrificing to some degree their own personal agenda. There is not always enough time to specialize on issues dear to the heart.

> Mary McClure
> Vice Chairman, Council of State Governments
> *The Journal of State Government*,
> September/October 1987

A well-worn precept of the British Navy was that the difficult was done at once; the impossible took a little longer.

> P. McCutchan
> *Shard calls Tune*, 1981
> *Oxford Dictionary of Proverbs*

What business you're in is what you do should do when you walk into the office in the morning.... The trick is to decide what is the thrust of your business at that particular time.

> William G. McGowan
> Chairman, MCI Communications Corp.
> *Inc. Magazine*, August 1986

I must govern the clock, not be governed by it.

> Golda Meir, 1989–1978
> Prime Minister of Israel
> Fallaci, *L'Eoropeo*, 1973

Even an angel can't do two things at the same time.

> Midrash Genesis Rabbah

I've been on a calendar, but never on time.

> Marilyn Monroe, 1926–1962
> American movie star
> *Look*, January 16, 1962

The most striking difference between the outlooks of European and American [managers] lies in their orientation towards time. It is as if they were standing back to back, with the European inclined to look at the past and the present and the American seeing the present and the future.

> Otto Nowotny
> *Harvard Business Review*, March/April 1964

Do nothing in great haste, except catching fleas and running from a mad dog.

> *Old Farmer's Almanac* (1811)

Other people's time, like your time, is limited.

> William Oncken, Jr.
> Management author
> *Success*, February 1988

Beside the task of acquiring the ability to organize a day's work, all you will ever learn about management is child's play.

> E. B. Osborn
> President, Economics Laboratory, Inc.
> *Executive Development Manual* (ELI, 1959)

Time flies.
[*Tempus fugit.*]

> Ovid, 14 B.C.–c. A.D. 17
> Roman poet
> *Fasti*

The time spent on any matter is usually inversely proportional to its importance.

C. Northcote Parkinson
University of Malaya
*Parkinson's Law and Other Studies
in Administration*, 1957

Work expands so as to fill the time available for its completion.... The thing to be done swells in importance and complexity in a direct ratio with the time to be spent.

C. Northcote Parkinson
University of Malaya
*Parkinson's Law and Other Studies
in Administration*, 1957

[L]ate hours, like gray hairs, are among the penalties of success.

C. Northcote Parkinson
University of Malaya
*Parkinson's Law and Other Studies
in Administration*, 1957

If you put off everything till you're sure of it, you'll get nothing done.

Normal Vincent Peale
Clergyman and inspirational speaker
Reader's Digest, January 1972

Delay is the deadliest form of denial.

John Peers
President, Logical Machine Corp.
1,001 Logical Laws (Doubleday, 1979)

The only one who got anything done by Friday was Robinson Crusoe.

John Peers
President, Logical Machine Corp.
1,001 Logical Laws (Doubleday, 1979)

There is nothing of which we are apt to be so lavish as of time, and about which we ought to be more solicitous; since without it we can do nothing in this world.

William Penn, 1644–1718
Founder of Pennsylvania
Prochnow, *The Toastmaster's Treasure Chest*
(Harper & Row, 1979)

I was so busy doing things I should have delegated, I didn't have time to manage.

Charles Percy
President, Bell & Howell, and U. S. Senator
Mackenzie, *The Time Trap*
(McGraw-Hill, 1972)

It takes five years to develop a new car in this country. Heck, we won World War II in four years.

H. Ross Perot
Founder, Electronic Data Systems
Peters, *Thriving on Chaos* (Knopf, 1987)

Be ruled by time, the wisest counsellor of all.

Plutarch, c. 46–c. 120
Greek biographer and philosopher
The Parallel Lives: Pericles

One of these days is none of these days.

Barber, *The Book of 1000 Proverbs*, 1876

While we stop to think, we often miss our opportunity.

Publilius Syrus, c. 42 B.C.
Roman writer
Maxims

Nothing can be done at once hastily and prudently.

Publilius Syrus, c. 42 B.C.
Roman writer
Maxims

Nothing is so dear and precious as time.

> François Rabelais, 1494–1547
> French physician, humorist, and satirist
> *Works*

People who employ their minds too much with trifles often make themselves incapable of doing anything serious or great.

> François de La Rochefoucauld, 1613–1680
> French politician, writer, and philanthropist
> *Reflections, or Sentences and Moral Maxims*

Nine-tenths of wisdom is being wise in time.

> Theodore Roosevelt, 1858–1919
> Twenty-sixth President of the United States
> Speech, Lincoln, Nebraska, 1917

The first step toward saving time ... is to find out how you've been spending it.

> William Ruchti
> American Management Association
> *Leadership in the Office* (AMACOM, 1963)

We don't want to spend a lot of management time on things that don't fit our growth scenario.

> Peter L. Scott
> Chairman, Emhart Corp.
> *Sky*, August 1, 1987

The hour has come, but not the man.

> Walter Scott, 1771–1832
> Scottish poet, novelist, and biographer
> *Guy Mannering*

We slip our opportunities; and if they be not caught in the very *nick*, they are irrevocably lost.

> Seneca, 4 B.C.–A.D. 65
> Roman writer and rhetorician
> *Epistles to Lucilius*

The time isn't there.

> Dorothy Servello
> Personnel Specialist, General Foods
> *The New York Times,* April 27, 1988

Therefore,—since brevity is the soul of wit,
And tediousness the limbs and outward flourishes,—
I will be brief.

> William Shakespeare, 1564–1616
> English dramatist and poet
> *Hamlet*

Better three hours too soon than a minute too late.

> William Shakespeare, 1564–1616
> English dramatist and poet
> *The Merry Wives of Windsor*

Time travels in divers paces with divers persons. I'll tell you who Time ambles withal, who Time trots withal, who Time gallops withal, and who he stands still withal.

> William Shakespeare, 1564–1616
> English dramatist & poet
> *As You Like It*

Everything happens to everybody sooner of later if there is time enough.

> George Bernard Shaw, 1856–1950
> Nobel laureate in literature
> *Back to Methuselah*

The calendar doesn't care how you spend your time.

> Carlton Sheets
> Real estate developer
> *Carlton Sheets on Investment* (TV program),
> December 20, 1987

I make lists every day, and when I finish something on my list I cross it out. I feel very good when I see the list all crossed out. I look at my list of things to do and I can plan my time realistically.

> Sonja R. Siegel
> Manager, Software Applications
> Development, Data Sciences, Inc.
> Late one night

The shortest way to do many things is to do one thing at a time.

> Samuel Smiles, 1812–1904
> Scottish physician and biographer
> *Self-Help*

Know the true value of time; snatch, seize, and enjoy every moment of it. No idleness; no laziness, no procrastination: never put off till tomorrow what you can do today.

> Philip Dormer Stanhope, 1694–1773
> English Secretary of State
> *Letters of Lord Chesterfield to his Son*

Despatch is the soul of business.

> Philip Dormer Stanhope, 1694–1773
> English Secretary of State
> *Letters of Lord Chesterfield to His Son*

No one can be provident of his time who is not prudent in the choice of his company.

> Jeremy Taylor, 1613–1667
> English clergyman and writer
> *Holy Living and Dying*

Time is the most valuable thing that a man can spend.

> Theophrastus, 371–287 B.C.
> Greek philosopher
> Quoted by Diogenes Laertius, *Theophrastus*

But with unhurrying chase,
And unperturbed pace,
Deliberate speed, majestic instancy, ...

> Francis Thompson, 1859–1907
> English poet, critic, and biographer
> *The Hound of Heaven*

There is only one time that is important— NOW! It is the most important time because it is the only time that we have any power.

> Leo Tolstoi, 1828–1910
> Russian novelist
> *Twenty-Three Tales*

Devote 100% of your time to the critical issue.

> Robert Townsend
> Former CEO, Avis
> *Up The Organization* (Knopf, 1975)

Time is
Too Slow for those who Wait,
Too Swift for those who Fear,
Too Long for those who Grieve,
Too Short for those who Rejoice,
But for those who Love
Time is not.

> Henry Van Dyke
> *For Katrina's Sun-Dial*

Patience is the art of hoping.

> Marquis de Vauvenargues, 1715–1747
> French soldier and moralist
> *Reflections and Maxims*

When time flies it cannot be recalled.
[*Fugit irreparable tempus.*]

> Virgil, 70–19 B.C.
> Roman poet
> *Georgics*

If you're there before it's over, you're on time.

> James J. "Jimmy" Walker, 1881–1946
> "The Midnight Mayor" of New York City
> Prochnow, *The Toastmaster's Treasure Chest*
> (Harper & Row, 1979)

Sleep on it and then decide, unless you have a competitor who doesn't need the sleep.

> Theodore Waller
> Vice President, Grollier, Inc.
> Staff meeting, 1968

The inevitability of gradualness cannot fully be appreciated.

> Sidney Webb, 1859–1947
> English socialist and writer
> Presidential address, British Labour Party,
> June 28, 1923

When the whistle blows, you have only a limited amount of time to do what you have to do. You either do it then or you don't do it at all.

> Byron R. "Whizzer" White
> U. S. Supreme Court Justice
> and college football All-American
> Prochnow, *The Toastmaster's Treasure Chest*
> (Harper & Row, 1979)

There isn't any time for him to work harder. He's already working 18 hours a day.

> Q. T. Wiles
> Turnaround Operations consultant
> *Inc. Magazine*, February 1988

Procrastination is the thief of time.

> Edward Young, 1683–1765
> English poet
> *Night Thoughts*

Talk of nothing but business, and dispatch that business quickly.

> Anonymous
> Sign in general store
> Kresgeville, Pennsylvania

Work smarter and harder.

> Anonymous

Work smarter, not harder.

> Anonymous

[It is a function of the executive] ... to reflect sadly that one could have done it right in 20 minutes, and now one has to spend two days to find out why it has taken three weeks for someone else to do it wrong.

> Anonymous Document
> "Functions of the Executive"
> Mackenzie, *The Time Trap*
> (McGraw-Hill, 1972)

Thank God for the last minute. Otherwise nothing would ever get done.

> Anonymous

Definition of a manager: A man who never puts off till tomorrow that which he can get someone else to do today.

> Anonymous

47
Training

You are only as good as the people you train.

The conventional definition of management is getting work done through people, but real management is developing people through work.

Agha Hasan Abedi
President, Bank of Credit & Commerce
International (Luxembourg)
Leaders, July 1984

Training is the teaching of specific skills. It should result in the employee having the ability to do something he or she could not do before.

Mary Ann Allison
Vice President, Citicorp.
and Eric Anderson
Financial planner
Managing Up, Managing Down
(Simon & Schuster, 1984)

Diligence is a great teacher.

Arabic proverb

You cannot make a crab walk straight.

Aristophanes, c. 448–c. 380 B. C.
Athenian comic playwright
The Peace

Learning is more important than practice because it leads to practice.

Babylonian Talmud, Megillah

How to educate broad-guaged professionals for the public service; how to keep professional specialists accountable to politically responsible generalists within the executive and legislative branches; these are at present and prospectively among the most important unresolved issues of public management.

Stephan K. Bailey
President,
American Society of Public Administration
Agenda For the Nation
(The Brookings Institution, 1968)

486

Trainers can now manage learning just as their counterparts in accounting manage accounts receiveable.

Janet Bensu
President, Janet Bensu Associates
Training, November 1986

The costs of pre-service training are so high that rapid turnover results in unacceptable costs for academy training and lost time of personnel in training.

L. Cary Bittick
Executive Director,
National Sheriffs' Association
The National Sheriff, October/November 1986

What they [managers] do, they do well, but they feel inadequate to teach it to others.

Kenneth H. Blanchard
Chairman, Blanchard Training & Development
Training, November 1986

Training isn't a quick fix.

Kenneth H. Blanchard
Chairman, Blanchard Training & Development
Training, November 1986

We are forced to rely on people, which is why we put so much emphasis on training them.

Henry Block
CEO, H&R Block
Inc. Magazine, December 1987

One indicator will tell executives a great deal about whether or not they have got the right heir for their business wisdom. When the pairing was a mistake, even moderately so, the senior partner felt it to be ... "a drain, " "a chore," "a one-way street." That is a signal that must not be ignored, and for a very good reason. For more than 25 centuries, great

teachers have always learned as much from their best students as the other way around.

Srully Blotnick
Management consultant
The Corporate Steeplechase
(Facts On File, 1984)

A student who gives a particular answer merely because that is the one the teacher reinforces has not learned a subject.

John W. Blythe
Hamilton College
The Educational Record, 1960

I learned how to get things done on time, because you had to get the papers delivered.

Paul Brayton
President, Brayton International
The Hawk Eye (Burlington, Iowa),
July 10, 1987

When a fixed procedure is too long to be memorized economically, job aids in the form of check lists or some other cuing mechanism are provided to enable the man to become familiar with the task during training and to perform it dependably in the field situation.

Leslie J. Briggs
Training and human factors psychologist
*Problems in Stimulation and Programming
in the Design of Complex Trainers*
Paper read at the Annual Meeting of the
American Psychological Association, 1959

Repair shops have been built for electric motors, but we scrap men.

Heywood Campbell Broun, 1888–1939
American journalist
Prochnow, *The Toastmaster's Treasure Chest*
(Harper & Row, 1979)

People have to be willing to be retrained.

> Walton Burdick
> Human Resources Manager, IBM
> Tomasko, *Downsizing* (AMACOM, 1987)

The grand Instructor, Time.

> Edmund Burke, 1729–1797
> English statesman, orator and writer
> Letter to H. Langrishe, May 26, 1795

Example is the school of mankind, and they will learn at no other.

> Edmund Burke, 1729–1797
> English statesman, orator, and writer
> *On a Regicide Peace*

Set a beggar on horseback and he will ride a gallop.

> Robert Burton, 1577–1640
> Vicar of St. Thomas's, Oxford
> *The Anatomy of Melancholy*

Perhaps the most well established and universally observed experimental fact about extinction is that it occurs more slowly after partial reinforcement than after continuous reinforcement.

> Robert R. Bush
> University of Pennsylvania
> *Developments in Mathematical Psychology*
> (The Free Press, 1960)

An art [skill] can only be learned in the workshop of those who are winning their bread by it.

> Samuel Butler, 1835–1902
> English novelist and translator
> *Erewhon*

Because the importance of training is so commonly underestimated, the manager who wants to make a dramatic improvement in or-ganizational effectiveness without challenging the status quo will find a training program a good way to start.

> Theodore Caplow
> *Managing an Organization*
> (CBS College Publishing, 1983)

Organizational values are best transmitted when they are acted out, and not merely announced, by the people responsible for training, or by the people who become role-models for recruits. The manager of an organization is a role-model *ex officio* and may have an astonishing ability to communicate organizational values to recruits in fleeting contacts with them. That is the age-old secret of successful generalship, and it is applied every day by charismatic leaders in other fields, whose commitments to their roles is so dramatic that they strike awe into the recruits who observe them in action.

> Theodore Caplow
> *Managing an Organization*
> (CBS College Publishing, 1983)

Not only is there an art in knowing a thing, but also a certain art in teaching it.

> Cicero, 106–43 B.C.
> Roman orator and statesman
> *De Legibus*

Training frequently fails to pay off in behavioral changes on the job: Trainees go back to work and do it the way they've always done it instead of the way you taught them to do it.

> Ruth Colvin Clark
> Manager, Training and Information Services,
> California Edison Co.
> *Training*, November 1986

The people in charge of training should have access to top management's strategic plans for the future so that appropriate training will be in place when needed.

Ruth Colvin Clark
Manager, Training and Information Services,
California Edison Co.
Training, November 1986

Through training your employees you can have a greater degree of confidence that the work will progress through a pattern you designed.

William F. Cone
Manager of Professional Development,
Hughes Aircraft
Supervising Employees Effectively
(Addison-Wesley, 1974)

Virtually all the computer based instruction around is little more than electronic page turning. That wouldn't be so bad if the pages represented decent training materials. But tragically they most often consist of material which, if presented via any other medium, would be intolerable. Soon after the learner gets past the excitement of the blinking screens, he is faced with the sad truth.

Donald Cook
Training Psychologist
Speech, Washington, D.C., September 1984

Employees usually perceive training as either a punishment or a reward. Trainers should, therefore, ask themselves whether the way they use training tells employees that they recognize their potential and want to provide them with an opportunity to grow and realize that potential, or whether it tells employees that they consider them to be inadequate.

Dan L. Costley and Faye A. Moore
New Mexico State University
Personnel Journal, March 1986

The biggest cost in training may be time.

Linda Grist Cunningham
Executive Editor, Trenton (New Jersey) *Times*
Presstime, March 1988

First study the science, and then practice the art which is born of that science.

Leonardo da Vinci, 1452–1519
Italian artist, inventor, and scientist
Treatise on Painting

When asked what learning was most necessary, he said, "Not to unlearn what you have learned."

Diogenes Laertius, c. 200–250
Greek historian and writer
*Lives and Opinions of Eminent Philosophers:
Antisthenes*

Practice is everything.

Diogenes Laertius, c. 200–250
Greek historian and writer
*Lives and Opinions of Eminent Philosophers:
Periander*

Experience is the child of Thought, and Thought is the child of Action. We can not learn men from books.

Benjamin Disraeli, 1804–1881
English Prime Minister and novelist
Vivian Grey

One of the major tasks of the people moving into managerial positions today is going to be just helping everyone learn enough, fast enough, to keep up with the business or specialty involved.

Sharon Kirkman Donegan
President, Boyle/Kirkman Associates
Training, November 1986

Top management ... cannot tell the trainer how to train. All it can do is get another trainer if it feels that the present one does not know his job.

> Peter F. Drucker
> Management consultant and writer
> *Management in Turbulent Times*
> (Harper & Row, 1980)

Thomas Watson [IBM's founder] trained, and trained, and trained.

> Peter F. Drucker
> Management consultant and writer
> *Washington Business Journal*,
> October 12, 1987

A job in which young people are not given real training—though, of course, the training need not be a formal "training program"—does not measure up to what they have a right and a duty to expect.

> Peter F. Drucker
> Management consultant and writer
> *People and Performance*
> (Harper & Row, 1977)

It makes little sense to subject all employees to training programs, to personnel policies, and to supervision designed for one group of employees, and in particular designed, as so many of the policies are, for yesterday's typical entrant into the labor force—the fifteen or sixteen year old without any experience. More and more we will have to have personnel policies that fit the person rather than bureaucratic convenience or tradition.

> Peter F. Drucker
> Management consultant and writer
> *Management in Turbulent Times*
> (Harper & Row, 1980)

When a subject becomes totally obsolete, we make it a required course.

> Peter F. Drucker
> Management consultant and writer
> Prochnow, *The Toastmaster's Treasure Chest*
> (Harper & Row, 1979)

Genius must be born, and never can be taught.

> John Dryden, 1631–1700
> English poet
> *Epistle to Congreve*

In analyzing the cost of any on-the-job training program, one usually finds that the largest single factor is the trainees themselves; they are being paid while they are being trained. Therefore ... the cost of relatively esoteric and expensive equipment can be rationalized if there would be a corresponding savings in training time.

> Lewis D. Eigen
> Executive Vice President,
> University Research Corp.
> *Improving Human Performance Quarterly*,
> Spring 1978

Skill to do comes of doing; knowledge comes by eyes always open, and working hands; and there is no knowledge that is not power.

> Ralph Waldo Emerson, 1803–1882
> American essayist aand poet
> *Old Age*

The world can never be learned by learning all its details.

> Ralph Waldo Emerson, 1803–1882
> American essayist and poet
> *Journals*

Each mind has its own method.

> Ralph Waldo Emerson, 1803–1882
> American essayist and poet
> *Essays*

Practice yourself in little things; and thence proceed to greater.

> Epictetus, c. 60
> Greek philosopher
> *Discourses*

The faculty of doubting is rare among men. A few choice spirits carry the germs of it in them, but these do not develop without training.

Anatole France, 1844–1924
French novelist
Penguin Island

Instruction does not prevent waste of time or mistakes; and mistakes themselves are often the best teachers of all.

James Anthony Froude, 1818–1894
Oxford University
Short Studies on Great Subjects

The lowest morale in the plant was found among those men whose supervisors were rated *between* the democratic and authoritarian extremes.... [T]hese foremen may have varied inconsistently in their tactics, permissive at one moment and hardfisted the next, in a way that left their men frustrated and unable to anticipate how they would be treated. The naturally autocratic supervisor who is exposed to human relations training ... may make him harder to work for than he was before being "enlightened."

Saul W. Gellerman
University of Dallas School of Management
Motivation and Productivity
(AMACOM, 1963)

Leadership cannot really be taught. It can only be learned.

Harold Geneen
CEO, IT&T
Managing (Doubleday, 1984)

People learn from their failures. Seldom do they learn anything from success.

Harold Geneen
CEO, IT&T
Managing (Doubleday, 1984)

The mistakes of others can be good teachers.

German proverb

You [the trainer] should begin with the most trustworthy facilities you have. First use your common sense; next, use the approximations to principles of adult educational programming that have been set down be a few people. Remember, these people probably are not more expert than you, only more audacious. They may be mostly wrong. Use their principles only as a starting place.

Thomas F. Gilbert
President, Praxis, Inc.
*On the Relevance of Laboratory
Investigation of Learning to
Self-Instructional Programming*
Paper read at the Annual Meeting of the
American Psychological Association, 1959

Where several years ago we saw training used as a form of personal growth, in recent years we've seen an increasing emphasis on training activities designed to meet corporate objectives that not uncommonly revolve around the issue of productivity.

Jack Gordon
Editor, *Training*
Training, November 1986

Cultivate those who can teach you.

Baltasar Gracián, 1601–1658
Spanish priest and popular writer
Oraculo Manual

Rotating people and letting them work in different assignments is an excellent way to keep a person's work interesting. In addition, it serves to enrich and develop the employees' skills. It's a pity that it isn't practiced more broadly.

Andrew S. Grove
CEO, Intel Corp.
One-On-One With Andy Grove
(G. P. Putnam's Sons, 1987)

491

There is a remarkable agreement upon the definition of learning as being reflected in a change of behavior as the result of experience.

E. A. Haggard
Quoted in *Readings in Human Learning*
(McKay, 1963)

Everyone we hire will have to be retrained three or four times during the normal employment period. The alternative ... is constant turnover, replacing the work force every five years or so.

Jeffrey Hallett
Business consultant
Nation's Business, February 1988

We teach everybody accounting and marketing but not enough about the world in which executives must operate.

Donald L. Harnett
Indiana University
Working Woman, March 1988

The training director must see line management, and particularly top management, as the clients to be served by the entire training function. The training participants (the ultimate "consumers") must be distinguished from the real client, top management.

Richard D. Hays
President,
Organizational Management Associates
Training and Development Journal,
June 1984

You are only as good as the people you train.

Lonear Heard
President, James T. Heard Management Corp.
(McDonald's franchisee)
Black Enterprise, September 1987

A dwarf on a giant's shoulder, sees further of the two.

George Herbert, 1593–1632
English clergyman and poet
Jacula Prudentum

Woe be to him who reads but one book.

George Herbert, 1593–1632
English clergyman and poet
Jacula Prudentum

In every art it is good to have a master.

George Herbert, 1593–1633
English clergyman and poet
Jacula Prudentum

I'm critical of sensitivity training and human relations programs. They prostitute human relations and prostitute human decency.

Frederick Herzberg
University of Utah
The Managerial Choice
(Dow Jones-Irwin, 1976)

Emulation is good for mankind.

Hesiod, eighth century B.C.
Greek poet
Works and Days

Leaders, troop leader, finance chairman, computer specialist—it doesn't matter what your job is; we try to design training for you.

Frances Hesselbein
Executive Director, Girl Scouts U.S.A.
Management Review, April 1987

The shy man will not learn; the impatient man should not teach. Ask and learn.

Hillel the Elder, c. 30 B.C.–c. A.D. 25
Jewish sage and teacher
Sayings of the Fathers

Knowledge and timber shouldn't be used till they are seasoned.

> Oliver Wendell Holmes, 1809–1894
> American physician and popular writer
> *The Autocrat of the Breakfast Table*

The five steps in teaching an employee new skills are preparation, explanation, showing, observation and supervision.

> Harold S. Hook
> Chairman and CEO, American General Corp.
> *Forbes*, October 19, 1987

Some experience of popular lecturing had convinced me that the necessity of making things plain to uninstructed people was one of the very best means of clearing up the obscure corners in one's own mind.

> Thomas Henry Huxley, 1825–1895
> English biologist
> *Man's Place in Nature*

Perhaps the most valuable result of all education is the ability to make yourself do the thing you have to do, when it ought to be done, whether you like it or not.

> Thomas Henry Huxley, 1825–1895
> English biologist
> *Technical Education*

Doing depends upon learning, not learning upon doing. [Therefore] learning must precede practice.

> Jerusalem Talmud, Pesahim

Example is always more efficacious than precept.

> Samuel Johnson, 1709–1784
> English lexicographer and writer
> *Rasselas*

I cannot see that lectures can do so much good as reading the books from which the lectures are taken.

> Samuel Johnson, 1709–1784
> English lexicographer and writer
> *Boswell's Life of Dr. Johnson*

Knowledge is of two kinds: we know a subject ourselves, or we know where we can find information upon it.

> Samuel Johnson, 1709–1784
> English lexicographer and writer
> *Boswell's Life of Dr. Johnson*

You can change behavior in an entire organization, provided you treat training as a process rather than an event.

> Edward W. Jones
> Training Director,
> General Cinema Beverages, Inc.
> *Training*, December 1986

To teach is to learn twice.

> Joseph Joubert, 1754–1824
> French moralist and critic
> *Thoughts*

Technique is hardly worth talking about unless it's used for something worth doing.

> Pauline Kael
> American film critic
> *Going Steady*

Model first, teach second.

> Dennis C. Kinslaw
> President, Developmental Products, Inc.
> and Donna Christensen, Consultant
> *Training*, December 1986

Training is probably the most important aspect of buying a computer system.

> Barry Knowles
> Owner, Valcom Computer Center
> *Inc. Magazine*, November 1987

Practice is the best master.
[*Exercitatio optimus est magister.*]

> Latin proverb

You will always find some Eskimos ready to instruct the Congolese on how to cope with heat waves.

> Stanislaw J. Lec
> Polish writer and aphorist
> *Unkempt Thoughts* (St. Martin's Press, 1962)

You must learn from the mistakes of others. You can't possibly live long enough to make them all yourself.

> Sam Levenson, 1911–1980
> Teacher and comedian
> *You Don't Have to be in Who's Who to Know What's What* (Simon & Shuster, 1979)

We must further individualize our training efforts because the job needs of our people will become more unique, and we will find a rising proportion of training assignments involving a single individual, or at most a very limited number.

> Jerome P. Lysaught
> Training Psychologist, Eastman Kodak Co.
> Margulies and Eigen, *Applied Programmed Instruction* (John Wiley & Sons, 1962)

[Question put to the West Point Military Academy adjutant when MacArthur became Superintendent in 1919:] How long are we going on preparing for the War of 1812?

> Douglas MacArthur, 1880–1964
> Five-star General of the U. S. Army
> Quoted in *American Heritage,* April 1988

Learning is for the future; that is, the object of instruction is to facilitate some form of behavior at a point after the instruction has been completed.

> Robert F. Mager
> Psychologist and educational technologist
> *Developing Attitude Toward Learning*
> (Fearon, 1968)

Order and simplification are the first steps toward the mastery of a subject—the actual enemy is the unknown.

> Thomas Mann, 1875–1955
> German novelist and essayist
> *The Magic Mountain*

Do not think that what is hard for thee to master is impossible for man; but if a thing is possible and proper to man, deem it attainable by thee.

> Marcus Aurelius, 121–180
> Roman Emperor and Stoic philosopher
> *Meditations*

If the only tool you have is a hammer, you treat everything like a nail.

> Abraham Maslow, 1908–1970
> Humanistic psychologist
> Lecture to Graduate Psychology Club,
> Brandeis University, Spring 1966

If you make an honest mistake, the company will be very forgiving. Treat it as a training expense and learn from it.

> Konosuke Matsushita
> Founder, Matsushita Electric Co. (Japan)
> *Cherry Blossoms and Robotics*
> (Young Presidents' Organization, 1983)

Effective training programs are essential to identify needs for improvement wherever they might occur, and develop solutions to the concerns that we discover ... before they become problems.

T. Allen McArtor
Administrator, FAA
Speech, Washington, D.C., August 18, 1987

In training salesman to master sales talks for several different products ... the trainer should require thorough mastery and use of one before going on to learning the next. If the talks are only partially learned, parts of one talk will intrude into another.

N. MaGehee and P. W. Thayer
Training in Business and Industry
(John Wiley & Sons, 1961)

[T]he trainer must be alert to the fact that he will tend to discontinue reinforcement as the trainee becomes more skilled. He will be tempted to assume that the trainee knows what he is supposed to do now so he needs no attention. If this occurs, motivation may drop, and the lack of motivation can lead to extinction. The decline in motivation may be offset in a number of ways, such as by an indication that less close supervision by the trainer is a sign of real progress on the trainee's part. Reinforcement cannot be eliminated completely, but must be reduced gradually and supplanted by intrinsic task reinforcement.

N. McGehee and P. W. Thayer
Training in Business and Industry
(John Wiley & Sons, 1961)

Young people who really wanted a challenge went in and they looked around and found there was nothing they could decide, because everything had been decided for them. And a lot of young people would not tolerate that.... They simply left. And for those who stayed, they were trained not to make a decision. So when the time came that they moved up a bit and there was really something to be decided, they were lost, because they had never practiced on small decisions, and they had never made a mistake. So they figured out ways to

continue not making decisions, to continue avoiding mistakes.

William G. McGowan
Chairman, MCI Communications Corp.
Inc. Magazine, August 1986

The future of work consists of *learning* a living.

Marshall McLuhan, 1911–1980
University of Toronto
Understanding Media: The Extensions of Man
(McGraw-Hill, 1964)

Managers are busy people.... Either positively or by default, they're constantly involved in training.

Philip W. Metzger
Computer analyst and management writer
Managing Programming People
(Prentice-Hall, 1987)

One of management's most important functions is to train people for their jobs.

Philip W. Metzger
Computer analyst and management writer
Managing Programming People
(Prentice-Hall, 1987)

It is one thing to be proficient in a job and quite another to know how to develop someone else to do a similar job.

James C. Miller
Personnel Development Manager,
Standard Brands, Inc.
Leadership in the Office (AMACOM, 1963)

The case study method [for management training] probably came into wide use because management schools tacitly recognized that they were not able to teach the specific managerial talents. They could only help to accelerate the learning that might otherwise take place on the job.

Henry Mintzberg
McGill University School of Management
The Nature of Managerial Work
(Harper & Row, 1973)

In training, I use and teach all ... types of visual aids. Times have changed. We're in a visual world. People expect more, and like more visual appeal today. Objects, graphs, charts, posters all help an audience learn more, learn faster and maintain interest in the speaker and the message as well as help the speaker be more confident.

Robert L. Montgomery
President, R. L. Montgomery & Associates
How to Sell in the 1980's
(Prentice-Hall, 1980)

Human Resource Development or training programs are defined as (1) a series of organized activities, (2) conducted within a specified time, and (3) designed to produce behavioral change.

Leonard Nadler
The George Washington University
Developing Human Resources
(Learning Concepts, 1979)

The big challenge of the 1980s is not the retraining of workers, but the retraining of managers.

John Naisbett and Patricia Aburdene
Business writers and social researchers
Re-inventing the Corporation (Warner, 1985)

Training and education programs within American business are so vast, so extensive, that they represent in effect an alternative system to the nation's public and private schools, colleges and universities.

John Naisbett and Patricia Aburdene
Business writers and social researchers
Re-inventing the Corporation (Warner, 1985)

A man has no ears for that which experience has given him no access.

Georg Wilhelm Nietzsche, 1844–1900
German philosopher
Ecce Homo

[In developing managers:] Although conferences and courses can help, most observers agree that major emphasis should be on systematic coaching and carefully-planned job assignments.

George S. Odiorne
University of Massachusetts
How Managers Make Things Happen
(Prentice-Hall, 1982)

Never chide for Anger, but *Instruction*.

William Penn, 1644–1718
Founder of Pennsylvania
Fruits of Solitude in Reflections and Maxims

The neglect of training is but one outcropping of our favoring of hardware vs. humans.... Review the training budget before the capital budget—and spend at least as much time in your strategic review on human capital issues.

Tom Peters
Business writer
Washington Business Journal,
October 12, 1987

Train everyone—lavishly.... You can't overspend on training.

Tom Peters
Business writer
Thriving on Chaos (Knopf, 1987)

Indeed, what is there that does not appear marvelous when it comes to our knowledge for the first time.

Pliny the Elder, 23 –79
Roman writer
Natural History

American business spends more on training its employees than is spent by the entire higher education establishment in this country.

> Curtis E. Plott
> Executive Vice President,
> American Society of Training Directors
> *Training*, November 1986

Demosthenes overcame and rendered more distinct his inarticulate and stammering pronunciation by speaking with pebbles in his mouth.

> Plutarch, c. 46–c. 120
> Greek biographer and philosopher
> *The Parallel Lives: Demosthenes*

Men must be taught as if you taught them not, and things unknown proposed as things forgot.

> Alexander Pope, 1688–1744
> English poet
> *An Essay on Criticism*

In order for contingencies of reinforcement to be effective, certain conditions must be met: (a) Reinforcement must take place *immediately* after a response has been made. A time interval ... greatly reduces the effectiveness of the reinforcement. (b) The reinforcement must be made *precisely contingent* upon performance of the behavior being taught. (c) A sufficient *number* of reinforcements must be given.

> Douglas Porter
> Psychologist and training scientist
> *Bulletin of the Harvard Graduate School of Education*, March, 1978

One bad example spoils many good precepts.

> Barber, *The Book of 1000 Proverbs*, 1876

'Tis harder to unlearn than learn.

> Barber, *The Book of 1000 Proverbs*, 1876

Practice is the best of all instructors.

> Publilius Syrus, c. 42 B.C.
> Roman writer
> *Maxims*

No one knows what he can do till he tries.

> Publilius Syrus, c. 42 B.C.
> Roman writer
> *Maxims*

It is better, of course, to know useless things than to know nothing.

> Publilius Syrus, c. 42 B.C.
> Roman writer
> *Maxims*

Do nothing you don't understand.

> Pythagoras, c. 500 B.C.
> Greek philosopher and mathematician
> Quoted in *Ethical Sentences from Stoboeus*

Knowledge about training's impact can come only from observing and analyzing the subsequent performance of the trainees as they function on the job.

> Elaine Radloff
> Manager of Training and Education,
> Detroit-Macomb Hospital Corp.
> *Personnel Journal,* March 1988

Japan is a country committed to learning. The United States isn't—and it shows.

> Thomas P. Rohlen
> Stanford University
> *Harvard Business Review*,
> September/October 1987

The skills that make technical professional competent in their specialties are not necessarily the same ones that make them successful within their organizations.

Bernard Rosenbaum
President, MOHR Development, Inc.
Training, November 1986

The training which makes men happiest in themselves also makes them most serviceable to others.

John Ruskin, 1819–1900
English art critic and historian
Sesame and Lilies

Our educational system imparts mostly academic values, which emphasize optimum solutions, while putting little emphasis on such considerations as speed, cost, and customer satisfaction—the values of the marketplace.

Roland Schmitt
Vice President and Chief Scientist,
General Electric Co.
High Technology, April 1987

The short-term and frequently shortsighted positions win out with disturbing regularity because American business is top-heavy with the ever expanding numbers of business school graduates who are trained advocates of the short-term profit.

Michael P. Schulhof
Executive Vice President, Sony of America
The New York Times, February 1, 1981

For it is not enough to remember and to understand, unless we do what we know.

Seneca, 4 B.C.–A.D. 65
Roman writer and rhetorician
Epistles to Lucilius

Some people are *excited* about learning a new piece of software. Other people get very

depressed. Good managers anticipate *both* situations—they involve the persons to be affected in the process of selecting a particular program, and they provide time and resources for training. Training is the key in both cases.

Jonathan P. Siegel
Information Communications Associates
Communications, January 1988

Learning does not occur because behavior has been primed [stimulated]; it occurs because behavior, primed or not, is *reinforced*.

B. F. Skinner
Harvard University
Beyond Freedom and Dignity (Knopf, 1971)

People learn what you teach them; not what you intend to teach them.

B. F. Skinner
Harvard University
Speech, New York City, September 1959

A great point to be aimed at is to get the working quality well trained. Facility will come with labor.

Samuel Smiles, 1812–1904
Scottish physician and biographer
Self-Help

The demand for men, like that of any other commodity, necessarily regulates the production of men.

Adam Smith, 1723–1790
Scottish political economist
Inquiry into the ... Wealth of Nations

One must learn by doing the thing;
for though you think you know it
You have no certainty, until you try.

Sophocles, c. 496–406 B.C.
Greek tragic playwright
Trachiniae

Though a man be wise, it is no shame for him to live and learn.

> Sophocles, c. 496–406 B.C.
> Greek tragic playwright
> *Antigone*

The more intelligible a thing is, the more easily it is retained in the memory, and contrariwise, the less intelligible it is, the more easily we forget it.

> Benedict Spinoza, 1632–1677
> Dutch philosopher and oculist
> *Ethics*

This company took off with a great team of class A players. Now if we want class A people, we have to hire class C's and make them into class A's.

> Edward Staley, Jr.
> CEO, Commonwealth
> *Inc. Magazine*, December 1987

We are more than half of what we are by imitation. The great point is to choose good models and to study them with care.

> Philip Dormer Stanhope, 1694–1773
> English Secretary of State
> *Letters of Lord Chesterfield to His Son*

[In teaching quantitative management techniques] ... simple examples are used to facilitate the learning process. More realistic applications reflecting actual applications would be so complex that they would not be very helpful in learning a technique.

> Bernard W. Taylor III
> Virginia Polytechnic Institute
> *Introduction to Management Science*
> (William C. Brown, 1986)

Everyone can improve, but not everyone can become world class.

> Noel Tichy
> University of Michigan
> *Fortune,* September 28, 1987

I'll learn him or kill him.

> Mark Twain
> (Samuel Langhorne Clemens), 1835–1910
> American author and riverboat captain
> *Life on the Mississippi*

There is no disgrace in not knowing when knowledge does not rest with you; the disgrace is in being unwilling to learn.

> Benedetto Varchi, c. 1502–1565
> Italian poet and historian
> *L'Ercolano*

Happy is he who has been able to learn the causes of things.
[*Felix qui potuit rerum cognoscere causas.*]

> Virgil, 70–19 B.C.
> Roman poet
> *Georgics*

There are truths which are not for all men, nor for all times.

> François Marie Voltaire, 1694–1778
> French writer
> Letter to Cardinal de Bernis

My God-given talent is my ability to stick with it [training] longer than anybody else.

> Hershel Walker
> Professional football player
> Garfield, *Peak Performers* (Avon, 1986)

Ah, you may say, but can't people be trained to modify their behavior? The key questions for an employer are: How completely? For how long? At what cost?

Alan Weiss
President, Summit Consulting Group, Inc.
Success, February 1988

Hiring and training are costlybut it is infinitely more costly to have a marginal or barely average on the company rolls for 30 years.

Gordon W. Wheeling
Personnel Manager, Beckman & Whitley
Leadership in the Office (AMACOM, 1963)

We are living in the first period of human history for which the assumption that the time-span of major cultural change is greater than the life-span of an individual is false. Today this time-span is considerably shorter than that of human life, and accordingly our training must prepare individuals to face a novelty of conditions.

Alfred North Whitehead, 1861–1947
English mathematician and philosopher
Introduction to Donam, *Business Adrift*

The expense isn't what it costs to train employees. It's what it costs *not* to train them.

Philip Wilber
President, Drug Emporium, Inc.
Inc. Magazine, December 1987

The way to get higher productivity is to train better managers and have fewer of them.

William Woodside
Chairman, Primerica
Peters, *Thriving on Chaos* (Knopf, 1987)

Training won't cover up for poor equipment and outmoded methods. It won't offset mediocre products or deteriorating markets. It won't compensate for poor compensation or abusive supervisory or management practices. And training definitely won't turn the unwilling and uncaring in your organization into motivated, devoted, gung-ho fireballs.

Ron Zemke
President, Performance Research Associates
Training, November 1986

[Assessing the value of a training course:] It comes at least 20 years too late.

Anonymous trainee
Training, November 1986

Definition of a good executive: A man who has successfully trained others to discharge his responsibilities.

Anonymous

On Indexes

So essential did I consider an index to be to every book, that I proposed to bring a bill into Parliament to deprive an author who publishes a book without an index of the privelege of copyright, and, moreover, to subject him for his offense to a pecuniary penalty.

John Campbell, 1779–1861
Lord Chancellor of England
Lives of the Chief Justices of England

An index is a necessary implement.... Without this, a large author is but a labyrinth without a clue to direct the readers within.

Thomas Fuller, 1608–1661
Chaplain in extraordinary to Charles II
The Worthies of England

I can tell where that saying was born.

William Shakespeare, 1564–1616
English dramatist and poet
Twelfth Night

Index

This Index contains all the persons, organizations, and sources quoted in this book. The numbers in the Index refer to **chapter numbers** and not pages. Within each chapter, the quotations are arranged alphabetically. Anonymous quotations appear at the end of each chapter.

C

D

E

G

H

M

N

O

P

T

W

Y

Z

Miscellaneous